PRETRIAL

ASPEN PUBLISHERS

PRETRIAL

Seventh Edition

THOMAS A. MAUET
Director of Trial Advocacy
and Riepe Professor of Law
University of Arizona

Wolters Kluwer
Law & Business

AUSTIN   BOSTON   CHICAGO   NEW YORK   THE NETHERLANDS

Aspen Publishers
Attn: Permissions Department
76 Ninth Avenue, 7th Floor
New York, NY 10011-5201

To contact Customer Care, e-mail customer.care@aspenpublishers.com, call 1-800-234-1660, fax 1-800-901-9075, or mail correspondence to:

Aspen Publishers
Attn: Order Department
PO Box 990
Frederick, MD 21705

Printed in the United States of America.

1 2 3 4 5 6 7 8 9 0

ISBN 978-0-7355-7203-4

Library of Congress Cataloging-in-Publication Data

Mauet, Thomas A.
   Pretrial / Thomas A. Mauet. –7th ed.
      p. cm.
   Includes index.
   ISBN 978-0-7355-7203-4
   1. Pre-trial procedure–United States.   I. Title.

   KF8900.M386 2008
   347.73′72 — dc22   2008012094

About Wolters Kluwer Law & Business

Wolters Kluwer Law & Business is a leading provider of research information and workflow solutions in key specialty areas. The strengths of the individual brands of Aspen Publishers, CCH, Kluwer Law International and Loislaw are aligned within Wolters Kluwer Law & Business to provide comprehensive, in-depth solutions and expert-authored content for the legal, professional and education markets.

CCH was founded in 1913 and has served more than four generations of business professionals and their clients. The CCH products in the Wolters Kluwer Law & Business group are highly regarded electronic and print resources for legal, securities, antitrust and trade regulation, government contracting, banking, pension, payroll, employment and labor, and healthcare reimbursement and compliance professionals.

Aspen Publishers is a leading information provider for attorneys, business professionals and law students. Written by preeminent authorities, Aspen products offer analytical and practical information in a range of specialty practice areas from securities law and intellectual property to mergers and acquisitions and pension/benefits. Aspen's trusted legal education resources provide professors and students with high-quality, up-to-date and effective resources for successful instruction and study in all areas of the law.

Kluwer Law International supplies the global business community with comprehensive English-language international legal information. Legal practitioners, corporate counsel and business executives around the world rely on the Kluwer Law International journals, loose-leafs, books and electronic products for authoritative information in many areas of international legal practice.

Loislaw is a premier provider of digitized legal content to small law firm practitioners of various specializations. Loislaw provides attorneys with the ability to quickly and efficiently find the necessary legal information they need, when and where they need it, by facilitating access to primary law as well as state-specific law, records, forms and treatises.

Wolters Kluwer Law & Business, a unit of Wolters Kluwer, is headquartered in New York and Riverwoods, Illinois. Wolters Kluwer is a leading multinational publisher and information services company.

This book is dedicated to my father,
Rudolf B. Mauet

SUMMARY OF CONTENTS

CONTENTS

IV. CASE EVALUATION AND STRATEGY

PART B
CONDUCTING THE LITIGATION   115

V. PLEADINGS

VI.   DISCOVERY

VII. MOTIONS

PREFACE

New litigation lawyers are quickly faced with an uncomfortable reality: Civil litigation is vastly different from studying civil procedure in law school. For civil litigators the procedural rules are primarily functional tools that regulate the pretrial stage of the litigation process. The new litigator's primary concern is not to "miss the boat."

Helping that litigator not to miss the boat is this book's purpose. Whether a third-year law student in a clinical program or a litigator in the first years of practice, you must approach every lawsuit systematically to make sure that you think through the important considerations and take all timely steps during the investigation, pleading, discovery, and motion practice stages of the pretrial process. Only then have you adequately prepared for settlement or trial.

This text approaches litigation the same way. It presents a methodology for preparation, and reviews the procedural rules and thought processes a litigator should utilize before and during each stage of the process. In addition, it discusses and gives examples of how these litigation skills translate into pleadings, discovery, and motions. In litigation, as in trials, there is no one "right way" to litigate. Consequently, while the text presents standard ways of drafting pleadings and motions and of conducting discovery, there are actually numerous ways of effectively conducting pretrial litigation. The examples set forth in the text are only one approach and are there to illustrate how these steps, in recurring situations, can be accomplished.

This text is of necessity an overview of the basic steps in the civil litigation process. Because any single-volume work must limit how much space can be devoted to any specific topic, compromises and hard choices were inevitable. In making them, I followed a basic rule: Provide an overview that gives inexperienced litigators the basic information they need to handle routine civil cases. What they *need* was arrived at by reflecting on my beginning years as a litigator and by discussing the book's scope with a number of inexperienced litigators. Sometimes their suggestions were surprising. For example, almost all recommended an overview of joinder, jurisdiction, and venue, since these are such complex, technical areas. They did not mean to suggest that some topics were more important than others; rather these inexperienced litigators felt they were weak in some areas and stronger in others. In many ways their suggestions corresponded with my experiences and account in large measure for the text's coverage.

The text focuses on federal district court practice and the Federal Rules of Civil Procedure. This is done for two reasons. First, the federal rules have been adopted by many state jurisdictions. Most other states have modern code pleading rules that are very similar to the federal rules. Second, solid planning, investigation, and drafting are essential skills regardless of the particular jurisdiction, and the text's emphasis is on those skills. Hence, the book is designed to be a basic resource regardless of where a case is to be litigated.

Rather than using case references, this text cites the treatises commonly used by litigators. These are Wright; James & Hazard; Friedenthal, Kane & Miller; Moore's Manual; the Manual of Federal Practice; Moore's Federal Practice; and Wright & Miller. The citations to these treatises should be much more useful in researching legal issues that may arise than individual case citations. Most topics discussed in this text begin with a footnote that provides citations to the relevant portions of these treatises. The citations generally appear in this order.

What's New in the Seventh Edition

The big change since the last edition, of course, has been the adoption of the new Federal Rules of Civil Procedure governing electronic discovery. The new rules, effective in December 2006, introduced a new term to civil litigators: "electronically stored information," or ESI. The changes, found in Rules 16, 26, 33, 34, 37, and 45, now establish comprehensive procedures governing the discovery of ESI. These rules are important because they substantially change the timing and procedures for discovering ESI, and ESI is increasingly the place where the principal discovery battles are being fought. Section 6.8 has been completely rewritten to detail the rules changes and discuss how the rules affect the pretrial process in general and the discovery process in particular. Since the adoption of the new federal rules, several states have also adopted their own version of e-discovery rules, and a number of states are studying the issue.

In addition, the Supreme Court's decision in Bell Atlantic v. Twombly, 127 S. Ct. 1955 (2007) may have a significant effect on how complaints are drafted and may make Rule 12(b)(6) motions to dismiss a more important pleading response. Sections 5.2–5.4 have been revised to incorporate the holding of Bell Atlantic v. Twombly. The Class Action Fairness Act significantly changed the basis for removing class actions to federal court, and these changes are reflected in §§3.5 and 5.12. The tax consequences of settlements in the personal injury field are constantly changing, and §8.3 has been revised to reflect the most recent statutory changes and cases. Finally, the text incorporates other statutory changes and Supreme Court decisions since 2004.

As with the sixth edition, this edition comes with a CD version of *Materials in Pretrial Litigation*, which contains six tort and contract case files that can be used in a course on pretrial litigation. The witness materials for these case files are contained in the *Teacher's Manual*, also on a CD, which course instructors may obtain from Aspen Publishers.

Thomas A. Mauet

Tucson, Arizona
January 2008

CITATIONS

For ease in citing, the text uses the following abbreviated citations:

Wright

Law of Federal Courts, Charles Alan Wright & Mary Kay Kane (6th ed. 2002)

James & Hazard

Civil Procedure, Fleming James, Jr., Geoffrey C. Hazard, Jr. & John Leubsdorf (5th ed. 2001)

Friedenthal

Civil Procedure, Jack H. Friedenthal, Mary Kay Kane & Arthur R. Miller (4th ed. 2005)

Moore's Manual

Moore's Manual — Federal Practice and Procedure, James W. Moore, Allan D. Vestal & Philip B. Kurland (supplemented annually)

Manual of Federal Practice

Manual of Federal Practice, Richard A. Givens (5th ed.), which is part of Trial Practice Series (supplemented annually)

Moore's Federal Practice

Moore's Federal Practice, James W. Moore, et al. (3d ed.) (updated quarterly)

Wright & Miller

Federal Practice and Procedure: Civil, Charles Alan Wright, Arthur R. Miller, and E.H. Cooper (updated monthly)

PRETRIAL

Part A
INVESTIGATING AND PLANNING THE LITIGATION

I

INTRODUCTION TO LITIGATION PLANNING

§1.1. Introduction

You have just been called into the office of a partner in the firm that recently hired you. The partner tells you that a prospective client will be coming to the office shortly who has a "problem" that might lead to litigation. The partner tells you that this problem appears to be just right for you to manage. With a smile, he hands you a note containing the prospective client's name and appointment time. Apprehensively you walk out of his office, thinking: "My God. What do I do now?"

What you do, when you do it, how you do it, and why you do it is what this book on civil pretrial litigation is all about. This first chapter is an overview of the litigation process, and discusses how to organize a coordinated litigation plan. Each step in the plan will be discussed in detail in the other chapters.

§1.2. Organizing litigation planning

Litigation planning deals with two basic questions. First, what overall litigation strategy will best serve the client's realistically attainable goals? Second, how does each piece of the litigation plan contribute toward achieving those goals? Addressing these two questions early, and constantly keeping the answers to them in mind, will do much to develop and implement an intelligent, realistic, and cost-effective litigation plan.

An effective litigation plan obviously requires structure. That structure should trigger the important thinking, at the right times, so that you will not "miss the boat" during any step in the litigation process. The basic steps in this plan are listed here followed by a discussion of each step.

1. Establish the terms of the attorney-client relationship
2. Determine the client's needs and priorities
3. Determine the elements of potential claims, remedies, defenses, and counterclaims

4.   Identify likely sources of proof
5.   Determine what informal fact investigation is necessary
6.   Determine what formal discovery is necessary
7.   Identify solutions
8.   Develop a litigation strategy
9.   Make litigation cost and timetable estimates
10.   Use a litigation file system

1.   Establish the terms of the attorney-client relationship

The first step in any litigation plan is to formally establish the attorney-client relationship. This must be done in writing, unless the client is a regular client with whom you have an established business relationship, because an attorney-client agreement is a contract between the attorney and client, and general contract principles apply.

The agreement should spell out who the client is, who will do the work for the client, what work will be done, how you will be compensated, and when the client will be billed for costs and legal work. All too often either a clear understanding with the client is never reached or all likely issues are not covered, causing serious problems later. Representing a client in litigation is difficult enough without having client relationship problems adding to the difficulties.

Before entering into an agreement, of course, you must first decide if you should take the case. In a simple case you can frequently make an intelligent decision after interviewing the potential client and reviewing available records. For example, in a personal injury case arising out of an automobile accident, you can probably determine whether the client's case has merit by interviewing the client to get the history of what happened and by reviewing available records, such as police reports and medical records. In more complicated cases, substantial factual and legal investigation may be necessary. For example, in a medical malpractice or product liability case, the common practice is to send all the records about the patient or product to an appropriate expert for evaluation before deciding whether to take the case.

Establishing the attorney-client agreement is discussed in §4.3.

2.   Determine the client's needs and priorities

People seek out lawyers when they have problems that need to be managed and solved. The lawyer, therefore, should first identify the client's problems and needs, viewing them broadly. The client's needs, seen from his perspective, may well be in conflict with possible solutions; however, finding out what the client wants to have happen is the beginning step in dealing with the problems that brought him to a lawyer in the first place.

Keep in mind that the client's needs must be considered in the long-term as well as the immediate sense. Clients often demand a lawsuit against every imagined wrongdoer, when any lawsuit may be against the client's best interests. You need to assess what can be gained by a lawsuit and then see how a suit would affect the client in the long term. For example, consider the frequently encountered situation of a client who wishes to sue another party with whom there is an ongoing business relationship. While the particular matter may have merit, suing the other party may put in jeopardy that valuable relationship and adversely affect current deals with that party. A lawsuit that may vindicate the client on one deal may not make sense when viewed in light of the overall picture.

You will also need to assess the client's priorities. Clients rarely get everything they want, so they must develop a scale of priorities that will help you fashion the litigation strategy. For example, suppose your client wants to sue another party over a contract dispute. Does she want a quick, inexpensive resolution to preserve an ongoing relationship? Does she simply want the other party to live up to the agreement, or is she primarily interested in money damages because she considers the relationship destroyed? These possibilities must be arranged to reflect their relative importance to the client before you can sensibly decide how best to help that client.

Determining the client's needs and priorities is discussed in §2.3.

3. Determine the elements of potential claims, remedies, defenses, and counterclaims

The initial client interview will often identify the legal areas involved. At this early stage, however, it is better to think expansively and consider all legal theories that might apply to the case. For example, while a "contract case" will obviously involve contract claims, it might also involve UCC claims, state and federal statutory claims such as securities and product safety statutes, and business torts. It's best to include all of them in your initial thinking.

After you have identified the possible applicable legal theories, determine what the legal requirements are for each theory. This is best done by looking at the applicable jurisdiction's jury instructions. Most jurisdictions have approved pattern jury instructions for commonly asserted claims and defenses. These will tell you what the required "elements" are for a particular claim or defense. If pattern instructions are unavailable, you should consult practice manuals that cover the particular field or research the cases and statutes to learn the elements for the applicable law.

The same type of analysis must be made for remedies. The availability of remedies is related to the choice of claims, and some remedies are broader than others. For example, in a contract dispute, contract damages will be an available remedy. However, if the dispute has fraud aspects, you may be able to bring a business tort claim and have broader damages rules apply. If statutory claims can be made, they may permit the prevailing party to recover attorney's fees and costs. In litigation, particularly complex litigation, the nature of the remedies is frequently a compelling reason a particular claim is, or is not, raised in the pleadings.

Potential counterclaims must also be considered. Before bringing a lawsuit, always check on what the other side has against your client. This is particularly important in commercial litigation, where the parties have dealt with each other many times over a period of time. There is little point in starting a lawsuit if it succeeds in provoking a large, previously dormant counterclaim.

Evaluating potential claims, remedies, defenses, and counterclaims is discussed in §3.3.

After you have identified the possible applicable legal theories and the elements for each of them, it's best to set up some type of litigation chart, or diagram, to list the theories and elements. For experienced ligators planning routine cases, this may not be necessary. New litigators, however, should develop a chart system to systematically analyze cases from the beginning by correlating the elements of claims, defenses and counterclaims, sources of proof, informal fact investigation, and formal discovery. When fully developed, the litigation chart will form the basis for your trial chart, should the case eventually go to trial.[1] For now, the chart will be the basis for your strategic litigation planning. Litigation charts are commonly organized like the one below.

Example:

You represent the plaintiff in an automobile negligence case.[2]

LITIGATION CHART

Elements of Claims, Defenses, and Counterclaims	Sources of Proof	Informal Fact Investigation	Formal Discovery
1. Negligence			
(a) negligence			
(b) causation			
(c) damages			
(1) lost income			
(2) med. expenses			
(3) disability			
(4) pain and suffering			

The chart should be continued for each potential claim, defense, and counterclaim. Developing a litigation chart is discussed in §2.2.

4.   Identify likely sources of proof

Most litigation involves events or transactions that have occurred in the past. The likely sources of proof will be centered on those witnesses who

---

1. See T. Mauet, Trials §2.3 (2005).
2. The elements of negligence claims are duty, breach of duty, proximate cause, injury, and damages. Duty is a legal question, however, so the terminology used here fits more to the trial proof.

have some knowledge of, and exhibits that contain information about, past events or transactions.

The usual witness sources include your client, other witnesses to the events or transactions, the opposing parties, witnesses who have no direct knowledge of the events or transactions but may have useful circumstantial information, and experts. Exhibit sources include physical objects, photographs, police reports, business records, transaction documents, and any other paperwork that has a bearing on the events or transactions involved. At this stage it is best to think expansively. Develop a long, thorough list early and refine it over time.

Finally, list the likely sources of proof of the elements of each possible legal theory on your developing litigation chart.

Example:

LITIGATION CHART

Elements of Claims, Defenses, and Counterclaims	Sources of Proof	Informal Fact Investigation	Formal Discovery
1. Negligence			
(a) negligence	plaintiff police officers bystanders defendant		
(b) causation	plaintiff defendant treating doctors police officers police reports		
(c) damages			
(1) lost income	plaintiff employer employment records		
(2) med. expenses	med. bills treating doctors pharmacy bills		
(3) disability	plaintiff treating doctors employment records		
(4) pain and suffering	plaintiff treating doctors		

Identifying the likely sources of proof is discussed in §2.2.4.

5.   Determine what informal fact investigation is necessary

Once you have identified the likely sources of proof, you then need to decide how to acquire information from those sources. Your choices are twofold: informal fact investigation and formal discovery.

Inexperienced litigators frequently use formal discovery as the principal fact-gathering method. This is often a serious mistake. It is vitally important to acquire as much information as possible *before* filing suit when formal discovery methods usually are unavailable. As a defendant, you will most likely begin the investigation after the suit has been filed, but you should still consider informal sources of proof. Rule 11 of the Federal Rules of Civil Procedure requires that a lawyer make a "reasonable inquiry" to determine if a pleading is well grounded in fact before signing the pleading.

Informal fact investigations are principally conducted by interviewing witnesses and obtaining documents, records, and other data from willing sources, and getting expert reviews of the case. These investigations have advantages and disadvantages. On the plus side, they are relatively quick and inexpensive and can be done without other parties being present. This is important because evidence can become lost unless identified and obtained quickly. On the negative side, while such investigations can yield important information, it is usually not developed in a way that makes it directly admissible at trial. For example, taking a written statement from a witness during an interview does not normally create a statement that is admissible as an exhibit at trial. At best, the statement is useful for impeachment.

When you have identified the witnesses and exhibits that are best reached through informal investigations, note on your litigation chart how you plan on getting the necessary information from those sources.

Example:

LITIGATION CHART

Elements of Claims, Defenses, and Counterclaims	Sources of Proof	Informal Fact Investigation	Formal Discovery
1. Negligence			
(a) negligence	plaintiff police officers bystanders defendant	interview interview interview	
(b) causation	plaintiff defendant	interview	
	treating doctors police officers police reports	interview interview request letter	

(c) damages			
(1) lost income	plaintiff employer employment records	interview interview request letter	
(2) med. expenses	med. bills treating doctors pharmacy bills	pl. possession interview pl. possession	
(3) disability	plaintiff treating doctors employment records	interview interview request letter	
(4) pain and suffering	plaintiff treating doctors	interview interview	

Informal fact investigations are discussed in Chapter 2.

6. Determine what formal discovery is necessary

Formal discovery can ordinarily be used only after suit has been filed. For that reason, it is the last stage of the fact-gathering process. It also has benefits and risks. On the plus side, it is usually the only way to get information from the opposing party and other hostile or uncooperative witnesses. In addition, the information is often in a form that makes it admissible at trial. For example, obtaining business records from an opposing party or a nonparty will generate an exhibit that will usually be admissible at trial. On the negative side, formal discovery is time consuming and expensive. In a case with a modest litigation budget, formal discovery may be substantially curtailed because of its cost.

Once you have decided which witnesses and exhibits must be reached through formal discovery, you have to decide which of the discovery methods are best suited to obtaining the necessary information. Each of the formal discovery methods — initial disclosures, interrogatories, documents requests, depositions, physical and mental examinations, and requests to admit facts — is particularly suited to obtaining certain types of information. To be both effective and cost efficient in obtaining the missing information, the methods must be carefully selected and used in the proper sequence.

Formal discovery serves two purposes: obtaining information you need to get but don't have and pinning down your opponent and other witnesses on facts you already have. You will need to use formal discovery to obtain missing information from your opponent and uncooperative witnesses and other sources. You will want to pin down your opponent to learn where the key factual disputes in the case will be and to make your proof easier if the case later goes to trial. Although there is some overlap, each discovery method is particularly suited for certain kinds of information.

The Federal Rules of Civil Procedure recognize six discovery methods:

1. Initial disclosures — Rule 26
2. Interrogatories — Rule 33
3. Requests to produce documents, electronically stored information, and tangible things — Rule 34
4. Depositions — Rule 30
5. Physical and mental examinations — Rule 35
6. Requests to admit facts and genuineness of documents — Rule 36

Initial disclosures, part of the required disclosures, govern four categories of information: the identity of persons likely to have discoverable information; the production of documents, data compilations, and tangible things; a computation of claimed damages; and the production of insurance agreements. Initial disclosures are automatic and do not require a request or any action from the other side.

Interrogatories are most effective for obtaining basic factual data from other parties, such as the identity of proper parties, agents, employees, witnesses, and experts, and the identity, description, and location of documents, records, and tangible evidence. They may be useful in obtaining other parties' positions on disputed facts. On the other hand, interrogatories are not usually effective instruments for getting detailed impressions and versions of events.

A request to produce documents, electronically stroed information, and tangible things is the discovery method by which one obtains from another party or a nonparty witness copies of records, documents, data, and other tangible things for inspection, copying, and testing. Such a request also permits an entry on another person's land or property to inspect, photograph, and analyze things on it. This is the only discovery device that forces another person actually to produce records and things or to permit entry onto his property to copy, photograph, or study evidence found there.

Depositions can be used on nonparty witnesses as well as parties. They are most effective in obtaining details, tying down parties and witnesses to details, and discovering everything they know pertinent to the case. It is the only discovery vehicle that permits you to assess how good a witness a person is likely to be at trial. It is an excellent vehicle to secure admissions or other evidence favorable to your side. Further, a deposition is the only method that preserves testimony if a witness becomes unavailable for trial.

A physical and mental examination of a party can be obtained by court order when the physical or mental condition of that party is in issue, a situation most common in personal injury cases. While other discovery methods can be used to get records of past examinations, this is the only means of forcing a party to be examined and tested prospectively. For that reason it is the best method for evaluating a party on such damages elements as permanence and extent of injury and medical prognosis.

Finally, a request to admit facts is the method that forces a party to admit or deny facts or a document's genuineness. Requests to admit are used principally to pin down the other party to specific facts to learn what facts will be conceded or disputed at trial. An admitted fact is deemed conclusively admitted for the purpose of the pending trial. This method is effective if limited to simple factual data, such as someone's employment on a specific date, or the genuineness of signatures on a contract. It is not a good method for dealing with opinions or evaluative information.

When you have identified the witnesses and exhibits that must be reached through formal discovery methods, note on your litigation chart what discovery methods you plan to use to obtain the missing information. You might also annotate your litigation chart by putting question marks next to topics that you are unsure of or by writing in numbers to reflect your planned discovery sequence.

Example:

LITIGATION CHART

Elements of Claims, Defenses, and Counterclaims	Sources of Proof	Informal Fact Investigation	Formal Discovery
1. Negligence			
(a) negligence	plaintiff police officers bystanders defendant	interview interview interview	deposition? deposition & interrogatories
(b) causation	plaintiff defendant treating doctors police officers police reports	interview interview interview request letter	 deposition deposition?
(c) damages			

(1) lost income	plaintiff
	employer
	employment
	  records
		interview
		interview
		
		request letter
			
			request to
			  admit

(2) med. expenses	med. bills treating doctors pharmacy bills	pl. possession interview pl. possession	 deposition? request to admit
(3) disability	plaintiff treating doctors employment records	interview interview request letter	 deposition?
(4) pain and suffering	plaintiff treating doctors	interview interview	deposition?

Formal discovery is discussed in Chapter 6.

7.   Identify solutions

There are many ways to deal with conflict, and litigation is only one of them. Before a decision to litigate is made, a client's problems should be considered in broad terms to determine what approach will best serve the client's immediate and long-term interests. The best approach must be arrived at through discussion with the client, with whom the decision about what to do ultimately rests. There are several basic possibilities:

1.   Do nothing
2.   Seek an informal resolution
3.   Seek formal dispute resolution
4.   Litigate

Doing nothing should always be considered. The case may simply be a high-risk case. The amount realistically recoverable may not be enough to justify the financial cost of seeking it. In addition, the noneconomic costs should always be assessed. Your client may not have the resolve to get involved in a lengthy fight. He may not want to take his time, and that of others, away from other pressing concerns. He may have more important ongoing business, professional, or personal relationships with the adversary. Finally, negative publicity surrounding the disputed matter may make litigation prohibitive. If you decide nothing should be done, let the client know and get his agreement in writing so you can formally end the case and your representation.

If your client decides to push ahead, you should always consider resolving the dispute informally. Your adversary may also wish to avoid a lengthy, expensive battle. He may admit liability, and dispute only damages. It is always worthwhile to look at informal solutions before battle lines are drawn.

If informal solutions are impossible, think next about alternative dispute resolution, such as mediation, arbitration, and summary trials. These can be relatively quick and inexpensive, and frequently are required in commercial contracts. By getting an impartial, experienced outside party involved, the adversaries can frequently get advisory opinions or binding decisions on both liability and damages.

The last possibility is formal litigation. Keep in mind that litigation is expensive and time-consuming and that even the winning litigant is rarely made whole. These realities must be driven home to the client. The worst thing that can happen is for a lawyer to quickly yield to a client's insistence to sue, only to have that client become disinterested, then uncooperative, as the realities of litigation set in. The only safe way to do this is to develop a litigation strategy, litigation budget, and litigation timetable and have your client approve them before starting the lawsuit.

Identifying solutions is discussed in §4.5.

8.   Develop a litigation strategy

Up to now you have been thinking expansively, to ensure you are not "missing the boat" on anything that might influence the case. If you and the client have decided that litigation is the only solution, it is time to focus your thinking and begin making choices.

Assume that your client has valid claims, that attempts to resolve them informally have failed, and that the client agrees that the only recourse is formal litigation. What do you do now?

Everything you do in litigation must have a purpose. A common mistake inexperienced litigators make is to conduct litigation mechanically so that it becomes an end unto itself, rather than becoming a means to an end. Always ask yourself two questions. What are my client's goals in this lawsuit? How does each thing I do help achieve those goals? Only if you constantly focus on the desired result will the individual steps in the process help achieve it. Perhaps the easiest way to think of litigation strategy is to consider its principal parts:

1.   Where can I file the lawsuit?
2.   What claims, defenses, or counterclaims should I plead?
3.   How extensive should discovery be?
4.   What motions should I plan?
5.   When should I explore settlement?

First, where can you bring the lawsuit? Can you bring the case in federal court, state court, or both? Some types of claims can only be brought in federal court, some can only be brought in state court, and still others can be brought in both federal and state courts. There are advantages and disadvantages that you must consider when you have a choice. While this choice is mainly the plaintiff's, the defendant may be able to remove the case from state to federal court.

Second, how "big" a lawsuit do you want? This decision comes at the pleading stage. There is a world of difference between a simple contract case involving two parties and a complex commercial case involving multiple parties. You have to keep in mind the consequences of your pleadings. Multiple claims frequently require multiple parties, which in turn usually generate extensive pleadings, discovery, and motions; just because the claims are there does not necessarily require that you assert them. Also, litigation must be cost conscious. Inexperienced litigators sometimes allege every conceivable claim, with the result that the client becomes immersed in expensive, time-consuming litigation, which may not be in his best interests. This is the time to review your litigation chart, see which claims and remedies are the most meritorious, and structure a lawsuit that will serve the client's objectives and that is feasible in light of the client's economic resources.

As plaintiff, when you have decided on appropriate claims and remedies, you must determine where, and against whom, you can bring the suit. In federal district court, as well as in state court, there are several procedural issues that must be considered:

1.   What parties must or can I join?
2.   Will I have subject matter jurisdiction over the claims?
3.   Will I have personal jurisdiction over the parties?
4.   Where will proper venue lie?

Asking and answering these questions is critical because they determine what actions can properly be brought in a particular court. The questions are interrelated. For example, choosing the claims and parties is affected by whether you have subject matter jurisdiction over these claims in a particular court. The choice of parties is necessarily related to the question of whether you can get personal jurisdiction over them. These decisions in turn influence the determination of where venue is proper. In short, each of these questions is to varying degrees dependent on the others.

Second, once you have decided on the pleadings, you need to select the discovery that is appropriate for your case and your purposes. What do you need to know that you don't already know or can find out through informal fact investigation? What witnesses do you need to pin down with depositions? What are your cost constraints? What order, and when, should you engage in formal discovery? How extensive should each discovery method be? Again, many inexperienced litigators mechanically begin a standard discovery sequence — initial disclosures, interrogatories, documents production, depositions, physical examination, and requests to admit — without a clear idea of what information is needed and how best to get it. Without a consistent overall litigation strategy, the case then bogs down as discovery assumes a life of its own.

Third, what motions should you plan? Your motions strategy must be part of, and coordinated with, your overall litigation plan. For instance, if you plan on moving for summary judgment on some counts, or some issues, your discovery must be focused on getting the facts that will support your motion. Now is the time to plan on making those dispositive motions and to make sure that your litigation plan, principally the pleadings and discovery, is thought through to support those motions.

Finally, when should you explore settlement, if your opposing party doesn't? Since over 95 percent of civil cases are settled before trial, you need to think through what your position on settlement should be at those points when the issue is likely to come up. This includes assessing the "value" of the case at various times, as well as the financial and emotional benefits of settlement. The likelihood of a settlement, particularly an early one, will also affect your handling of the litigation and the relationship with your adversary.

Devising a litigation strategy is discussed in §4.5.

9.   Make litigation cost and timetable estimates

A litigation cost estimate is something every litigator should make in every case. The client, particularly a sophisticated one, will always ask: "How much is this going to cost me?" All clients, except those whose cases are on a contingency fee basis, will ask this question sooner or later. You should give your client an estimate of likely costs *before* starting the litigation and get the client's approval, keeping in mind that you are dealing with an estimate, not a guarantee, and that you do not have complete control over costs.

Creating a litigation budget forces you to develop a realistic litigation plan and assess the tasks required at the beginning of the case. Over time, you will become more accurate in estimating how much time and cost the various parts of the process will likely require in a particular type of case. Many law firms use task-based litigation software that does this systematically, and many sophisticated clients will expect such an analysis when they send out requests for proposals to law firms interested in handling a substantial matter. The amount of detail these clients will expect in the litigation budget depends on the complexity of the lawsuit.

The cost estimate should be broken down by basic litigation categories. For example, in a simple personal injury case your estimate may be as follows:

Litigation Cost Estimate

Fact and legal investigation	15 hrs.
Pleadings	5 hrs.
Discovery	50 hrs.
Motions	20 hrs.
Pretrial memorandum and settlement	20 hrs.
Trial preparation and trial	60 hrs.

The total estimated time before trial totals 110 hours; trial preparation and trial will add another 60 hours. As defense counsel, if you are billing at $100 per hour, the likely cost if the case settles after the pretrial conference is $11,000; a trial will add another $6,000. Expenses, such as for experts, depositions, and travel costs, might add a few thousand dollars.

The client may not like the estimated litigation costs, but what they are and whether your client wants you to limit costs (for example, by restricting formal discovery or limiting the number of experts) must be discussed before plowing ahead. Explain the assumptions on which the cost estimate is based, and emphasize that it is only an estimate based on facts presently known.

As plaintiff's lawyer, even though you will usually handle a personal injury case on a contingency fee basis, preparing a cost estimate is still useful to determine if taking the case makes economic sense to you.

The last step in the litigation plan is to create a realistic timetable that will control the litigation. As plaintiff, you have substantial flexibility. Unless there is a statute of limitations problem, a short notice of claim period, or a particular reason to file suit quickly, you will have the advantage of time to think through your litigation plan before filing the complaint. Once the complaint is filed, the litigation timetable is largely controlled by procedural rules and judges' practices. Judges will usually hold a scheduling conference after the pleadings are filed to establish a timetable for discovery, motions, and the final pretrial conference. For example, a judge may order that all discovery be concluded within 6 months and that any dispositive motions be filed within 30 days of the discovery cut-off date, and then schedule a pretrial conference 60 days later. Even where the judge does not establish a timetable, every jurisdiction has an informal set of expectations in routine cases that you should usually follow.

When you have structured a realistic timetable for your litigation plan, it is best to plot it out on a calendar to ensure that you don't omit any steps or lose track of when particular steps should be taken.

Example (plaintiff):

Litigation Timetable

1/1 (today)	Client interview
by 2/1	Interview bystander witnesses Get pl.'s medical records Get pl.'s employment records Get police reports Interview police officers
by 3/1	File complaint
by 4/1	Interrogatories to def. Documents request to def. Deposition notice to def.
by 6/1	Depose def.
by 7/1	Depose other witnesses? Depose physicians?
by 8/1	Requests to admit to def.
by 10/1	Prepare pretrial memorandum
11/1	Pretrial conference
12/1	Anticipated initial trial date

Every client will ask: "How long is my case going to take?" Keeping in mind that your timetable is an estimate, not a guarantee, you should let the client know what your best estimate is, revising it later if necessary.

Devising a litigation timetable is discussed in §4.5.

10. Use a litigation file system

The last step is to develop and use a system for organizing your litigation files. There is no magic in doing this. All law firms have systems for the types of cases they routinely handle. Those systems include both litigation software systems that organize all electronic data in a case as well as manual file systems that organize all hard copies. The important point is that your system must be logical and clearly indexed to reflect the kinds of materials your cases will generate. It should be in place when litigation starts. The more lawyers and paralegals that work on one case, the more important it is to use a good file system.

Litigation files are usually divided into several categories. The files should have tabbed dividers for each category, and categories may be further divided. For example, discovery is frequently divided into initial disclosures, interrogatories, documents requests, depositions, mental and physical examinations, experts, and requests to admit facts.

The following file organization and categories are commonly used in routine civil cases:

1. Court documents
   a. pleadings
   b. discovery
   c. motions
   d. orders
   e. subpoenas
   f. pretrial memoranda
2. Attorney's records
   a. chronological litigation history
   b. case summary
   c. client agreement, time sheets, bills, costs, billings
   d. correspondence with client and lawyers
   e. legal research
   f. miscellaneous notes and memos
3. Evidence
   a. bills, invoices, statements, receipts
   b. correspondence between parties and with nonparties
   c. business records and public records
   d. photographs, diagrams, maps, charts
   e. physical evidence (needs to be safeguarded in secure location)

Certain paperwork, such as pleadings, orders, and correspondence, should be clipped together in chronological order with the most recent on top. Original evidence, such as bills and correspondence, should be put in clear plastic sheet protectors so that the originals will not be marked during the litigation process.

§1.3. Conclusion

This overview chapter has discussed the basic sequential steps in litigation planning. The critical concept is that every step of that plan is interdependent with every other. Each step you take influences what happens later, and the various steps you take will make sense only if they are part of an overall plan. When you are immersed in the technical details of any particular step in the process, it is easy to lose sight of that overall plan. Consequently, before doing anything, always ask yourself two questions.

Why am I doing this? How does it promote my overall litigation plan? If you never lose sight of the big picture and keep your long-term objectives in mind, you will have a much better chance to conclude your litigation with satisfactory results.

II

INFORMAL FACT INVESTIGATION

§2.1. Introduction

Preparation and planning for litigation are the critical initial components of the litigation process. Too many lawyers, however, rush to court and file a complaint to get the process started without thoroughly investigating the facts and the law and without devising a coordinated litigation strategy. Small wonder, then, that the results are frequently disappointing.

Most cases are decided by facts, not law. Litigation outcomes are usually decided according to which party's version of disputed events the fact finder accepts as true. Hence, litigators spend much of their time identifying and acquiring admissible evidence that supports their contentions and evidence that refutes the other side's contentions. That evidence at trial will be witness testimony and exhibits. Hence, the fact investigation principally involves finding and acquiring "people and paper," which means following the people trail and the paper trail. The party that is more successful in doing this will have a better chance of convincing the fact finder that its version of the facts is what "really happened."

§2.2. Structuring fact investigations

There are two ways of "getting the facts." You can get the facts informally before filing suit, and you can get them through formal discovery after suit is filed. A common mistake inexperienced litigators make is using the informal investigation, such as an initial client interview and the reviewing of an accident report, only to decide whether to take the case, and using formal discovery methods as the principal fact-gathering method. This is a serious mistake. First, information is power, and the party that has a better grasp of the favorable and unfavorable facts is in a stronger position to accurately evaluate the case. Second, information obtained early on, particularly from witnesses, is more likely to be accurate and complete. Third, information sought before the action is formalized is more likely to be obtained, since a lawsuit often makes people cautious or uncooperative. Fourth, information obtained before suit has been filed is less expensive to acquire. Formal discovery is the most expensive way to get information. It is usually more effective and less expensive to use informal discovery before filing suit and to use formal discovery methods to obtain missing information, pin down witnesses, obtain specific information and records from the opposing party, and for other such focused purposes. Fifth, Rule 11 of the Federal Rules of Civil Procedure requires that a lawyer conduct a reasonable inquiry into the facts to ensure that a pleading is well grounded. Finally, you can get information informally without the opposing parties participating, or even being aware that you are conducting an investigation. For all these reasons, then, you should use informal discovery as much as possible.

1.   When do I start?

The best time to start is immediately, particularly in cases that are based primarily on eyewitness testimony. For example, a personal injury case should be investigated as soon after the accident as possible. Witnesses forget, or have second thoughts about being interviewed; witnesses move away and disappear; physical evidence can be lost, altered, or destroyed. In this type of case, where liability will be determined largely by eyewitness testimony, it is best to start quickly.

On the other hand, an immediate investigation is not always required. For example, in contract and commercial cases, where the evidence will primarily consist of documents, correspondence, and other business records, and there is no danger that records will be lost or will disappear mysteriously, a prompt fact investigation may not be essential. Contract and commercial cases may have complex legal questions that must be researched and resolved before you can start an intelligently structured fact investigation. In addition, delay sometimes helps. For a defendant who expects to be sued, starting an investigation may only serve to stimulate the other side into investigating the case. Unless the defendant needs to investigate an affirmative defense or counterclaim, a sound approach may be simply to wait for the other side to do something.

2.   What facts do I need to get?

Your job as a litigator is to obtain enough admissible evidence to prove your claims and disprove the other side's claims. Therefore, you need to identify what you must prove or disprove. This is determined by the substantive law underlying the claims, remedies, defenses, and counterclaims in the case. However, how do you research that law if you do not yet know what the pleadings will allege? What do you research first, the facts or the law?

There is no easy answer here. In litigation, the facts and law are intertwined. The investigation of one affects the investigation of the other. You will usually go back and forth periodically as you develop your theory of the case.

Example:

> You have what appears to be a routine personal injury case. From your initial interview of the client it appears to be a simple negligence case against the other driver. You do preliminary research on the negligence claim to see if the damages are sufficient to warrant litigation. You then continue your fact investigation and discover that the defendant is uninsured. Because of this, you start wondering if there may be a claim against the municipality for not maintaining intersection markings and safe road conditions. Of course you need to research the law here. If there is a legal theory supporting such a claim, you then need to go back and see if there are facts that support that theory. Back and forth you go between getting the facts and researching the law until you have identified those legal theories that have factual support. This process, going back and forth between investigating the facts and researching the law, is ongoing and is how you will develop your "theory of the case," what really happened from your side's point of view.

3.   How do I structure my fact investigation?

The easiest way to give structure to your investigation is to use a system of organizing the law and facts based on what you will need to prove if your case goes to trial. In short, this is a good time to start a "litigation chart."[1] A litigation chart is simply a diagram that sets out what you need to prove or disprove in a case and how you will do it. The chart is a graphic way of identifying four major components of the litigation plan:

1.   Elements of claims, remedies, defenses, and counterclaims
2.   Sources of proof
3.   Informal fact investigation
4.   Formal discovery

Start with the "elements" of each potential claim and remedy in the case. Most jurisdictions have pattern jury instructions for commonly tried claims, such as negligence, products liability, and contract claims. The elements instructions will itemize what must be proved for each claim, remedy, or defense. If pattern jury instructions don't exist, more basic research will be necessary. If the claim is based on a statute, read the statute and look at the case annotations that deal with elements and jury instructions. If the claim is based on common law, consult treatises covering the claim and research the recent case law in the applicable jurisdiction. Regardless of where the applicable law is, you must find it and determine what the specific elements are. When you have done this, you will have completed the first step on your litigation chart.

---

1. The litigation chart will become a "trial chart" if the case is ultimately tried. See T. Mauet, Trials §2.3 (2005); F. Lane, Goldstein Trial Technique chs. 2–4 (3d ed. 1995).

Example:

> You represent the plaintiff in a potential contract case. Your client says she obtained goods from a seller and paid for them, but the goods were defective. From your initial client interview, and from reviewing the documents and records she provided, you decided to bring a contract claim against the defendant. Your jurisdiction's pattern jury instructions for contract claims list the elements you must prove to establish liability and damages.

LITIGATION CHART

Elements of Claims	Sources of Proof	Informal Fact Investigation	Formal Discovery
1. Contract			
(a) contract executed			
(b) pl.'s performance			
(c) def.'s breach			
(d) pl.'s damages			

This approach should be used for every other possible claim. For example, since the contract is for the sale of goods, a claim based on UCC warranties may be appropriate. If so, you should put the elements of this claim on your litigation chart. Most lawyers also use the chart for potential defenses and counterclaims.

The litigation chart has two principal benefits. First, it helps you identify what you have to prove or disprove so that you can focus your fact investigation on getting admissible evidence for each required element. Second, a litigation chart helps you pinpoint the strengths and weaknesses of your case as well as your opponent's case. In most trials the side that wins is the one that convinces the fact finder to resolve disputed issues in its favor. The litigation chart will help you identify the disputed matters on which you will need to develop additional admissible evidence to strengthen your version and rebut the other party's version.

Notice that the grid structure of your chart is just a simple spreadsheet. There are commercially available case management software programs that allow you to create and use customized fields. In addition to the four fields in the litigation chart, you can add fields for questions, favorable/unfavorable facts, lawyer assigned, and so on. You can create hyperlinks to exhibits and witness testimony. You can export facts to create chronologies. Extending the fields using a case management program allows you to use the database for evidence analysis, discovery planning, and trial preparation. Some of these programs are powerful and flexible and are extremely useful, particularly in large or complex litigation.

4.   What are the likely sources of proof?

Facts come from five basic sources: the client, exhibits, witnesses, experts, and the opposing party. Of these categories, most can often be reached by informal investigations. The client, of course, must be interviewed. Whenever possible obtain exhibits in your client's possession, and other evidence such as physical objects, photographs, documents, and records in the possession of third parties. Witnesses can frequently be interviewed. You can hire consulting experts to help analyze and prepare your case.

On the other hand, formal discovery may sometimes be the only way to get essential information. For example, important witnesses may be uncooperative and need to be deposed. Exhibits in the possession of uncooperative third parties may need to be subpoenaed. Information from the opposing party can usually be obtained only through initial disclosures, interrogatories, depositions, and other discovery methods. However, it is always worthwhile to try the informal approach first, since it is quicker, less expensive, and may be more accurate and complete.

You can interview any person willing to be interviewed, unless you know that person is represented by counsel. In that situation, ethics rules prevent you from interviewing any person known to be represented by counsel in the matter, unless the counsel gives you consent. The rule applies to employees of corporations and other organizations known to be represented by counsel. It also applies to certain former employees of corporations and other organizations.[2]

While informal fact investigations should always be conducted, their usefulness depends significantly on the particular case at hand. Some cases can be almost completely investigated through informal means, while others must rely principally on formal discovery. For example, in a routine personal injury case based on an automobile accident, you should be able to get all the basic information informally, since the principal sources will be your client, police officers, police reports, medical reports, and disinterested nonparty witnesses. By contrast, in a products liability case brought against the manufacturer of a consumer product, most of the information about the product's design, manufacture, distribution, and safety history will be in the possession of the defendant manufacturer and can be obtained only through formal discovery methods.

Regardless of the type of case, you must first identify the likely sources of proof, then decide how that proof can be obtained. The second step on your developing litigation chart is to list the likely sources of proof and correlate them to the required elements of the claims.

Example:

> In a contract case, determine the witnesses and exhibits that will provide the facts about the case. Your client, the plaintiff, is an obvious witness, and the contract is a central exhibit. Other than these

2. See Model Rules of Professional Conduct, Rule 4.2 and Comment to the rule; see also §2.5.

obvious sources, where else can you go for proof? For example, what proof is there that the plaintiff performed his obligations under the contract? The plaintiff is again a source of proof. In addition, the plaintiff may have business records showing his performance. The defendant may have written letters acknowledging the plaintiff's performance. The defendant may have business records proving performance. There may also be nonparty witnesses who have knowledge of the plaintiff's performance.

Continue this type of analysis of each element of every claim you are considering, and put those sources on your developing litigation chart.

Example:

LITIGATION CHART

Elements of Claims	Sources of Proof	Informal Fact Investigation	Formal Discovery
1. Contract			
(a) contract executed	plaintiff defendant contract pl.'s secretary		
(b) pl. performed	plaintiff pl.'s records def.'s records		
(c) def. breached	plaintiff pl.'s correspondence def.'s correspondence pl.'s records def.'s records experts		
(d) pl.'s damages	plaintiff pl.'s records replacement vendor replacement vendor's records experts		

The third step is to determine whether these sources of proof can be reached by informal fact investigation and, if so, what method is best suited to getting the necessary information. Witnesses can be interviewed;

exhibits in your client's possession should be obtained and reviewed; exhibits possessed by nonparties can frequently be obtained from friendly or neutral nonparties simply by requesting them; experts can be interviewed, and you can sometimes obtain their reports. Once again, think expansively here, since obtaining information informally is quicker, less expensive, frequently more candid and accurate, and can be obtained without the opposing party participating or perhaps even being aware that you are investigating the case. Put the methods by which you plan to obtain the information on the litigation chart.

Example:

LITIGATION CHART

Elements of Claims	Sources of Proof	Informal Fact Investigation	Formal Discovery
1. Contract			
(a) contract executed	plaintiff defendant contract pl.'s secretary	interview obtained from pl. interview	
(b) pl. performed	plaintiff pl.'s records def.'s records	interview obtained from pl.	
(c) def. breached	plaintiff pl.'s correspondence def.'s correspondence pl.'s records def.'s records experts	interview obtained from pl. obtained from pl. interview	
(d) pl.'s damages	plaintiff pl.'s records replacement vendor replacement vendor's records experts	interview obtained from pl. interview request letter interview	

The last step is to decide what to use formal discovery methods for, and how and when to use them. These considerations are discussed in Chapters 4 and 6.

5.   What is my litigation budget?

You can't buy a Cadillac on a Ford budget, and the same holds true for litigation. The client's financial resources are an important consideration. The "value" of the case, the amount you can reasonably expect in a jury verdict, is another. The amount of work the case requires for adequate preparation is a third consideration. Consequently, you need to estimate how much work the case will require, and see if it is feasible that you can accomplish the work given the resources involved. You need to prepare a litigation budget.

How do you do it? First, you need to estimate how much time you can devote to the case and whether the case can be adequately handled within that time. If a client has a limit on what she can spend, that is the outside limit. Simply divide your hourly rate — if you are billing by the hour — into the fee limit, and you will know the total number of hours you can devote to this case. If your fee is a contingency fee, you should still do the same type of calculation. Start with the dollar amount of a reasonably expected verdict after a successful trial. Reduce that amount by the likelihood that liability will not be proved. For instance, if you have a 50 percent likelihood of proving liability, reduce the expected verdict by that percentage, then divide that dollar amount by your usual hourly rate, and you will again determine the total hours you can devote to the case and still reasonably compensate yourself. Once you determine the total hours, estimate the time you will need to spend on each part of the litigation process: preliminary investigation, pleadings, discovery, motions, and trial.

Think you can't do it? You'd better start. Insurance companies and businesses, knowing that litigation makes sense only if it is cost-effective, regularly require lawyers to prepare detailed litigation budgets. Keep in mind that your time *estimates* are only that, and it is sometimes appropriate to have a range for your estimates.

Example:

> You represent the plaintiff in an automobile accident case. Your fee is one-third of any recovery. Assume that if you win at trial, your client can realistically expect a verdict of about $90,000. However, you estimate your chances of proving liability at 50 percent. This reduces the "value" of the case to about $45,000, of which you will earn $15,000. Your time is presently billed at $100 per hour. This means you can devote up to 150 hours on the case and still be paid a fee equal to your hourly rate.
>
> The case will take approximately two days to try and require about four days of trial preparations, for an estimated total of 48 hours. How do you allocate the remaining 102 hours? Your prefiling investigation — client interviews, witness interviews, exhibits acquisition, legal research, and just plain thinking about the case — may require about 25 hours. Preparing and responding to pleadings may take about 10 hours. Preparing and responding to discovery

will require the largest amount of time, approximately 50 hours.[3]
Making and responding to motions may take another 15 hours.
Preparing pretrial memoranda and attending pretrial conferences
may require 15 hours. How does your budget add up?

Investigation	25 hrs.
Pleadings	10 hrs.
Discovery	50 hrs.
Motions	15 hrs.
Pretrials	<u>15 hrs.</u>
	115 hrs.

You didn't come within the allocated 102 hours, but your initial time estimates are reasonably within range. With experience, you will become more
accurate in estimating time requirements of particular cases and in estimating the likelihood and amounts of a recovery. This will help you determine
if you should take a case to begin with, and, if you do, how much time you
can realistically expect to devote to the various stages of its preparation
and trial.

However, always keep in mind that your ethical obligations to the
client must ultimately control your handling of the client's case. You
have an obligation to handle the case competently; your performance is
determined by the requirements of the case, not the anticipated fee.[4]

6. What sources should I investigate?

The basic sources for informal investigations are fourfold: the client,
exhibits, witnesses, and experts. Your litigation chart will provide the direc-
tions for your informal fact investigation. That investigation should focus
on obtaining basic facts — favorable and unfavorable — about the case
and identifying credible, admissible evidence for each claim you are
considering.

How extensive should your fact investigation be? It needs to be
thorough enough to fill out your litigation chart, to the extent that you
can do so through informal fact investigation, while meeting the cost constraints you have established. Practically, this means several things. First,
the client must be interviewed as often as necessary to learn everything she
knows about the case. You will also need to interview her periodically as you
gather additional information from other sources.

---

3. Determining how to allocate these 50 hours among the various discovery methods is discussed in detail in §6.3.
4. See Model Rules of Professional Conduct, Rule 1.1.

Second, you should try to obtain all key documents, records, and other exhibits. In a personal injury case, this includes the police accident reports, hospital and doctor's records, insurance claims records, and employment history. These can often be obtained informally, and many jurisdictions have statutes that require they be released to the client on request. In a contract case, this includes the contract, correspondence, invoices, shipping records, and related business records. Where physical evidence is important, it should be safeguarded or photographed before such evidence is altered or possibly lost.

Third, witnesses usually need to be identified, located, and interviewed, although what you do will depend on the particular case. In most cases, what witnesses say is critical. For example, in a personal injury case, where the plaintiff and defendant are likely to have contradictory versions of how the accident happened, the testimony of neutral witnesses will frequently control the liability issue. You need to identify, locate, and interview them whenever possible. On the other hand, witness testimony is not invariably critical at trial. For example, in a contract or commercial case, the issues are frequently decided by the documents, records, or substantive law. In such a case there may be no advantage in interviewing witnesses quickly.

Finally, in some cases you will need to consult appropriate experts early in your investigation. For example, in medical malpractice and products liability cases, plaintiff's lawyers usually have the case reviewed by a physician and a technical expert before filing suit. You might as well see what a qualified expert thinks of the strengths and weaknesses of your case now.

§2.3.   *Client interviews*[5]

The initial meeting between client and lawyer may be the most important meeting in the client's life. How it goes will largely determine the nature of that relationship during the course of the litigation. Understanding what is involved in that meeting is critically important.

Client interviewing has two components: what information to get, and how to get it. What to get will be determined by your litigation chart. How to get it is based on interviewing techniques that must be fully understood in order to get the important information from the client.

1.   Client attitudes and disclosure

The typical client is unsure of his rights and obligations, and a lawyer's office is an unfamiliar, imposing environment. The lawyer who empathizes with the client's psychological needs and knows the factors that promote and inhibit client disclosure will be more successful in getting an accurate picture of the problems that brought the client to a lawyer in the first place.

---

5. There are several excellent texts that discuss and illustrate in detail the dynamics of client interviewing. See, e.g., D. Binder & S. Price, Legal Interviewing and Counseling (1993); S. Krieger et al., Essential Lawyering Skills (1999).

A client comes to a lawyer to determine if there are actual legal issues relative to his problems and, if so, how to deal with them. The lawyer needs to interview the client so she can identify the legal issues, get all relevant available information, and discuss with the client how the problems can best be handled. How does a lawyer go about getting that information from the client?

There are several factors that can inhibit a client from a full disclosure of information. First, a client being interviewed often feels that he is being judged. This causes the client to withhold or distort facts that may create negative impressions about the client or his case. Second, a client being interviewed often tries to satisfy what he feels are the lawyer's expectations. This causes the client to tell the lawyer what he thinks will be a pleasing story and, again, to withhold negative and contradictory facts. Third, a client may have a variety of internal reasons, such as embarrassment, modesty, and fear that, once again, prevent him from disclosing all information.

On the other side, there are positive factors that promote full disclosure. First, a client is more likely to disclose fully if he feels that the lawyer has a personal interest in him. A friendly, sympathetic lawyer is more likely to get "all the facts" from a client. Second, a client is more likely to disclose fully if he senses that the lawyer is identifying with him. The lawyer who lets the client know that "she's been there too," or is familiar with and understands the client's situation, is more likely to draw out all the facts. Third, some clients enjoy being the center of attention. Supplying critical information makes the client feel important and may stimulate his supplying more information. Fourth, a client enjoys feeling that he is doing the right thing. The lawyer who can instill the feeling that full disclosure is the proper, decent approach is more likely to achieve it.

Lawyers will obtain the fullest possible disclosure by stressing the positive psychological influences and by understanding and minimizing negative influences that inhibit disclosure. Lawyers who create a comfortable physical environment and show an understanding and appreciation of the client will be more successful in obtaining "all the facts," both good and bad. This sensitivity will establish a positive context for client relations during the course of the litigation process.

2.   Interview environment

Creating a positive interview environment has several components. What kind of physical setting should you have? How will you record what the client says? What should the client do to prepare for the interview? What topics will you cover during the actual interview?

Many clients will be uncertain and insecure during the interview. After all, it may be the first time they have ever been to a lawyer's office. A physical setting that is informal, friendly, and private will help make a client feel relaxed and comfortable. A lawyer's private office is a good place to conduct an interview; a small conference room is another.

Strive for informality. Sit in a place other than behind your desk, have coffee and soft drinks available, perhaps play quiet background music. Avoid interruptions. Leave the telephone alone, and close the door to keep others out. Schedule the interview so that you will have enough time to accomplish what you have planned. An interview with a client can easily take one or two hours, but perhaps much more. If possible, schedule client interviews as the last appointment for the day, provided you are still mentally sharp at that time. This will allow you to continue the interview without running out of time because of other appointments. Remember that as you are sizing up the client, the client is sizing you up as a lawyer.

A principal function of a client interview, in addition to establishing rapport and gaining the client's trust, is to obtain information. This information needs to be recorded and there are several ways to do this. First, you can take notes yourself. This has the advantage of allowing for privacy, but has the disadvantage of interfering with your interview. Second, you can have someone else, a secretary, clerk, or paralegal, take notes. Here the advantage is that you are relieved of note taking, but it puts a third person into the interview environment, which may be an inhibiting influence, particularly during the client's first interview. Third, you can tape record the interview with the client's permission. Here the advantage is completeness. However, you will still need to make a summary of the interview, and many clients are uncomfortable having their statements recorded. Fourth, you can avoid taking notes altogether and dictate notes immediately following the interview. This has the advantage of conducting the interview without distractions, but has the disadvantage that your notes of the interview may not be as complete as they otherwise would be.

The paramount consideration is creating an atmosphere in which the client feels comfortable and tells everything she knows about the problems that brought her there. Most lawyers conduct the initial part of the interview without note taking. After the client becomes comfortable with you and the interview environment and you begin to get the details of her story, you can discuss the need to record what she says and then ask her if she will feel comfortable with the method you suggest. Once you explain why it is so important for you to have an accurate record of what she says and how the attorney-client privilege will prevent anyone else from getting it, the client will usually agree.

What can you have the client do to prepare for the first interview? First, the client should be told to collect all available paperwork, such as letters, documents, bills, and other records. Second, many lawyers ask the client to write down everything she can remember about the legal problems, particularly if they involve a recent event, list the names of all persons involved, and create a chronology of events. If the client's memo is directed to the lawyer, and no one outside the lawyer's staff is permitted to see it, the memo should be protected by the attorney-client privilege, even though the attorney-client relationship may not yet formally exist.[6] The records and memo should be brought to the initial interview.

Some lawyers, particularly plaintiff's personal injury lawyers, frequently use paralegals to screen prospective clients by conducting the "intake interviews." The interviewing techniques discussed here

6. See Wright & Miller §2017; McCormick on Evidence §§88–89 (5th ed. 1999); Fed. R. Civ. P. 26.

obviously have equal applicability regardless of who does the initial client interview.

3. Initial client interview

The initial client interview should have several objectives, although accomplishing all of them may require more than one session. First, conduct yourself in a manner that establishes a good working relationship. When the client arrives at your office, don't make him wait. Greet him personally. Have the client make himself comfortable in your office or conference room, and spend a little time making small talk—about traffic or the weather, for instance. Offer him coffee or a soft drink. Remember that the client is sizing you up both as a lawyer and as a person. Second, spend a few minutes learning about the client's background. This shows the client that you see him as a human being and not just as another case. It also helps you evaluate the client as a witness and provides important biographical and financial information. Third, let the client know what is going to happen during the interview, what you need to accomplish, and the reasons for it. Explain that you need to get all the important facts in order to intelligently identify and analyze his legal problems. Stress the importance of candor and completeness. Give the client an overview of the litigation process and why this interview is an important part of it. Tell the client that his conversations with you and your staff are private and protected (privileged), so long as the client does not tell anyone else about the conversations (which would waive the privilege).

Fourth, have the client identify the general nature of his problems. You will usually have a general idea—a "car accident," a "contract problem"—when the client makes the appointment. However, it is always useful to have the client initially tell his story his own way, without interruptions, sizing him up as a trial witness. You may also discover facts you might never otherwise have stumbled upon, and it allows the prospective client to get the matter off his chest in his own words. These considerations are well worth "wasting time" on, even if the client talks about seemingly irrelevant things. The usual way to get the client to tell the story his way is to ask open-ended, nonleading questions. For example, simply asking, "I know you were in an accident. Why don't you tell me what happened in your own words?" will usually get the client started. While the client tells his story, listen not only to what he says but also note things he omits, things that would usually be mentioned. When the client is done, you can paraphrase what he has said. This serves as a check on accuracy and shows the client that you have been listening carefully.

Fifth, after the client has told his story, you need to get a detailed chronological history of the events and other background facts. It is frequently advantageous to make an outline or checklist so that you do not overlook important topics. Your litigation chart, setting out the elements of the claims you are considering, should provide a start. Get a set of your jurisdiction's uniform or pattern interrogatories for this kind of case. (These will be sent to your client to answer after the lawsuit is filed, so you might as well get the information you will need to answer them now.) It is sometimes useful to look at deposition checklists for this type of case and witness.[7] These may help you develop ideas for the topics and necessary details as you go through the history of the case. However, don't use a checklist as a questionnaire, since your interview will quickly lose the personal touch. The standard method is to use the chronological storytelling approach. Most people think chronologically, and that is usually the best way to elicit details. While your checklist should be tailored to fit the particular case involved, you will usually cover the same basic topics regardless.[8]

Sixth, you need to ask follow-up questions on potential problem areas. Here it is best to use specific, focused questions that bear on potential claims, remedies, defenses, and counterclaims (although most lawyers avoid aggressively cross-examining clients during the first meeting). A client naturally wants to impress his lawyer and convince her that the case is a good one, so he will often give only "his version" of what are disputed facts and omit altogether the unfavorable ones. It is always better to get the bad news early. Remind the client that your job is to get all the facts, both good and bad, so you can accurately assess the case and represent him effectively.[9] Remind him that the opposing lawyers will discover the bad facts soon enough, so it is better to deal with them now. This will usually keep him from adopting an "I thought the lawyer was on my side" attitude.

Where do you probe? Look for information that might adversely affect the client's credibility. Are there problems with the client's background? Is there a spotty work history? Are there prior convictions or other such trouble with the law? Clients frequently omit negative facts in their background. Therefore, you should be looking for the gaps and asking what the client has left out of the story. For example, in an automobile accident case, has the client omitted the fact that he was given a traffic citation? Was driving with a suspended license? Was drinking? Had just left a bar before the accident happened? Or was using a car without permission? A useful device in getting out these kinds of facts, without directly suggesting to the client that you don't believe his story, is to get the client to be a kind of devil's advocate. Ask him what the other side is probably going to say to his lawyer about the event. This will frequently draw out the "other side's version" of the disputed facts. Keep in mind that under Rule 11 it is at your peril that you accept your client's version of the facts. The client needs to be pushed, probed, even cross-examined to test the facts he gives you. You may need to verify his version of the facts with an independent investigation.

The usual topics you will need to discuss with the client during the initial interview include the following.

---

7. See, e.g., D. Danner, Pattern Discovery (series 1981–1996).

8. See D. Baum, Preparation of the Case §§1.10–1.21 (Art of Advocacy Series 1984); J. DeMay, The Plaintiff's Personal Injury Case: Its Preparation, Trial and Settlement (1977); R. McCullough & J. Underwood, Civil Trial Manual II 57–72 (1980); J. Werchick, California Preparation and Trial §§1.2–1.6 (1981).

9. This is required in any event by Rule 11's "reasonable inquiry" duty.

a. Statute of limitations

Determine when the statute of limitations begins to run on all potential claims, and when it ends. If the time to file a lawsuit is about to end, you will need to file a complaint quickly to toll the statute and protect the client's rights.

b. Liability

Facts bearing on the liability of all parties must be developed fully. Details are critical. For example, in an automobile accident case, you will need to explore how the accident happened step by step. You need to get a detailed description of the scene of the collision. Diagrams and charts are very helpful. You need to establish the location of each car involved before the collision occurred, at the point of impact, and after the accident had run its course. You need to get details on speed, distance, time, and relationship to road markings. In a contract case, you will need to get a detailed chronology of all contacts between the parties before the contract was executed, when it was executed, and all events that have happened since it was executed.

c. Damages

Damages information must be obtained, for both your client and all other parties, for each possible claim. For example, in an automobile collision case, damages should include out-of-pocket expenses, lost income, future expenses, and future lost income, as well as intangible damages such as permanence of injury, and pain and suffering. Find out if the client suffered an injury, the extent of it, how she was treated, how she felt then and feels now, and how the injury has affected her life. Find out if she had a preexisting condition that could affect damages. You should also explore insurance coverage for all parties, as well as collateral sources such as health insurance, employer benefits, and government entitlements (e.g., Social Security and Veterans Administration benefits). In contract and commercial cases, and cases in which equitable relief is sought, you need to determine if the injuries to the client can be measured in monetary terms.

You must determine if the defendant has the ability to pay a judgment. Find out if the defendant has insurance, the amount of the policy's coverage, and if the policy covers the event or transaction. Determine the defendant's income sources and assets, particularly those that can easily be attached to collect a judgment. When representing a defendant, determine if the defendant has any insurance policies that may cover some or all of the claims against the defendant, and notify the insurance companies of the claims. Failure to do so in a timely manner may affect the insurance coverage and the insurance company's duty to defend.

d. Client background

Your client's background is important for several reasons. The client's personal background — education, employment, family history — is important for assessing the client's credibility as a trial witness. His financial background — income and assets — is important for assessing damages. Finally, the client's financial picture bears on a mundane but obviously important question: Does he have the ability to pay you? You need to get this background information from the client early on, but be sure you let the client know why this personal information is important for your evaluation of the case.

After you have obtained your client's background information, consider corroborating it. Obtain a claims check on the client to see if he has sued, or been sued, previously. Obtain a credit check to evaluate the client's financial condition. Do a background check for any criminal convictions and bankruptcies. The Internet can be a useful source for information, particularly about corporate clients.

e. Parties

It is frequently difficult to ascertain who all the parties to an event or transaction are and, if businesses are involved, their proper legal identities. Often the client does not know and has given little thought to this aspect of the case. Now is the time to begin obtaining the facts that will help you identify those parties. Once again, Rule 11 requirements must be kept in mind. For example, in an automobile accident case you will need to know not only who the other driver was, but also who owns the other vehicle and whether it is a business or rental vehicle, or was loaned or stolen. You will also need to know where the accident occurred and need to determine who owns, or is in control of, the accident location, since that entity may be responsible for designing, building, and maintaining the roadways. If a workplace accident is involved and state law bars bringing an action against the employer because of the workers' compensation act, look for other potential defendants, such as manufacturers of equipment or independent contractors.

From your fact investigation you will usually be able to identify the parties you will want to name in your lawsuit. However, identifying parties is not the same thing as learning the proper technical identity of parties. For example, just because the truck that ran into your client had the name "Johnson Gas" on its side does not necessarily mean that the Johnson Gas Company is a properly named party. The potentially liable party may be a sole proprietorship or a corporation with a different name entirely. You need to find this out.

For individuals, learn their correct full names. For corporations, partnerships, unincorporated businesses, and other artificial entities, you must not only learn the proper names, but also whether they are subsidiaries of other entities that should be brought in as parties. Each state's Secretary of State or Corporation Commission usually has a list of domestic and foreign corporations licensed to do business within that state. Such lists usually show the state of incorporation and principal place of business, which is useful for determining if diversity jurisdiction exists, and state who the resident agent is for service of process. If the party is an unincorporated business operating under an assumed name, you may be able to determine the true owners and properly named parties by consulting an assumed-name index, required by many jurisdictions.[10]

f. Defenses, counterclaims, and third-party claims

Plaintiffs and defendants alike must look closely at a frequently over-looked area: What do they have on us? And who else can be brought into the case? Cases are legion where a plaintiff has filed an action only to be hit with a much larger, previously dormant, counterclaim. Think expansively, particularly in the commercial area, since the parties usually will have had previous dealings that could give rise to counterclaims or third-party claims. You should look at both related and unrelated transactions, since liberal joinder rules usually permit raising unrelated claims in the same action.

g. Witnesses

The client must be questioned on all possible information sources, whether eyewitnesses, experts, or anyone else who possibly has useful information. Get names and information that will help to identify and locate people with information. Think expansively here, and don't be concerned with the admissibility of testimony at this point. Find out who your client has already talked to about the case, what he has said, and whether he has signed any written statements, reports, or claim forms.

h. Records

The client should bring to the interview all paperwork in her possession, such as accident reports, insurance claims and policies, bills, checks, personal records, medical records, tax records, business records, and correspondence. If the client does not bring them, have her do so as soon as possible. You should keep these records; if the client needs them, make photocopies for her. Learn what other records may exist and who has them, so that these can be obtained now, or later through discovery.

i. Physical evidence

Does the case involve objects such as vehicles, machinery, or consumer products? While most common in negligence and products liability cases, such evidence can exist in other cases as well. How to locate, obtain, and preserve physical evidence is discussed in §2.4.

---

10. The capacity of individuals, corporations, and unincorporated associations to sue is governed by Rule 17, which refers to state law. Hence, you must always check state law to determine whether a party has capacity to sue or be sued, and what the technically proper party is.

j. Other lawyers

Clients often shop around for lawyers. While a client has a perfect right to talk to more than one lawyer about taking a case, there are always clients who go from door to door until they find a lawyer willing to take it. It is important to find out if the client has seen other lawyers about the case. On the theory that lawyers turn down cases because the cases lack merit, you should be appropriately cautious.

k. Client goals

What does the client really want? In some cases, such as personal injury, the answer is often simple. The plaintiff basically wants money damages and the defendant wants to avoid paying them. But even then it is important to probe deeper. What does the client view as a favorable outcome? Does he want the case to go to trial, or is he willing to have it settled? Is he looking for vindication, revenge, or other satisfaction not related to money damages? In other cases, such as contract and commercial disputes involving businesses, the answer may be difficult to discern. Money damages is not always what the client wants or needs. The dispute may be with another business with which the client has an ongoing relationship, and that relationship may be more important than the money damages. Perhaps relief such as specific performance is more important than money damages. Now is the time to find out what the client thinks he wants and begin assessing whether his expectations are realistic or need to be modified.

Avoid predicting what the case is "worth," or when the client will get any money. These are questions that all clients ask sooner or later, usually sooner. Explain that you cannot at this early stage make any such predictions and that it would be foolish to do so before you have gathered more information, researched the applicable law, and are then in a position to make an informed analysis of the strengths and weaknesses of the case. Consider putting this in writing in a follow-up letter to the client. When the case reaches the settlement stage, some clients always think that the settlement amount is much less than what the lawyer earlier "said the case was worth."

l. Next steps

Following a client interview, write a short memo evaluating the client and her story. It is easy to forget your specific impressions of a client, yet her credibility as a trial witness will often be critical to her case's success. This is particularly important where more than one lawyer will work on the file.

If you conclude from the initial client interview that you will take the case, you will need to discuss the details of a contractual relationship, including fees, and you should let the client know what steps you will take concerning her problem and what she will need to do to help you. These are discussed in §4.3.

4. Follow-up client interviews

Many things should be done during the initial interview of the client. Some cases are relatively simple, and interviewing a well-prepared client can take less than an hour. Many cases, however, will require more than one session to collect the basic information. Accordingly, you might use the first session just to build rapport with the client, get the client's story out, and compile a chronology of events. A second session could then be used to review the client's records and ask focused follow-up questions about problem areas. In more complicated cases, it may take several client interviews to acquire the necessary information.

Follow-up interviews will also be periodically necessary during the litigation process. Whenever you receive additional information, through informal fact investigation or during formal discovery, you should review it with the client. The new information may differ from what the client previously told you. Obviously the contradictory information must be evaluated, discussed with the client, and dealt with. In some cases the client may admit that what he previously told you was not entirely true, and change his story. In others, he may deny the new information and stick to his version of the facts. Whatever the client's position, the new information, if it is at odds with the client's story, must be dealt with. Is it true? Is it more accurate? What does the new information do to the client's story? This is an ongoing process, but the key point to remember is that the client must be kept informed as the fact-gathering process progresses.

§2.4. *Exhibits acquisition*

Your interviews with the client should also identify future exhibits. These include the scene, physical evidence, documents, and records. In addition, interviews with witnesses and your review of exhibits when you get them, particularly documents and business records, may disclose additional exhibits.

You need to acquire these exhibits, get copies of them, or protect them from being lost or altered. The order in which you do things will depend on how important it is to obtain the particular exhibits. For example, physical evidence, such as the condition of a vehicle, machine, or consumer product, should be acquired quickly, before it is repaired, altered, destroyed, or becomes lost. Some records, such as a police accident report, are essential for you to begin your investigation.

The basic types of exhibits are the following.

1. Scene

If a lawsuit involves an event, such as an automobile accident, investigating the scene is vital. Whenever possible, the lawyer should visit the scene, even if someone else will do the technical investigation. That should include taking photographs of all locations from a variety of perspectives and making all necessary measurements so that you can make scale diagrams. Photographs should be both in black and white and in color and be enlarged to 8 inches × 10 inches for courtroom use. Diagrams for courtroom use should be at least 30 inches × 40 inches. While photographic enlargements and courtroom diagrams need not be made until shortly before trial, the necessary preparations should be made now. You should visit the scene at the same time and day of week on which the event occurred, so your photographs will accurately show the relevant lighting, traffic, and other conditions. You might also find additional witnesses to the event — people who are there each day at that time.

If you are reasonably proficient in taking photographs and have the equipment to take photographs that can be processed and enlarged with sufficient quality to make effective courtroom exhibits, you can take them yourself. This will not create a problem for you, a lawyer in the case, becoming a witness, since any person familiar with how the scene looked at the relevant time is a competent qualifying witness. However, where you will be the only person who can qualify the admission of the photographs, obviously someone else must come along because the lawyer cannot usually be a witness in a case she is trying. If you are not a proficient photographer, hire a commercial photographer to accompany you. You must tell the photographer specifically what pictures you will need.

Numerous photographs should be taken from a variety of perspectives. For example, in an intersection collision case, you will normally want pictures of how the intersection looked to each of the drivers as they approached it. Accordingly, pictures should be taken in the road from the appropriate lane, with the camera held the same distance above the road as the driver's head. Several pictures should be taken, starting from perhaps 300 feet away, then moving to 150 feet, and so on. The photographs will then show what each driver saw as he approached the intersection. In addition, photographs should be taken from where other eyewitnesses, such as other drivers and pedestrians, were when the crash occurred. Finally, if there are nearby buildings, it's always useful to have overhead, bird's-eye-view pictures taken that will show lane markings, pedestrian walkways, traffic signs, and signals in the intersection. You must review witness statements beforehand to know where the witnesses were, and what they saw and did, before you can know what photographs you will need.

Diagrams present a different problem. Since the person who took the measurements and made a scale diagram is often the only witness who can qualify the diagram for admission in evidence, it is better to have someone other than the lawyer do this.

2. Physical evidence

Physical evidence, such as vehicles, machinery, and consumer products, if not already in the possession of police, other investigative agencies, or your client, must be obtained and preserved for possible use at trial. This includes not only locating them, but also keeping them in the same condition and establishing chains of custody. This is particularly important if the evidence will be tested by experts before trial. When you cannot take or move evidence for safekeeping, take a thorough series of photographs and sufficient measurements so that you can make accurate diagrams and models for trial.

Preserving physical evidence often requires that you act quickly. In an automobile accident case, for example, skid marks and the condition of the vehicles involved will be lost as the skid marks wear off and the vehicles are repaired. In these situations you must take immediate steps to prevent the loss, destruction, or alteration of the evidence and ensure a chain of custody when such a chain will be an admissibility requirement.[11] Have someone such as an investigator do this, since he may be a necessary witness at trial.

How do you actually "preserve" physical evidence? Two concerns are involved. First, you must gain actual physical possession of the objects so that they are kept in the same condition until the trial. Second, you must either label the objects or, if they cannot readily be labeled, put them in a container that can be sealed and labeled. Both of these steps ensure admissibility at trial by establishing the two basic requirements — identity and same condition. The usual way to accomplish this is to have someone like an investigator, who can serve as a trial witness, get the objects from wherever they are, label or put them in a container that is sealed and labeled, and have them taken to your office for safekeeping. This label should describe the object, show where it came from, who obtained it, when it was taken, and who received it at your office.

Evidence is frequently in the possession of nonparties, such as police departments and repair shops. If the evidence does not belong to your client, the nonparties are probably under no legal obligation to preserve the evidence for you. However, most will be cooperative when they learn that what they have is important evidence. They will usually keep the evidence in an unaltered condition until you have had an opportunity to photograph and measure it. You should check if someone else, such as an investigator from the police department or insurance company, has already taken these steps. Finally, a nonparty will sometimes agree to preserve evidence until you can serve him with a subpoena, or have the court issue a protective order.

Many times, of course, a client comes to a lawyer too late to take these steps, and the evidence will be lost. If the client comes to you shortly after the event, however, you should always act quickly to preserve the evidence. Many cases, particularly in the personal injury and products liability areas, are won or lost on this type of evidence.

3. Records

You should obtain all available documents and records from your client. You may as well obtain everything your client has because once suit is filed

---

11. See McCormick on Evidence §212 (5th ed. 1999); T. Mauet, Trials §7.5 (2005).

the opposing party will be able to discover from your client anything that is relevant and not privileged. If important documents and records are in the hands of other persons, see if those persons will voluntarily turn them over or provide copies. Public records are usually available on request. In many jurisdictions persons have a statutory right to obtain certain records on demand, such as their own medical reports. A written demand on behalf of the client, coupled with her written authorization, will usually suffice. If not, contact the sources to learn the required procedure for obtaining the records. These records are, of course, usually available by subpoena after suit is filed, but it is better to get them as soon as possible, since the records may be essential to evaluate the case before suit is filed. For example, in a personal injury case, you will need to review police accident reports, doctor's reports, hospital records, employment records, and perhaps others.[12] In a contract action, you will need to get the contract itself, and records that bear on the performance and nonperformance of the parties, such as orders, shipping documents, invoices, and payment records.

If you can get these kinds of records from others, maintain them properly. Keep the records you receive together, in order, and do not mark them. Keep a record of how, from whom, and when you got them, since these persons may be necessary foundation witnesses if the case later is tried. Make additional copies that you can mark up and use during client and witness interviews.

4. Electronic research

Never overlook information that may be available on the Internet. You can find and locate people, learn about corporations and other business organizations, acquire information about products, and get medical information about diseases, hospitals, and doctors. You can obtain financial information from government and private databases, identify experts and their backgrounds, learn about business competitors and suppliers, and research opposing lawyers. Don't overlook public records that may be available online or through Freedom of Information Act requests (or its state counterpart) to the appropriate federal or state agency.

§2.5. *Witness interviews*

After you have interviewed your client, and obtained the available exhibits, the next stage of your informal fact investigation is interviewing witnesses. Here a great deal of flexibility is possible, and it is particularly important to plan ahead.

---

12. Since some records, such as hospital reports, will be technical, get a good dictionary or encyclopedia to help you understand them or use a consulting expert to evaluate them for you.

1.   Who and when to interview

The more you know, the more accurately you can assess the strengths and weaknesses of your case. It makes sense, then, to interview every witness, favorable, neutral, and unfavorable, to find out what each knows. The benefits of interviewing everyone, however, are always tempered by economic realities. There are few cases in which you can simply interview everyone regardless of expense. On the other hand, every case has critical witnesses that you must try to interview regardless of the cost. In addition, once taken, the case must be handled competently regardless of cost constraints. Between these two extremes, you need to decide whether you should try to interview a particular known witness and attempt to identify and interview others. For example, suppose you represent a party in an automobile collision case. From your client and the accident reports, you learn what other persons were present. If a police report identifies an eyewitness, you need to interview him; but what else should you do? Should you interview the police officer who wrote the report and other officers present who did not write reports? Should you try to locate bystanders who were present but have not been identified?

How far you go is determined by three basic considerations. First, you need to interview all critical witnesses regardless of cost. A competent lawyer simply must always do this. The critical witnesses are the eyewitnesses to an event, the participants to a business transaction, and other persons such as the principal investigating officers. Such witnesses will probably be witnesses at trial. In the above hypothetical, this would mean interviewing the known eyewitness, the police officer who prepared the accident report, and other eyewitnesses whose identity you are able to learn. Second, with witnesses who are not critical, interviewing *is* influenced by your cost constraints. For example, canvassing homes and stores near the accident scene may turn up someone else who saw the accident; however, doing this is expensive and may produce nothing useful. Attempting to identify and interview such possible witnesses may be worthwhile in a $200,000 lawsuit in which liability is unclear, but cannot be done in a $20,000 case where liability is clear. Third, how far you go in locating and interviewing witnesses depends on what you have developed so far. For example, if your client and two solid eyewitnesses clearly establish liability, it may not make sense to find other eyewitnesses who can corroborate the client. On the other hand, if your client's version is contradicted by one eyewitness, it is obviously important to locate and interview other witnesses to see which version they support.

When you have decided on the witnesses you need to interview, you must decide the order in which to interview them. Here again flexibility is required. It is frequently better to interview favorable and neutral witnesses first, before you interview the unfavorable ones, since you will have better success in pinpointing the differences in their stories. Identifying and interviewing the favorable and neutral witnesses first will give you the basis for your side's version of any disputed events and will help you identify the areas of disagreement when you interview the unfavorable witnesses. These areas can then be explored in detail. Frequently, however, you won't know for sure whether a given witness will be favorable.

On the other hand, there are advantages in interviewing unfavorable witnesses early before their attitudes and recall have solidified. For example, in an accident case you know a witness will be unfavorable because that witness is quoted in a police accident report. It may be useful to interview that witness quickly. He may change his mind, or tell you that he "didn't really see it happen," or "isn't sure" about important facts. You may minimize the impact of the witness through an early interview.

Are there limits on who you can interview?[13] Ethical rules control here. Under Model Rules 4.2 and 4.3, you can interview any person *not* known to be represented by counsel. (That person, of course, has a right not to talk to you.) You *cannot* interview any person *known* to be represented by counsel in the matter, unless the counsel gives you consent or you are authorized by law. This clearly means that you cannot communicate with the opposing party if you know the opposing party is represented by counsel in the matter. This rule applies even though a lawsuit has not yet been filed.

Difficult questions arise when the opposing party is a corporation or other artificial entity. The only persons who can "speak" for the corporation are its employees and agents. The Comment to Rule 4.2 sets out three categories of employees of an organization you may *not* communicate with: (1) any person having managerial responsibility on behalf of the organization; (2) any person whose act or omission may be imputed to the organization; and (3) any person whose statement may constitute an admission on behalf of the organization.

Most states have adopted some version of Model Rule 4.2. However, while all apply it to current employees, they differ in applying it to former employees. Are former employees now nonparties, so that the rule does not apply, or are they still employees for purposes of the rule? Case law in the various jurisdictions differs. Some jurisdictions follow the Comment to Model Rule 4.2, but others reject it, particularly in the third category. In this situation, jurisdiction-specific research will be necessary.

If you can properly interview a witness, what must you disclose to him? Under Model Rule 4.1, you cannot knowingly misrepresent material facts or applicable law. You must disclose that you are a lawyer representing a party, that you do not represent the witness's interests, that you are trying to gather information to help your party in a particular matter, and that the witness has the right to talk, or not to talk, to you.

13. See Model Rules of Professional Conduct, Rule 4.2; Wyeth, Talking to the Other Side's Employees and Ex-employees, 15 Litig. (no. 4, Summer 1989); J. Iole & J. Goetz, Ethics or Procedure? A Discovery Based Approach to Ex Parte Contacts with Former Employees of a Corporate Adversary, 68 Notre Dame L. Rev. 81 (1992); Restatement (Third) of the Law: The Law Governing Lawyers §§99, 100 (2000).

2.   Who should do the interviewing?

Either the lawyer or an investigator should conduct the actual interviews. There are advantages and disadvantages with each approach. If the lawyer interviews, the advantages are that no additional investigator costs are incurred, and he can get a first-hand impression of the person as a trial witness. This is particularly important with key witnesses. On the other hand, lawyer interviews can create impeachment problems. If at trial the witness denies making a statement to the lawyer, which is inconsistent with his testimony, the lawyer will have to be a prove-up witness. This puts the lawyer in conflict with ethical rules that generally prevent a lawyer from being a witness in a trial in which the lawyer represents a party.[14] A common approach is to have the lawyer personally interview witnesses known to be favorable, but have another person present when interviewing neutral or unfavorable witnesses. That person can then prove up impeachment at trial if necessary.

If an investigator interviews witnesses, the advantages are economic and practical. An investigator's time will usually be less expensive than the lawyer's, so there may be cost savings for the client. However, the time saving may be minimal, since the lawyer must spend time educating the investigator about the known facts, the issues, and about what direction the interviews should take. The principal benefits of a properly experienced investigator are that she will probably be better at locating witnesses and will be an available impeachment prove-up witness at trial.

When hiring an appropriate investigator, you should establish a contractual relationship and give her specific instructions. A contract with the investigator will prevent misunderstandings about what work will be required, what the cost limitations of the case are, and how the investigator will be paid. The contract should expressly state that the investigator will be an employee of the lawyer, and that everything the investigator learns and obtains during the investigation will be reported only to the lawyer and will otherwise be kept confidential. This will improve the chances that the investigative reports will be protected from disclosure by the attorney's work-product doctrine.[15] As always, it is best to put the agreement in writing, either in a simple contract or in a letter to the investigator.

3.   Locating witnesses

Lawyers are perfectly capable of locating many witnesses. The client frequently knows the important ones. Records, such as business records and accident reports, will usually identify others. When their names are known, it is surprising how many witnesses can be located over the telephone or by checking basic, available sources. The telephone book, neighbors at a previous address, workers at a former job, friends, and relatives are all good

---

14. See Model Rules of Professional Conduct, Rule 3.7.

15. See Rule 26(b)(3). A lawyer's notes summarizing a witness interview are usually not discoverable under Rule 26(b)(3).

sources in locating a known witness. It is often the case that a witness has merely changed a telephone number, moved to a different apartment, or changed jobs, and tracking her down is relatively simple. If these leads do not work, check with the post office, voter registration and motor vehicle departments, utility companies, and other government agencies such as the Veterans Administration, Social Security office, and unemployment and welfare agencies. If the witness is important to you and cannot be located through these types of leads, you may need an experienced investigator.

4.   Purposes of the interview

There are several purposes you should try to accomplish during a witness interview. These purposes usually should be pursued in the following order. First, learn everything the witness knows and does not know that is relevant to the case. Have the witness tell what he knows by using open-ended questions. These can be followed later with specific, focused questions; however, you want details only of the critical events and transactions, not everything the witness knows that may possibly be relevant. When learning what the witness knows, make sure you pinpoint the admissible facts based on first-hand knowledge, separating them from opinion, speculation, and hearsay. With witnesses who have unfavorable information, you should try to limit the damage by limiting the witness' testimony. Find out what the witness does not know, is not sure of, is only guessing about, or has only second-hand information about.

Second, pin the witness down. This means going beyond generalizations and getting to specific, admissible facts. For example, "driving fast" should be changed to an approximation of speed in miles per hour. "He looked drunk" should be pursued to get the details underlying the conclusion, such as "staggering, glassy eyed, and smelling of alcohol." Getting only generalizations and conclusions makes it easy for a witness to change his testimony later.

Third, get admissions. With unfavorable witnesses, having the witness admit that he "isn't sure," "didn't really see it," "was only guessing," or "was told" all serve to prevent the witness from changing or expanding his testimony at trial.

Fourth, get information that might be used for impeachment. If an unfavorable witness says something that later may be useful to impeach him, pin him down. For example, if an unfavorable witness to an accident says he was 200 feet away when it happened, make sure you commit him to that fact. Use "200 feet" in other questions, and recommit him to that fact, since at trial he may claim that the distance was shorter.

Fifth, get leads to other witnesses and information. It is surprising how often a witness will name other witnesses or divulge information not previously mentioned in any report. For example, asking a witness if anyone else was present at an accident scene will sometimes get a response like: "Sure, Ellen, my sister, was standing right next to me and saw the whole thing."

Finally, try to record the interview or get some type of written statement. How to do this is discussed later in this section.

5.   Arranging the interview

Often the most difficult part of witness interviews is getting witnesses to agree to be interviewed in the first place. With favorable witnesses this is not usually a problem, and selecting a convenient time and place for the interview is a routine matter. Unfavorable witnesses, however, are frequently reluctant. Here you can take either of two approaches: attempt to arrange an interview, or attempt a surprise interview. A reluctant witness may agree to be interviewed at a convenient time and place, where privacy is assured, and if the interview won't take too long. Let such a witness know that cooperating now may eliminate the need to be deposed later, and suggest that an interview at home would be both convenient and private. Tell the witness that you need and appreciate her help in understanding what really happened, and that her information may help resolve the case more quickly.

If a witness will not agree to an arranged interview, the only alternative is the unannounced interview. Frequently, a witness who doesn't want to be bothered or "get involved" will nevertheless agree to talk when an investigator "pops into" the witness' office or "stops by" the house. Again, it may help to reassure the witness that the questions won't take long and may eliminate the need for further involvement. However, a witness has a perfect right to refuse to be interviewed, and you cannot harass or badger the witness hoping to change her mind. The only alternative is to depose the witness after the lawsuit has been filed.

Whenever you interview a witness, you must tell her that you are a lawyer, that you represent one of the parties in a dispute, and that you represent only that party. Tell the witness what you want to talk to her about. These disclosures are clearly required by Model Rules 4.1 and 4.3.

6.   Structuring the interview

How do you go about structuring a witness interview? First, review the case file, which should contain client interviews, exhibits such as police reports, perhaps other witness interviews, and the developing litigation chart. Second, get copies of any diagrams, photographs, and records you may use during the interview. Third, decide if and how you will record the interview. Finally, prepare an outline for the interview. A frequently followed order for witness interviews is the following:

1.   Witness background
2.   Story in witness's own words
3.   Detailed chronological story
4.   Questions focused on your theory of the case

First, witness background is important for assessing witness credibility and determining if there is any bias, interest, or other facts that affect credibility. Most witnesses don't mind talking about their work, family, and home. Asking these background questions usually puts witnesses at ease. Some witnesses, however, may resent what they consider to be intrusions into their private lives. In such cases you may want to slip the background information later into the interview, or simply touch on it at the end. Second, let the witness tell her story in her own words, even at the price of hearing irrelevant facts. It gives you a good picture of the kind of witness she will be at trial, and you may discover important facts that would never have come to light. Third, go over the story in chronological order and in detail. Get specifics on what the witness saw, heard, and did at all important times, and what she saw others do and say. Find out what exhibits the witness knows of, and other witnesses she is aware of. Find out what the witness personally knows and what is only opinion, speculation, or hearsay. Find out to whom the witness has talked or given statements. Finally, ask focused questions based on your theory of the case. For example, if the witness gives information that contradicts your version of the events, see how you can minimize its effect. If the witness is "not sure," "guessing," "didn't see it myself," or says other things that lessen the damage, make sure you note it. In addition, see if the witness can corroborate something useful to your side. Witnesses are rarely completely unfavorable; a little searching will often turn up something positive.

7.   Recording the interview

Regardless of the witness, you should make a record of the interview. There are several possibilities:

1.   Use a court reporter
2.   Make a tape recording, with the witness' consent
3.   Obtain a written, signed statement
4.   Take notes during the interview
5.   Have another person take notes during the interview
6.   Make notes after the interview

The approach you use depends on what will best serve your interests and what the witness will permit. If you expect the witness to give favorable information and be cooperative, a short, written, and signed statement is often best. After interviewing the witness, simply type a summary of his story and ask him to sign it. The statement should be from the witness' point of view (e.g., "I was standing on the corner of Main and Elm when I saw . . ."). Have the witness draw and label a diagram showing where he was and what he saw. Another method is to send the witness a confirming letter summarizing what he said, and ask the witness to sign and return a copy acknowledging its accuracy. This will lock a favorable witness into his basic story, and there is no damage if the opposing side obtains the statement during discovery.[16] With unfavorable witnesses, it is often advantageous to

---

16. While a lawyer's notes summarizing a witness interview are usually not discoverable, under Rule 26(b)(3) even trial preparation materials are not absolutely protected from discovery. Upon a showing of substantial need and undue hardship, such materials are discoverable, except that "mental impressions, conclusions, opinions, or legal theories of an attorney or other representative of a party" are always protected from disclosure.

get a detailed statement. This improves your chances of getting contradictions, admissions, and impeachment that may be valuable at trial. Using a court reporter or a tape recorder is probably the most reliable method. Get the witness' permission if you plan to tape record, since surreptitious recordings are illegal in some jurisdictions. Avoid later criticism that the recording does not include everything the witness said by being mindful of when conversation is off the record.

What is best, and what a witness is willing to do, are two different things. Many witnesses are reluctant to talk, and they are usually under no legal obligation to talk to anyone, unless compelled by legal process. Of those willing to talk, many are understandably reluctant to give a signed statement or to have their statements recorded or reduced to a writing. Hence, your priority should be to get the witness to tell what he knows so you will learn what his trial testimony is likely to be, and get leads on other witnesses and evidence. Only then should you try to get the most reliable type of statement the witness agrees to give. In short, it is usually better to conduct an interview without any recording than to have no interview at all. You can always dictate immediately afterwards what the witness has said.

Whether a record of a witness interview is discoverable depends on the kind of record involved. Under Rule 26(b)(3), a "statement" is discoverable if it is "a written statement signed or otherwise adopted or approved by the person making it, or a stenographic, mechanical, electrical, or other recording, or a transcription thereof, which is a substantially verbatim recital of an oral statement by the person making it and contemporaneously recorded." If what the witness says is helpful, taking a discoverable statement usually creates no problems if the other side obtains it later, and the statement can be used to refresh memory or impeach if the witness testifies inconsistently at trial. If, however, what the witness says is unfavorable, there is usually no point in creating a discoverable statement that will only educate the other side to the fact that a good witness for them exists.

8.   Interviewing techniques[17]

Every witness is influenced by both positive and negative factors that affect her willingness to be interviewed and disclose what she knows. An interviewer, therefore, should understand these factors and use them to accomplish his primary purpose of finding out what the witness knows. These factors bear on both friendly and hostile witnesses. Hostile witnesses may be unwilling to talk at all; friendly witnesses, although willing to talk, may be influenced by a variety of negative and positive factors.

Negative factors inhibit witness disclosure. Some witnesses feel that they are being judged by the interviewer. Others tell the interviewer what he apparently wants to hear. Still others become inhibited by emotions such as fear or embarrassment. The interviewer must learn to recognize

17. See D. Binder & S. Price, Legal Interviewing and Counseling (1993); S. Krieger et al., Essential Lawyering Skills (1999).

situations in which these factors exist and use interviewing techniques that reduce their effect.

Positive factors promote disclosure. Witnesses usually respond favorably when the interviewer shows a personal interest in them. Witnesses like to feel that they are doing the decent thing by talking to the interviewer. They tend to identify with the side that values their testimony. Witnesses enjoy feeling important and may be more likely to help if they feel that the information they can provide is important to resolve a dispute fairly. Positive reinforcement is a strong motivator.

Getting witnesses to disclose fully and accurately is best achieved by minimizing the negative factors and reinforcing the positive ones. Accordingly, pick a convenient time and place for the interview. When scheduling the interview, remind the witness that it's always better to talk when the events are fresh in her mind. Remind her that it is natural to want to help others, and that her disclosing information will help ensure a just and accurate result. Point out what other witnesses have said about the case so as to give her an opportunity to correct inaccuracies. Finally, show interest in the witness. Empathy is also a strong motivator; a witness naturally will want to please someone who appears interested in her.

An interviewer can use either open- or closed-ended questions to achieve desired results. Use open-ended, direct-examination questions to get the witness talking, to obtain the basic story, and to pursue leads. For example, questions in a "describe how" and "tell me" format will force the witness to give descriptive answers. But use closed, leading cross-examination questions to pin the witness down and develop potential impeachment. This question form can focus on specific, isolated facts. For example, ask: "You're sure the car was going 40 mph?" and "She couldn't have been going faster than that, could she?"

The content of questions can also effectively influence responses. Let the witness know your attitude on the matter being discussed, since she has a psychological interest in satisfying her listener's expectations. For example, telling a witness that you feel badly about your client having been cheated by the defendant may get a more sympathetic story from the witness. Second, word choices can influence responses. For example, it is well known that using the phrase "how fast" rather than "how slowly" will increase estimations of speed. Third, leading questions are more likely to get the kind of answer you want. For example, asking a witness, "That car was going faster than the speed limit, wasn't it?" is more likely to elicit a "yes" response. Fourth, knowing what other people have said or what other evidence has already shown can influence witnesses, since witnesses prefer consistency and disdain conflict. For example, telling a witness that another eyewitness has already stated that the car was speeding will often influence the witness.

9.   Evaluating witnesses

Following a witness interview, write a short memo evaluating the witness and her information. It is easy to forget your impressions of the witness, yet witness credibility is frequently the critical component in case evaluation. The memo is particularly important if more than one lawyer will work on the file. The memo should evaluate the witness' credibility and effectiveness as a trial witness, note the witness' attitude toward the case, and summarize where the witness' anticipated testimony will help and hurt your case.[18] When evaluating witnesses, it is also a good idea to do a computer search to learn more about witnesses' backgrounds. Web sites such as MySpace can reveal things witnesses have written about themselves that reflect on their credibility.

§2.6. *Expert reviews*

Wrongful death, medical malpractice, product liability, major negligence, and commercial cases almost always use expert witnesses at trial. The plaintiff's case will probably require expert testimony to establish a prima facie case on liability and causation and to make out a solid case on damages. The defense case will probably have opposing experts. Accordingly, your investigation is frequently incomplete unless you have the file reviewed by appropriate experts.

You may need two experts: one to review the file and consult with you in order to develop facts and theories for trial, the other to be a trial witness. Of course, one expert can and sometimes does perform both roles. Remember, however, that under Rule 26(b)(4) the facts and opinions of a consulting expert are usually protected from discovery, absent exceptional circumstances, but the identity and substance of facts and opinions of experts expected to be witnesses at trial are discoverable. Hence, having a separate consulting expert will usually limit what is discoverable by other parties and should be valuable in developing theories and evidence for trial. Make sure that your agreement with the consulting expert clearly shows her status and requires that she communicate only with you, so that her work comes under the Rule 26 protection. Some lawyers require in the agreement that the client is responsible for paying the expert's fees. Doing this should not change the protection of the work-product doctrine.

If a case is complex and will involve substantial work, it may be advisable to insist that the case be reviewed by an expert before you agree to take it. The cost of the review should be paid by the prospective client. While the lawyer can usually advance the cost of the review, requiring the client to pay for the review in advance is often an effective way of weeding out clients who already know they have a weak case. Such clients will often refuse to pay for the review, which should make you think carefully about taking the case in the first place, particularly where the client has the ability to pay. This is a sensible approach whenever you have a case that will require expert witnesses. Regardless of how the review comes out, both you and

---

18. Such a memo should also be absolutely privileged as work product and therefore not discoverable. See Rule 26(b)(3).

the client will benefit. If the case is complex and will require expert witnesses, Rule 11 may require an expert's review before filing suit. Some jurisdictions require, in certain types of cases such as medical malpractice, that you have an expert who has reviewed the case and is of the opinion that it has merit, before you can file suit.

Do not send out a file for expert review until you have collected the reports and records the expert will inevitably need. Make sure the written materials you send her give a complete and neutral picture of the case, but do not give the expert privileged materials. Keep in mind that an expert who becomes the testifying expert at trial can under Rule 26(b)(4) be deposed and forced during cross-examination to produce all materials she received for her review. Materials that the lawyer gives to the expert are usually not protected by the work product privilege;[19] therefore, do not give an expert any materials that contain your mental impressions and thought processes. In addition, have the expert review the file generally, and direct the expert to specific areas where you see potential problems. This is best done in conversations with the expert, after you have sent her the necessary materials. For example, in a medical malpractice case you might ask the expert to evaluate whether the anesthetic was improperly administered, and ask the expert if the standard of reasonable care was breached. A focused review is usually more productive.

While Rule 26 makes important discovery distinctions between consulting and testifying experts, hiring an expert as a consultant does not prevent you from using her as an expert at trial. That decision may have to be made at the discovery stage, however, since the required disclosures require that you identify all experts expected to testify at trial. Again, if you list the consulting expert as a trial witness, she can be deposed and forced to produce all materials she has reviewed and, probably, disclose all communications she has had with you, even before the time she was designated as a testifying expert.

Because an expert is so important, and because a consulting expert may later be the testifying expert at trial, you must be careful in selecting one. Perhaps the best way to select an expert is simply to ask litigators you know to recommend one who is knowledgeable in the subject area of your case, is willing to work with and educate you, and will be an effective trial witness. If this fails, or you need an expert in an extremely specialized area, some lawyers' groups, such as the American Association for Justice and Defense Research Institute, maintain expert directories, and law libraries sometimes have directories for various specialties.[20]

---

19. See, e.g., Bogosian v. Gulf Oil Corp., 738 F.2d 587 (3d Cir. 1984); FRE 612.
20. See, e.g., H. Philo et al., Lawyers Desk Reference, which lists experts by category and is revised periodically. TASA, the Technical Advisory Service for Attorneys, is one of several organizations that refers experts in numerous fields. Many legal newspapers and journals also contain listings and information about experts. Local universities are a good source as well.

§2.7. The "small" case

This book discusses how to organize and investigate a case using the litigation chart method. This approach integrates the legal and fact investigations so that you can intelligently plan the litigation before filing suit, or responding to one. These are steps that every litigator should take when handling any litigation matter.

When a case is sufficiently large, perhaps with over $100,000 in issue, it makes economic sense for the litigants to devote substantial legal resources to achieve the best possible result. In such cases, the lawyers representing the parties will usually be able to do all the things a conscientious litigator should do, without being seriously constrained by cost. However, consider the client with a "small" case, involving less than $10,000, who comes to you. His case, although appearing to have merit, involves so little money that it is not economically possible to handle it competently and receive adequate compensation for the work involved. What do you do?

This is hardly a theoretical question. The "average" case filed in courts today involves approximately $50,000.[21] If that is the typical case, there are obviously numerous cases involving smaller amounts. Automobile accidents involving a few hundred dollars in direct losses, and consumer contract matters involving similarly small sums, are common disputes, and some are litigated.

The inherent conflict can be stated simply. On the one hand, every lawyer has a professional obligation to represent each client competently. On the other hand, a lawyer needs to be compensated to stay in business. How do you resolve this conflict?

The very small cases present less difficulty. Most jurisdictions have small claims courts in which the litigants can represent themselves at trial. Many jurisdictions do not allow lawyers in small claims courts, and judges hear the cases informally without adhering to strict rules of procedure or evidence. They frequently have brochures that explain how to bring a claim in small claims court and how the case will be heard. In addition, some jurisdictions have special procedures for other small cases. These frequently include restriction or elimination of discovery. The intent of both types of procedures is to bring down the cost of trying a case so that it makes economic sense to bring a lawsuit to enforce a claim in the first place. The cases that are too large to be brought as small claims, yet too small to make normal litigation cost-effective, cause the greatest problems. What can you do when presented with such cases? These small cases are particularly problematical, because a case that is small in dollar amounts may be just as legally and factually complex as a larger case.

21. See Trubek, et al., The Costs of Ordinary Litigation, 31 U.C.L.A. L. Rev. 72 (1983). The authors conducted a study of approximately 1600 civil cases in five federal districts in 1978; half were state cases, half federal. They found that over two-thirds of the cases involved tort and contract claims, and the average amount at stake was approximately $10,000 (in 1978 dollars). Over 90 percent of the cases settled before trial. The median amount of time a lawyer devoted to a single case was 30.4 hours. A 2000 study of state court jury verdicts showed a median award in automobile cases of $29,000; in all tort cases of $51,000; in medical malpractice cases of $201,000.

However, keeping several concepts in mind can at least reduce the concerns.[22]

First, screening small cases is particularly important. This involves carefully assessing liability, damages, and the other party's ability to pay a judgment. There is nothing more unproductive than taking a small case with questionable liability or filing an action against a party who is effectively judgment proof. Small cases must be screened quickly before any substantial investment in time is made.

Second, the client must understand what you can realistically do given the size of the case, and agree to your approach. For example, if the case is not worth the filing of a suit, perhaps you can attempt to get a settlement or resolve it through an alternative dispute resolution method. If the case is large enough to bring suit, but formal litigation would be prohibitively expensive, perhaps you can handle this particular case without formal discovery or with limited discovery. Whatever your approach, make sure the client knows what it will be and the reasons for it, and also agrees to it in writing.

Third, make sure you get your costs covered in advance, and let the client know the overall anticipated costs. A client who has paid the anticipated costs in advance has a direct financial interest in the litigation and will usually be more cooperative and realistic. A client who understands how costs, such as a medical expert's fee, can devour any recovery will have a better grasp of what can realistically be done.

Fourth, get the client to do as much work as possible, such as obtaining documents and records and locating witnesses. This can substantially reduce costs. You can also tell the client that you will not take the case until he has done this kind of preliminary work. Again, this not only reduces expenses but also involves the client in the litigation.

Fifth, you can sometimes economize without seriously compromising the preparation of the case. The largest savings can be made in the area of formal discovery, particularly depositions. Sometimes depositions need not be transcribed. Sometimes you can avoid depositions of witnesses entirely and rely on witness statements. Sometimes the opposing lawyer will agree to reciprocal informal interviews of parties in place of depositions. These savings, of course, must be discussed with the client, and he must agree to the procedures you take.

Sixth, the paramount rule, regardless of the size of the lawsuit, is always the same: The client's case must be competently handled.[23] This means that you must do whatever is necessary to uncover the important facts and witnesses, even if it is not cost-effective. If the opposing lawyer will not agree to informal interviews of the parties and you do not know what the opposing party will say at trial, you simply must depose that party. If the case cannot be settled short of trial, you simply must try the case. Lawyers, wittingly or not, sometimes take cases that are uneconomic from the lawyer's point of view. Once taken, however, the lawyer has the same

---

22. See Adelman & Halderman, The Dog Case, 10 Litig. (no. 3, Spring 1984).
23. See Model Rules of Professional Conduct, Model Rule 1.1.

professional obligation to prepare that case competently as he has for any other case.

Finally, keep in mind that when lawyers take cases, they frequently do so for reasons other than the compensation they will directly receive from that particular case. In small cases, accept the fact that you simply will not be paid at your usual rate. However, that fact alone should not prevent you from taking certain cases. The case may be from a regular client, whom you want to ensure remains satisfied with your overall representation. The case may come from a new client who may become a regular client if he is satisfied with the way in which you handle a small matter. The case may be legally or factually challenging. The case may be a high profile case that will enhance your reputation among lawyers and in the community. The case may be a new type of case and involve an area you have become interested in. Finally, you may decide to take a case to meet your pro bono obligations as a lawyer.

The high cost of litigation is a serious concern in our society and has sparked considerable discussion among the public, government, and the organized bar. Litigation procedures have become more streamlined in small cases; proposals to curtail formal discovery—or to eliminate it altogether in certain types of cases—are frequently made; alternative dispute resolution is becoming common; judges are taking a more active role in litigation management and settlement discussions. If a lawyer decides to take a case, however, the cardinal rule is that he always has a professional obligation to represent a client competently. That the client's matter is a small case cannot serve as an excuse for the lawyer to avoid professional obligations. The realities of your professional life as a lawyer are that once you agree to take a case, adequate planning and preparation are required to resolve the matter, regardless of its size. Accordingly, the basic steps discussed in this book must be followed to ensure that your representation is adequate.

III

LEGAL INVESTIGATION

§3.1. Introduction

As you conduct your informal fact investigation, you must also evaluate the various legal considerations that arise in every lawsuit. These include determining what jurisdiction's substantive law applies; what claims, remedies, or defenses to pursue; what parties must or can be joined; whether the court has subject matter jurisdiction over the claims; whether the court has personal jurisdiction over the parties; and where venue is proper. This chapter discusses the legal choices a plaintiff must make before filing a lawsuit, and a defendant must make before responding to one, as well as the interdependence of these legal considerations. While this discussion is based on federal district court litigation, the basic analytical sequence is also applicable to state court lawsuits.

A note of caution is in order. Issues dealing with choice of law, legal theories of claims and remedies, joinder, subject matter jurisdiction, personal jurisdiction, and venue can be complex and the literature about them is extensive. A single volume can hardly deal with these issues in depth, much less one chapter in a general text on pretrial techniques. This discussion's purpose is necessarily limited to getting the new litigator to think intelligently about these legal considerations in broad terms to avoid "missing the boat" on vital issues. Where a serious legal issue exists, it must always be researched thoroughly before filing suit. As always, remember that Rule 11 requires that a lawyer conduct a reasonable inquiry into the law and determine that the pleading has evidentiary support and is not frivolous before presenting the pleading to the court. The rule, in short, requires that you do your homework.

§3.2. Choice of law[1]

Before you can determine what claims, remedies, or defenses you can raise in your case, you need to know which jurisdiction's substantive law applies. In federal court, where plaintiff brings a claim under the court's federal question jurisdiction, the resolution is simple: federal substantive law applies.[2] However, if plaintiff brings a claim under the court's diversity jurisdiction, and the claim is based on a substantive right created by state law, two types of choice-of-law questions arise.

1.   When will a state's substantive law apply in federal court?

The question of when state law will be considered "substantive" and be applied in federal court is the so-called *Erie* problem, based on the landmark case of Erie R.R. Co. v. Tompkins, 304 U.S. 64 (1938). In *Erie* the Supreme Court held that whenever a federal court applies state substantive law, it must apply not only its statutory law, but its case law as well. The principal impact of *Erie* is on diversity cases, where a federal court must apply the appropriate state's substantive law.

The question of what is substantive law, as opposed to procedural, is unfortunately not always clear. For example, a state's basic negligence law is clearly substantive, and its discovery rules in civil procedure acts are clearly procedural. However, matters such as statutes of limitations, privileges, and burdens of proof can arguably be both. The Supreme Court has periodically grappled with the substantive-procedural distinction since deciding *Erie*.

In Guaranty Trust Co. v. York, 326 U.S. 99 (1945), the Court announced what has come to be called the "outcome determinative" test. When a state law, if applied in federal court, would substantially affect the outcome of the case, the state law is substantive and must be applied. In later cases, however, the Court modified the outcome-determinative test. For example, in Byrd v. Blue Ridge Rural Electric Cooperative, 356 U.S. 525 (1958), the Court held that the federal right to a jury trial on a claim prevailed over a contrary state rule; in Hanna v. Plumer, 380 U.S. 460 (1955), the Court applied the federal service-of-process rules over a conflicting state rule; in Walker v. Armco Steel Corp., 446 U.S. 740 (1980), the Court applied a state rule defining how an action is to be commenced for statute of limitations purposes over the conflicting Rule 3 in the Federal Rules of Civil Procedure; and in Stewart Organization v. Ricoh Corp., 487 U.S. 22 (1988), the Court held that the federal change of venue statute governs whether a federal court should give effect to a contractual forum selection clause.

It should be obvious that the question of whether a federal court will apply a state's substantive law is a complex one with which the United States

1. James & Hazard §§2.33–2.37; Friedenthal §§4.1–4.7; Moore's Manual §§3.01–3.05; Moore's Federal Practice §§0.301 et seq.; Wright & Miller §§4501 et seq.

2. In some instances, as with the Federal Tort Claims Act, the federal substantive law refers to the forum state's substantive law.

Supreme Court continues to grapple. Accordingly, any lawyer faced with an *Erie*-type question must thoroughly research the decided cases to determine how the issue is likely to be resolved in a particular case.

2. What is the state's substantive law?

The second choice-of-law issue deals with multistate events and transactions. If, for example, an Arizona driver is suing a California driver over an automobile accident in Nevada and brings a diversity action in federal court, which state's tort law applies? Does it matter where the action is filed?

The Supreme Court in Klaxon Co. v. Stentor Electric Manufacturing Co., 313 U.S. 487 (1941), held that in a federal diversity action the forum state's conflict-of-law rules govern in determining which state's substantive law will apply. In the above example, if plaintiff brings suit in federal district court in Arizona, then Arizona's conflicts-of-law rules govern. While the rule attempts to restrict shopping between federal and state forums, a plaintiff who can bring an action in more than one venue may still be able to acquire a more advantageous forum. For example, if the Arizona plaintiff can file suit in Arizona, the Arizona conflicts rules govern, which may result in Arizona substantive law being applied, since Arizona has an interest in applying its own law to its own citizens. If the Arizona plaintiff can file suit in Nevada, the Nevada conflicts rules govern and Nevada may apply its substantive law, since the accident occurred within its borders. If Arizona and Nevada tort law differ and the plaintiff has a choice of forums in which to bring suit, he will obviously pick the more advantageous one.

When the choice-of-law issue has been resolved, it is sometimes difficult to determine what the applicable state's substantive law actually is. State law, of course, is what a particular state's legislature and supreme court have declared it to be. What happens, however, if there is no controlling statute and the state's high court has not spoken on a particular question of law? How should a federal district court decide what the applicable state law is? The Supreme Court has held that in such cases a state appellate court decision will be highly persuasive, although not binding.[3] If there is no appellate court decision, the district court can certify the question to the state supreme court. If there is no such procedure, the district court can look at any available sources to determine what the state law is likely to be were the state courts presented with the question. Finally, if the district court feels that an antiquated state law would no longer be followed, the court may determine that it is not bound by precedent and can instead fashion a rule that the state courts would likely create if again faced with the issue.[4] In such circumstances, of course, thorough research is required.[5]

---

3. Commissioner v. Estate of Bosch, 387 U.S. 456 (1967).

4. Bernhardt v. Polygraphic Co. of Am., 350 U.S. 198 (1956).

5. See Friedenthal §4.6 for an excellent discussion of how a district court determines applicable state law.

§3.3. *Legal theories for claims, remedies, and defenses*

One or two theories for claims or defenses probably provided the initial direction for your fact investigation. Before filing suit or responding to one, however, you should always explore whether the presently available facts will support other legal claims or defenses. There are dangers in prematurely labeling a client's legal problems. Think expansively, so that all reasonably assertable claims are considered before deciding which ones to raise in your initial pleading. However, there are contrary considerations that must be remembered. Rule 11 provides sanctions for improper pleadings when the attorney has not conducted a "reasonable inquiry" of the facts and law, or has filed for any improper purpose.[6] In addition, more claims usually create a more complex and costly lawsuit, something that may not be appropriate in a particular case.

This discussion obviously cannot review the numerous legal theories on which claims and defenses can be brought. However, it is always useful to review checklists of potential theories for claims and defenses before filing the initial pleading. Doing so will at least get you to consider other similar theories, both statutory and common law; to review the required elements of each theory; and to analyze the advantages and disadvantages of each in light of the existing facts.[7] This review must be broad. Research to see if any federal and state statutes create a basis for claims and defenses, even if there is a common law basis for the lawsuit. For example, a claim against a railroad arising out of a collision at a grade crossing will obviously be based on a common law negligence theory. However, since railroads are a heavily regulated industry, check if any federal statutes such as the Grade Crossing Safety Act of 1994 apply, and if any state statutes apply, such as requiring quadrant gates at certain crossings. In short, always do a broad common law and statutory search as part of the overall legal research of the case. Each of these theories, with its required elements, should be put on your litigation chart.

When you have identified all possible theories of claims or defenses, how do you find the "elements" for each of them? Perhaps the best place to start is with the pattern jury instructions used in the applicable jurisdiction. These usually exist for common claims and defenses with the required elements of a prima facie case itemized. Additional research will usually be necessary, particularly if the claims or defenses are not based on routine tort or contract theories. For common law claims and defenses, the best starting point is usually a hornbook or treatise on the substantive area involved. For statutory claims, you should obviously start with the statute involved and check the case annotations for elements and jury instructions. After checking these basic sources, check the recent cases interpreting and applying the substantive law. Computer searches on LEXIS or Westlaw are frequently useful. Finally, many states have practice manuals that cover types of litigation that are common to the jurisdiction; frequently these prove to be excellent practical reviews. With this type of research, you should have enough to "mull over" the pros and cons of the various legal theories that can be supported by the available facts.

6. See discussion of Rule 11 in §5.2(f).
7. See, e.g., Actions and Remedies (C. Friend ed. 1985).

For example, assume you represent the plaintiff in a personal injury case arising out of an automobile accident. You consider, of course, a negligence claim against the other driver and a claim based on violating the "rules of the road." However, is there a claim based on negligent maintenance of the defendant's vehicle? If the defendant had been drinking, can the drinking support a negligence or statutory claim? Again, the point is to think expansively so that you consider every theory of recovery that can be supported by provable facts.

What claims you decide to bring in a lawsuit are influenced not only by theories of recovery, but also by the remedies permitted under each legal theory. Your choice of remedies will significantly influence what proof is relevant at trial and the scope of discovery.[8]

Under the Federal Rules of Civil Procedure, a party is not usually limited to the relief requested, and pleadings can ordinarily be amended. Nevertheless, it is always preferable to frame your pleadings so that they accurately reflect all the types of relief to which your client may be entitled. In addition, the remedies you seek will, like all the allegations in the pleadings, determine what will be relevant for discovery purposes. The distinction between legal and equitable actions no longer controls what remedies are permissible, since federal courts, like most jurisdictions, have merged courts of law and equity and have power to order any appropriate relief. Hence, it is important to review all potentially available remedies, legal and equitable, and request all that are proper. The simplest way to look at remedies is to review first the general types of legal and equitable relief, then relate that relief to the specific claims you are considering, and finally review any statutes and court rules that permit additional relief.

First, legal remedies (historically, those remedies permitted for actions in a court of law) include money damages, restitution, and recision. Money damages, the most frequently sought relief, can be compensatory, consequential, or punitive. While compensatory damages are always permitted, consequential or punitive damages are usually permitted only where statutes or case law permit them. Equitable remedies (historically, those remedies granted by a court of chancery when legal remedies were inadequate or inflexible) include injunctions, specific performance, reformation, unjust enrichment, accounting, constructive trust, equitable lien, and reclamation. Any of these remedies should be requested if appropriate to the circumstances, regardless of the kind of claims brought.

Second, the precise measure of the allowable money damages, frequently controlled both by statute and case law, depends on the type of claim being asserted. For example, damages for breach of contract depend on whether the contract involves land, personal property, construction, or employment. Tort damages also vary considerably, depending on whether the claim is based on personal injury, survival, wrongful death, undue influence, fraud, defamation, intentional tort, or statutory actions. Where a claim is statutory, the allowable damages are frequently specified in the statute.

Third, you must check to see if there are any statutory provisions for allowing recoveries for other damages, court costs, and attorney's fees. This

8. The leading treatise on remedies is Dobbs, Law of Remedies (2d ed. 1993).

includes checking not only the statutes providing for specific causes of action, but also federal and state procedural rules.[9] State civil practice rules often have provisions for costs and fees that, if viewed as substantive, may be applied in federal diversity actions.

For example, assume you represent the plaintiff in a contract dispute over the sale of goods. The plaintiff delivered the goods but has not been paid. Certainly, the plaintiff can receive compensatory damages, but are other remedies possibly available? Can the plaintiff support a claim for consequential damages? Is the defendant guilty of bad faith, or is there some other basis for a punitive damages claim? Are there any statutory means by which you can recover the plaintiff's attorney's fees and other costs? Once again, the point is to think expansively so that you consider every remedy that the law provides in your case.

Remedies issues should always be researched carefully to learn the full measure of damages permitted for the claims involved. A good place to start is with the damages instructions in those jurisdictions that have pattern jury instructions.

§3.4. *Joinder of parties and claims*

Joinder-of-parties issues are best addressed by asking a series of questions that parallel the analytical sequence involved. These are:

1. Who is the real party in interest?
2. Does that party have capacity to sue?
3. Is joinder of parties required?
4. Is joinder of parties permitted?
5. Do any special pleading rules apply?
6. Is joinder of claims permitted?

1. Real party in interest[10]

Rule 17(a) requires that an action be brought "in the name of the real party in interest." That party is the one who, under applicable substantive law, has the right that the lawsuit seeks to enforce. The purpose of the rule is to ensure that the parties with the real interests are the ones actually

9. There are over 100 federal statutes that permit awarding attorney's fees and other costs to the successful litigant. Common examples include §1983 civil rights actions, employment discrimination actions under Title VII of the 1964 Civil Rights Act, consumer products warranty actions under the Magnuson-Moss Warranty Act, and actions under the Freedom of Information Act. See E. R. Larson, Federal Court Awards of Attorney's Fees (1981); Dobbs, Awarding Attorney Fees Against Adversaries: Introducing the Problem (1986); Duke L.J. 435.

10. Wright §70; James & Hazard §10.3; Friedenthal §6.3; Moore's Manual §13.01; Manual of Federal Practice §§3.106–3.110; Moore's Federal Practice §§17.07–17.15; Wright & Miller §§1543–1558.

prosecuting cases. Potential issues arise when personal representatives are named parties. For diversity jurisdiction purposes, the citizenship of the real party in interest is controlling.

Rule 17(a) also specifies exceptions to the general rule by providing that an "executor, administrator, guardian, bailee, trustee of an express trust, a party with whom or in whose name a contract has been made for the benefit of another, or a party authorized by statute" may sue in his own name. While the plaintiff has the burden of showing he is the proper real party in interest, the exceptions to Rule 17(a) have largely eliminated controversy in this area. The only areas where disputes still arise are assignments and subrogation. While a complete assignment makes the assignee the real party in interest, 28 U.S.C. §1359 expressly provides that such an assignment cannot be used to "create" diversity where it would otherwise not exist. If an assignment or subrogation is only partial, both parties to the assignment or subrogation are usually considered real parties in interest.[11]

If the wrong party is sued, Rule 17(a) provides that no dismissal should be entered unless after a reasonable time following an objection a proper substitution of parties is not made or the real party in interest ratifies the action.

2. Capacity to sue[12]

A lawsuit must be brought by and against parties that have a legal capacity to sue. Capacity to sue is governed by Rule 17(b), which in turn refers to state law. In the case of an individual, capacity to sue is determined by the state law of the individual's domicile. For corporations, capacity is determined by the law of the state of incorporation. In other cases, including those involving representatives, the law of the forum state controls capacity to sue. The forum state's laws control partnerships and unincorporated associations, except that, regardless of the forum law, partnerships and unincorporated associations always have capacity to sue over substantive federal rights. Finally, under Rule 17(a) an infant or incompetent can sue or be sued in the name of a representative. If no representative has been appointed, a guardian ad litem can bring suit or be appointed for the sued party.

If a defendant wishes to challenge plaintiff's claim of capacity to sue, the defendant must, under Rule 9, deny the claim "with particularity." Failing to make the denial in a responsive pleading will usually result in any error being deemed waived.

---

11. Wright §70; James & Hazard §§10.4–10.5; Moore's Manual §13.01; Manual of Federal Practice §3.109; Moore's Federal Practice §17.05; Wright & Miller §§1545, 1546.
12. Wright §70; James & Hazard §10.7; Friedenthal §6.3; Moore's Manual §13.02; Manual of Federal Practice §§3.111–3.117; Moore's Federal Practice §§17.16–17.27; Wright & Miller §§1559–1573.

3. Required joinder of parties[13]

Joinder of parties is governed by Rules 19 and 20. The joinder rules address a basic question: What parties must, should, or may be, brought into the lawsuit so that the plaintiff's claims can be properly decided? What parties must, or should be, joined is governed by Rule 19; what parties may be brought in is governed by Rule 20.[14]

Needless to say, these esoteric distinctions have been the source of much debate and litigation over the years. The present joinder rules are an attempt to get away from rigid labels and move toward a pragmatic analysis of the competing interests involved. On the one hand, there are legal and social interests in giving every party an opportunity to litigate and at the same time avoiding multiple suits over the same issues. On the other hand, there are corresponding interests in permitting some claims to be adjudicated, rather than none. The modern approach to joinder, as represented by Rules 19 and 20, is to resolve joinder issues by focusing on those competing interests.

Rule 19, dealing with required joinder, is divided into two basic rules. Rule 19(a) governs what parties are to be joined "if feasible"; Rule 19(b) governs what the court should do if all required parties cannot be joined.

Under Rule 19(a), a party should be joined if that party's presence is (1) required to grant "complete relief," or (2) the party has an interest in the action so that the party's presence is, practically speaking, necessary to protect his interest, or the party's absence may expose other parties to double or inconsistent obligations. Such a party should be joined unless he cannot be served with process, or the party's joinder would defeat federal subject matter jurisdiction. While the rule appears complex, in practice its application is not particularly problematical. As a practical matter, a plaintiff should join any potentially liable party who can be served, if the party's joinder will not defeat subject matter jurisdiction (and, of course, the Rule 11 requirements are met).

Rule 19(b) governs the situation where a party who should be joined cannot be because the party cannot be served with process, or because the party's joinder would defeat federal jurisdiction. The issue before the court then is whether to proceed without the party or dismiss the action. Rule 19(b) states four factors the court must balance in reaching an equitable decision: (1) whether nonjoined and existing parties will be prejudiced, (2) whether an order can minimize any potential prejudice, (3) whether any judgment without the absent party can be adequate, and (4) whether the plaintiff will have an adequate remedy if the action is dismissed.

These practical concerns frequently compete with each other, but certain conclusions are likely. First, if the consequence of a dismissal is

---

13. Wright §71; James & Hazard §§10.11–10.15; Friedenthal §6.5; Moore's Manual §§13.04–13.07; Manual of Federal Practice §§3.120–3.124; Moore's Federal Practice §§19.05–19.21; Wright & Miller §§1601–1624.

14. The "must-should" categories roughly approximate the traditional "indispensable-necessary" distinction, the "may" category approximates the traditional "proper" label. These traditional terms are now considered outdated.

that the plaintiff is left without any state forum in which to pursue claims against all parties, it is highly unlikely that the court will dismiss the action. Second, if an absent party can be brought in as a third-party defendant, there is strong ground for rejecting a present defendant's claim of potential prejudice. The possibility of intervention is also a strong ground for rejecting the claim of prejudice to an absent party. Third, the possibility of incomplete relief to the plaintiff will usually be rejected as a reason for dismissal, since that result alone prejudices no one. In short, the judicial tendency has been to retain federal jurisdiction rather than dismiss the case.

In community property states, additional joinder issues arise because spouses may be liable as joint obligors since a spouse's activities that form the basis for the lawsuit are frequently viewed as benefiting the marital community. For example, a spouse who causes an automobile collision on the way to work is usually viewed as engaging in an activity that benefits the marital community because driving to work is part of earning money for the marital community. In such situations, the other spouse should be joined as an additional defendant in the complaint.

4. Permissive joinder of parties[15]

Permissive joinder, governed by Rule 20, resolves the question of who may be joined as a proper party. Rule 20 provides two tests, both of which must be met before joinder will be permitted. First, there must be a question of law or fact common to all parties arising out of the action. Second, each plaintiff must have a right of relief, either jointly, severally, or alternatively against each defendant based on the same occurrences or transactions, or series of transactions or occurrences.

The language of Rule 20 is broad and permits joinder whenever there is a legal or factual relationship between the parties making it sensible to have all these parties present in one lawsuit. On the other hand, permissive joinder can operate to delay the litigation and make it unfairly expensive and burdensome on certain parties. For that reason, Rule 20(b) gives the court broad regulatory powers, including the power to order separate trials to prevent any unfairness.

Where there is improper joinder, Rule 21 provides simply that the case cannot be dismissed. Rather, the misjoined parties are dropped and non-joined parties added by court order.

5. Special pleadings rules

Required and permissive joinder rules, set forth in Rules 19 and 20, are not the only rules that regulate whether parties can be joined in a lawsuit.

---

15. Wright §71; James & Hazard §§9.7–9.8; Friedenthal §6.4; Moore's Manual §14.01; Manual of Federal Practice §§3.118–3.119; Moore's Federal Practice §§20.05–20.08; Wright & Miller §§1651–1660.

There are several pleading rules that govern a number of special types of actions. These are:

Rule 13 — counterclaims
Rule 13(g) — cross-claims
Rule 14 — impleader
Rule 22 — interpleader
Rule 24 — intervention
Rule 23 — class actions
Rule 23.1 — shareholder derivative suits

These pleadings, and their special requirements, are discussed in Chapter 5.

6. Joinder of claims[16]

Joinder of claims, governed by Rule 18, is always permissive. Each party can bring as many claims as the party has against every other party. These include both present and contingent claims. Deciding what claims to bring against another party is principally a practical matter.[17]

§3.5.   *Subject matter jurisdiction in district courts*

Subject matter jurisdiction refers to the power of a court to hear particular matters. Federal district courts are courts of limited jurisdiction and cannot hear a case unless it falls within their power, as defined in Article III of the United States Constitution, and Congress has extended jurisdiction over the particular type of case.

Because federal district courts are courts of limited jurisdiction, a party seeking to invoke the court's jurisdiction must affirmatively plead and demonstrate proper subject matter jurisdiction.[18] The basis for jurisdiction must appear on the face of a well-pleaded complaint and cannot rest on counterclaims, defenses, or anticipated defenses. On the other hand, any party or the court can raise lack of subject matter jurisdiction. Although most commonly raised in the defendant's answer or by a Rule 12 motion to dismiss, it can be raised at any time, even after judgment or on appeal. If the court has no jurisdiction over the subject matter, the case must be dismissed.

---

16. Wright §§13, 78; James & Hazard §9.4; Friedenthal §§6.3, 6.6; Moore's Manual §10.06; Manual of Federal Practice §§3.163–3.166; Moore's Federal Practice §§18.03–18.11; Wright & Miller §§1581–1594.
    17. See §4.5.
    18. See §5.2.

1. "Case or controversy" and standing[19]

The court must have an actual "case or controversy" that is ripe for adjudication. Put another way, the court will not hear moot or collusive cases, render advisory opinions, or hear controversies that are essentially political or administrative issues. This requirement limits cases to those involving real controversies in which parties have a direct stake in the outcome and will actively represent their interests.

A party must also have "standing" to sue. The standing doctrine is derived from the "case or controversy" requirement and limits the kinds of cases that can be brought in federal courts. To have standing, a plaintiff must show that the challenged conduct of the defendant has caused an "injury" in fact and that the interest which the suit seeks to protect is within the "zone of protection" guaranteed by the statute or constitutional provision in question. The Supreme Court has considered the standing issue many times and has not yet articulated a test that will easily resolve standing issues in particular circumstances.[20]

The question of whether there is an actual case or controversy, and the related issue of standing, arises frequently in public interest, constitutional, and administrative litigation. For example, a suit to enjoin enforcement of a city regulatory code provision, brought by a local resident, will raise both issues. In private litigation, there will ordinarily be an obvious controversy, with the parties having obvious standing. In public interest litigation, on the other hand, these issues are common as well as complex and must be researched thoroughly, particularly when the plaintiff is an organization or association bringing suit on behalf of its members or third parties.

2. Federal question jurisdiction[21]

28 U.S.C. §1331 provides that "district courts shall have original jurisdiction of all civil actions arising under the constitution, laws, or treaties of the United States." Section 1331 is generally referred to as conferring "general" federal question jurisdiction. This distinguishes §1331 from other "specific" grants of jurisdiction found in §§1333 et seq. and from other non-Title 28 grants.

19. Wright §12; Moore's Manual §1.01(1); Manual of Federal Practice §1.4; Wright & Miller §3529.

20. See Wright §13; Friedenthal §6.3; the standing test comes from Association of Data Processing Service Organizations v. Camp, 397 U.S. 150 (1970), and its companion case, Barlow v. Collins, 397 U.S. 159 (1970). See also Sierra Club v. Morton, 405 U.S. 727 (1972); United States v. Students Challenging Regulatory Agency Procedures, 412 U.S. 669 (1973); and Warth v. Seldin, 422 U.S. 490 (1975) on the "injury" part of the standing test. Recent Supreme Court cases include Raines v. Byrd, 521 U.S. 811 (1997); National Credit Union Admin. v. First National Bank & Trust Co., 522 U.S. 479 (1998); Federal Election Commission v. Akins, 524 U.S. 11 (1998); Allen v. Wright, 525 U.S. 946 (1998).

21. Wright §§17–22; James & Hazard §2.5; Friedenthal §2.3; Moore's Manual §§5.02–5.05; Manual of Federal Practice §§1.59–1.66; Moore's Federal Practice §0.62(2.1); Wright & Miller §§3561–3567.2.

The general-versus-specific distinction is important because of the requirement that a party invoking the court's jurisdiction must affirmatively show the basis for jurisdiction. Issues over jurisdiction seldom arise when the basis is a specific grant in a statutory provision. Problems frequently exist, however, when the basis for jurisdiction is the general grant under §1331.

a. *"Arising under"*[22]

Jurisdictional issues occur under §1331 because its "arising under" language is so general. Section 1331 creates jurisdiction over civil actions "arising under the Constitution, laws or treaties of the United States." The constitutional provisions are contained in Article III, §§1 and 2. However, §1331, which contains the same language as Article III, §2, has been interpreted much more narrowly than the parallel constitutional language.

The basic requirements for jurisdiction under §1331 are that the claim be based on federal law, which must be demonstrated in the complaint, and that the federal claim be substantial rather than frivolous.[23] For example, plaintiff brings an action for patent infringement. This raises federal question jurisdiction because it is brought under the Patent Act. Another plaintiff brings an action for an unlawful search of his house. This raises federal question jurisdiction because it is brought under the Fourth Amendment of the U.S. Constitution. Where federal law expressly creates a remedy, jurisdiction will be found. However, where a federal statute, although declaring rights, does not expressly confer a remedy, complex issues exist, and they center on whether an implied remedy exists that is recognizable under §1331. On these issues the courts are frequently divided; therefore, the law must be thoroughly researched.

b. *Specific grants of jurisdiction*

There are several other sections of Title 28 that grant federal courts jurisdiction to hear particular matters. These include:

§1333 — admiralty
§1334 — bankruptcy
§1336 — ICC/commerce
§1337 — commerce/antitrust
§1338 — patent, copyright, trademark, unfair competition
§1339 — postal
§1340 — IRS/customs
§§1341–1364 — miscellaneous provisions

---

22. Moore's Manual §5.02–5.03; James & Hazard §2.6; Friedenthal §2.3; Manual of Federal Practice §§1.60–1.66, §§1.80–1.108; Moore's Federal Practice §0.62(2.1); Wright & Miller §3562.

23. Since the complaint must affirmatively show that federal jurisdiction exists, it follows that raising a defense based on federal law cannot create jurisdiction. Nor can a counterclaim create federal jurisdiction; see Holmes Group v. Yornado Air Circulation Systems, 535 U.S. 826 (2002).

Finally, there are numerous statutory provisions outside of Title 28 that also confer jurisdiction on district courts. The more important ones are:

Jones Act, 46 U.S.C. §688
Federal Employer's Liability Act, 45 U.S.C. §56
Securities Act, 15 U.S.C. §77
Civil Rights Act, 42 U.S.C. §1983

Where jurisdiction is based on these specific grants, the same pleading requirements apply: A plaintiff wishing to invoke the court's jurisdiction must always affirmatively plead a proper jurisdictional basis.

Keep in mind that these federal grants of jurisdiction can be exclusive or concurrent with state courts. In several areas, notably admiralty, bankruptcy, and patent and copyright cases, the district courts have exclusive jurisdiction.

c. Pendent jurisdiction[24]

A claim can properly be brought in federal court if the basis for jurisdiction is a federal question. What happens, however, if plaintiff has other claims, not based on federal question jurisdiction? Can these be brought with the federal claim? If the other claims each have a separate proper basis for federal jurisdiction, such as diversity jurisdiction, no problems arise. However, if there is no such basis for the claims, the question arises of whether the other claims can be "joined" to the federal claim.

The concept of "pendent jurisdiction" addresses this question and strikes a compromise between the usual requirement that federal jurisdiction must be strictly construed and the obvious advantage of hearing at one time all claims that can be brought by one party against another. A simple solution is to deny federal jurisdiction on the non-federal claims, the result being that a plaintiff who wants to pursue all claims in one action must do so in a state court. However, this option is not available when the federal claim is one over which federal courts have exclusive jurisdiction. In this situation the options are to try all claims in federal court or to split the claims between federal and state courts.

The term "pendent jurisdiction," and the closely related term "ancillary jurisdiction," have been replaced by a comprehensive statute, 28 U.S.C. §1367, which controls what is now called "supplemental jurisdiction." Supplemental jurisdiction and the statute are discussed in subsection 4 below.

d. The United States as a party[25]

When the United States is a plaintiff, no special jurisdictional problems arise. However, the United States cannot be sued unless it has waived

---

24. Wright §19; James & Hazard §2.7; Friedenthal §2.13; Moore's Manual §5.15; Manual of Federal Practice §§1.109–1.112; Moore's Federal Practice §18.07(1.2); Wright & Miller §§3567, 3937.

25. Wright §22; James & Hazard §2.5; Friedenthal §2.10; Moore's Manual §13,078; Manual of Federal Practice §§1.128–1.135; Moore's Federal Practice §17.24; Wright & Miller §§3651–3660.

its sovereign immunity and consented to be sued. A plaintiff suing the United States, therefore, must expressly demonstrate the statutory basis under which the government has consented to be sued. The most frequently used grounds are the Court of Claims Act,[26] Tucker Act,[27] and Federal Tort Claims Act.[28]

Frequently, however, a plaintiff may wish or need to sue a federal official or federal administrative agency, rather than the United States directly. In this situation there must be a specific statute that permits suit against the agency or a named federal official. Such statutes frequently permit suits brought to challenge administrative agency decisions. For example, suit is frequently brought against the Secretary of Housing and Urban Development for denial of claimed Social Security benefits.[29] Where there is no statute permitting suit against a federal official or agency, it is still sometimes possible to sue an official individually for an alleged improper act. Finally, there are a number of federal entities, which may be incorporated or unincorporated, of which the United States is whole or part owner. Examples include the Federal Deposit Insurance Corporation and Federal Housing Authority. Whether such quasi-governmental entities can be sued in federal court is heavily regulated by statute and, sometimes, by case law.

3. Diversity jurisdiction[30]

Section 1332 provides for the jurisdiction of federal courts in civil actions involving diversity of citizenship, and parallels the constitutional grant of power found in Article III, §2 of the Constitution. Section 1332 sets out four categories of actions for which diversity jurisdiction is proper:

1. Between citizens of different states
2. Between citizens of a state and citizens or subjects of a foreign state
3. Between citizens of different states and in which citizens or subjects of a foreign state are additional parties
4. Between a foreign state as plaintiff and citizens of a state or of different states

Of these four categories, the first is the predominantly used section. The other three are usually referred to as the alienage sections. Diversity jurisdiction does not apply to domestic relations and probate matters, which are considered local matters properly raised only in state courts.

---

26. 28 U.S.C. §1491.
27. 28 U.S.C. §1346(a).
28. 28 U.S.C. §1346(b).
29. 42 U.S.C. §405.
30. Wright §§23–31; James & Hazard §2.5; Friedenthal §§2.5–2.7; Moore's Manual §5.06; Manual of Federal Practice §§1.19–1.58; Moore's Federal Practice §§0.71–0.85; Wright & Miller §§3601–3610.

a. *"Citizenship" requirement*[31]

Section 1332 is based on "citizenship," an imprecise term. The citizenship of natural persons is the state of domicile, and no person can have more than one domicile at a time. The citizenship of corporations is both the state where incorporated and the state where it has its principal place of business, which is usually defined as where a majority of its business is conducted or, if that is unclear, where the corporate headquarters is located. The citizenship of the legal representative of a decedent, infant, or incompetent is deemed to be the same state as the decedent's, infant's, or incompetent's citizenship. A permanent resident alien is deemed to be a citizen of the state where domiciled. (Other legal representatives, not mentioned in §1332, presumably retain their own citizenship for diversity purposes.) In direct actions against liability insurers, the insurer is considered a citizen of the state where the insured is domiciled,[32] as well as the state where incorporated and where its principal place of business is located. Unincorporated associations present particular difficulties. If the association is not an entity entitled by state law to sue or be sued in its own name, its citizenship is that of each of its members. If the association is an entity entitled to sue or be sued, the prevailing rule is that here also the association is considered to be a citizen of each state of which a member is a citizen.

Needless to say, what constitutes citizenship for diversity purposes when artificial entities are involved can be a complex issue involving law that is frequently unsettled; thorough research is essential.

b. *Complete diversity requirement*[33]

The requirement that diversity must be "complete" in order for the federal district courts to have jurisdiction means that each plaintiff must have a different state citizenship from each defendant. Stated another way, if any plaintiff and any defendant are citizens of the same state, diversity will not be complete. For example, if citizens of Illinois and California sue citizens of Maine and Vermont, complete diversity exists. If citizens of Illinois and California sue citizens of Maine, Vermont, Connecticut, and California, complete diversity does not exist.

The complete diversity requirement applies to every party that is actually joined, regardless of whether that party is required or permissive. To retain the required complete diversity, a plaintiff can dismiss all but indispensable parties from the action. In addition, a plaintiff may manipulate the parties to create complete diversity. Because of this, a party's

---

31. Wright §§24, 26; James & Hazard §2.5; Friedenthal §2.6; Moore's Manual §5.06; Manual of Federal Practice §§1.24–1.33; Moore's Federal Practice §0.74; Wright & Miller §§3601–3642.

32. Some states have so-called direct action statutes that permit suits to be brought directly against an insurance company The typical situation is an automobile accident involving the insured.

33. Wright §§23–31; James & Hazard §2.5; Friedenthal §2.6; Moore's Manual §5.06; Manual of Federal Practice §1.34; Wright & Miller §3605.

characterization as a plaintiff or defendant in the complaint is not controlling. Parties will be realigned as plaintiffs or defendants, and nominal or formal parties will be ignored, to determine if complete diversity actually exists. In the case of legal representatives of decedents, infants, and incompetents, the citizenship of the representative is deemed to be the same state as the decedent's, infant's, or incompetent's citizenship. Where the legal representative is nominal, such as with a guardian ad litem, the citizenship of the represented party is also determinative for diversity purposes. Collusive assignments, made solely to create diversity, are also ignored.[34]

The complete diversity rule is somewhat misleading because it applies to the original plaintiffs' claims against original defendants and does not apply to many other situations. The concept of ancillary jurisdiction, which applies to counterclaims, cross-claims, impleader, and interventions as of right, significantly modifies the complete diversity requirement.

Complete diversity is determined according to the citizenship of parties at the time the initial complaint was filed. Later changes in citizenship by a party will not defeat jurisdiction.

c. Jurisdictional amount requirement[35]

Section 1332(a) requires that the "matter in controversy exceeds the sum or value of $75,000, exclusive of interest and costs." The plaintiff's complaint is the sole basis for determining if the requirement has been met. The allegations are controlling unless there is a "legal certainty" that the jurisdictional amount cannot be obtained. This will occur only when plaintiff requests damages, such as punitive damages, to which he is not entitled under the applicable substantive law, and those damages are necessary to reach the jurisdictional amount.

The principal issue in this area involves the problem of valuation, particularly where equitable relief is requested. With injunctions, where this problem most frequently occurs, the measure of damages is the value of the right sought to be enforced or the value of the avoided injury. The value may be different, depending on whether it is measured from the plaintiff's or the defendant's perspective. The courts are divided on which view of the measure of damages is appropriate, although more appear to use the plaintiff's loss approach. For example, suppose the plaintiff brings suit to enjoin the enforcement of certain statutes, such as zoning ordinances or health regulations, and to have them declared unconstitutional. The court must look to see what the amount of the loss to the plaintiff would be if the statutes continue to be enforced.

Another issue involves aggregation of claims to meet the jurisdictional amount. Here there are four basic situations. First, where there is one plaintiff and one defendant, the plaintiff can aggregate all claims against the defendant to meet the jurisdictional amount requirement. For

---

34. See 28 U.S.C. §1359.

35. Wright §§32–37; James & Hazard §2.5; Friedenthal §2.8; Moore's Manual §§5.07–5.14; Manual of Federal Practice §§1.72–1.79; Moore's Federal Practice §§0.90–0.99; Wright & Miller §§3701–3712.

example, a plaintiff has two claims, each involving $40,000, against one defendant; the claims involve two separate, unrelated contracts. The plaintiff can properly aggregate the claims. Second, where there is one plaintiff and multiple defendants, plaintiff can aggregate claims only if the claims are joint rather than several and distinct. For example, a plaintiff has two claims, each involving $40,000, against two defendants; the claims involve two separate, unrelated contracts. The plaintiff cannot aggregate these claims. However, if the liability is joint, as would be the case if the defendants are partners jointly liable on a partnership obligation, aggregation is proper. Third, where there are multiple plaintiffs and one defendant, the plaintiffs cannot aggregate separate and distinct claims. The plaintiffs can aggregate only if the claims are undivided and a single title or right is involved. For example, two plaintiffs each have a $40,000 claim against one defendant; the claims involve two separate, unrelated contracts. The plaintiffs cannot aggregate these claims; however, if the two plaintiffs are partners suing to recover a debt owed to the partnership, aggregation is proper. Finally, where there are multiple plaintiffs and multiple defendants, the above analysis applies to the individual claims.

Interest and costs raise fewer questions. Costs include attorneys' fees only if a contract or statute permits them. Interest, which is ordinarily incidental to the action, is included for purposes of determining if the jurisdictional amount is met only if the interest itself is the basis of the action.

4. Supplemental jurisdiction[36]

Because federal courts are courts of limited jurisdiction, the question arises of whether a federal court can have jurisdiction over claims for which no federal jurisdiction exists. The concept of "pendent jurisdiction" principally addresses the question of what happens when a plaintiff, properly in federal court because one of the claims has federal question jurisdiction, also brings other claims, based on the same conduct, not having independent grounds for federal jurisdiction. The closely related concept of "ancillary jurisdiction" principally addresses the question of what happens when a plaintiff is properly in federal court because the claim has a proper federal jurisdictional basis, and another party wishes to bring a counterclaim, cross-claim, or third-party complaint, but this new claim does not have an independent federal jurisdictional basis.

The concerns in both situations are similar. On the one hand, both the litigants and the court have an interest in avoiding piecemeal litigation, in which some claims between the parties can be brought in federal court, while others must be brought in state court. On the other hand, allowing state claims to be brought in federal court, through the concepts of

---

36. Wright §9; James & Hazard §2.7; Friedenthal §2.14; Moore's Manual §5.15; Manual of Federal Practice §§1.109–1.112; Moore's Federal Practice §8.07(5); Wright & Miller §§3523, 3567.

pendent and ancillary jurisdiction, must be consistent with Article III of the U.S. Constitution as well as statutory grants of power to the federal courts.

The concepts of pendent and ancillary jurisdiction, being judicial creations, enjoyed a rich judicial history, producing leading cases such as United Mine Workers of America v. Gibbs, 383 U.S. 715 (1966), and Owen Equipment & Erection Co. v. Kroger, 437 U.S. 365 (1978). Following the much criticized case of Finley v. United States, 490 U.S. 545 (1989), Congress in 1990 enacted a statute which codifies pendent and ancillary jurisdiction under the new name of "supplemental jurisdiction" (and overrules the holding in *Finley*). While retaining most of the former concepts, the statute modifies them in certain respects.

28 U.S.C. §1367, has three principal provisions:

(a) Except as provided in subsections (b) and (c) or as expressly provided otherwise by Federal statute, in any civil action of which the district courts have original jurisdiction, the district courts shall have supplemental jurisdiction over all other claims that are so related to claims in the action within such original jurisdiction that they form part of the same case or controversy under Article III of the United States Constitution. Such supplemental jurisdiction shall include claims that involve the joinder or intervention of additional parties.

(b) In any civil action of which the district courts have original jurisdiction founded solely on section 1332 of this title, the district courts shall not have supplemental jurisdiction under subsection (a) over claims by plaintiffs against persons made parties under Rules 14, 19, 20, or 24 of the Federal Rules of Civil Procedure, or over claims by persons proposed to be joined as plaintiffs under Rule 19 of such rules, or seeking to intervene as plaintiffs under Rule 24 of such rules, when exercising supplemental jurisdiction over such claims would be inconsistent with the jurisdictional requirements of section 1332.

(c) The district courts may decline to exercise supplemental jurisdiction over a claim under subsection (a) if—

(1) the claim raises a novel or complex issue of State law,

(2) the claim substantially predominates over the claim or claims over which the district court has original jurisdiction,

(3) the district court has dismissed all claims over which it has original jurisdiction, or

(4) in exceptional circumstances, there are other compelling reasons for declining jurisdiction.

Under the statute, subsection (a) confers on the district court mandatory supplemental jurisdiction over all other claims that are so related to the original claim that they form part of the same case or controversy, unless the court exercises its discretion under the circumstances set forth in subsection (c) and declines supplemental jurisdiction. The use of the phrase "case or controversy" is intended to extend to the constitutional limits of federal court power.

Subsection (b) creates several exceptions to deal with situations in which a plaintiff in diversity cases might otherwise bring into the case claims against certain other parties that it would not be able to bring because of the lack of subject matter jurisdiction. This section does not restrict the use of supplemental jurisdiction by defendants in recognized and accepted circumstances, such as compulsory counterclaims, cross-claims, interpleader, intervention of right, and impleader. Such pleadings commonly involve indemnity. For example, consider a plaintiff who properly brings a claim in federal court that has proper subject matter jurisdiction. The defendant wishes to bring in a third-party defendant on an indemnification theory. Indemnification raises no federal questions, however, and since the defendant and third-party defendant are citizens of the same state, diversity is lacking. Yet, in this situation the court will have ancillary jurisdiction over the third-party claim.

In 2005, the Supreme Court expanded supplemental jurisdiction under §1367. In Exxon Mobil Corp. v. Allapattah Services, 545 U.S. 546 (2005), the Court held that where complete diversity exists and at least one named plaintiff satisfies the amount in controversy requirement, the district court has supplemental jurisdiction over the claims of the other plaintiffs that do not meet the amount in controversy requirement, so long as all claims arise out of the same case or controversy. The decision applies to individual cases as well as class actions.

5. Removal jurisdiction[37]

The right to remove cases from state to federal courts protects nonresident parties from perceived local prejudices. The removal jurisdiction of federal district courts is governed by 28 U.S.C. §§1441–1452. Since it is a jurisdictional statute, it is strictly construed and its requirements must be followed closely to ensure that removal is properly made.

Removal is the procedure in which a case, already filed in a state court, is transferred to the federal district court for the same district in which the state action is pending. The first requirement, then, is that the case has already been filed in state court. To determine if removal is proper, you must look to the complaint at the time the removal petition is filed. The removal cannot be based on defenses or counterclaims.[38]

The removal statute permits the removal of otherwise nonremoveable claims if those claims are joined with other claims over which the federal court has proper jurisdiction under §1331, the general federal question jurisdiction statute. In addition, a federal court can retain a removed case over which it has proper subject matter jurisdiction, even if the state court did not have proper personal jurisdiction over the defendant.

---

37. Wright §§38–41; James & Hazard §2.9; Friedenthal §2.11; Moore's Manual §§8.01–8.13, Manual of Federal Practice §§1.149–1.173; Moore's Federal Practice §0.155; Wright & Miller §§3721–3740. The mechanics of the removal procedure are discussed in §7.6.

38. See Rivet v. Regions Bank, 522 U.S. 470 (1999); Beneficial National Bank v. Anderson, 539 U.S. 1 (2003).

Second, all defendants — except nominal, unknown, or fraudulently joined ones or ones who were not served with process prior to the filing of the notice — must join in the notice of removal. Since removal is for the benefit of defendants, each must agree to the removal; a "defendant" for removal purposes is each party against whom the original plaintiff brought a claim in state court.

Third, under §1446(b), the notice of removal must be filed within 30 days of the time the defendant receives formal service of plaintiff's initial pleading in state court, or within 30 days of receiving summons if the initial pleading under state practice is not required to be served on the defendant, whichever is shorter.[39] If a case is not initially removable but later becomes so (such as by dropping a nondiverse defendant), defendant may file a notice of removal within 30 days of receiving a court paper that first reveals that removal is now proper. There is also an absolute one-year limitation on removing cases based on §1332 jurisdiction. The time period, like all the removal requirements, is strictly enforced. Once the petition is filed, it operates as a stay on any state court proceedings.

Fourth, removal is generally proper if the federal district court could have had jurisdiction over the action had it been filed originally in federal court. For this reason you must determine if the federal district could have had proper subject matter jurisdiction over the plaintiff's original complaint.

There are three basic grounds for removal: diversity, federal question, and special removal statutes. Under §1441, removal jurisdiction can be based on diversity; this is usually proper when each plaintiff has a different citizenship from each defendant.[40] The complete diversity rule for removal has one important exception: §1441(b) prevents removal if any proper defendant is a citizen of the state where the action was brought. (The citizenship of defendants sued under fictitious names is disregarded.) This exception is based on the notion that a principal reason for permitting removal in diversity of citizenship cases is the possibility of local prejudice against noncitizen defendants, which fails if a defendant is a citizen of the forum state. Accordingly, the diversity jurisdiction for removal is narrower than diversity for original diversity jurisdiction purposes. In addition, complete diversity must exist both when plaintiff's original action was filed in state court and when the removal petition is filed.

Removal can also be based on federal question jurisdiction. If an action could have been brought in district court on federal question grounds, it can ordinarily be removed, and the citizenship of the parties is disregarded. Removal generally cannot be allowed unless the claim could be brought as an original action in federal court.

The removal sections also provide for removal in certain special circumstances. These include:

§1441(d) — civil actions against foreign states
§1442 — federal officers or agencies sued or prosecuted

---

39. See Murphy Bros. v. Michette Pipestringing, 526 U.S. 344 (1999).
40. See Lincoln Property Co. v. Roche, 546 U.S. 1 (2005), regarding the diversity of citizenship basis for removal.

§1442a — members of armed forces
§1443 — civil rights actions
§1444 — foreclosure against the United States

The Class Action Fairness Act of 2005 (28 U.S.C. §1332(d) and §1453) changed the rules governing the removal of class actions to federal court. CAFA permits removal of a class action without regard to whether any defendant is a citizen of the state in which the action is brought. It allows removal by any defendant without the consent of all defendants, and it overturns the rule requiring actions to be removed within one year. These changes make it much easier for a defendant to remove a class action to federal court.

Section 1445 makes certain actions nonremovable. These include actions under state workers' compensation acts; actions against railroads, their receivers, or trustees; and actions against a common carrier, its receivers, or trustees, arising under specific federal statutes.

A case removed to federal court may be remanded back to the original state court under §1447. A motion to remand based on defects in the removal procedure must be made within 30 days of the filing of the notice of removal. A remand based on lack of subject matter jurisdiction may be made at any time before final judgment. While a court in a contested removal case will usually decide issues of subject matter jurisdiction before issues of personal jurisdiction, there is no requirement that it always proceeds in this order.[41]

A plaintiff who wishes to file and keep a lawsuit in state court can use certain strategies to defeat removal. First, where diversity would otherwise permit removal, plaintiff can add a defendant who either is not diverse from the plaintiff or is a citizen of the forum state. So long as such a joinder is not fraudulent in the sense that plaintiff does not really wish to prosecute a claim against that party, it will defeat removal. Second, where diversity does not exist, plaintiff can draft the complaint to avoid pleading a claim that would permit removal based on federal question jurisdiction. Where plaintiff has decided that a state forum is preferable, it is often possible to structure the claims and select the defendants to prevent removal.

The mechanics of the removal procedure are discussed in §7.6.

§3.6. Personal jurisdiction[42]

Personal jurisdiction refers to the power of a court to bring a party before it. A judgment is not enforceable against a party unless that party can lawfully be brought into court and has received notice of the lawsuit. Thus, constitutional concepts of due process underlie this requirement.

Jurisdiction to adjudicate can be in personam, in rem, or quasi in rem. An in personam jurisdiction over a party is necessary for full enforcement

41. See Ruhrgas v. Marathon Gas, 526 U.S. 574 (1999).
42. Wright §§64–65; James & Hazard §§2.14–2.25; Friedenthal §§3.1–3.28; Moore's Manual §§6.01–6.19; Moore's Federal Practice §§0.219–0.229; Wright & Miller §§1061–1075.

of a judgment against a party and for the concepts of res judicata and collateral estoppel (now called claim preclusion and issue preclusion) to operate. An in rem action is one that involves property over which the parties have some dispute, and jurisdiction over the party exists by virtue of the party's ownership of the property. Finally, a quasi in rem action refers to an action brought to subject only certain property to the claims asserted. This is frequently done by seeking to attach property of a known party to satisfy a future judgment. These distinctions have less significance today at the federal court level, where the critical concerns involve the constitutional limits of personal jurisdiction and the issue of whether service was properly made. Hence, issues surrounding personal jurisdiction involve two separate questions:

1. Can the defendant constitutionally be subject to the court's jurisdiction?
2. Was service of process on the defendant proper?

The first question involves the due process limitations on personal jurisdiction, and the second involves the service-of-process requirements of Rule 4.

1.   Due process requirements

Due process issues do not arise for plaintiffs, since by initiating suit a plaintiff is considered to have voluntarily submitted to the court's jurisdiction for all purposes, including being required to respond to counterclaims and other claims brought in that action. Where a defendant is a resident of the forum state, due process problems do not arise, since by virtue of residency it is fair to require the defendant to defend against an action in the forum state. When a nonresident defendant, however, is sued in the forum state and does not consent to the jurisdiction of the court, due process problems may prevent that defendant from being required to defend there. Determining what the due process limitations are is a difficult question that the Supreme Court has frequently considered. The question is raised with increasing frequency as more businesses engage in national and international commerce and in e-commerce on the Internet.[43]

The leading constitutional cases include International Shoe Co. v. State of Washington, 326 U.S. 310 (1945), Hanson v. Denckla, 357 U.S. 235 (1958), and World-Wide Volkswagen Corp. v. Woodson, 444 U.S. 286 (1980). Recent significant Supreme Court cases are Burger King Corp. v. Rudzewicz, 471 U.S. 462 (1985), Asahi Metal Industry Co. v. Superior Court, 480 U.S. 102 (1987), and Burnham v. Superior Court, 495 U.S. 604 (1990).

---

43. The issue rarely arises in tort litigation, because a tort is usually seen as an event caused by a defendant that subjects him to the court's jurisdiction, and because state automobile statutes usually impose a "consent to be sued" fiction on out-of-state motorists.

In *International Shoe* the Court addressed the question of what activities by a corporation within a particular state will subject it to suit within that state consistent with due process concepts. It held that where a corporation's "minimum contacts" in the forum state were such that being forced to defend a suit in that state would not offend "traditional notions of fair play and substantial justice," jurisdiction was proper. Many subsequent decisions, of course, expounded on what minimum contacts satisfied due process. In *World-Wide Volkswagen,* the Court rejected the argument that an out-of-state seller should be subjected to suit in another state simply because it was foreseeable that the vehicle sold might be involved in a collision in another state. Instead, the Court stressed that minimum contacts protect a defendant from being sued in a remote or inconvenient forum, and that foreseeability does not by itself create such contacts as would satisfy due process requirements. Requiring a defendant to defend in the forum state, the Court held, must be fair and not impose unreasonable burdens on the defendant.[44]

In *Asahi Metal* a divided court held that merely placing a product into the stream of commerce is not an act that will subject a party to the forum state's jurisdiction, even if the party was aware that the stream of commerce would sweep the product into the forum state. Minimum contacts requires some action purposely directed toward the forum state.

Personal jurisdiction issues are common, particularly in lawsuits involving defendants engaged in interstate business activities. The most recent issues center on e-commerce activities on the Internet. Businesses are increasingly using their web sites for a range of activities, from advertising and informational purposes to conducting commercial sales and transmitting products. When litigation, whether based on contract or tort claims, springs from such uses, the question also arises whether these kinds of activities can subject a nonresident defendant to in personam jurisdiction in the state to which its web site activities reach. In due process terms, are these business uses of the Internet adequate "minimum contacts," did the defendant "purposely avail" itself of the privilege of conducting business in the state, or did the defendant "purposely direct" its activities to residents of the state, so that the nonresident defendant can "reasonably" be required to defend itself in the forum state? Case law, not surprisingly, is hardly uniform, as courts grapple with applying the Supreme Court's personal jurisdiction jurisprudence to doing business on the Internet.[45]

---

44. In *Burnham* the Court held that personal service within a forum state satisfies due process requirements.

45. See Robert W. Hamilton and Gregory A. Castanias, Tangled Web: Personal Jurisdiction and the Internet, 24 Litigation 27-35 (No 2, Winter 1998); Ira S. Nathenson, Showdown at the Domain Name Corral: Property Rights and Personal Jurisdiction Over Squatters, Poachers and Other Parasites, 58 U. Pitt. L. Rev. 911 (Summer 1997); Mane D'Amico, A Survey of the Current Cases of Personal Jurisdiction and the Internet, 1 J. of Internet Law 8 (1998); Sarah K. Jezairian, Lost in the Virtual Mall: Is Traditional Jurisdiction Analysis Applicable to E-Commerce Cases?, 24 Ariz. L. Rev. 965 (2000); 155 A.L.R. Fed. 535 (1999).

The minimum-contacts analysis applies with equal force to in rem and quasi in rem actions.[46] Because of this, distinctions such as in rem or quasi in rem have no direct bearing on the due process question of a defendant's amenability to suit in a particular forum. However, the distinctions are still important for determining the enforceability of judgments.

2. Service-of-process requirements

It is important to keep in mind that amenability to process is different from, and independent of, the adequacy of service of process. If a party is not constitutionally amenable to process, any service on that party will have no effect unless the party waives objections to the service. If a party is amenable to process, service of process on that party must still be properly made.

Service must be properly made because due process considerations require that service be made in a manner that is reasonably calculated to put a defendant on notice that he has been sued.[47] Since Rule 4(e) now permits service by any method allowed by the state law in which the district court is sitting, this means, in practical terms, that an out-of-state defendant can be served under the forum state's long-arm statutes. Alternatively, a defendant can be served pursuant to the law of the state in which service is effected.

Service of process under Rule 4 is discussed in §5.3.

§3.7. Venue[48]

A lawsuit must be filed in a proper place. Where a lawsuit can be filed is governed by venue statutes. Those statutes determine the geographic districts where the case can properly be heard.

Since venue provisions are designed in part to protect a defendant from being forced to litigate in an "unfair" forum, it follows that a defendant can waive the benefits of the venue rules. Hence, a defendant must raise improper venue in a timely manner, either by a Rule 12 motion or in the answer, otherwise objections will be deemed waived.

Because a plaintiff may sometimes have more than one available venue, the question of which venue to choose may arise. This question involves both practical and legal considerations. On the practical side, convenience and the cost to the plaintiff, the plaintiff's lawyer, and

---

46. The Supreme Court so held in Shaffer v. Heitner, 433 U.S. 186 (1977), deciding that a defendant's ownership of property by itself did not establish such contacts as would create proper personal jurisdiction over the defendant, where the claims were not related to the property.

47. See Mullane v. Central Hanover Bank, 339 U.S. 306 (1950); Dusenberg v. United States, 534 U.S. 161 (2002).

48. Wright §§42–44; James & Hazard §§2.10–2.11; Friedenthal §§2.15–2.17; Moore's Manual §§7.01–7.15; Manual of Federal Practice §§2.1–2.78; Moore's Federal Practice §§0.140–0.148; Wright & Miller §§3801–3868.

witnesses will frequently dominate the decision. The plaintiff's own district will often be the choice, if it is available. If the plaintiff's principal witnesses are in another district, that should be considered. On the legal side, choice-of-law decisions may be critical, since applicable substantive law may differ for such matters as statutes of limitations, elements of claims, and allowable damages. Further, since the subpoena power of a district is generally limited to its geographical boundaries, if uncooperative witnesses are out-of-state, you may need to choose another available forum to reach these witnesses. Finally, considerations such as the choice of judges, the desirability of prospective jury pools, and length of time until trial should all be considered.

1. Determining venue[49]

The general venue statute for federal district courts is §1391. Under §1391(a), if jurisdiction is based solely on diversity, venue is proper in

> (1) a judicial district where any defendant resides, if all defendants reside in the same state, (2) a judicial district in which a substantial part of the events or omissions giving rise to the claim occurred, or a substantial part of property which is the subject of the action is situated, or (3) a judicial district in which any defendant is subject to personal jurisdiction at the time the action is commenced, if there is no district in which the action may otherwise be brought.

Under §1391(b), if jurisdiction is based other than solely on diversity, venue is proper only in

> (1) a judicial district where any defendant resides, if all defendants reside in the same state, (2) a judicial district in which a substantial part of the events or omissions giving use to the claim occurred, or a substantial part of property that is the subject of the action is situated, or (3) a judicial district in which any defendant may be found, if there is no district in which the action may otherwise be brought.

However, there are numerous special venue statutes, both in the Title 28 venue section and elsewhere, that control venue in special kinds of cases. The special provisions begin with §1394. Other venue provisions are scattered throughout the United States Code, usually as part of the substantive statute that creates a cause of action.[50] Consequently, you must always check whether a special venue statute exists that overrides the general provisions of §1391.

In addition, §1392 governs venue in "local" actions that are actions involving property. Whether the action is in rem, so that §1392 applies, is

---

49. Wright §42; James & Hazard §2.10; Friedenthal §2.15; Moore's Manual §§7.02–7.11; Manual of Federal Practice §§2.1–2.12; Wright & Miller §3801.
50. For a list of such venue statutes, see Moore's Federal Practice §0.142.

controlled by the nature of the remedy sought. Ordinarily, if the remedy is specific to the property, the action will be local, and §1392 makes the venue that of the res involved.

Once the applicable statutes are determined, the question of a party's residence arises, since §1391 is based on residence. An individual's residence is where the individual is domiciled. A corporation under §1391(c) is considered a resident of any district "in which it is subject to personal jurisdiction at the time the action is commenced." Unincorporated associations, if they have no capacity to sue under state law, are residents of each district in which any member of the association resides. If the association is an entity entitled to sue under state law, the association is a citizen of the district where it conducts its business. Aliens under §1391(d) can be sued in any district. Finally, where a defendant is the United States, its agencies, officers, or employees, §1391(e) controls and provides that venue is generally proper — unless law provides otherwise — in a district where the defendant resides, where a substantial part of the events or omissions giving rise to the claim occurred, where a substantial part of property involved in the action is located, or where the plaintiff resides if no property is involved.

The venue provisions control where a plaintiff files the initial complaint against the original defendants. They do not apply to counterclaims, cross-claims, or third-party claims, since these are seen as ancillary to the initial suit and hence raise no additional venue issues.

2. Change of venue[51]

A change of venue can be based on three grounds: improper venue, governed by §1406; inconvenient venue, governed by §1404; and the doctrine of forum non conveniens. Under §1406, the court has discretion either to dismiss or to transfer to a proper venue any case that has been filed in an improper venue. Since the statute encourages transfers "if it be in the interest of justice," this is the usual approach. Keep in mind that proper venue is a personal right. A plaintiff, by filing an action in an improper venue, waives the right to object to it. A defendant must raise any venue objection either by a Rule 12 motion or in the defendant's answer, otherwise objections will usually be considered waived.

Under §1404(a), the court may transfer a case from a proper venue to another venue, "where it might have been brought," "for the convenience of parties and witnesses, in the interest of justice." This section recognizes that a plaintiff frequently has venue choices, and that the plaintiff's choice, while proper, may not be the most convenient forum for the case seen as a whole. If this situation exists, the court can transfer the case to the more convenient forum, the only restriction being that the new forum must be in

---

51. Wright §44; James & Hazard §2.11; Friedenthal §2.17; Moore's Manual §7.12; Manual of Federal Practice §§2.52–2.74; Moore's Federal Practice §§0.145–0.148; Wright & Miller §§3841–3855.

a district in which the plaintiff could have filed the action and where the court could have obtained personal jurisdiction over the defendants.

When a case is transferred from one venue to another, the substantive law follows the case. This is important in diversity cases, where the forum state's substantive law, including its conflicts of law rules, is applied. When a case is transferred to another district, in another state, the original substantive law is still applied to the case. This rule avoids forum shopping by the defense in an attempt to get more favorable law applied to the case.

The doctrine of forum non conveniens recognizes that there may be instances in which a court may dismiss an action because the selected forum, while proper, is inconvenient. The leading case is Gulf Oil Corp. v. Gilbert, 330 U.S. 501 (1947). Today most cases are decided under the venue transfer rule, §1404(a). However, the forum non conveniens doctrine is still used, particularly in cases in which the events on which the action is based occurred in a foreign country.[52]

---

52. See In re Union Carbide Gas Plant Explosion, 809 F.2d 195 (2d Cir. 1987).

IV
CASE EVALUATION AND STRATEGY

§4.1. Introduction

Case evaluation requires that you gather enough facts and consider sufficiently the legal issues to decide intelligently whether to take the case. Then, if you decide to take it, the evaluation requires that you devise a realistic, cost-effective litigation plan. This chapter discusses making the initial decision to take a case, establishing the attorney-client relationship, developing a litigation strategy, and completing prefiling requirements.

§4.2. Taking the case

You should take those cases that have factual and legal merit and are economically feasible, and you should usually decline the others. But just how and when do you decide if you should take a case?

First, always check for conflicts of interest with existing and former clients. A lawyer's relationship with a client is based on two key duties: loyalty and confidentiality. Both duties may be breached in the litigation environment if a lawyer represents multiple clients on the same matter if the interests of the clients are directly adverse, or represents a client against a former client on a substantially related matter in which the client's interests are materially adverse to the interests of the former client. A law firm and its lawyers are generally viewed as a single entity, and for conflicts purposes lawyers generally carry their former clients from former firms and government offices to their present firms. Hence, a conflict of interest may disqualify an entire firm, not just a lawyer within the firm. The bigger the firm, the more likely conflicts of interest will arise with present and former clients. The time to determine if a conflict of interest exists, and whether it bars representation of the client, is now, not when an opposing party moves to disqualify you or your firm.[1]

Law firms must have conflicts procedures to screen new matters for potential conflicts. These procedures include circulating a new client or new matter memorandum to all lawyers in the firm, using a docket or conflicts clerk to check for potential conflicts with existing or former clients in the firm's client data base, and having new lawyers list all former clients and matters they worked on at previous firms or government offices so that these can be entered into the conflicts data base. Developing a conflicts search procedure and following it carefully for every new client and matter will identify possible problems so that they can be analyzed and resolved before litigation is underway.

A conflict of interest situation in litigation arises when, simply stated, a law firm (1) represents a new client against another current client in the same or an unrelated matter, (2) represents a new client against a former client in the same or a substantially related matter, or (3) represents two clients in the same matter. When such a situation arises, it must be resolved under the applicable ethics rules.

If representing a client will be "directly adverse" to another client, the law firm cannot undertake the representation unless, following the requirements of Model Rule 1.7(a), the lawyer reasonably believes the representation will not adversely affect the relationship with the other client, and each client consents after consultation.

If representing a client "may be materially limited" by the lawyer's responsibilities to another client, a third person, or the lawyer's own interests, the law firm cannot undertake the representation unless, following the requirements of Model Rule 1.7(b), the law firm reasonably believes the representation would not be adversely affected, and the client consents after consultation. If multiple clients in a single matter are involved, that consultation must include explaining the implications of the common representation and the advantages and risks involved.

The usual way to raise this is to send a "conflict waiver" letter both to the existing client and the potential client. The letter should set out the requirements of Model Rule 1.7; state your belief, based on the presently known facts, that joint representation is not precluded by the rule because the two parties do not have interests that are directly adverse to each other within the meaning of the rule; explain the advantages of joint representation (primarily cost savings and a united stance during the litigation); explain the risks of joint representation (primarily that a settlement offer to one party may create a conflict, a judgment against one party may create indemnification and contribution claims, and that the attorney-client privilege may be affected); explain what may happen if claims do arise between the two parties (which usually means that you must drop the new party and continue representing only the original party); and remind the party that he has the right to consult with independent counsel on these matters. Finally, the letter should provide that, if the party consents

---

1. The controlling conflicts rules are Rules 1.7 through 1.12 of the Model Rules of Professional Conduct.

to the joint representation, he should sign the original of the letter, indicating his consent and opportunity to consult with independent counsel, and return it to you. Once you receive the signed consents from both parties, you can then begin to jointly represent them.

The question of whether a conflict exists and, if so, whether and how it can be resolved can be complicated and requires knowledge of all the applicable ethics rules, opinions, and case law in that jurisdiction. Because of this, most law firms, as part of their conflicts-check procedures, have an experienced partner available to review all new matters in which a possible conflict of interest may exist. In difficult situations, outside counsel may be necessary to review the question of whether a conflict exists and whether it can be waived.

Consider, for example, the common situation in which a driver and passenger in a car, involved in a collision with another car, seek a lawyer to sue the driver of the other car. Since the passenger could potentially sue the driver of the car in which she was riding (if there is any evidence of that driver's negligence), as well as the driver of the other car, a conflict of interest may exist between the passenger and her driver. In this situation, the passenger must be fully informed of her right to sue her own driver and the consequences if she decides not to sue, and must have the opportunity to consult further about the situation. If the passenger waives her right to sue her driver, the conflict disappears, and the lawyer can represent both the passenger and her driver in a lawsuit against the driver of the other car. (Note, however, that other conflicts may arise, such as whether to accept a proposed aggregate settlement, in which case Model Rule 1.8(g) must be followed.)

Second, your litigation chart, which sets out the potential legal claims and required elements of proof for each claim, provided the direction for your factual and legal investigation. This provides the framework from which to analyze the case. In addition, keep in mind Rule 11, which provides that an attorney's signature on a pleading constitutes a verification that the attorney has conducted a "reasonable inquiry" into the facts and law.[2] Hence, you cannot plead claims, remedies, or defenses that you have not adequately investigated to determine whether they are well grounded.

As the lawyer for a prospective plaintiff, you should take a case only if you can realistically expect to prove a prima facie case on at least one theory of recovery. You should already have some admissible proof for each element of each asserted claim or have a reasonable basis for believing you will get such missing proof during formal discovery. In addition, the potential recovery must be large enough to justify the work and risks of litigation. Many lawyers, for example, refuse even a simple case on a contingency fee basis unless a realistic recovery is at least in the $20,000 range because the fee, usually one-third of any recovery, will simply not provide reasonable compensation for the work and risks involved. In a complex case, such as a medical malpractice claim, the realistic damages may have to be at least in the $500,000 range to make it economically feasible to take the case.

2. See discussion of Rule 11 in §5.2.4.

When to decide, as a plaintiff's lawyer, to accept or decline a case depends on the type of case and the factual and legal issues involved. For example, you might accept a simple automobile collision case not involving a serious injury after interviewing the client and reviewing the police accident report. Sometimes such a limited investigation will be enough to assess whether the client "has a case," whether, economically speaking, the damages are substantial enough to make it worth pursuing, and whether a judgment can actually be collected. In more complex matters, however, such as serious personal injury, medical malpractice, products liability, or commercial cases, you may need to do substantial legal research, extensive factual investigation, and have an expert review the case before you can make this decision. The basic question is always the same: Do I know enough from my fact investigation and legal research to conclude that the client has a provable case with substantial damages that can be collected? If the case appears weak on liability or damages, involves a great deal of work, and would be taken on a contingency fee basis, the best time to turn it down is now. Cases rarely look better than when they first walk in the door. Every lawyer has taken cases and later regretted it. The best way to avoid this is by rejecting the marginal cases early.

There are exceptions. First, where a plaintiff is in imminent danger of having an applicable statute of limitations run, your first obligation is to file a claim to prevent the statute from running, even though you have not had an opportunity to investigate the facts and research the law. Protecting the plaintiff's claim from a limitations bar must take precedence over other considerations.[3] Second, keep in mind that lawyers frequently take cases for reasons other than the income that the case will produce.[4]

If you decide to take a case, you need to enter into an agreement with the client. If you turn down the case, you need to send the client a letter declining representation. These steps are discussed in the following sections.

As a defendant's lawyer, the decision whether to take a case is in one way easier and in another way more difficult. It is easier from the economic point of view, since defendant's cases are not taken on a contingency basis. So long as the defendant agrees on how to pay the lawyer for the legal services, and the defendant is able and willing to pay, there are no economic risks in taking a weak case. However, the decision is more difficult in the sense that the lawyer and the defendant must agree on how best to defend the case. If the client realizes the case is not defensible on the merits, the client may try to pressure the lawyer to drag out the case or file unfounded defenses, counterclaims, or third-party claims. But a defense lawyer has the same obligations, under ethics rules as well as under Rule 11, as the plaintiff's lawyer. Such conflicts are best handled at the outset by letting the client know what you can and cannot do in defending the case and by reaching agreement on how you plan to defend.

3. Protecting the plaintiff's claim under these circumstances should not constitute a Rule 11 violation. See Boone v. Superior Ct., 145 Ariz. 235, 700 P.2d 1335 (1985).
4. See §2.7.

§4.3.   Establishing the terms of the attorney-client agreement

The attorney-client relationship should be formally established with a written agreement. There are several reasons for this. First, any contractual relationship is best established by a written instrument. Second, the agreement will prove the existence of an attorney-client relationship for privilege purposes. Third, it will establish the work to be done, what will not be done, and the basis for compensation, all of which are necessary for a good working relationship with the client. Fourth, Model Rule 1.5 requires that a client be informed in writing of how the fee is set and of all the material facts concerning the representation. Although a written agreement signed by the client is required only in contingency and referral cases, good practice dictates its use in all cases. For all these reasons, you need a written agreement with the client.

Unless your client is sophisticated and has experience working with lawyers, the client will have little understanding of the legal work involved in litigation and the various fee arrangements that can be made. It is in everyone's best interests that the client be educated on these matters. You should discuss how you set your fees, and the expected costs, with the client.

Lawyers most commonly incorporate the terms of the representation in a letter from the lawyer to the client, usually called an engagement letter. The letter and a copy are sent to the client, who signs the copy to show approval of the terms and returns it to the lawyer. Written contracts are sometimes used, particularly with contingency fee agreements and institutional clients. Regardless of which method is used, it should be sufficiently detailed to cover all aspects of the relationship. Unfortunately, disputes between lawyers and clients are common, but they can largely be avoided by making sure that the agreement is drafted in clear and simple English, covers all likely issues, and specifies what is not covered. In disputes between lawyers and their clients, ambiguities and omissions in attorney-client agreements will usually be strictly construed against the lawyer.[5] The agreement should cover the following basic subjects.

1.   Work covered

The agreement should specify what work will be performed and what will not be. For example, the agreement might be to prosecute a negligence claim arising out of a car accident through settlement or trial. If you will not handle any appeal or postjudgment proceedings to collect a judgment, or if there will be an additional charge for any such work, the agreement should specify this. If you will not handle a workers' compensation claim, insurance claim, or other related matters, the agreement should say so. In general, you must guard against a client thinking that you would do more than you agreed to do. Spelling out what is not covered should prevent

---

5. See R. Rossi, Attorney's Fees (2d ed. 1995).

this from happening. It is also a good idea, especially as the plaintiff in personal injury cases, to state explicitly that you have not guaranteed any particular outcome.

2. Who will do the work?

The agreement should specify who will do the work, unless the lawyer is a solo practitioner or it is clear that the entire law firm will collectively do the work. Clients usually think that they are hiring a particular lawyer to do all the necessary work on their problem. Clients today will not tolerate a bill that shows several other lawyers in a firm working on their problem, when they have never met these lawyers and were never told they would be involved. Consequently, particularly when the client is sophisticated and the matter complex, the agreement should specify who the supervising lawyer will be and how the matter will be staffed with other partners, associates, paralegals, and support staff.

3. Lawyer's fee[6]

A lawyer's fee is the compensation the lawyer will receive for professional services rendered on behalf of the client. The amount of the lawyer's fee, the way it will be determined, and when it will be paid must be spelled out. The total fee must be reasonable in light of the work to be done, the difficulty of the work, the amount of time it will involve, and the customary range of fees for similar work in your locality.

The agreement should specify how the fee will be determined. Three approaches are commonly employed: an hourly rate (common in corporate, commercial, and insurance defense cases), a fixed flat fee (common in criminal defense and family law cases), and the contingency fee (common in plaintiff's personal injury cases). Obviously the agreement can specify any number of combinations or modifications of these basic approaches, unless the fee is regulated or set by rule or statute. For example, agreements frequently specify a minimum retainer fee, paid up front, that is credited against an hourly billing rate. The agreement might use more recent approaches such as capped fees, or incentive billing and defense contingency fees, which base the fee in part on obtaining favorable results. When the fee is based on an hourly rate, the client must understand that what is being paid for is the lawyer's expertise and time. Hence, any time expended on a client's case will be billed to the client, regardless of whether the time is spent on court appearances, conferences, research, drafting documents, or making telephone calls.

The agreement should define how the fee amount is determined and when it should be paid. For instance, in personal injury cases where the plaintiff's attorney's fees are usually a percentage of any recovery, the

---

6. See Model Rules of Professional Conduct, Rule 1.5.

agreement must specify whether the percentage is computed before or after expenses are deducted and that the fee is due when any judgment is actually collected. If the fee is on an hourly basis, it's a good idea to estimate the fee range, since a common misunderstanding with clients is what the total fee is likely to be.

If a fee will be shared with another lawyer outside the principal lawyer's firm, you must disclose this fact to the client and obtain his consent. The division of fees must be proportionate to the work done by each lawyer, or each lawyer assumes joint responsibility for the representation and the client agrees in writing.[7]

A lawyer has an ethical duty to make the fee reasonable. This may mean that the lawyer must review the fee at the end of the representation, even in a contingent fee situation, to make sure it is in fact reasonable before submitting it to or collecting it from the client.[8] A fee agreement that was reasonable when made may no longer be reasonable at the end of the representation.

Many statutes and rules regulate and limit attorney's fees. For example, statutory causes of action frequently either limit attorney's fees or make them subject to court approval.[9] Make sure that your agreement complies with any applicable statutes and rules.

An attorney's lien, the right of a lawyer to hold or retain money or property until all proper charges have been paid or adjusted, can usually be imposed on a judgment to ensure payment of the fee. This is frequently done in contingent fee situations. In some jurisdictions an attorney's lien is only enforceable if the client expressly agrees to it. Hence, it is good practice to discuss the lien with the client and have the written agreement state that the client agrees to it.

4.   Retainers

In some situations a lawyer should insist on a retainer to ensure payment of the fee and other costs. A retainer is simply a cash payment of a sum of money to the lawyer before work begins on the client's case. This makes sure that the lawyer will get paid for the work and that costs the lawyer advances will be reimbursed. A common arrangement is to insist on a retainer, and then periodically deduct fees and costs as they are incurred. Regardless of the precise arrangement, the agreement must specify the amount of the retainer, when it must be remitted, and what fees and costs will be deducted from it.

Whenever a lawyer receives advanced funds from a client, the funds must be put in a separate client trust account. Under no circumstances can any client's funds be commingled with the lawyer's funds.[10] Funds of all of

---

7. See Model Rules of Professional Conduct, Rule 1.5(e).

8. See, e.g., In the Matter of Schwartz, 686 P.2d 1236 (Ariz. 1984).

9. See, e.g., Federal Tort Claims Act, 28 U.S.C. §2678; M. F. Derfner & A. D. Wolfe, Court Awarded Attorney Fees (1983).

10. See Model Rules of Professional Conduct, Rule 1.15.

a lawyer's clients can be held in one trust account; however, a separate ledger must be kept for each client showing receipts and disbursements. Most states have adopted, through statutes or court rules, the Interest on Lawyer's Trust Accounts (IOLTA) system, which requires holding client funds in interest-bearing accounts.[11]

5. Costs

The agreement should distinguish between fees due the lawyer for professional representation and the costs and expenses incurred during the course of that representation. The agreement should note anticipated costs, such as filing fees and other court costs; expert witness fees and expenses; court reporter fees; travel expenses; photocopying, mailing, and long distance calls. It is sometimes a good idea to estimate the usual costs for the type of case involved. In some cases, such as commercial, medical malpractice, and products liability cases, the costs of paralegals, experts, travel, and other expenses can exceed the lawyer's fee. The agreement should also specify when the costs will be paid; customarily the client is billed at regular intervals, such as monthly or quarterly. The agreement should make clear that costs are the client's obligation, even if no recovery is obtained.

Plaintiff's personal injury cases present a special situation. The reason for permitting a contingency fee arrangement—that the client is otherwise unable to pay for legal representation—also bears on the propriety of advancing costs. A lawyer may advance costs, such as court costs, deposition expenses, investigator fees, and expert witness fees; however, the client ultimately is still responsible for paying those costs. The most common approach is to reimburse costs to the lawyer when a judgment is actually paid. If there is no recovery, the client is still responsible for paying the costs, although a client without money will probably not be able to reimburse the lawyer. For this reason, some lawyers accept contingency fee arrangements for cases that will have substantial costs only if the client advances a sum of money sufficient to cover the expected costs. Requiring a client to advance expected costs has another benefit: It tends to weed out weak cases. A prospective client who knows his case is weak often will refuse to advance costs for an expert review before filing suit or will refuse to pay a retainer. Clients who, though able, refuse to invest in their lawsuits are usually clients to avoid.

11. In Brown v. Legal Foundation of Washington, 538 U.S. 216 (2003), the Supreme Court held that interest earned on IOLTA funds was not a compensable regulatory taking for 5th Amendment purposes since the client suffered no financial loss, because the client's funds, if deposited in an individual account, would have earned no interest.

6.   Billings

The agreement should specify when fees and costs will be billed. While monthly billing is normally best for both lawyer and client, less frequent billings are sometimes appropriate, particularly for regular business clients, or if little work is done in any given month.

If the client is new, or has a spotty payment history, consider advising the client of your intent to stop work on the case if your bills are not paid and charging interest on late payments. You should also obtain the client's consent to withdraw in the event of non-payment, regardless of the status of the case.

7.   Authorization to file suit and withdraw

The agreement should contain a statement that authorizes the lawyer to file suit on behalf of the client or, if a defendant, authorizes the lawyer to defend the suit. The client should also be told that you have a right to withdraw from the case in case of non-payment of fees, or if later developments show that the matter has no merit. However, keep in mind that you must receive permission from the court before which the case is pending, and your withdrawal cannot prejudice the client.[12]

The terms of the agreement should then be put in writing, either in a letter to the client or in a written agreement. If a contingency fee agreement, it must be in writing and signed by the client. As with any legal document, it should be written in plain English, not legalese.

Example (hourly fee agreement letter):

Dear Mr. Jones:

As we discussed in my office yesterday, I have agreed to represent you in the divorce proceedings recently started by your wife Joan. I will handle all negotiations necessary to attempt a property settlement before trial. If a trial becomes necessary, I will represent you to the conclusion of the trial and until the court enters a final divorce decree.

Fees for representing you will be based on the time expended on your case. My present hourly rate is $100 per hour. You have agreed to provide a retainer of $1,500 within one week. Based on what you have told me, I estimate the fee in your matter will be in the $3,000 to $5,000 range, although circumstances may change this estimate. The total fee will depend on the particular facts and circumstances of your situation and the time necessary to represent you to the conclusion of your divorce.

In addition to my fee, there will also be certain costs expended on your case, such as court filing fees, court reporter fees, long

---

12. See Model Rules of Professional Conduct, Rule 1.16(b).

distance telephone and photocopying charges. You will be responsible for paying all such costs. Costs in divorce cases vary but usually fall in the $200 to $400 range.

I will send you an itemized statement each month showing the time I have spent on your case and the other costs that have been incurred. I will subtract each monthly statement from the $1,500 retainer until it has been used up. I will then bill you directly, and you have agreed to pay those monthly statements in full when you receive them. In the event that my bills are not paid promptly, you agree that I may withdraw from representing you in this matter.

Please confirm that this letter correctly reflects the terms of our agreement by signing and dating the enclosed copy of this letter on the spaces provided and returning the copy to me. If any of this is unclear, or you have other questions about this agreement, please call me as soon as possible.

Upon receipt of the signed letter and a check for the $1,500 retainer, I will begin to represent you and work on your case. If I do not receive the signed letter and check within ten days, I will assume that you have decided to retain another lawyer to represent you in this matter.

Sincerely,

/s/ John Smith

Agreed: _____
        John Jones

Dated: _____

Example (contingency fee agreement):

AGREEMENT

Date: _____

I agree to employ the law firm of Smith & Smith as my attorneys to investigate and, if warranted, prosecute all claims for damages against Frank Johnson and all other persons or entities that may be liable on account of an automobile collision that occurred on June 1, 2005, at approximately 3:00 P.M., near the intersection of Maple and Elm Streets in this city. I authorize you to file suit on my behalf.

I agree to pay Smith & Smith a fee that will be one-third (33⅓ percent) of any sum recovered in this case, regardless of whether received through a settlement, lawsuit, or any other way. The fee will be calculated on the sum recovered, after costs and expenses have been deducted. The fee will be paid when any moneys are actually received in this case. I agree that Smith & Smith has an express attorney's lien on any recovery to ensure that their fee is paid. I agree that no representations or guarantees of a recovery, or amount of any recovery, have been made.

I agree to pay all necessary costs and expenses, such as court filing fees, court reporter fees, expert witness fees and expenses, travel expenses, long distance telephone costs, and photocopying charges, but these costs and expenses will not be due until a recovery is actually received in this case. I understand that I am also responsible for paying these costs and expenses, even if no recovery is received.

I agree that this agreement does *not* cover matters other than those described above. It does not cover an appeal from any judgment entered, any efforts necessary to collect money due because of a judgment entered, or any efforts necessary to obtain other benefits such as insurance, employment, Social Security and Veteran's Administration benefits.

I understand that I have the right to discharge Smith & Smith at any time. In that event, I agree to pay Smith & Smith for the reasonable value of its services up to the date of the discharge. The reasonable value of its services shall be made on the basis of a professional evaluation of its services to the ultimate recovery or results in the case.

If in the opinion of Smith & Smith the claims no longer appear to have merit, or a change in circumstances occurs, so that reasonable prospects no longer exist for receiving or collecting a judgment, Smith & Smith has the right to cancel this agreement and withdraw from representing me. In that event, Smith & Smith agrees to turn over to me all papers relating to this claim, and Smith & Smith is still entitled to reimbursement for reasonable costs and expenses it has incurred.

Agreed: _____
           John Jones

I agree to represent John Jones in the matter described above. I will receive no fee unless a recovery is obtained. If a recovery is actually received, I will receive a fee as described above.

I agree to notify John Jones of all developments in this matter promptly, and will make no settlement of this matter without his consent.

Agreed: _____
           John Smith for
           Smith & Smith

8. Next steps

Once you have decided to take the case and have reached an agreement with the client, there are several steps you should take to get the new relationship started on the right track and make sure that it stays on that track. First, if your agreement includes an express attorney's lien, send a notice of your attorney's lien to the opposing party's lawyer and any insurance companies. Some jurisdictions have standard attorney's lien forms used in litigation. Sending out the notices will ensure that your fee is paid when any judgment is paid.

Second, you should have the client sign authorization forms that will allow you to obtain certain records before filing suit. Depending on your jurisdiction's laws and practice, you may need signed authorizations to get police reports and motor vehicle records; hospital, doctor, employment, and insurance records; Social Security, Veterans Administration, and other governmental records. Find out what type of authorization is necessary, and become familiar with the statutes requiring that such documents be made available to the client or his lawyer on request. You can also call the particular agency to learn its requirements and procedures. Some agencies have standard authorization forms.

Third, your client needs advice on what he should and should not do. He should be told not to talk to anyone other than you about the matter. Explain that persons may try to interview him or get him to make or sign statements. He should tell such persons that he is represented by a lawyer and cannot talk to them, and he should notify you of all such attempts. Explain that he is generally not required to talk to anyone unless required through the formal discovery process; he should direct all requests for information to you. He should not sign anything without first discussing it with you. Other persons may try to give him money. He should refuse any such attempts, and report them to you. He should be told to save and collect all relevant records, documents, bills, checks, and paperwork of any kind in his possession and deliver them to you; he should send records and documents that subsequently come into his possession to you as well.

Fourth, your client needs a blueprint for the future, since he may have little idea how civil litigation is actually conducted. He should be told what needs to be done before suit is filed, what happens during the pleadings, discovery, and motion practice stages of the litigation process, and what his role in this process will be. He should have some idea of how much time each of these stages takes and how far in the future any trial is likely to be; at the same time he should be aware that most cases are settled before trial. He also needs to be reminded of the risks and costs of any lawsuit, including the risk of an adverse verdict after trial. A well-informed client will understand the process he is a part of and will be likely to assist you throughout. Many lawyers use a follow-up letter or brochure that repeats this advice and contains a chronology of likely events. This is a sound practice that can easily be tailored to your litigation practice.

This is a good time, particularly for the defense side, to have a serious talk with the client who likely will, and probably ought to, lose. Such a client needs a dose of reality early, before he develops an unrealistic set of expectations about what you can do and about how the case will probably turn out. Such a client needs to be told clearly and regularly what you can do, as well as what you cannot do, to defend the case. It is difficult enough defending a weak case; a difficult client, with unrealistic hopes and expectations about litigation, only compounds the problems.

Finally, maintain communication with your client. Litigation goes in spurts; a period of activity is often followed by weeks of inactivity. If your client has not heard from you recently, he may erroneously conclude that you don't care about him or have lost interest in his case. Accordingly, make sure you maintain contact. Send him copies of all pleadings, discovery, motions, and other court papers. Write him periodically to let him know what is going on in the case. If nothing is happening, let him know and explain why. A well-informed client will usually be a cooperative, satisfied client.

§4.4.   Declining representation

A lawyer may not always be able to take a case. The matter may not be within the lawyer's expertise. It may not have merit or be large enough to justify a suit, or the defendant may not be able to pay a judgment. The lawyer may be too busy or have a conflict of interest. Or the lawyer may be unable to agree with the client on a fee. Whatever the reason, when a lawyer declines a potential case, it should be put in writing, usually in a letter to the prospective client.

Where a lawyer represents one party but cannot represent a related party because of a potential conflict of interest, the related party, who may be expecting representation, should be sent a letter in which the lawyer declines employment. Also, if an attorney withdraws from representing a client, an appropriate letter should be sent. It is important to make a decision and send the notification promptly, since a person's rights may be affected by any delay.

The letter declining the case ensures that the party clearly understands that you will not be representing her, and can help resolve any question about whether the attorney had a duty to protect the party's interests even though she was never a client.[13] If you decide not to represent a party, you nevertheless have an obligation to warn her if a statute of limitations or other notice statute may run shortly, so that she can get another lawyer in time.[14]

Example (letter):

Dear Mr. Jones:

As we discussed in my office yesterday, I will not be able to represent you for any claims you may have based on an automobile collision that occurred near the intersection of Maple and Elm Streets in this city on June 1, 2005, at approximately 3:00 P.M.

Since I cannot take your case, you may wish to see another lawyer about handling this matter for you. As we discussed yesterday, if you wish to have another lawyer represent you, you

13. See J. M. Smith & R. E. Mallen, Preventing Legal Malpractice 4–5 (2d ed. 1996).

14. See, e.g., Togstad v. Vesely, 291 N.W.2d 686 (Minn. 1980).

should do so promptly. If you do not, there may be legal problems, such as a statute of limitations bar, that might prevent you from pursuing your claims. Since your accident happened on June 1, 2005, and the statute of limitations for tort claims in this state is two years, if you wish to file a lawsuit you must do so *before* June 1, 2007. To avoid such problems, I recommend that you find another lawyer promptly, so any rights you have can be protected.

Enclosed are the originals of the police reports and insurance claim forms you brought to my office.

Sincerely yours,

/s/ *John Smith*

Make sure that the statute of limitations computation is correct and, if there is a shorter statutory or contractual notice requirement which applies, that this is stated and computed correctly as well. If you are not sure of the computation period, do not state the date, since an incorrect statement could subject you to liability.

The letter should be sent by registered mail, return receipt by addressee only requested. When you get the signed return receipt, staple it to the copy of your letter. This will be persuasive evidence to rebut any later claim that you never actually declined the case.

§4.5. *Planning the litigation*

Assume you have accumulated the facts available through informal discovery; researched the possible legal claims, remedies, defenses, and counterclaims; put them on your litigation chart; researched other procedural questions; reached an agreement with the client to represent him; and have no timing problems. Now is the time, before filing your initial pleading, to structure a litigation plan.

A litigation plan consists of defining the client's objectives and developing a strategy to achieve those objectives. Once you develop a strategy in broad terms, you can then divide the strategy into its component, chronological parts.

Even if you think a litigation plan can't be developed, your client will think it can, and he's right. Sophisticated commercial clients, such as insurance companies and corporations, usually require a litigation plan before authorizing a lawsuit or, if a defendant, after receiving the complaint. The litigation plan requirements usually include an explanation of what claims, remedies, or defenses you will raise; a description of the basic facts, including the anticipated factual issues; an explanation of the planned discovery; a description of anticipated legal issues; an assessment of settlement possibilities; an assessment of the likely trial outcome; and cost projections for each stage of the plan. If sophisticated users of legal services have found that a detailed litigation plan promotes cost-effective representation, doesn't it make sense to make such a plan in every kind of case?

After you have completed your informal investigation, the basic steps in developing a litigation plan are the following:

1.   Reevaluate the client's objectives, priorities, and cost constraints
2.   Define the client's litigation objectives
3.   Develop a "theory of the case"
4.   Plan the pleadings and jury demand
5.   Plan the discovery
6.   Plan the dispositive motions
7.   Plan the settlement approach
8.   Develop a litigation timetable

1.   Reevaluate the client's objectives, priorities, and cost constraints

When the client first came to you for legal advice, he had one or more "problems" he told you about. One of your first steps was to identify his legal problems and objectives, and develop a scale of priorities for those objectives. Now is the time to reassess those problems and objectives. You will have the benefit of your partially completed litigation chart showing the fruits of your research and informal fact investigation. You will also know the client's cost constraints. Finally, time has passed. All of these may influence what the client's current objectives and priorities are. You need to sit down with the client, review what you have done to date, determine if the client's thinking is the same or has changed, and analyze those objectives and priorities to see if they still make sense in light of what you now know about the case.[15]

2.   Define the client's litigation objectives

If the client's thinking is unchanged and the dispute cannot be resolved short of litigation, you next need to decide on broad litigation objectives that serve the client's overall objectives and priorities. Always remember that the client controls the objectives of the litigation, and the lawyer decides on the means to achieve those objectives. For example, suppose that your plaintiff-client wants to settle early in the case and to keep expenses at a minimum. Your strategy may be to keep the pleadings simple, to push for focused discovery, and then to start early settlement discussions. On the other hand, suppose that you anticipate that a trial will be necessary. Your strategy may be to use broad pleadings with alternative theories of recovery, to engage in extensive discovery, and to prepare thoroughly for trial. Your litigation objectives will then form the basis for the remainder of your litigation plan.

15. Model Rules of Professional Conduct, Rule 1.2(a), provides that the client decides the objectives of the representation, subject to certain limitations.

3.   Develop a "theory of the case"

Your side's "story" is a critical part of the litigation plan. You need to review what you presently know about the uncontested and contested facts, and ask some basic questions. Is your side's story complete or are there significant missing pieces? Are your client and witnesses reliable? Do their stories make sense? Is your side's story one that has jury appeal? Where does your side's version and the other side's version of the facts clash? How do you plan to win the credibility battle over the disputed facts?

Trial lawyers frequently call their side's position the "theory of the case."[16] Those with experience know that most trials are won on the facts, not the law. Find the winning story that shows the other side acted unfairly and that an injustice exists that needs to be fixed. The winning side usually organizes credible witnesses and exhibits into a believable story, and wins the war over the disputed facts by presenting more persuasive evidence on its side of the dispute. This will only happen if you take the time to develop a coherent, persuasive theory of the case before drafting the pleadings.

4.   Plan the pleadings and jury demand

Pleadings are the vehicle by which you bring your theory of the case to court. Seen this way, you will not make the mistake of (and violate Rule 11 by) raising a number of allegations in your pleadings and then wondering how you can find facts that fit into the theories of recovery.

What claims, remedies, or defenses should you assert? Inexperienced litigators often "throw the book at them" and plead every conceivable claim, remedy, or defense that meets Rule 11 requirements. This illusion of safety can come at a high price. By adding claims, a case becomes more complex, with its additional costs and time requirements. Adding claims frequently results in adding parties, again making the litigation more involved. Adding claims also broadens the scope of discovery with the danger that discovery, always expensive and time consuming, may escalate out of control. While you must protect the client's legal interests by advancing essential claims, you should also consider the costs and disadvantages of pursuing every supportable claim against every proper party.

The better approach is to begin with your theory of the case. What claims, remedies, or defenses are reasonably supported by the facts that you have obtained through informal discovery or that you reasonably can expect to support with the fruits of formal discovery? Beyond that, do you have a realistic ability to prevail on each legal theory?

Once you have determined which legal theories can be supported, it's time to decide which ones to raise in a pleading. You again need to reflect on your overall litigation objectives. For example, if an objective is to hold down litigation costs, it may make little sense to raise numerous legal theories. Simplicity in the pleadings will better serve your objective.

16. See T. Mauet, Trials §1.5 (2005). See also D. Binder & P. Bergman, Fact Investigation: From Hypothesis to Proof ch. 9 (1984); J. McElhaney, "The Theory of the Case," in Trial Notebook (3d ed. 1994).

What do your proposed pleadings do to your discovery plan? The more complex the pleadings, the more expansive and expensive the permissible discovery. The scope of the pleadings controls the scope of discovery, and often its costs, because anything relevant, that is not privileged, is discoverable; so the more things that are raised by the pleadings, the greater the areas that are now relevant for discovery purposes. There is little point in pleading a variety of legal theories, just to be "safe," only to have the litigation get out of control. For example, consider a plaintiff who wishes to bring a negligence claim against a trucking company because of a vehicle collision. The plaintiff is considering whether to plead a claim for punitive damages. Doing so, however, will greatly expand the relevant scope of discovery, since the defendant's financial and safety history will now be discoverable. If the likelihood of getting punitive damages is small, does it really make sense to push such a claim? You may well be undertaking substantial additional work without a corresponding benefit to your client. On the other hand, plaintiffs frequently want broad discovery, at least compared to defendants. By adding peripheral parties, consistent with Rule 11 requirements, you make discovery easier, since discovery can be more broadly applied to parties than nonparties.

When you have decided which of the possible legal theories to raise in the initial pleading, you will still need to consider the related legal issues. The plaintiff must appreciate how the choice of claims will affect such issues as the choice of parties that must be brought into the suit, whether subject matter jurisdiction exists for each claim, whether personal jurisdiction exists for each defendant, where venue is proper and, if more than one venue, where the best place to file suit is. These questions are all interrelated, and substantial legal research will be necessary when the issues are complex. The time to research is now, not when you are suddenly faced with a motion to dismiss for lack of subject matter jurisdiction or for failure to join an indispensible party.

A plaintiff must always balance the pros and cons of adding additional parties as defendants. This is particularly true when the potential additional party is an employee of a named defendant. The typical situation arises when a plaintiff, suing a trucking company or other commercial entity, must decide whether to name the company's driver as an additional defendant. The advantages are that discovery is easier if an employee is a named defendant and an employee is usually happy to testify to agency and scope of employment issues favorable to the plaintiff. The disadvantages are that the case becomes more complex, with more parties, sometimes more lawyers, and more work, and that the idea of driving a wedge between the driver and company will usually fail because both will probably be represented by the same lawyer (unless a conflict arises). In many cases, there is no point in naming the driver as an additional defendant, particularly where employment and scope of employment are not in dispute, although plaintiffs sometimes name the driver as an additional defendant to obtain discovery advantages, then dismiss the driver as a named party before trial. On the other hand, if there is an issue as to whether the driver is an employee or an independent contractor, or was acting outside the scope of his employ, the driver must be named as a defendant.

Finally, decide if you want a jury trial.[17] If so, a jury demand must be made with a party's first pleading, either the complaint or answer, or else under federal practice the right to a jury trial will be deemed waived. No hard and fast rules exist. Decisions must be made on a case-by-case basis, in consultation with the client. On the plus side, cases that have emotionally compelling witnesses and stories, where the client is sympathetic or the underdog, where the jury will want to do what's fair despite the law, and where the jury pool is favorable for your side, should be tried to a jury. On the other hand, not requesting a jury should always be considered. A bench trial will usually be cheaper, faster, simpler, often get an earlier trial date, and be preferable if your side involves dry, technical evidence and has a client and witnesses with little jury appeal.

5. Plan the discovery

The discovery stage is usually the largest part of the litigation process, the one that consumes the most time and money. Hence, it is particularly important to plan discovery to serve your client's overall objectives and cost considerations. Without planning, discovery usually becomes unfocused and expensive — two disasters you should avoid.

Planning discovery is essentially a seven-step process:

1.   What facts do I need to establish a winning case on my claims (or to defeat the opponent's claims)?
2.   What facts have I already obtained through informal fact investigation?
3.   What "missing" facts do I still need to obtain through formal discovery?

The answers to the above questions should already be established on your litigation chart. You must consider four other questions:

4.   What discovery methods are the most effective for obtaining the missing facts?
5.   What facts and witnesses, that you already know through informal investigation, do you need to "pin down" by using formal discovery methods?
6.   What restrictions does your litigation budget place on your discovery plan?
7.   Finally, in what order should you execute your discovery plan?

These questions obviously require some time to think through. When you have decided on what discovery methods to use for particular information, exhibits, and witnesses, put them on your litigation chart and your litigation timetable.[18]

---

17. See T. Mauet, Trial Techniques §2.2 (7th ed. 2007); P. Taskier, Judge or Jury? 24 Litigation (No. 1, Fall 1997).

18. This process is discussed in detail in §§6.3, 6.4.

6. Plan the dispositive motions

What dispositive motions, such as summary judgment, should you plan? Will your planned discovery provide the basis for succeeding on those motions? On the other hand, if the other side will be making the motions, what discovery have you planned that will defeat them? The motions stage of the litigation process will only be successful if you have coordinated your discovery with your motions plan. This means that you must look down the road before filing the pleadings to see what motions will be realistic and use discovery to obtain the facts necessary to prevail when the motions are later made.

7. Plan the settlement approach

Your sense of when to discuss the possibility of settlement with the opposing party must be part of your overall litigation plan. When the client's objective is to settle quickly and keep costs down, you might consider discussing settlement early, such as before filing suit, after the pleadings have been closed, or after a critical witness has been deposed. Otherwise, you will probably want to consider settlement after discovery is closed, after dispositive motions have been ruled on, or when you are preparing for the final pretrial conference. At these later stages you will have a better grasp of the case's strengths and weaknesses, but you will have incurred substantial litigation expenses.

8. Develop a litigation timetable

After developing and coordinating each of the preceding steps in your litigation plan, you should draw up a realistic timetable. For this you need to consider the case's complexity, the likely responses of the opposing party, and the usual time between the filing of a complaint and trial date in the jurisdiction where the case is brought. You can then put the steps into a chronological sequence, and include them on your master calendar to remind yourself of the due date for each step in this particular case. Keep in mind that the court under Rule 16(b) will usually enter a scheduling order that will control that timetable.

The master calendar for this case, and all other open cases, becomes the firm's docket control system. Although a few lawyers still use a paper calendar system, nearly all firms today use docket-control software. The software system contains each date for each case in which some activity is scheduled or planned, such as court hearings, depositions, trial dates, and filing deadlines. It also contains reminders that important deadlines are approaching, such as the due date for serving interrogatory answers or expert witness reports. The system generates a daily schedule of events for all open cases, noting the time, location, and assigned lawyer for each scheduled event. For example, the daily activity printout would show that Smith v. Jones, Case No. 05 C 4332, office file number 05-121, assigned to John Burns, has a deposition of the defendant scheduled in Burns' office at 2:00 P.M. When court, deposition, or other dates change, it is your responsibility to make sure that the docket system reflects the changes. Keep in mind that such a system is only as good as the information with which it is provided. Such a docket control system is also essential for conflicts of interest checks, quality control, and malpractice prevention.

The planning of litigation must be an integrated, creative, flexible, continuing process. The plan needs to be integrated because each step should be tailored to achieving your client's litigation objectives while keeping in mind that each step influences the other steps. It should be creative because every case is different and must be planned out to account for the conditions of the particular case, rather than plugging the conditions into a standard formula. Finally, it must be flexible and continuing because developments invariably occur during the litigation process that require changes in your plan.

§4.6. *Example of litigation planning:* Novelty Products, Inc. v. Gift Ideas, Inc.

The following example illustrates the thought process that is involved in each step of a coordinated litigation plan.

Facts

Novelty Products, Inc. ("Novelty") is a New York corporation that manufactures novelty items that are sold to gift shops throughout the United States. Its corporate headquarters and manufacturing plant are in Buffalo, New York. Gift Ideas, Inc. ("Gift") is a California corporation that owns a chain of gift shops located throughout California. Its corporate headquarters is in Los Angeles.

Over the past five years Gift has periodically ordered products from Novelty under an established procedure. Gift's purchasing department places orders over the telephone, and Novelty sends a written confirmation of the order before delivering it. Gift then pays for each shipment within 30 days of receipt.

One of the items Gift has ordered from Novelty during that time is a patented tabletop electric cigarette lighter called the "Magic Lite." Gift has ordered the lighter, in increasingly large shipments, approximately every six months. The lighter now accounts for about half of all sales from Novelty to Gift. The latest lighter order, for $80,000, was made the usual way, and was shipped last month.

A few days ago Gift notified Novelty that the latest shipment of lighters would be returned unpaid. Gift has just decided to make and market a table-top electric cigarette lighter itself, and from now on its shops will only carry its own lighter. The Gift lighter, called the "Magic Flame," is almost identical in appearance and design to the Novelty lighter. A few months ago Novelty's design chief left the company and began working for Gift.

The shipment of lighters has been returned to Novelty, but Novelty has been unable to find another buyer for the lighters. Since

Novelty will soon be marketing an improved version of the lighter, finding a buyer seems unlikely.

The president of Novelty now comes to you for help.

Assume you have researched potential claims against Gift, determined the elements of those claims, identified the sources of proof, and completed an informal fact investigation. You have interviewed your client and appropriate employees, and have reviewed your client's records and correspondence along with what you could obtain from other nonparty sources. You have also checked on the historical relationship between Novelty and Gift, and have concluded that there is no likelihood that Gift can file any counterclaims against Novelty. At this time your litigation chart (for the contract claim) appears as follows:

LITIGATION CHART

Elements of Claims	Sources of Proof	Informal Fact Investigation	Formal Discovery
1. Contract			
(a) contract executed	pl.'s records pl.'s witness def.'s records def.'s witnesses	obtained from client interviews	request to produce depositions, interrogatories, request to admit
(b) pl.'s performance	pl.'s records pl.'s witness def.'s records def.'s witnesses	obtained from client interviews	initial disclosures, request to produce depositions, interrogatories, request to admit
(c) def.'s breach (nonpayment & return of goods)	pl.'s records pl.'s witness def.'s records def.'s witnesses shippers	obtained from client interviews	initial disclosures, request to produce depositions, request to admit subpoenas
(d) pl.'s damages	pl.'s records pl.'s witness 3d parties who rejected lighters	obtained from client interviews interviews	subpoenas

The litigation chart would be continued for every other potential claim you have been considering. In Novelty's case, these would include:

2. Bad faith
3. Theft of trade secret
4. Trademark infringement
5. Patent infringement
6. Unfair competition

Now is the time to develop the litigation plan. The steps are:

1. Reevaluate the client's objectives, priorities, and cost constraints
2. Define the client's litigation objectives
3. Develop a "theory of the case"
4. Plan the pleadings
5. Plan the discovery
6. Plan the dispositive motions
7. Plan the settlement approach
8. Develop a litigation timetable

1. Reevaluate the client's objectives, priorities, and cost constraints

From your interviews with Novelty's president, the company's objectives have become clear: Novelty wants to be paid the $80,000 due under the contract, yet it also wants to maintain its other ongoing business with Gift. It wants to accomplish these dual objectives quickly at a minimum cost. After your demand that Gift pay the contract amount has been rejected, Novelty's president agrees that litigation will be necessary. The president still hopes that litigation, if kept simple, will not destroy Novelty's ongoing business relationship with Gift. These client objectives remain unchanged.

2. Define the client's litigation objectives

Since Novelty's president has authorized litigation, you need to decide on the basic litigation objectives and then get the client's approval. In this case Novelty has three possible approaches: it can keep the case simple and bring only a contract claim against Gift; it can bring the former design chief in as a defendant by alleging theft of a trade secret; or it can expand the case against Gift by alleging bad faith, copyright, trademark, and unfair competition claims. Which one of these litigation objectives will best serve Novelty's overall objectives?

You first recommend not pursuing a case against the former design chief, since he was not under contract with Novelty, and you have no proof that he helped Gift design its new lighter. Pressing a theft-of-trade-secrets claim against him has Rule 11 problems and runs counter to the client's preference for handling the case simply, quickly, and cheaply.

You next recommend not pursuing the complex case involving the patent, trademark, and unfair competition claims. You have doubts that Novelty will prevail on these claims on both legal and factual grounds. In addition, such claims would undoubtedly destroy the continuing business dealings between Novelty and Gift, which remain important to Novelty. The claims would also create lengthy, expensive, and publicity-generating litigation, all things Novelty needs to avoid. Novelty could always decide to bring a separate suit on these claims if circumstances require it, since joinder of claims is always permissive and there are no statute of limitations that are about to run.

This leaves the basic contract claim against Gift, based on common law and the UCC sales provisions. The advantages of taking this approach are that you have an excellent chance of winning on the merits, and the case can be handled relatively quickly and inexpensively. The disadvantages are that damages may be low since a party has a duty to mitigate damages. However, to date Novelty has been unable to resell the returned lighters, so damages near the contract price may be appropriate. You also consider adding a bad faith claim, which, if permitted under the applicable jurisdiction's substantive tort law, might permit compensatory or punitive damages. Your thinking is that Gift is more likely to settle the case for the contract price when faced with a bad faith claim. However, your research of current bad faith law, under both New York and California law, reveals that such a claim probably cannot be brought in a contract case under your facts. Bringing such a claim probably would violate Rule 11 and destroy Novelty's hopes of preserving its business relationship with Gift.

You then develop a litigation budget for the proposed contract claim against Gift. You project the following amounts of time will be necessary:

Fact and legal investigation	15 hrs.
Pleadings	5 hrs.
Discovery	50 hrs.
Motions	15 hrs.
Pretrial conference	15 hrs.
Trial and trial preparation	50 hrs.

The total projected time remaining, without a trial, is about 100 hours; with a trial, the total time will be about 150 hours. Your hourly rate is presently $100. Accordingly, the legal fee to the client for resolving the dispute through a trial should be around $15,000. Since the contract case will not require experts, and the only significant costs will be deposition expenses, litigation costs should be in the $2,000 to $3,000 range. Since you feel the contract claim is strong and that under the circumstances getting $80,000 in damages is realistic, bringing the case—and trying it if necessary—still makes economic sense to the client. This holds even though Novelty will have to bear its own legal expenses, based on your research finding that no applicable law permits the recovery of attorney's fees in this situation.

While not part of this budget, every litigated case will require client time. In commercial cases, this means the time of the company's management and those employees involved in the transaction on which the litigation is based. This time is a real cost to the company. Estimate how much time will be required from the company during the litigation, and make sure the client understands this and commits to it.

You meet with Novelty's president and present the above analysis and litigation budget to him. You remind him that this is your projected budget based on the facts presently known, and that unforeseen circumstances often arise, which can increase the budget. He agrees with it, and authorizes you to file suit against Gift on the contract claim. He again reminds you of his wish to settle quickly if possible and to keep the tone of the litigation as a simple dispute between two businesses over which one will bear the loss for an improperly canceled order.

3.   Develop a "theory of the case"

Before dealing with the pleadings, you need to consider what Novelty's theory of the case should be. You decide to portray Novelty as a small company that had ongoing business dealings with Gift, a larger corporate chain. The specific transaction was a routine one where Gift made an oral order and Novelty sent a confirming letter, shipped the lighters, and sent a bill. Gift refused to pay for the lighters, but had no valid reason to do so. Gift simply changed its mind after agreeing to buy because it was going to market its own lighter. When the lighters were returned, Novelty could not resell them because it was preparing to market an improved version of the original lighter. In short, according to your theory, Gift welshed on the deal, and therefore owes Novelty the full $80,000. You feel that this theory will both be simple and have jury appeal.

4.   Plan the pleadings

So far, you have decided to bring a contract action against Gift; however, many important questions must still be answered. First, what substantive law will apply? Novelty, the plaintiff, is in Buffalo, New York; Gift is based in Los Angeles, California. The offer was made from Los Angeles and accepted in Buffalo. Since the contract was completed in New York and the place of contracting under the standard interests analysis usually controls the choice of the applicable substantive law, New York law will probably be applied, regardless of whether the action is filed in New York or California. Filing the action in New York will also help, since it is the plaintiff's home state.

Since you have decided to sue only Gift, proper parties are not a concern. However, if you file in federal district court, will the court have subject matter jurisdiction over the claims? In this case, jurisdiction can properly be based on the court's diversity jurisdiction under 28 U.S.C. §1332; since the plaintiff is a citizen of New York and the defendant is a citizen of California, complete diversity exists, and the claim is in excess of the required jurisdictional amount of $75,000.

Can you get personal jurisdiction over Gift? If suit is filed in California, service of process on Gift will be easy, since Gift's corporate headquarters is in Los Angeles. If suit is filed in New York, can Gift be forced to defend a lawsuit there and can Gift be properly served with process? Your research indicates that Gift's dealings with Novelty are adequate "minimum contracts" such that Gift can be required to defend in New York. Moreover, since provisions of Rule 4 of the Federal Rule of Civil Procedure allow for service under the forum state's long-arm statute, you should be able to properly serve Gift if suit is filed in New York.

Finally, where is venue proper? Under 28 U.S.C. §1391, New York (the Western District) is a proper place to bring suit. Since the Western District of New York has such obvious advantages to Novelty, suit, if brought in federal court, should be brought there.

The other possibility, of course, is to file the complaint in state court. New York (Buffalo) is the obvious choice, and you should be able to serve Gift under the state long-arm statute. However, because the federal court will get the case to trial sooner, and because federal judges are more actively involved in the settlement process, you decide to file in federal court.

5.   Plan the discovery

The client has two basic objectives: keep it simple and inexpensive, and try to settle it quickly. The first objective was served by keeping the pleadings simple. The second objective must be remembered when planning the discovery, as well as in the later steps of your litigation plan, since your litigation budget allocates just 50 hours to discovery.

Consult your litigation chart. At this stage the facts you have gathered came principally from Novelty's employees and business records. In a contract case, this is to be expected. The untapped sources, then, Gift's employees and records, must be reached through formal discovery.

Since a basic objective is an early settlement, you don't want to get mired in lengthy discovery. You decide to ask for limited and accelerated discovery at the planning meeting and the Rule 16 pretrial conference. In addition, you have decided to move for partial summary judgment on liability as soon as possible. These objectives — getting the missing information, getting evidence for your summary judgment motion, and pushing for early settlement — can be served by a carefully designed discovery plan.

For example, you decide to use discovery only to get Gift's records and witness testimony that deal with the specific transaction involved. You decide that the evidence of an established course of dealings between Novelty and Gift, which would be necessary at trial to prove the contract terms, can be established by Novelty's records and witnesses. Second, you decide to focus on the contract and its breach, not contract damages, which you can again prove through Novelty's records and witnesses.

This will give you the information necessary for your motion for partial summary judgment on liability.

What remains to be decided is which discovery methods to use to execute the plan and what order to use them in. Initial disclosures are automatic and required. You decide to send a set of interrogatories to Gift dealing with the basic chronological events involved in the transaction. You also decide to send Gift a request to produce all records dealing with the specific transaction. These should, among other things, identify the Gift employees who handled the transaction and were involved in the decision to return the lighters. Finally, you decide to depose those same essential Gift employees in succession, during one or two days, to minimize their contact with each other. When this is done, you will send a request to admit facts that covers the liability facts of the case.

The last decision is when to take these steps. Ordinarily you will want to move quickly to stay ahead of the other side. Here you decide to send out the interrogatories and requests to produce records at the earliest permitted time, and to send out the deposition notices for the necessary depositions as soon as you receive adequate answers to your interrogatories and documents requests. The request to admit facts can then follow on the heels of the depositions.

6. Plan the dispositive motions

Your overall litigation objective is to seek an early settlement, preferably after pleadings are filed or discovery has begun. If this does not work, you plan to move for partial summary judgment on liability as soon as discovery is completed. You will then have the information necessary to support your motion and to create additional pressure for a settlement.

7. Plan the settlement approach

Early settlement has always been a priority in your case. Accordingly, you plan to make settlement overtures, if Gift does not initiate them, after the pleadings are filed, after discovery is well under way and also when completed, after the motion for partial summary judgment is heard, and at the final pretrial conference.

Your approach has been to use focused discovery, particularly the request to admit facts, and the partial summary judgment motion to eliminate liability from the settlement discussions and put pressure on Gift. Since Novelty has been unable to resell the lighters, there is no mitigation of damages problem and damages are likely to be the full contract price. You decide that, with Novelty's consent, you will agree to settle for an amount close to the contract price, minus your total litigation expenses. This puts the settlement "value" of the case in the range of $65,000 to $80,000, depending on how early the case is settled.

8.   Develop a litigation timetable

Now that you have developed a litigation plan that will realistically serve the client's objectives and priorities, you need to put the basic components on a timetable. Your basic timetable for Novelty is:

Litigation Timetable

1/1 (today)	Complete litigation plan
by 2/1	File complaint
by 3/1	Initial disclosure
by 4/1	Interrogatories, production requests to def.
by 5/1	Deposition notices to def. witnesses
by 6/1	Depose def. witnesses (same day if possible)
by 7/1	Requests to admit facts to def.
by 9/1	Motion for partial summary judgment on liability
by 10/1	Prepare pretrial memorandum
by 11/1	Pretrial conference
12/1	Initial trial date

You plan to recommend this schedule to the lawyer for Gift when you meet and confer to develop a discovery plan under Rule 26(f) and propose it to the trial judge when you meet for the pretrial conference under Rule 16. These dates can then be put on your general docket calendar to remind you when the basic steps in this case should be completed.

§4.7.   Prefiling requirements

Are you finally ready to begin drafting the pleadings? Not quite. There are still a few matters you need to consider before plunging ahead.

1.   Statutory notice requirements

Some actions, primarily claims against governmental bodies such as municipalities, often have statutory notice requirements that must be complied with or else suit will be barred. These statutes usually have time limitations substantially shorter than the applicable statute of limitations, often as short as six months or less, and usually have detailed fact requirements. These statutes are usually strictly construed, so each statutory requirement must be closely followed.

2.   Contract requirements

Many contracts, particularly insurance and employment contracts and contracts with governmental bodies, have notice and claims provisions that are drafted as conditions precedent. These provisions usually require notice of intent to sue, or presentation of claims before filing suit, and require that notice be given within a short period of time, usually much shorter than the applicable statute of limitations period. Make sure you comply with the conditions precedent required by the contract before filing suit.

3.   Mediation, arbitration, and review requirements

By statute or contract, many disputes must be submitted to binding or nonbinding mediation or arbitration before suit can be brought. For example, construction contracts frequently have arbitration clauses. Many states require by statute that medical malpractice claims must first be presented to a medical review panel or that plaintiff must have an appropriately qualified expert who will testify that the defendant breached the applicable standard of care.

4.   Administrative procedure requirements

Claims against governmental bodies usually cannot be brought in court until administrative procedures have been followed and exhausted. Sometimes this exhaustion requirement is statutory; sometimes it is judicially created. For example, claims for benefits from the Social Security and Veterans Administrations must ordinarily be pursued through the administrative process before resort to the judicial system is permitted.[19] Accordingly, determine what applicable administrative procedure statutes and case law apply to your claim, and make sure that they have been followed and exhausted before filing suit.

5.   Appointment of legal guardian

Some individuals are incompetent to sue in their own name and must have a legal representative or specially appointed guardian litigate for them. Capacity to sue is governed by Rule 17, which generally defers to state law in determining both capacity to sue and the appropriate representative party.[20] Minors and incompetents, for example, can only sue through their legal guardians or conservators. Appropriate state court appointments of guardians, or other legal representatives, must be obtained before suit can properly be brought. When the statute of limitations will run shortly, this is a serious concern since obtaining such appointments may take time.

---

19. See 42 U.S.C. §421(c); Administrative Procedure Act, 5 U.S.C. §§551 et seq.
20. See §3.4.

6. Lis pendens

Some jurisdictions require the filing of a lis pendens notice and service on all interested parties whenever a suit involves an interest in real property or tangible personal property. The notice is filed in the public records, usually property and title records. This gives notice of the pending litigation to parties having an interest in the property. Once notified, any interest in the property they acquire is subject to any judgment that may be entered in that particular litigation. Where your suit involves real or personal property, you should always check to see if any lis pendens rules apply; if so, follow them so that a judgment will be valid and enforceable against such parties. State lis pendens notice requirements are applicable to federal cases involving real estate.[21]

7. Attachment

Attachment is the legal process in which someone's property is seized to satisfy a judgment not yet rendered. While there are no federal attachment statutes, Rule 64 makes available the attachment procedures allowed under the forum state's law. State statutes often provide for attachment of a debtor's property interest under certain defined circumstances and usually specify the procedures, including service of process and bonds, that must be followed. Some jurisdictions also provide for prefiling attachment or garnishment procedures that may be used to freeze assets that may satisfy any future judgment. There are remedies for wrongful attachment, however, so caution is obviously in order.

8. Temporary restraining orders

If you are seeking injunctive relief, you may be able to obtain a temporary restraining order (TRO) to prevent immediate irreparable injury to your client's interests. A TRO may be obtained under specified conditions for a strictly limited period of time, until a hearing for a preliminary injunction can be scheduled.[22] While it is difficult to obtain a TRO, there will be times when seeking a TRO is essential to preserve a client's rights.[23]

9. Discovery before suit

Upon filing a verified petition that complies with Rule 27's requirements, you may depose a person before suit is filed to perpetuate that person's testimony. This should be considered in two situations. First, if you cannot get enough pre-filing factual information to comply with the Rule 11

21. See Rule 64, 28 U.S.C. §1964.
22. See Rule 65.
23. Obtaining a TRO or preliminary injunction is discussed in §7.5.

requirements, using Rule 27 may be your only recourse. Second, if an important witness is old, sick, or is about to leave the jurisdiction, Rule 27 can be used to depose that person to perpetuate the testimony.

10.   Demand letters

While not legally required, demand letters, which state a party's claim against another party, are frequently used, particularly in tort, contract, and commercial cases. For instance, in anticipatory breach situations it is advantageous to send a demand letter asserting that the other side appears to be in breach and requesting assurances of performance. Such letters, if not responded to, may constitute admissions by silence.

Demand letters also serve practical purposes. In small disputes, where a compromise is possible, a demand letter that notifies the other side of your intent to sue unless an acceptable settlement is reached can often trigger settlement discussions. Including a draft of your proposed complaint shows the other side that you are serious. A demand letter will often generate a denial letter stating the basis for rejecting your claim, and is sometimes a good indication of what defenses will be raised if suit is brought later.

In some cases, where your ability to get the facts is limited because the important records are all in your opponent's possession, it may also be appropriate to send a draft of your complaint to your opponent and await a response. The opponent may respond by giving you information that will affect your decision to file the lawsuit or will affect the claims that you ultimately bring.

Example:

Re: Martha Wilde construction contract dated January 15, 2005

Dear Mr. Johnson:

We represent Martha Wilde, the owner of the home at 1822 Forest Lane. On January 15, 2005, your company, Johnson Construction, Inc., entered into a contract with Ms. Wilde to do certain renovations in her home. Under the contract, the work was to have begun on or before March 1, 2005, and completed on or before May 1, 2005. As you knew, the completion date was an important and material provision of the contract since Ms. Wilde was hiring you to do the renovations because she was planning to put her home up for sale on May 1, the beginning of the summer selling season, and the renovations were essential for that purpose. Ms. Wilde entered into the contract with your company relying on your assurances that the work would be completed by May 1.

The present date is June 15, 2005, and your company has yet to begin work under the contract. This constitutes a breach of a material term of the contract. Since you have breached the contract, it is hereby terminated, and Ms. Wilde is no longer required to perform any obligations under the contract. Furthermore, your breach of the contract has caused damages to Ms. Wilde that you knew she would incur if the contract were not performed in timely fashion. Because of your breach of the contract, Ms. Wilde has been unable to sell her home and has suffered other losses.

Accordingly, demand is hereby made upon Johnson Construction, Inc., to pay the sum of $25,000 for damages caused to Ms. Wilde because of your breach of the contract. Unless Johnson Construction, Inc., pays that amount by certified check to Ms. Wilde on or before July 1, 2005, we have been authorized to file suit on her behalf to recover all damages, expenses, attorneys' fees, and court costs incurred by Ms. Wilde as a result of your breach. We are prepared to file the attached complaint in Superior Court without further notice in the event you do not make the payment demanded and resolve this matter by that date.

Since we represent Ms. Wilde, please direct all future communications in this matter to me rather than to Ms. Wilde. I await a call from you or your legal representative.

11. Preservation letters

When litigation is pending or reasonably anticipated, a party has a duty to preserve evidence in the party's possession, custody, or control when the party has notice or knowledge that the information may be relevant to the litigation. There is always a danger that a party will destroy documents, records, and data to keep the opposing party from obtaining it. This concern is even greater if that evidence is generated and stored electronically. As plaintiff, if you are concerned that the defendant may alter or destroy evidence, you should put the defendant on notice, before filing the lawsuit, that you will be seeking both paper and electronic evidence and that the defendant has a duty to preserve all such evidence. This is done by sending a "preservation letter" to the party or, if you know the party is represented by counsel, to the lawyer. This is discussed in §6.8.

12. Litigation holds

Your client has the same preservation obligations as the opposing party: to preserve documents, electronically stored information, and things relevant to the pending or reasonably anticipated lawsuit that are in your client's possession, custody, or control. Hence, you need to advise your client of the preservation obligation when the obligation first arises and to make sure that the obligation is in fact implemented. This is usually done by sending the client a "litigation hold letter," which spells out the preservation obligations, and then following up to ensure compliance. Litigation holds are discussed in §6.8.

13.   Physical examinations

As plaintiff in a personal injury case, consider offering to have your client examined by a defense doctor before filing suit. There are several reasons to consider this. First, the defense is entitled to such an examination after suit is filed, under Rule 35. Second, the plaintiff's injuries will be more apparent at this time. Third, such an offer lets the defense know you're prepared and confident about your case. Fourth, it may pave the way to an earlier settlement of the case.

Part B
CONDUCTING THE LITIGATION

V

PLEADINGS

§5.1. *Introduction*

Pleadings get the lawsuit started, usually stop the running of the statute of limitations, and frame the issues involved in the lawsuit. However, modern pleading rules essentially limit the purpose of pleadings to notice of claims and defenses. Former purposes that included discovering facts, sharpening issues, and disposing of frivolous claims are now controlled by discovery and motion practice. Under modern rules, claims and factual issues will rarely be resolved at the pleadings stage. Hence, don't expect the pleadings to accomplish more than what they are designed to do.

Federal pleadings rules are principally contained in the Federal Rules of Civil Procedure, although other sources exist and must always be kept in mind. Under Rule 83 district courts can create local rules governing litigation in that district. Most have done so. Local rules generally do not affect the substance of pleadings, but ordinarily control mechanics such as the number of copies filed, size of paper, format, bindings, and whether papers can be filed by facsimile or other electronic means. Particular federal statutory actions, such as bankruptcy and copyright, may also have special procedure rules. Finally, specialized federal courts, such as bankruptcy and claims courts, may have special statutory and local procedural rules. Hence, you should always check procedural statutes and local rules in addition to the Federal Rules of Civil Procedure to determine what rules apply to your particular case.

Good pleadings practice is a combination of two things: a solid litigation plan and technically precise drafting. The litigation plan, which you have already developed, will control the claims and remedies (if a plaintiff), or the defenses, counterclaims, cross-claims, and third-party claims (if a defendant). The drafting of pleadings then becomes the primary concern, since pleadings that are technically precise will avoid attacks by motions and eliminate the need to file amended pleadings to cure defects that should have been avoided in the first place.

§5.2. *General pleading requirements*

The Federal Rules of Civil Procedure have made simplicity and limited purpose the touchstones of the pleadings stage of the litigation process. Under Rule 2, all actions are "civil actions," and under Rule 7(a) the only basic pleadings allowed are complaints, answers, and replies.

1. General "notice" requirements for claims[1]

Rule 8(a) permits four forms of claims:

1. complaint — claim brought by plaintiff against defendant
2. counterclaim — claim brought by defendant against plaintiff
3. cross-claim — claim brought by one defendant against another defendant
4. third-party complaint — claim brought by an original defendant against a new party (third-party defendant)

All forms are actually complaints, since each asks for relief of some kind, but the various labels designate which party is bringing the claim. Since they are all complaints, however, their requirements are the same. Rule 8 requires only a "short and plain statement of the claim showing the pleader is entitled to relief." This commonly, although perhaps inaccurately, is labeled "notice pleading."

Under "notice pleading," the only requirement is that the pleading contain enough information to fairly notify the opposing party of the basis of the claim. It does not require an elaborate narration of facts, nor does it require that a legal theory of recovery or relief be set forth. Previous distinctions about whether a pleading was of fact, law, or conclusion of law now have no significance. Hence, for most allegations the only requirement is a "short and plain statement" that gives fair notice of your claims to the opposing side. Forms 2 through 23 in the Appendix of Forms to the Federal Rules of Civil Procedure contain a variety of legally sufficient pleadings. The safest pleadings approach is to use the forms and modify them to meet the specific requirements of your case. The standard drafting technique is to state enough facts to identify the events or transactions that your claim is based on and the legal theory of recovery. These techniques are detailed in §5.3.

However, in 2007 the Supreme Court decided Bell Atlantic Corp. v. Twombly, ___ U.S. ___, 127 S. Ct. 1955 (2007), holding that a pleading,

---

1. Wright §68; James & Hazard §3.8; Friedenthal §5.7; Moore's Manual §901; Manual of Federal Practice §3.5; Wright & Miller §§1182–1192; Moore's Federal Practice §§8.02–8.06.

to be adequate under the "plain statement" requirement of Rule 8(a)(2), must furnish factual "allegations plausibly suggesting (not merely consistent with)" an "entitlement to relief." Mere "labels and conclusions, and a formulaic recitation of the elements of a cause of action will not do." A plaintiff must allege "only enough facts to state a claim for relief that is plausible on its face." This plausibility requirement is new, and how courts will apply it is uncertain.

Bell Atlantic was a class action antitrust case, and the complaint merely alleged, based on information and belief, that the defendants had conspired to prevent competitive entry in certain telephone and Internet markets, without setting out any facts supporting that conclusion. The Supreme Court held this pleading inadequate, since there were no factual allegations plausibly suggesting the conclusion that the antitrust laws were violated. Given the Bell Atlantic holding, the safer course is to allege more facts in the complaint (but not to the level of Rule 9, which requires that certain claims "shall be stated with particularity") and avoid pleading mere legal conclusions, particularly in complex cases such as securities and antitrust where courts can be understandably reluctant to let a massive case proceed on factually threadbare allegations.

The only exception to the notice pleading requirement is Rule 9, which requires that certain matters, including capacity and authority to sue, fraud, mistake, and special damages, be alleged specifically and particularly. This type of pleading is also discussed in §5.3. Note also that Rule 5.1 imposes additional procedural requirements if a pleading, motion, or other court paper draws into question the constitutionality of a federal or state statute.

Rule 26(a) provides for automatic initial disclosure of basic information that "the disclosing party may use to support its claims and defenses," and Rule 26(b) permits discovery of "any matter, not privileged, that is relevant to the claim or defense of any party." A party may create discovery benefits by alleging specific facts in the pleadings to make it harder for the opposing party to avoid making the required initial disclosures, or arguing that discovery seeks irrelevant matter. This is discussed in §§5.3 and 6.4.

2. Alternative and inconsistent pleadings[2]

Rule 8(e)(2) allows a party to plead multiple claims or defenses in alternative or hypothetical form, either in one or in separate counts or defenses. In practice, each claim is usually put in a separate count and each defense is designated separately. Keep in mind, however, that since pleadings can be used during trial, alternative or inconsistent pleadings may cast the party in a poor light. Hence, drafting must also be done with an eye toward the impression the pleading will have on the jurors.

---

2. Friedenthal §§5.12–5.13; Moore's Manual §§9.05–9.06; Manual of Federal Practice §372.

3. Format requirements[3]

Format requirements are set forth in Rules 10 and 11. There are several that must be followed for every pleading. Local rules may also specify additional requirements.

a. Caption

The caption of a case refers to the names of the parties, the court in which the case is being filed, and the case number. Every pleading must have a caption containing this information.

b. File number

The file number is the case number that is stamped on the complaint when it is first filed with the clerk of the court. It must appear on all successive pleadings and other court papers. Although not required, the designation "Civil Action" is usually placed below the file number.

c. Parties to action

The complaint caption must list all the parties to the action. Subsequent pleadings need only list the first plaintiff and first defendant, with an appropriate reference to additional parties, such as "et al."

Make sure that your caption correctly states the proper name and legal description of each party. Under Rule 17, every action must be brought in the name of the real party in interest; and, according to this Rule, the capacity to sue or be sued is controlled by the law of domicile, incorporation, or forum.[4] You must always check Rule 17(b) and (c) to see if a party has capacity to sue or be sued and that the correct person or entity is designated as a party. Common designations include the following:

- John Smith
- Sharon Jones, as guardian of the Estate of Robert Jones, a minor
- Robert Smith, as conservator of the Estate of Ellen Smith, an incompetent
- Frank Watson, as executor of the Estate of James Morley, deceased
- Barbara Myers, as trustee in bankruptcy of the Estate of Robert Jackson, bankrupt
- R. J. Smith Company, a corporation
- Johnson Hospital, a not-for-profit corporation
- Robert Smith, d/b/a Smith Cleaners
- Barnett and Lynch, a partnership
- Western Ranches Association, an unincorporated association

---

3. Friedenthal §5.14.
4. See §3.4.

Where a party is being sued both individually and in a representative capacity, it should be spelled out.

Example:

> John Smith, individually and as administrator of the Estate of Franklin Smith, deceased

The caption, then, simply lists each party and what side of the action each is on.

Example:

UNITED STATES DISTRICT COURT
FOR THE NORTHERN DISTRICT OF NEW YORK

Rebecca Smith, and J. W. Smith Company, a corporation, Plaintiffs	
v.	No. _____
Randolph Construction, a corporation, and William Johnson, d/b/a Solar Consultants, Defendants	Civil Action

Sometimes it is impossible to identify a proper party by name before filing. In many state courts you can designate a party as "John Doe, the true name being presently unknown," and pursue the identity of the party through formal discovery. This sometimes happens when a plaintiff has been able to identify some but not all liable parties. The advantage of doing this is that plaintiff can get the case started against the known defendants and amend the complaint to add the additional parties when their identity is discovered (and the statute of limitations has not yet run as to the additional parties). However, in federal court the use of fictitious parties is prohibited, although some local rules provide for permitting the use of fictitious parties if ordered by the court.

Keep in mind, however, that naming John or Jane Doe defendants, when permitted, to attempt to toll the applicable statute of limitations under the concept of relation back will probably be ineffective, unless the person properly named later as a defendant had actual notice of the suit before the statute of limitations ran.[5]

---

5. See §5.13; Schiavone v. Fortune, Inc., 477 U.S. 21 (1986).

d. Designation

Each pleading should be labeled to show what type it is, such as a complaint, counterclaim, cross-claim, third-party complaint, answer, or reply. Where multiple parties are involved, it is useful to show against whom the pleading is directed.

Examples:

COMPLAINT

DEFENDANT SMITH COMPANY'S
ANSWER TO CROSS-CLAIM OF DEFENDANT
FRANKLIN CORPORATION

THIRD-PARTY COMPLAINT AGAINST
JONES CONSTRUCTION COMPANY

e. Signing pleadings

Every pleading, or other court paper, must be signed by one of the party's lawyers. The signing must be by an individual, not a law firm, although in practice the lawyer's firm is frequently shown as "of counsel." The pleading must also contain the lawyer's address and telephone number.

Under the federal rules pleadings are not "verified" — that is, signed under oath by the parties and notarized — although this remains proper procedure in many state jurisdictions. Verification is still appropriate in a few special circumstances, most commonly in applications for a TRO under Rule 65(b).

f. Disclosure statement

Under Rule 7.1, a nongovernmental corporate party must file a disclosure statement that "identifies any parent corporation and any publically held corporation that owns 10% or more of its stock or states that there is no such corporation." This disclosure statement helps the judge to whom the case is assigned determine if she has a financial interest, usually stock ownership, in any party, and will need to recuse herself.

4. Rule 11[6]

Under Rule 11, a lawyer's presentation to the court of a pleading, written motion, or other court paper (except discovery disclosures, requests, responses, objections, and motions, which are covered under the certification sanctions of Rule 26(g) and Rule 37) automatically constitutes a

---

6. Friedenthal §5.11; Moore's Manual §3.70; Moore's Federal Practice §11.02; Wright & Miller §§1331 et seq.

certification that to the best of the lawyer's knowledge, information, and belief the pleading has evidentiary support or is likely to have evidentiary support after reasonable investigation, is supported by existing law or can be supported by a nonfrivolous argument for a change in law, and is not being filed for delay, harassment, or some other improper purpose.[7] A presentation to the court means signing, filing, submitting, or later advocating a paper. Under Rule 11(b), "later advocating" a position in a previously presented paper is considered a presentation to the court.

Rule 11(a) requires that every pleading, written motion, and other paper be signed by an attorney of record or by the unrepresented party filing it. Each paper must provide the address and telephone number of the signer. If not signed, the paper "shall" be stricken unless corrected promptly after being called to the signer's attention.

Rule 11(b) imposes significant obligations on the lawyer. A subjective good faith belief that the pleading is well founded is no longer sufficient; a lawyer must make a "reasonable inquiry" into the law and facts, and have concluded that there is a sound basis in law and fact for each allegation against each party in the pleading. The rule applies to every lawyer signing any pleading, written motion, or other court paper, even if the actual research and drafting was done by another lawyer, law firm, or in-house counsel. In short, local counsel cannot assume that work done by other lawyers meets the requirements of the rule. Rule 11(b) also imposes the same obligations on the client, since a party, even if represented by counsel, can incur penalties if the party presents a paper to the court by signing, filing, submitting, or later advocating in violation of the rule's standards.

What is a reasonable inquiry depends on the facts and circumstances that existed at the time the pleading was made.[8] Among the factors to be considered are the amount of time available to investigate the law and facts, the reliability of the client as a source of facts, and the extent to which an investigation could corroborate or alter those facts.

Can you rely on your client as the sole source for critical facts? This depends on whether it is reasonable under the circumstances. You must consider whether the client's story can be corroborated by information available from other independent sources, the cost of seeking such corroboration, whether the client has actual firsthand knowledge of the critical facts, how well you know the client, how reliable the client has been in the past, and whether the client's story is inherently plausible.[9] The reasonableness of the pleading or other court paper is measured at the time of its filing; Rule 11(b) does not impose a requirement to amend on discovering errors, although other practice rules do. However, if evidentiary support for a claim or defense is not obtained after a reasonable opportunity for

---

7. Rule 11 parallels the applicable ethics considerations. See Model Rules of Professional Conduct, Rule 3.1.

8. See Stempel, Sanctions, Symmetry and Safe Harbors: Limiting Misapplication of Rule 11 by Harmonizing It with Pre-Verdict Dismissal Devices, 60 Fordham L. Rev 257 (1991); Ward, Rule 11 and Factually Frivolous Claims — The Goal of Cost Minimization and the Client's Duty to Investigate, 44 Vand. L. Rev 1165 (1991).

9. See Lyles v. K Mart Corp., 703 F. Supp. 435 (W.D.N.C. 1989).

investigation, Rule 11(b) calls upon the litigant not to advocate such claims or defenses.

Can you allege facts without first having evidentiary support for those allegations? Rule 11 does not prohibit filing a pleading or other court paper simply because the information you have may not yet be in admissible form. On the other hand, a mere hunch that the client may have a good claim is inadequate. You must have some reasonably reliable information that the client has a proper claim. The court can also consider whether you were on notice that your investigation, both legal and factual, was inadequate or incorrect. Arguments for the extension, modification, or reversal of existing law, or for the establishment of new law, are not violations of the rule so long as the arguments are "nonfrivolous."

If a pleading is signed in violation of Rule 11(b), the court "may" impose sanctions against the lawyer who signed the pleading, the law firm for whom the lawyer works, the party, or all three. A law firm is generally jointly responsible for the conduct of its partners, associates, and employees. Rule 11(c) does not provide factors a court should consider when deciding to impose sanctions, but gives considerable discretion to the court. Sanctions can include costs and attorney's fees where they are directly incurred as a result of the violation, as well as nonmonetary sanctions such as striking the challenged paper or requiring participation in educational programs. Sanctions are limited to what is sufficient to deter repetition of the conduct or similar conduct by others in the same situation, and are proper even though there was no subjective bad faith or harassment.[10]

The court can impose sanctions in response to a formal motion for sanctions.[11] Such a motion is to be served separately from other motions and must describe the specific conduct alleged to violate the rule. However, under Rule 11(c) a motion for sanctions cannot be filed or presented to the court unless the challenged paper, claim, defense, contention, allegation, or denial is not withdrawn or corrected within 21 days of service of the motion. This is the so-called "safe harbor" provision; a timely withdrawal of a contention will protect the party against a motion for sanctions. The court can shorten or alter the 21-day rule.

The court can also act on its own, but only after notice and an opportunity to respond. The court will issue an "order to show cause" specifically describing the conduct in question and directing an attorney, law firm, or party to show why it has not violated Rule 11(b). When the court acts on its own, there is no "safe harbor"; there is no opportunity for the litigant to withdraw or correct a challenged paper, but such a withdrawal or correction is a factor that the court may consider in determining whether to impose sanctions. In addition, monetary sanctions against a represented party for frivolous legal positions may not be awarded on the court's own initiative, and monetary sanctions generally may not be awarded unless the order to show cause is issued before a voluntary dismissal or

---

10. See Cruz v. Savage, 896 F.2d 626 (1st Cir. 1990); Cabell v. Petty, 810 F.2d 463 (4th Cir. 1987).
11. See In re Itel Sec. Litig., 791 F.2d 672 (9th Cir. 1986).

settlement of the claims made by or against the litigant. When awarded, a monetary sanction will usually be limited to a penalty payable to the court; a monetary award to an injured party will be allowed only in unusual circumstances.

Sanctions should be no more severe than necessary to deter the same or similar conduct in the future. Factors the court will consider include whether the misconduct was willful or repeated, its effect on the pleadings and the litigation, and what amount will serve to deter this person, as well as other litigants, in the future. The court can impose sanctions without holding a hearing in every instance. However, the pleading or other court paper must be signed before the court can impose sanctions on the signer.

Rule 11 is not self-enforcing. It is the responsibility of the bench and bar to ensure that sanctions are imposed where appropriate. Rule 11 is not to be used as a tactical weapon or a vehicle for fee-shifting. In fact, a motion for sanctions improperly brought is itself subject to Rule 11 sanctions.

To avoid Rule 11 problems, conduct an adequate prefiling factual and legal investigation. Personally interview the client, critically analyze the client's information, interview corroborating witnesses, obtain and review relevant documents, and research the applicable law. Make sure that each allegation, against each defendant, meets the "reasonable inquiry" standard. In short, do your homework first, think, reflect, get second opinions when in doubt, and then file.

The message of Rule 11 should be abundantly clear: Gone are the days when a lawyer could, with little preparation, file an action containing a variety of claims against a multitude of defendants and later simply dismiss those claims and defendants that never should have been raised or brought into the case in the first place. Rule 11's reasonable inquiry requirement has teeth, and judges now impose significant sanctions for violations.[12]

Rule 11 has spawned substantial satellite litigation, and the Supreme Court has decided several cases in this area in recent years. These include Pavelic & LeFlore v. Marvel Entertainment Group, 493 U.S. 120 (1989); Cooter & Gell v. Hartmarx Corp., 496 U.S. 384 (1990); Business Guides, Inc. v. Chromatic Communications Enterprises, Inc., 498 U.S. 533 (1991); Chambers v. NASCO, Inc., 501 U.S. 32 (1991); and Willy v. Coastal Corp., 503 U.S. 131 (1992).

In *Pavelic*, the Court held that because Rule 11 requires that pleadings and other papers shall be signed in the individual attorney's name, sanctions for violations of the rule could only be imposed on the individual lawyer signing, not on the lawyer's law firm. This holding was modified by the 1993 amendments to Rule 11. If a motion for sanctions is filed under this rule, Rule 11(c)(1)(A) makes it clear that a law firm is held jointly responsible when one of its partners, associates, or employees is determined to have violated the rule, absent exceptional circumstances. This is because such a motion can only be filed if the offending paper is not withdrawn or corrected within 21 days after service of the motion. Since the

---

12. See Brandt v. Schal Assocs., 960 F.2d 640 (7th Cir. 1992), where the court upheld the imposition of a $443,564.66 sanction.

law firm is on notice of an alleged violation, sanctions may be appropriate. The court may consider whether other attorneys in the firm, co-counsel, or other law firms should be held accountable for their part in causing a violation. In *Cooter & Gell*, the Supreme Court ruled that a voluntary dismissal of an action does not deprive the court of jurisdiction over a Rule 11 motion, since a Rule 11 violation is complete once the improper court paper is filed. In *Business Guides*, the Court held that Rule 11 applies to parties who sign pleadings, even if they are represented by counsel. In *Chambers*, the trial court imposed sanctions on the defendant for bad faith conduct under the court's "inherent power" to control the conduct of parties who appear before it. The Court upheld the trial court, noting that the availability of Rule 11 or other sanctions do not preclude imposing sanctions under the court's inherent powers. Finally, in *Willy*, the Court held that Rule 11 sanctions can be imposed on lawyers and their clients even if the trial court is later found not to have had proper subject matter jurisdiction over the case when the offensive conduct was committed.

5. Service and filing

Whenever a pleading is created — whether a complaint, answer, or reply — two things must happen. First, it must be properly served on the other parties. Second, it must be filed with the court. How service is accomplished depends on which pleading is being served.

a. Service of original complaint and summons on defendant

Service of an original complaint and summons on a defendant must be done in accordance with the provisions of Rule 4. If a served defendant decides to bring a third-party complaint against a new defendant, the new defendant also must be served with the third-party complaint in accordance with the provisions of Rule 4. In these situations, the formality of service under Rule 4 is necessary to put the new defendant on notice that he has been sued and to obtain a lawyer and defend against the lawsuit. Service under Rule 4 is discussed further in §5.3.

b. Service of all other pleadings on existing parties

After the original complaint and summons have been served on the defendant, service of any subsequent pleadings — an answer, reply, and amended pleadings — on existing parties must be done in accordance with the provisions of Rule 5. This is because fairness requires that all parties presently in the case receive notice of everything that is happening in the case, beginning with the pleadings. When a party is represented by a lawyer, service is made on the lawyer. If a party is not represented by a lawyer, service is made on the party. Rule 5 permits several methods of service, but the common ones are personal delivery, mail delivery, or delivery at the lawyer's office to a person in charge. Rule 5(b) also permits service by electronic means if consented to in writing.

c. Filing and proof of service

Pleadings must, in addition to being served on the parties, be filed with the clerk of the court. The original complaint must be filed with the clerk before service of the complaint and summons can be made. Other pleadings must be filed with the clerk either before service on the parties or within a reasonable time after service. Filing of other pleadings is usually done at the same time the pleading is being served on the other lawyers or parties. The usual practice is to take the original and an appropriate number of copies of the pleading to the clerk's office for filing. Make sure you get a copy stamped "filed" and dated as proof of filing for your own files. Under Rule 5(e) filing can also be made by electronic means if permitted by local rules.

Finally, whenever service is made, you should attach a "proof of service" to the pleading. Proof of service of the complaint is made on the summons form. Local rules usually specify how proof of service of other pleadings is made. The usual practice is to have a certificate or affidavit of service attached to the end of the answer, reply, or amended pleading that shows when and how service was made, which includes the signature of the lawyer or the notarized signature of a member of the lawyer's staff.

§5.3. Complaints

The complaint is the plaintiff's initial pleading, which, when filed with the clerk of the court, starts the litigation. There are three essential components of every complaint required by Rule 8(a):

1. Statement showing subject matter jurisdiction
2. Statement of claims
3. Statement of relief requested

In addition, the complaint should contain a jury demand, if plaintiff wants a jury trial, must be signed by the lawyer, filed with the clerk of the court, and served with summons on the defendant. Beyond these requirements, how the complaint is organized is largely a matter of logic and clarity. Many lawyers organize a complaint by using introductory headings, such as "jurisdictional allegation," "parties," "facts common to all counts," "demand for relief," and "jury demand."

1. Subject matter jurisdiction[13]

Since federal courts are courts of limited jurisdiction, jurisdiction must be alleged in the complaint; and since jurisdiction cannot be assumed, it must

---

13. Wright §69; James & Hazard §3.24; Friedenthal §5.14; Moore's Manual §10.03; Manual of Federal Practice §3.6; Moore's Federal Practice §§8.07–8.11; Wright & Miller §§1206, 1208–1209.

be affirmatively demonstrated. Care as well as particularity is required. The jurisdictional allegation is usually the first part of a complaint and is customarily labeled as such. There are two principal ways that subject matter jurisdiction can be acquired in federal court.

a.   *Federal question jurisdiction*[14]

Federal jurisdiction can be based on a federal statute, constitutional provision, or treaty. The general federal question statute is 28 U.S.C. §1331. To establish jurisdiction in this way, the complaint should cite the particular statute, constitutional provision, or treaty, and perhaps quote the operative wording or paraphrase it. Failure to do so is not fatal, since jurisdictional allegations can be amended;[15] however, citing a federal statute, constitutional provision, or treaty will not conclusively confer jurisdiction, since facts alleged in the complaint can contradict and disprove the jurisdictional allegation. As always, the safest pleading approach is to track the language of the Appendix of Forms to the Federal Rules of Civil Procedure.

Example:

[Caption]

COMPLAINT

Plaintiff Ralph Johnson complains against Defendant Wilbur Jackson as follows:

Jurisdictional Allegation

1. Jurisdiction in this case is based on the existence of a federal question. This action arises under [the Constitution of the United States, Amendment _____, §_____] [or the Act of _____, _____ Stat. _____, _____ U.S.C. §_____] [or the Treaty of the United States _____], as is shown more fully in this complaint.

b.   *Diversity jurisdiction*[16]

Federal jurisdiction can also be based on diversity of citizenship. The diversity statute is 18 U.S.C. §1332. The jurisdictional allegation must affirmatively show complete diversity of each plaintiff and each defendant (and

---

14. See §3.5.
15. See 28 U.S.C. §1653.
16. See §3.5.

allege the required amount in controversy). The essential requirement is citizenship, not residence. An individual has only one state of citizenship. A permanent resident alien is treated, for jurisdictional purposes, as a citizen of the state where domiciled. (A nonresident alien is presumably still treated as if a citizen of the foreign country of which he is a national.) A corporation, for jurisdictional purposes, is deemed a citizen of both the state where incorporated and the state where it has its principal place of business.

Example (individuals):

Jurisdictional Allegation

Jurisdiction in this case is based on diversity of citizenship of the parties and the amount in controversy. Plaintiff is a citizen of the State of California. Defendant is a citizen of the State of Oregon.

Example (corporations):

Jurisdictional Allegation

Jurisdiction in this case is based on diversity of citizenship of the parties and the amount in controversy. Plaintiff is a corporation incorporated under the laws of the State of Delaware having its principal place of business in the State of New York. Defendant is a corporation incorporated under the laws of the State of Georgia having its principal place of business in the State of Florida.

Where the party is a legally recognized unincorporated association, such as a labor union or service organization, it is a citizen of every state of which any of its members is a citizen. Partnerships are considered citizens of each state where a general partner is a citizen. For legal representatives — such as a guardian of a minor, executor or administrator of an estate, and representative of an incompetent — the minor, deceased, or incompetent's citizenship is controlling for diversity purposes, although there may be exceptions in special circumstances.[17]

Diversity jurisdiction under 28 U.S.C. §1332 also requires that the "matter in controversy exceeds the sum or value of $75,000, exclusive of interest and costs."[18] Since the jurisdictional amount must be alleged in the pleadings, it is customary to simply paraphrase the statute at the end of the jurisdictional allegation.

---

17. See Wright §29; Wright & Miller §3606.
18. See §3.5. The $75,000 matter in controversy requirement applies to diversity cases under 28 U.S.C. §1332; since 1980, it no longer applies to federal question cases under 28 U.S.C. §1331.

Example:

<u>Jurisdictional Allegation</u>

. . . The amount in controversy exceeds the sum of seventy-five thousand dollars ($75,000), exclusive of interest and costs.

Where a statute makes notice of a claim a prerequisite to suit, some courts have held that the fact that notice was given is a jurisdictional requirement that must be alleged in the complaint.[19]

Because state trial courts are usually courts of general jurisdiction, a specific jurisdictional allegation in complaints brought in state courts is usually unnecessary.

2.   Statement of claims[20]

Rule 8(a) requires that a pleading contain a "short and plain statement of the claim showing that the pleader is entitled to relief." Rule 8(e) states that each allegation in the pleading shall be "simple, concise and direct"; only a few claims, principally fraud and mistake, must be pleaded with particularity. In short, technical requirements have been discarded, the sole requirement now being that enough be pleaded that the other party has fair notice of the claims presented sufficient to defend itself.

Since the requirements for the statement of claims are usually rosy to meet, great latitude in drafting exists. Hence, the more significant drafting questions are: What is the most effective way to make a statement of the claim in a complaint? Are there any general drafting "rules" that apply?

a.   Use plain English

In recent years the trend in legal drafting has been away from legalese in favor of plain English. The same approach should be applied when drafting pleadings. Commonly used words, short sentences of simple construction, active verbs, and a preference for nouns and verbs over adjectives and adverbs create clear and forceful language. This benefits everyone in litigation — parties, lawyers, judge, and jury.

b.   Keep it simple

Pleadings are not the place to disclose the detailed facts on which you base your claims, nor the place to elaborate on your theories of recovery. The Rules require only a "short and plain statement." You need only allege enough to put the opposing party on fair notice of what your claims against

---

19. See Manual of Federal Practice §3.6.

20. Wright §68; James & Hazard §§3.14–3.20; Friedenthal §5.15; Moore's Manual §10.14; Manual of Federal Practice §3.17; Moore's Federal Practice §§8.12–8.17; Wright & Miller §§1215–1254.

him are. While this must be read in the light of the complexity of the case, with complex cases requiring more detailed allegations, the preference should still be for simplicity. Adding more than the pleading rules require is usually surplusage that does not improve the legal adequacy of the complaint.

However, the Supreme Court in 2007 signaled a partial return to fact pleading. In Bell Atlantic v. Twombly, ___U.S. ___, 127 S. Ct. 1995 (2007), a class action antitrust case, the Court held that a pleading, to be adequate under the "plain statement" requirement of Rule 8(a)(2), must furnish factual "allegations plausibly suggesting (not merely consistent with) an "entitlement to relief," and not mere "labels and conclusions and a formulaic recitation of the elements of a cause of action." There must be enough facts alleged to "nudge [a] claim across the line from conceivable to plausible." This plausibility requirement is new, and how courts will apply it is uncertain. The Court also rejected the long-standing rule (established in Conley v. Gibson, 355 U.S. 41 (1957)) that "a complaint is not to be dismissed for failure to state a claim unless it appears beyond doubt that the plaintiff can prove no set of facts in support of his claim which would entitle him to relief." The Court found the "no set of facts" standard to be overly broad, since it would allow wholly conclusory allegations to survive a motion to dismiss. Where does Bell Atlantic now put pleading standards? The safer course is to allege more facts in the complaint and avoid pleading mere legal conclusions, particularly in complex cases.

Two sources should always be consulted when drafting complaints. First, check the wording of the elements instruction for each theory of recovery that will be given to the jury if the case goes to trial. Second, the official Appendix of Forms gives excellent examples of complaints in common situations that, by virtue of Rule 84, are legally adequate, yet use simple English. The safest approach in drafting pleadings is to modify these forms to your claims whenever practical.

Example (negligence):

1. On August 1, 2005, at approximately 3:00 P.M., plaintiff Jones and defendant Smith were driving automobiles on Elm Street, near Maple Avenue, in Chicago, Illinois.
2. Smith negligently crossed the center lane of Elm Street with his automobile, striking Jones' automobile.
3. As a result Jones received facial injuries, a broken arm, and other injuries, experienced pain and suffering, incurred medical expenses, lost substantial income, and will incur more medical expenses and lost income in the future.

Example (contract):

1. On August 1, 2005, plaintiff Jones and defendant Smith entered into a contract. A copy of the contract is attached to this complaint as Exhibit A.

2. Jones paid Smith $80,000 and has performed all of her obligations under the contract.

3. Smith failed to repair Jones' house as he was required to do under the contract.

On the other hand, there are times when making more detailed or specific factual allegations than required under Rule 8(a) can be effective. First, specific factual allegations are harder for the defendant to deny. Second, a specific allegation can be used to support a later specific discovery request. If the defendant denies the allegation in the complaint, she can hardly object to discovery methods that are directed to uncovering the denied fact. Rule 26 makes this substantially more important. Rule 26(a) requires automatic initial disclosure of facts and documents "the disclosing party may use to support its claims or defenses," and Rule 26(b) provides that parties "may obtain discovery regarding any matter, not privileged, that is relevant to the claim or defense of any party." Hence, alleging specific events such as meetings, conversations, and transactions and referring to specific records and documents in a pleading will make it more difficult for the responding party to deny those allegations and to avoid disclosing facts and documents relevant to the pleading. Seen in this light, the complaint can be plaintiff's first discovery device, since detailed allegations will trigger the automatic disclosure requirements and support later discovery requests. Third, if plaintiff has a compelling story to tell, setting that story out in the complaint for both the judge and later the jury to read can be an effective approach, particularly if you are seeking an early settlement of the case.

The preference for using simple English should also apply to naming parties. Use names rather than the pleading's designations, such as plaintiff, defendant, cross-claimant, or third-party defendant or other legal designations, such as trustee, drawer, or obligor, unless a local pleading rule requires the designation of the party. Using names keeps things clear, particularly where multiple parties are involved.

A common practice is to set out the full name of each party the first time it is used, then show in parentheses how you will refer to that party from then on.

Example:

Defendant William B. Jones (hereafter "Jones") . . .

The International Business Machines Corporation ("IBM") . . .

c. *Plead "special matters" with particularity*

Rule 9 is an exception to the general "notice pleading" approach of the federal rules. Under Rule 9, certain allegations must be pleaded "specifically" and "with particularity." These include fraud, mistake, and special damages.[21]

---

21. Subject matter jurisdiction must also be pleaded specifically. See §3.5.

While capacity and authority to sue and conditions precedent can be pleaded generally, denials must be made specifically and with particularity.

What constitutes appropriate specificity and particularity in pleading these special matters is unclear.[22] It is safer as well as proper to set forth the specific elements of the special matter being pleaded. This will ensure that the requisite particularity has been established.

Example (fraud):

> 1. On August 1, 2005, plaintiff Jones and defendant Smith entered into a contract. A copy of the contract is attached to this complaint as Exhibit A.
>
> 2. Under the contract, Jones agreed to pay Smith $80,000, and Smith agreed to sell Jones a parcel of land in Atlanta, Georgia. The precise location and description of the parcel are set out in the contract, attached as Exhibit A.
>
> 3. Before executing this contract, Smith represented that he had legal title to the parcel, that the parcel had no encumbrances of any kind, such as mortgages, tax liens, or judgment liens, and that Smith would be able to have the property rezoned to a B-2 zoning.
>
> 4. Those representations were false and fraudulent, Smith knew they were false and fraudulent when made, and Smith made them to induce Jones to enter into the contract.
>
> 5. Jones relied on Smith's representations and was damaged.

d.   Use separate paragraphs

The rules require a separate paragraph for a "single set of circumstances" whenever practicable — admittedly an imprecise standard. When in doubt, it is probably better to use paragraphs liberally, since this usually makes the pleadings simpler to follow. Keep each paragraph to a simple point, and avoid colorful characterizations. More important, it makes the complaint easier to answer and will minimize the likelihood that an answer will admit part and deny part of a single paragraph. As a result the positions of the parties will be clearer, benefiting everyone.

Example:

> 1. On June 1, 2005, plaintiff Jones and defendant Smith entered into a contract, a copy of which is attached as Exhibit A.
>
> 2. On June 15, 2005, Jones paid Smith $80,000 as required by the contract.
>
> 3. Jones has performed each of her obligations under the contract.
>
> 4. Smith failed to deliver 1,000 folding chairs to Jones by June 30, 2005, and has failed to perform his obligations under the contract.

---

22. See Moore's Manual §9.07.

In some jurisdictions the practice is to number the paragraphs with Arabic numbers; others use Roman numerals.

e. *Use separate counts*

Although not required by the rules, it is customary to state each claim involving a separate theory of recovery in a separate count, even if all are based on the same occurrence or transaction. This has the advantage of setting out clearly each legal theory that forms a basis for recovery.

Since setting out different theories of recovery in different counts usually requires restating some allegations, it is efficient and proper under Rule 10(c) to incorporate into the later count by reference those allegations made in earlier counts.

Example:

<u>Count II</u>

1-15. Plaintiff adopts Par. 1-15 of Count I as Par. 1-15 of this Count.

16. . . .

17. . . .

It is better to number all the paragraphs in all the counts of the complaint sequentially, rather than to begin each count with a Par. 1. This avoids confusion and makes it easier for the defendant to respond to each paragraph in the answer.

It is also useful to label the legal theory for each count and, where different counts are against different parties, show which parties are involved in each count.

Example:

<u>Count I — Contract</u>

(against defendants Jones and Roberts)

1. . . .

2. . . .

3. . . .

<u>Count II — Implied Warranties</u>

(against defendant Roberts only)

7. . . .

8. . . .

9. . . .

If the complaint alleges several theories of recovery, but the facts are common to all the counts, lawyers frequently set out the common facts separately and label them appropriately.

Example:

<u>Factual Allegations</u>

    1. . . .
    2. . . .
    3. . . .

Example:

<u>Allegations Common to All Counts</u>

    1. . . .
    2. . . .
    3. . . .

When this approach is used, the common allegations will immediately follow the jurisdictional allegation section.

f. Use exhibits

Rule 10(c) permits attaching exhibits to pleadings. This is most commonly done in contract cases, where a copy of the contract that forms the basis for the claim is attached to the complaint. When attached to the pleading, the exhibit becomes an integral part of it. This is sometimes a more efficient way of stating a claim than setting out the exhibit's contents in the body of the complaint.

Example:

1. Plaintiff Jones and defendant Smith entered into a contract on June 1, 2005. A copy of this contract is attached as Exhibit A.

Example:

8. The employee manual sets forth some of the terms of the employment contract entered into by Jones and Smith. A copy of this employee manual is attached as Exhibit B.

If the exhibit is lengthy, however, it may be easier to set out the key language in the pleading, rather than attach the exhibit to the pleading. Courts dislike lengthy attachments to pleadings.

3. Prayer for relief[23]

Rule 8(a) requires a pleading to make a "demand for judgment for the relief the pleader seeks. Relief in the alternative or of several different types may be demanded." The Rule makes no distinction between legal and equitable relief.

Care in pleading relief is important for two reasons. First, since under federal law the nature of the remedy sought is often controlling on the question of the right to a jury trial,[24] the demand for relief should be drafted to ensure the right to a jury trial, or to avoid it, as the case may be. Second, where a default judgment is requested, the method under which default can be obtained is affected by the type of relief sought, and the relief granted is limited to that requested in the pleadings.[25] Since default is always a possibility, you should always draft the prayer carefully. Third, if jurisdiction is based on diversity, make sure the prayer for relief asks for a sum in excess of $75,000, exclusive of interest and costs, as required by 28 U.S.C. §1332.

The demand for relief should specify the types of relief sought, including legal and equitable remedies, interest, costs, attorney's fees, and any special damages, with sufficient detail. Where several specific types of relief are sought, the better practice is to itemize and number them.

Example:

> WHEREFORE, plaintiff demands judgment against defendant for the sum of $80,000, with interest and costs.

> WHEREFORE, plaintiff demands a preliminary and permanent injunction, an accounting for all damages, and interest and costs.

Example:

DEMAND FOR RELIEF

Plaintiff demands:

1. That defendant pay damages in excess of the sum of $80,000;
2. That defendant be specifically ordered to perform his obligations under the contract;
3. That defendant pay interest, costs, and reasonable attorney's fees incurred by plaintiff.

---

23. Wright §68; James & Hazard §§3.21–3.22; Friedenthal §5.15; Moore's Manual §10.15; Manual of Federal Practice §3.8; Moore's Federal Practice §8.18; Wright & Miller §§1255–1260.
    24. See §3.3.
    25. See Rules 54 and 55; Sec. 79.

Do you need a prayer for relief for each claim, or only one prayer for the complaint as a whole? Rule 8 does not specify, and local practices vary, so practical concerns should provide the answer. If each claim raised has different allowable damages, you may want to have a prayer for relief after each count for clarity's sake. However, if your claims all have the same allowable damages — when all claims seek negligence damages, for example — have one prayer for relief at the end of the complaint.

Can you ask for a specific dollar amount in damages? In some jurisdictions, local rules bar asking for specific amounts. This rule prevents lawyers from asking for large amounts to generate publicity for the lawsuit and the lawyer. In such jurisdictions the usual allegation is that plaintiff seeks damages "in excess of the jurisdictional amount of $75,000." If allowed, you should still be careful not to exaggerate your damages claims. In some jurisdictions pleadings can be read to the jury, and exaggerated claims will make you look greedy and unrealistic. Finally, if you anticipate that the defendant may not defend the case, a specific dollar amount in a damages claim may make it easier to obtain a default judgment under Rule 41. (See §7.9.)

4. Jury demand[26]

Under Rule 38, a party may demand a jury trial, on any claim triable as of right by a jury, in writing at any time after the complaint is filed and "not later than 10 days after the service of the last pleading directed to such issue." To be effective, the jury trial demand must be served on the other parties and filed with the court. The party may specify in the demand which claims he wishes tried to a jury. The rule permits the jury demand to be placed on the pleading itself, and this is the customary method of making the demand. A common practice is to place "<u>JURY TRIAL DEMANDED</u>" below the case number, and "<u>PLAINTIFF DEMANDS TRIAL BY JURY</u>" at the end of the complaint. Another common practice is to use a separate heading for the jury demand.

Example:

<u>JURY DEMAND</u>

Plaintiff demands a trial by jury on all claims on which she has the right to trial by jury.

Local rules usually have additional requirements, such as the filing of jury demand forms and the payment of fees.

If one party makes a jury demand, the other parties are entitled to rely on it. However, if a party makes a jury demand on only some counts, the

---

26. Wright §92; Friedenthal §11.9; Moore's Manual §9.10; Manual of Federal Practice §§7.20–7.21; Moore's Federal Practice §§38.07–38.46; Wright & Miller §§2318–2322.

other parties must make a timely jury demand on other counts. Failure to make a timely demand for a jury trial constitutes a waiver of the right under Rule 38(d), and courts have taken a strict view on waiver and only rarely exercise their discretion and permit a belated demand.[27]

5. Signature

Under Rule 11, every complaint must be signed by the lawyer preparing it, and that lawyer must be authorized to appear in the court in which the case is being filed. Signing the complaint triggers the Rule 11(b) certification about the complaint. The rule also requires that the lawyer's address and telephone number be shown. Since the rule requires the signature of an individual lawyer, a common practice is to show the lawyer's firm as "of counsel." Finally, a complaint in a federal court need not be verified or supported by affidavit. Verification is still a common requirement in some state jurisdictions for certain kinds of complaints.

Example:

Dated this 3rd day of June, 2005.

                                      _____

Jane Smith Johnson
Attorney for Plaintiff
Suite 1400
100 Madison Avenue
Chicago, IL 60601
(312) 807-9000

6. Common problems

The complaint is one of the most important documents in the litigation process. A complaint, in addition to getting the litigation started, sends messages to the defense about you: how well you have researched the facts and law, how well you have analyzed and made decisions about them, and how knowledgable you are about litigation. A well-planned and drafted complaint sends a clear message that you are competent and prepared to move the litigation ahead. Accordingly, unless there is a pressing need to file quickly, usually because of a statute of limitations deadline, it makes sense to draft the complaint carefully, have others review it, and make revisions before filing.

Problems in preparing complaints usually fall into three categories. First, the complaint is not well thought out. Many lawyers make complaints unnecessarily complex, having too many parties and alternative theories of

---

27. See Wright §92.

recovery. Remember that complex complaints usually generate complex, lengthy, expensive litigation, which may not be in the client's best interest. Most plaintiffs want a speedy, inexpensive, and favorable outcome. A good general rule is to file the simplest complaint that will serve the client's litigation objectives.

Second, the complaint is not well drafted. Remember that a complaint should be factually and legally clear. Use headings to break the complaint into its logical components, such as jurisdiction, parties, facts, counts, and relief. Make sure that the jurisdictional allegation properly alleges the basis for federal jurisdiction and that the facts demonstrate it. Make sure the allegations show that venue is proper. Keep the factual paragraphs simple, limited to a single point, and avoid unnecessary characterizations. Decide if you want a "bare bones" approach or whether you want more specific and detailed factual allegations. Make sure that the counts clearly set forth the required elements of each of the legal claims. Make sure that the prayer for relief contains all the kinds of relief to which you may be entitled, and avoids requesting unsupportable dollar amounts. Finally, if you want a jury trial, make sure that the complaint contains a jury demand.

Third, the complaint only alleges legal conclusions without any supporting facts. Remember that in Bell Atlantic v. Twombly, __ U.S. __, 127 S. Ct. 1995 (2007) the Supreme Court held that complaints, to meet the requirements of Rule 8(a)(2) and to survive a Rule 12(b)(6) motion to dismiss, must allege enough facts to "nudge a claim across the line from conceivable to plausible." This plausibility requirement is new, and plaintiffs should make sure that their complaints are not "mere labels and conclusions and a formulaic recitation of the elements of a cause of action."

7. Filing and service of summons[28]

Under Rule 3, a federal action is commenced when the complaint is filed with the clerk of the court, and commencement is significant for statute of limitations purposes. In federal question cases, the filing of the complaint tolls the statute of limitations. In diversity cases, however, state law controls, and if state law requires something more than the mere filing of the complaint — usually actual service of summons on the defendant — state law must be complied with fully before the statute of limitations is tolled.[29]

After the action is commenced, the complaint must be served on each defendant. Under Rule 4, detailed service of summons rules control how the complaint and summons are to be served on defendants. There are several steps involved, and you should check local rules for any additional filing and service of summons requirements. For example, most districts require designation or civil cover sheets and appearance forms to be filed with the complaint and summons.

28. Wright §§64–65; Moore's Manual §§6.01–6.19; Manual of Federal Practice §§3.80–3.94; Moore's Federal Practice §§4.02–4.46; Wright & Miller §§1061–1153.
29. See Wright §64.

a. Issuing the summons

Under Rule 4(b), the plaintiff must prepare the summons and present it to the clerk after filing the complaint. If the summons is in proper form, the clerk is directed to issue it to the plaintiff. In practice, the summons form, which is available from the clerk's office, is usually filled out in advance and taken to the clerk's office when the complaint is filed. To assist in service it is useful to list on the form where and when service on each defendant can most likely be made. For example, if the service is to be made at the defendant's work address, it is useful to put down the working hours and where on the premises the defendant actually works. The clerk then "issues" the summons by signing and stamping it with the court seal, the date, and the case file number. In the case of multiple defendants, the plaintiff has two options: he can secure issuance of a separate original summons for each defendant or he can serve copies of a single original that names all of the defendants. Make sure you have enough copies of the complaint and summons for the clerk's administrative needs, for service on each defendant, and for your own files.

b. Summons content

Rule 4(a) controls the summons content. The following example contains the standard elements of a summons.

Example:

SUMMONS

To:_____ *(defendant)* _____

You are hereby summoned and required to serve upon_____
_____, plaintiff's attorney, whose address is _____
_____, an answer to the complaint that is hereby served upon you, within 20 days after service upon you, exclusive of the day of service.

If you fail to do so, judgment by default will be taken against you for the relief demanded in the complaint.

_____
Clerk fo Court

[Seal of the U.S. District Court]

Dated: _____

If there is a technical defect in the summons, such as the misspelling of the defendant's name, the court, in its discretion, may allow an amendment of the summons.

The federal summons is used even if service is effected under state service rules.

c. *Persons who may serve the summons*

As a general rule, the complaint and summons can be served by any person who is not a party and is at least 18 years old. Service by the U.S. Marshal is now required only in limited circumstances specified in Rule 4(c)(2) — for actions brought in forma pauperis and for actions brought by a seaman. On motion of a plaintiff, the court may appoint a process server.

d. *Methods of service*

How service of summons may be made depends on the entity being served, and is governed by Rule 4(c)-(j).

i. Individuals

An individual under Rule 4(e) can be served a summons in several ways. First, service can be made by personally giving the individual a copy of the complaint and summons. Second, it can be made by leaving a copy of the complaint and summons "at the individual's dwelling house or usual place of abode" with a person of suitable age and discretion residing there. Third, service can be made on an agent authorized by appointment or law to receive process. Fourth, where the individual is out of state, service may be made when any federal statute authorizes out-of-state service, pursuant to the laws of the state in which service is effected, and when a statute of the state in which the district court sits permits out-of-state service. These are the state long-arm statutes, which provide for extraterritorial service on any defendant who has had constitutionally sufficient contacts with that state.[30]

Finally, Rule 4(d) allows the plaintiff to request that the defendant waive formal service of the summons. Individuals, corporations, and associations that receive such a request for waiver of service then have a duty to avoid unnecessary service costs. The rule contains an incentive for a defendant to comply with the request by signing and returning it in a timely manner: additional time to answer the complaint. If defendant does not comply, he becomes responsible for the costs of formal service. This request and waiver, coupled with mail service, has become the predominant method under which individuals (and domestic and foreign corporations, partnerships, and unincorporated associations) are served.

Under Rule 4(d)(2), valid service is accomplished by using first class mail or other reliable means such as messenger or fax to deliver to the defendant two copies of a notice of commencement of the action and request for waiver of service, a copy of the complaint, notice to the defendant of

---

30. See §3.6.

the duty to avoid unnecessary costs of service and the penalties for non-compliance, and two copies of a waiver form and prepaid means of compliance (such as a return envelope, postage prepaid). The request must state the date on which it was sent. Forms 1A and IB in the Appendix of Forms to the Federal Rules of Civil Procedure illustrate the text of the requirements for this rule. The person served then completes and signs one copy of the notice and waiver and returns it to the sender, who is ordinarily the plaintiff's lawyer. Note that sending the summons and complaint by registered or certified mail does not eliminate the requirement that the sender receive a signed acknowledgment of service from the person served. This method of service can be used for those defendants who reside in the forum state, those who reside outside the forum state, and even those who reside in foreign countries.

If the sender does not receive the completed waiver of service within 30 days (60 days in the case of foreign defendants) of the date the request is sent, service of the complaint and summons must be made under Rule 4(e), (f), or (h), which, in the case of individuals, is effected by the means mentioned above. If this method of service becomes necessary, the court shall order the costs incurred in effecting service, and the costs (including attorney's fees) of any motion to collect the cost of service to be paid by the person served.

The intent and effect of the service by mail and waiver of formal service rules are clear. Service by mail is easier, quicker, and less expensive, and the requirement of the signed waiver returned to the sender eliminates the need for the traditional proof of service. Only if the person served by mail refuses or fails to return the signed waiver within the 30-day period is the sender then obligated to use other methods of service and the person served obligated to bear the actual cost of service.

The waiver of formal service rules is attractive, but it has one important caveat. If the case is in federal court based on diversity jurisdiction, state law will control what needs to be done to toll the running of the statute of limitations. Some states require not only filing of the complaint, but also require actual proper service of the complaint and summons on the defendant. If the defendant refuses to sign the waiver of formal service and return it to the plaintiff, and the statute of limitations runs before the plaintiff properly serves the defendant through one of the other methods permitted by Rule 4, the lawsuit will be time-barred. Accordingly, a plaintiff should always serve the defendant with the complaint and summons through another method when faced with an imminent running of the statute of limitations.

ii.   Infants and incompetents

Service on infants and incompetents is made in the same manner as service would be made under the law of the state in which service is to be made. While state laws vary, they usually require service on a parent or a legal guardian of the infant or incompetent.

Service can also be made upon infants and incompetents in foreign countries under Rule 4(g). In such a case, service would be made according to the law of the foreign country or as the court directs.

iii.   Corporations, partnerships, and associations

Service on domestic and foreign corporations, partnerships, and unincorporated associations that can be sued in their own name can be made several ways under Rule 4(h). First, service can be made by personal delivery to an officer, manager, or general agent. Second, service can be made to an agent authorized to receive service of process; the list of domestic and foreign corporations, usually compiled by each state's Secretary of State or Corporation Commission, should show the authorized agent for service of process. Third, when the corporation is out of state, service can be made under any federal statute providing for service or under any method permitted by a statute of the state in which the district court sits — principally the state's long-arm statute — or service can be made pursuant to the law of the state in which service is effected. Finally, service can be made by mail using the procedure set forth by Rule 4(d)(2). This mail service procedure, which is the same as permitted for individuals, described above, is now the most common way corporations are served with a complaint and summons.

iv.   Officers and agencies of the United States, foreign, state, and local governments

Rule 4(i) details the requirements for service on the United States and its federal agencies and employees, and Rule 4(j) details the requirements for foreign, state, and local governments. The requirements are technical, and the Rule should always be reviewed before attempting service.

e.   *Territorial limits of service*

The geographical scope of service is governed by Rule 4(k). There are four basic precepts.

i.   Statewide service

Summons may be served anywhere within the state in which the district court sits.

ii.   The 100-mile "bulge" rule

The 100-mile "bulge" provision provides for some service within 100 miles of the place where the original action commenced, even if state lines are crossed. However, this rule applies only to parties brought in as third-party defendants under Rule 14, or as additional necessary parties to a counterclaim or cross-claim under Rules 13 and 19.

The purpose of the rule is to permit service of process on additional parties that are brought into the action after the original suit is filed and are necessary for a fair and complete disposition of the action. This is an important rule for multi-party litigation in large metropolitan areas such as New York, Chicago, and Washington, D.C., which cover several jurisdictions, since otherwise it would often be difficult to serve every party in the suit.

iii.   State long-arm statutes

Rule 4(e) provides for service on parties outside the state in which the district court sits whenever that state permits out-of-state service. The Rule refers, of course, to state long-arm statutes and attachment procedures that create quasi in rem jurisdiction.[31] It puts federal and state process on essentially the same footing as far as territorial limits are concerned.

iv.   Federal statute or court order

Whenever a federal statute or court order authorizes service on a party outside the state in which the district court sits, service may be made in accordance with the statute or order.

If the Rule 4(k) requirements are met, proper service of summons or filing a waiver of service is deemed to establish personal jurisdiction over a defendant. Under Rule 4(k)(2), if the exercise of jurisdiction over the defendant is constitutionally proper, service of summons or filing a waiver of service is also effective to confer personal jurisdiction over a defendant as to any federal claims, even if the defendant is not subject to personal jurisdiction in any state courts.

Finally, keep in mind that under Rule 4(d)(1) a waiver of service of summons does not constitute a waiver of objections to the jurisdiction of the court over the defendant or to venue. A defendant can waive service of summons and thereafter contest personal jurisdiction and venue in a Rule 12(b) motion or in the answer.

f.   *Timeliness of service*

Under Rule 4(m) service of the complaint and summons must be carried out within 120 days after filing of the complaint. Unless good cause can be shown for not having carried out service in time, the action will be dismissed without prejudice as to the unserved defendant.

The complaint, of course, may be refiled against that same party. Refiling after the statute of limitations has run should not create a problem, so long as the original action was properly filed within the limitations period. The reasoning for this is similar to the "relation back" analysis for amended and supplemental pleadings.[32] However, when a state

---

31. See §3.6.
32. See §5.13.

cause of action is asserted and state law requires more than the mere filing of the complaint to satisfy the state statute of limitations, such as actual service of summons, these additional requirements must be met within the limitations period.[33]

g. *Proof of service*

As discussed above, the complaint and summons are served most commonly today by mail service under the waiver rules of Rule 4(d). The proof of service will be the Notice and Waiver of Service of Summons (Forms 1A and 1B in the Appendix of Forms) that the served party signs and returns to the sender, who is usually the plaintiff's lawyer.

When the complaint and summons are served through a process server, Rule 4(1) requires that the person serving process establish proof of service promptly and in any event within the time during which the party served has to respond to the process. If process is served by anyone other than the U.S. marshal, proof must be in affidavit form. In practice, the proof-of-service affidavit is usually found on the summons form.

Example:

AFFIDAVIT OF SERVICE

I, _____, having been first duly sworn, state that I served a copy of the summons and complaint on _____(defendant)_____ by _____(method of service)_____ at __(address)__ on ____(date)____.

_____(signature)_____

Signed and sworn to before me on: _____

_____
Notary Public

My commission expires on _____

h. *Informal service*

Sometimes you will know the lawyer who will represent the defendant in the lawsuit. You may have already had contact with the defendant's lawyer before filing suit, or you may know the lawyer who regularly handles the defendant's legal matters. In such instances, a good practice is to call

33. See Wright §64; Wright & Miller §1057. The leading case is Ragan v. Merchants Transfer & Warehouse Co., 337 U.S. 530 (1949).

the lawyer and let her know you are about to file suit. Ask her if she will accept service of process on behalf of the defendant. If so, simply deliver or mail the complaint and summons to her. However, because Rule 4 requires that the defendant sign and return the notice and waiver of service of summons within 30 days of service (60 days for foreign defendants), make sure that the defendant's lawyer gets the signed waiver from her client and delivers it to you within that time period. Mail service is not deemed effective unless the defendant signs and returns the waiver form.

If you think the defendant will try to avoid service of process, or will contest the validity of service, serve the defendant formally under one of the methods permitted by Rule 4. Otherwise, informal service can be a convenient approach; it is frequently used in commercial litigation with corporate parties.

§5.4.   *Rule 12 responses*[34]

When a complaint and summons have been properly served on a defendant, he can respond in two basic ways. First, he can answer the complaint. Ordinarily, the defendant must answer within 20 days of service. If formal service was timely waived by the defendant, the defendant has 60 days from the date the request was mailed to serve an answer (90 days in the case of foreign defendants).

Second, before filing an answer the defendant can make any of three motions attacking claimed defects in the complaint.[35] These are a motion to strike, a motion for a more definite statement, and a motion to dismiss, all of which are governed by Rule 12. Where a defendant decides to attack the complaint with a Rule 12 motion, he must do so within the time permitted for his answer, ordinarily within 20 days of service of the complaint.[36]

1.   Motion to strike[37]

Under Rule 12(f), if the complaint contains "any redundant, immaterial, impertinent or scandalous matter," it can be stricken upon motion.

---

34. Wright §66; James & Hazard §4.2; Friedenthal §§5.22–5.24; Moore's Manual §§11.01–11.07; Manual of Federal Practice §§3.38–3.44, 4.2–4.34; Moore's Federal Practice §§12.05–12.23; Wright & Miller §§1341–1397.

35. See §5.3 for the requirements of a complaint.

36. If a Rule 12 motion is denied, a defendant generally has 10 days from the denial of the motion to answer the complaint. See Rule 6 for how time periods are computed.

37. Wright §66; James & Hazard §4.2; Friedenthal §5.24; Moore's Manual §11.05; Manual of Federal Practice §§4.20–4.22; Moore's Federal Practice §12.21; Wright & Miller §§1380–1383.

While such a motion is not frequently made, it should be considered where there is a possibility that the complaint will be read to the jury during trial.

Example:

[Caption]

MOTION TO STRIKE

Defendant Johnson Corporation moves under Rule 12(f) for an order striking certain immaterial and scandalous matters from the complaint. In support of its motion defendant states:

1. Par. 2 of the complaint alleges that the "Johnson Corporation had gross receipts of $102,436,000 for fiscal year 2005." This allegation is immaterial to a contract action and should be stricken.

2. Par. 7 of the complaint alleges that the "Johnson Corporation is an international cartel that dominates the furniture polish industry." This allegation is impertinent and scandalous and should be stricken.

WHEREFORE, defendant Johnson Corporation requests that the court enter an order striking these parts of plaintiff's complaint and requiring plaintiff to file an amended complaint that deletes the stricken matter within 10 days.

2. Motion for a more definite statement[38]

Under Rule 12(e), if the complaint is "so vague or ambiguous" that the defendant cannot respond to it, the defendant may move for a more definite statement. The motion must point out the defects and specify the details that are needed. However, since the complaint need only be a "short and plain statement," and pleadings generally should be "simple, concise and direct," and because discovery is the preferred method for flushing out details, such motions are disfavored and infrequently granted. A more commonly used approach is to move to dismiss under Rule 12(b)(6) for failure to state a claim on which relief can be granted.

On the other hand, since Rule 26(a) requires initial disclosures for facts and documents that "the disclosing party may use to support its claims and defenses," lawyers may use the motion to try to obtain more details about the pleadings before the initial disclosures are due.

---

38. Wright §66; James & Hazard §4.2; Friedenthal §5.23; Moore's Manual §11.07; Manual of Federal Practice §§4.18–4.20; Moore's Federal Practice §§12.17–12.19; Wright & Miller §§1374–1379.

Example:

[Caption]

MOTION FOR A MORE DEFINITE STATEMENT

Defendant Johnson Corporation moves under Rule 12(e) for an order requiring plaintiff to provide a more definite statement. In support of its motion defendant states:

      1. Par. 3 of the complaint alleges that "plaintiff and defendant and others entered into an agreement in 2002 under which defendant was obligated to deliver such amounts of furniture polish as plaintiff may from time to time request."

      2. Nowhere else in the complaint is greater detail provided, and no copy of any contract is attached to the complaint. Without additional details, defendant cannot respond to this allegation.

      WHEREFORE, defendant Johnson Corporation requests that the court enter an order requiring defendant to serve and file a more definite statement within 10 days showing what date this alleged contract was entered into, where it was entered into, every party to it, the requirements under the contract, and, if in writing, a copy of the alleged contract.

3.   Motion to dismiss under Rule 12(b)[39]

Under Rule 12(b), the defendant may raise certain defenses either in the answer or by a motion to dismiss. This is the predominant motion for attacking the complaint, and it has several important characteristics.

a.   *The one motion requirement*

If you decide to respond to the complaint with a motion to dismiss on Rule 12(b) grounds, the Rule requires that you present all defenses that can be raised in one motion to dismiss. In other words, you must consolidate all available Rule 12(b) defenses into one motion. This requirement prevents attacking the complaint on a piecemeal basis.

b.   *Rule 12(b) defenses*

The following defenses may be raised in a motion to dismiss:

1. Lack of subject matter jurisdiction
2. Lack of jurisdiction over the person
3. Improper venue

---

39. Wright §66; James & Hazard §4.2; Friedenthal §5.22; Moore's Manual §11.06; Manual of Federal Practice §§3.38–3.44, 4.23–4.30; Moore's Federal Practice §§12.07–12.14, 12.22–12.23; Wright & Miller §§1347–1366.

4. Insufficiency of process
5. Insufficiency of service of process
6. Failure to state a claim upon which relief can be granted
7. Failure to join a party under Rule 19

In addition, there is some case law holding that affirmative defenses in Rule 8(c) may be asserted in a Rule 12(b) motion to dismiss.[40]

Federal practice has eliminated the need for special appearances to contest personal jurisdiction, since under Rule 12(g) the joinder of defenses does not create a waiver of any of them. Hence, a defendant can raise any of the Rule 12(b) defenses by motion and is not held to have waived the right to assert lack of personal jurisdiction.[41]

c. Waiver

Under Rule 12(g) and (h), defenses not consolidated into one motion to dismiss may be waived, but the waiver rules depend on the defense involved. Lack of jurisdiction over the person, improper venue, insufficiency of process, and insufficiency of service of process are all waived if not included in a motion to dismiss or, if no motion is made, in the answer. Hence, if any of these grounds are raised in a motion to dismiss, the others must be raised then as well, or they will be waived. Failure to state a claim and failure to join an indispensable party, however, may be raised in the answer, in a motion for judgment on the pleadings, or at trial. Finally, lack of subject matter jurisdiction is never waived and can be raised at any time.

The waiver rules create two categories of defenses to a claim. The procedural irregularity defenses are waived unless timely presented, while substantive defenses to a valid judgment cannot be so waived.

d. Practice approach

The underlying theory of Rule 12 must be kept in mind when deciding whether to present Rule 12(b) defenses in a motion to dismiss or in the answer. The Rule permits certain defenses that may terminate the litigation to be presented and heard early in the litigation process. This is obviously an efficient way to deal with a defective or meritless complaint. If you decide to assert a defense in a motion to dismiss, you should raise the other Rule 12(b) defenses available and assert them in one consolidated motion, because most of those defenses are waived if not raised then.

Second, consider the types of defenses that can be raised. Three of the grounds, lack of jurisdiction over the person, insufficiency of process, and insufficiency of service of process, are essentially procedural defects that usually can be cured. Since the plaintiff can ordinarily file an amended complaint or serve process on the defendant again, there may be little point in raising these defenses if the plaintiff can easily cure them.

40. See Moore's Manual §1606(3); Manual of Federal Practice §3.41.
41. See Manual of Federal Practice §3.41.

For example, where there is no proper personal jurisdiction over the defendant because of a defect in the service of process, but it is obvious that the defendant can be properly served later, there may be little point in raising these defenses even though they are technically available. On the other hand, where personal jurisdiction over the defendant does not properly exist, and probably cannot be obtained, the motion should be made.

If the defense is improper venue, the defense is waived if not included in a motion to dismiss that raises other 12(b) defenses.[42] Hence, if venue is in fact improper under venue rules, and the present venue is a logistically inconvenient location for the defendant, the motion should be made. If granted, the probable result will not be dismissal, but transfer to a proper venue.[43]

Finally, where the defenses are lack of subject matter jurisdiction, failure to state a claim upon which relief can be granted, and failure to join an indispensable party, the defendant has more flexibility since these may be made either in the answer or by a motion for judgment on the pleadings, even if a motion to dismiss based on other Rule 12(b) grounds has been made. Hence, the defendant has the option of including these grounds in a motion to dismiss or raising them later. Raising them by motion to dismiss, of course, will get the issue resolved sooner than by including them in the answer. Regardless of which approach is taken, however, the plaintiff is on notice of a possible defect in his pleading and can usually file an amended complaint correcting the defect.

The history of Rule 12(b) shows that motions to dismiss rarely result in the final disposition of a lawsuit.[44] Indeed, federal pleadings are designed to frame issues, not resolve disputes. Hence, the trend in litigation practice has been to make fewer motions under Rule 12 and to raise those defenses instead in the answer; that is, to raise those defenses in a motion to dismiss only when there is a clear strategic reason to do so, not simply because the Rules permit it.

A motion to dismiss based on Rule 12(b) should clearly set out the defenses being asserted in separate paragraphs.

Example:

[Caption]

MOTION TO DISMISS

Defendant Jones moves under Rule 12(b) for an order dismissing the complaint. In support of his motion defendant states:

1. The court lacks jurisdiction over the subject matter of this action because it appears from the complaint that the alleged claim does not arise under the Constitution of the United States, any Act of Congress, or treaties of the United States.

---

42. See §3.7; 28 U.S.C. §§1391 et seq.
43. See §3.7; 28 U.S.C. §§1404, 1406.
44. See Wright §66.

2. The court lacks jurisdiction over the subject matter of this action because the controversy is not between citizens of different states, and because the amount in controversy between the plaintiff and this defendant is less than $75,000, exclusive of interest and costs.

3. The court lacks jurisdiction over the defendant because the defendant is a corporation incorporated under the laws of the State of Delaware, has its principal place of business in Delaware, and is not subject to service in the State of Maryland where service was attempted.

4. This action has been brought in an improper district, since the complaint alleges that jurisdiction is based on diversity of citizenship, plaintiff is a citizen of the State of California, defendant is a citizen of the State of Nevada, and the claims arose in the State of Nevada. Venue in the district of Arizona is therefore improper.

5. Service of process on the defendant was insufficient because service was made on the defendant's business partner at his place of business, as shown by the proof of service for the summons.

6. The complaint fails to state a claim against this defendant on which relief can be granted.

7. The complaint fails to join all indispensable parties as required by Rule 19 because the Phillips Corporation is an indispensable party, has not been joined as a party, and if brought within this court's jurisdiction would destroy this court's jurisdiction since complete diversity would be lacking.

WHEREFORE, defendant Jones requests that the court enter an order dismissing the complaint.

The basic allegations of Rule 12(b) grounds should be developed both factually and legally. Where facts are necessary, statements in affidavit form and exhibits should be attached to the motion, although the court under the Rule can then treat the motion as one for summary judgment. If case law is pertinent, it should be contained in a memorandum of law accompanying the motion.

The most commonly raised ground for dismissal, of course, is Rule 12(b)(6), failure to state a claim upon which relief can be granted. In 2007, the Supreme Court in Bell Atlantic v. Twombly, ___ U.S. ___, 127 S. Ct. 1955 (2007), held that it would no longer follow the rule established 50 years ago in Conley v. Gibson, 355 U.S. 41 (1957), that complaints should not be dismissed under Rule 12(b)(6) "unless it appears beyond doubt that the plaintiff can prove no set of facts in support of his claim which would entitle him to relief." This standard is "retired." Instead, to survive a motion to dismiss, a complaint now needs to allege enough facts to create "plausible grounds to infer" that the claims can be proven and "to raise a reasonable expectation that discovery will reveal evidence" that supports the claims in the complaint. The decision did not detail what quantum of facts is necessary to "nudge [a] claim across the line from the [merely] conceivable" to "plausible," although the decision did make it clear that detailed factual allegations are not required and that the particularity requirement in pleading special matters under Rule 9 would not be read into the Rule 8 requirements.

What is clear is that *Bell Atlantic* breathed new life into Rule 12(b)(6) motions, and defendants can be expected to make such motions more frequently, especially in complex cases, where the complaint fails to allege any facts plausibly supporting the claims and the complaint is little more than a conclusory recitation of the legal elements of the claims. Such motions are also likely to be made in cases where the defendant is in possession of most of the discoverable evidence, such as employment discrimination cases and cases in which the defendant's mental state is in issue, such as fraud and conspiracy cases. In those types of cases it may be difficult for the plaintiff to learn and allege enough facts to state a plausible claim without the benefit of pretrial discovery.

The motion is conceptually limited to matters alleged in the complaint. If facts outside the pleadings are presented at a hearing on the motion, the court should treat the motion as one for summary judgment and proceed in accordance with Rule 56. If the motion is granted, plaintiff will routinely be given leave to file an amended complaint. However, if the plaintiff is acting in bad faith, has repeatedly failed to amend properly, or obviously cannot amend properly, leave to amend should be denied.[45]

Service of the motion must be made in one of the ways permitted under Rule 5 on every other party presently in the case. The most common methods are service by mail or personal service, although service by electronic means is now permitted. The motion with proof of service must be filed with the clerk of court or, if permitted by local rules, with the judge.

§5.5. *Answers*[46]

When the plaintiff's complaint has been properly served on a defendant, that defendant must respond, either by filing a Rule 12 motion, discussed in the preceding section, or by answering the complaint. The answer, like any other pleading and court paper, must comply with the requirements of Rule 11, under which a lawyer signing the answer thereby certifies that the denials of factual contentions are warranted on the evidence and that there are no frivolous legal arguments.

1. Timing

As a general rule, under Rule 12(a) the defendant must serve an answer within 20 days of service of the complaint and summons. Different deadlines may apply if the U.S. government is a defendant, or if a specific

---

45. Foman v. Davis, 371 U.S. 178 (1962).
46. Wright §66; James & Hazard §§4.4–4.8; Friedenthal §§5.17–5.20; Moore's Manual §11.08; Manual of Federal Practice §§3.28–3.44; Moore's Federal Practice §§8.21–8.29, 12.05–12.07; Wright & Miller §§1261–1279, 1347–1348.

federal statute applies. In addition, if formal service was timely waived by the defendant, the defendant has 60 days from the date the request was mailed to serve an answer (90 days in the case of foreign defendants). This additional time is an added inducement to defendants to waive service by following the waiver provisions of Rule 4(d). Where the defendant first responds with a Rule 12 motion, the answer is due within 10 days after the defendant receives notice of the court's action on the motion or within 10 days after service of a more definite statement.

2.   General requirements

There are several rules that regulate the form and content of the answer. Rule 8(b) requires that an answer shall "state in short and plain terms" the defenses asserted. It must either admit or deny the allegations, or state that the defendant is without knowledge or information sufficient to form a belief as to their truth. Under Rule 8(c), affirmative defenses must be set out in the answer, and under Rule 12(b), the specified defenses may be set out as well. The defenses may be set out alternatively, inconsistently, and hypothetically. A hypothetical defense can be raised to an allegation in a complaint if it is found to be true, thus permitting a response that both denies the allegation and raises a hypothetical defense to it.

Since a complaint must be answered, failing to answer will constitute an admission of all facts alleged in the complaint; this does not apply, however, to the prayer for relief. Answering with a simple "admit," "deny," or "no knowledge or belief" is usually sufficient. Under Rule 9(a), however, where the answer raises an issue as to the "legal existence of any party or the capacity of any party to sue or be sued or the authority of a party to sue or be sued in a representative capacity," the denials must be made with particularity.

To parallel the complaint, the answer must be organized in paragraphs and by counts, setting out separate defenses in separate paragraphs. Where there is only one defendant the answer is simply titled "<u>ANSWER</u>." If there are multiple defendants, however, the title should specify the party answering, for example, "<u>ANSWER OF DEFENDANT ACME TOOL COR-PORATION</u>." If a defendant demands a jury trial, the "<u>JURY TRIAL DEMANDED</u>" notice should appear in the caption of the answer, and the words "<u>DEFENDANT DEMANDS TRIAL BY JURY</u>" at the end of the answer. Finally, the answer, like every pleading, must be signed by the lawyer; this signature constitutes a certification that the pleading is made in accordance with Rule 11.

The answer, therefore, may have three parts: responses to the complaint's allegations, affirmative defenses, and Rule 12(b) defenses. A well-drafted answer will set out each part clearly.

3.   Responses

Rule 8(b) permits three types of responses to the complaint's allegations. The answer may either admit or deny the allegations, or state that the party is without knowledge or information sufficient to form a belief as to their truth. The format, whether informally brief or more formal, is largely a matter of local custom, although the trend is toward brief responses. Instead of referring to the "defendant," use the defendant's name after the introductory statement. This personalizes the party in the answer.

Example:

[Caption]

ANSWER

Defendant Jones answers the complaint as follows:

Count I

1. Admits.
2. Jones admits the allegations in Par. 2.
3. Denies.
4. Jones denies the allegations in Par. 4.
5. No knowledge or belief.
6. Jones states that she is without knowledge or information sufficient to form a belief as to the truth of the allegations in Par. 6, and therefore denies them.

If the response is "no knowledge or belief," this must be based on good faith. Such a response should not be available on matters that are common knowledge or that can easily be learned by the defendant.[47] For example, if the complaint alleges that the defendant corporation had "gross receipts during 2002 in the amount of $6,450,000," the defendant's lawyer cannot answer "no knowledge or belief" since the lawyer can easily find out if the allegation is true or not.

The answer may admit only part of an allegation and deny the remainder, or may admit having no knowledge or information as to the remainder, as the case may be. Each paragraph of the complaint must be responded to individually, unless the defendant can in good faith collectively deny every allegation of the complaint.

Example:

1. Jones admits he is a citizen of the State of California, but denies the remaining allegations in Par. 1.
2. Jones admits he entered into a written contract with plaintiff on June 1, 2005, but denies that the contract was modified by agreement on August 1, 2005, or on any other date.
3. Jones denies he owned and operated a business known as Jones Excavating in 2005 or any other year. Jones does not have

47. See Moore's Manual §11.08(2).

sufficient knowledge or information to form a belief as to the truth of the other allegations in Par. 3, and therefore denies them.

Within these guidelines the rules permit considerable drafting flexibility. The modern trend is toward brevity and conciseness. The standard approach is to simply have counts and numbered paragraphs corresponding to the counts and paragraphs of the complaint. However, it is just as effective to set out admissions, denials, and no-knowledge-or-information responses collectively when the situation is appropriate.

Example:

Count I

    1. Jones admits the allegations of Pars. 1, 2, 3, 4, 5, and 6 of the complaint.
    2. Jones denies the allegations of Pars. 8, 9, and 10 of the complaint.
    3. Jones states she does not have sufficient knowledge or information to form a belief as to the truth of the allegations in Par. 7, and therefore denies them.
    4. Jones denies all other allegations of Count I not specifically admitted.

Count II

    1. Jones incorporates her answers to Pars. 1-3 of Count I.
    2. Jones denies all other allegations of Count II.

Denying all allegations not specifically admitted is a safe practice, since this prevents a typographical error in the answer from prejudicing the defendant.

Claims under Rule 9(a) of no capacity or authority and claims under Rule 9(c) that conditions precedent have not been performed are raised by denials, but must be particularly specified.

Example:

    1. Jones denies that plaintiff is a legal entity that has capacity to sue in its own name, and specifically denies that plaintiff has any legal existence that permits it to pursue this action in the name of "John Smith Corporation."
    2. Jones denies that plaintiff has performed all conditions precedent as required under the contract, and specifically denies that plaintiff delivered a copy of the contract to Jones within 30 days of execution, although plaintiff was required to do so before the contract would be in force.

Not every allegation in the complaint must be responded to, since not every count, or every paragraph in a count, will contain an allegation directed at your defendant. Where you represent one defendant in a case that has multiple defendants, and some counts or paragraphs do not apply to your defendant, the usual practice is to point this out in your answer. This avoids the possibility of "silence" in your answer being interpreted as an admission.

Example:

Count II

The allegations in this count are not directed to this defendant.

Example:

12. The allegations in Par. 12 of plaintiff's complaint are not directed toward this defendant, so this defendant makes no answer to the allegations.

4.   Rule 12(b) defenses

As discussed previously,[48] the defendant can raise Rule 12(b) defenses in a pre-answer motion to dismiss or can include them in the answer. If the defenses are raised in the answer, each should be labeled separately to refer to the specific defense being asserted, preferably by tracking the language of Rule 12(b) and elaborating where necessary.

Example:

FIRST DEFENSE

The complaint fails to state a claim against the defendant on which relief can be granted.

SECOND DEFENSE

This court lacks jurisdiction over the subject matter of this action, since the complaint alleges that jurisdiction is based on diversity of citizenship and there is no allegation that the amount in controversy exceeds $75,000, exclusive of interest and costs.

What is a "defense"? The safe approach is to list as a defense anything that might defeat part or all of any claim or request for damages in the plaintiff's complaint. For example, in a contract case the answer might list

---

48. See §5.4.

as a defense that plaintiff is not entitled to any damages that are not consequential damages. There is no penalty for incorrectly characterizing something as a defense; there is a risk that something not raised as a defense in the answer will be deemed waived because it is a defense that should have been raised.

5. Affirmative defenses

Rule 8(c) sets forth what it characterizes as affirmative defenses:

> accord and satisfaction, arbitration and award, assumption of risk, contributory negligence, discharge in bankruptcy, duress, estoppel, failure of consideration, fraud, illegality, injury by fellow servant, laches, license, payment, release, res judicata, statute of frauds, statute of limitations, waiver, and any other matter constituting an avoidance or affirmative defense.

Keep in mind that other defenses have also been characterized as affirmative defenses.[49] An affirmative defense is generally one in which a defendant has a burden of raising in the answer, and on which a defendant has a burden of proving at trial, unless in diversity cases applicable state law holds otherwise. When answering the complaint, the usual practice is to label each affirmative defense separately, and clearly describe the affirmative defense being asserted, preferably by using the language of Rule 8(c) and elaborating where necessary.

Example:

FIRST AFFIRMATIVE DEFENSE

plaintiff's claim set out in the complaint did not occur within two years before commencement of this action, and is barred by the applicable statute of limitations.

SECOND AFFIRMATIVE DEFENSE

plaintiff's claim is barred by defendant's discharge in bankruptcy.

Affirmative defenses are usually considered substantive. In diversity cases, therefore, the trial court will apply the substantive law of the state in which it is sitting.[50] That forum state's law must be researched for the substantive law that will apply under its conflict of law rules and for the recognized defenses. However, under state law an affirmative defense may not necessarily be one that the defendant has the burden of pleading. The danger in asserting such a defense as an affirmative defense in the answer is

---

49. See Manual of Federal Practice §3.35.
50. This is the rule of Erie R.R. Co. v. Tompkins, 304 U.S. 64 (1938). See §3.2.

that the defendant may be held to have undertaken the burden of proof. On the other hand, failing to raise in the answer all affirmative defenses mentioned in Rule 8(c) runs the risk that the defenses will be waived.[51] The safer course is to raise the defense and make it clear that you do not intend to assume a burden of proof not existing under state law.

Example:

THIRD AFFIRMATIVE DEFENSE

Plaintiff was contributorily negligent in sustaining the injuries complained of in her complaint. By raising the defense of contributory negligence, however, defendant expressly does not assume any burden of proof that applicable substantive law may place on plaintiff.

6.   Practice approach

Drafting answers to complaints involves two basic considerations. First, make sure you respond to every allegation in every paragraph of every count of the complaint, since any allegation not responded to is deemed admitted. A safe practice is to deny all allegations not specifically admitted or otherwise answered. Where the allegations are admitted in part and denied in part, make sure the answer clearly states the facts being admitted and clearly denies all remaining allegations. Clear, simple language is critical here.

There may be times, however, when you may wish to admit an allegation even though you are not required to admit it. Remember that pleadings are always interrelated with discovery. If a fact alleged is denied, a plaintiff will invariably focus some of his discovery efforts on the denied fact. On the other hand, admitting a fact may have the effect of preventing further discovery of information that would prove the fact. When that information contains harmful or embarrassing facts, it may make sense to simply admit the allegation in your answer, although you could have — consistent with Rule 11 — denied it.

Second, set out all Rule 12(b) defenses and affirmative defenses that you can raise in good faith; it is best to list and label them separately. There is no penalty for raising inconsistent, hypothetical, or alternative defenses. If you are in doubt whether a defense is considered an affirmative defense, the safer course is to raise it in the answer. The real danger is that you will fail to raise a defense with the result that it will be waived. If you need additional time to study potential defenses, it is better to move for additional time to respond than to serve a hastily considered answer.

If the plaintiff has not made a jury demand with the complaint and you want a jury trial, you must make an appropriate jury demand on the answer.

---

51. See Manual of Federal Practice §3.37; Moore's Manual §11.08(4).

If the plaintiff has made a jury demand on the complaint, you need not make one, although the safer approach is to make the demand on the answer as well. If the plaintiff has made a jury demand on some counts of the complaint and you want a jury on any of the remaining counts, you must make the jury demand on those counts on the answer. The jury demand is usually made by putting the words "<u>JURY TRIAL DEMANDED</u>" below the case number and the words "<u>DEFENDANT DEMANDS TRIAL BY JURY</u>" at the end of the answer. Local rules usually have additional requirements, such as jury demand forms and fees.

Service of the answer must be made in one of the ways permitted by Rule 5 on every other party presently in the case. The most common methods are service by mail or personal service on each party's lawyer, although service by electronic means is now permitted. The answer with proof of service must be filed with the clerk of the court or, if permitted by local rules, with the judge.

The answer must have a proof of service showing that the answer was actually served on each party's lawyer. While local rules usually specify how proof of service should be made, the usual practice is to have a certificate from a lawyer or an affidavit from a nonlawyer state how and when service was actually made. The signed certificate or signed and notarized affidavit is then filed with the clerk of the court.

Example:

CERTIFICATE OF SERVICE

I, _____(attorney)_____, state that I served the above by mailing a copy to the attorneys for _____(plaintiff/defendant)_____, at _____(state address)_____, on _____(date)_____.

Dated:_____   _____
                                     Name of attorney
                                     Address
                                     Tel. No.

AFFIDAVIT OF SERVICE

I,_____(name)_____ having been first duly sworn, state that I served the above by mailing a copy to the attorneys for the other parties at their addresses of record in this case.

                                     _____
                                     Name

Signed and subscribed to before me on ___(date)___.

_____
Notary Public

My commission expires on ___(date)___.

§5.6.   Counterclaims[52]

In addition to Rule 12 motions and the answer, both of which are responses to the complaint, a defendant can also counterclaim. This is a pleading brought against a plaintiff within the time the defendant has to answer. The counterclaim is functionally identical to a complaint and is made part of the answer. As such, the analytical approach and the pleading strategy for the counterclaim are the same as for a complaint. The plaintiff must respond to the counterclaim, either with Rule 12 motions or a reply, within the usual time limits. Counterclaims are either compulsory or permissive, and substantially different rules apply to each.

1.   Compulsory counterclaims

Compulsory counterclaims, governed by Rule 13(a), are claims that a defendant is required to bring against the plaintiff. The purpose of the compulsory counterclaim rule is clear: If the court already has jurisdiction over the plaintiff, the defendant, and the subject matter of the lawsuit, it makes sense to hear and adjudicate at one time all claims related to the occurrence or transaction involved.

A claim is compulsory if four requirements are met:

1.   the claim must already exist when the defendant is required to answer the complaint;
2.   the claim must arise out of the same transaction or occurrence on which the complaint is based;
3.   the court must be able to obtain jurisdiction over any necessary additional parties; and
4.   the counterclaim must not be the subject of a pending action.[53]

No jurisdictional dollar amount is necessary. The court has ancillary jurisdiction over the counterclaim even if the plaintiff voluntarily dismisses the complaint. However, if the complaint is dismissed for jurisdictional defects, the counterclaim will be dismissed unless it has an independent jurisdictional basis.

The principal difficulty with compulsory counterclaims is in determining if the defendant's claim involves the same transaction or occurrence that gave rise to the plaintiff's claim. While this is often easy to determine in tort claims, such as an automobile accident, it is often a difficult question in the corporate and commercial area where numerous lengthy transactions are often involved. Courts have devised several approaches for determining whether the "same transaction or occurrence" is involved. These include deciding whether the legal or factual issues are the same, whether

---

52. Wright §79; James & Hazard §4.8; Friedenthal §6.7; Moore's Manual §11.09; Manual of Federal Practice §§3.45–3.50; Moore's Federal Practice §§13.02–13.41; Wright & Miller §§1401–1430.
53. See Moore's Manual §11.09(2).

the trial would involve the same proof, and whether the complaint and counterclaim are logically related. The purpose of Rule 13(a) is to promote fairness and efficiency by having related claims heard in one trial to achieve consistent results. Accordingly, the phrase in general has been broadly interpreted. The "logical relation" test, the most flexible approach, has the support of most of the treatises on the topic.[54]

Keep in mind that where there is proper jurisdiction over the plaintiff's complaint, the court will also have ancillary jurisdiction over the compulsory counterclaims. In addition, since the plaintiff selected the venue by filing the original complaint, the plaintiff cannot complain about the same venue for the defendant's counterclaim. Hence, there are no basic jurisdiction or venue problems associated with bringing compulsory counterclaims.[55]

2. Permissive counterclaims

Permissive counterclaims, governed by Rule 13(b), are claims that a defendant may bring, but is not required to bring, against a plaintiff in the pending lawsuit. A counterclaim is permissive if it does not arise out of the transaction or occurrence on which the plaintiff's complaint is based.

A permissive counterclaim, because it is a claim asserting different grounds than the complaint, must have a separate jurisdictional basis. The reasoning behind the requirement is that a defendant cannot use a counterclaim to bring another claim into federal court that could not have been filed there as an original claim. A permissive counterclaim, in other words, cannot enlarge federal jurisdiction. If the permissive counterclaim has an independent jurisdictional basis, but no proper venue exists in the district where the plaintiff's complaint was filed, it also cannot be brought.[56] Both independent jurisdiction and proper venue must exist before the defendant can bring a permissive counterclaim.

The concept behind the permissive counterclaim rule is fairness. Since a plaintiff has total freedom to bring unrelated claims against the defendant in one lawsuit, the defendant should have the same freedom, restricted only by the independent jurisdiction and venue requirements. If the counterclaims make the case too complex, the court can order separate trials on the counterclaims.

3. The United States as plaintiff

When the United States is a plaintiff, Rule 13(d) applies special rules. As a sovereign power, the United States has immunity from suit unless it has waived that immunity and has consented to be sued. No procedural rule can enlarge the types of suits that can be brought against the United States. Accordingly, no counterclaim can be asserted against the United States

---

54. See Manual of Federal Practice §3.46; Moore's Manual §11.09(3); Wright §79.
55. See Moore's Manual §11.09(5); Wright §79.
56. See Manual of Federal Practice §3.47; Moore's Manual §§11.09(9) and (10).

unless the government has expressly consented to be sued on that type of claim. The only exception is recoupment, which can be asserted as a counterclaim to reduce or defeat a claim.[57] This rule does not work the other way around; when the United States is a defendant, there is no equivalent restriction on its right to bring any proper counterclaim against the plaintiff.

4.   Statutes of limitations

Statutes of limitations are usually considered substantive law. Federal statutes of limitations apply to federal claims, and state statutes apply to state claims brought under diversity jurisdiction. A counterclaim, like a complaint, must be filed within the applicable statutory period, or it will usually be barred.[58]

5.   Waiver and amended pleadings

Failure to plead a compulsory counterclaim bars the defendant from asserting the claim later in another action. Rule 13(a) operates like a statutory bar in both federal and state courts.[59]

If a counterclaim was omitted through "oversight, inadvertence or excusable neglect, or when justice requires," the court may permit an amended answer to include the omitted counterclaim. However, the court cannot allow such a counterclaim if the statute of limitations has run because the concept of relation back applies only to amended pleadings, and a new counterclaim in an amended answer is viewed as a new pleading.[60]

Under Rule 13(e), a counterclaim that matures or accrues after the defendant serves his answer may, in the court's discretion, be raised through a supplemental answer. If the court denies it, no prejudice should occur because such a counterclaim by definition cannot be compulsory and the defendant can always assert it later as an independent claim. Of course, where the defendant requests leave to file a supplemental pleading early in the litigation process and the counterclaim is based on the same transaction or occurrence as the plaintiff's complaint, leave will usually be granted.

6.   Practice approach

A counterclaim is simply a complaint brought by a defendant against a plaintiff in a pending suit. In format, content, and signing the counterclaim

---

57. See Moore's Manual §11.09(20); Manual of Federal Practice §3.49.

58. See Moore's Manual §11.09(18); Wright §79. An exception is recoupment, which only diminishes or defeats the plaintiff's claim and is usually viewed as arising out of the same transaction.

59. See Wright §79; this bar is frequently characterized as res judicata, waiver, or estoppel.

60. See Moore's Manual §11.09(17).

should be drafted like a complaint.[61] The only difference is that the counterclaim is made part of the defendant's answer and is served on the plaintiff's attorney like any post-complaint pleading, motion, or discovery. It is usually titled "<u>ANSWER AND COUNTERCLAIM</u>," with separate headings and sections for each. If there are several plaintiffs against whom counterclaims are brought, the titles should be specific.

If the counterclaim is not included in the answer, it may be waived. To set it off from the answer, it should be clearly labeled a counterclaim; if you are unsure whether the claim is in fact a counterclaim, the safe course is to label it as such, since there are no penalties for an incorrect designation. If you are unsure whether your counterclaim is compulsory or permissive, the safe course again is to assert the counterclaim to avoid a possible waiver. Finally, since a counterclaim is analogous to a complaint, you should make a jury demand on those counterclaims that you want tried to a jury, since failure to do so may constitute a waiver. The plaintiff's demand for a jury trial will not extend to the defendant's counterclaims.

Example:

COUNTERCLAIM

Defendant Acme Manufacturing complains of plaintiff Wilbur Johnson as follows:
1. [If the counterclaim is permissive, you must allege the jurisdictional basis for bringing the claim in federal court.]
2. [Draft the pleading in the same manner as any complaint.]

7. Plaintiff's responses

The plaintiff must consider how best to respond to the answer and counterclaim. If the answer merely admits or denies the complaint's allegations, the plaintiff ordinarily need do nothing. However, if the answer contains redundant, immaterial, impertinent, or scandalous matters, plaintiff can move to strike. If the answer contains Rule 12(b) defenses or affirmative defenses, plaintiff may move to strike "any insufficient defense." In short, plaintiff can make any of the Rule 12 motions that are available when responding to a complaint. The plaintiff's responses to an answer that includes a counterclaim are discussed in the next section.

§5.7. Replies[62]

The plaintiff under Rule 7(a) must reply to a "counterclaim denominated as such." There must be a counterclaim in fact, and it must be labeled a counterclaim on the defendant's answer. Only if both requirements are

---

61. See §5.3.
62. Wright §66; James & Hazard §4.9; Friedenthal §5.21; Moore's Manual §12.03; Manual of Federal Practice §3.55; Moore's Federal Practice §7.03; Wright & Miller §§1184, 1188.

met must plaintiff reply. These requirements relieve the plaintiff of the burden of correctly guessing if the defendant's pleading is a counterclaim or an affirmative defense, since the distinction as a matter of substantive law is not always clear. However, a careful plaintiff will reply to any responsive pleading that may be a counterclaim, even to those not so labeled, since pleadings may be read to the jury during trial.

Since a counterclaim is the functional equivalent of a complaint, the plaintiff in responding is in the same position a defendant is in when responding to the original complaint. Hence, the plaintiff can respond to the counterclaim with any Rule 12 motions or may respond with a reply. The reply itself can answer the counterclaim, assert Rule 12 defenses, and raise Rule 8(c) affirmative defenses.[63]

Because a reply is simply an answer to a counterclaim, the reply should be drafted in the same manner as an answer[64] and should be titled "<u>REPLY</u>." When a plaintiff must respond to more than one counterclaim, the reply should show in the title which counterclaim is being responded to.

Example:

[Caption]

<u>REPLY</u>

Plaintiff Wilbur Johnson replies to Defendant Acme Manufacturing's counterclaim as follows:
1. Johnson admits the allegations in Par. 1 of the counterclaim.
2. . . .
3. . . .
WHEREFORE. . . .

Under Rule 12(a), plaintiff must reply to a counterclaim within 20 days after service of the answer containing the counterclaim. Service of the reply must be made in one of the ways permitted by Rule 5 on every party presently in the case. The most common methods are service by mail or personal service, although service by electronic means is now permitted. The reply with proof of service must be filed with the clerk of court or, if permitted by local rules, with the judge.

§5.8.   *Cross-claims*[65]

A cross-claim is essentially a complaint brought by one codefendant against another codefendant. Rule 13(g) permits a cross-claim if the claim arises out of the same transaction or occurrence that is the subject matter of the

---

63. There is some case law permitting a compulsory counterclaim in the reply as well. See Moore's Manual §12.04.

64. See §5.5.

65. Wright §80; James & Hazard §9.12; Friedenthal §6.8; Moore's Manual §14.04; Manual of Federal Practice §3.51; Moore's Federal Practice §§13.34–13.35; Wright & Miller §§1431–1433.

original complaint or relates to any property that is the subject matter of the original action. If a counterclaim has been brought against two or more plaintiffs, those plaintiffs may cross-claim against each other. Also, if a defendant has brought third-party complaints against additional parties, those third-party defendants may cross-claim against each other.

There are several cross-claim rules that must be understood.

1. Discretionary pleading

Cross-claims are always discretionary. A cross-claimant may, but is not required to, bring his claim in the pending action. The cross-claimant can always bring the claim as a separate action. Hence, there are no waiver dangers involved in this decision.

2. Subject matter

A cross-claim must be based on the subject matter of the original complaint, a counterclaim, or property involved in the original complaint. This restriction is designed to protect the original plaintiff from being unfairly forced into litigation that involves a matter totally different from the matters raised in the original complaint and one in which he may not have any interest. Requiring the cross-claim to arise out of the same transaction or occurrence as the complaint, or counterclaim, or the property involved in the complaint involves the same test and analysis used for compulsory counterclaims.[66]

The rule allows both matured and contingent cross-claims. Accordingly, claims that the codefendant "is or may be liable" for all or part of plaintiff's claim against him are properly raised in the cross-claim. In fact, most cross-claims raise just such issues, usually based on active-passive negligence, indemnity, or contribution.

3. When made

Rule 13(g) requires that the cross-claim be made in a party's responsive pleading, usually the answer. Accordingly, just as a counterclaim must be made when answering a complaint, a cross-claim also must be made at that time. This promotes efficient and orderly pleadings.

4. Jurisdiction, venue, and joinder

Since cross-claims must involve the same subject matter as the original complaint or of a counterclaim, jurisdiction over the cross-claim is considered ancillary and venue is considered already established by the original pleading. Hence, there are no jurisdiction or venue problems relative to

---

66. See §5.6.1.

cross-claims. If the original complaint is dismissed, however, the cross-claim will also be dismissed, unless it has an independent jurisdictional basis.

Difficulties may arise in a related area, however. Rule 13(h) applies the joinder requirements of Rules 19 and 20 to cross-claims as well as to counterclaims. While Rule 13(g) requires that a cross-claim be brought against a coparty, usually a codefendant, additional parties that are indispensable to the cross-claim must be joined. Where an indispensable party cannot be brought in because jurisdiction over the person cannot be obtained, the cross-claim must be dismissed, although the dismissal will necessarily be without prejudice. The cross-claim can always be brought as an independent action later. Further, if the addition of cross-claims makes the trial too complex, the court can order separate trials under Rule 13(i).

5.   Cross-claims against the United States

Cross-claims against the United States cannot enlarge the scope of claims on which the United States as a sovereign power has consented to be sued. The cross-claim, like counterclaims, must be based on a claim that could have been independently brought against the United States. This result appears required by the concept of sovereign immunity, although Rule 13 explicitly requires this only for counterclaims, not cross-claims.

6.   Practice approach

The cross-claim, like a counterclaim, must be part of the defendant's answer. It must be served with the answer on existing parties in the same way any pleadings, motions, or discovery are served.

The cross-claim, like a complaint,[67] counterclaim, or third-party complaint, is a pleading that asks for relief. Hence, it should be drafted like a complaint. The prayer for relief will ordinarily reflect the contingent liability position of the cross-claiming party.

Example:

CROSS-CLAIM AGAINST DEFENDANT JONES

Defendant John Smith cross-claims against Defendant James Jones as follows:

    1. . . .

    2. . . .

WHEREFORE, in the event that Defendant Smith is liable to Plaintiff, Defendant Smith demands judgment against codefendant Jones in the same amount, plus interest and costs.

---

67. See §5.3.

7. Responses to cross-claims

When a cross-claim has been served on a coparty, that party can respond with any of the responses permitted to a complaint. The party can make any of the Rule 12 motions or can answer the cross-claim and raise Rule 12(b) defenses and affirmative defenses. The party responding to the cross-claim must do so by motion or answer within the required time for answering, normally 20 days.

§5.9. Impleader (third-party practice)[68]

Impleader, also called third-party practice, is governed by Rule 14. It is a method for bringing into the action new parties who may be liable to a defendant for some or all of the judgment that the plaintiff may obtain against the defendant. The original defendant becomes a "third-party plaintiff" filing a complaint against a new party, the "third-party defendant."

Impleader must be distinguished from the filing of counterclaims and cross-claims, both of which involve new claims between original parties to the action. Impleader, by contrast, is a procedure by which new parties, the third-party defendants, are added to the action. The process helps carry out one of the principal purposes of federal pleadings rules: Whenever possible, consistent with jurisdictional limitations, a court should hear all related claims in one action because this is an efficient way to resolve multiparty disputes and obtain consistent results.

There are several rules for impleader actions that must be understood. The terms usually employed to identify the parties in impleader situations are the original plaintiff; the original defendant, who is now also a third-party plaintiff; and the third-party defendant.

1. Discretionary pleading

Under Rule 14(a), an original defendant can serve a third-party complaint on a third-party defendant without leave of court so long as it is done within 10 days of serving the original answer to plaintiff's complaint. After that time the defendant must obtain the court's permission to do so. The original plaintiff, if served with a counterclaim, may under Rule 14(b) also bring in a third-party defendant.

The court retains discretion to allow or deny impleader, and any party may move to strike a third-party claim.[69] In deciding whether to allow impleader, the court must balance the preference for complete resolution of all related issues with any possible prejudice to the plaintiff. Ordinarily the court should permit impleader; if the case then becomes too complex, it can simply order separate trials on the third-party claims. If the court

68. Wright §76; James & Hazard §10.18; Friedenthal §6.9; Moore's Manual §§14.02–14.03; Manual of Federal Practice §§3.125–3.134; Moore's Federal Practice §§14.02–14.37; Wright & Miller §§1441–1465.
69. See Wright §76.

denies impleader, the third-party claim can usually be brought as an independent action.

2.   Subject matter

An original defendant, as a third-party plaintiff, may include in his third-party complaint any claim that asserts that the third-party defendant "is or may be liable to the third-party plaintiff for all or part of the plaintiff's claim against the third-party plaintiff." However, the original defendant's right to bring third-party claims is broader than would first appear from Rule 14. There are four types of claims that can be brought under the impleader rule.

First, and most commonly, an original defendant can bring an impleader action based on indemnity, contribution, active-passive negligence, subrogation, or any other theory that passes part or all of the defendant's liability to one or more new parties. Second, the original defendant can bring a contingent claim against the third-party defendant. The "is or may be liable" language in the Rule permits accelerated contingent liability claims. Third, the original defendant may be able to bring an independent claim against a third-party defendant, since under Rule 18(a) any party can join claims against another. So long as the defendant has one claim against a third-party defendant that is proper under Rule 14(a), any other independent claims proper under the joinder rules can be added. Finally, the original defendant can bring a claim against the third-party defendant that the original plaintiff could not bring directly against the third-party defendant.

3.   Jurisdiction and venue

Impleader necessarily involves two related questions: whether the new action is proper under impleader rules and whether there is proper jurisdiction and venue over the new action. Although an impleader action may be proper under Rule 14, this does not necessarily mean that jurisdiction and venue properly exist.

Where impleader is based on an indemnity type of claim, for instance, ancillary jurisdiction exists and there will be no jurisdiction or venue problems. This situation is much like that which exists with the filing of compulsory counterclaims. Where impleader is based on a claim that is independent of the original plaintiff's claim against the original defendant, however, there must be an independent basis for jurisdiction.[70] This situation is much like that involving permissive counterclaims.

4.   Statutes of limitations

As with any complaint, a third-party complaint is subject to all applicable statutes of limitations. In addition, if the original plaintiff files an amended

---

70. The leading case is Owens Equip. Co. v. Kroger, 437 U.S. 365 (1978). See Wright §76.

complaint directly against a third-party defendant, it is considered a new cause of action to which the relevant statute applies. The concept of relation back, applicable to amended pleadings, does not apply here.[71]

5.   Practice approach

A third-party complaint under Rule 14 is the fourth type of complaint permitted by the federal rules, in addition to complaints, counterclaims, and cross-claims. As such, it should have the three basic parts of any complaint: a jurisdictional allegation, a statement of claims, and a prayer for relief. In short, the approach to drafting a third-party complaint is essentially identical to that of the original complaint, although it should recite the circumstances of the already pending original complaint. The document itself is entitled "<u>THIRD-PARTY COMPLAINT</u>." The caption should clearly show the status of the various parties.

Since a third-party complaint brings new parties into the suit, each new third-party defendant must be served with the third-party complaint and summons, as required by Rule 4.

Where leave of court is required, the defendant must move for permission to bring the third-party complaint against the new party. The usual procedure is to attach the proposed pleading to the motion.

Example:

[Caption]

<u>DEFENDANT JOHNSON'S MOTION TO BRING IN THIRD-PARTY DEFENDANT</u>

Defendant Thomas Johnson requests permission to proceed as a third-party plaintiff against Frank Jones. A copy of the proposed third-party complaint is attached to this motion as Exhibit A. In support of his motion Defendant Johnson states:

　　1. . . .

　　2. . . .

WHEREFORE, Defendant Johnson requests that an order be entered permitting him to proceed as third-party plaintiff against Frank Jones, file the third-party complaint (Exhibit A), and to have that complaint and summons served upon Frank Jones as third-party defendant.

　　　　　　　　　　　　　　　　　　_____
　　　　　　　　　　　　　　　　　　Attorney for
　　　　　　　　　　　　　　　　　　Defendant Johnson

---

71. See §5.13.

Example:

UNITED STATES DISTRICT COURT
FOR THE DISTRICT OF VERMONT

Rebecca Smith, Plaintiff	

v.
Thomas Johnson,
    Defendant and Third-
    Party Plaintiff
	No. 05 C 100
	
	Civil Action

v. Frank Jones, Third-Party Defendant	

<u>THIRD-PARTY COMPLAINT</u>

Defendant Johnson complains of Third-Party Defendant Frank Jones as follows:

1. Plaintiff Smith has previously filed a complaint against defendant Johnson. A copy of that complaint is attached as Exhibit A.

2. . . .

3. . . .

WHEREFORE, Defendant Johnson demands judgment against Third-Party Defendant Jones for all sums that Plaintiff may receive in judgment against Defendant Johnson.

6.   Third-party defendant responses

A third-party defendant who has been served with a third-party complaint can choose any of the responses of any party served with a complaint. He may make Rule 12 motions, or he may answer the third-party complaint. He can also assert any defenses the original defendant may have against the original plaintiff. This protects the third-party defendant who might otherwise be prejudiced by the original defendant's failure to assert all available defenses against the original plaintiff.

Further, a third-party defendant can counterclaim against the original plaintiff directly, so long as that counterclaim involves the same transaction or occurrence that is the basis for plaintiff's claim against the original defendant. The court will have ancillary jurisdiction over such a counterclaim. He can also assert cross-claims against other third-party defendants under Rule 13.

Finally, a third-party defendant can also bring a third-party complaint against a new party who in turn may be liable to him for all or part of the original third-party complaint filed by the original defendant.

The approach for drafting each of these responses is essentially identical to the approach for responses discussed earlier in this chapter. Make sure that the particular response chosen bears a title that makes clear what type of response it is and identifies the pleading to which it is responding. Where ancillary jurisdiction does not attach to a third-party claim, an independent jurisdictional basis must exist, and there must be personal jurisdiction over the new parties.

While the pleading possibilities under Rule 14 appear complex, its underlying philosophy is simple: The federal rules broadly permit adding parties and claims so that all parties and all aspects of a dispute can be disposed of in one consolidated proceeding that produces consistent results. If the pleadings make the case too complex, the court can always order separate trials. This in fact is frequently done. The court will try the claims between the original plaintiff and original defendant first. The third-party claims can then be tried later if necessary. Ordering separate trials for the original claims and the subsequent third-party claims will also protect the original plaintiff from any unfairness that might be caused by the addition of the third-party claims.

7. Original plaintiff responses

Under Rule 14(a), after a third-party complaint has been filed, the original plaintiff can file an amended complaint directly against a third-party defendant. This in effect allows the plaintiff to do what could have, and perhaps should have, been done in the first place. However, there must be an independent jurisdictional basis for the amended complaint. If a third-party defendant has counterclaimed directly against the original plaintiff, that plaintiff must reply to the counterclaim within the usual time limits.

§5.10. Interpleader[72]

Interpleader is the procedure that allows a party, called a "stakeholder," who is or may be subjected to double liability because two or more claimants are making competing claims on a fund or property, to ask a court to determine proper ownership of or interest in the disputed fund or property. The standard situation involves multiple claims on the proceeds of an insurance policy. If the insurance company does not know who should get the proceeds, it may pay the wrong person and later be forced to pay a second time. In an interpleader action the stakeholder is the plaintiff, and the competing claimants become the defendants.

---

72. Wright §74; James & Hazard §10.19; Friedenthal §§16.10–16.13; Moore's Manual §14.06; Manual of Federal Practice §§1.98, 3.135; Moore's Federal Practice §§22.02–22.17; Wright & Miller §§1701–1721.

There are two types of federal interpleader: Rule 22 interpleader, and so-called statutory interpleader under 28 U.S.C. §1335. Each must be considered separately, since substantial differences exist.

1.   Rule 22 interpleader

Rule 22 interpleader is in some respects broad, in others restrictive. It is broad because it allows interpleading claims that "do not have a common origin, or are not identical but are adverse to and independent of one another." It also allows the defense that the plaintiff-stakeholder is "not liable in whole or in part to any or all of the claimants." Accordingly, the plaintiff need not deposit the fund in issue with the clerk of the court or post an equivalent bond. The rule allows a defendant in a pending suit to plead interpleader in a counterclaim or cross-claim.

On the other hand, Rule 22 interpleader is restrictive since the usual jurisdiction and venue rules apply. This means that where federal jurisdiction is based on diversity of citizenship under 28 U.S.C. §1332, there must be complete diversity between a plaintiff-stakeholder and each defendant-claimant, a situation that in interpleader cases will rarely exist. The amount in controversy must also exceed $75,000, a determination based on the amount of the fund or value of the property involved. Proper venue is determined under the general venue statute, 28 U.S.C. §1391.

2.   28 U.S.C. §1335 interpleader

Statutory interpleader under §1335, while conceptually identical to Rule 22 interpleader, has significant procedural advantages. First, §1335 relaxes the diversity requirement by requiring that only two of the defendant-claimants have diverse citizenship. Plaintiff's citizenship is not considered. This relaxed diversity requirement allows most interpleader actions to be filed in federal court. Venue under §1397 is proper in any district where one or more of the defendant-claimants resides. Second, the amount in controversy need only exceed $500. Third, under §2361 the court may issue an injunction against any defendant-claimant pursuing another action involving the same fund or property in state or federal courts. Finally, statutory interpleader under §2361 permits nationwide service of process.

Section 1335 requires that the claims be "adverse to and independent of one another," but the claims need not have a common origin or be identical in type. However, the plaintiff must deposit the fund or property with the clerk of the court or post a bond in the amount of the fund or property.

Further, while §1335 itself is silent on whether to allow a statutory interpleader to be asserted in a counterclaim or cross-claim, most courts permit it.[73]

---

73. See Wright §74.

3.   Practice approach

An interpleader complaint based on either Rule 22 or §1335 should have all the components of an ordinary complaint: a jurisdictional statement, a statement of claims, and a prayer for relief. Under §1335, the jurisdictional statement should state whether the fund has been deposited with the court or a bond has been posted in the appropriate amount payable to the clerk. The prayer for relief should ask for all relief that is appropriate, including a determination of the amount of liability, if any; a determination of which claimants are entitled to the fund or property and in what amounts; an injunction against any claimants pursuing other actions in state or federal courts based on this claim; and fees and costs, including attorney's fees where permitted.[74]

Example:

Whole Life Insurance Co., a corporation, Plaintiff	No. _____
v.	
Thomas Smith and James Smith, Defendants	Civil Action

COMPLAINT FOR INTERPLEADER

Plaintiff Whole Life Insurance Co. complains of defendants Thomas Smith and James Smith as follows:

Jurisdictional Allegation

1. Jurisdiction in this action is based on 28 U.S.C. §1335. Defendant Thomas Smith is a citizen of the State of Maine. Defendant James Smith is a citizen of the State of Vermont. The amount in controversy exceeds the sum of $500, exclusive of interest and costs.

or

---

74. Attorney's fees are permitted where the plaintiff is a passive litigant not disputing that it owes a set amount to someone. See Moore's Manual §14.06(2).

1. Jurisdiction is based on Rule 22 of the Federal Rules of Civil Procedure and 28 U.S.C. §1332. Plaintiff is a citizen of the State of New York. Defendant Thomas Smith is a citizen of the State of Maine. Defendant James Smith is a citizen of the State of Vermont. The amount in controversy exceeds the sum of $75,000, exclusive of interest and costs.

2. On June 1, 2005, plaintiff issued a life insurance policy on the life of Franklin Smith. A copy of that policy is attached as Exhibit A.

3. . . .

4. . . .

5. By reason of the defendants' conflicting claims, plaintiff cannot determine with certainty which defendant [, if either,] is entitled to any proceeds of the policy [or, if either is entitled, in what amount].

6. Plaintiff has deposited the face amount of the policy, $80,000, with the clerk of the court. [Required only under §1335 interpleader.]

WHEREFORE, plaintiff requests that the court enter a judgment finding that:

(1) Neither defendant is entitled to recover any money from the policy [permitted only under Rule 22 interpleader];

(2) Each defendant is permanently enjoined from pursuing any other actions or claims on this policy [permitted only under §1335 interpleader];

(3) If this court finds the policy in force at the time of Franklin Smith's death, that the defendants be required to interplead and settle their claims on the policy between themselves, and that plaintiff be discharged from any liability except to any person in such amount as the court adjudges plaintiff is liable;

(4) Plaintiff is entitled to costs [and reasonable attorney's fees if a passive litigant].

Since an interpleader brings new parties into the lawsuit, each defendant must be served with the complaint and summons, as required by Rule 4.

§5.11.   *Intervention*[75]

Intervention, governed by Rule 24, is the procedure by which a nonparty having an interest in a pending action can protect its rights by becoming an additional party and presenting a claim or defense. The Rule closely parallels the joinder rules by allowing two types of intervention, intervention of right and permissive intervention.

---

75. Wright §75; James & Hazard §10.17; Friedenthal §6.10; Moore's Manual §14.05; Manual of Federal Practice §§3.148–3.155; Moore's Federal Practice §§24.02–24.20; Wright & Miller §§1901–1913.

1. Intervention of right

Rule 24(a) permits two bases for intervention of right. The seldom-used basis is if "a statute of the United States confers an unconditional right to intervene."[76] The frequently used basis is Rule 24(a)(2), which sets forth three requirements for intervention of right.

First, the intervenor must claim "an interest relating to the property or transaction which is the subject of the action" pending. What is a sufficient "interest" remains unsettled, since the case law is hardly uniform. Various courts have held that the intervenor's interest must be "direct," "substantial," or "significantly protectable."[77] An analysis of the intervenor's claimed interest, of the relief sought, and of the nature of the claims and defenses asserted in the pending action is required.

Second, the intervenor must be "so situated that the disposition of the action may as a practical matter impair or impede his ability to protect that interest." The critical term "as a practical matter" was included to make clear that this determination should not be limited to legal bars such as res judicata, but should include any substantial functional difficulties that might adversely affect the intervenor's interests.

Third, the intervenor must not be "adequately represented by existing parties." This requires a comparison of the interests of the existing parties with the claimed interests of the intervenor to determine how closely they are related. If the intervenor's interests are essentially identical to those of an existing party, so that the existing party will necessarily assert the same positions as the intervenor would, intervention should be denied.

2. Permissive intervention

Rule 24(b) permits two bases for permissive intervention. The seldom-used basis is if "a statute of the United States confers a conditional right to intervene." The usual situation for such a basis is where the federal or a state government can intervene in a case involving the constitutionality or interpretation of a statute.[78]

The frequently used basis for permissive intervention is Rule 24(b)(2), which permits intervention "when the applicant's claim or defense and the main action have a question of law or fact in common." This involves an analysis similar to that made for the permissive joinder of parties under Rule 20(a). This request to intervene is addressed to the court's discretion, and the court may deny it where the intervenor's request would "delay or prejudice" the rights of the pending parties or inject unimportant issues into the case. If a court denies intervention, there are no adverse legal consequences since res judicata will not apply to the unsuccessful intervenor. The common situation where

---

76. A list of such statutes is found at Moore's Federal Practice §24.06.
77. See Wright & Miller §1908.
78. See Moore's Federal Practice §24.10.

intervention is permitted is where the intervenor has a claim against the defendant that is factually and legally similar to the plaintiff's pending claim against the defendant.

3. Timing

A prospective intervenor must move to intervene in a timely fashion, regardless of whether the intervention sought is of right or is permissive. Both Rule 24(a) and (b) require a "timely application," but where intervention of right is requested, it will ordinarily be permitted, regardless of when the application is made, since the intervenor's right might otherwise be adversely affected. Despite this, it is possible to seek intervention of right so late in the pending action that it is considered untimely and is therefore denied.

When permissive intervention is sought, the court must consider "whether the intervention will unduly delay or prejudice the adjudication of the rights of the original parties." This requires analyzing the relief the intervenor wants, whether the intervenor will be an active or passive party, and particularly the stage that the pending action is in. Intervention obviously will be more favorably viewed when sought early in the pleading stage than if substantial discovery has already been taken.

4. Jurisdiction

The intervenor's addition to the pending action must meet jurisdiction and venue requirements. Where intervention of right is requested, the intervenor's claim is necessarily closely related to the original action and ancillary jurisdiction will attach. On the other hand, if intervention is not based on Rule 24(b)(1), independent jurisdictional grounds must exist.[79]

Venue should not be an issue, since it is viewed as a personal right and the intervenor is generally held to accept the venue that has already been established.

5. Practice approach

Rule 24(c) requires that the intervenor make a timely motion to intervene in the district in which the original action is pending. It must attach an appropriate pleading to the motion. The motion, which must be served on all existing parties, should state the reason why intervention is appropriate under the circumstances.

---

79. See Wright §75.

Example:

Frank Johnson,
          Plaintiff

v.   No. 05 C 100

Wilma Smith,   Civil Action
          Defendant,

Jacob Franklin,
          Intervenor

MOTION TO INTERVENE AS A DEFENDANT

Jacob Franklin moves for leave to intervene as a defendant in this action. A copy of his proposed answer is attached as Exhibit A. In support of his motion Franklin states:
1. Intervention is appropriate because . . .
2. . . . .

WHEREFORE, Jacob Franklin requests that he be permitted to intervene as a defendant, file his answer to the complaint, and participate in this action as a party defendant.

ANSWER OF DEFENDANT-INTERVENOR FRANKLIN

Defendant Franklin answers the complaint as follows:
1. . . .
2. . . .

If the motion to intervene is granted, the intervenor becomes a party and has the rights of any party. The intervenor usually cannot contest past orders, but can counterclaim and cross-claim, present any appropriate motions, and fully participate in discovery. Keep in mind, however, that the court has power to limit intervention to certain matters if permissive intervention has been granted.

The denial of a motion to intervene raises the difficult issue of whether the ruling is final and appealable.[80] While there is a split in authority on this question, it appears that a motion for intervention of right is appealable if denied, but the denial of a motion to intervene permissively is appealable only where an abuse of discretion is shown. If the motion to intervene is granted, it is not an appealable order.

---

80. See Moore's Manual §14.05(6); Moore's Federal Practice §24.15.

§5.12.   Class actions[81]

The topic of class actions by itself can fill volumes, and literature on the subject in treatises, cases, and journals is extensive. It is obviously a complicated area, one in which the inexperienced litigator should tread cautiously if at all. Hence, this section is limited to a brief overview of the class-action requirements and the initial considerations and steps in such suits. The principal concern of the inexperienced litigator should be determining whether a case can be pursued as a class action. (The initial fight is usually over class certification and the scope of discovery that will be permitted on the certification question.) Assistance from someone with experience in class action litigation should be sought.

1.   General class requirements

Class actions are governed by Rule 23, which was significantly amended in 2003. Rule 23(a) sets out four class requirements that must be met before the action can proceed as a class action. These are frequently referred to as the requirements of numerosity, commonality, typicality, and adequate representation. These apply regardless of whether the class involves the plaintiff or the defendant. Courts usually analyze the Rule 23 requirements rigorously before certifying a class, and the party seeking certification has the burden of showing that certification is proper.

First, the class must be so "numerous that joinder of all members is impracticable." The Rule itself does not define what a class is or how its members should be determined. Impracticability depends on the type of claims asserted and the persons asserting those claims. Because of this, the numbers necessary for a class action are quite flexible, and the ultimate decision whether a class action is the preferred method of dealing with a claim is left to the discretion of the trial court. While it is usually clear that hundreds of potential plaintiffs or defendants make the action suitable for class-action treatment, and that fewer than 30 ordinarily is not enough, the case law on class numbers in the middle range — perhaps 30 to 50 members — shows no particular pattern. Some of such classes have been held to be of an appropriate number, others not.[82] The outcome is as dependent on other considerations as it is on the number of class members.

Second, there must be "questions of law or fact common to the class." This requires the same type of analysis required for joinder and intervention requests.[83]

Third, the "claims or defenses of the representative parties" must be "typical of the claims or defenses of the class." Also, the representatives must be actual members of the class. In addition, the claims or defenses of

---

81. Wright §72; James & Hazard §§10.20–10.23; Friedenthal §§16.1–16.19; Manual of Federal Practice §§3.138–3.147; Moore's Manual §14.07; Moore's Federal Practice §§23.01–23.97; Wright & Miller §§1751–1803.
82. See Moore's Manual §14.07(1); Wright & Miller §1762.
83. See §3.4.

the class must be reviewed, and there must be enough representative parties to ensure that each claim or defense is represented fairly. This obviously requires that the lawyers closely analyze the facts before selecting actual parties and initiating suit.

Finally, the representative parties must "fairly and adequately protect the interests of the class." This requirement is directed to both the representative parties and their lawyers. The interests of the representatives must be scrutinized to determine if conflicting interests exist. If they do, a possible solution is to certify separate classes. In addition, the lawyers must have sufficient ability and experience to represent the class competently.

2. General facts requirements

Rule 23(b) sets out three fact situations in which a class action is appropriate.

First, it is appropriate where separate actions would "create a risk of inconsistent or varying adjudications" that would "establish incompatible standards of conduct" for the party opposing the class, or where separate adjudications would "as a practical matter be dispositive of the interests of the others" in the class who are not parties to that adjudication. The former is commonly relied upon in actions against governmental entities to declare actions invalid, such as expenditures and bond issues. The latter is frequently relied upon in shareholder actions against corporations, such as to compel declaration of a dividend.

Second, a class action is appropriate where the party opposing the class has "acted or refused to act on grounds generally applicable to the class." Many of the cases brought on this basis are civil rights actions in which a party is asking for injunctive or other equitable relief under Title VII of the 1964 Act, and some employment discrimination cases.

Third, a class action is appropriate where "questions of law or fact common to the members of the class predominate over any questions affecting only individual members" and a class action is the superior method for handling the entire controversy. This has become the most common basis for class actions, and one that is frequently relied upon in antitrust and securities fraud cases. However, a class action under this Rule — Rule 23(b)(3) — is rarely permitted in mass tort cases because the plaintiffs' claims are usually seen as too diverse to justify class action treatment.[84]

3. Jurisdiction

In 2005, Congress overhauled diversity jurisdiction for class actions in the Class Action Fairness Act (CAFA), which amended 28 U.S.C. §1332 and

---

84. See Amchem Products v. Windsor, 521 U.S. 591 (1997), holding that a class for settlement purposes only was not appropriate in an asbestos exposure case brought under Rule 23(b)(3); Ortiz v. Fiberboard, 527 U.S. 815 (1999), holding that a class in a limited fund situation in an asbestos exposure case was not an appropriate class under Rule 23(b)(1).

added §1453. The current statutory requirements for class actions are complex, and courts have just begun to resolve some of their ambiguities. The basics are as follows. CAFA adopted a "minimum diversity" standard for federal jurisdiction. Generally, federal jurisdiction exists if at least one class member is diverse from at least one defendant, and defendants can remove class actions that satisfy the minimum diversity requirements. There are several exceptions, however, to this minimal diversity requirement. For example, if two-thirds or more of the class members come from the same state as a primary defendant, the district court must decline jurisdiction. Also, a district court may, in its discretion, decline jurisdiction if more than one-third but fewer than two-thirds of the class members come from the same state as a primary defendant. Other exceptions exist, and an inexperienced litigator should carefully consult the diversity jurisdiction statute to determine which diversity of citizenship requirement applies in a particular case.[85] These rules replaced the former requirement that each named class representative be diverse from each defendant.

Congress also replaced the usual amount in controversy requirement for class actions. Claims of individual class members are aggregated, and the class as a whole must allege a sum that exceeds $5,000,000. This rule replaced the former requirement that each named class representative meet the usual $75,000 threshold.

Congress left federal question jurisdiction untouched, so the same rules apply to these class actions as to any other case.

4. Procedure

Rule 23(c) governs the initial procedures in a class action. The first two steps are critical. First, the court must determine at "an early practicable time" if the action can be brought as a class action. This necessarily requires an evaluation of the Rule 23(a) and (b) requirements, a determination of what issues can be tried as a class action, and a determination of what the class or classes will be. Rule 23(f) provides that a court of appeals may in its discretion permit an appeal from a district court order granting or denying class certification.

Second, in an action under Rule 23(b)(3), the most frequently used section, the court must direct the "best notice practicable under the circumstances," which includes "individual notice to all members who can be identified through reasonable effort." Under Rule 23(c)(3), class notices must be written "in plain, easily understood language." Notice can be an expensive undertaking, sometimes prohibitively so. For class members whose identity can be ascertained with reasonable effort, notice by first class mail is usually required; for unknown class members, some form of notice by publication is required. Since each side must bear its costs of litigation, the expense of actually notifying the

---

85. See generally Vance, A Primer on the Class Action Fairness Act of 2005, 80 Tul. L. Rev. 1617 (2006).

individual class members can effectively prevent a claim from being pursued as a class action.[86]

Rule 23(g) governs the selection and appointment of class counsel. It authorizes the appointment of interim class counsel before certification and sets forth the standards the court must consider in selecting class counsel. Rule 23(h) authorizes the court to address the issue of fees in an action certified as a class action when class counsel is first appointed.

§5.13. *Amendments of pleadings and supplemental pleadings*[87]

The principal concepts behind the federal rules' pleading requirements are that pleadings should accurately notify the parties of the claims involved and that enough flexibility should be permitted so that substantial justice is achieved in every case. Rule 15, the amendments rule, reflects these concerns. Amended pleadings should be freely allowed when fairness requires it; that is, whenever an amendment would create a more accurate or complete pleading and the opposing parties will not be substantially prejudiced. The Rule applies to all pleadings — complaints, answers, and replies.

1. Amendments as of right

Any party has a right to amend a pleading once, at any time before a responsive pleading is made. If no responsive pleading is permitted, an amendment by right can be made within 20 days after service, unless the case is already on the trial calendar. A motion that attacks a pleading is not considered a responsive pleading. If an amendment is by right, it is simply served on the other parties and no court action is needed.

When the amended pleading seeks to add new parties, Rule 15(a), permitting timely amendments of right, seems to conflict with Rule 21, which permits additions of parties only by leave of court. Courts have ruled both ways on this issue, some holding that leave is always required, others not.[88]

There is also some conflict between Rule 15(c) and state statutes of limitations, which apply in diversity cases. In circumstances where the federal rule would permit an amended complaint but the complaint would be barred by the applicable state statute, courts have held that Rule 15 controls and permits the amendment.[89]

---

86. The Supreme Court has held that in class action suits brought under Rule 23(c)(2) the party seeking the class action must bear the costs of actual notice to the reasonably identifiable class members. Eisen v. Carlisle & Jacquelin, et al., 417 U.S. 156 (1974).

87. Wright §§66, 68–69; James & Hazard §§4.11–4.17; Friedenthal §§5.26–5.28; Moore's Manual §§9.09–9.11; Manual of Federal Practice §§3.58–3.65; Moore's Federal Practice §§15.02–15.16; Wright & Miller §§1471–1510.

88. See Moore's Manual §909(2).

89. See Wright §59.

2. Amendments by leave of court

Rule 15(a) permits amendments by leave of court. The Rule expressly provides that "leave shall be freely given when justice so requires." The amended pleading can change the jurisdictional allegations, factual claims, legal theories of recovery, events and transactions involved, and even parties to the action.[90] Yet the courts have been indulgent in permitting amendments, and grounds such as oversight, error, or delay by themselves are generally held insufficient to deny leave to amend.[91]

Courts may exercise their discretion and deny leave to amend when, in addition to delay or neglect, there is some actual prejudice to the opposing party. In other situations, the court may grant leave to amend while restricting it to particular matters so that prejudice to an opposing party is minimized. Obviously, the amending party should seek leave to amend as early in the litigation process as possible to minimize prejudice. A motion during the pleading stage will in all likelihood be granted. One made after discovery is underway, however, may well encounter difficulties.[92]

When a motion for leave to amend is made after a motion to dismiss for failure to state a claim on which relief can be granted, some courts will not grant leave if it appears certain that plaintiff cannot, under the existing facts, state a proper claim.[93] Courts often look to see if the proposed amended complaint properly states a claim before granting leave to amend. If it does not, leave can properly be denied.

3. Statutes of limitations and "relation back"

An important concern in amending pleadings is whether the statute of limitations applies to amended pleadings. This question arises only if the amended pleading is filed after the applicable statute of limitations has run on a particular claim. Whether the statute will bar the amended pleading depends on whether the concept of "relation back," set out in Rule 15(c), will apply. The two principal types of amendments—changing facts and legal theories, and changing parties—must be considered separately.

a. Changing facts and theories

Rule 15(c) states that if the amended pleading's claims or defenses "arose out of" the same "conduct, transaction or occurrence set forth or attempted to be set forth" in the original pleading, the amendment will relate back to the date the original pleading was filed so that the statute of

---

90. 28 U.S.C. §1653 provides that "defective allegations of jurisdiction may be amended, upon terms, in the trial or appellate courts."

91. See Moore's Manual §9.09(3).

92. See Nelson v. Adams, 529 U.S. 460 (2000), holding that a postjudgment amendment of pleadings, while proper under Rule 15, violated due process.

93. See Manual of Federal Practice §3.60.

limitations will not operate as a bar. When the amended pleading alleges an entirely new claim, the concept of relation back will not apply. Whether the claims or defenses in the amended pleading "arose out of the same conduct, transaction or occurrence set forth or attempted to be set forth" in the original pleading is an imprecise standard, but courts have been reasonably lenient in permitting amendments, particularly when only a change in legal theory is involved.[94]

b. Changing parties

The more difficult situation concerns changing parties with an amended pleading. Rule 15(c) permits relation back to avoid a limitations bar where the new party added by amendment either actually knew of the suit and would not be prejudiced, or knew or should have known that, but for a mistake in identifying the proper party, he would have been sued.

The first situation involves actual knowledge of the action by the new party. The second involves a misnomer of a proper party, where the proper party knew or should be held to know that it was the target party all along. This is a common problem when commercial parties or the United States government is involved, where determining the technically proper defendants is difficult and sometimes impossible prior to discovery. Cases that have dealt with the question of when a party "should have known" it was the intended party are hardly uniform and should be thoroughly researched.[95]

4. Supplemental pleadings

Under Rule 15(d), a party may move to file a supplemental pleading alleging transactions, occurrences, and events that have occurred since the time the original pleading was served. Permitting the motion is discretionary with the court, which can impose any reasonable terms to protect the other parties.

Since a supplemental pleading by definition raises new matters that have arisen since the original pleading was filed, statute of limitations and relation back issues will rarely be involved.

5. Practice approach

A motion for leave to amend, like any other motion, must meet the Rule 7(b) requirements. The motion must state with particularity the grounds

---

94. See Wright §66.
95. See Manual of Federal Practice §3.61; Schiavone v. Fortune, Inc., 477 U.S. 21 (1986), is a leading case on the "identity of interest" exception. However, Rule 15(c) was amended in 1991 to change the result of the holding in *Schiavone*. Rule 15(c)(3) provides that relation back is proper when the amendment of a pleading adds a new party if that added party received notice of the institution of the action within the time provided for service under Rule 4, and knew or should have known that, "but for a mistake concerning the identity of the proper party, the action would have been brought against the party."

for the motion and the relief sought. Timely notice must be sent to other parties. The better practice is to attach the amended pleading as an exhibit to the motion. In addition, it is both more convenient and a safer practice to have a complete amended pleading, rather than incorporate by reference parts of the original pleading. It is simply easier to deal with a complete pleading, and responses will likely be more accurate.

Example:

[Caption]

MOTION FOR LEAVE TO FILE AMENDED COMPLAINT

Plaintiff moves for an order permitting plaintiff to file an amended complaint. A copy of the amended complaint is attached to this motion as Exhibit A. In support of this motion plaintiff states:

1. Plaintiff's original complaint was against one defendant, William Smith, and alleged one theory of liability based on negligence.

2. New information, based on both informal fact investigation and discovery, has revealed that another party, Acme Motors, may be liable to plaintiff and that a valid claim against Acme may exist, based on products liability and implied warranty.

WHEREFORE, plaintiff requests that an order be entered permitting plaintiff to file the amended complaint attached as Exhibit A, which adds Acme Motors as a defendant and alleges two additional counts, based on products liability and implied warranty, against Acme Motors.

_____
Attorney for Plaintiff

If the motion is allowed, or the amended pleading is of right, a party that is required to respond to the amended pleading must do so either within the time remaining to respond to the original pleading or within 10 days of service of the amended pleading, whichever is greater.

Many motions to permit an amended pleading are made after an opposing party has been granted a motion to dismiss under Rule 12. Here the dismissed party should move for leave to file an amended pleading within 10 days of dismissal.[96] The better and more common practice, however, is to move for leave to file an amended pleading and have the motion granted at the hearing on the motion to dismiss, if that motion is granted. In this way the order granting the motion to dismiss will also contain an order permitting the amended pleading.

96. See Moore's Manual §9.09(5).

VI

DISCOVERY

§6.1. Introduction

Discovery is the principal fact-gathering method in the formal litigation process. In today's litigation environment, the discovery stage is where most of the battles are fought, most of the litigation costs are incurred, and where the war is often won or lost. Consequently, understanding discovery so that you can effectively and efficiently use the permissible discovery methods as tactical and strategic tools is critical for every litigator.

Federal discovery has several principal characteristics. First, it is largely a self-executing process. For the most part, lawyers conduct discovery without prior judicial approval, although in recent years courts are increasingly supervising and even dictating the order and timing of discovery. Second, the discovery rules are flexible and usually permit any order, and sometimes repeated use, of the various discovery methods subject only to the court's approved discovery plan and court protection against abuse. Third, orders regulating discovery are usually not final appealable orders. Since discovery issues will often be moot by the time a final judgment is entered in the case, appeals are relatively infrequent. This means that issues concerning discovery are principally resolved at the trial court level.

Recent years have seen numerous changes to the discovery rules, principally brought about by increasing pressure for discovery reform. Many judges, litigators, legislators, and the public see civil litigation as unnecessarily complicated, slow, and expensive; and Rules 26 through 37, the discovery rules, are usually identified as the worst offenders. Hence, recent years have seen repeated efforts to simplify discovery, make the discovery rules reflect changes in technology, and impose effective sanctions for discovery abuse.

Keep in mind that ethics rules apply to discovery. Model Rule 3.4(d) commands that a "lawyer shall not . . . make a frivolous discovery request or fail to make a reasonably diligent effort to comply with a legally proper discovery request by an opposing party."

§6.2.   Scope of discovery[1]

Rule 26 is the basic discovery rule that controls the scope of discovery. This section discusses what "relevance" means in the discovery context and reviews specialized areas expressly regulated by Rule 26: insurance, statements, experts, privileges, and work product.

1.   Relevance

Relevance for discovery purposes is broad, although it was narrowed by the 2000 amendments to Rule 26. Under Rule 26(b)(1), parties may discover "any matter, not privileged, that is relevant to the claim or defense of any party, including the existence, description, nature, custody, condition, and location of any books, documents, or other tangible things and the identity and location of persons having knowledge of any discoverable matter." In addition, "for good cause, the court may order discovery of any matter relevant to the subject matter involved in the action." The term "relevance" has a special meaning for discovery purposes. "Relevant information need not be admissible at the trial if the discovery appears reasonably calculated to lead to the discovery of admissible evidence."[2]

Rule 26 creates two levels of discoverable material: discovery by right, as to matters relevant to claims and defenses, and discretionary broader discovery, as to matters relevant to the subject matter of the litigation.

The effect of the 2000 amendments are twofold: First, more detailed allegations in the claims and defenses in the pleadings may be useful to trigger discovery of relevant facts. Second, the parties probably can't use discovery to develop new claims and defenses not already raised in the pleadings.

Relevant matter may be obtained from other parties and, sometimes, non-parties, through six discovery methods:

- Required disclosures — Rule 26(a)
- Interrogatories — Rule 33

---

1. Wright §81; James & Hazard §5.8; Friedenthal §7.2; Moore's Manual §15.02; Manual of Federal Practice §5.1 et seq.; Moore's Federal Practice §26.55; Wright & Miller §2007.

2. Wright §81; Moore's Manual §15.02; Manual of Federal Practice §5.24; Moore's Federal Practice §26.56(1); Wright & Miller §2008.

- Requests to produce documents, electronically stored information, and things — Rule 34
- Depositions — Rules 27-32
- Physical and mental examinations — Rule 35
- Requests for admissions — Rule 36

Each of these discovery methods will be discussed in detail in this chapter.

2. Insurance agreements[3]

Rule 26(a)(1)(D) makes discoverable any insurance agreement held by any person which "may be liable to satisfy part or all of a judgment," or "indemnify or reimburse for payments made to satisfy the judgment." This information is critical for assessing the "value" of the case and the defendant's ability to pay a judgment.

3. Statements[4]

A "statement" for discovery purposes is defined by Rule 26(b)(3) to include "(A) a written statement signed or otherwise adopted or approved by the person making it, or (B) a stenographic, mechanical, electrical, or other recording, or a transcription thereof, which is a substantially verbatim recital of an oral statement by the person making it and contemporaneously recorded." This means that if a witness has been interviewed, but nothing tangible was produced, such as a written statement, recording, or transcript, there is no "statement" in existence that can be discovered. It also means that if a lawyer, after interviewing a witness, later makes notes summarizing the interview, but the notes are not substantially verbatim, the lawyer's notes of the witness interview are not discoverable, and fall within the Rule 26(b)(3) work-product doctrine.

A party is entitled to obtain a copy of his prior statement in the possession of anyone else upon demand, without a court order or a showing of need. A party is considered to have a right to his own written or recorded statements. Statements made by a party to his own lawyer are not discoverable, principally because the attorney-client privilege will apply to such communications.

A witness is also entitled to obtain a copy of his prior statement. Note that the rule does not expressly allow discovery of a witness's statement. Only the witness himself has a right to obtain a copy of his own statement. A lawyer, however, can always urge a witness to ask for a copy of his own statement and then obtain it from the witness. Because it is so easy to obtain

---

3. Wright §81; James & Hazard §5.7; Friedenthal §7.2; Moore's Manual §15.02(1)(c); Manual of Federal Practice §5.37; Moore's Federal Practice §26.62; Wright & Miller §2010.

4. Wright §82; James & Hazard §5.8; Friedenthal §7.5; Moore's Manual §15.02(4); Moore's Federal Practice §26.65; Wright & Miller §§2027, 2028.

the statement indirectly, many lawyers, and some courts, view witness statements as being discoverable directly.

4. Experts[5]

There are three basic kinds of experts: testifying experts, consulting experts, and informally consulted experts. Different rules govern the discoverability of their identity, opinions, reports, and background information. There are also experts who are employees of a party and were involved in the events on which the litigation is based, but they are treated like any fact witness.

Rule 26(a)(2) governs the disclosures of expert witnesses expected to testify at trial. Required to be disclosed are the "identity of any person who may be used at trial to present evidence" as an expert under the Federal Rules of Evidence. Also required to be disclosed is a signed written report of "a witness who is retained or specially employed to provide expert testimony in the case, or whose duties as an employee of the party regularly involve giving expert testimony." The report must contain "a complete statement of" all opinions to be expressed and the reasons for those opinions, the data and other information considered to form those opinions, exhibits to be used to support the opinions, the expert's qualifications, including all publications within 10 years, the expert's compensation, and a list of all cases in which the expert has testified at trial or by deposition within four years. Rule 26(b) allows a party to depose such an expert as of right.

Rule 26(b) also governs consulting experts, those who have been retained or employed to help the lawyer during the litigation process, but are not expected to be witnesses at trial. Such experts ordinarily cannot be subjected to the discovery process, unless a requesting party can show "exceptional circumstances under which it is impracticable . . . to obtain facts or opinions on the same subject by other means." The rule in effect establishes a qualified privilege for the work of a consulting expert, one akin to that for a lawyer's trial preparation materials. The only exception is Rule 35(b), which makes the reports of a suitably licensed or certified examiner's mental or physical examination of a party discoverable in certain circumstances.[6]

Informally consulted experts, those experts who have not been employed or retained by the lawyer but have provided information, are not governed by the discovery rules. Therefore, neither the existence, identity, nor opinions of such an expert is discoverable. This prevents experts with minimal or incidental contact with the lawyer from being drawn into the discovery process.

---

5. Wright §81; James & Hazard §5.11; Friedenthal §7.6; Moore's Manual §15.02(5); Manual of Federal Practice §5.36; Moore's Federal Practice §26.66; Wright & Miller §§2029–2034.

6. See §6.10.

5.   Privileges[7]

Rule 26(b)(1) excludes privileged matter from being discoverable. Federal privileges are controlled by Rule 501 of the Federal Rules of Evidence.

The first question to ask regarding this aspect of discovery is: What privilege law applies? Rule 501 provides that federal privileges, as developed by the courts, will apply. The exception is that in civil cases for which state law "provides the rule of reason" as to an element of a claim or defense, state privileges will apply. This essentially means that in federal criminal cases and federal civil cases based on federal question jurisdiction, federal privilege law will apply. However, in federal civil cases based on diversity jurisdiction, state privileges rules will apply. Which state's privileges rules will apply is determined by the forum state's choice-of-law rules. Where a privilege is based on the U.S. Constitution, such as the Fifth Amendment's self-incrimination clause, it applies regardless of the type of federal case involved.

The second question that must be asked is: What is the applicable federal or state privilege law? When the Federal Rules of Evidence were enacted, Congress chose not to codify federal common law privileges, preferring to let federal privileges continue to develop in the courts. Therefore, care must always be taken to research the law of the appropriate jurisdiction, because privilege law can vary.

State privileges, by contrast, are developed by both the courts and the legislatures, although in recent years the trend has been to codify privileges. Keep in mind that state jurisdictions vary widely in their privilege law. While all states recognize frequently used privileges such as marital, attorney-client, and doctor-patient, they vary substantially in their recognition of others such as the privilege for accountants, reporter's informants, and governmental secrets. The scope of any privilege, and whether it applies in civil or criminal cases, also varies significantly. This is an area of evidence law that, when joined with choice of law issues, always requires substantial research.

The third question that must be asked is: What is the proper procedure for asserting a privilege claim? Rule 26(b)(5) requires that when a party wishes to withhold discoverable materials based on a claim of privilege, the claim must be made expressly, and the party claiming the privilege must describe the nature of the documents, communications, or things "in a manner that, without revealing information itself privileged or protected, will enable other parties to assess the applicability of the privilege or protection." Failure to comply with the notice requirement may be viewed as a waiver of the privilege.

This collection of descriptions and documents for which a privilege is claimed is commonly called a "privilege log." The documents themselves, of course, must be segregated from other discoverable documents and may

---

7. Wright §81; James & Hazard §5.9; Friedenthal §§7.4–7.5; Moore's Manual §15.02(2); Manual of Federal Practice §§5.30–5.34; Moore's Federal Practice §§26.60–26.61; Wright & Miller §§2016–2020; T. Mauet & W. Wolfson, Trial Evidence §§8.8–8.14 (3d ed. 2005).

later need to be presented to the court for an in camera inspection if the requesting party moves to compel the production of those documents.

6.   Trial preparation materials[8]

Ever since the Supreme Court decided Hickman v. Taylor, 329 U.S. 495 (1947), federal courts have recognized a two-tier privilege rule applicable to an attorney's work product; that rule, with some changes and added details, is now incorporated in Rule 26(b)(3).

The attorney's work product, now called "trial preparation materials," is protected by a qualified privilege. Trial preparation materials include "documents and tangible things" that were "prepared in anticipation of litigation" by another party or that party's "representative." A representative includes not only the lawyer but may include the lawyer's employees and agents such as an investigator. The party must expressly claim the privilege under Rule 26(b)(5).

If the privilege attaches, it is only a qualified privilege. The rule permits a party seeking discovery to obtain protected documents and tangible things upon a showing of "substantial need" because the party cannot obtain the "substantial equivalent" by other means without "undue hardship." Under the provisions of the rule, it is clear that undue hardship cannot be shown simply by demonstrating added expense or inconvenience. With witness statements, the area where this issue most frequently arises, there must be some demonstrable reason why the requesting party cannot get the substantial equivalent of the statement himself before production can be ordered.[9]

§6.3.   Discovery strategy

The discovery rules in the Federal Rules of Civil Procedure are both broad and extensive, and in most cases they permit more discovery than either party will wish to make. Consequently, your overriding concern at the discovery stage is: What will be an effective discovery strategy for this particular case? As outlined previously, discovery planning is essentially a seven-step process.[10]

---

8. Wright §82; James & Hazard §5.10; Friedenthal §7.5; Moore's Manual §15.02(4); Manual of Federal Practice §§5.35, 5.175; Moore's Federal Practice §26.57(2); Wright & Miller §§2021–2028; E. Epstein, The Attorney-Client Privilege and the Work-Product Doctrine, Section of Litigation, ABA (4th ed. 2001); see United States v. Adlman, 134 F.3d 1194 (2d Cir. 1998), for an expansive view of the "prepared in anticipation of litigation" requirement.

9. Wright §82; Manual of Federal Practice §§5.35, 5.175; Moore's Manual §15.02(4); Moore's Federal Practice §26.64(3); Wright & Miller §2025.

10. See §4.5.5.

1.   **What facts do I need to establish a winning case on my claims (or to defeat the opponent's claims)?**

Remember that under the 2000 amendments to Rule 26, the scope of relevant discovery is based on the claims and defenses raised in the pleadings. Before starting discovery, review your pleadings and amend them if necessary.

2.   **What facts have I already obtained through informal fact investigation?**

These questions should already be answered in your developing litigation chart.

3.   **What "missing" facts do I still need to obtain through formal discovery?**

Discovery is the vehicle you use to force other parties, and nonparties, to disclose information they have which is relevant to the litigation. Your first question, therefore, should be: What information do I need to know, that I do not already know from my informal investigation and have not been admitted in the pleadings, so that I can properly prepare the case for a possible trial? While the answer will vary with each case, it will usually include most of the following:

1.   Identity of proper parties
2.   Defendant's ability to pay a judgment (insurance coverage and fiscal condition)
3.   Identity of agents and employees
4.   Opponent's factual basis for legal claims
5.   Opponent's position on factual issues
6.   Identity and location of witnesses
7.   Prospective testimony of adverse parties, agents, and employees
8.   Prospective testimony of witnesses
9.   Identity, opinions, reasoning, and backgrounds of experts
10. Prospective testimony of experts
11. Tangible evidence
12. Documents
13. Records
14. Electronic evidence
15. Statements of parties and witnesses
16. Deposition testimony of favorable witnesses that may become unavailable for trial

Not all of this information is necessarily discoverable. However, you should always compile a similar roster for each case — using your litigation chart — since it will control the information you will try to discover.

Think in terms of evidence, not just in terms of information, and think how the formal discovery rules can be used to create evidence that later will be admissible at trial.

4.   What discovery methods are most effective for obtaining the "missing" facts?

There are six methods of discovery permitted under the federal rules: required disclosures, interrogatories, requests to produce documents, depositions, physical and mental examinations, and requests to admit facts. Although there is some overlap, each method is particularly well suited for certain kinds of information.

Initial disclosures, part of the required disclosures under Rule 26(a)(1), is the automatic discovery method by which parties must disclose, early in the litigation, basic information they have about the case, including identity of witnesses, identity or disclosure of documents and tangible things, computation of damages and the sources of those computations, and insurance agreements which may pay part or all of any judgment.

Interrogatories are most effective for obtaining basic factual data from other parties, such as the identity of proper parties, agents, employees, witnesses, and experts, and the identity and location of documents, records, and tangible evidence, and sometimes financial and statistical data. They can be useful in obtaining other parties' positions on disputed facts. On the other hand, interrogatories are not usually effective instruments for getting detailed facts, impressions, or versions of events.

A request to produce documents and tangible things is the discovery method by which one obtains from another party copies of records, documents, electronically stored information, and other tangible things for inspection, copying, and testing. Such a request also permits an entry on another person's land or property to inspect, photograph, and analyze things on it. This is the only discovery device that forces another party actually to produce records and things, and to permit entry onto someone else's property to copy, photograph, or study evidence. A subpoena to a nonparty witness can obtain the same information.

Depositions are most effective in tying down parties, nonparty witnesses, and experts to details, and in discovering everything they know pertinent to the case. It is the only discovery vehicle that permits you to assess how good a witness a person is likely to be at trial. It is an excellent vehicle to secure admissions or other evidence favorable to your side. Further, a deposition is the only method to preserve testimony if a witness will become unavailable for trial.

A physical and mental examination of a party can be obtained by court order when the physical or mental condition of that party is in issue, a situation most common in personal injury cases. While other discovery methods can be used to get records of past examinations, this is the only means of forcing a party to be examined and tested prospectively. For that reason it is the best method for evaluating a party on such damages elements as permanence and extent of injury, and medical prognosis.

Finally, requests to admit facts is the method that forces a party to admit or deny facts or a document's genuineness. An admitted fact is deemed conclusively admitted for the purpose of the pending trial. This method is effective if limited to simple factual data, such as someone's employment on a specific date, or the genuineness of signatures on a contract. It is not a good method for dealing with opinions or evaluative information.

There are three more areas where, upon motion and court order, you may obtain additional discovery.

Under Rule 26(b)(1), you may be able to obtain discovery of "any matter relevant to the subject matter involved in the action" if the court orders it for good cause. This is broader than the scope of discovery by right rule, which permits discovery of any matter "relevant to the claim or defense of any party."

Under Rule 26(b)(4)(B), you can obtain discovery of your opponent's consulting expert only on a showing of "exceptional circumstances under which it is impractical . . . to obtain facts or opinions on the same subject by other means." While this is obviously a difficult standard, the Rule contemplates those rare cases where relevant expert information is solely in the possession of one party's expert, such as where a consulting expert has engaged in destructive testing of a product.

Finally, under Rule 26(b)(3), trial preparation materials, which are protected from disclosure by a qualified privilege, can be obtained from an opponent "only upon a showing of substantial need." The party seeking production must also be "unable without undue hardship to obtain the substantial equivalent of the materials by other means." This exception to the attorney's work product rule arises most often in regard to nonverbatim memos of witness interviews, which are not usually discoverable. Where one side has interviewed a witness who now refuses to talk to other lawyers, who cannot be subpoenaed, or who has a lapse of memory, and the substantial equivalent of the statement cannot be obtained, the court may order the production of the memorandum.

5.   What facts and witnesses, that I already know of through informal investigation, do I need to "pin down" by using formal discovery?

There is little point in using formal discovery methods with your favorable witnesses, unless those witnesses are old, sick, or are likely to move away. If this is the case, you will want to take the witness' deposition to preserve the testimony for trial, since the transcript will usually qualify as former testimony.[11]

With unfavorable, hostile, or adverse witnesses and parties, however, there are good reasons for deposing them, even if you already know from your informal fact investigation what they will say at trial. First, there are always benefits in learning in detail what those witnesses will say. Second,

---

11. See Rule 32; FRE 804(b)(1).

witnesses may testify inconsistently with their previous statements, or inconsistently with each other. Third, you may be able to limit the witnesses' trial testimony by getting the witnesses to admit to topics they have no firsthand knowledge of, are not sure of, or are only approximating or guessing at. All of these are good reasons for deposing important, unfavorable, or adverse witnesses you expect will testify for the opposing party at trial.

6. What restrictions does my litigation budget place on my discovery plan?

Information gathering, especially formal discovery, is expensive, and any discovery strategy must necessarily consider the expenses involved. While your litigation budget, which you have already prepared, will have analyzed the amount of time you will allocate to discovery, at this point you should give the discovery portion a second look. This should be done for three reasons. First, the pleadings, now completed, may force changes in your discovery strategy. Second, since discovery will usually consume the majority of your pretrial time allotment, it is particularly important to review it. Third, discovery can easily escalate out of control, so staying with your game plan is essential.

Most formal discovery methods are expensive, and responding to discovery, particularly interrogatories and documents requests, can become expensive because of the time involved in researching and preparing responses and reviewing the necessary documents. Depositions are an expensive discovery method, and it is here that cost effectiveness is particularly important. Deposition costs include the lawyer's time, witness fees, the court reporter's attendance fees, and transcript costs. Assuming a one-hour deposition, the witness, reporter, and transcript costs will probably exceed $200. A lawyer may need two hours to prepare for the deposition and one hour after the deposition to make a summary of her impressions. Even a short deposition, then, will cost the client several hundred dollars.

Deposition costs, therefore, require that you use this discovery method cautiously. You will probably need to depose your adverse party and critical witnesses in every case. However, you can often postpone depositions of experts and rely on expert's reports, initial disclosures, interrogatory answers and various records for settlement purposes, deposing your adversary's experts only when a trial becomes a realistic possibility. In some situations, such as the plaintiff's medical expert in a personal injury case, you may not always need to depose the doctor if his written report sufficiently details his opinions, bases for the opinions, supporting records, and other background information. Similarly, consider moving for a physical examination of the opposing party only when a trial becomes likely. Also, use investigators to interview nonparty witnesses who are not central to the case. There are often other ways of getting the essence of a witness' testimony short of a deposition, and you must always balance the additional benefit of depositions with their cost in all cases where litigation costs are a concern.

Example:

Consider a typical automobile accident case, in which you represent the plaintiff. You previously estimated the "value" of plaintiff's case at $90,000, of which you will earn about $30,000 with a successful conclusion. You have made various estimates of time requirements, and have allocated 60 hours to preparing and responding to discovery. How do you estimate how much time you should plan spending on the various discovery methods?

Start by breaking down formal discovery into its component parts to consider what discovery is essential. First, you will need to confer with your opposing counsel to develop a proposed discovery plan, attend a pretrial conference with the judge, and prepare initial disclosures required under Rule 26(a)(1). You estimate these steps will take five hours.

Second, you will need to submit interrogatories to the defendant and answer the defendant's interrogatories. In automobile cases involving only negligence claims, many jurisdictions use standard interrogatories. Sending interrogatories to the defendant, answering the defendant's, and reviewing the defendant's answers for sufficiency will probably take only a few hours, particularly if you have done your informal fact investigation before filing suit. You estimate interrogatories will take five hours.

Third, you will need to depose the critical witnesses: These will include the parties and occurrence witnesses. You will need to depose the defendant and one bystander, and to prepare your plaintiff for deposition, since the defendant will certainly depose him. In a simple automobile case, the plaintiff's deposition will probably take two or three hours, the defendant's and bystander's will perhaps take one hour each. Preparation for each deposition will probably take at least as long as the deposition itself. In addition, you will need to prepare a summary of each deposition immediately afterward and review the transcript of the plaintiff's testimony for accuracy. Accordingly, you estimate that these depositions will take approximately 20 hours.

Fourth, you will need to send requests to produce documents to the defendant and nonparties, and answer the defendant's production requests. You will also need to organize and review all the documents and records you receive. These will include hospital records, physician records, employment records, vehicle repair records, police reports, and insurance reports. You estimate that this work will take 10 hours.

Fifth, the defendant may want to have the plaintiff medically examined, particularly if plaintiff is claiming any permanent physical injuries. You will need to review the information that is developed through that examination, which is usually disclosed through interrogatory answers and the report of the examining doctor. You estimate this will require five hours.

Sixth, plaintiff and defendant will probably depose each other's medical experts. Defendant will want to depose plaintiff's treating physician and plaintiff will want to depose the defendant's examining physician. Preparing, taking, and summarizing these medical-expert depositions will take substantial time. You estimate this will take 15 hours.

Finally, you may want to send a request to admit facts to the defendant, and you may have to respond to the defendant's. You estimate this will take four hours.

Notice that this time estimate already adds up to over 60 hours, and not all the variables that exist have been taken into consideration. On the positive side, both parties may agree not to depose each other's experts, or the case may settle early. On the negative side, you may need to depose additional witnesses, and you may need to file motions to enforce or protect your discovery rights. The point, however, is to analyze the cost considerations as you develop your discovery strategy, because the two must be consistent with each other.

7. In what order should I execute my discovery plan?

Formal discovery should be used as a progressive device in which each discovery method is used as a sequential building block. Under Rule 26(d), there is no required sequence, except that before any discovery requests can be made, you must first confer with the opposing lawyer to develop a proposed discovery plan and make the initial disclosures required by Rule 26(a). After this point, the parties can engage in discovery to the extent permitted by the Rules, and consistent with the court's scheduling order setting forth the discovery plan. Under Rule 16, the judge may, and many do, hold a scheduling conference with the parties to decide how to regulate and expedite the case, particularly the discovery phase. At the conference, the judge will have the report of the parties on their proposed discovery plan. After the conference, the judge will enter an order that will control the remainder of the litigation. For example, the court may order that any interrogatories and documents requests be served within 60 days, answered within 30 days of service; that depositions of nonexperts be completed within six months; and that experts be deposed within nine months. The court will probably set a "discovery cutoff" date, when all discovery must be completed.

The only limitations on discovery should not be confining, and if the facts of the case make the limits imposed by the Rules unrealistic, the court has discretion to modify them. In addition, the court has power under Rules 26(c) and 37 to issue orders to compel and impose sanctions for failure to comply with the required disclosure rules and for other abuse of discovery. Finally, under Rule 29 the parties may, and frequently do, stipulate to modify certain discovery procedures without court approval, unless the stipulation would interfere with other court-ordered time limits and schedules. In that event, court approval is necessary.

Because the discovery process is so flexible, the relevant questions are: When should I start discovery? In what order should it be carried out?

The initial question can be answered simply. You should start discovery as soon as the Rules permit and as soon as practical. If you have done your pre-filing investigation and preparation work, you should be able to begin discovery as soon as you have conferred with your opponent to develop a proposed discovery plan. Although the parties may agree to begin, or the court or local rules may permit, discovery prior to this meeting, the meeting may help eliminate some unnecessary discovery and provide a clearer focus for the discovery plan.

The following is a common discovery sequence:

1. discovery planning conference and pretrial scheduling conference
2. required initial disclosures
3. interrogatories
4. requests to produce documents, electronically stored information, and things, and subpoenas
5. depositions of parties and witnesses
6. physical and mental examinations
7. expert disclosures and depositions
8. requests to admit facts
9. pretrial disclosures

This sequence utilizes the building block approach to discovery. Once the initial disclosures are received, you can serve interrogatories and requests to produce on parties and subpoenas on nonparty witnesses in order to obtain the additional information and documents, records, and other evidence identified in the interrogatory answers. After you have received this information you are ready to take depositions of parties, witnesses, and experts. In personal injury cases the physical and mental examinations of parties are ordinarily conducted later in the litigation process, since these examinations usually focus on such issues as permanence of injury, prognosis, and loss of earning capacity. Once these steps have been completed, notices to admit can further pinpoint areas of dispute and eliminate the need to prove uncontested facts at trial.

This sequence, of course, can be and often is modified. Amended, supplemental, or additional pleadings may be filed that will necessarily alter the course of discovery. In addition, there may be tactical benefits in changing the usual sequence or in serving more than one discovery device at the same time. Keep in mind that the discovery process educates your opponents as well as yourself. Lawyers sometimes take the deposition of an adverse party early, before interrogatories or notices to produce have been sent out, on the theory that the adverse party will have neither the time nor the inclination to prepare thoroughly by collecting and reviewing all the pertinent records beforehand. Lawyers frequently couple interrogatories requesting the identification of documents with a request to produce the documents identified, and use early requests to admit facts in order to narrow the scope of discovery.

There is no magic formula for deciding on the best sequence for discovery. This should be tailored to the specific needs and circumstances of each case. An important point to remember, however, is that discovery should not be used simply because it is available. Each step must have a specific purpose and be part of an overall discovery strategy.

In addition to this basic seven-step process, there are two additional considerations you should always keep in mind.

8. How can I conduct discovery informally?

The federal rules prescribe how discovery should be conducted, and a procedurally safe approach to discovery is to always do it "by the book." However, life doesn't always go by the book, nor does discovery in the litigation world. Litigation lawyers usually try to arrange things between themselves informally. This applies to all phases of the litigation process and is permitted and encouraged under Rule 29.

What aspects of discovery can be handled informally? The simple task of scheduling depositions can be. Instead of simply serving notice on your party opponent for his deposition, why not contact the other party's lawyer and try to arrange a mutually agreeable date and time? This will probably avoid any motions to reschedule the deposition, and will usually result in the same courtesy being extended to you in the future. Serve a notice of deposition after you have worked out the arrangement.

With nonparty deponents, whom you must subpoena and usually depose in the location convenient to that deponent, informal accommodations can be made. Serve the subpoena first, then see if the deponent is willing to come to your office. Offering to pay the witness' reasonable, legitimately incurred expenses in coming to your office, rather than following the formal Rule 45 procedures, frequently benefits everyone.[12]

It is also common to work out the mechanics of documents production informally. Why not call the other party's lawyer and work out how, when, where, and in what order each party will produce the requested documents, and electronic data, along with how they will be copied and who will pay for the charges. Another area where "working it out" informally is a common practice is in arranging to depose each other's experts.

While there are many other areas where the informal resolutions of problems are common, the point is the same: Whenever possible, it makes sense to try to work out the mechanics and details of discovery with the other side and with nonparties. Courtesy and reasonableness somehow make the world work better, and discovery in the litigation process is no different.

9. How can I limit discovery against my party?

As the lawyer for a party, you often have an interest in limiting the discovery of your case, unless your case is so strong that you don't want to limit it, or where

---

12. See §6.9.1(c).

early complete disclosure will force a favorable settlement. There are three basic areas where you can affect whether information can be discovered.

First, if your client is a business entity, take immediate steps to control the paperwork and e-mail and other electronic information generated in the business that has any bearing on the litigation: If it is not written down, it cannot be turned over under a request to produce. Have the business' employees communicate directly to you about the pending litigation, rather than to supervisors, since this may afford the advantage of bringing the communications under the attorney-client privilege protection.[13]

Second, again, if your client is a business entity, make sure that employees notify you if anyone tries to interview any of them about the case. Since any statements made by the employees may be admissions that are admissible against the business employer under FRE 801, you are probably entitled to treat such an employee as a party. This means that no one can interview the employee without your permission, and you can represent the employee at his deposition. It also means that communications between the employee and you may be protected by the attorney-client privilege.[14]

Third, obtain statements from witnesses that bring the statements under the qualified trial preparation materials doctrine or, better yet, under the absolute attorney's mental impressions privilege. Verbatim signed statements from adverse witnesses are useful, since they can be used to impeach. They may be dangerous, however, when taken from favorable witnesses, and so it is safer to have your investigator — or for you yourself to — interview the witness, then prepare a summary of the witness' information with observations on how strong or weak the witness is, what kind of witness she will make at trial, and how her testimony fits into the theory of the case, along with other pertinent mental impressions. You will then have a useful record of the witness, which will probably be protected from disclosure. Even if the other side does obtain it through a showing of substantial need, it will not include any verbatim statements usable to impeach. The observations about the witness, however, should be absolutely protected as the lawyer's work product.

Finally, consider ways in which you can protect your testifying expert during the discovery process.[15] Rule 26(a)(2) requires that each party disclose the identity of each expert expected to testify at trial, and a report containing a "complete statement of all opinions to be expressed," the "data or other information considered by the witness in forming the opinion," and other background information about the expert.

13. See Upjohn Co. v. United States, 449 U.S. 383 (1981). *Upjohn* rejected the "control group" test for determining which corporate employees' communications with corporate counsel will be protected by the attorney-client privilege. Any employee who has information necessary for the corporate counsel to evaluate will have those communications to corporate counsel protected by the privilege. However, state laws on the scope of the attorney-client privilege for corporate employees vary widely, so thorough research of the applicable jurisdiction's law is always necessary. T. Mauet & W. Wolfson, Trial Evidence §8.12 (3d ed. 2005).

14. See §2.5, discussing the rules that govern interviews of employees and former employees of a party.

15. See §2.6, discussing expert review of cases before filing suit.

How detailed should your disclosures be? While you may frequently want to minimize discovery, remember that the opposing party can always move to compel more detailed information. It is often a sound strategy to provide broad disclosure to other parties. This can provide substantial benefits in the future. First, it can forestall motions to compel full and complete disclosure. Second, it gives you a stronger position from which to resist motions for discretionary additional discovery. Third, providing complete responses puts you in a stronger position if you are seeking more expert discovery from other parties. Courts quite naturally are inclined to look at scope-of-discovery issues as a two-way street. Fourth, providing detailed disclosures may sometimes cause your opponent to forego taking the expert's deposition before trial.

Finally, maintain a professional relationship with your testifying expert to minimize the danger of disclosing matters that might otherwise be protected by the attorney-client privilege and work product doctrine. Allowing your experts to communicate directly with your client is dangerous. Disclosing information to your expert that is work product runs the danger that it may end up being discovered. But since the expert must have sufficient information on which to evaluate the case and develop opinions, the question becomes how to best convey the necessary information to your expert. The safe approach is to give your expert only those materials that are discoverable by other parties anyway. Assume that any communications you have with the expert at any time, both oral and written, will be discoverable and admissible at trial. This will minimize the danger of having your case hurt or of your being embarrassed at trial.

§6.4. Discovery planning meeting and pretrial scheduling conference

Before formal discovery can begin, the parties must complete three steps: confer to plan discovery, submit a written report to the court, and attend a pretrial scheduling conference with the judge. These are controlled by Rules 26(f) and 16(b).

1. Law[16]

Rule 26(f) requires that the parties that have appeared in the case confer "as soon as practicable" and in any event at least 21 days before a scheduling conference is held or scheduling order is due, to discuss the pleadings and the possibility of settlement, and to develop a proposed discovery plan. This is the "meet and confer" requirement. The discovery plan should contain the parties' views on the following topics:

1. changes to and timing of initial disclosures;
2. the subjects of, timing for, and order of other discovery;

---

16. Wright §83A; Manual of Federal Practice §5.2; Moore's Federal Practice §§26.01 et seq.

3. issues relating to disclosure or discovery of electronically stored information and the forms in which it should be produced;
4. issues relating to claims of privilege or protection of trial-preparation materials;
5. whether discovery limits should be modified;
6. need for protective orders or pretrial conference orders.

The parties are under an obligation to make good faith efforts to agree on a proposed discovery plan. Within 14 days after the conference, the parties must submit to the court a written report outlining the discovery plan.

Rule 16(b) requires that the court enter a scheduling order, after receiving the parties' written report of their planning conference. The order shall be issued "as soon as practicable" but in any event within 90 days after the appearance of a defendant and within 120 days after the complaint has been served on a defendant." The usual procedure is that the district judge, or a magistrate judge, sets a scheduling conference with the parties and receives the parties' written report at least seven days before the conference. At the scheduling conference, the judge will discuss the case with the lawyers and fashion a sequence and timing for discovery and other matters, such as amending pleadings, scheduling expert disclosures, dispositive motions, pretrial disclosures, and settlement conferences.

2. Practice approach

a. Timing

When should the lawyers hold their discovery planning conference? Rule 26(f) merely provides that it be held "as soon as practicable" and at least 21 days before the pretrial scheduling conference or order. Hence, you need to know when the judge has, or probably will, set a date for the scheduling conference and work backwards from that date.

Most judges will hold the scheduling conference shortly after the defendants have appeared and answered the complaint. At this time, the judge, and parties, can get a general picture of the case, what's in issue, how "big" the case is, and accordingly what the discovery needs are.

Complications can arise. What happens if not all defendants named in the complaint have been served? What happens if defendants file Rule 12(b) motions? What if defendants bring in third-party defendants? In these situations, the "as soon as practicable" language controls. Since the principal purpose of the parties' planning meeting and the court's scheduling conference is to set a realistic discovery plan, this cannot be accomplished when the pleadings are still substantially incomplete. Accordingly, most judges will wait until all parties have appeared and answered the complaint. On the other hand, if all but one defendant have appeared, and the unserved defendant is either not a critical party, or may never be served, the judge will probably still set an early scheduling conference date. Every judge has her own preferences; many have standing orders on when the conference will be held. Check with the judge's clerk after the case has been assigned if you don't know the judge's practice.

Since you must confer with the other parties to develop a proposed discovery plan, contact the other lawyers after they have appeared in the case. Rule 26(f) holds each party responsible for arranging and participating in the planning conference, and "attempting in good faith to agree on the proposed discovery plan." Hence, you must attempt to schedule the conference, even if the other side is uncooperative.

At the conference the parties should discuss amending the pleadings, the possibility of settlement, the details of the proposed discovery plan, and other matters such as the preservation of physical evidence and electronic data from inadvertent or intentional destruction, and the need for protective orders for trade secrets and other proprietary or confidential information. Aside from these matters, the conference, whether in person or by telephone, often accomplishes another intended purpose: getting the lawyers to meet in an informal setting. The reality is that if lawyers actually communicate directly, early in the litigation, to discuss their needs and concerns, the litigation process, particularly discovery, will be more efficient and less contentious.

Agreeing on a proposed discovery plan frequently creates conflict, particularly in larger cases. As a general rule, plaintiffs usually prefer quick and broad discovery, while defendants usually prefer more measured and focused discovery. For example, in a products liability case, plaintiff will want broad discovery to get at the defendant manufacturer's records, which will detail the design, manufacturing, marketing, and safety history of the product; defendant will want discovery to target the plaintiff's claimed damages and causation evidence, and defer discovery on other issues. After the meeting with the parties, consider writing a letter summarizing what happened at the meeting. Make sure it accurately sets out what was agreed on and where the parties disagree. This letter can later form the basis of the written discovery plan. If another party sends you such a letter, make sure it is accurate and, if not, send a letter identifying the inaccuracies.

Absent the court entering a case management or discovery scheduling order under Rule 16, the parties are generally free to conduct the discovery they want when they want it. However, courts are increasingly willing, in large or complex cases, to enter such orders and limit discovery to successive, focused issues. For example, the court may direct that plaintiff designate an expert on causation and submit the expert's report, followed by the expert's deposition, and then schedule a *Daubert* hearing on the admissibility of the expert's opinions. This can be followed by discovery directed to the defendant's design and manufacture of the product. Thereafter, discovery can be directed to punitive damages evidence. Be prepared, at the pretrial conference, to argue for a discovery plan that serves your client's interests.

b.   Written report of proposed discovery plan

Rule 26(f) requires that the parties submit a written report of their conference and proposed discovery plan to the court within 14 days of the conference. This requirement gives the judge time to review the report before meeting with the parties at the scheduling conference.

The report should itemize the decisions, and disagreements, of the parties on each of the major components of the litigation process: pleadings, discovery, dispositive motions, settlement, and trial. Form 35 in the Appendix of Forms is a useful guide for what the court expects the written report to contain. Keep in mind that the judge may have a standing order on how the written report should be organized and what it should contain.

Example:

[Caption]

REPORT OF PARTIES' PLANNING MEETING

The parties submit the following written report, pursuant to Rule 26(f):

1. Meeting. A meeting was held on June 1, 2005, at the offices of Johnson & Barnes, 100 Main Street, Boise, Idaho. Present were William Johnson, plaintiff's attorney, and Sarah Anton, defendant's attorney. The parties jointly propose to the court the following:

2. Scheduling conference. The parties request a scheduling conference before the entry of a scheduling order.

3. Pleadings. Plaintiff should have until July 1, 2005, to add additional parties and amend pleadings. Defendant should have until August 1, 2005, to add additional parties and amend pleadings.

4. Discovery.
   a. Initial disclosures under Rule 26(a)(1) will be exchanged by June 15, 2005.
   b. Discovery will be needed on the following subjects: plaintiff's and defendant's conduct before, during, and after the collision; plaintiff's medical treatment, plaintiff's future medical needs, plaintiff's present and future lost income, and other claimed damages.
   c. Interrogatories will be limited to 20 by each party to another party, and will be served by July 15, 2005. Responses are due 30 days after service.
   d. Documents requests will be limited to 20 by each party to another party, and will be served by September 15, 2005. Responses are due 30 days after service.

e. Disclosure or discovery of electronically stored information should be handled in accordance with the proposal attached to this report.

f. The parties have agreed to an order regarding claims of privilege and protection as trial-preparation materials asserted after production. The proposed order is attached to this report.

g. Depositions of non-experts will be limited to 8 by each party, and will be taken by December 1, 2005. Each deposition will be limited to 3 hours, unless extended by agreement of the parties.

h. Written reports from plaintiff's retained experts under Rule 26(a)(2) are due December 15, 2005. Written reports from defendant's retained experts are due January 15, 2006.

i. Depositions of experts will be limited to 2 by each party, and will be taken between December 15, 2005, and February 15, 2006. Each deposition will be limited to 4 hours, unless extended by agreement of the parties.

j. Requests to admit will be limited to 15 by each party to another party, and will be served by March 1, 2006. Responses are due 30 days after service.

k. Supplementation under Rule 26(e) is due by April 1, 2006.

l. Discovery cut-off date is April 1, 2006.

5. <u>Dispositive motions.</u> Dispositive motions will be served and filed by April 15, 2006. Responses are due by May 15, 2006.

6. <u>Settlement.</u> Settlement cannot be evaluated until after the experts' reports have been received. The parties request that the court schedule a conference to discuss settlement after February 15, 2006.

7. <u>Trial.</u>

a. Witness and exhibits lists under Rule 26(b)(3) should be due from plaintiff by May 1, 2006, and from defendant by May 15, 2006.

b. Parties should have 15 days after service of witness and exhibits lists to specify objections under Rule 26(a)(3).

c. The case should be ready for trial by July 1, 2006. The trial is expected to take approximately 4 days.

Respectfully submitted,

_____

William Johnson, attorney for
    plaintiff

_____

Sarah Anton, attorney for
    defendant

If the parties cannot agree on certain matters, the written report should state what the disagreements are and the basis for them.

Example:

> 6. Settlement. The parties cannot agree on when a conference to discuss settlement should be held. Plaintiff prefers a conference after initial disclosures have been served. Defendant prefers a date after experts have been deposed.

Finally, if the other party has failed to participate in the planning meeting, this must be reported to the court, since the failure to meet can subject that party to sanctions under Rule 37(g).

c. *Scheduling conference*

Under Rule 16(b), the court is required only to enter a scheduling order. A scheduling conference is optional, although many judges hold scheduling conferences in all cases, or delegate it to a magistrate judge. Some judges, however, will not hold a conference if the case appears routine, and the parties' written report shows no serious disagreements and proposes a reasonable chronology of events. At the conference, the judge will have the parties' written report containing their proposed discovery plan.

Your purpose at the scheduling conference is twofold: convince the judge to accept the agreed parts of the written report and your side of the matters on which the parties disagree. Remember that the judge will have attitudes about how litigation should be handled and about the pace, sequence, and discovery complexity that is appropriate to certain kinds of cases. A diversity personal injury case or simple contract dispute is different from, and has different needs from, an antitrust or multiparty building construction case. Hence, the judge may routinely ratify the parties' written report without much discussion in routine cases, but go over the report in detail in large or complex cases. The more complicated the case, and the more contentious the parties, the more likely the judge will actively control the litigation, beginning with a Rule 16 scheduling conference. In some districts, cases are divided into routine and complex cases. If routine, the judge may put the case on a "fast track," and schedule discovery so that it is completed within a few months.

After the scheduling conference, the judge will enter a scheduling order, which will usually cover the same subjects as the parties' written report. The order controls what discovery will take place and when it will be completed, unless the judge later modifies the order.

Because the scheduling order is so important, make sure you "get it right" the first time. This means that your conference with other parties to make a discovery plan must be candid and realistic and achieve a compromise between the parties' preferences and the likely attitude of the judge. This also means that the lawyers must "educate the judge" about the unusual circumstances that justify a discovery schedule different from what the judge will expect in this kind of case. Only when there is candid, open communication among the parties and judge will the result be mutually beneficial: a scheduling order that realistically and efficiently regulates the remainder of the litigation process.

§6.5. *Required disclosures*

Rule 26(a) creates three categories of required disclosures: initial disclosures, expert disclosures, and pretrial disclosures. Disclosures are mandatory, except that certain types of cases, set forth in Rule 26(a)(1)(E), are exempt from the initial disclosures requirement.

All disclosures shall be made in writing, signed, and served on all other parties unless the court orders otherwise. The disclosures shall be made at the times provided by Rule 26. The times for initial disclosures can be modified by agreement of the parties or by court order. The times for expert disclosures and pretrial disclosures can be modified only by court order.

1. Initial disclosures[17]

Under Rule 26(a)(1), each party must make initial disclosures to the other side, without a discovery request, in four categories of "core" information: witnesses, documents, damages, and insurance.

1. The name and, if known, the address, and telephone number of each individual likely to have discoverable information that the disclosing party may use to support its claims or defenses, unless solely for impeachment, identifying the subjects of the information;
2. A copy of, or a description by category and location of, all documents, electronically stored information, and tangible things that are in the possession, custody, or control of the party and that the disclosing party may use to support its claims or defenses, unless solely for impeachment;
3. A computation of any category of damages claimed by the disclosing party, making available for inspection and copying as under Rule 34 the documents or other evidentiary material, not privileged or protected from disclosure, on which such computation is based, including materials bearing on the nature and extent of injuries suffered;
4. For inspection and copying as under Rule 34 any insurance agreement under which any person carrying on an insurance business may be liable to satisfy part or all of a judgment which may be entered in the action or to indemnify or reimburse for payments made to satisfy the judgment.

A party must make the disclosures based on the information "then reasonably available to it" and cannot fail to make disclosures because its investigation of the case is not complete or it is challenging the adequacy of the other party's disclosure. A party is under a duty to supplement and

---

17. See Wright §83A; Manual of Federal Practice §5.2; Moore's Federal Practice §§26.01 et seq.

correct disclosures if it learns that the disclosure was in "some material respect incomplete or incorrect."

The timing of the initial disclosures is controlled by Rule 26(a) and (f). The parties must confer to develop a discovery plan "as soon as practicable" and at least 21 days before the pretrial conference. No discovery can be done until after this conference. Initial disclosures are due within 14 days of the parties' conference, unless the parties stipulate otherwise, or a court order or local rule provide otherwise.

Initial disclosures have three basic consequences. First, this discovery is automatic, requiring no triggering request or action from the other parties, and will occur sooner than other discovery. Second, initial disclosures should partially replace the first set of interrogatories and documents requests that invariably sought the same basic information now required to be disclosed automatically. Third, the production of documents is required only of those documents the disclosing party "may use to support its claims or defenses," that is, the disclosing party's helpful documents. To obtain the documents that *hurt* the disclosing party, you must serve a Rule 34 request on that party.

Initial disclosures, being automatic, are a departure from traditional discovery, which required a party to produce information only when served with a specific request. Initial disclosures change how lawyers litigate. First, since a lawyer is required to disclose information automatically to the other side, if it is "discoverable information that the disclosing party may use to support its claims and defenses, unless used solely for impeachment," the scope of the required initial disclosures may be influenced by the specificity of the allegations in the pleadings. This may cause lawyers to make their complaints and answers more fact-specific, although not required under "notice" pleading. Second, lawyers may more frequently move for a more definite statement under Rule 12(e) to identify what the case is about and hence what is required to be disclosed in the initial disclosures. Third, Rule 26(a) requires a party to make initial disclosures "based on the information then reasonably available to it" and cannot avoid making disclosures because it has not completed its investigation of the case.

Finally, keep in mind that a party has a duty to supplement its disclosures. Rule 26(e) requires supplementation "at appropriate intervals" if a party's disclosure is "in some material respect" incomplete or incorrect and the other parties were not made aware of it. The sanctions for violating Rule 26 are severe. The court must, under Rule 37(c), exclude from trial a witness or information not listed or produced in the initial disclosures, if the failure to disclose was "without substantial justification" and was not "harmless."

2. Expert disclosures

Under Rule 26(a)(2), each party must also make expert disclosures. The disclosure includes the "identity of any person who may be used at trial to present evidence" as an expert. This includes computer forensic experts who will testify about electronic evidence and systems. Also required is disclosure of a written signed report of "a witness who is retained or specially employed to provide expert testimony in the case, or whose duties as an employee of the party regularly involve giving expert testimony." The report must contain a "complete statement" of all opinions and bases; the "data or other information considered" to reach the opinions; summary exhibits; witness qualifications; all publications within 10 years; compensation; and other cases in which the witness has testified at trial or deposition within 4 years. Rule 26(e) requires supplementation "at appropriate intervals" if the disclosure is in some material respect incomplete or incorrect and the other parties were not made aware of it.

Expert disclosures are due at least 90 days before trial, or 30 days if the expert is solely a rebuttal witness, unless the court directs or the parties stipulate otherwise. The 90-day rule can create problems, since there will be no information provided to the other parties about the testifying experts until that time. When expert disclosures should be due must be taken up at the Rule 16 scheduling conference.

Expert witness discovery is broad. Rule 26(a)(2) requires a "complete statement" of all opinions and bases for the opinions, the data and information relied on, and the background of the expert. Rule 26(b)(4) provides for depositions of testifying experts as of right. Between the two provisions, parties can now get essentially unlimited information about, and from, the other party's testifying experts.

Note that an "expert" is someone who will give testimony under Rules 702, 703, and 705 of the Federal Rules of Evidence. Rules 701 and 702 were amended in 2000 to make it clear that all testifying experts, regardless of what forms their testimony take, must be qualified under Rule 702.

3. Pretrial disclosures

Under Rule 26(a)(3) each party must make pretrial disclosures in the following categories of evidence:

1. witnesses who are expected to testify at trial
2. witnesses who may be called "if the need arises"
3. witnesses who are expected to be presented through depositions (and a transcript of pertinent portions of the testimony)
4. each exhibit expected to be offered at trial
5. each exhibit that may be offered "if the need arises"

Pretrial disclosures are due at least 30 days before trial, unless the court directs otherwise. Objections to depositions and exhibits must be made at least 14 days before trial. Failure to object will be deemed a waiver of all objections except relevance.

The requirement of disclosing witnesses called and exhibits offered "if the need arises" includes rebuttal witnesses and exhibits. However, the rule specifically excludes evidence that will be used "solely for impeachment."

These pretrial disclosures are usually made as part of the more comprehensive joint pretrial memorandum. This is discussed in §8.2.

4. Practice approach to initial disclosures

Initial disclosures are required, unless the proceeding is of a kind that is exempted by Rule 26(a)(1)(E). A lawyer preparing initial disclosures should ask three questions: When must I serve initial disclosures on the other parties? What must I disclose? How should I organize and draft my initial disclosures?

a. Timing

Under Rule 26(f), the parties must confer to develop a discovery plan as soon as practicable, and in any event at least 21 days before the court holds a scheduling conference under Rule 16. The parties must submit a written report outlining their discovery plan within 14 days after they confer.

The logical time to have this conference is shortly after the defendant has answered the complaint or, if the answer contains counterclaims, cross-claims, or third-party complaints, when the plaintiff has replied or other parties have answered. At this time, the claims and defenses will be reasonably clear, and the parties should be able to confer and develop a realistic discovery plan and schedule they can present to the court. The court may, of course, schedule an early pretrial conference, and that will trigger the due dates of the lawyers' conference and submission of the discovery plan.

b. Topics

Rule 26(a)(1) clearly sets forth the required topics in the initial disclosures and the details within each topic. Required are four types of disclosures: witnesses, documents, damages, and insurance.

1. The name, address, and telephone number, if known, of each individual "likely to have discoverable information that the disclosing party may use to support its claims or defenses, unless solely for impeachment";
2. The description and location of documents, electronically stored information, and tangible things, or copies of them, in the possession, custody, or control of the party that the disclosing party "may use to support its claims or defenses, unless solely for impeachment";
3. The computation of damages, making available for inspection and copying the documents on which the computation is based;
4. Insurance agreements, making them available for inspection and copying, that may be liable for all or part of any judgment.

Note that disclosure is required of evidence a "party may use to support its claims or defenses." This language, from the 2000 amendment to the rule, replaced previous broader language ("disputed facts alleged with particularity in the pleadings"), which had triggered much disagreement and controversy.

c. Drafting the initial disclosures

Drafting initial disclosures requires that you make disclosures based on the information "then reasonably available." A party cannot avoid disclosures because its investigation is not yet complete, a situation that will more frequently apply to defendants. A party must disclose the core evidence it may use to support the claims and defenses raised in its own pleading.

Keep in mind that a threadbare disclosure will probably result in motions to compel as well as follow-up interrogatories and documents requests. Moreover, Rule 26(e) requires supplementation of initial disclosures "at appropriate intervals" when the party learns that its disclosures "in some material respect" are "incomplete or incorrect," and the additional and corrective information has not been made known to the other parties.

The message should be clear: draft the initial disclosures carefully and completely the first time. It sends a message to the opposing party that you have done your homework, understand the issues and the facts, and are fully prepared to litigate. This is an important message to send early in the litigation process, and a detailed initial disclosure does just that.

i. Heading

An initial disclosure, like any court document, must contain a caption showing the court, parties, and civil case number. It should contain a heading that identifies which party is making the initial disclosure.

Example:

[Caption]

PLAINTIFF'S INITIAL DISCLOSURES

Plaintiff Johnson makes the following initial disclosures, pursuant to Rule 26(a)(1) of the Federal Rules of Civil Procedure:

ii. Content

Rule 26(a)(1) requires four categories of information, and drafting the actual information is simply a matter of carefully following the rule so that you provide what is required.

(1) *Witnesses.* The first category is the name and, if known, the address and telephone number of each individual "likely to have discoverable information that the disclosing party may use to support its claims or defenses, unless solely for impeachment," and "identifying the subjects of the information."

Example:

> A. The following individuals are likely to have discoverable information that the plaintiff may use to support its claims:
>
> 1. William Dawes (occurrence witness)
>   483 Bright Street
>   Wilmington, NC
>   677-4123
> 2. Ellen Johnson (occurrence witness)
>   address and telephone unknown
> 3. Mary Wilson, RN (nurse at emergency room)
>   Mercy General Hospital
>   Wilmington, NC
>   447-7000

(2) *Documents.* The second category is a description and location of documents, electronically stored information (ESI), and tangible things, or copies of them, in the possession, custody, or control of the party that "the disclosing party may use to support its claims or defenses, unless solely for impeachment." While an itemized list of each document and ESI is not required, enough of a description is required to allow the other parties to make informed decisions about which documents and ESI to inspect and copy and to draft a documents request directed to those documents and ESI. An adequate description of the documents and ESI should probably include the type of document and ESI, its date, and the general subject matter of its contents. The disclosing party can always decide to provide actual copies of the documents and ESI with the initial disclosure.

Example:

> The following records, electronically stored information, and tangible things are in the possession, custody, or control of the plaintiff and may be used to support the plaintiff's claims:
>
> 1. 1998 Honda Civic automobile, presently in possession of plaintiff at plaintiff's residence.
> 2. Mercy Hospital medical records, in the possession of both Mercy Hospital and plaintiff's attorney (electronic copy attached).
> 3. Wilmington Police Department accident report, in the possession of both the Wilmington Police Department and plaintiff's attorney (hard copy attached).

(3) *Damages.* The third category is a computation of any category of damages, making available for inspection and copying the documents on which the damages are computed. The disclosing party can always decide to provide copies of the documents with the initial disclosure.

Example:

Plaintiff's present damages are as follows and are based on the following records, which are in the possession of plaintiff's attorney and can be inspected and copied at any mutually convenient time:

1. hospital expenses (Mercy Hospital)	$2,498.71
2. doctor's expenses (Dr. Albert Rosen)	3,433.80
3. drugs (Walgreen's Pharmacy)	126.00
4. vehicle repair (Dobbs Honda)	2,135.00
5. rental vehicle (Hertz Car Rental)	288.39
6. lost wages (Montgomery Ward)	3,122.00
7. past pain & suffering	50,000.00
8. future pain & suffering	30,000.00

(4) *Insurance.* The fourth category is any insurance agreements that may be liable for all or part of any judgment, making them available for inspection and copying. The disclosing party can always decide to provide copies of the agreements with the initial disclosure.

Example:

Defendant was insured under a general casualty insurance policy issued by Allstate Insurance, Policy No. 4522147. A copy of the policy is attached.

iii.   Signing and serving

The initial disclosures must be signed by the party's lawyer and served on every other party. Service is made by any permitted method under Rule 5, most commonly by mailing a copy to the lawyers for the other parties. However, under Rule 5(d) initial disclosures are not to be filed with the court until they are used in the proceeding or the court orders filing. (This saves space in the clerk's office.)

d.   *Effect of initial disclosures*

Initial disclosures have changed how litigation is conducted in federal courts. First, initial disclosures partially replace the boilerplate interrogatories and documents requests that customarily sought the basic information now required to be automatically disclosed under Rule 26(a)(1). This basic information will be available sooner than was previously the case. This means that interrogatories and documents requests will be used as supplemental methods to get missing information and to pin down the other party to specific facts and positions. Second, since the rule refers to "discoverable information that the disclosing party may use to support its claims or defenses," parties may draft their pleadings with more care and factual detail, since the claims and defenses control the scope of the initial disclosures. Third, since the rules now also contain limits on the number of depositions and interrogatories, parties are more likely to move to compel more complete responses to the initial disclosures before pursuing the information through other discovery devices. Fourth, parties may be able to depose witnesses and parties sooner, if the initial disclosures have provided an adequate factual and documentary setting. Finally, initial disclosures may result in more motions for sanctions and other relief for failing to make adequate timely disclosure of required information. Lawyers will undoubtedly ask that witnesses and exhibits be precluded from trial if they were not properly and timely disclosed.

5. Practice approach to expert disclosures

A lawyer preparing expert disclosures should ask three basic questions: When must I make the disclosures? What must I disclose? How should I organize and draft the disclosures?

a. Timing

Under Rule 26(a)(2), expert disclosures are due at least 90 days before trial, or 30 days if the expert is solely a rebuttal witness, unless the court directs otherwise. Keep in mind that the court may have entered a pretrial order under Rule 16 establishing shorter time limits for the expert disclosures.

b. Topics

Under Rule 26(a)(2), each party must disclose "the identity of any person who may be used at trial to present evidence" as an expert under FRE 702, 703, or 705. It also requires a written signed report for a "witness who is retained or specifically employed to provide expert testimony, or whose duties as an employee of the party regularly involve giving expert testimony." The latter category includes witnesses such as design engineers for manufacturers and research chemists for pharmaceutical companies. The written report must contain:

1. a complete statement of all opinions to be expressed and the basis and reasons therefor;
2. the data or other information considered by the witness in forming the opinions;
3. any exhibits to be used as a summary of or support for the opinions;
4. the qualifications of the witness, including a list of all publications authored by the witness within the preceding 10 years;
5. the compensation to be paid for the study and testimony;
6. a listing of any other cases in which the witness has testified as an expert at trial or by deposition within the preceding 4 years.

An expert witness can be deposed as of right under Rule 26(b)(4), but only if the expert has first provided his written report.

c. Drafting the expert disclosure

Drafting the expert disclosure is just a matter of following the language of the rule and making sure that you provide all the required information.

i. Heading

The expert disclosure must contain a caption showing the court, parties, and civil case number. It should contain a heading that identifies which party is making the expert disclosure.

Example:

[Caption]

PLAINTIFF'S DISCLOSURE OF EXPERT TESTIMONY

Plaintiff Johnson makes the following disclosure of expert testimony, pursuant to Rule 26(a)(2). The following experts are expected to testify on behalf of the plaintiff at trial:

ii. Content

By tracking the requirements of the Rule, making the required disclosure is simple.

Example:

1. Emily Lieberman, M.D.
   a. Dr. Lieberman's opinions, the bases for her opinions, and the data and information she considered to reach her opinions are contained in her signed written report dated June 1, 2005, a copy of which is attached.
   b. Dr. Lieberman will use no summary exhibits during her testimony.
   c. Dr. Lieberman's professional qualifications, including her publications within the last 10 years, are contained on her current curriculum vitae, a copy of which is attached.
   d. Dr. Lieberman is being compensated for her study and testimony at the rate of $300 per hour.
   e. Dr. Lieberman has testified as an expert at trial or deposition a total of 6 times within the last 4 years. A list of those 6 cases is attached.

iii. Expert report

Rule 26(a)(2) requires disclosure of a signed written report from an expert who may testify at trial, and the report must include a "complete statement of all opinions to be expressed and the basis and reasons therefor." How do you get such a report from the expert that meets the requirements of the rule?

It goes without saying that the report should be prepared and written by the expert, who must sign it and who is responsible for its content. On the other hand, the expert needs to know the requirements of the rule, and the topics on which the expert will be asked to give opinions. The usual practice is that the lawyer and expert meet to discuss the issues; the lawyer explains the issues on which he needs expert opinions; and the expert explains whether he can give opinions on those issues and what the opinions will be. Sometimes the lawyer may ask the expert to assume certain facts as true and provide a factual summary with, preferably, the underlying source of the facts. The expert later drafts a written report of his evaluation of the issues, his opinions, and the reasons for them, and submits it to the lawyer, who reviews it for completeness and notes any errors and omissions. The expert then submits the final report to the lawyer.

How the expert's report looks when complete varies according to the circumstances, but most are organized along the following lines:

Example:

EXPERT REPORT

by

Mary G. Smith, M.D.

Case: Williams v. Johnson
        No. 05 C 1287

1. Introduction
I have been retained as an expert by counsel for the plaintiff in the above-captioned litigation.

I have been asked to express opinions on . . .

I am being compensated for my time spent studying this matter and any time spent testifying at the rate of $300 per hour.

2. Professional qualifications
I am a medical doctor and have been licensed to practice medicine since 1980 . . .

Attached is a curriculum vitae detailing my professional background.

3. Matters considered
As part of my review I have requested, received, and reviewed the following materials:

I have also conducted an examination of the plaintiff . . .

I have ordered and received the following tests . . .

4. Factual background
On June 1, 2005, . . .

5. Opinions
I have reached the following opinions:

6. Bases for the opinions
    My opinions are based on the following:
7. Conclusion
    For the foregoing reasons . . .

Date: _____   _____

                                         Mary G. Smith, M.D.

Keep in mind that under Rule 26(a)(2)(B), instructions, conversations, letters, and any other communications between the lawyer and expert, records and documents sent to the expert, and earlier drafts of the expert's report and working notes are usually discoverable and admissible at trial. This is because most courts hold there is no work-product doctrine protection between the lawyer and the testifying expert. Destruction of drafts of the expert's report may be considered spoliation. You can ask an expert to avoid creating drafts, but you cannot tell an expert to destroy drafts. Conduct yourself accordingly. Make sure you send to the expert only those things that would be discoverable anyway. Make sure the report is the expert's work. Lawyers who actively participate in creating and drafting an expert's report make themselves, their experts, and their case vulnerable at trial.

d.   Effect of expert disclosure

Rule 26(a)(2), controlling expert disclosure, and Rule 26(b)(4), permitting expert depositions as of right, have substantially changed discovery practice directed to experts. First, expert discovery is often likely to be sooner, because expert disclosure is required at least 90 days before trial. This rule change reduces the expert disclosure delaying games some lawyers played as the case moved closer to trial, and no disclosure was made until just before trial. However, expert disclosure may also come later, since no expert discovery is required until 90 days before trial. Most lawyers ask the court to accelerate the expert disclosure dates during the Rule 16 scheduling conference. Second, pre-deposition discovery of experts is significantly expanded, now requiring a "complete statement" of the opinions, basis, and data, as well as a complete biographical picture of the witness. This is much more than was previously obtained through interrogatories directed to information about experts. Since expert disclosure must be made before the expert can be deposed, there may be more motion practice directed to the completeness of the disclosed information. Third, not taking an expert's deposition may be a realistic option in some cases, saving the lawyers time and the clients money. For example, the defense may not always need to take the deposition of plaintiff's emergency room treating physician, if expert disclosure is complete and the emergency room records have been obtained, particularly since the party taking the deposition of an adversary's expert is required to reimburse the expert "a reasonable fee for the time spent responding to the discovery." Even when the expert is deposed, the actual deposition may be significantly shorter because of the required expert disclosure.

6.   Practice approach to pretrial disclosures

Pretrial disclosures, governed by Rule 26(a)(3), are discussed in §8.2.

§6.6.   Interrogatories

Interrogatories are frequently the second step in the discovery process because they provide the best method for getting basic facts about the other side's case not already obtained from the other party's initial disclosures. In states that do not have initial disclosures, interrogatories are usually the first discovery method employed. Further discovery can develop the information received in the interrogatory answers.

1.   Law[18]

Although interrogatories are governed by Rule 33, that Rule is often supplemented by local rules. Some districts have approved pattern interrogatories for common cases such as automobile personal injury suits. Hence, you should always check the local rules for the particular jurisdiction.

Interrogatories may be used to learn basic facts; identify witnesses and experts; and identify documents and other tangible things. They can be used to get information about "any matter, not privileged, that is relevant to the claim or defense of any party," the scope of discovery defined by Rule 26(b). Interrogatories can ask for "an opinion or contention that relates to fact or the application of law to fact." The line between what is "opinion" and what is a question of "pure law" is admittedly imprecise and has generated substantial litigation.[19] Because such issues usually become either clearer or moot as discovery progresses, the court may order that such interrogatories remain unanswered until a later time.

Interrogatories can be served by any party on any other party at any time after the parties have conferred to develop a discovery plan as required under Rule 26(f). In practice, interrogatories are frequently served after the parties have served their initial disclosures and reviewed the other party's initial disclosures.

The role of interrogatories in the discovery process was significantly changed by the amendments to the Rules in 1993. First, initial disclosures under Rule 26(a)(1) have, as they were intended to, substantially replaced the boilerplate pattern interrogatories that asked for basic information from the other parties. Interrogatories in federal court are now used in a more focused way: to target information not revealed, and to clarify information revealed, in the initial disclosures.

---

18. Wright §86; James & Hazard §5.4; Friedenthal §7.9; Moore's Manual §15.09; Shepard's Manual §§5.10, 5.126–5.144; Moore's Federal Practice §33; Wright & Miller §§2161–2182.

19. Moore's Manual §15.09; Shepard's Manual §5.137; Moore's Federal Practice §33.17; Wright & Miller §2167.

Second, any party can serve on any other party interrogatories "not exceeding 25 in number including all discrete subparts," unless the parties stipulate in writing or the court orders otherwise. The parties can ask for leave of court to serve more interrogatories. The question of whether an interrogatory is a single interrogatory or whether it is a compound interrogatory that attempts to get around interrogatory limits frequently arises.[20] The Committee Notes to Rule 33 make it clear that the "including all discrete subparts" language bars a single interrogatory that requests information about discrete separate subjects from counting as one interrogatory. On the other hand, an interrogatory that seeks information about one subject but asks that information about the subject be broken down into categories should be considered one interrogatory. As always, you need to know how your judge will count interrogatories, since it may affect how you draft them.

Third, objections to interrogatories must be stated and the answering party must answer any part of an interrogatory to which there is no objection. Objections must be stated "with specificity," and grounds not stated in a timely objection will generally be deemed waived.

Answers are due within 30 days of service of the interrogatories, unless a different time is set by court order or by written stipulation between the parties. The answer must respond to each interrogatory separately with either an answer or an objection. An answer must be a "full" answer that fairly meets the substance of the interrogatory. The answering party has an obligation to find the information if it is within the party's possession, even if not within the personal knowledge of the actual person answering.[21]

Under Rule 33(d) the answering party may specify business records and electronically stored information (ESI) from which an answer may be derived or ascertained, instead of giving a direct answer, if the "burden of deriving or ascertaining the answer is substantially the same for the party serving the interrogatory as for the party served." Where this is the case, the answer need only specify the records and ESI in sufficient detail to allow the requesting party to locate and identify the records and ESI and to give the requesting party a reasonable opportunity to inspect and copy them.

An answer must be signed under oath by the party making it. If any interrogatories are objected to, the lawyer making the objection must sign as well.

Finally, an answering party has a continuing obligation to "seasonably" supplement certain answers. Rule 26(e) requires supplementation of responses, even though complete when made, if "the party learns that the response is in some material respect incomplete or incorrect and if the additional or corrective information has not otherwise been made known to the other parties during the discovery process or in writing." Hence, unless the other parties have obtained the corrective information through other discovery or have been provided with that information in writing, the

---

20. See Wright & Miller §2168.
21. Moore's Manual §15.09; Shepard's Manual, §§5.141, 5.155; Moore's Federal Practice §33.26; Wright & Miller §2177.

answering party must amend its answers within a reasonable time. Failing to do this will, on motion, subject the answering party to Rule 37 sanctions.

2.   Practice approach

A lawyer preparing to send interrogatories to another party must ask three basic questions: When should I send out interrogatories? What kind of information should I seek? How should I organize and draft interrogatories to get the desired information?

a.   Timing

Interrogatories can be served on any other party once the parties have had their discovery planning conference required under Rule 26(f). However, the better approach is to wait until you have received the other party's initial disclosures and attended the pretrial conference under Rule 16. This will give you an opportunity to review the other party's initial disclosures and learn how the judge intends to schedule and regulate the discovery process in this case. This will allow your interrogatories to be more focused, an important consideration since interrogatories are now limited to 25 without leave of court or written stipulation of the parties.

In state courts that do not use initial disclosures, interrogatories are commonly sent out as soon as the initial pleadings have been made. For example, plaintiffs usually serve interrogatories on the defendant shortly after the defendant has answered the complaint; defendants frequently serve interrogatories on the plaintiff with their initial response (an answer or Rule 12 motion) to the complaint.

Sending interrogatories out quickly accomplishes two important things. First, it gets the discovery process started, which is particularly important since using the other discovery methods often depends on the interrogatory answers. With court-imposed discovery cutoff dates increasingly a part of the litigation process, efficiency is important. Second, it lets other parties know that you intend to litigate actively, an important message to send to your adversaries early on.

b.   Topics

Before drafting the interrogatories, ask yourself: What information do I want now so that I can use subsequent discovery methods to develop the information more fully? If you have thought through your discovery strategy,[22] you should know what information you need that is well suited to obtaining through interrogatories. Other parties should have provided much of this information in their initial disclosures. However, even if you have received the initial disclosures (or you are in a state court that does not recognize initial disclosures as a discovery method) you should be

---

22. See §6.3.

sure that you always know or, if you don't know, get the following information.

i.   Identity of parties, agents, and employees

Frequently in commercial litigation, you may not know the proper formal names of parties, parent corporations, or subsidiaries; where they are incorporated or licensed to do business; or the type of legal entities they are or their relationships to other parties. You need to know this information for a variety of purposes, relating to jurisdictional and joinder issues, for instance. You will also need to learn the identity of all agents and employees, and their relationships to the party. Interrogatories are the best method for getting this information.

ii.   Identity of witnesses

Almost every lawsuit will have witnesses to the events and transactions on which the claims are based. Interrogatories are a good method for obtaining the witnesses' identities, locations, and relationships to the parties.

iii.   Identity of documents and tangible things

Similarly, almost every lawsuit will have certain documents, records, and other tangible things on which the claims are based, or that are relevant to the claims. Interrogatories are the best method for identifying and locating these, for determining who has custody or control of them, and for determining if they are in paper or electronic form.

iv.   Identity of experts, facts, and opinions

Under Rule 26(a)(2), the expert disclosure rule, the other parties must disclose the identify and written reports of their testifying experts. The reports must contain a "complete statement" of all the experts' opinions, bases and supporting data for the opinions, and information about the experts' professional backgrounds. In state courts not recognizing initial disclosures, interrogatories will be the usual method to obtain much of this information.

Keep in mind, however, that Rule 26 only requires expert disclosures 90 days before the trial date, and the court under Rule 16 will probably have entered a pretrial order that controls when expert disclosures must be made. At this early stage in the litigation process, the parties may not yet have selected the experts who will ultimately be the testifying experts at trial. If you seek this information through interrogatories, the response will frequently be "not yet known." Nevertheless, many lawyers ask for expert disclosure early, because it makes an early record of the request. Keep in mind that Rule 26(e) requires that a party "seasonably" amend a discovery answer if the party learns it is incomplete or incorrect and the requesting party has not been provided with the additional or corrective information during the discovery process or in writing. Some lawyers, however, ask for expert information in a later interrogatory, after a substantial amount of discovery has been taken, the theory being that a useful answer is more likely to be received at that time.

v.   Details and sequences of events and transactions

Interrogatories are a useful method for obtaining concrete facts underlying vague or generalized claims. For this reason they are particularly useful in the commercial litigation area where lawsuits are frequently based on a series of events and transactions spread out over time, but are not detailed in any way in the pleadings.

vi.   Technical and statistical data

Interrogatories are a good method to identify and obtain technical and statistical data, such as financial statements, accounting information, sales data, and similar information.

vii.   Damages information and insurance coverage

The plaintiff's complaint will often contain only a general request for damages "in excess of $75,000," the minimum jurisdictional amount in diversity cases. Damages interrogatories to the plaintiff are useful for drawing out the specific legal theories of recovery the plaintiff is asserting, the dollar amount claimed for each element of damages, and the basis for each claim.

Since it is vitally important for a plaintiff to determine the defendant's ability to pay a judgment, a standard interrogatory should ask about insurance policies that may cover the event or transactions on which the lawsuit is based, and for the details of the coverage. Rule 26(b)(2) expressly makes this information discoverable. If the pleadings, such as a punitive damages claim, make the defendant's financial condition relevant, this information should also be requested. Defendant, however, will usually object to any discovery of its financial condition or ask that such discovery be stayed until the court has heard and ruled on a summary judgment motion attacking the punitive damages claim. If you suspect that the defendant's insurer may be defending under a reservation of rights, you should try to obtain this information through an interrogatory because this fact will influence how you, and the defense, conduct the litigation.

viii.   Identity of persons who prepared
answers and of sources used

Where interrogatories are served on a corporate party, they should ask for the identity of each person who participated in preparing the answers, and ask for the identity of the documents used to prepare each answer. This information will be important in deciding whom to depose and what documents to request.

ix.   Positions on issues, opinions of fact, and contentions

Interrogatories that ask for "opinions," "contentions relating to facts," or the "application of law to facts" are usually proper. On the other hand, interrogatories that ask for matters of "pure law" are objectionable. The dividing line is unclear, and many discovery motions deal with this problem.[23] Where a pleading is vague, however, a proper interrogatory can prove to be a useful request. For example, it is proper in a negligence action to ask what specific conduct plaintiff claims constituted the negligence, just as in a contract action it is proper to ask what conduct plaintiff claims constituted a breach. Of course, contention interrogatories also have the practical effect of forcing the opposing party to focus on its evidence and strategy.

The court has the power under Rule 33(c) to postpone answering such interrogatories. Accordingly, many lawyers avoid such requests in the initial interrogatories, since it may trigger objections and delay receiving answers to the more basic interrogatories.

Keep in mind that interrogatories, while important, are frequently overused. They are a "low yield" discovery method. Interrogatories take time to prepare and answer, and the answers limit the amount of information disclosed. The amount of information actually produced through interrogatories is frequently low. Therefore, focused interrogatories, which ask only for basic factual data, are usually more effective. Interrogatories should be used in a more selective and focused way: to target the "missing gaps" in the opposing party's initial disclosures or to pin down the opposing party on specific facts that may be used at trial for impeachment if the party that signed the interrogatory testifies inconsistently at trial.

c.   Drafting the interrogatories

The drafting lawyer's principal task is to prepare a set of interrogatories that will successfully elicit the desired information. The questions must be drafted so as to force the answering party to respond to them squarely and to eliminate the possibility of evasive, though superficially responsive, answers. (Always ask yourself: If I received this interrogatory, could I avoid giving a meaningful answer because of the way the interrogatory is worded? If so,

---

23. Moore's Manual §15.09; Manual of Federal Practice §5.137; Moore's Federal Practice §§33.12, 33.17; Wright & Miller §2167.

redraft the interrogatory.) Also, the questions must be organized sequentially to make sure that all desired topics are covered. Basic interrogatories for recurrent types of actions are frequently stored in a law firm's computer data base, making them easy to modify for a specific case. In addition, many jurisdictions have approved pattern or uniform interrogatories which, if appropriate for the case, should be submitted verbatim to the other side. Finally, make sure you do not exceed or violate the requirement that interrogatories served on any party not exceed "25 in number including all discrete subparts."

i.   Headings

An interrogatory, like any court document, must contain a caption showing the court, parties, and civil case number. Further, the interrogatories should include a heading that identifies which party is submitting the interrogatories to which other party. It is also a good practice to label them "First Set," "Second Set," and so on, and to number them sequentially with a later set picking up where the previous set left off. This avoids confusion when references are later made to interrogatories and answers.

Example:

[Caption]

PLAINTIFF JOHNSON'S INTERROGATORIES TO DEFENDANT ACME CORPORATION

(First Set)

Plaintiff Johnson requests that defendant Acme Corporation, through an officer or authorized agent of the corporation, answer the following interrogatories under oath and serve them upon plaintiff within 30 days, pursuant to Rule 33 of the Federal Rules of Civil Procedure:
 1. . . .
 2. . . .
 3. . . .

Example:

[Caption]

PLAINTIFF JOHNSON'S INTERROGATORIES TO DEFENDANT ACME CORPORATION

(Second Set)

Plaintiff Johnson requests that. . . .
 15. . . .
 16. . . .
 17. . . .

Consider using headings for related sections of the interrogatories, such as "parties," "collision," "medical history," "contract," and "damages," particularly in more complex cases. These make the interrogatories easier to understand and answer.

ii.   Definitions and instructions

A common practice in more complex interrogatories is to have the actual interrogatories preceded by a definitions and instructions section. Terms used repeatedly in the interrogatories can be defined, making the interrogatories easier to follow, while deterring evasive answers. Terms commonly defined in interrogatories include "record," "agreement," "document," "electronically stored information," "communication," "witness," "participate," "transaction," "occurrence," "collision," "state," "knowledge," "describe," and "identify." Use broad descriptions of these basic terms so that the answering party cannot give a superficially accurate but effectively unresponsive answer. Make sure the definitions of records and documents includes paper, handwritten, and electronic data.

Example:

DEFINITIONS

The following terms used in these interrogatories have the following meanings:

1. To "identify" means to (a) state a person's full name, home address, business address, and present and past relationship to any party; (b) state the title of any document, who prepared it, when it was prepared, where it is located, and who its custodian is.
2. A "document" means any legal documents, business records, letters, memoranda, notes, work papers, drafts, copies, interoffice and intraoffice communications and messages, drawings, and graphic material, whether created or stored in handwritten, printed, tangible, electronic, mechanical, or electrical form of any kind, including material on computer hard drives, tapes, disks, files, and other memories, backup copies and "deleted" files, whether located on-site or off-site.
3. A "communication" means all oral conversations, discussions, letters, telegrams, memoranda, e-mail, facsimile transmissions, and any other transmission of information in any form, both oral and written.

It is sometimes useful to have an instruction section detail how interrogatories should be answered. Again, it makes the particular interrogatories easier to understand.

Example:

<u>INSTRUCTIONS</u>

In answering each interrogatory:
(a) state whether the answer is within the personal knowledge of the person answering the interrogatory and, if not, identify each person known to have personal knowledge of the answer;
(b) identify each document that was used in any way to formulate the answer.

Finally, in cases where a series of events or transactions is involved, it may be useful to state the time frame the interrogatories are intended to cover.

Example:

Unless expressly stated otherwise, each interrogatory relates to the time period beginning June 1, 2005, through and including the date on which answers to these interrogatories are signed.

Keep in mind, however, that such preambles are useful only in more complex interrogatories. For instance, they are frequently employed in commercial cases. In other cases, such as simple contract or personal injury actions, they are usually unnecessary because they make the interrogatories more complex than they need to be. If interrogatories are drafted in clear, plain English, there should be no need to add definitions and instructions. If the definitions and instructions are too lengthy and detailed, and the case is a relatively simple one, the answering party may object that the interrogatories are unduly burdensome and ask the court to strike the interrogatories and sanction the requesting party.

In addition, keep in mind that clear, simple interrogatories are more likely to yield clear, simple answers that will provide information that is actually useful. This makes the questions and answers much more effective if they are used during trial, such as admissions and impeachment. The more complex the interrogatories, the more complex and less useful the answers are likely to be. Accordingly, it is usually better to err on the side of simplicity.

iii.   Interrogatory style

Interrogatories must be clear and must adequately cover the necessary subjects. The interrogatories are usually drafted as imperatives, not as actual questions, since the imperative form affirmatively requires the answering party to supply information.

The first purpose of interrogatories is to identify parties, witnesses, documents, and experts.

Example (parties and agents):

> 1. State the full name of the defendant, where and when incorporated, where and when licensed to do business, where it has its principal place of business, and all names under which it does business.
>
> 2. Identify each officer and director of the defendant during the time period of June 1, 2005, through the date answers to these interrogatories are signed.
>
> 3. Identify each company, subdivision, and subsidiary in which the defendant has any ownership, control, or interest of any kind for the period referred to in Interrogatory #2 above.

Example (witnesses):

> 1. Identify each person who was present during the execution of the contract that forms the basis of Count I of plaintiff's complaint.
>
> 2. Identify each person who participated in or was present during any of the negotiations of the contract executed by plaintiff and defendant on June 1, 2005.
>
> 3. State the full name and address of each person who witnessed, or claims to have witnessed, the collision between vehicles driven by the plaintiff and defendant occurring on June 1, 2005.
>
> 4. State the full name and address of each person who was present, or claims to have been present, at the scene of the collision during and after the collision, other than the persons identified in Interrogatory #3 above.
>
> 5. State the full name and address of each person who has any knowledge of the facts of the collision, other than those persons already identified in Interrogatories #3 and 4 above.

Note that rather than ask for witnesses in a general way, the interrogatories first focus on witnesses to a particular transaction or event, then expand the scope in subsequent questions to ensure that all possible known witnesses are identified. This organizes the information into useful categories.

Example (documents):

> 1. Identify each document that relates to the shipping of the machinery by plaintiff to defendant on or about June 1, 2005.
>
> 2. Identify each document in your possession and control that refers to the plaintiff's employment termination that is the basis for plaintiff's complaint.
>
> 3. Identify each document that you contend put the defendant on notice of a dangerous condition existing on the roadway at the intersection of Main and Elm Streets on or about June 1, 2005.

A common practice is to combine an interrogatory that asks for the identity of documents and electronically stored information (ESI) with a request to produce all documents and ESI identified in the interrogatory answer. This has the advantage of getting copies of the identified documents and ESI more quickly.[24]

Interrogatories can also obtain information about experts expected to testify at trial. The use of a basic imperative with subsections is recommended.

Example (experts):

> 1. As to each expert expected to testify at trial, state:
>   a. the expert's full name, address, and professional qualifications;
>   b. the subject matter on which the expert is expected to testify;
>   c. the facts and opinions to which the expert is expected to testify; and
>   d. the grounds of each opinion.

However, remember that Rule 26(a)(2) governs disclosure of expert witness information that is substantially broader than what Rule 33 formerly permitted. Hence, expert disclosures, not interrogatories, are the preferred method for obtaining information about the other party's testifying experts. However, in state courts not having expert disclosure rules, interrogatories are still the method for obtaining information about the other parties' experts.

The above interrogatories are all directed toward obtaining the identity of parties and agents, witnesses, documents, and experts, and are a part of almost every interrogatory set. These questions obtain the hard data that will provide the springboard for further investigation and discovery.

Interrogatories should also ask for the specific facts on which the pleadings are based. This is particularly important since, due to the minimal requirements of federal "notice pleading," the pleadings frequently contain general language that gives little information about the facts on which claims, defenses, or damages are based. Interrogatories should develop the basic facts so that the parties can focus on specific facts underlying the legal claims.

Example (facts underlying complaint in personal injury action):

> 1. Describe the personal injuries you received as a result of this occurrence.
> 2. If you were hospitalized as a result of this occurrence, state the name and address of each such hospital or clinic, the

---

24. See §§6.6 and 6.7 on drafting documents requests.

dates of your hospitalization at each facility, and the amount of each facility's bill.

If a single interrogatory asks for several categories of information, it is more effective to set out those categories in lettered subsections. This makes it clear what information you want, and makes it more likely that you will elicit complete answers. Since each subpart relates to the same subject, it should count as a single interrogatory under Rule 33, an important consideration since the rule limits interrogatories to 25 unless more are permitted by court order or written stipulation of the parties.

Example:

> 3. If you were treated by any physicians as a result of this occurrence, state:
>   a.   the name and address of each such physician;
>   b.   each physician's areas of specialty;
>   c.   the dates of each examination, consultation, or appointment; and
>   d.   the amount of each physician's bill.
> 4. If you were unable to work as a result of this occurrence, state:
>   a.   the dates during which you were unable to work;
>   b.   your employers during those dates;
>   c.   the type of work you were unable to do; and
>   d.   the amount of lost wages or income.
> 5. State any other losses or expenses you claim resulted from this occurrence, other than those already stated above.
> 6. During the past 10 years, have you suffered any other personal injuries? If so, state:
>   a.   when, where, and how you were injured;
>   b.   the nature and extent of the injuries;
>   c.   the name and address of each medical facility where you were treated; and
>   d.   each physician by whom you were treated for those injuries.
> 7. During the past 10 years, have you been hospitalized, treated, examined, or tested at any hospital, clinic, or physician's office for any medical condition other than personal injuries? If so, state:
>   a.   the name and address of each such medical facility and physician;
>   b.   the dates such services were provided; and
>   c.   the medical conditions involved.

These kinds of questions serve to systematically discover the facts on which the plaintiff's case is based, and the answers will point to the areas that need to be explored in greater detail.

Finally, interrogatories should be used to identify the facts on which specific claims are based. Complaints commonly allege in general fashion that the defendant "breached the contract" or "negligently operated a motor vehicle." An interrogatory is an effective means of developing the facts that the other party claims support the legal contentions. These are commonly called "contention interrogatories." Keep in mind, however, that such contention interrogatories are frequently objected to on the ground that they are overly broad, so particular care must be used in drafting them. In addition, the court may order that such contention interrogatories need not be answered until a later time, when more facts are known to the answering party.

Examples:

> 1.   State the basis upon which you claim that defendant acted negligently.
> 2.   State the conduct by the plaintiff and any of its officers, employees, or agents that you claim constituted a breach of the contract.
> 3.   Do you contend that Samuel Jones lacked authority to enter into a contract on behalf of the defendant corporation? If so:
>> (a) state each fact on which this contention is based;
>> (b) identify each person having knowledge of each fact;
>> (c) identify each document containing information of each fact.

What are the common problems that arise when drafting interrogatories? Remember that the skill in drafting interrogatories is in finding a clear, simple way to elicit the information you need, and are entitled to get, without making the interrogatories unduly burdensome. A common problem is interrogatories that are overly broad. For example, interrogatories that ask "Identify in detail each and every fact that relates to your claim in Count I," "Identify all documents that relate to your complaint," "State in detail everything you did on May 1, 2005," and "State every fact on which you base your denial that the defendant was negligent" are probably overly broad. The answering party will either object or provide a brief summary of the relevant facts. Remember that interrogatories are effective in obtaining basic information. They are not usually effective in obtaining details of events, descriptions, or mental impressions.

Another common problem is interrogatories that are premature. For example, interrogatories that ask "Identify each witness that you expect to call at trial," and "Identify each exhibit you intend to introduce at trial" are premature. These ask for information that is probably not yet known or has not yet been decided, and is usually disclosed when the pretrial memorandum is due, which is at least 30 days before trial. The answering party will usually object or answer, "Not known at present; investigation continues," or give a partial answer to the extent it can, such as "Other than the plaintiff, plaintiff's employer, and treating physician, plaintiff has not yet determined who her trial witnesses will be."

A third common problem is interrogatories that ask for facts only, rather than also request the identity of documents that contain the facts and persons having knowledge of the facts. For example, an interrogatory that asks "Identify all persons who attended the May 1, 2005, meeting" is proper, but should also be combined with an interrogatory that asks "Identify each record, memorandum, and document of any kind that states the persons who attended the May 1, 2005, meeting." Asking for facts and documents, while obviously overlapping, is the better approach, since you later will want to send a request to produce the documents identified in the interrogatory answer, or combine documents requests with your interrogatories.

Finally, a common problem is interrogatories that are drafted so that the answer can give literally true but misleading answers. For example, asking "Identify each eyewitness to the collision other than the plaintiff and defendant" may get a literally true answer that none are known. A broader interrogatory asking "Identify each person who was at or near the scene during or after the collision" or "Identify each person who has knowledge of the collision" may yield more useful information.

iv. Signing and serving

The interrogatories must be signed by a lawyer and served on every other party. Service is made by any permitted method under Rule 5, most commonly by mailing a copy to the lawyers for the other parties. However, under Rule 5(d) interrogatories are not to be filed with the court until they are used in the proceeding or the court orders otherwise. (This saves space in the clerk's office.)

d. *Responses to interrogatories*

A party must usually answer interrogatories within 30 days of service of the interrogatories. Since they frequently require a substantial amount of work, information necessary to prepare the answers must be obtained reasonably quickly. If the client is out of town and unavailable, or the interrogatories are lengthy, move for additional time to answer. It is usually a good idea to call the opposing lawyer, explain your problem, and ask the lawyer to agree not to oppose your motion for additional time.

i. Researching and preparing answers

A common procedure in answering interrogatories is to send the interrogatories to the client and ask her to respond to the request for information from her own records and from personal recall and to then return the information to you, her lawyer. You then draft the actual answers. After the client reviews the answers for accuracy and completeness, the client must sign the answer and notarize her signature and return it to you. This procedure works well with individual clients. When the interrogatories are complicated, the client and lawyer must work together on preparing the answers.

Corporate parties and other artificial entities, however, present special considerations. First, the lawyer representing the corporation must decide who in the corporation should answer the interrogatories. Ordinarily a corporate officer who has personal knowledge of the transactions involved, or who has knowledge of the corporate record-keeping system, is an appropriate choice. The selection of the person is not as significant as might first appear, however, because although whoever provides the answer will be bound by it, the answer will also be imputed to the corporate party.

Second, the corporate party has an obligation to investigate files, records, and computer systems that are in its possession or control, to collect the requested information, and to put that information in the answer. Records are considered in a party's possession or control if they are records that are kept at the company's offices or in its computer systems, or if they are physically in the possession of another, like an accountant or a storage company, but the party has the power to get the records returned. The corporation's duty to investigate is limited only by the extent of its own records, but there is no duty to conduct an independent outside investigation.[25] A corporate party cannot avoid answering a proper interrogatory through the device of selecting someone to answer the interrogatories who has no personal knowledge of any relevant facts.

Third, under Rule 33(d) a party can answer an interrogatory by specifying the business records and electronically stored information from which the requested information can be derived if the burden of obtaining the desired information from those sources is substantially the same for either party. This is a most useful device, because it avoids "doing the homework" for the requesting party and permits answers to be made more quickly.

ii. Objections

A party on whom interrogatories have been served has two possible responses: an answer or an objection. If the response is an objection, simply state the objection as your answer to a particular interrogatory. All grounds for the objection must be stated "with specificity." If part of an interrogatory is objectionable, the part not objected to must still be answered. There are several bases for objecting.

First, a party may object on the basis that the information sought is irrelevant. However, since the Rule 26(b)(1) definition of relevance for discovery purposes is quite broad, such an objection is difficult to make successfully. In addition, the court can impose sanctions for frivolous objections. Second, a party may object on the ground of privilege, relying on either the privilege for qualified trial preparation materials and absolute mental impressions under Rule 26(b) or on the privileges under

---

25. Moore's Federal Practice §33.07; Wright & Miller §2171.

Rule 501 of the Federal Rules of Evidence. Rule 26(b)(5) requires that a claim of privilege be made expressly and shall describe the nature of the matters claimed to be privileged in a manner that, "without revealing information itself privileged or protected, will enable other parties to assess the applicability of the privilege." Third, an objection can be made to interrogatories that ask for information that cannot be obtained by interrogatories, such as an interrogatory that demands the production of records. Fourth, an objection can be made on the basis that the interrogatory is annoying, embarrassing, oppressive, overly broad, unduly burdensome, and expensive. This is probably the most frequently raised objection, one that has generated a substantial body of case law. Where such an objection is raised, the answering party should also move for a protective order under Rule 26(c).[26] The claim that an interrogatory is unduly burdensome requires under Rule 26(b)(2) that the court balance the burden of collecting the information requested with the benefit to the requesting party. Where the work involved in obtaining the information is enormous and the benefit to the requesting party is small in light of the issues in the case, an objection to the interrogatory should be sustained.[27]

Where an objection exists, it should be made on the interrogatory answer. Draft the objection so that the opposing lawyer (and the judge, if there is a later motion to compel) knows that you are serious and have a well-founded basis for your objection. This will frequently cause the opposing lawyer not to file a motion to compel answers.

The usual practice is to repeat the interrogatory and then state your answer.

Example:

> Interrogatory No. 8: State which officers were involved in the sale of forklift trucks to the XYZ Corporation on August 1, 2005.
>
> Answer: Defendant objects to Interrogatory No. 8 on the ground that it asks for information that is irrelevant because it pertains to a transaction with a nonparty, the XYZ Corporation, that has no relevance to the controversy between the plaintiff and defendant.
>
> Interrogatory No. 9: Identify all conversations between defendant's employees and defendant's corporate counsel between August 1, 2005, and the present date.
>
> Answer: Defendant objects to Interrogatory No. 9 on the ground that it asks for material that is privileged under the attorney-client privilege.
>
> Interrogatory No. 10: Identify all witnesses you have interviewed or from whom you have taken statements.

---

26. See §6.6.1.
27. See Wright & Miller §2174.

Answer: Defendant objects to Interrogatory No. 10. While plaintiff has a right to ask for the identity of all witnesses to the collision, asking for the identity of witnesses interviewed, or from whom statements have been taken, asks for work product of the attorney and is protected from disclosure under Rule 26(b)(3).

If a proper objection exists, consider making the appropriate objection but also answering the interrogatory to the extent appropriate.

Example:

Interrogatory No. 10: Identify all witnesses you have interviewed or from whom you have taken statements.

Answer: Defendant objects to Interrogatory No. 10, since it asks for work product of the attorney and is protected from disclosure under Rule 26(b)(3). However, since an interrogatory asking for the identity of all witnesses to the collision would be proper, defendant in the spirit of cooperation answers as follows:
The only known witnesses to the collision, other than the plaintiff and defendant, are Jennifer Jones, 200 Elm St., Dallas, Texas, and Wilbur Johnson, 400 Maple St., Ft. Worth, Texas.

Answering in this way should not be deemed a waiver of an otherwise proper objection, and again often results in the party not moving to compel answers. If the answer contains any objections, Rule 33 (b) requires that the lawyer making the objections must sign the answer.

iii.   Answers

The other possible response is to answer the interrogatory. There are three basic types of responses.

First, the party can answer the interrogatory by supplying the requested information if it is either known or ascertainable from the party's personal knowledge or records. The answer should be brief, since you ordinarily don't want to volunteer information that has not been requested. On the other hand, you must answer with the essential facts at your disposal, since failing to disclose can subject you to serious sanctions. In addition, if you have a strong case and are looking toward an early settlement, you may want to volunteer information. You need to ask yourself: What message do I want to send to the other side? Full answers say that you have good evidence to support your claims or defenses and that you are confident in the merits of your case. Finally, keep in mind that interrogatories and answers can be used by the opposing party at trial, since a party's answers are admissions or, if the party testifies, can be used as impeachment. The lawyer's task in answering interrogatories is to strike an appropriate balance between the advantages of brevity and a full, detailed answer.

Example:

Interrogatory No. 2: Identify each person who was present during the execution of the contract that forms the basis of Count I of plaintiff's complaint.

Answer: John Marlowe and Phillip Johnson.

Interrogatory No. 3: Identify each physician who treated you as a result of this occurrence.

Answer: Dr. William Jackson, Mercy Hospital, Seattle, Washington; Dr. Erica Olson, 3420 Cascades Highway, Seattle, Washington; possibly other physicians at Mercy Hospital, whose names are unknown; investigation continues.

Interrogatory No. 4: State the name and address of each person who was present or claims to have been present during the collision.

Answer: Mary Jones, 2440 Congress St, Tucson, Arizona; Frank Wilson, 1831 N. Campbell Ave., Tucson, Arizona; Abby Jones, 2440 Congress St., Tucson, Arizona; Jennifer Jones, 2440 Congress St., Tucson, Arizona; in addition, there were several other pedestrians in the vicinity, but the names and addresses of such persons are presently unknown; investigation continues.

Where the interrogatory asks for information on which the answering party has some personal knowledge but not to the detail requested, and no records exist that can supply those details, the answer should accurately reflect this situation.

Example:

Interrogatory No. 6: Identify each communication between John Marlowe and Phillip Johnson that relates to the contract that forms the basis of Count I of plaintiff's complaint.

Answer: There were several telephone conversations between Marlowe and Johnson during a period of approximately four weeks preceding the execution of the contract. The exact dates and substance of each of these conversations are unknown.

This type of answer is satisfactory when the answer cannot state facts that are not within the knowledge or recall of the answering party and no records exist to supply the details. The better practice is to follow up on this type of response through depositions, which allow the extent and details of the party's recall to be explored and developed.

Where an interrogatory asks for a party's contentions, a more complete answer is called for since the answering party does not wish to limit its proof or theories of liability.

Example:

> Interrogatory No. 4: State the basis on which you claim that defendant acted negligently at the time of the collision.

> Answer: Defendant (1) drove in excess of the posted speed limit; (2) drove in excess of a reasonable speed under the existing conditions and circumstances; (3) failed to keep a proper lookout to ensure the safety of others; (4) failed to keep his vehicle in the proper lane; (5) failed to yield the right of way; and (6) failed to obey traffic signals, markers, and "rules of the road." Investigation continues.

In this type of answer the "investigation continues" response is important because additional investigation and discovery may develop additional facts to support the negligence claim.

A second type of response is simply to state "no knowledge" where this is accurate. Keep in mind that an answering party must search his own records to determine if the information exists, and, if it does, use the information to answer the interrogatory.

Example:

> Interrogatory No. 4: State if any witnesses to the collision prepared written reports of any kind regarding the collision.

> Answer: No knowledge of any such reports.

Rule 26(e) imposes a continuing duty to amend interrogatory answers "seasonally" if the answering party learns that its response is "in some material respect incomplete or incorrect" and the "additional or corrective information has not otherwise been made known to the other parties during the discovery process or in writing." A common response in interrogatory answers is to answer based on present knowledge and acknowledge the continuing duty under the rule.

Example:

> Interrogatory No. 2: Identify each person who saw or heard the collision.

> Answer: Other than plaintiff and defendant, none presently known; investigation continues.

> Interrogatory No. 3: Identify each person who was present at or near the collision when it happened, other than the persons already identified in your answer to Interrogatory No. 2.

> Answer: None at present; plaintiff is aware of her continuing duty to supplement responses under Rule 26(e).

The third type of answer is to identify business records and electronically stored information (ESI) that provide the answers. Rule 33 (d) requires only that the answer specify the records and give the requesting party a reasonable opportunity to examine and copy them. Actual production with the interrogatory answer is not required; however, such records and ESI are always discoverable through a request to produce under Rule 34. For this reason, many lawyers simply attach copies of the pertinent documents and ESI as exhibits to the interrogatory answers.

Examples:

> Interrogatory No. 5: Identify each communication between Phillip Johnson and Jane East between June 1, 2005, and August 4, 2005, relating to the contract that forms the basis of Count I of plaintiff's complaint.
>
> Answer: Any such communications are kept in the defendant's telephone logbook, the pertinent dates of which may be examined and copied at a reasonable time at the defendant's place of business.
>
> Interrogatory No. 6: Identify each sales transaction entered into between plaintiff and defendant for the period of January 1, 2005, through August 4, 2005.
>
> Answer: These transactions are recorded on the defendant's Sales Records, which are computerized after sales transactions are completed. A printout of these transactions is attached as Exhibit A.

Interrogatories are frequently coupled with a document request directed to any records and ESI identified in the interrogatory answers.

Example:

> Interrogatory No. 4: If any witnesses to the collision prepared written accounts of any kind regarding the collision, identify each witness and the location of the written account. If your answer to this interrogatory identifies any such written accounts, pursuant to Rule 34 you are hereby requested to make available for copying, within 30 days of service of this interrogatory and documents request, any such written accounts within your possession, custody, and control.
>
> Answer: The only witness known to have prepared a written account of the collision is William Morris, 123 Elm Street, Boston, MA. A copy of his written account is in the possession of plaintiff's attorney, and a copy of which is attached as Exhibit A.

The standard approach in drafting interrogatory answers is to draft the shortest answer that fairly provides the information requested. Keep in mind, however, that, as with all court papers, your answers send messages to your opponent and the court. If your own answers to interrogatories are threadbare, the court will hardly be responsive if you complain that the other side's interrogatory answers are inadequate. Answering interrogatories more fully than expected sends positive signals about your case, signals that you are well prepared, know the facts, and have a winning case.

iv.   Signing, serving, and filing

The format for interrogatory answers, like any other court document, should have the case caption and title of the document. The answers must be signed and sworn to by the party making them. The signature of the party's lawyer does *not* comply with the rule. If any interrogatories are objected to, the attorney must sign as to the objections.

The completed interrogatory answers must then be served on each party. Service is made by any proper method under Rule 5, most commonly by mailing a copy to the lawyers for the other parties. However, under Rule 5(d), interrogatory answers are not to be filed with the court until they are used in the proceeding or the court orders filing. (This saves space in the clerk's office.)

Example:

[Caption]

DEFENDANT ACME CORPORATION'S ANSWERS TO PLAINTIFF'S INTERROGATORIES

Defendant Acme Corporation answers the first set of interrogatories put forth by plaintiff as follows:

Interrogatory No. 1: . . .
Answer: . . .

Acme Corporation

By _____
William Phillips
   Vice President for Administration
   of Acme Corporation

As to the interrogatories to which objections have been made:

By _____
Attorney for defendant

State of Arizona
County of Pima.   SS.

William Phillips, after being first duly sworn, states that he is an officer of Acme Corporation and is authorized to make the above interrogatory answers on behalf of Acme Corporation, that the above answers have been prepared with the assistance of counsel, that the answers are based either on his personal knowledge, the personal knowledge of Acme Corporation employees, or on information obtained from Acme Corporation records, and that the answers are true to the best of his knowledge, information and belief.

_____

William Phillips

Signed and sworn to before me on this _____ day of _____, _____

_____

Notary Public

My commission expires on _____

§6.7. *Requests to produce and subpoenas*

After answers to interrogatories have been received you will usually have enough detailed information to ask for copies of identified documents and electronically stored information not already obtained as part of the other party's initial disclosures under Rule 26(a)(1), through a request to produce. Hence, requests to produce are usually the next step in the discovery process, although requests to produce are also frequently served with interrogatories.

This section discusses the production of documents and things. The next section, §6.8, discusses the new rules that govern the production of "electronically stored information."

1. Law[28]

Requests to produce documents, electronically stored information, and things for inspection and copying and for entry upon land to inspect tangible things are governed by Rule 34. A request to produce can only be served upon parties. The scope of the request, like other discovery, is controlled by Rule 26(b), which permits the discovery of any "matter, not privileged, that is relevant to the claim or defense of any party." The rule expressly requires that the items to be inspected must be set forth with "reasonable particularity."

---

28. Wright §87; James & Hazard §5.5; Friedenthal §7.11; Moore's Manual §15.10; Manual of Federal Practice §§5.161–5.194; Moore's Federal Practice §§34.01–34.22; Wright & Miller §§2201–2218.

Under Rule 34(c), a nonparty's books, documents, electronically stored information, and tangible things can also be subpoenaed for production, inspection, and copying. This process, controlled by Rule 45(a), is discussed later in this section.

Rule 34 permits requests to produce for four things:

1. Documents (including writings, drawings, graphs, charts, photographs, sound recordings, images, and other data or other data compilations) for inspection and copying
2. Electronically stored information (see §6.8)
3. Tangible things for inspection, copying, and testing
4. Entry on land or property for inspection and testing

Of these, production of documents is a principal use of Rule 34 requests. The rule requires a party to produce all documents that are in that party's "possession, custody or control." This obligates a party to produce all relevant documents, even those not in the party's actual possession, if the party has a lawful right to get them from another person or entity.[29] In short, a party cannot avoid production through the simple device of transferring the documents to another person or entity such as the party's lawyer, accountant, insurer, or corporate subsidiary. When this avoidance device is used the party is deemed to have retained "control" of the documents and is required to get them returned in order to comply with the production request. On the other hand, the mere fact that a party *can* obtain documents from a third person or entity usually does not mean that the documents are in the party's control. To hold otherwise would allow a litigant to shift the cost and effort of investigation to the other side.

A request to produce may be served at any time after the parties hold the conference to develop a discovery plan required under Rule 26(f), and must describe each item or category to be produced with "reasonable particularity." This is usually read to require that, in the context of the case and the overall nature of the documents involved, a responding party must reasonably be able to determine what particular documents are called for.[30]

Rule 34 requires that the documents produced for inspection must be produced in either the same order as they are normally kept, or in the order, with labels, that corresponds with the categories of the request. The producing party cannot purposefully disorganize documents and records to make them more difficult to comprehend. The producing party must make the originals available for inspection and copying. Most courts take the view that the producing party has the choice of complying either by producing the records in the same order as they are ordinarily kept, or by producing them in the order that corresponds to the categories of the request; the requesting party cannot insist on the method of complying.

29. Moore's Manual §15.10; Manual of Federal Practice §5.172; Moore's Federal Practice §34.17; Wright & Miller §2210.

30. Moore's Manual §15.10; Manual of Federal Practice §5.168; Moore's Federal Practice §34.07; Wright & Miller §2211.

Some courts, however, take the position that a producing party cannot produce a mass of jumbled documents, even if that is the way they were ordinarily kept; they must be organized in a useful way.[31] Further, the request to produce must specify a "reasonable time, place, and manner" for the inspection. The responding party must serve a written response for each category requested, usually within 30 days of service of the request, stating whether he objects, with reasons for the objection, or will comply.

Note the broad language of Rule 34(a). It provides that a request to produce can be directed to "any designated documents or electronically stored information — including writings, drawings, graphs, charts, photographs, sound recordings, images, and other data or data compilations stored in any medium from which information can be obtained." The terms "documents" and "electronically stored information" collectively encompass information of any kind stored in any medium. And courts usually consider "deleted" documents in computer databases as documents under the rule.[32]

2. Practice approach

a. Timing

Before serving a request to produce documents or a request for entry upon land to inspect, you need to know what documents you want produced and what things you want to inspect. If you have received the other party's initial disclosures under Rule 26(a)(1), you will probably already have copies of some of those documents or descriptions of them. If you have drafted your interrogatories carefully, and have asked for descriptions of relevant documents and for the identity of those persons whose custody those documents are in, answers to the interrogatories should provide sufficient detail to meet the particularity requirement for production requests. Hence, requests to produce should normally be served as soon as possible after the answers to interrogatories have been received.

This timetable presumes that the party has adequately, and in a timely fashion, made initial disclosures and answered your interrogatories. If the answering party has objected, failed to answer, or served evasive or incomplete answers, you must resolve the problems through appropriate discovery motions.[33] Doing this, however, will necessarily delay serving the requests to produce. In this situation you should consider serving a request to produce anyway, since you can ordinarily determine in a general way what documents the other party is likely to have and describe them sufficiently by topic or subject matter to meet the particularity requirement. It is easy for discovery to become sidetracked or to stall completely. In these

31. See Cagan, Rule 34(b): Who's Organizing this Production, 20 Litigation No. 2 (Winter 1994); Moore's Federal Practice, §34.05; Wright & Miller, §2213.

32. See J. Flynn & S. Finkelstein, A Primer on "E-*vide*n.c.e.," 28 Litigation 34 (Winter 2002).

33. See §6.12.

situations you must weigh the benefits and liabilities of waiting or going ahead in light of your overall discovery strategy.

Of course, in some cases you will know what documents you want from the other side and can describe them with reasonable particularity when the parties make their initial disclosures. If that is the case, most lawyers will then serve interrogatories and requests to produce on the opposing party at the same time. This frequently shortens the discovery process by several weeks.

b. *Organization*

Before actually drafting the request to produce, you need to organize your thoughts on what you want from the other party. If you have intelligently thought through your discovery strategy, received initial disclosures, submitted your interrogatories to and received answers from that party, then the bulk of your work is already done. You will know in sufficient detail what documents you want, what documents the answering party admits having, how those documents are described or labeled, and who their custodian is. However, be careful when reviewing the other side's initial disclosures made under Rule 26 since that rule requires the disclosing party to provide a copy or description of only those documents that it "may use to support its claims or defenses." You will need to use the Rule 34 requests to obtain the other relevant documents in the disclosing party's possession, especially those documents that hurt the disclosing party. It is also useful to review your party's records and documents, because this helps you identify what records and documents you will need from the other side.

If you have not yet received interrogatory answers but have decided to send out requests to produce anyway, you will have to evaluate what documents the other party is likely to have, how they are likely to be labeled and organized, and who their custodian is. If this is difficult or impossible to do, you should consider deposing that party at an early date in order to question the deponent about his records. In the case of a corporate party, you should also consider deposing the party's custodian of records. This will help you determine what kind of records the corporation generates and maintains, how they are organized and stored, where they are stored, and who their custodian is, which will help you draft a more focused documents request.

Watch making overly broad requests. Copying, filing, numbering, and indexing documents can be expensive. If the case is a commercial or products liability case large enough to warrant using an electronic litigation support system that stores and cross-indexes the documents, the cost of such a system can be several dollars per document. If you are not sure of the volume of documents you are requesting, use interrogatories or depositions to find out before plunging ahead.

c. *Drafting requests to produce*
i. Heading

A request to produce should be drafted like any other court document. It must have a caption showing the court, case title, and docket number and be properly labeled. Where a case has several parties, it is useful to designate which party is sending the request to which other party; otherwise, the simple title "<u>REQUEST TO PRODUCE</u>" will suffice.

Example:

[Caption]

<u>PLAINTIFF JOHNSON'S REQUEST TO PRODUCE</u>
<u>TO DEFENDANT ACME CORPORATION</u>

Plaintiff Johnson requests defendant Acme Corporation to produce the documents and things listed below, pursuant to Rule 34 of the Federal Rules of Civil Procedure:
1. . . .
2. . . .
3. . . .

ii.   Definitions

Requests to produce present the same problems concerning definitions as interrogatories. Accordingly, terms and phrases frequently used, such as "document," "record," "relating to," "transaction," "communication," and "occurrence," should be defined if the complexity of the case warrants their use. If so, it is best to use definitions identical to those used in the interrogatories.[34]

Example:

<u>DEFINITIONS</u>

The following terms used in this request to produce have the following meanings:
1. A "document" means all writings of any kind, including all handwritten, typed, printed, or otherwise visually produced or recorded materials, whether originals, copies, nonidentical copies, annotated copies, or drafts, in your possession, custody, or control. A "document" includes, but is not limited to, records, reports, studies, contracts, agreements, letters and other correspondence, memoranda, notes, diaries, minutes, notations, drawings, blueprints, sketches, charts, statistics, summaries, bills, invoices, statements, checks, receipts, emails, telegrams, other wire and wireless communications, telephone records, notes and notations of telephone calls, voice mail, instant and text messaging, conversations and other communications,

---

34. See §6.4.

photographs, slides, photographic negatives, microfilm records, movies, videotapes, and published material of any kind. A "document" includes anything which is encompassed by the term "document" as used in the Federal Rules of Civil Procedure.

2. "Electronically stored information" means . . .

Another method is to incorporate by reference definitions already used in interrogatories.

Example:

DEFINITIONS

Plaintiff incorporates by reference each of the definitions in plaintiff's interrogatories previously served on defendant.

Yet another method is to incorporate by reference your opponent's definitions previously used in the opponent's interrogatories or requests to produce. He will be hard pressed to object to your use of his definitions.

Finally, make sure your definitions of records, documents, and the like are sufficiently broad. They should always specifically include handwritten and electronically created and stored records.

iii.   Drafting requests

Rule 34 permits three kinds of requests: to inspect and copy documents and electronically stored information, to inspect and examine tangible things, and to enter upon land to inspect and examine things.

The requests to produce must specify a reasonable date, time, and place for the production or entry. Rule 34 requires only that this be "reasonable," which must necessarily take into account the volume and complexity of the records sought. Since the Rule requires a response within 30 days of service, the date set for the production should be a longer time period.

Example:

A. Plaintiff requests that defendant produce the following documents and electronically stored information for inspection and copying at the offices of Mary Anton, plaintiff's attorney, 200 Main Street, Suite 400, Tucson, Arizona, on August 21, 2005, at 2:00 P.M.:

1. . . .

B. Plaintiff requests that defendant produce the following things for inspection, copying, and testing at the offices of Independent Testing, 2000 Main Street, Tucson, Arizona, on August 22, 2005, at 9:00 A.M.:

1. . . .

C. Plaintiff requests that defendant permit plaintiff to enter defendant's lumber yard located at 4000 Monroe Street, Tucson,

Arizona, for the purpose of inspecting, photographing, and measuring the premises on August 23, 2005, at 2:00 P.M.

Most requests to produce involve documents and electronically stored information. There are several ways to draft requests that will meet Rule 34's particularity requirement.

First, you can use the other party's initial disclosures and interrogatory answers. If those answers have listed and described a variety of documents, referring to the descriptions should be adequate. The responding party will be in a poor position to claim that a description it furnished is now suddenly insufficient.

Example:

1. Each document and electronically stored information identified in defendant's answer to Interrogatory No. 6 in plaintiff's first set of interrogatories.

Second, ask for all documents and electronically stored information that relate to a specific transaction, event, or date. By making the request specific, it should not be challenged on the grounds of being too vague.

Example:

2. All documents and electronically stored information relating to the sale of the property located at 4931 Sunrise St., Tucson, Arizona, entered into between plaintiff and defendant on July 31, 2005.

Third, you can ask for specific types of documents and electronically stored information that relate to a more general time frame or course of conduct.

Example:

3. All bills of lading, invoices, and shipping confirmation notices for all goods shipped from plaintiff to defendant during the period from January 1, 2005, through April 30, 2005.

In each of the above examples, the party responding to the request to admit should not have difficulty in either understanding the request or identifying the documents requested. In contrast, a request calling for the production of "all documents relating to the allegations in plaintiff's complaint," "all documents which support your claim in Count I," or similarly vague language is probably defective and unenforceable since it does not meet Rule 34's reasonable particularity requirement. A request calling for the production of "all documents you intend to introduce at trial" is improperly premature, since you are not required to disclose this information until the pretrial disclosures are due.

It is possible that the responding party will not object to a general request, but, regardless, it is usually not an effective approach for discovery. Requests to produce should balance the safety of inclusiveness with the utility of a more focused request. A request that is too broad may result in a huge volume of paperwork being deposited in your office; you may have neither the time nor assistance to review all of it in order to extract the few documents that are relevant to your case.

Fourth, it is always useful to ask for the identity of any documents that existed at one time but have since been destroyed. This prevents the literally true but misleading response that there are "no records" of the description requested.

Finally, consider sequencing your documents requests to progress from the more specific to the more general. For example, requests might seek (1) all medical records relating to plaintiff's treatment of her knees and all other injuries following the collision; (2) all medical records relating to plaintiff's treatment for any knee conditions before the collision date; (3) all medical records relating to plaintiff's treatment for any orthopedic conditions for a period of five years preceding the collision date; and (4) all medical records relating to plaintiff's treatment for any medical condition for a period of five years preceding the collision date. This strategy often obtains more useful information than does one generally worded request.

iv. Signing and serving

The request to produce should be signed by the lawyer and served on each party. Service is made by any permitted method under Rule 5, most commonly by mailing a copy to the lawyers for the other parties. However, under Rule 5(d), requests to produce are not to be filed with the court until they are used in the proceeding or the court orders otherwise. (This saves space in the clerk's office.)

d. *Common problems*

What are the common problems that arise when drafting documents requests? Remember that the skill in drafting documents requests, like interrogatories, is in finding a clear, simple way to get the documents you need, and are entitled to get, without making the requests overly burdensome and at the same time meeting the rule's "reasonable particularity" requirement.

A common problem is that documents requests are overly broad. For example, a documents request that asks to produce "all records relating to plaintiff's allegation that defendant breached the contract" is overly broad, and does not meet the particularity requirement. The rule requires that the documents be identified, either individually or by category, with sufficient particularity that the responding party can reasonably identify which documents are being requested. A good technique is using the responding party's answers to interrogatories in describing the documents. If the answering party described documents in its interrogatory answers, it will be hard pressed to claim that the same description in documents requests is now insufficient to understand what documents are being sought.

Another common problem is documents requests that do not adequately define what is being sought, so that the responding party can give literally true but evasive responses. For example, asking a party to produce "all documents relating to the board meeting on June 1, 2005" may not get a fruitful response, unless "documents" is broadly defined to include all paper records, handwritten records, handwritten notes, electronic records, correspondence, e-mail, voice mail, and so forth. Documents requests should define commonly used terms such as "records," "documents," and "communications" expansively so that the responding party cannot evade the request.

Another common problem is failing to couple with a documents request an interrogatory asking about records that once existed but have been destroyed, discarded, lost, or sent to another party. Such an interrogatory should ask "If your response to any documents request is that none exist or none are presently in your possession, state whether such documents were ever in existence, where and in whose possession they are now, who prepared the documents, who was custodian of the documents, who made the decision to destroy or send away the documents, when that decision was made, and any other reasons and circumstances why such records no longer exist." Asking about destroyed records through a broadly worded interrogatory is a good way to begin tracking down possible "smoking guns."

Finally, documents requests are sometimes premature. Asking a party to "produce all documents you intend to introduce as exhibits at trial" is premature, since such information is usually disclosed only when the pretrial disclosures are due. Asking for that information now will get either an objection or a response of "not known at present; investigation continues."

e. Responses to requests to produce

A party served with a request to produce usually must respond in writing within 30 days of service of the request. Even though the lawyers for the requesting and responding parties frequently reach an informal agreement on how and when to produce documents and conduct inspections,[35] the responding party should serve and file a written response, since this is required by Rule 34.

i. Researching and preparing responses

If the preliminary investigation has been done, and answers to interrogatories have been prepared and served, you already will have done most of the initial work involved in responding to requests to produce.

---

35. See §6.3.8.

In addition, you should always send the requests to your client and ask the client a couple of questions about the requests. First, does the client know what the requests actually call for? If not, you may want to object on grounds of vagueness. Second, how much effort will be required to collect the documents and electronically stored information requested? If it is substantial and the case is not complex, you may be able to object on the grounds that the requests are unduly burdensome and move for a protective order, or at least for additional time to respond.

When you receive a broadly worded request, particularly when directed to a business, you need to search not only the paper records but also the computer databases. You will probably need to work with employees who operate the business's computer systems to learn how records, e-mail, and the like are created, stored, and retrieved.

After your party has collected the documents and electronically stored information, review the material to determine if all of it is relevant. Make sure that those documents are in fact all the available documents your party has in his possession, custody, or control. You can be sure that your party, and other witnesses, will be questioned about the completeness of the tendered documents during their depositions. Now is the time to review the documents for completeness with your party.

Review the documents collected to see if any are privileged. Since privileges are usually deemed waived unless an objection to their production is timely asserted, this must be done first. The most common privilege is the attorney-client privilege, which protects all confidential communications, relating to the providing of legal services, made between a client (its directors and officers, and certain employees, depending on the breadth of the applicable privilege) and its in-house and outside counsel.

When thousands of documents are involved, it is easy for a privileged document to be overlooked and inadvertently disclosed to the other party. The question then becomes: does inadvertent disclosure waive the privilege? Courts have taken three approaches: (a) always yes; (b) usually no; and (c) it depends on a case-by-case analysis, considering the reasonableness of the precautions taken, the efforts necessary to undo the problem, the scope of the discovery involved, the extent of the disclosed information, and basic fairness. Most courts probably follow the case-by-case approach. The best way to avoid this issue is to prevent it from arising in the first place — by carefully reviewing each document for privileges and then physically segregating the privileged documents from the properly discoverable documents. You can then create a "privilege log" that lists each document and describes it generically (e.g., "letter dated 6/1/05 by Tom Wolfe, CEO of Acme Manufacturing, to Jean Smith, attorney for Acme Manufacturing, regarding contract negotiations"). Such a privilege log will be necessary if disputes arise over whether a particular document is actually privileged and protected from disclosure.

Finally, review the documents collected to see if any contain confidential information. While these will be discoverable if relevant to the claims and defenses, a business has a legitimate interest in keeping certain information confidential, such as financial records, future plans, customer lists, production processes, patented information, and the like. In this situation, you will need to move the court for an appropriate protective order, or at least reach an agreement in writing with the opposing lawyer and party in advance of any disclosures. (In practice, the need for such protective orders is usually discussed and resolved as part of the parties' initial pretrial conference and written report of a discovery plan required under Rule 26(f).)

ii.   Objections

As with interrogatories, a party on whom requests to produce have been served has two possible responses: an answer or an objection. If the response is an objection, there are several possible bases. First, an objection may be made on the ground that the documents sought are irrelevant. However, since Rule 26 has such a broad definition of relevance for discovery purposes, this is a difficult ground on which to prevail. Moreover, this ground will probably have been ruled on if the same objection was made to the interrogatory that asked for the identity of the documents. Second, an objection can be based on a privilege, either the protection for trial preparation materials and mental impressions under Rule 26(b), or the privileges recognized under Rule 501 of the Federal Rules of Evidence. Under Rule 26(b)(5), the privilege must be expressly asserted and "shall describe the nature of the documents, communications, or things not produced or disclosed in a manner that, without revealing information itself privileged or protected, will enable other parties to assess the applicability of the privilege or protection." In practice, lawyers usually prepare a "privilege log" containing a generic description of each document for which a privilege is claimed and the particular privilege being asserted for that document, and a copy of each document. If the requesting party later moves to compel production, the privilege log and accompanying documents can, if necessary, be tendered to the court for an in camera inspection. Third, an objection can be based on the request being annoying, embarrassing, oppressive, or unduly burdensome and expensive. Here the answering party should seek a protective order under Rule 26(c); still, an objection to a request to produce should be made on the response.[36]

Example:

[Caption]

<u>RESPONSE TO PLAINTIFF'S REQUEST TO PRODUCE</u>

Defendant Acme Corporation responds to plaintiff's Request to Produce as follows:

1. Acme objects to plaintiff's Request No. 1 on the ground that it requests documents the disclosure of which would violate the attorney-client privilege, since the request on its face asks for the

---

36. See §6.4.2.

production of "all correspondence from corporate officers to corporate counsel regarding the contract dated July 1, 2005."

Frequently a request may be objectionable in part. Where this is so, the response should make clear what part is being objected to and what the responding party agrees to produce. Such an objection is a common response to a broad request asking for a variety of documents, some of which may be privileged.

Example:

> 2. Acme objects to plaintiff's Request No. 2 to the extent it asks for privileged communications protected by the attorney-client privilege. Plaintiff's Request No. 2 asks for the production of "all memoranda by defendant's subsidiary, Acme Productions, relating to a bid on U.S. Government Contract No. 97-3287, commonly known as the 'Tristar Contract.'" These memoranda include documents prepared by Acme Productions officers and employees, documents prepared at the request of and sent to Acme Corporation's General Counsel, which relate to the pending litigation and are protected from disclosure by the attorney-client privilege. Acme will produce the non-privileged memoranda at the requested time and place.

iii.   Answers

If a request to produce is not objected to, it must be answered. An answer involves two considerations: the formal response, and the practical concerns involved in arranging for the actual production of the documents. There should be a formal answer even if, as is often the case, the production is worked out informally between the attorneys, since Rule 34 requires a written response. In some jurisdictions, the practice is to set out each request with your response (like interrogatory answers); in others the practice is to state only your responses (like the answer to a complaint).

Example:

[Caption]

RESPONSE TO PLAINTIFF'S REQUEST FOR PRODUCTION AND INSPECTION

Defendant Acme Corporation responds to plaintiff's Request for Production and Inspection as follows:

1–8. Acme agrees to produce the documents and electronically stored information requested in plaintiff's Request Nos. 1 through 8 at the offices of plaintiff's attorney on or before August 15, 2005.

9. Acme agrees to permit the inspection of the items described in plaintiff's Request No. 9 at its manufacturing plant

located at 9000 Main St., Tucson, Arizona, at a mutually agreed upon date and time, but not later than August 31, 2005.

_____

Attorney for Defendant Acme Corporation

If the request is for documents that are already in the lawyer's possession, they can be attached to the response.

Example:

3. Acme agrees to produce the contract requested in plaintiff's Request No. 3. A copy is attached to this response.

If records requested do not exist, the response should clearly establish this fact.

Example:

3. There are no documents in the possession, custody, or control of defendant Acme Corporation requested by plaintiff's Request No. 3.

Most requests to produce are worked out informally between the lawyers, who usually call each other and agree on the mechanics of delivering and copying the pertinent records. This will usually include when and where the documents will be produced, how the documents will be organized, and who will perform and pay for the actual copying. The usual procedure is for the documents to be produced at, or delivered to, the requesting attorney's offices on an agreed-upon date. The responding party has the option of producing the records either in the order in which they are ordinarily kept, or labeled to correspond to the categories of the request. Since most production requests overlap on particulars to ensure completeness, a common approach in responding is to produce the documents in their usual order since this is easier for the responding party.

Regarding an informal agreement on the mechanics of reproducing the records, the rule requires only production — not copying — by the responding party. However, it is important for the responding party to make copies so as to retain possession of the original documents. For this reason it is common for the responding party to make copies of the records that comply with the requests and number ("Bates" stamp, a stamped page number, named after the company that makes the devices that stamp consecutive numbers on documents) the pages. The usual rule is that the responding party bears the cost of copying, unless the parties have reached an agreement on how copying costs will be allocated or the court has entered an order allocating production costs. Make sure that the copies you receive are clear and show any handwritten notes legibly; if not, insist on examining the originals. As the lawyer for the answering party, make sure you keep a copy of everything submitted to the opposing side so that no issues arise later over what was actually delivered.

When the documents involved are so voluminous that copying all of them would be prohibitively expensive, a common solution is to have the lawyer for the requesting party review the documents at the offices of either the responding party or the responding party's lawyer. The requesting lawyer can then select the relevant documents for photocopying. The copying is then done by the responding party or a commercial copy service.

Always index, bind, and "Bates" stamp every document you send or receive to create a clear record of what, when, and to or from whom, documents were sent or received. Always make sure you keep a copy of what you have sent to the other parties in the litigation. Disputes frequently arise over whether certain documents were sent or received, and clear, complete records are necessary to resolve these disputes.

iv.   Signing and serving

The response to requests to produce must be signed and served on every other party. Service is made by any permitted method under Rule 5, most commonly by mailing a copy to the lawyers for the other parties. However, under Rule 5(d), responses to requests to produce are not to be filed with the court until they are used in the proceeding or the court orders otherwise. (This saves space in the clerk's office.)

3.   Documents subpoenas to nonparties

Rule 34(c) provides that subpoenas can be issued to command any person "to produce documents and things or to submit to an inspection." Rule 45 provides a vehicle for obtaining documents, electronically stored information, and things directly from nonparties, without also requiring the attendance of the nonparty at a deposition. The subpoena must be issued for the court of the district in which the production will be made. The documents and things sought should be described with the same particularity required of requests to produce. If the subpoena is unreasonable or oppressive, the court can on motion quash it or require that the party issuing the subpoena pay in advance the reasonable cost of complying with the subpoena.

§6.8.   *Electronically Stored Information*

The computer era has changed the way business and personal matters are conducted. Business records, formerly created only on paper, are now routinely created and stored in electronic media, and hard copies are frequently destroyed. E-mail, voice mail, and instant messaging have become important communication methods and often show who knew what and when and what those persons were doing, thinking, and saying. Cellular telephones and pagers record calling information, take photographs, and perform other functions. Personal digital assistants such as Palm and BlackBerry contain appointment calendars, address books, and memo pads. Digital cameras now take photographs that can be stored on computers. The ease, speed, and low cost of saving digital information now permits the warehousing of vast amounts of data. Information no longer in the main computer system may remain on laptop computers and other backup and storage systems.

In today's world, it has become largely unnecessary to print documents, records, and data that have been generated and distributed electronically. Electronic information is both more fragile, because it can be modified and deleted easily, and more durable, because it is usually sent to, copied, and stored in multiple locations and is difficult to erase completely. This explosion of electronic information has changed civil litigation. Consequently, a thorough discovery plan always includes a plan to identify and obtain electronic information from the other parties, as well as a plan to respond to electronic information requests.

1. Law[37]

In December, 2006, the Federal Rules of Civil Procedure were significantly amended to provide a comprehensive set of procedural rules to govern the discovery of a new category: "electronically stored information" (ESI). The principal changes were the following.

Rule 16 — Pretrial conferences; scheduling; management

Rule 16(b) was amended to provide that the judge's pretrial scheduling order, which regulates the discovery process, may include "provisions for disclosure or discovery of electronically stored information," and "any agreements the parties reach for asserting claims of privilege or of protection as trial-preparation material after production."

Rule 26 — General provisions governing discovery; duty of disclosure

Rule 26(f) was amended to provide that the parties' "meet and confer" conference must "discuss any issues relating to preserving discoverable information." In addition, the parties' proposed discovery plan shall include the parties' views and proposals concerning "(3) any issues relating to the disclosure or discovery of electronically stored information, including the form or forms in which it should be produced; (4) any issues relating to claims of privilege or of protection as trial-preparation materials, including — if the parties agree on a procedure to assert such claims after production — whether to ask the court to include their agreement in an order." Form 35, the report of the parties' planning meeting, was also

37. E-Discovery, ABA Section of Litigation, 2007; The Discovery Revolution, George L. Paul & Bruce H. Nearon, ABA (2006); Electronic Evidence and Discovery: What Every Lawyer Should Know, Kristin M. Nimsger & Michele C. S. Lange, ABA (2004).

amended to reflect how the parties propose to handle the discovery of ESI. This amendment, coupled with the amendment to Rule 16(b), effectively forces the parties to discuss ESI and privilege and work-product issues at their Rule 26(f) conference.

Rule 26(b)(2)(B), a new subsection, provides: "(B) A party need not provide discovery of electronically stored information from sources that the party identifies as not reasonably accessible because of undue burden or cost. On motion to compel discovery or for a protective order, the party from whom discovery is sought must show that the information is not reasonably accessible because of undue burden or cost. If that showing is made, the court may nonetheless order discovery from such sources if the requesting party shows good cause, considering the limitations of Rule 26(b)(2)(C). The court may specify conditions for the discovery." This new subsection sets out the procedure to be followed when the responding party claims that the requested ESI is not reasonably accessible.

Rule 26(b)(5)(B), also a new subsection, provides: "(B) If information is produced in discovery that is subject to a claim of privilege or of protection as trial-preparation materials, the party making the claim may notify any party that received the information of the claim and the basis for it. After being notified, a party must promptly return, sequester, or destroy the specified information and any copies it has and may not use or disclose the information until the claim is resolved. A receiving party may promptly present the information to the court under seal for a determination of the claim. If the receiving party disclosed the information before being notified, it must take reasonable steps to retrieve it. The producing party must preserve the information until the claim is resolved." This new subsection sets out the procedure to be followed when privileged information is inadvertently disclosed, provides for the disclosure of privileged materials without waiving the privilege, and provides for the return of such information under certain circumstances. Whether these procedures will preserve privilege against claims of nonparties to this litigation is questionable under current law.

Rule 33 — Interrogatories to parties

Rule 33(d) was amended to provide that an interrogatory answer can specify ESI from which the answer can be derived in the same way that business records can be specified from which the answer can be derived.

Rule 34 — Production of documents, electronically stored information, and things and entry upon land for inspection and other purposes

Rule 34's title was amended to expressly include "Electronically Stored Information." Rule 34(a) was amended to make clear that a documents request can include "electronically stored information" and other data compilations "stored in any medium."

Rule 34(b) was amended to provide that a documents request "may specify the form or forms in which electronically stored information is to be produced." The responding party can object to the request, "including an objection to the requested form or forms for producing electronically stored information. . . . If objection is made to the requested form or forms for producing electronically stored information — or if no form was specified in the request — the responding party must state the form or forms it intends to use." Finally, "unless the parties otherwise agree, or the court otherwise orders . . . if a request does not specify the form or forms for producing electronically stored information, a responding party must produce the information in a form or forms in which it is ordinarily maintained or in a form or forms that are reasonably usable; and a party need not produce the same electronically stored information in more than one form." This amendment sets out the procedure for discovering ESI and the forms in which ESI is to be produced.

Rule 37 — Failure to make disclosure or cooperate in discovery; sanctions

Rule 37(f), a new subsection, provides: "(f) Electronically stored information. Absent exceptional circumstances, a court may not impose sanctions under these rules on a party for failing to provide electronically stored information lost as a result of the routine, good-faith operation of an electronics information system." This new subsection provides for a "safe harbor" for a party losing ESI because of a reasonable ESI destruction program.

Rule 45 — Subpoena

Rule 45 was amended to provide that a subpoena issued to a nonparty "may specify the form or forms in which electronically stored information is to be produced." The amendment makes it clear that nonparties can be compelled to provide ESI and parallels the changes in Rules 26 and 34.

2. Practice

The new discovery rules governing ESI are the most significant changes to the Federal Rules of Civil Procedure since 1993. Lawyers need to familiarize themselves with the rules, understand how courts will apply them, and use that knowledge in their litigation practices. The best way to understand the new rules is to look at the sequential steps the rules require in the litigation process.

a. *Initiate a "litigation hold" with your party and the opposing parties and learn about your party's ESI and key IT personnel.*

Initiating a "litigation hold" on your party is now the first step in the litigation process. There is a duty to preserve information relevant to the claims and defenses raised in the pending or contemplated lawsuit. It is imposed on both the lawyer and the lawyer's party. That duty arises from statutes, ethics rules, and case law. Some statutes, such as the Sarbanes Oxley Act, 18 U.S.C. 1519, impose a duty on corporations to preserve certain records for certain periods of time. Model Rule 3.4 of the Model Rules of Professional Conduct provides that "A lawyer shall not: (a) unlawfully obstruct another party's access to evidence or unlawfully alter, destroy or conceal a document or other material having potential evidentiary value." Modern case law — the leading case is Zubulake v. UBS Warburg, 220 F.R.D. 212 (S.D.N.Y. 2003), commonly referred to as *Zubulake IV* — recognizes the common law obligation to preserve evidence and holds that when a party reasonably anticipates litigation, it has a duty to suspend its documents destruction policies and impose a litigation hold to preserve relevant documents and ESI. This duty to preserve may arise even before a complaint is filed and served. For example, sending a demand letter to a future defendant, filing a discrimination allegation with the employer or the EEOC, or having notice that a company driver was involved in an accident that injured another person, usually trigger the duty to preserve. In short, whenever a party — plaintiff and defendant — first becomes aware of an event or issue that may later lead to litigation, that knowledge triggers the obligation to initiate a litigation hold.

As plaintiff, when you are first brought into the matter and become aware that litigation may follow, you need to impose a litigation hold on your party's relevant information to make sure it is neither altered nor destroyed. The duty to preserve falls first on the lawyer, who is held to know this duty, and then on the lawyer's party, who the lawyer must educate about the duty. This means that you need to meet with your party — in the case of a company, its key officers — and inform the party of what a litigation hold is and why it needs to be imposed immediately. It means you need to advise the company, and in particular its officers and information technology (IT) personnel, about the scope of the contemplated lawsuit, the scope of information relevant to the lawsuit, and ensure that no documents retention policies destroy or alter any relevant information. And it means that you must make sure that key information relevant to the lawsuit is backed up and secured electronically. Finally, document the steps you take to impose a litigation hold on your party's information. This includes sending your party a "litigation hold letter" detailing the party's obligation to preserve information and making sure that your office records detail the steps you have taken to ensure that your party understands and follows the requirements of a litigation hold. Doing anything less may expose you, as well as your party, to spoliation claims and sanctions.

As plaintiff, consider sending the parties you contemplate suing a "preservation letter" that will put those parties on notice of the possible lawsuit. This is particularly important with defendants who are not frequently involved in litigation, who may not be aware of the duty to preserve relevant information, and whose records are important for plaintiff to obtain. If the defendants are corporations or other artificial entities, the letter should be sent to the highest officers of the corporation. Of course, if you know the corporation is represented by counsel, ethics rules require that you send the letter to the general counsel or outside counsel.

A preservation letter will be much more explicit than a typical demand letter. It should set out the possible claims, the key dates, persons, and events involved, the time frame of relevant evidence, and the kinds of documentary and ESI involved. Make sure the letter is reasonable in its requests and tailored to the discovery needs of the lawsuit. A well-crafted preservation letter shows the opposing party that you are professional, knowledgeable, and focused, and a court later is more likely to find that your letter triggered a duty for the opposing party to preserve all relevant information. However, make sure that you do not demand more from the opposing party than you demand of your own party. A good way to do this is to have the preservation letter to the opposing party use the same language as your litigation hold letter to your own party, and use the same language you will later use in your Rule 34 requests.

Example:

> Please take notice that the ABC Company is considering bringing a lawsuit against the XYZ Company based on your failure to perform your obligations under a contract you entered into with the ABC Company on June 1, 2007. A copy of that contract is attached. The claims include breach of contract and fraud, and the time frame of the claims covers the period from approximately January 15, 2007, when the ABC Company first contacted the XYZ Company, to the present date. I represent the ABC Company. Please direct all your future communications about this matter to me.
>
> Federal and state case law both require that a "litigation hold" be put in place when any entity reasonably anticipates becoming involved in litigation. Accordingly, we request the following:
>
> (1) You immediately stop any destruction or alteration of documents or electronically stored information in your possession, custody, or control, including e-mail, instant messaging, voice mail, electronic calendars, telephone logs, photographs, word processing documents, spreadsheets, and databases, including all underlying metadata, that may be relevant to the above described lawsuit, and that you immediately notify your directors, officers, and IT personnel of this legal obligation;
>
> (2) You immediately instruct all employees not to destroy or alter any documents or electronically stored information in their possession, custody, or control, including all notes, memoranda, calendars, e-mails, instant messages, and photographs, that may be contained on laptops, home computers, zip drives, CDs, PDAs, cellular telephones, and other storage media, that may be relevant to the above described lawsuit;
>
> (3) You immediately take steps to secure and preserve any backup tapes, hard drives, CDs, paper and other archival storage media in your possession, custody, or control, including those provided by third-party vendors, that may be relevant to the above described lawsuit.
>
> If you will be represented by a lawyer in this matter, please have your lawyer contact me as soon as possible to make sure that you have complied with the requirements of this litigation hold. If you will be handling this matter yourself, please contact me as soon as possible.

If important information is in the possession of a nonparty, consider sending the nonparty an appropriate preservation letter.

Once the lawsuit is underway, and before the parties' Rule 26(f) conference, consider making a motion for a protective order. The order will be helpful if you later seek sanctions if the opposing party fails to preserve all relevant information.

As defendant, your duty to preserve information also arises when you reasonably anticipate litigation. Sometimes this will happen only when your client is served with a complaint and summons. However, a defendant frequently knows of a current dispute that may lead to future litigation, and the duty to preserve relevant information arises from the time of an event, such as the filing of a grievance against an employer, that triggers the duty.

Regardless of whether you represent plaintiff or defendant, you must learn from your party how its paper records and ESI are generated and stored, what computer hardware, software, storage, and backup systems it uses, what retention policies it has in place, how those retention policies work and whether they are followed, and who the key IT personnel are that make the systems function. You should also learn what ESI is regularly used and is readily obtainable, and what ESI is not readily accessible, and how much time and expense will be involved in locating, retrieving, and reviewing both categories of ESI. This means that you will need to meet with those officers and IT personnel to educate yourself about your party's systems and satisfy yourself that the party's personnel understand and follow the requirements of a litigation hold. This also means that you should put the party's legal obligations and the legal consequences of failing to preserve information in a litigation hold letter and send it to the party's directors, officers, IT personnel, and other employees that have access to the information. It may mean that you will need to obtain copies of the relevant documents and ESI and safeguard them in your office. Remember that you, the lawyer, are responsible for seeing that your party understands and complies with the litigation hold. Some lawyers now include the requirements of a litigation hold in the client engagement letter and have the client specifically agree to follow those requirements.

Consider hiring an experienced technical expert early in the process if you anticipate that the case will involve substantial ESI and the party you represent does not have the appropriate expert. That expert can help on several fronts. First, the expert can help you identify the likely sources of relevant information from the opposing party. If you need to depose the opposing party's IT manager to learn about its computer systems before serving a Rule 34 request, the expert can help you ask the proper questions to get the necessary technical information. Second, the expert can help you draft the technical language of the Rule 34 request that will most accurately describe the information you are trying to get and the systems in which that information typically will be found. Third, the expert can help you organize, encode, and store the information after you receive it. Fourth, the expert can help you access and understand the metadata behind the information without altering the information during the process. Finally, the expert may become a witness in pretrial discovery hearings and a trial witness on chain of custody issues and other technical matters.

   b.   "Meet and confer" under Rule 26(f) with opposing counsel about ESI
      discovery issues, including whether to enter into a "clawback"
      agreement to govern privileged and trial-preparation material.

Rule 26 requires that the parties meet and confer to develop a discovery plan and present that plan during the Rule 16 scheduling conference with the court. This meeting must be held "as soon as practicable" but in any event at least 21 days before the scheduling conference. The court's scheduling order must be issued "within 90 days after the appearance of a defendant and within 120 days after the complaint has been served on a defendant." These time requirements mean that the parties must meet and confer within a few weeks after a defendant has been formally brought into the lawsuit.

The court's scheduling order may include "(5) provisions for disclosure or discovery of electronically stored information" and "(6) any agreements the parties reach for asserting claims of privilege or of protection as trial-preparation materials after production."

As plaintiff or defendant, you need to determine the scope of what you want to discover from the other party. This should include determining the time frame for discoverable information, determining the kinds of ESI involved, and the hardware, software, storage, and backup systems the parties use, and who the key IT personnel are. Remember that the most common dispute is over whether requested ESI discovery is overly broad in terms of time frame and the kinds of ESI sought so that the time and expense of the requested discovery is unreasonable. If both sides during the Rule 26 meet and confer have a candid discussion of their ESI systems, and cooperate in producing relevant ESI, this will go a long way to streamlining discovery and making it less contentious and costly. The meet and confer works best when both parties, such as businesses, have similar ESI and cost issues and mutual interests in seeing that discovery is focused and efficient.

In addition, you need to discuss four things. First, determine if there will be disputes over whether your party's or the opposing party's ESI is "not reasonably accessible because of undue burden or cost." The new discovery rules create two categories of information: ESI that is reasonably accessible is discoverable (if relevant and not privileged); ESI that is not reasonably accessible is not discoverable unless the court rules otherwise. A major issue in many cases will be whether ESI in the possession of the parties as well as third-parties is reasonably accessible and, if not, whether production should nonetheless be required. Making these determinations may require the participation of the parties' IT personnel.

Second, determine if you want to enter into a "clawback" agreement to govern privileged and trial-preparation materials and whether you want the court to include such an agreement in the court's scheduling order. Reviewing documents and ESI for privilege and trial-preparation materials is both time-consuming and expensive, and lawyers have looked for ways to make the process more efficient and less expensive. When documents and ESI number in the hundreds of thousands or millions of documents, a thorough review can be prohibitively expensive, although search software is constantly improving and making such reviews more efficient.

Rule 26(b)(5) controls the procedure for dealing with privileged and trial-preparation materials that have been turned over to the other side during discovery. Under the rule, a party making the claim of privilege must notify any party that received the privileged materials of the claim and the basis for it. The party that received the privileged materials must then "promptly return, sequester, or destroy the specified information and any copies it has and may not use or disclose the information until the claim is resolved." The receiving party may also present the materials to the court for resolution of the claim. In effect, the rule freezes the materials until the court can determine if the privilege claim has merit. However, Rule 26(b)(5) is procedural only; it does not control the question of whether the claim of privilege will be upheld. That is controlled by substantive law, and the law varies depending on the jurisdiction. For that reason, in recent years parties have sometimes entered into agreements on privilege and trial-preparation issues and have asked the court to incorporate such agreements into the pretrial discovery order.

A clawback agreement is an agreement between the parties that if a party inadvertently turns over privileged or trial-preparation documents or ESI, the receiving party will notify the producing party of this fact and will return the documents or ESI promptly and not attempt to use them later as evidence. In addition, the parties agree that the inadvertent production will not be deemed a waiver of the privilege or trial-preparation protection. In this way the parties can turn over large volumes of documents and ESI without waiving their privilege and trial-preparation protection. While such an agreement will make production more efficient and less expensive, it has a downside. A party that has received the other party's privileged and trial-preparation material may gain an advantage because it may learn what the other party is thinking, doing, or planning in the litigation. In addition, there is a serious question whether such an agreement will be enforceable against third parties who later make demands for the same material.

The common law rule on waiver is that any disclosure of privileged or protected material triggers a complete waiver. Some courts follow the strict common law rule. Other courts have adopted a more permissive approach, ruling that a waiver occurs only if the production was grossly negligent. The most common approach is between the two extremes, where courts consider the totality of the circumstances in determining whether a waiver occurs, including the amount of information disclosed, the scope of discovery, the reasonableness of precautionary measures taken to avoid inadvertent disclosure, the amount of time taken to correct the mistake, and fundamental fairness. In this uncertain environment, whether a clawback agreement will be enforceable against third parties is uncertain. Rule 16 provides that the court's scheduling order may include the parties' clawback agreement, but it is uncertain whether such an order makes a clawback agreement enforceable against third parties. (There also is a pending proposal to enact a new Rule 502 to the Federal Rules of Evidence that would make clawback agreements enforceable against third parties in both federal and state courts, but it has not yet been adopted.)

Third, determine the form or forms in which you want the ESI to be produced, and determine if the opposing party will object to those forms.

Determine if you will object to the form or forms in which the opposing party wants your ESI to be produced.

Fourth, determine how long it will realistically take for you and the opposing party to accumulate, Bates stamp, review, copy, and actually turn over the ESI that is discoverable. Remember that in most cases discovery is a two-way street. A party that makes sweeping demands for ESI can expect the other side to do the same thing. Focused requests are usually in both sides' best interests.

After the parties meet and confer about discovery issues, they must present their proposed discovery plan, those matters on which they agree and disagree, to the court. Courts usually require that the parties present their plan in writing sufficiently in advance of the Rule 16 conference that the court has time to review it. Form 35 in the Appendix of Forms to the Federal Rules of Civil Procedure sets forth the format for the report of the parties' planning meeting.

What happens if one of the parties does not participate in a Rule 26(f) conference? This sometimes happens when a defendant has not meaningfully responded to the lawsuit, it is likely that the defendant will not defend against the lawsuit, and ultimately will have a default judgment entered against it. In such a situation, plaintiff should recite those facts in a written discovery plan and present the plan in timely fashion.

> c. *Attend the Rule 16 conference to discuss the parties' discovery plan with the court, and argue for your approach in disputed areas.*

The Rule 16 conference with the court is a key event in the litigation because it will control the discovery process (and other matters set forth in Rule 16(b)), which is usually the most time-consuming and expensive part of the litigation. This makes it imperative that you prepare seriously for the conference. Once the court enters the scheduling order, it controls motions and discovery, and the order cannot be modified without a showing of good cause and the court's agreement.

At the conference, be prepared to explain to the court why the agreed-on matters are reasonable and why the court should adopt the parties' plan. The court will usually accept discovery plans that the parties have agreed on. More importantly, where the parties disagree on discovery issues — most commonly, the time frame and breadth of the ESI search and how to handle privilege issues — be prepared to argue why your position is the more reasonable. You can only do this if you are knowledgeable about your party and the opposing party's claims and defenses, what information will be relevant to those claims and defenses, and the parties' ESI, its hardware and software systems that need to be mined for relevant information.

> d. *Make sure your initial disclosures under Rule 26(a) include required ESI disclosures.*

Amended Rule 26(a)(1)(B) now provides that initial disclosures must include "a copy of, or a description by category and location of, all documents, electronically stored information, and tangible things that are in the possession, custody, or control of the party and that the disclosing party may use to support its claims or defenses, unless solely for impeachment." In short, your initial disclosures now must include your party's ESI relevant to the lawsuit. This puts ESI on the same footing as documents in the initial disclosures.

e. Consider using ESI to answer Rule 33 interrogatories.

Amended Rule 33(d) now provides that a party answering interrogatories can answer by designating ESI from which the answer can be ascertained, provided that the burden of ascertaining the answer is substantially the same for the party serving the interrogatory as for the party served. This puts ESI on the same footing as business records in interrogatory answers.

f. As the requesting party, for your Rule 34 requests to produce and Rule 45 subpoenas, determine the form or forms in which you want the requested ESI to be produced. Consider early interrogatories and depositions of opposing parties' IT personnel to learn details of their ESI systems.

Amended Rules 34 and 45 now expressly include ESI and provide that "the request may specify the form or forms in which electronically stored information is to be produced." This is important, because if you do not specify the form or forms, the "responding party must produce the information in a form or forms in which it is ordinarily maintained or in a form or forms that are reasonably usable." Once the responding party has produced the information in accordance with the rule, a court will hardly be sympathetic to a belated request to have the information produced in another format.

You cannot formulate a sensible Rule 34 request until you know the formats in which the opposing party generates and maintains its ESI. You should have received some useful information during the parties' "meet and confer" under Rule 26(f) and from the opposing party's initial disclosures under Rule 26(a). In addition, your party's IT personnel and the opposing party's former employees (if they can be interviewed under Model Rule 4.2, which depends on how that rule is interpreted in the applicable jurisdiction; see §2.5.1) should be able to give you valuable advice on how the opposing party likely maintains its ESI. In many cases, these sources will be adequate for you to draft focused and technically precise Rule 34 requests that set out the form or forms in which you want the ESI produced.

In other cases, you may need to submit interrogatories to the opposing party and depose the opposing party's key IT personnel to acquire the detailed information about the opposing party's computer systems and how it organizes its ESI before you can draft effective Rule 34 requests. In still other cases, you may need to hire an experienced IT expert early in the litigation to help you draft focused, specific, and technically accurate requests. In short, you must learn how your opposing party generates and maintains each type of electronic information, both on its main computer systems and its backup systems.

What are the options you have in requesting ESI under Rule 34? First, you can still request that if the information exists on paper it be produced in paper form. The advantage is that paper is easy to review and sequentially number using the common Bates stamp. The disadvantage is that paper is cumbersome if the volume is great, and paper gives you only the paper itself, not the underlying information (the metadata). In addition, you cannot use a computer's search capabilities if the information is not in electronic form.

Second, you can request the information in TIFF or PDF images. The advantages are that the images cannot be altered and they can easily be Bates numbered. The disadvantage is that images do not contain metadata, and there can be problems with searching through the data and accessing attachments.

Third, you can request ESI in "native format." Native format refers to the format in which the ESI was created and is maintained. For example, if a business record is created in Word and stored in Word, that is the record's native format. Most of the time you will want ESI produced in native format, particularly when it is based on popularly used software such as Word, WordPerfect, and Excel. Make sure that you also specifically request the metadata, the data underlying the creation of the record. For example, a business record in Word will have metadata that discloses when changes in the record were made, who made the changes, who received copies of the changes, and when these events took place. The disadvantage of native format is that it is difficult to Bates stamp, and the data can easily be altered.

Example:

> Responsive documents that comprise electronically stored information (ESI) are to be produced in the native format in which such responsive documents are ordinarily maintained on an appropriate medium such as CDs or DVDs.

Make sure you also request a copy of the software used to create the ESI if it is not commonly used software. For example, if a party creates spreadsheets using proprietary software, you will need to get not only the data but also the software in order to access and analyze the data.

Finally, always ask for "deleted" and "erased" information, since information no longer on a computer's hard drive may still exist on backup systems or on paper. Always couple the Rule 34 requests with an interrogatory that asks for all relevant information about any deleted or erased information, including when and by whom the information was first created, where it was stored before it was deleted or erased, why it was deleted or erased, who authorized or caused its deletion or erasure, any policies that apply to the deletion and erasure of the information, and whether the information or drafts of the information exist in any form.

Example (interrogatory):

> If any such document or electronically stored information (ESI) was, but is no longer, in your possession, custody, or control, state what disposition was made of it, explain the circumstances surrounding its disposition, the authorization for such disposition, and identify any person or entity now in possession of such document or ESI.

Follow up on the interrogatory answers when you depose the officers, IT personnel, and other employees of the party. The information you pursue and obtain can be the "smoking gun" and may form the basis for a spoliation claim.

The common practice in Rule 34 requests is to define ESI broadly, the same way that "documents" is usually defined broadly.

Example:

> "Electronically stored information" (ESI) includes documents, records, files, memoranda, contracts, agreements, notes, work papers, diagrams, charts, preliminary material, drafts, summaries, calendars, drawings, graphics, e-mail, voice mail, text and instant messaging, and data compilations of any kind, whether in electronic, mechanical, electric, digital, or any other form, and any other information stored on computer systems, hard drives, tapes, disks, backup devices and systems, laptops, PDAs, cellular telephones and pagers, and any other electronic devices and systems, both on-site and off-site, that can store information. ESI includes all metadata and all deleted or erased files on a computer or any other storage device.

Another approach is to be simple, because the term ESI in Rule 34 is intended to be all encompassing.

Example:

> The term "Electronically stored information" (ESI) includes all "documents," as defined above, and all data or data compilations of any kind stored in any medium from which information can be obtained and that are in your possession, custody, or control. The term ESI also includes active data (information readily available and accessible to users), replicate data (clone files created by automatic backup features), archival data (information copied to removable media to provide access to data in the event of a system failure), residual data (information that has been deleted but is still recoverable from a computer system), metadata, and source code to software creating such information. The term ESI also includes anything else that is encompassed by the term "electronically stored information" as used in Rule 34 of the Federal Rules of Civil Procedure.

> g. *As the producing party, determine if you will object to a request or subpoena for ESI on the grounds that (a) the requested ESI is "not reasonably accessible," or (b) the requested form of production is improper and suggest another form.*

When there is no dispute over whether the requested ESI is reasonably accessible (and is relevant and not privileged), it must be produced. However, when you receive a Rule 34 request, you can object, by moving for a protective order, on the ground that the ESI is "not reasonably accessible because of undue burden or cost." A large part of this analysis will necessarily focus on the formats and systems in which the ESI is stored. Active data, such as information that is stored on a computer hard drive, or data that can quickly and easily be retrieved from storage systems such as magnetic tapes or CDs, are usually considered reasonably accessible. Erased and fragmented information, backup tapes, and data in obsolete systems are usually considered not reasonably accessible, because such information cannot be read with current software and must be restored before it is usable. If requested information is not reasonably accessible, it does not mean it is not discoverable; it simply means if the requesting party insists that the information should nevertheless be produced, the producing party has the burden to demonstrate why production should not be compelled.

The producing party can also object to the form or forms of the requested production of ESI and suggest an alternative form. The usual basis for such an objection is that the ESI is reasonably accessible in a certain format but that the requesting party wants the ESI produced in a different format without having a sufficient justification for the request.

Rule 45, governing subpoenas to a nonparty, was amended to parallel the changes to Rule 34. You can send a preservation letter to a nonparty, which will trigger the duty to preserve relevant information. You can meet and confer with the nonparty over discovery issues. You can send the non-party a subpoena that designates the form or forms in which ESI is to be produced. The nonparty can object to an ESI request on the same grounds that a party can object. The nonparty can ask the court to bar discovery because it is overly broad and ask the court to shift some or all of the cost of complying with an ESI request to the requesting party. Courts recognize that discovery of ESI from a nonparty sometimes involves considerable time and expense, and courts under these circumstances are more willing to shift those costs to the requesting party.

> h. *As the requesting party, if the court rules that the requested ESI is not reasonably accessible, be prepared to show that good cause exists to require that the ESI still be produced.*

Whether requested ESI is not reasonably accessible will come before the court if either the requesting party moves to compel production or the producing party moves for a protective order to bar production. Either way, the court will first need to determine if the requested ESI is in fact not reasonably accessible and then, if so, whether the information should nevertheless be produced. This involves a cost-benefit analysis, with the producing party having the burden of showing that the cost exceeds the benefit. On the benefit side, how much information is there that is not obtainable from other sources, and how significant is that information to the litigation? On the cost side, what will be the cost, in terms of time and money, necessary to retrieve the requested information? This conflict frequently arises when a party seeks to obtain the opposing party's e-mails. In this situation the court must compare the likelihood of discovering relevant e-mails against the cost of retrieving the e-mails from backup or archival sources. Courts have sometimes ordered "sampling," where selected databases are examined to determine how much useful information is obtained and the cost of retrieval.

    i. As the producing party, if the court orders discovery of ESI that is not reasonably accessible, be prepared to show that cost-shifting is warranted because the request creates an undue burden or cost.

The traditional view of discovery costs is that the producing party bears the costs of producing the requested information. This is the general rule for paper discovery, and it remains the general rule for ESI. When documents, records, and data are on a computer system's hard drive, they usually can be copied quickly and inexpensively, and that is a reasonable cost that the producing party should bear. Even when the retrieval costs are more substantial, the producing party ordinarily still bears the costs. Many courts take the position that a party cannot reap the benefits of computerization and at the same time use the technology to argue that it should be protected from the costs of searching its computers to comply with a discovery request. Put another way, a party cannot select a storage system and then complain about the costs associated with retrieving data from the storage system it selected.

However, what happens if a Rule 34 request asks for electronic information that does not reside on a computer hard drive or other easily accessible location? What if the information sought cannot be extracted from computerized storage systems without expending substantial time and incurring substantial expense? For example, retailers, banks, and other financial institutions generate vast amounts of transactions data that are warehoused in large storage facilities. Trying to find and copy only certain transactions records from such warehoused data can be a daunting technical task that will involve time, expense, and expertise. As another example, large businesses create large numbers of e-mails on a daily basis, and searching for specific e-mails by subjects, dates, and senders can require extensive effort. If the court determines that the transactions data or e-mails are not reasonably accessible but should nonetheless be produced, the producing party can ask the court to shift some or all of the costs of production onto the requesting party.

In recent years courts have begun to soften the traditional rule that the responding party always bears the costs of complying with a reasonable request for electronic information. When the information sought is unique and not in an easily retrievable form, and the costs of obtaining the information are high, courts have begun to examine such requests more closely and shift the costs of production partly or entirely onto the requesting party. The analysis is essentially a balancing test, balancing the significance of the information sought with the cost of obtaining it.

The most-cited case is Zubulake v. USB Warburg, 217 F.R.D. 309, (S.D.N.Y. 2003), commonly called *Zubulake I*. In *Zubulake I*, involving a documents request for e-mails in a gender discrimination and wrongful retaliation case, the court set forth a seven-part test on cost-shifting, with the most important factor at the top and decreasing in importance:

1. The extent to which a discovery request is specifically tailored to discover relevant information;
2. The availability of such information from other sources;
3. The total cost of production compared to the amount in controversy;
4. The cost of production compared to the parties' available resources;
5. The relative ability of each party to control costs and its incentive to do so;
6. The importance of the issues at stake in the litigation;
7. The relative benefits to the parties of obtaining the information.

Another frequently cited case, Rowe Entertainment v. William Morris Agency, 205 F.R.D. 421 (S.D.N.Y. 2002) uses a similar eight-point analysis.

Note that the cost to the responding party for screening the electronic information for privileged communications is *not* a factor. Courts generally reason that, whether the information is in paper or electronic form, the responding party will still need to screen for privilege, a cost the responding party should bear.

If the court rules that ESI must be produced even though it is not reasonably accessible, and the court shifts some or all of the cost of retrieval on the requesting party, that party must then decide whether to go ahead with the request and pay those costs. If the projected costs are high, and the likelihood of obtaining significant information is low, the requesting party may decide to forgo obtaining this information.

> j. As the requesting party, if the responding party has altered or destroyed ESI after the time that party knew or should have known of its obligation to preserve ESI, determine if Rule 37 sanctions for spoliation are appropriate because the destruction of ESI was not the "result of the routine, good-faith operation of an electronic information system."

"Spoliation" refers to the alteration or destruction of evidence by parties to the litigation. In the computer age, it is easy to delete vast quantities of information quickly, and recovering that information is usually costly, time-consuming, and not always possible. If records are destroyed *before* the party had notice or should have known that particular information may be relevant to a dispute, this does not constitute spoliation. However, once a party has notice, the party has a duty to preserve relevant information. Whenever a party intentionally destroys or alters such information *after* being on notice, such as by shredding paper records, deleting computer records, e-mails, and other data, or erasing backup computer tapes, the party is obviously acting in bad faith, and this constitutes spoliation.

The more common situation occurs when a party has notice and its records are destroyed or altered through inaction or negligence. In today's business world, many businesses have "document retention" policies, which are in reality document destruction policies. What happens if relevant documents, records, or data are destroyed because of such a policy? For example, many businesses have policies in which certain electronic records, such as e-mails, are routinely deleted or overwritten at regular intervals, such as every 30 days. This obviously saves the business money by reusing its storage capacity, but it also means that information relevant to future litigation will be systematically purged.

Courts appear willing to accept selective retention policies for electronic documents to the same extent that such policies have been allowed for paper records. However, the policy must be made in good faith, must be reasonable, and must comply with applicable statutes and regulations. In addition, the policies should provide for an effective means of promptly stopping the destruction or alteration of relevant data when notice of a dispute is received. When a document retention policy is simply a thinly veiled attempt to purge a business of records and data that an opponent would want to discover whenever litigation arises, courts have not been hesitant to find that spoliation of evidence has occurred.

Rule 37 (f) is a new subsection that provides: "Electronically Stored Information. Absent exceptional circumstances, a court may not impose sanctions under these rules on a party for failing to provide electronically stored information lost as a result of the routine, good-faith operation of an electronic information system." This is sometimes called the "safe harbor" provision, but the rule is more limited than that label suggests. Sanctions cannot be imposed for the routine, good-faith destruction of ESI. The emphasis, of course, is on good-faith. A party cannot let its ESI be deleted or altered by inaction when it knows or should have known that the ESI is relevant to actual or reasonably anticipated litigation, because it is not acting in good faith. In such a situation, a party has an affirmative obligation to timely modify or suspend the routine destruction features of its computer systems.

When courts impose sanctions on a party for destroying or failing to prevent the destruction of ESI, they usually focus on three factors: (1) the nature and extent of the destruction, (2) whether the destruction was made in bad faith, and (3) whether the requesting party was significantly prejudiced. Sanctions should be commensurate with the degree of the violation. Courts have imposed sanctions such as fines, awarding attorney's fees, shifting costs, admitting evidence of spoliation during trial, giving the jury during trial an adverse inference instruction, precluding evidence, and entering judgment on a claim or even all claims against the violating party.

k.   As the responding party, if no prior agreement exists, screen your ESI for privileged and confidential information.

Unless you have entered into a clawback agreement with the opposing party, you need to screen all your party's documents and ESI for privilege and trial-preparation materials before turning it over to the requesting party. The usual way this is done is that each paper document or ESI and its underlying metadata is reviewed and, if it is a privileged communication or trial-preparation material, it must be segregated and recorded in a "privilege log." (Today many lawyers and clients label their written communications "Privileged Communication" or "Attorney-client Privileged Materials" so that a word search of a database will quickly identify most of the privileged communications.) The privilege log records the basic information of each document or ESI, such as the date, person who made the communication, the recipients of the communication, and the general nature of the communication (but not in such detail that a waiver occurs). Spreadsheet programs work well for this purpose. The opposing party gets the privilege log, but not the privileged materials. If there is a dispute whether a particular document or ESI is actually privileged, the court usually inspects the disputed material in camera.

Do the same review for confidential information such as trade secrets, customer lists, and financial data, which should be put under a protective order early in the litigation to ensure that the opposing side does not misuse the information or disseminate it to other persons.

l.   The producing and requesting parties must work out the mechanics for producing the discoverable ESI.

Use your party's IT director to identify, locate, and copy the ESI called for in the Rule 34 request. You must search for ESI in every location where it may be stored. Determine whether no ESI exists that complies with a request. If ESI once existed but now no longer exists, find out why it no longer exists.

When you have gathered the ESI that is responsive to the request, you need to work out the mechanics for delivering it to the requesting party. The most common arrangement is to put the ESI, in the form or forms requested, on tapes or CDs and deliver them to the opposing party by the required date. Most lawyers will also create a TIFF or PDF version of the ESI that is Bates numbered and give one copy to the opposing party and keep the other copy. In this way there will be no question what was given to the opposing party. A good practice is to have your written response to the Rule 34 request spell out exactly what you are producing and when and how you are producing it. If the requesting party has requested ESI that does not exist or no longer exists, your written response to the Rule 34 request should spell this out as well.

Consider an agreement under which all the parties agree to deposit all discovery materials into a central depository organized and managed by a professional vendor that specializes in this work. All the lawyers and parties can be given passwords and can then access the central depository from remote locations at any time during the litigation.

§6.9.   *Depositions*

Depositions are usually taken after both interrogatory answers and responses to documents requests have been received, since those answers and documents will usually be necessary to plan an intelligent deposition. Although depositions are both expensive and time consuming, they are essential for assessing witness credibility, learning what witnesses know and don't know, getting details, and pinning witnesses down. They can be used on parties and nonparties, and are the only method in which the opposing counsel does not directly control the responses. For these reasons, depositions play a critical role in the discovery plan of virtually every case.

Rules 27 through 32 govern depositions. Rule 30, which regulates oral depositions, is the principal one, however, since oral depositions are the predominant way in which depositions are taken.[38] Rule 45 controls deposition subpoenas directed to nonparties.

1.   Law[39]

a.   *Timing*

Oral depositions may be taken of any party or nonparty, and can be taken after the parties meet to develop a discovery plan under Rule 26(f). Leave of court is not necessary to take a deposition before the meeting if the deposition notice certifies, and provides supporting facts, that the deponent is expected to leave the country and will thereafter be unavailable for examination. Court approval is required under Rule 30(a) if the person to be deposed is confined in prison.

b.   *Number and length of depositions*

Each side — plaintiffs, defendants, or third-party defendants — has a presumptive limit of 10 depositions. Under Rule 30(a), that number can be enlarged by court order or written stipulation of the parties. This means that when a case has multiple plaintiffs or defendants, the plaintiffs or defendants must get together and decide how to use their 10 depositions most effectively. It also means that the court, under Rule 26(b)(2), will be more actively involved in determining the number and order of depositions. While a deposition is normally considered to be of one person, Rule 30(b)(6) permits a deposition to be directed to corporations and other entities, and the corporation or other entity must designate one or more persons to testify on its behalf. Under these circumstances, a single deposition may be taken of more than one person and still count as one deposition for purposes of the 10-deposition limit.

---

38. Depositions on written questions, governed by Rule 31, are rarely utilized.

39. Wright §84; James & Hazard §5.3; Friedenthal §7.7; Moore's Manual §15.06; Manual of Federal Practice §§5.55–5.117; Moore's Federal Practice §§30.01–30.64; Wright & Miller §§2071–2157; Henry L. Hecht, Effective Depositions, Section of Litigation, ABA, 1997.

Under Rule 30(d), a deposition of a person is limited to one day of seven hours, unless the court orders otherwise or the parties stipulate otherwise. Lunch and other breaks do not count in computing the seven hours. No person can be deposed more than once without court order or written stipulation of the parties. However, Rule 30(d)(2) also provides that "the court must allow additional time consistent with Rule 26(b)(2) if needed for a fair examination of the deponent or if the deponent or another person, or other circumstance, impedes or delays the examination." If you think you need more than seven hours (which should happen rarely), ask the other side in advance to agree to reasonable additional time, or get a court order. Don't assume that you can go past the seven-hour limit and then seek additional time.

c. *Notice*

Whenever a deposition will be taken, the party taking the deposition must give "reasonable" notice to every party to the action. Rule 30(b) does not specify what is reasonable, although some local rules specify minimum requirements, frequently five days. Also, many courts have addressed the question, most finding that reasonable notice is a flexible standard that depends on the nature of the case and the deponent involved.[40]

The notice must state the name and address of each person to be deposed. If the name is not known, the notice must describe the person to be deposed in sufficient detail to identify that person individually or as part of a class or group. This is frequently the case with corporations and other artificial entities, where the actual name of the proper person to be deposed is unknown. In such a case, under Rule 30(b)(6), the corporation or other entity must designate an officer, director, managing agent, or other person to testify on its behalf. The notice must also state the time and place for the deposition.

Notice to a party deponent can be accompanied by a document request that complies with the requirements of Rule 34. A subpoena to a nonparty can also command the nonparty deponent to produce designated materials at the deposition. In this situation, notice to the parties must include a designation of the materials the nonparty deponent has been directed to produce at the deposition. The easy way to do this is to attach a copy of the subpoena to the notices. You should, however, always have the necessary documents of the party or nonparty witness before taking the deposition, unless you plan to catch the party or witness unprepared, before he has had time to collect and review the relevant documents and records.

The notice of deposition must designate how the deposition will be recorded, which includes sound and video recording as well as stenographic means. Any other party can designate by notice other means of recording, each party bearing the cost of its method of recording.

---

40. Wright §84; Moore's Manual §15.06; Manual of Federal Practice §5.82; Moore's Federal Practice §§30.56–30.57; Wright & Miller §2106.

In addition to the notice to other parties, of course, the person to be deposed must also be notified. Where the deponent is also a party, the notice of deposition is sufficient. Where the deponent is a nonparty, he must be subpoenaed in accordance with Rule 45.

Subpoenas can be issued directly by the attorneys as officers of the court. The attorney simply fills out a blank subpoena form issued by the clerk of the appropriate court, or the attorney as an officer of the court can also issue and sign a subpoena on behalf of the court, if authorized to practice law in the court in which the case is pending. The subpoena shall issue from the court for the district in which the deposition is to be taken or the production or inspection is to be made. The subpoena can be served anywhere within the district from which it was issued, within 100 miles of the place of the taking of the deposition or production of documents if outside the district, or anywhere in the state if a state rule allows such subpoena service. If a federal statute provides for it, the court may authorize service of a subpoena in any other place. In short, by permitting attorneys to issue subpoenas directly, the administrative aspects of issuing subpoenas have been substantially eased.

The witness attendance fee and transportation costs must accompany the subpoena. These fees are set by 28 U.S.C. §1821. The common practice is to attach a check to the subpoena for one day's witness attendance fee and the transportation costs incurred by the deponent travelling to and from the place where the deposition is to be held.

If the terms of the notice of deposition or subpoena are unreasonable or oppressive, make your objection known to the other parties. If the dispute cannot be worked out informally, file a motion for a protective order or, if representing a nonparty deponent, move to quash the subpoena or for a protective order.

d. Location

Rule 30 does not specify where a deposition may be conducted. Accordingly, the deposition of a party can be held anywhere. If for some reason the location is unreasonable, the deposed party must seek a protective order under Rule 26(c).[41] The deposition of a nonparty must meet the requirements of Rule 45, discussed above.

e. Persons present

Who may be present at a deposition? The usual persons are the person being deposed, the parties' lawyers, and the court reporter. If the deposition will be videotaped, a videotape operator will also be there.

Parties usually have the right to be present at any deposition, although they infrequently appear. However, if a party's appearance is for an improper purpose, such as intimidation or harassment of a deponent, you must seek a protective order from the court. Nonparties and members

---

41. See §6.12.1.

of the media are usually held to have no right to attend depositions, since a deposition, unlike a trial, is not considered to be a public forum.

f. Recording

Under Rule 28, a deposition must be taken in the presence of someone authorized to administer oaths. Invariably, a certified court reporter who will stenographically record the testimony is also a notary public and therefore able to perform both functions. Rule 30(b)(2) allows the deposition to be recorded by sound, videotape, or stenographically. Rule 30(b)(7) also authorizes depositions to be taken by telephone or "other remote electronic means." While the predominant means of recording remains the court reporter, since this method produces a written transcript, the other methods are being utilized more as ways to reduce costs or to make a more vivid re-creation of the deponent's testimony. These other methods, particularly videotaping, have become a common way of recording experts' depositions when the experts are not expected to testify at trial and their depositions will be introduced in evidence during the trial. Video depositions are also a good idea if the opposing counsel is unduly interfering when you are taking the deposition, such as by repeatedly making objections that serve no proper purpose and are made only to coach the witness on a desirable response.

g. Signing and correcting

There is no requirement that a deposition be transcribed. Under Rule 30(e), the deponent or any party is entitled to a transcript of the deposition. The deponent has the right to review the transcript for accuracy and sign it; and any party may also request that the deponent review and sign, so long as the request is made before the deposition is completed. This is commonly called the "read and sign" right. The deponent has 30 days after receiving notice that the transcript is ready to review it and, if there are any changes, to make and sign a statement noting the changes and the reasons for them. That statement will then be appended to the deposition transcript.

The reporter must certify that the witness was sworn and that the transcript is accurate. The reporter should then seal the original, which should include any exhibits that were marked and used during the deposition, and promptly send it to the lawyer who arranged for the transcript to be made. That lawyer has the obligation to store the transcript "under conditions that will protect it against loss, destruction, tampering, or deterioration." Under Rule 5(d), depositions are not to be filed with the court until they are used in the proceeding or the court orders otherwise. (This saves space in the clerk's office.)

h. Objections

Rule 30(c) provides that the reporter shall note on the deposition all objections to the qualifications of the reporter or other officer, to the procedure, evidence, and conduct of parties, as well as any other objections. The Rule states that testimony objected to shall be "taken subject to the objections," the intent being that the witness should answer the questions asked with all objections being noted. This permits a judge to rule on the objections later, in the event that any party wishes to use the transcript at trial.

Rule 30(d)(1) governs the conduct of attorneys making objections during the deposition. Any objections must be "stated concisely and in a non-argumentative and non-suggestive manner. A person may instruct a deponent not to answer only when necessary to preserve a privilege, to enforce a limitation directed by the court, or to present a motion" to limit or terminate the examination.

Rule 32(d) provides that objections to a witness' competency, or the materiality or relevance of the testimony, need not be made during the taking of the deposition, unless the ground for the objection could have been eliminated if made known at that time. However, objections to the form of questions, and other errors that might have been cured if the objection had been made, are waived unless timely made.

Rule 30 addresses the special problems concerning privilege objections. The usual procedure of requiring answers "subject to the objection" will not work. If the answer is privileged, providing the answer will constitute a waiver of the privilege. Therefore, a timely objection must be made, and if the deponent is represented by a lawyer, the deponent's lawyer can instruct the deponent not to answer pursuant to Rule 30(d)(1).[42] The party taking the deposition then has the option of moving for an order to compel discovery under Rule 37.

If the examination is being conducted in bad faith to annoy, embarrass, or harass the deponent, then a party or the deponent can demand that the deposition be suspended so that the party or deponent can move for a protective order under Rule 30(d) to terminate or limit the examination.

---

42. The problem is more complicated with nonparty witnesses who are not represented by counsel. Can a lawyer for a party make an objection for the witness? Under Model Rule 3.4(f), the usual answer is no. Since a party's lawyer does not represent the witness, the lawyer ordinarily cannot give legal advice to the witness other than recommending that the witness get advice, particularly since the witness may have interests that are, or may be, adverse to the party's. However, there is nothing improper in objecting to a question on behalf of your client; state the basis of your objection, and suggest that the witness talk to a lawyer before answering the question. There is nothing wrong in suggesting to anyone that he ought to talk to his own lawyer and get proper legal advice.

The problem also arises with employees of business entities. The lawyer for the business will usually treat the employee as her client and represent the employee at the employee's deposition. The theory is that since the employee's statements may be admissible at trial as admissions against the business, the lawyer for the business has a right to represent him (unless, of course, the employee is also a party or has his own lawyer). In some situations a former employee may be treated as a client, particularly where the former employee was a management level employee and was involved in acts that are the basis of the lawsuit. See §6.3.9.

i.   Conferring with counsel during the deposition

Can the deponent confer with his lawyer during the deposition? You can confer with your client during the deposition to determine whether to assert a privilege. However, in most jurisdictions you cannot confer with a client while a question is pending (unless a privilege issue is involved). Some courts bar any conferring during a deposition (except for privilege issues) and require that the atmosphere and conduct of the lawyers during a deposition resemble that of a trial. Other courts expressly permit conferring during a deposition, particularly during breaks. Check the local rules, the informal practices of the lawyers, and whether the judge has any standing orders on how depositions are to be conducted.

2.   Practice approach

Deposition rules are sufficiently broad that they rarely restrict the deposition process in any meaningful way. Since the rules permit such latitude, the principal concerns are the practical ones of using depositions effectively as part of your overall discovery strategy. There are several questions that you should always ask.

a.   Should I take a deposition?

Depositions are probably both the most effective discovery vehicle when used properly and the most ineffective one when misused. You should consider the pros and cons of depositions in general and weigh these considerations when deciding if a particular witness should be deposed.

On the plus side, depositions are by far the most effective discovery device for obtaining detailed information, primarily since the deposition is taken in question and answer form, which permits follow-up questioning on promising topics. Depositions allow you to learn the information and where it is, and what this witness knows and doesn't know. Second, a deposition commits the deponent to the details of his story. This will tell you what the witness is going to say at trial, and gives you an opportunity to investigate those facts to see if contrary evidence can be obtained to refute the testimony. Third, the deposition gives you an opportunity to develop specific facts that may be used as admissions and impeachment at trial. Fourth, a deposition is in many respects a trial simulation, so you can evaluate the deponent as a trial witness. Finally, opposing counsel has only limited objection rights, making depositions the only discovery method in which counsel does not prepare the responses.

On the minus side, depositions are expensive. Even a short deposition will cost hundreds of dollars in lawyer's fees, reporter's fees, video operator costs, transcript costs, and possibly the witness' lodging and mileage fees. Where the amount at issue in a dispute is modest, costs are usually the primary reason for limiting the use of depositions. Second, depositions can perpetuate unfavorable testimony. Taking a deposition simply to find out what a witness will say can come at a price, if that witness is unfavorable and later becomes unavailable for trial. Third, a deposition educates your opponents as much as it educates you. Where you believe your opponent will learn more from the deposition than you, or you can get the same information informally such as by having an investigator interview the witness, taking the deposition can be counterproductive. Fourth, taking depositions may motivate an inactive opponent to prepare and pursue discovery. Unless your opponent has been using delaying tactics, motivating an opponent rarely does you any good.

b. *Whose deposition should I take?*

The cost-benefit factors discussed above must be used in deciding which witnesses to depose. In addition, keep in mind that each side under Rule 30(a) cannot take more than 10 depositions, or take a second deposition of a person, without a court order or written stipulation of the parties. There are three basic categories of witnesses you need to consider.

First, the opposing parties should always be deposed. You obviously will want to tie them down to the detailed facts and their versions of disputed events and transactions, and evaluate them as potential witnesses. The only exception might be nominal parties, such as a guardian or administrator of an estate. When the party is an artificial entity like a corporation, the officers and employees directly involved in the transactions and events at issue should be deposed.

Second, consider deposing the principal nonparty witnesses you have identified. In personal injury cases, this would include eyewitnesses to the event involved, as well as witnesses to the major damages elements. In contract and commercial cases, it would include the witnesses to the conversations, agreements, and conduct that are relevant to the transactions involved, and witnesses to any breaches and resulting damages.

The nonparty witnesses category obviously has the potential to be the largest one, and it is here that you need to consider how far to go in keeping with cost-effectiveness. While you obviously need to learn what the testimony of important witnesses will be, there comes a point at which the information obtained from witnesses who are merely corroborative and peripheral is not worth pursuing through depositions.

A good rule of thumb for depositions is that you should depose your opponent's witnesses, not your own, since there is usually no benefit in deposing witnesses you know will be favorable. However, where such a witness is elderly or in poor health, or may leave the jurisdiction and be unavailable for trial, you should always consider taking the witness' deposition to preserve the testimony. Hence, at the beginning of the depositions stage, lawyers will usually depose a favorable witness that is known to have strong testimony in order to guard against disaster. If the witness becomes unavailable, a deposition will usually qualify as former testimony under Rule 804(b)(1) of the Federal Rules of Evidence. If this is your purpose, make sure that the deposition is conducted so that the transcript is clear and complete. Consider taking a videotaped deposition, since this is probably the most effective method of presenting former testimony to a jury.

Third, consider what experts you need to depose.[43] Under Rule 30(b)(4), any party can depose any expert identified as an expert whose opinions may be presented at trial. From the experts' written reports, you will have a substantial amount of information about the other party's experts, including their opinions, bases for the opinions, data relied upon, exhibits to be used, and background information about the witness. In some cases, it may not be essential to depose the other party's expert. For example, in a personal injury case the information you will have from the expert disclosure, medical records, and other information obtained through interrogatories, documents requests, and depositions of other witnesses will sometimes be adequate to know what the plaintiff's treating doctor will say at trial.

In most cases, an expert deposition will be essential. The amount of information you receive about the other party's experts may be inadequate to learn what the witness will say at trial. If the case depends in large part on the relative persuasiveness of the experts, you will need to depose the other party's expert to get a good feel for the kind of witness she will make at trial. The point is that you need not depose every expert in every case. Deposing experts is expensive and time consuming, particularly since under Rule 26(b)(4)(C) the party deposing the expert must pay the expert's reasonable fees, and should be done only when there is a clear need in doing so.

Where the expert is outside the court's jurisdiction and the expert will not come forward voluntarily to testify at trial, the expert will usually be "unavailable" for the purposes of Rule 804(a)(5). Since the expert cannot be compelled to testify at trial, the expert's deposition can be admitted at trial as former testimony under Rule 32 and Rule 804(b)(1). For this reason, the deposition of such an expert should be taken to ensure that the questions and answers will be available for admission at trial. It is particularly important that an "unavailable" expert's testimony be clear and complete. A videotaped deposition should be considered here for this purpose. A video deposition has the advantage of presenting a vivid re-creation of the deponent's testimony to the jury, and is particularly useful where the expert will use exhibits, visual aids, and demonstrations during her testimony. Its disadvantage is that taking the deposition and then editing out objectionable questions and answers is expensive. Nevertheless, a video deposition of an expert, if done carefully, is a vastly superior method of presenting the absent expert's testimony.

Keep in mind that talking a deposition can benefit your opponent as well as you. Once taken, if the witness later becomes unavailable, the deposition probably will qualify for admission at trial under Rule 804(b)(1). Where you suspect this may happen, and the witness is unfavorable, consider taking only a short deposition to learn the basics of what the witness has to say. If the witness is one of your opponent's expert witnesses, and you suspect the expert may be unavailable at trial, consider not asking background qualifications questions. (Of course, nothing will prevent your opponent from asking the qualifications questions.)

---

43. See §6.3.9.

c. When should I take depositions?

Since under Rule 30(a) oral depositions can be taken any time after the parties confer to plan discovery under Rule 26(f), the timing of depositions is determined primarily by tactical considerations.

First, depositions can be taken before an action has been commenced if Rule 27(a) requirements are met. Those requirements are technical and detailed; they include drawing up a verified petition that sets out the facts of the anticipated suit, the details expected from the witness, and the reasons a deposition is necessary. The petition must be served, with a notice of deposition, to each anticipated adverse party that can be found. The amount of work required under Rule 27(a) is at least as much as is required to prepare, file, and serve a complaint and summons. For that reason, Rule 27(a) is ordinarily used only in those circumstances where service on the adverse party cannot be made quickly.

Second, another possibility is to depose your opponent as soon as permitted after the suit has been commenced. This may be necessary in certain situations, such as when you need facts to support a jurisdictional motion, or when you need to learn the identity of proper parties and officers and agents of such parties, or when you want to depose a custodian of records to learn about your opponent's records so that you can prepare a more focused documents request.

An early deposition may also catch your opponent unprepared, not yet having collected and reviewed records and documents, and result in a more useful deposition. The witness may disclaim knowledge of certain facts, or assert facts that can be disproved. These can be used as admissions and for impeachment at trial.

On the other hand, there are obvious risks. Without interrogatory answers and documents received through documents requests, your preparation cannot be nearly as thorough as it should be. Rule 30(a) bars a second deposition of a person without a court order or written stipulation of the parties. If any party objects, you may be prevented from taking a second deposition. In short, taking an early deposition with the idea of taking a second detailed one later involves risks.

Third, the usual approach is to take depositions after initial disclosures, interrogatory answers, and documents have been received. Only then will you have the necessary facts and documents to prepare thoroughly and take the kind of detailed, complete deposition you will want to take. This is particularly important when deposing adverse parties, where the party can only be pinned down when you have the preliminary discovery on hand.

Deciding when to take a deposition can only be done on a case-by-case basis. Your decision must balance the benefits of an early deposition against a later one based on the extent of your knowledge from your pre-filing investigation and existing discovery. The important concept to keep in mind is that the question of when to take a particular deposition should never be a routine matter, but should always be decided by weighing the benefits, disadvantages, and risks of a particular course of action.

d. What order of depositions should I use?

There are several approaches to establishing the order of depositions, and the approach that will be effective in a given case depends on the issues, parties, and witnesses involved.

First, continuing with the concept that discovery should be a building process, a common approach is to depose neutral and unfavorable witnesses first, then adverse employees, officers, and parties to the action, and finally, the adverse parties' experts. Arranging the depositions in this order allows you to use information obtained from witnesses to prepare for depositions of parties to the action and, in turn, the experts. This approach, however, has built-in disadvantages, since every deposition educates both you and the other parties. Every witness deposition you take before taking the adverse party's deposition functions to prepare that party to be deposed.

The second approach, therefore, is to reverse the order and depose adverse parties first, then the nonparty witnesses. This has the advantage of pinning down the adverse parties to detailed testimony before hearing other witnesses, who may have conflicting testimony.

The third possibility is to schedule a series of depositions back to back so that later deponents do not have time to review the transcripts of the earlier depositions. This works well with unfavorable witnesses and adverse parties, who might otherwise try to find out what an earlier witness said and then tell a consistent story. If you see a danger of this happening in a particular case, simply schedule the first deposition for the morning, the second for early afternoon, and so on, allowing enough time so that you can realistically keep to the schedule. For example, when deposing corporate employees, it is often effective to schedule them back to back, starting at the bottom and working up to management. You are more likely to get inconsistencies this way.

As with the decision on when to depose, a decision on the order of depositions can only be made on a case-by-case basis. Deciding on the order should not be a routine matter, but should always involve weighing the advantages, disadvantages, and risks of a particular approach.

e. What must I do to schedule a deposition?

Scheduling a deposition involves two decisions: when and where. When has been discussed above. Where depends on your personal preference and what the Rules allow. Rule 30 does not deal with location, so it leaves the choice up to the party taking the deposition of another party. However, Rule 45 has specific location rules for deposing nonparty witnesses. Such witnesses can be deposed anywhere within the district from which the subpoena was issued, or any place within 100 miles of the place where the subpoena was issued, even if outside the district, or anywhere in the state if a state rule allows such subpoena service. In addition, under Rule 30(b)(7) a deposition can, by court order or written stipulation of the parties, be taken by telephone or other remote electronic means.

The usual location for deposing a party is in your own offices. You will be comfortable there, have your files with you, and have your deponent away from familiar surroundings. If you have previously obtained responses to your documents requests, there should be no need to be at the deponent's place of business.

To depose a distant nonparty witness, you will often have to go to the witness, unless you can get the witness to come to you. While Rule 45 is designed to convenience nonparty witnesses, it can have the effect of inconveniencing everyone else. Therefore, it is usually a good idea to try to have the witness come to you. If, in addition to the mileage and witness fees, you offer to compensate the witness for actual travel expenses and lost wages, the witness may be more likely to come to your offices to be deposed. (If you do this, and most jurisdictions permit it, notify the other lawyers that you are compensating the witness for actual lost wages or time.)

To depose experts, it is frequently better to visit the experts at their offices. It will be convenient for the expert, and you will have access to the expert's reports, records, and reference material. This will avoid what otherwise is a common problem: the expert who, for one reason or another, fails to bring all necessary paperwork, thereby making a thorough deposition impossible. Make sure, however, that you bring everything you need to the expert's office.

Regardless of where the expert will be deposed, make sure you have previously obtained, either from the opposing party or through subpoenas, all records you will need for the deposition. Before deposing a doctor, for example, make sure you have the relevant hospital records as well as the doctor's own medical records. In addition, under Rule 26(b)(4) you must obtain the expert's report from the testifying expert before you can depose the expert. It is simply impossible to take a good deposition of an expert without first obtaining and reviewing all relevant reports.

After you have selected a time and place for the depositions, you must do the following:

1. Send notices to parties
2. Serve subpoenas and witness fees on nonparty witnesses
3. Reserve a suitable room for the deposition
4. Arrange for a court reporter and video operator
5. Reconfirm deposition date and attendance

The notices to parties and subpoenas to witnesses should be served with a reasonable lead time. Given the busy schedules of most people, 20 or 30 days' notice is certainly appropriate. When deposing a party, it is always a good practice to call that party's lawyer and select a mutually convenient time before preparing the notices. This avoids delays, avoids motions to reset deposition dates, and generally helps create good working relationships between lawyers, which benefits everyone. With nonparty witnesses, it is frequently a good idea to serve a subpoena first, and subsequently try to arrange for the witness to travel to your office.

The notices must be sent to every party to the action. If the deposition is for a party, nothing else need be done. If the deposition is for a nonparty, you also must serve a subpoena on that witness which complies with the requirements of Rule 45. Such subpoena forms are usually available from the clerk of the court. The notice must state how the deposition will be recorded. Other parties may choose to record the deposition by other means, at their expense.

Example:

[Caption]

NOTICE OF DEPOSITION

To: *(defendant's attorney)*
Please take notice that I will take the deposition of Rudolf Watson, defendant, before a notary public, or any other authorized officer, on August 30, 2005, at 2:00 P.M., at Room 201, 400 Elm St., Chicago, Illinois, pursuant to Rule 30 of the Federal Rules of Civil Procedure. You are required to have the deponent present at that date, time, and place for oral examination. The deposition will also be recorded by videotape.

_____
Attorney for Plaintiff

If you wish to have the party deponent produce records and documents at the deposition, the notice can be accompanied by a statement directing that certain records and documents be produced at that time. The documents and records must be described with reasonable particularity in compliance with Rule 34. However, the better practice is to get all the necessary records and documents from the party before noticing the party's deposition. It is also a good practice to send a copy of the notice to the court reporter who is scheduled to take the deposition. The subpoena for a nonparty will be on a standard form issued by the appropriate clerk's office. It also can command the production of documents and things at the deposition. Make sure you attach a check for the necessary witness fees.[44]

Example:

[Caption]

SUBPOENA

To: *(name and address of deponent)*
YOU ARE COMMANDED to appear at the place, date, and time specified below to testify at the taking of a deposition in the above case.

Place of deposition _____   *Date and Time* _____

---

44. 28 U.S.C. §§1821 et seq. provides for a daily attendance fee, actual expenses of travel or mileage fee, and a subsistence fee.

YOU ARE COMMANDED to produce and permit inspection and copying of the following documents or objects at the place, date, and time specified below (list documents or objects):

Place _____   *Date and Time* _____

_____   _____
Issuing officer signature and tide   Date
  (indicate if attorney for
  plaintiff or defendant)

Issuing officer's signature and title:

_____

(See Rule 45, FRCP, Parts C & D on Reverse)

After the notice and subpoena have been served, arrange for a suitable room in which to take the deposition. Make sure a court reporter is scheduled and told where and when the deposition will be held. Schedule a videographer if you plan to videotape the deposition. Those who should be present include the deponent, the court reporter, the lawyers for the parties, and perhaps the parties themselves. A conference room or private office in your law office suite is usually the best place to take the deposition. You will be comfortable there and have all your files available. However, if you want to be particularly accommodating to a witness for tactical reasons, use a location convenient for the witness. If the deponent is required to produce documents and you are afraid she will not fully comply, depose her where the records are kept.

Finally, it is always a good idea to reconfirm the deposition with the parties, lawyers, witnesses, and court reporter involved shortly before the deposition date. Rule 30 allows the court to order the deposing party to pay reasonable expenses, including attorney's fees, to the other parties and lawyers if the party giving notice fails to attend the scheduled deposition, or fails to serve a subpoena on a witness and fails to notify the other parties of this fact. Hence, if your conduct causes another party or lawyer to attend a scheduled deposition, and those parties or lawyers were not notified of your failure to subpoena a witness, they are entitled to recover reasonable expenses incurred by attending that deposition. Whenever a scheduled deposition is canceled for any reason, notify everyone entitled to notice immediately.

f. How should I prepare for taking a deposition?

Taking a good deposition obviously requires preparation. You must collect all the documentation that has any bearing on the witness' anticipated testimony, review it, and have copies available for use during the deposition. A copy can be marked by the witness during the deposition, in which case it should be given to the court reporter to attach as an exhibit to the deposition transcript.

This documentation includes all documents and records where the witness is "down on paper" and includes any written or signed statements, oral interviews reduced to writing, police reports in which the witness is mentioned, and records created by or mentioning the witness. If the deponent is a party, this documentation should include the party's pleadings, the party's initial disclosures, interrogatory answers, responses to documents requests, and any affidavits that accompanied motions, since you will probably want to question the party about specific allegations and representations contained in the pleadings and discovery.

When you have reviewed the available material, you should begin to outline how you will take the particular deposition. This depends on several considerations: Is the deponent an adverse party, unfavorable witness, or friendly witness? What information do you need to obtain? What foundations for exhibits do you want to establish? What admissions or impeachment should you try to obtain? Are you taking the deposition only to discover information, or should you take it with an eye toward preserving the witness' testimony for possible later use, such as for a motion to preclude expert testimony, a motion for summary judgment, or for trial? What are the risks involved in deposing this person? These considerations must be evaluated so that you have good answers to the fundamental question you must ask yourself: Why am I taking this deposition?

These considerations affect how you will take a particular deposition. Regardless of your approach, your questioning should be thorough, because a basic purpose for depositions is to find out what the deponent knows. It is usually a good practice to make an outline of your anticipated topics with suitable references to the exhibits you will want to use. While such an outline must obviously be tailored to the facts of each case, certain general topics should usually be explored. There are numerous books available that contain checklists for various types of cases and witnesses. These are useful for considering the types of topics that can be explored and a sensible order for them, but such checklists should never be a substitute for tailoring your outline to the particular deponent.

Example (preliminary matters):

1. Background
   a. Name and address
   b. Personal and family history
   c. Education
   d. Job history
2. Preparation for deposition
   a. Documents witness has seen, at any time
   b. Who witness has talked to, at any time
   c. Any documents or papers witness has with him, other than subpoenaed documents
3. Documents and records
   a. Notice to produce and subpoenas
   b. Record keeping
   c. Records search

      d. Identifying produced records
      e. Identifying any destroyed records
      f. Names and addresses of other persons and entities that may have records related to case
  4. Identity of party
      a. Officers, directors, employees, agents
      b. Parent corporation and subsidiaries, licensees
      c. Incorporation and places of business
      d. Residence
      e. Place where licensed to do business
      f. Names used in business
  5. Witnesses
      a. Names and addresses of persons witnessing events and transactions
      b. Names and addresses of persons deponent has communicated with about case
      c. Names and addresses of persons who may know something about case

These background topics should usually be pursued regardless of the deponent. When the deponent is a party, most of this information should already have been received in the interrogatory answers, but you should have the deponent reconfirm the information and explain them in greater detail where necessary.

On the other hand, these background topics need not be the first matters covered in the deposition. It is often more effective to question the witness first about her personal knowledge, then ask about the background and documents later. In this way you will find out what the witness knows, then find out what the witness can say about the documents. This approach often works well if the case involves numerous documents. This approach also works well with experts, who can be questioned about their opinions first, then the bases for their opinions, and, last, about their professional backgrounds. Keep in mind that depositions are limited to one day of seven hours, which means that you must make sure you get to the important matters quickly.

Once you have organized your preliminary matters, you should outline the substantive areas, which depend on the type of case, legal and factual issues, and the witness' relationship to them. The key to the deposition here is detail. You need to make sure that the outline covers all the topics and is logically organized — usually chronologically — which helps you to be thorough and avoid mistakes. Sometimes, however, it may be useful to vary your topics from a strictly chronological order so that the deponent cannot anticipate questions.

The deposition should extract from the witness what the witness knows that is pertinent to the case. Remind yourself that you usually get only one opportunity to depose a person, so you must be prepared to get the most out of that opportunity.

On the other hand, keep in mind that the basic purpose of any deposition is to learn what the witness knows and did, and what his trial testimony will be. Endless questioning, particularly if repetitive and argumentative, accomplishes nothing positive and only serves to educate the opposing lawyer and witness on what the content and tone of the cross-examination is likely to be at trial. There is a difference between finding out what you need to know, and finding out everything you can possibly know. Good trial lawyers know the difference.

Example (plaintiff in personal injury case):

1. Background questions
   a. (Preliminary matters as outlined previously)
   b. Health history before accident
2. Vehicles involved
   a. Make, year, registration
   b. Insurance
   c. Condition, inspection, repair records
3. Scene of collision
   a. Neighborhood
   b. Roads
   c. Traffic markings and controls
   d. Lighting
4. Weather and road conditions
5. Events before accident
   a. Activities earlier in day
   b. Food, alcohol, drugs, eyeglasses
   c. Physical condition at time
6. Events immediately before collision
   a. Location and direction of vehicles
   b. Passengers
   c. Traffic conditions
   d. Visibility
   e. Other distractions
   f. Where first saw defendant's car
   g. Marking diagrams and photographs
7. Collision
   a. Speed of cars before impact
   b. Traffic signals
   c. Braking and other conduct of plaintiff
   d. Braking and other conduct of defendant
   e. Point of impact
   f. Where cars ended up
   g. Marking diagrams and photographs
8. Events after collision
   a. Bystander activities
   b. Police activities
   c. What plaintiff and defendant did
   d. What plaintiff and defendant said
   e. Plaintiff's and defendant's condition after collision
   f. Ambulance

9. Medical treatment
   a. At hospital — diagnosis and treatment
   b. Doctor's visits after discharge — treatments
   c. Medication, therapy
10. Present physical condition
    a. Any physical limitations
    b. Any mental conditions
    c. Medication
11. Damages
    a. Vehicle
    b. Hospital expenses
    c. Doctor's bills
    d. Lost wages
    e. Insurance payments
    f. Other claimed losses

Example (corporate plaintiff in contract breach case):

1. Background questions
   a. (Preliminary matters as outlined previously)
2. First contact with defendant
   a. Reasons — how came about
   b. Persons involved
3. Course of dealing up to contract
   a. Types of business conducted
   b. Business practices
   c. Specific contracts entered into
   d. Performance history
4. Negotiations leading up to contract
   a. Dates, times, places, participants
   b. All communications
5. Contract execution
   a. Date, time, place, participants
6. Conduct following execution
   a. Performance by each party
7. Breach claimed
   a. When, what
   b. Witnesses
8. Conduct following breach
   a. Attempts to mitigate
9. Damages claimed
   a. Breach damages
   b. Consequential damages

Example (treating physician in personal injury case):

1. Professional background
   a. Education
   b. Internship and residency

      c. Licenses and specialty boards
      d. Description of practice
      e. Experience in type of injury involved here
  2. Physician's medical records and reports
      a. Identify them
      b. Treatises he relies on
      c. Consultations
  3. First contact with plaintiff at hospital
      a. Where and when
      b. History
      c. Symptoms
      d. Examination and findings
      e. Tests
      f. Diagnosis
      g. Treatment
  4. Subsequent contacts with plaintiff
      a. Where and when
      b. Symptoms
      c. Examinations and findings
      d. Tests
      e. Prognosis
  5. Opinions and conclusions
      a. Extent of injuries
      b. Permanence of injuries
      c. Effect on plaintiff
      d. Causation
      e. Why physician disagrees with other experts
  6. Fees
      a. How much
      b. Future fees

   g. How should I prepare to take the deposition of a testifying expert?

Depositions of testifying experts require additional preparation. Under Rule 26(b), you may depose as of right any expert "whose opinions may be presented at trial." However, you may depose the expert only after the expert is disclosed as a testifying expert and has submitted his signed, written report in accordance with Rule 26(a)(2). The written report is due at least 90 days before trial, unless the court orders otherwise, and the report must, under Rule 26(e), be supplemented "at appropriate intervals" if it is incomplete or incorrect in some material respect, and the other parties have not been made known of the additional or corrective information during the discovery process or in writing.

When you subpoena the expert for his deposition under Rule 45, have the subpoena direct the expert to produce his written report, all earlier drafts of his report, all lab and field notes, all data the expert considered in reaching his opinions and conclusions, the expert's engagement agreement with the lawyer, all written communications with the engaging lawyer including letters and e-mails, and all payments received to date.

Most courts hold these are properly discoverable and are not protected by work-product claims. Since these may be voluminous, try to get them from the opposing lawyer before the deposition (but subpoena them for the deposition in any event). In practice, lawyers frequently work out reciprocal agreements, which are often incorporated into the court's pretrial scheduling order under Rule 16.

Talk to other lawyers who have deposed the expert or examined the expert at trial. Obtain transcripts of the expert's depositions and trial testimony. Talk to your own experts and client about the expert. These will give you a better feel for how the expert testifies and conducts himself during a deposition.

Obtain the expert's published books, articles, and speeches. Make sure that the expert's resume accurately details his education, training, employment history, teaching positions and status, licenses, memberships, and honors. Look for gaps in the history that may hide negative events in the expert's past. Research on the Internet can be effective here.

As with any witness, prepare an outline of your anticipated topics with suitable references to the exhibits you plan to use. Most expert depositions will explore the following topics:

Example (testifying expert):

1. Professional background
    a.   Education
    b.   Training
    c.   Job history and experience
    d.   Experience as expert
    e.   Experience as testifying expert
    f.   Any facts *not* on resume
2. Expert engagement
    a.   Date hired
    b.   What told and given by lawyer
    c.   What asked to do
    d.   Any written agreement with lawyer
    e.   All communications of any kind with lawyer
    f.   History of relationship with lawyer
3. Compensation
    a.   Basis of compensation, before and at trial
    b.   Payments received to date
    c.   Expected additional payments in future
4. Subpoena
    a.   Received subpoena with documents request
    b.   Itemize all documents produced
    c.   Any documents not yet produced
    d.   Any documents expert has with him not covered by subpoena
5. What expert did and how he did it
    a.   Tests and studies done — chronology of activities
    b.   Methods used

     c. Equipment used

     d. Others who helped or were consulted

     e. All data considered

     f. All data actually relied on

     g. What other tests could have been done but were not, and why

     h. What reasoning did expert use to go from the facts to his conclusions?

     i. What experience does expert have in doing this analysis?

     j. Has expert written and published articles about this analysis?

     k. Do other experts do the same kind of analysis?

     l. Is this analysis generally accepted by expert's peers?

6. Opinions

     a. All opinions reached

     b. Considering additional opinions

     c. Considering changing or modifying opinions reached

7. Bases for opinions

     a. All bases for each opinion reached

     b. Assumptions made

     c. What facts accepted and rejected

     d. Review opinions and bases with others

     e. Certainty of opinions

     f. Exhibits used as summary or support for opinions

8. Other reasonable opinions

     a. Read other experts' reports

     b. Other experts have different opinions

     c. Any criticisms of other experts' opinions and reasons, and why

     d. If other experts' opinions wrong or inaccurate, how did he analyze and find errors

9. Authorities in field

     a. Literature

     b. Experts — who would you hire

Note that under Rule 26(b)(4)(C) a party taking an expert's deposition is usually required to pay the expert "a reasonable fee for time spent in responding to discovery." The rule clearly applies to the deposition of experts retained as testifying experts. Courts are divided, however, over whether the rule applies to non-retained experts, such as treating physicians, but a growing number of courts hold that non-retained experts should also be compensated for their time when they are deposed.

h. How should I prepare for a Rule 30(b)(6) deposition?

Rule 30(b)(6) has special procedures that govern a deposition notice or subpoena that is directed to a corporation or other organization. This is an important rule, particularly in commercial litigation, because frequently you will not know which specific employee of a corporate party has the information you need to obtain. Rule 30(b)(6) requires that a corporation noticed or subpoenaed under the rule must designate one or more persons to testify as to "matters known or reasonably available to the organization." The persons can be employees or non-employees. The corporation cannot frustrate the deposition by designating a person who has no personal knowledge of the facts. Rather, the person designated must, if he does not know the information requested, get the information by obtaining the relevant documents and records and interviewing the employees who have knowledge of the relevant facts. The deposition of the corporation under this rule counts as one deposition, even if the corporation designates more than one person, and the seven-hour time limit for depositions applies to each person designated. A person deposed as the representative of the corporation under this rule can also be deposed again in his individual capacity.

The significance of Rule 30(b)(6) is that any person deposed under this rule is testifying in a representative capacity and making admissions that will be imputed to the corporation under Federal Rule of Evidence 801(d)(2). This makes it important for both the party taking the deposition and the responding corporation to proceed carefully and plan thoroughly.

Rule 30(b)(6) is a good vehicle to learn, in a corporation or other organization, who knows what, who did what and when, what former employees were involved, what documents and records exist, where these documents are and who made them, and what already obtained documents and records mean. It allows you to develop a blueprint of how the corporation is organized and of how records are generated and maintained, and to identify the key employees who were involved in the events and transactions underlying the lawsuit. It shifts the burden on the corporation to select and educate witnesses who need to acquire the specific information called for in the deposition notice. Accordingly, a deposition under this rule should be taken early in the discovery process since the whole point of the rule is to identify knowledgeable persons and documents early in the litigation. You can then serve more focused interrogatories and documents requests and consider follow-up depositions of key employees.

There are also some advantages in a Rule 30(b)(6) deposition for the corporation. It gets to select the representative witnesses who will appear at the deposition, so the corporation can pick witnesses who will make good impressions. Since the deposition notice must state with reasonable particularity the matters on which the deposition will be conducted, this allows the corporation to learn in advance the topics that will be covered during the deposition and prepare for them. Finally, the scope of the questions during the deposition are limited by the matters stated in the deposition notice, and the corporation can object if the questions to the witnesses go beyond the scope of the notice.

The notice or subpoena for a Rule 30(b)(6) deposition must designate the subject matter with "reasonable particularity." The more focused and detailed the notice, the better. Consider limiting the number of topics and categories of information on the notice. This will make it less likely that the corporation will object on the ground that the notice is unduly broad or burdensome, and more likely that the corporation will designate a person who is actually knowledgeable on those topics. Couple a Rule 34 documents request with the notice for the documents and records you will want at the deposition.

Example:

[Caption]

NOTICE OF RULE 30(B)(6) DEPOSITION

To: Blivitz Oil, Inc., plaintiff,
and its attorney of record:
Dominic Gianna
201 St. Charles Avenue
New Orleans, LA 70170

PLEASE TAKE NOTICE that defendant Luigi Oil Services, Inc., through its counsel, will take the deposition of Blivitz Oil, Inc., upon oral examination pursuant to Federal Rule of Civil Procedure 30(b)(6) as to the matters set forth below. Blivitz Oil, Inc. is required to designate one or more officers, directors, managing agents, or other persons to testify on its behalf who have knowledge of the matters specified below:

1. Blivitz Oil, Inc.'s calculations and substantiation of damages it claims it is due from defendant Luigi Oil Services, Inc., as set forth in Blivitz Oil, Inc.'s complaint.

2. The authenticity of the documents listed on and attached to Exhibit A, attached to this notice.

In accordance with Federal Rule of Civil Procedure 34, you are required to bring with you to the deposition:

1. All documents, records, writings, and calculations of any kind, both electronic and hard copy, evidencing the damages Blivitz Oil, Inc. claims it has sustained as set forth in its complaint.

The deposition will be held on June 1, 2005, at 9:00 A.M., at the offices of Gloria Torres, 123 Main Street, Tucson, AZ 85701, before an officer authorized to take depositions, and continuing until completed.

_____

Gloria Torres
123 Main Street
Tucson, AZ 85701
Attorney for defendant
Luigi Oil Services, Inc.

[Proof of service]

When the deposition notice (or subpoena to a nonparty) is served, the corporation is required to designate one or more appropriate persons to testify on its behalf. Rule 30(b)(6) requires only that the person designated be able to "testify as to matters known or reasonably available to the organization." That person must be knowledgeable as to the matters designated in the notice, but there is no requirement that the person designated is the most knowledgeable person. The corporation can designate an employee, the usual choice, or it can designate another person such as a former employee, so long as that person consents to testify on the corporation's behalf.

The corporation then has the obligation to prepare the designated witness so he can testify as to the collective corporate knowledge on the designated topics. This means that the witness must talk to the relevant employees and must review the relevant documents and records to acquire the necessary knowledge. It is improper and sanctionable for the corporation to designate a person who has little or no personal knowledge and to make no attempt to educate that person as to the collective corporate knowledge, so that the witness will simply say "I don't know" when questioned at the deposition. The corporation has the obligation to bring the designated person up to speed. When preparing that witness, make sure you show him documents and provide him with information that is not privileged since showing the witness privileged communications will probably constitute a waiver of the privilege.

Representing the corporation at the deposition can put the lawyer in an awkward position. As the corporate lawyer, you represent the corporation, not employees of the corporation. Therefore, your duty is to the corporation, not the employee who is appearing as the designated witness. The employee is not your client, and you should treat the employee as an unrepresented person under Model Rule 4.3. This needs to be explained to the employee. Trying to accommodate the employee by "representing" him at the deposition is in essence agreeing to jointly represent both the corporation and the employee, which can create conflicts. If there are any concerns, the employee should have his own lawyer present at the deposition.

When the deposition starts, make it clear that the witness is appearing in a representative, not individual, capacity. This is important because the corporation's collective knowledge is relevant at a Rule 30(b)(6) deposition, and the witness's statements of that corporate knowledge constitute admissions imputed to the corporation (if the witness testified in his individual capacity, his personal knowledge controls).

Depositions under Rule 30(b)(6) raise common problems. First, is the subject matter of the questions asked within the scope of the notice? As noted earlier, the deposition notice should be focused and detailed, but each specific topic should be described in the notice broadly enough so that the corporation will not be able to complain that the deposition questions exceeded the scope of the notice. Second, did the designated witness reasonably prepare for the deposition and get the necessary information to adequately represent the corporate knowledge of the designated topics? Remember that the witness must testify as to "matters known or reasonably available" to the corporation; the witness need not be the most knowledgeable person available. These two issues arise most commonly and, if counsel cannot resolve them, must be motioned up for resolution.

If the corporation fails to comply with the requirements of Rule 30(b)(6), you can ask for Rule 37 sanctions, and you can use the witness's deposition answers as party admissions at trial. These ordinarily operate as significant deterrents, and a corporation trying to shirk its obligations under Rule 30(b)(6) will usually pay a price for its conduct.

i.   How should I prepare for a videotaped deposition?

Rule 30(b) permits videotape depositions as of right, and depositions of lay and expert witnesses by videotape and video-conferencing are increasingly common. Videotaped depositions have benefits and costs. On the plus side, a videotape preserves deposition testimony much more vividly and has much more impact on a jury than a stenographic transcript. This is an important consideration if you plan to introduce the videotape during trial as former testimony under FRE 804(b)(1) or to use the videotape as impeachment with a prior inconsistent statement during trial. In addition, videotaping a deposition usually stops the kind of lawyer misconduct which has been all too common: improperly coaching a witness, making improper objections, and the like. This kind of misconduct will be recorded graphically on videotape. On the minus side, videotaping is expensive, involving a video operator and appropriate equipment, although many lawyers now have their own equipment and trained personnel. However, hiring an experienced professional videographer is usually money well spent.

Preparation for the deposition involves two principal concerns: preparing the setting for the deposition and preparing your party for the deposition. The setting for the videotaping is important, particularly when you want the deponent to look and sound persuasive. The video and sound equipment must be of professional quality. Have a running time and date clock visible on the tape throughout the taping. Decide if you want one or two cameras. If you use only one camera, the usual procedure is to start with a wide-angle shot showing all the participants in the deposition ("orientation shot") and, after the witness is sworn, the camera is brought closer and focuses on the head and upper body of the deponent, or the deponent and the examining lawyer. Watch using only close-ups of the witness, which can get too intense if uninterrupted. This process is repeated after each break. If you use two cameras, one camera can be a close-up of the deponent, the other a close-up of the questioning lawyer or a wide angle of all the participants. The two different shots can then be combined later. You must also work out how the deponent will handle exhibits and conduct any demonstrations. Take close-ups of each exhibit so they can be edited later into the videotape.

The lighting, background, and setting are critical in creating an attractive visual image. The lighting must be adequate to properly illuminate the participants, and should be diffused to avoid harsh shadows, particularly on the deponent's face. The background should be a light, softly textured wall or curtain with warm colors that will highlight the deponent. Avoid visual distractions such as plants, pictures, or windows. The setting should be a courtroom, conference room, or similar setting with a solid, stable chair and table. The deponent should have a wireless (lavaliere) microphone with excellent tone quality, and the lawyers should have a table microphone. An experienced videographer will be familiar with how to create a good visual and sound environment for a videotaped deposition and should be consulted in advance. You will probably also need to work out the logistics with opposing counsel in advance.

What do you do if your client is being deposed and it appears that the opposing lawyer is deliberately setting the stage to make the videotape of your client look bad? For example, if the visual background is distracting or jarring, or the lighting casts dark shadows on your client's face and makes him look sinister, what do you do? First, bring it to the attention of the opposing lawyer and ask him to fix the problem so that the videotape will be fair. Remind the opposing lawyer that Rule 30(b)(4) requires that "the appearance or demeanor of deponents or attorneys shall not be distorted through camera or sound-recording techniques." If that doesn't work, call the judge assigned to the case and explain the situation. If the staging is so unfair that you can credibly contend it is being done "in bad faith or in such manner as unreasonably to annoy, embarrass, or oppress the deponent or party," you can suspend the deposition and move the court for an appropriate protective order.

Preparing your client for a videotaped deposition includes all the steps involved in preparing a witness to testify at trial. The client must understand that in most cases the deposition *is* the trial, and he must look, act, and sound as if he is testifying at trial before a jury. Tell the client he's on stage, and his appearance and nonverbal behavior are key to projecting credibility and sincerity. He must be told how to dress, how to maintain eye contact with either the camera or the questioner, how to project his voice to sound confident, how to avoid long pauses that may suggest uncertainty, and how to control his body movements to develop reinforcing gestures and eliminate distracting mannerisms. This will obviously take time, and rehearsing on videotape is essential.

j. How do I start the deposition?

If all goes well, the parties' lawyers, the court reporter, video operator, and the deponent will all appear at the designated place, date, and time. You should also consider having your client attend, since this will educate the client. This is a particularly good idea when the deponent will testify to conversations and transactions with your client, in which case the deponent is more likely to be truthful and candid when your client is listening to the testimony. After routine introductions have been made, the participants have settled down in the deposition room, the court reporter has set up the stenographic equipment, and the video operator is ready. You are ready to begin the oral deposition. Start by giving the court reporter a copy of a pleading with a complete caption; also, the reporter should be given the correct spelling for the names of all persons present. Then proceed.

First, ask the court reporter to swear in the witness. Some lawyers have the transcript affirmatively show that the witness was sworn.

Second, make sure an introductory statement for the record identifies whose deposition it is, the date and place, and everyone present. Also, the statement should reflect that notice was given, that the deposition is being taken under the Federal Rules of Civil Procedure, and that the witness has been sworn. Rule 30(b) requires that the court reporter put these matters on the record, unless otherwise agreed by the parties. In many jurisdictions the lawyer taking the deposition makes the introductory statement on the record.

Example:

> Q. This is the deposition of the plaintiff, Margaret Singer, being taken in the case of Margaret Singer v. Robert Johnson, Case No. 05 C 483 in the United States District Court for the Northern District of Ohio. It is being held at the law offices of Marlyn Anders, 200 Main Street, Suite 400, Cleveland, Ohio. Today's date is August 15, 2005. Present in addition to Ms. Singer are myself, Marlyn Anders, attorney for defendant Johnson, Sharon Witts, attorney for plaintiff Singer, and Darlene Winters, a certified court reporter and notary public. Ms. Singer, you were just sworn to tell the truth by the court reporter, correct?
>
> A. That's right.

When the deponent is a party, he will usually have been prepared for the deposition, will know what to expect, and will be familiar with the procedure. When the deponent is a nonparty, however, this may not be the case, and it is sometimes worthwhile to explain the deposition procedure and its importance. This prevents a witness from later claiming, if impeached from the transcript, that he was confused or was being pressed by the lawyer.

Example:

> Q. Mr. Johnson, have you ever attended a deposition before?
> A. No.
> Q. Do you know how a deposition works?
> A. Not really.
> Q. Mr. Johnson, I'm going to ask you questions about this accident, and you'll have to answer them under oath. The other lawyers can also ask questions if they want to. Afterward the court reporter will type up everything said here today. That's called a transcript. Do you understand?
> A. Yes.
> Q. It's important that you understand the questions and give accurate answers. If there's anything you don't understand, or anything you don't know or aren't sure of, you let us know, all right?
> A. Yes.

Where the deponent is a party that has also been served with a request to produce, or the deponent is a witness that has been served with a subpoena duces tecum, have the deponent produce the records or documents on the record, even if he voluntarily sent them to you in advance. Identify them for the record, make copies of them and give the court reporter a copy to attach to the transcript, and mark them as exhibits.

Example:

> Q. Ms. Jones, you received a subpoena for certain records of your company along with the subpoena to appear, correct?
> A. Yes.
> Q. Did you comply and bring the records?
> A. Yes.
> Q. May I see them? (Lawyer obtains them from witness.) For the record, the witness has handed me photocopies totaling five pages. The court reporter will mark them Deposition Exhibit A. Page one is an invoice, page two is a bill of lading, page three is a shipping notice, and pages four and five are account ledgers. Each page bears the name of ABC Shipping Company. Ms. Jones, does that accurately describe these five pages?
> A. Yes.
> Q. These are all business records of ABC Shipping?
> A. Yes.
> Q. Did you search the company records for all records relating to the transaction described on the subpoena served on you?
> A. Yes.
> Q. These five pages are the only ones that exist?
> A. Yes.
> Q. Other than these records, does your company make other records for a transaction of this kind?
> A. No.

If you anticipate the need to introduce the records in evidence at trial, it is always a good procedure to qualify the witness as a "custodian or other qualified witness" and establish a business records foundation under Rule 803(6) of the Federal Rules of Evidence. If the witness is a party or agent of the party, the testimony will qualify as an admission; if a nonparty, the testimony should qualify as former testimony if the witness is unavailable at trial.

When you are examining the witness about documents, make sure that you have a good exhibit marking system when the depositions will involve numerous documents. Practices vary. For example, plaintiff may use numbers 1 to 300; defendant may use numbers 301 to 600. In this way, all deposition documents will be marked "Deposition exhibit no. _____ ." In some jurisdictions, the practice is for each side to designate its own deposition exhibits. For example, plaintiff will call its exhibits "Plaintiff deposition exhibit no. _____," the defense "Defendant deposition exhibit no. _____." Still others designate exhibits by the witness name.

For example, if a Shirley Williams is being deposed, the exhibits will be called "Williams exhibit no. _____ ." In other jurisdictions, the exhibits are only marked as "Exhibit no. _____ ," so that the same exhibit number will be used when the case is tried. The key concept is to have clarity in the marking system. You can then use the witness to establish the legal foundation for admissibility at trial for particular deposition exhibits. At the end of the deposition, make sure the court reporter has all the marked exhibits, which will later be attached to the deposition transcript.

Example:

> Q. Ms. Williams, you work for the defendant, the ABC Corporation?
> A. Yes.
> Q. You're the secretary to ABC's president, Mr. Greenberg?
> A. Yes.
> Q. You've been working for ABC and Mr. Greenberg since 2000?
> A. Yes.
> Q. Ms. Williams, you've seen Mr. Greenberg write his signature before, right?
> A. Of course.
> Q. About how many times?
> A. Certainly hundreds of times, maybe thousands.
> Q. And you've seen him write things out in longhand, right?
> A. Certainly.
> Q. Ms. Williams, I'm showing you a check which has been marked "Plaintiff's deposition exhibit no. 7." It's dated June 1, 2005, and is filled out by hand. Take a look at it.
> A. All right.
> Q. Have you seen that check before?
> A. I don't think so.
> Q. But you recognize the signature in the lower right hand corner of the check, right?
> A. Sure. That's Mr. Greenberg's signature.
> Q. Any doubt about that?
> A. No. I know Mr. Greenberg's signature. That's his.
> Q. Look at the rest of the face of the check. Is that also Mr. Greenberg's handwriting?
> A. Yes. It's all filled out by him.

Finally, good practice requires that you put any stipulations on the record and state expressly what they are. Parties frequently deal with the status of objections, sometimes stipulating that all objections are preserved or that all objections are preserved except those directed to the form of the question. This can be useful because it eliminates the need to make most objections during the deposition, allowing for a much clearer and shorter transcript. Objections can then be raised later if the transcript will be used during trial. However, agreeing to the "usual stipulations" is bad practice and should be avoided, particularly when you are outside your usual practice area. Find out what the usual stipulations are, and then decide whether to agree with them.

k. *What questioning styles should I use?*

The questioning style you employ during the deposition must be consistent with your purposes. Are you taking the deposition primarily to gather information from a witness? Are you taking a party's deposition to pin the party down on details, to obtain admissions, and to develop impeachment? Are you deposing a favorable witness to preserve the witness' testimony in the event he becomes unavailable for trial? The different purposes will affect how you conduct the deposition.[45]

Regardless of your purposes, you should always keep two concerns uppermost in your mind: Have I clearly and unambiguously stated questions and received answers? How will this sound if it is read to a jury during trial? Find out if the court reporter is using a real-time reporting system, where the questions and answers appear on a computer screen almost immediately. If you can tie into this system, you will be able to see your questions and the witness' answers and determine immediately if they are clear and usable as admissions or impeachment at trial. If not, you can rephrase and clarify as necessary.

i. Getting information

In many depositions your goal is to gather information that will support your theory of the case, support your story of what really happened, and prove the elements of your claims or defenses. When your principal goal during the deposition is to gather information, it is frequently a good approach to let the witness ramble on rather than control the witness with narrow, focused questions. Pause after the witness answers, in case the witness wants to provide additional information. You are more likely to have the witness volunteer useful information if you ask broad questions in a friendly, informal way. The "who, what, where, when, how, and why" questions work well here. You can always steer the witness to the topics that need to be covered and use follow-up questions to tie down the details. What is sometimes called the "funnel" approach works well here: For each topic, begin with an introductory question, follow that with a series of open-ended questions that draw everything possible out of the witness, and then recapitulate and summarize what the witness has just told you. Then move to the next topic. Whether the questions and answers violate evidentiary rules, such as leading or hearsay, is unimportant, if your only goal is to get information.

45. The actual questioning techniques for examining a deponent are much the same, and as varied, as conducting direct and cross-examinations of witnesses at trial. For a discussion of these techniques, see, e.g., T. Mauet, Trials (2005); P. Bergman, Trial Advocacy in a Nutshell (3d ed. 1997); J. Jeans, Handbook on Trial Advocacy (2d ed. 1993).

Just as important as finding out what the witness knows is finding out what the witness does *not* know or has no firsthand knowledge about. This will prevent the witness from adding to his testimony at trial, since you will be able to impeach the witness on these new points. If the witness says he doesn't know or doesn't remember and you want the information, use follow-up questions. Ask: Has he forgotten or doesn't know? Who does know? Where is the information? What would help the witness remember? Who has the witness talked to about the information? Where would you look? Who would you ask?

Find out what materials the witness reviewed to prepare for his testimony. Under FRE 612, if a witness used records and documents to refresh his recollection "before testifying," the adverse party may be entitled to see those records and documents. Most courts have held that this right trumps the lawyer's work-product doctrine, and some courts have held that this right prevails over claims that the records and documents are protected by a privilege.[46]

ii.   Eliciting detail and pinning down specific facts

When deposing an adverse party, you usually have dual purposes: finding out what the party knows in detail, and pinning the party down to specific, hopefully useful, facts. Ask open, nonleading questions to try to get the deponent to talk and to fully detail what he knows. Actively listen to the witness and use follow-up questions. Look and listen for verbal and nonverbal cues that you are probing in sensitive areas. If the opposing lawyer has done his homework, of course, the party will be loathe to volunteer information not specifically asked for. However, it is always good to use this approach since even a well-prepared party may sometimes divulge something you would never have uncovered.

The second purpose, pinning the party down, is usually accomplished by using leading, focused, cross-examination type questions. Your attitude and tone can be more forceful and adversarial. One of the most common mistakes is to let the witness give ambiguous or qualified answers that do not make for effective impeachment at trial. If the party hedges, ask follow-up questions that pin him down. If the party refuses, try to get him to admit that he is only "guessing," "approximating," or that he simply "doesn't know." Parties have a predictable talent for improving their recall of facts and details at trial. Therefore, getting an "I don't know" or an "I can only approximate" response can be useful for impeachment purposes if the party at trial claims to know specifically. Make the key questions self-contained, so that the individual questions and answers will make sense when used for impeachment.

A common avoidance method is the "I don't know" answer. When a witness frequently responds "I don't know," follow it up. If you don't know

46. See Sporck v. Piel, 759 F.2d 312 (3d Cir. 1985); Magee v. Paul Revere, 172 F.R.D. 647 (E.D.N.Y. 1997).

the information now, did you once know it? Who else would know it? What other employee should know it? Where would the information be recorded? Who would know if there is a record of that information? In short, let the witness realize that an "I don't know" answer will trigger a number of follow-up questions.

iii.   Preserving testimony

When deposing someone to preserve testimony for later admission at trial as former testimony under FRE 804(b)(1), your principal concern is to create clear, progressive testimony that will not run afoul of evidentiary rules. Keep in mind that, absent any contrary stipulations, Rule 32(d) preserves all objections to questions and answers except those directed to form or others that could have been cured had they been made promptly. Therefore, unless the witness is an adverse party or hostile witness, use nonleading questions. Have the witness paint verbal pictures of the events and transactions, the way you would at trial. Avoid objectionable forms of questions, such as those that can be considered leading, compound, argumentative, speculative, ambiguous, or narrative. Don't ask questions that call for hearsay or improper opinions.

Deposition purposes, of course, do not always separate out with such clear definition. For example, even when you are deposing a witness and are trying to pin the witness down with leading questions, you may want to use that witness to establish the foundations for records, documents, and other exhibits for possible use at trial.[47] If so, you must establish that the witness is a qualified witness, and state questions and get answers that meet the applicable evidentiary foundation requirements for each exhibit.

Some lawyers, at the end of a deposition, ask the deponent if he would like to correct anything he has said, or whether he has any additional information pertinent to the case that he has not been asked about. If the witness answers no, you can use this answer to impeach him at trial if he testifies inconsistently or testifies to new facts not previously disclosed, suggesting to the jury that the new or different testimony is a recent creation.

iv.   In what order should I cover my topics?

There are three basic approaches to ordering the topics you need to cover during a deposition: chronological, topical, and impact. The chronological approach is commonly used with witnesses to events where you want to find out everything the witness knows. The witness is simply directed to the beginning of the time line, and the questions move steadily from beginning to end. The topical approach is commonly used with witnesses to discrete transactions and events, where you can cover each

---

47. See T. Mauet, Trials, ch. 7 (2005) on establishing foundations for various types of exhibits.

transaction and event separately, and you do not need to cover them in order. It is also sometimes used with experts. The impact approach immediately confronts the witness on difficult matters. It is commonly used with adverse parties, where the lawyer immediately wants to create an atmosphere of control or uncertainty.

Regardless of your approach, examine the witness first, then the documents. Find out what the witness actually knows, and pin the witness down to what facts he actually knows. Only then should you explore the witness' opinions, beliefs, and other hearsay knowledge. Only then should you examine the witness about documents and records that may be relevant to his knowledge and the issues in the case.

v.   Common problems

Inexperienced litigators frequently experience problems while taking depositions. First, their time estimates are too short. Even a simple deposition will probably take half an hour; an eyewitness to a car crash may take an hour or more. If the deponent is a witness to a series of commercial transactions, or is an expert or a party in a medical or products liability case, the deposition may take a few hours. Keep in mind, however, that under Rule 30(d) the time limit on a deposition is one day of seven hours.

Second, their purposes are unclear. Depositions can be taken for one or more of three basic reasons: discovering information, pinning down for admissions and impeachment purposes, and for preserving testimony. You need to determine which of these three purposes are involved in every deposition and conduct yourself accordingly. If the latter two, you are creating a document—the transcript—that you will later use at trial. How it looks and reads is important. Follow your outline, and don't let the witness distract you from your purposes.

Third, their questioning forms are unclear. How you ask questions has much to do with what your deposition purposes are. If discovery, use non-leading questions that get the witness talking. If pinning down, use focused leading questions. If preserving testimony, use questions that you would use if you were conducting a direct examination of the witness at trial. Ambiguous, confusing questions serve no purpose well. Arguing with the witness, and letting your ego take over, never accomplishes anything positive. Nor does arguing with the opposing lawyer. Listen to the lawyer's objections, and adjust if necessary, but ignore the lawyer and focus on asking well-stated questions to the witness.

Fourth, necessary documentation is missing. You ordinarily cannot take a good deposition of a witness or represent your client at a deposition unless you have previously obtained all the documentation necessary for that deposition. If the party or witness was directed, by notice or subpoena, to bring such documentation to the deposition but doesn't, refuse to take the deposition under these circumstances and continue the deposition to another date.

Fifth, they explore unnecessary topics and details. This is a common problem with litigators who have little trial experience. Since they don't know what will be important if the case is finally tried, they cover all the bases by asking everything they can think of about every conceivable topic. This rarely accomplishes anything useful. The way to deal with this is to spend time beforehand planning the deposition and getting help from more experienced litigators who have trial experience.

l. How should I handle objections?

When you are taking depositions, there are three basic types of objections you can expect from the opposing lawyer.

First, an objection can be made to the form of the questions or answers; Rule 32 (d) requires that unless an objection is made promptly, it is waived. Even after a timely objection is made, the witness must still answer the question "subject to the objection." If you are taking the deposition only to gather information, you can safely ignore the objection. After the lawyer has made the objection, simply tell the witness: "Please answer the question." If you may use the transcript later at trial, however, determine if the objection has possible validity. If it does, rephrase the question properly to overcome the objection. Remember that you can never be totally sure that you will not need to use the transcript during trial.

Second, an objection can be made on evidentiary grounds other than privilege. However, since it is not necessary to object if the grounds are relevance, hearsay, or if the objection is not based on form, the other parties can reserve objections until such time as the deposition is used at trial. That is, if such an objection is not made at the deposition, it can still be made at trial — and this is the customary procedure. If made at the deposition, the deponent must still answer. Simply tell the witness: "Please answer the question." Again, however, if you plan to use the deposition at trial, and a proper objection is made, you should rephrase the question to eliminate the problem.

Third, an objection can be made on the grounds of privilege or harassment. If made on privilege grounds, the witness will probably refuse to answer, since the witness' lawyer will direct the witness not to answer the question.[48] If on harassment grounds, an objection can be made along with a demand under Rule 30(d) that the deposition be suspended in order to make a motion to limit or terminate the deposition. When objections are made on privilege or harassment grounds, the witness will probably refuse to answer, leaving you, the lawyer taking the deposition, with two options. First, you can terminate the examination and move to compel answers. Second, you can ask other questions not objected to and finish the examination to the extent possible.

Regardless of how you react to the witness' refusal, you must decide whether to seek an order compelling an answer. You can discuss the legal issue with the lawyer making the objection to learn the reason for it, and then either rephrase the question or ask the lawyer to withdraw the objection. If the witness persists in refusing to answer, the information you seek

48. See discussion in §6.2.

is important, and you wish to force the issue, you must make a clear record. The question, the witness' refusal to answer, and the grounds for the refusal should be clearly spelled out, since the court reporter must provide a transcript of that portion of the deposition that you will attach to your motion to compel discovery.[49]

Example:

> Q. Mr. Jones, you were the maintenance man at XYZ Leasing during this time, correct?
> A. Yes.
> Q. You talked to people about the problem, didn't you?
> A. Yes.
> Q. That included the company lawyer, Mr. Johnson?
> A. Yes.
> Q. Tell us what you told Mr. Johnson about the problem.
> Jones' Lawyer: Objection. Mr. Jones, don't answer that question. That question calls for the disclosure of attorney-client communications, which are privileged.
> Q. Mr. Jones, do you refuse to answer the question?
> A. Yes.
> Q. Your refusal is based on your assertion of the attorney-client privilege?
> A. Yes.

In this way you will have made a clear record of the witness' refusal to answer and the reason for it. Ask the court reporter to mark this part of the deposition and transcribe it later so you can attach it to your motion to compel.

Finally, it is an unfortunate fact in litigation that some lawyers misuse objections to coach the deponent into making more desirable responses. This conduct violates the express terms of Rule 30(d)(1), which provides that "any objection during a deposition shall be stated concisely and in a non-argumentative and non-suggestive manner." The purpose of this rule is clear. Lawyers cannot use objections to frustrate an otherwise proper deposition, such as by using objections to coach the witness on a desired response or to frustrate and impede the examining lawyer. Lawyers cannot instruct deponents not to answer a question unless necessary to preserve a privilege, to enforce a previous court-ordered limitation, or to make a motion to terminate the deposition because it is being taken in bad faith or is unreasonably annoying or oppressive. Such improper lawyer conduct unfortunately had become common in recent years, and the amendments to Rule 30 were made to clearly establish rules for lawyer conduct during depositions. Where this repeatedly occurs — such as a lawyer who makes constant

---

49. Asking the court reporter to "certify the question," while not necessary to raise the matter in a motion to compel answers, lets the court reporter know that this question should be on a list of questions the witness refused to answer that will be appended to the end of the deposition transcript. This is a common practice in state courts.

"clarification" or "if he knows" objections — you should note your objection to the opposing lawyer, warn him to stop his improper conduct, and make sure the court reporter records it. If this conduct persists, you may want to terminate the deposition and bring the matter to the court through a motion to compel discovery or for sanctions. If past experience with a particular lawyer suggests this may happen, it may be effective to take a video deposition, because it will graphically capture the lawyer's conduct and sometimes will even act as a deterrent to such conduct. The videotape will show the misconduct more vividly than a written transcript. Many courts limit or forbid consultation between the witness and her lawyer during questioning, requiring what amounts to a trial environment for the deposition. Make sure you know your judge's guidelines for taking depositions.

m.   How should I prepare and represent a deponent?

When you receive a notice for deposition of your client, preparing the client for the upcoming deposition may well be the most important single event in the litigation process. The opposing lawyers will use the deposition to determine what your client knows, develop admissions and impeachment, pin your client down to details about what he does or does not know, and generally size up your client as a trial witness. If the deposition goes well, the settlement value of the case will rise as well. Hence, preparation for the deposition is critical. Treat deposition preparation just like trial preparation. If the deposition will be videotaped, you must receive notice of the videotaping on the deposition notice since this is required under Rule 30(b)(2). If so, you must prepare the client not only on how to answer the questions but also on his appearance and non-verbal demeanor.

Shortly before the deposition date, have your client come to your office with enough time allocated to prepare him thoroughly. Scheduling this for the early afternoon, as the last appointment for the day, is a good idea since you will not be rushed by other appointments. On the other hand, some lawyers prefer to schedule such interviews in the morning, when they and the clients are fresh.

Create a positive atmosphere that relieves the client's anxiety and concerns. Many persons, especially those who have never been deposed before, are worried about how they will perform and what "the other lawyer" is like and what she will do. Tell the client his job is to give truthful, short answers to the questions, and you will take care of everything else. Witnesses do not perform well under stress. Ask the client directly about his concerns, then deal with them candidly.

First, have the pleadings, discovery, documents, records, reports, photographs, diagrams, and sketches available for the client to review. However, show the client only his statements, not those of others. Showing your client other persons' statements will always create the impression, particularly at trial, that your client has tailored his testimony to be consistent with other witnesses, or has used the other statements to acquire information he himself does not personally have. This may also make such statements disclosable at trial, since under Rule 612 of the Federal Rules of Evidence an adverse party may be able to obtain any documents used to refresh the witness' recollection, even if used before trial; the party may be able to use them during the witness' cross-examination and to introduce in evidence relevant portions of the documents. It is usually better to avoid this problem by not showing your client other witnesses' statements. You can always refer to reports and statements of other witnesses and still deal with any inconsistencies. Always assume that the opposing lawyer will ask the deponent what she did to prepare for the deposition and what materials she reviewed. Although your communications with your client are privileged, your communications with nonparty deponents, and what you show your client and other deponents, are usually not. Tell the deponent she may be questioned about these things. If you are representing an expert, make sure the expert has everything he "considered" in reaching his opinions and conclusions with him. Make sure you have a copy of everything he considered and that you have disclosed it to the other side.

Second, review what a deposition is, what its purpose is, why it is so critical, and what the procedure will be. Explain to the client that once the deposition begins, you will be relatively inactive, except to make objections to preserve error when necessary, or to instruct him not to answer if critical to do so.

Third, review the verbal and nonverbal considerations, particularly if the deposition will be videotaped. The nonverbal impression the client makes is as important as the words he says. He should be told to dress appropriately. For most witnesses this means a conservative suit or jacket and tie; if the witness usually wears a uniform, such as a police officer, he should wear the uniform if his testimony is based on his being a police officer. He should be told to maintain eye contact with the questioner, since looking down usually creates a negative impression. He should be instructed to sit comfortably in the chair, sit still, rest his hands comfortably and use them to gesture to emphasize his testimony when appropriate. Finally, he should be trained to use clear, simple, proper English and avoid speech forms that suggest hesitancy and uncertainty. Doing this will take time, but is necessary since preparing a witness for the nonverbal aspects of a deposition particularly if videotaped, is as important as his trial testimony.

Fourth, review how your client should answer questions accurately. Impress upon him that even though the atmosphere will probably be informal, he must answer carefully. Standard advice includes the following:

- Make sure you understand the question. If you don't, say so.
- If you know the answer, give it. If you don't know, say so. If you know but can't remember just then, say so. If you can only estimate or approximate, say so. However, give positive, truthful answers whenever possible.
- Answer only what the question specifically calls for. Don't exaggerate or speculate. Give the best short, accurate, truthful answer possible.
- Answer questions only with what you personally know, saw, heard, or did, unless the question asks otherwise.

- Be calm and serious at all times. Avoid arguing with the lawyers or getting upset over the questions. I will be there to protect you from unfair questions and procedures by making objections and instructing you on what to do and say.
- Bring nothing (notes, etc.) to the deposition.

Fifth, discuss how objections will be handled. Explain that most objections are made "for the record," and that usually the witness must answer despite the objection, which is made for possible later use at trial. However, be sure the client knows not to answer when an objection is made and you tell the client not to answer. This will be the case if the objection is based on privilege or harassment grounds, where answering the question may waive any error.

Sixth, review with the client what questions the lawyers are likely to ask. This involves creating a short outline as discussed previously. Make sure that the client can accurately respond to those expected questions in a positive, convincing manner whenever possible. Prepare the client, but don't coach him on what to say, and make sure the client uses his vocabulary, not yours. Let the client know that other lawyers present may ask additional questions, but that you will probably not ask questions unless necessary to correct a mistake or clarify something ambiguous.

Finally, explain that the client has a right to review the deposition if it is transcribed, noting any corrections and the reasons for them, and to sign it. Explain why that right to "read and sign" should not be waived, stressing the importance of correcting any errors in the transcript. Rule 30(e) requires the deponent to request a review of the transcript to record any changes, and the request must be made before the end of the deposition. The deponent has 30 days after being notified that the transcript is available for review to read, note corrections, and sign the transcript.

Lawyers use different methods to educate clients on what will happen during a deposition and on how important their depositions are. Many lawyers send the client a letter explaining the do's and don't's of depositions, which the client can then review before coming to your office for further preparation. Another common method is to send the client an audiotape or videotape containing the same advice and showing a deposition being taken. Some lawyers use commercially available videotapes; others make their own videotapes showing them representing a client at a deposition. These can all be helpful, but there is no substitute to your spending the necessary amount of time with the client to deal with the client's anxiety and concerns and prepare him to be an effective witness.

Above all, the client must understand that her deposition is a pivotal event in the litigation, one that will require time for preparation and practice. Many lawyers videotape the client's practice deposition, using another lawyer as the questioner, and play back the videotape for the client. This effectively demonstrates to the client the impression she is making during the deposition and sets the stage for further improvement.

How much time does all this preparation take? While many preparation sessions for a client take a few hours, they make take substantially more. For example, if your client is the CEO of a large corporation involved in a complex case, several sessions may be needed. One session may be a get-acquainted meeting to discuss the deposition process and its relationship to the overall case. The next session may be an overview of the anticipated main topics, to review documents, and see how the CEO answers questions. A third session may be a detailed practice session that will be videotaped and reviewed, and the CEO's content and delivery will be critiqued. A fourth session will be for final preparation and fine-tuning just before the actual deposition. The important point is that in most litigation, the deposition is the only time your client will testify, and how well she does will be an important influence on the outcome of that case.

n. After the deposition

When the deposition is completed, there are four things that still need to be done. First, decide if you want to order a transcript of the deposition. The party taking the deposition usually orders it; usually the other parties will want a copy as well. How long it takes to get the transcript depends on the court reporter, but it sometimes can take weeks. However, there is no requirement that you order a transcript of every deposition in the case. Transcripts usually cost at least three dollars per page, and typically run 40 to 50 pages for each hour the witness is being deposed. If the deposition provided nothing useful, or you are on a tight litigation budget, don't order the transcript until you know the case is going to be tried.

Second, dictate a memo recording your impressions of the witness immediately afterwards, when your impressions are still fresh. Include a summary of the kind of witness she will make at trial and how she helps or hurts your case. This is important, since a transcript does not give a good picture of the impression the witness made. Furthermore, the lawyer taking the deposition may not be the same lawyer who will later try the case.

Third, prepare a deposition summary when you get the transcript. A deposition summary, frequently prepared by paralegals, records in summary form the witness' testimony and correlates it to the transcript pages. It can also show subject matter and be cross-referenced, which is particularly useful if the summaries will be put into a computer database. There are three ways deposition summaries are organized: chronological, by page and line (see example); by topics (good for lawyers to review); and in narrative form based on the witness' answers (good for witnesses to review).

Example:

Ronald Smith

v.

James Woods

Case No. 05 C 1022
File No. 05-153

DEPOSITION SUMMARY OF MARIAN WELLS
JUNE 1, 2005

Page/Line	Subject	Text	References
8: 7-22	Address	Wells lives at 231 Barton, Dallas, Texas with husband, 3 children	
9: 12-34	Job	Works at IBM as computer programmer in R & D Division	IBM
10: 6-18	School	Graduated from Southern Methodist University in 1980, B.S. degree, math major	

The deposition summaries make it much more convenient for lawyers to review the depositions of witnesses, evaluate the case for settlement purposes, and prepare for trial.

Fourth, if the deponent is your party, arrange to have the party review the transcript for errors, and consider noting any errors and the reasons for them on the correction page (sometimes called the "errata sheet"). If the party makes any corrections, she must sign the correction page and return it to the court reporter. Under Rule 30(e), a witness has 30 days from the time the transcript is available in which to review the transcript and make any changes.

However, making corrections and signing the correction page has a downside: it commits the client to the corrected version and gives the other side additional impeachment at trial. For that reason, some lawyers never have their clients sign the correction sheet (unless making a correction is essential to avoid summary judgment).

Under Rule 5(d), depositions are not to be filed with the court until they are used in the proceeding or the court orders otherwise. (This saves space in the clerk's office.) Under Rule 30(f), the lawyer ordering the transcript receives the transcript under seal from the court reporter, and the lawyer is responsible for storing the transcript and protecting it from loss, destruction, tampering, and deterioration.

§6.10.   *Physical and mental examinations*

In some cases, primarily personal injury cases, the physical and mental condition of a party is a critical fact affecting both liability and damages. Under those circumstances, that party should be examined to evaluate the genuineness of the condition, its extent and causes, and to develop a prognosis. Rule 35 governs this process.

1.   Law[50]

Rule 35 applies to physical and mental examinations of a party and of a "person in the custody or under the legal control of a party." The Rule

---

50. Wright §88; James & Hazard §5.6; Friedenthal §7.12; Moore's Manual §15.11; Manual of Federal Practice §§5.195–5.198; Moore's Federal Practice §§35.01–35.07; Wright & Miller §§2231–2239.

clearly applies to minors and other legally incapacitated persons who are not the actual named parties, but are the real parties in interest.

A court order is required for such examinations, unless the person to be examined voluntarily agrees to the examination, which is permitted under Rule 29 so long as there is a written stipulation. In other situations you must move for a court order and give notice to the person and all parties. For the court to order an examination, the physical or mental condition of a party or related person must be "in controversy," and you must show "good cause" for requesting it.[51]

The good-cause requirement has sometimes caused difficulty. In most cases, however, typically personal injury cases or paternity cases where the physical condition of a party is important, there are few problems and the parties often informally arrange for the necessary examinations. In these types of cases the need for the examinations is apparent from the pleadings. However, issues such as testimonial competency will not be apparent from the pleadings; therefore, the moving party must make a sufficient showing of need in the motion to satisfy the good cause requirement.[52]

The court's order must specify the date, time, place, manner, conditions, and scope of the examination, as well as the person or persons who will perform it. The scope of the examination is determined by the nature of the claims, defenses, and facts and issues in controversy. Rule 35 provides only that the physical or mental examination be done by a "suitably licensed or certified examiner." In practice the moving party usually suggests a physician and the court ordinarily approves the selection unless another party, or the person to be examined, has a serious objection. The court has discretion to approve or disapprove, and some districts have local rules that provide for the selection of "impartial experts" from approved lists.[53]

The party moving for the examination must, upon request by the examined party, deliver to the examined party a detailed written report of the examining physician setting out findings, results of tests, diagnoses, and conclusions, as well as reports of all earlier examinations for the same conditions. The party moving for the examination can then, upon request, get any previous or future reports about the same person for the same condition, unless, where a nonparty is examined, the party shows he cannot obtain the report. This procedure essentially provides for reciprocal discovery when one side requests a report from the examining physician. When the party examined requests a copy of the report of the physician who examined him, this operates as a waiver of the doctor-patient privilege not only as to that physician, but also as to any other physician who has or may later examine him as to the same conditions.

These disclosure requirements and waiver effects apply regardless of whether the examinations are made pursuant to a court order or through

---

51. See Schlagenhauf v. Holder, 379 U.S. 104 (1964).

52. Moore's Manual §15.11; Manual of Federal Practice §5.196; Moore's Federal Practice §35.03(5); Wright & Miller §§2232, 2234.

53. Note that FRE 706 also gives the court authority to appoint and compensate experts.

agreement of the parties, unless that agreement expressly provides otherwise. In addition, the discovery permitted under Rule 35 does not restrict other permissible discovery. However, Rule 35 is the only rule that can compel discovery where otherwise the doctor-patient privilege would prevent disclosure.

2. Practice approach

Since the situations in which physical and mental examinations can be compelled are usually obvious, these examinations are frequently arranged informally between the parties. Even where there is an informal agreement, however, it is always a good idea to put it in a letter or, even better, in a stipulation under Rule 29 that is then filed with the court.

Where an arrangement cannot be worked out, you must move for a court order compelling the desired examination. To comply with Rule 35, the motion must (1) ask for the examination of a party or a person in the custody or control of the party, (2) allege a genuine controversy about that person's physical or mental condition, (3) demonstrate good cause for the examination, (4) request the date, time, place, manner, conditions, and scope of the examination, and (5) designate the examiner who should conduct it. In addition, the motion should reflect that the parties conferred and attempted to resolve their differences, but were unsuccessful, since Rules 26(c) and 37(a) require such a certification whenever discovery motions are brought.

Example:

[Caption]

MOTION FOR ORDER COMPELLING PLAINTIFF'S PHYSICAL EXAMINATION

Defendant moves under Rule 35 of the Federal Rules of Civil Procedure for an order compelling plaintiff to submit to a physical examination. In support of her motion defendant states:

1. Plaintiff's physical condition is genuinely in controversy, since plaintiff's complaint on its face alleges that "as a result of this collision, plaintiff has suffered severe and permanent injuries to his back and legs."

2. Since plaintiff alleges that his physical limitations are compensable, there exists good cause for a physical examination to evaluate the plaintiff's current physical condition, physical limitations, and prognosis.

3. William B. Rudolf, M.D., a board certified orthopedic surgeon, has agreed to examine the plaintiff at his offices at 200 Main Street, Suite 301, Washington, D.C., on August 15, 2005, at 4:00 P.M., or at another time if directed by this court.

4. The parties have conferred but are unable to agree on a physician to conduct the appropriate examination.

WHEREFORE, defendant requests that this court enter an order directing the plaintiff to be examined on the terms set forth above.

_____
Attorney for Defendant

If the court grants the motion, an order must be entered. In federal courts the practice is for the court clerk to prepare orders, which the judge then signs. Where permitted, however, it is always a useful approach to draft an appropriate order in situations where a nonparty, here the physician, is involved because the physician will want a copy of the order before conducting the examination.

Example:

[Caption]

ORDER

This matter being heard on defendant's motion to compel the physical examination of plaintiff, all parties having been given notice, and the court having heard arguments, it is hereby ordered that:

1. Plaintiff John Williams be examined by William B. Rudolf, M.D., at 200 Main Street, Suite 301, Washington, D.C., on August 15, 2005, at 4:00 P.M., unless the plaintiff and Dr. Rudolf mutually agree to an earlier date and time.

2. Plaintiff shall submit to such orthopedic examinations and tests as are necessary to diagnose and evaluate the plaintiff's back and legs, so that Dr. Rudolf may reach opinions and conclusions about the extent of any injuries, their origin, and prognosis.

3. Dr. Rudolf shall prepare a written report detailing his findings, test results, diagnosis and opinions, along with any earlier similar reports on the same conditions, and deliver it to defendant's attorneys on or before September 15, 2005.

Entered:

Dated:_____   _____
                                      United States District Judge

Finally, keep in mind the reciprocal discovery provisions of Rule 35(b)(1). If the examined party requests a copy of the examiner's report, the party moving for the examination has the right to receive from the examined party other reports dealing with the same conditions, regardless of when made; however, you must request those reports. Perhaps the safer approach is to send that party a document entitled "REQUEST FOR MEDICAL REPORTS," show that it is made under the provisions of Rule 35(b)(1), and file the request with the court. If the other party fails to deliver, or later attempts to use such reports, you have made a record of your request and can object to the introduction of those reports at trial because the party did not comply with Rule 35.

§6.11.   *Requests to admit facts*

Requests to admit facts and genuineness of documents are not designed to "discover." Up to now the parties have been acquiring information, through informal and formal discovery, and the information acquisition phase of the litigation process is essentially complete. The next step is to sift through all this acquired information and begin planning what you will introduce at trial and how you will do it. A request to admit (along with the pretrial statement and motions in limine) is a basic tool that you can use to streamline your proof at trial.

1.   Law[54]

Requests to admit facts and the genuineness of documents, governed by Rule 36, apply only to parties. Admissions made in response to the requests are conclusive admissions for the purposes of the pending action only and cannot be used for any other purposes. This encourages a party to admit facts without worrying about collateral consequences. Any matter admitted is deemed "conclusively established," which means the admitting party cannot at trial introduce evidence contradicting its earlier admission (unless the court allows the admission to be withdrawn or amended).

Requests may be served on other parties at any time after the parties meet to develop a discovery plan under Rule 26(f). Like other discovery provisions, requests can be employed essentially at any time during the litigation process.

A request can be directed to three categories: the truth of facts, the genuineness of documents, and the "application of law to fact." The general scope of these requests is the same as for discovery in general; they apply to anything that is relevant but not privileged. Each request must be separately stated.

After a request has been served on a party, that party must serve a response within 30 days or the matters requested will be deemed admitted, unless the court permits or a written agreement between the parties provides for a shorter or longer time. This automatic provision of Rule 36 makes it a formidable weapon because inertia or inattentiveness can have an automatic, and usually devastating, consequence. Hence, there is one cardinal rule for practice under this provision: Make sure you respond and serve the response within the 30-day period.

54. Wright §89; James & Hazard §5.7; Friedenthal §7.10; Moore's Manual §15.12; Manual of Federal Practice §§5.199–5.215; Moore's Federal Practice §§36.01–36.08; Wright & Miller §§2251–2265.

There are four basic responses permitted. First, you can object to a matter in the request. Second, you can admit the matter. Third, you can deny the matter. Fourth, you can neither admit nor deny because the matter is genuinely in dispute, or because after reasonable inquiry you do not have sufficient information to determine if the matter is true or not.

How you respond, and whether your response is justified under the circumstances, determines whether Rule 37 sanctions can be imposed. Rule 37(c) provides that the expenses — including attorney's fees — incurred in proving a denied matter can be taxed as costs against the losing party. However, if you neither admit nor deny on the basis of there being a genuine issue for trial, or because of genuine insufficient knowledge, Rule 37 sanctions cannot be imposed.[55]

Once a response has been received, you can move the court to review the adequacy of the objections and responses. The Rule requires that a response must specifically deny the matter or set forth in detail why the answering party cannot admit or deny after making a reasonable inquiry. A denial must fairly meet the substance of the requested admission. The better practice is to make a motion under Rule 36(a) to determine the sufficiency of an answer and see if the court will deem the matter admitted. This will avoid surprises at trial. The court can enter an order compelling an answer or amended answer if appropriate, order that the matter be deemed admitted, or continue the motion to the pretrial conference or to another date.

2.   Practice approach

Because the scope of Rule 36 is broad, using and responding to requests to admit are principally strategic concerns that must be coordinated with your overall trial strategy. Note the emphasis on trial strategy, not on discovery. Requests to admit do not "discover" additional information; they are used to sharpen trial issues, streamline the presentation of evidence, and eliminate the need to formally prove uncontroverted facts.[56] Hence, the question is not what you can get the other side to admit; the better question is: What do you want the other side to admit that ties in to your overall trial strategy?

a.   Timing

Rule 36 permits requests to admit at any time after the parties meet to plan discovery, so the decision on when to use it is controlled by practical considerations. However, the requests are most frequently used at the end of the discovery stage. When you have received initial disclosures, interrogatory answers, and records pursuant to document requests,

---

55. See Wright §90; Moore's Manual §15.13; Manual of Federal Practice §5.229; Moore's Federal Practice §§36.03(7), 36.07; Wright & Miller §§2265, 2288, 2290.

56. Some courts have held that since requests to admit are not true discovery devices, discovery cutoff dates do not apply to them.

have deposed the parties and necessary witnesses, and, where appropriate, have completed physical and mental examinations, discovery is essentially complete. Requests to admit are most commonly served at this point because the existing discovery will identify what still remains in issue. The requests should be served after other discovery has been completed but before the pretrial conference is scheduled or summary judgment motions are made. Requests to admit served at that time will help determine what facts the other side will concede, or contest if the case goes to trial.

Another approach is to serve requests to admit early in the discovery process, sometimes coupled with interrogatories and documents requests, to bring the potential Rule 37 sanctions into play. For example, if you have a strong case on liability and want to push for an early settlement, send the other side an early request to admit facts that prove liability. This forces your opponent to decide what facts and issues she intends to dispute and allows later discovery to become more focused. If a party denies a fact in a request to admit, without a substantial basis for the denial, and that fact is later proved at trial, the party proving the fact can receive as court costs the reasonable expense of proving the denied fact at trial, including attorney's fees. By making requests to admit early, you start the period for which you may be entitled to get Rule 37 costs. Where you think the opposing party will use dilatory tactics or avoid serious settlement discussions on a case that should be settled quickly, making a request to admit early raises the risks for the party using those tactics. This can be effective in forcing your opponent to admit facts.

b.   What to request

To determine what to request, look first at the elements of your claims and defenses. Second, analyze each "fact" you will need to prove to meet your burden of proof at trial on each element. This is what every trial lawyer must do in preparing for trial. Third, review the pleadings, to see what has been admitted, and your discovery results, to see what facts are conceded. Reviewing the discovery is particularly critical, since a fact, when conceded in interrogatory answers or in a party deposition, is only an admission by a party opponent, which is *not* the same thing as a conclusive admission. The party admitting a fact can still present contrary evidence at trial. To avoid this, focus on matters opposing parties have admitted in previous discovery. Those parties are likely to admit the facts in a request to admit if they have previously admitted them. The advantage is that when a matter is admitted under Rule 36, it is deemed conclusively established for purposes of that pending action, which bars that party from introducing contrary evidence at trial, unless the court permits amendment or withdrawal.

Fourth, think through your trial strategy. What witnesses and exhibits do you need to prove your case at trial? Where are your strengths and weaknesses? Is some of your evidence technical and likely to bore the jury? Is some of it costly to present? Is some of your testimony dramatic or emotional? Do some of your exhibits have significant visual impact? In short, don't ask the other side to admit something just because it's there;

ask the other side to admit it because it improves your case at trial. This means that you will *not* ask the other side to admit your most compelling, emotional, or dramatic evidence; that's exactly what you want the jury to hear and see. On the other hand, if the evidence is technical, boring but necessary, excessively expensive to present, or comes from a weak witness, that's the evidence you want admitted through requests to admit.

c. Drafting the requests

The cardinal rule for drafting requests to admit is to keep it simple and clear. A lengthy, complicated request practically begs to be denied, objected to, or responded to with a lengthy, equivocal response. This will merely generate further motions and probably achieve nothing.

Simplicity requires that a request be short and contain a single statement of fact. Such requests are difficult to quibble with, and they stand the best chance of being admitted outright. They should also comply with admissibility rules such as those concerning relevance, hearsay, and authentication.

Organize your requests into the three permitted categories:

1. truth of facts
2. genuineness of documents
3. opinions of fact and application of law to facts

When drafting requests to admit facts, ask that the facts be admitted as true.

Example (facts):

[Caption]

REQUESTS TO ADMIT FACTS AND
GENUINENESS OF DOCUMENTS

Plaintiff Ralph Johnson requests defendant Marion Smith to make the following admissions, within 30 days after service of this request, for the purposes of this action only:

Admit that each of the following facts is true:

1. On May 1, 2005, plaintiff had a valid driver's license issued by the state of Colorado.

2. On May 1, 2005, defendant was the owner of a Chevrolet sedan having a Colorado license no. BCD-437.

When drafting requests to admit the genuineness of documents, the usual request is to ask that attached documents are "genuine." Genuine means that the document is what it purports to be, that is, it was made by the person or entity it appears to be made by and, if signed, was signed by the person it appears to be signed by. Keep in mind, however, that a party admitting the genuineness of a document admits that and no more. That party may still raise other evidentiary objections, such as relevance or hearsay, to the document's admissibility at trial.

Example (genuineness of documents):

> Admit that each of the following documents is genuine:
>   3. The contract, attached as Exhibit A.
>   4. The check, attached as Exhibit B.

You can do much better than merely asking that a document be admitted as genuine, however. Always think about the evidentiary foundation necessary to get a particular document or record admitted at trial, then get the opposing party to admit the foundation requirements.

Example (foundation for documents):

> Admit that the following facts are true:
>   5. The contract, attached as Exhibit A, bears the signature of the defendant.
>   6. The defendant signed the original of Exhibit A on May 1, 2005.
>   7. The contract, attached as Exhibit A, is an accurate copy of the original contract signed by the defendant.
>   8. A bill of lading, attached as Exhibit B, is a business record of the XYZ Corporation under FRE 803(b).
>   9. The bill of lading, attached as Exhibit B, is an accurate copy (other than a possible change in size) of the original made by XYZ Corporation.

Keep in mind that a fact can be contained in a document, so you may want the other party to admit the fact, admit the genuineness of the document containing the fact, or both. Juries usually respond favorably to exhibits, so it's a sound idea to get the document before the jury at trial.

Requests to admit can also ask for "opinions of fact" and the "application of law to fact." This is a problematic area since questions of "pure law" cannot be asked. For instance, a request that asks a party to admit negligence or culpability is objectionable, and that will be a genuine issue at trial. Where the line is between "opinions of fact" and "application of law to fact," as against "pure law" remains unclear.[57] Regardless of where that line is, treading close to it will probably draw objections. Accordingly, it is usually better to be on the safe side and leave the legal disputes for resolution at trial. Common situations where the application of law to fact is raised are issues of title, ownership, agency, and employment.

---

57. See Wright §89; Moore's Manual §15.12; Moore's Federal Practice §36.04(4); Wright & Miller §§2255, 2256.

Example (application of law to fact):

> Admit that each of the following statements is true:
>
> 10. Defendant was the legal titleholder of a lot commonly known as 3401 Fifth Street, Tucson, Arizona, on August 1, 2005.
>
> 11. On August 1, 2005, William Oats was an employee of XYZ Corporation.
>
> 12. On August 1, 2005, William Oats was authorized to enter into sales contracts on behalf of XYZ Corporation.

Consider coupling requests to admit with interrogatories asking for the facts on which any response that does not admit a request is based. When the opposing party is faced with an interrogatory asking why a request to admit was not admitted, it makes it more difficult to deny the request in the first place. If the request is not admitted and the follow-up interrogatory is answered, you may have a better understanding of how the opposing side will attempt to deal with this issue at trial.

Example:

REQUESTS FOR ADMISSIONS

> 1. Admit that the defendant's car crossed the center lane and was in the plaintiff's lane of traffic when the collision happened.
>
> 2. . . .

INTERROGATORIES

> 1. If you failed to admit Request for Admissions No. 1:
>   (a) State the facts on which you base your denial;
>   (b) Identify all documents that support your denial;
>   (c) Identify each person that has information that supports your denial.
>
> 2. . . .

What are the common problems that arise when drafting requests to admit? Remember that the point of using requests to admit is to streamline the presentation of your case at trial by eliminating the need to present boring but necessary or expensive witnesses. The most common problem, therefore, is that requests to admit are not coordinated with your trial strategy. Always ask: What are the interesting and exciting parts of my case that I want the jury to hear? What parts of my case have no jury appeal and consist of boring or technical proof, which I would prefer to prove through a request to admit? In addition, your overall strategy may include making a summary judgment motion. The requests to admit should be considered in light of what you need to prove to win the motion.

Another common problem is that the requests to admit contain characterizations that the other party will be loathe to admit. For example, asking "Admit that there was no reason to believe that ABC Corporation would not deliver the goods by June 1, 2005," or "Admit that defendant harbored doubts about its denying the claim for benefits" will usually generate either a denial or a claim that this is a legitimate trial issue. Avoid characterizations—"quibble words"—in the requests. Simple requests, based on nouns and verbs, and avoiding adjectives and adverbs, are more likely to be admitted.

Another common problem is requesting that a fact be admitted, rather than asking that the foundation for the admissibility of a record or document containing the fact be admitted. Remember that visual exhibits have persuasive power. Jurors would much rather look at a key record or document, blown up as a courtroom exhibit, than listen to the judge instruct them that a certain fact will be deemed conclusively admitted.

Finally, keep in mind that requests to admit are designed to streamline the trial. Keep in mind that the request and response will be read to the jury during trial and that the judge will probably give a specific jury instruction based on the request and response. Always consider how the request will sound to the jurors. When using requests to provide the basis for admissibility of an exhibit at trial, always review what technical evidentiary foundation is necessary to get that particular exhibit admitted in evidence, and draft the request to admit accordingly.

The requests to admit should be signed by the lawyer and served on each party. Service is made by any permitted method under Rule 5, most commonly by mailing a copy to the lawyers of the other parties. However, under Rule 5(d) the requests to admit are not to be filed with the court until it is used in the proceeding or the court orders otherwise. (This saves space in the clerk's office.)

d. *Choosing a response*

A party on whom requests to admit have been served must respond, usually within 30 days of receiving the requests, or else the matters in the requests will automatically be deemed conclusively admitted for purposes of the pending action only. Therefore, it is *imperative* that you respond within the time limit. There are four basic responses to a request.

First, you can object to the request. As with discovery generally, you can object that the matter requested is irrelevant or privileged. In addition, you can seek a protective order if the request is unduly burdensome or harassing.

Second, you can admit the request. When you do so, you conclusively admit the matter for the purpose of the pending action only. Such an admission prevents you from presenting contrary evidence at trial.

Third, you can deny the request. The denial must be based on good faith. If the requesting party later proves the denied matter at trial, under Rule 37 that party may get reasonable expenses, including attorney's fees, involved in proving the matter. The response can, of course, admit some parts of a request and deny others.

Fourth, under certain circumstances you can "set forth in detail the reasons why the answering party cannot truthfully admit or deny the matter." This is allowed if the answering party has made a "reasonable inquiry" in an effort to acquire necessary information for responding to the request but is still unable to respond. In addition, if the answering party considers the requested matter to be a genuine trial issue, it can either deny or set forth reasons for neither admitting nor denying. In practice, lawyers deny such requests after detailing the reasons why the matter cannot be admitted or denied.

When you have decided what the appropriate response should be, actually drafting the response is very similar to drafting answers to complaints. However, the better format is that used for interrogatory answers, where the answers and interrogatories both appear together.

Example:

[Caption]

RESPONSE TO REQUESTS FOR ADMISSIONS

Defendant Marian Smith responds to plaintiff Ralph Johnson's requests for admissions as follows:

Request No. 1: A contract, attached as Exhibit A, is a true and accurate copy of the contract signed by plaintiff on August 1, 2005.

Answer: Admit.

Request No. 2: Plaintiff performed all his obligations under the contract.

Answer: Deny.

Request No. 3: On August 1, 2005, William Oats was authorized to enter into sales contracts on behalf of XYZ Corporation.

Answer: Objection. Responding to this request would disclose the substance of conversations between William Oats, an attorney, and the XYZ Corporation, which are protected from disclosure by the attorney-client privilege.

Request No. 4: Mary Doyle is the sole titleholder of a lot commonly known as 3401 Fifth Street, Seattle, Washington.

Answer: Defendant cannot truthfully admit or deny this request and therefore denies it. Public records neither confirm nor deny, and defendant has no access to any documents that could confirm or deny it.

The response to requests to admit should be signed by the party's lawyer and served on each party. Service is made by any permitted method under Rule 5, most commonly by mailing a copy to the lawyers for the other parties. However, under Rule 5(d) the response is not to be filed with the court until it is used in the proceeding or the court orders otherwise. (This saves space in the clerk's office.)

   e.   Requestor's responses

When a party has made and served responses to requests to admit on the requesting party, the requesting party can do two things: move to review the sufficiency of an answer, and move to review the propriety of an objection. Both of these are directed to the court's discretion. The court can enter any appropriate order, such as deeming a matter admitted, requiring an amended answer, or continuing the issue to the pretrial conference or other time.

When the answering party denies a request to admit facts, a good approach is to send the answering party interrogatories that ask for the basis of the denial. Another approach is to send "contention interrogatories" along with the requests to admit, again asking for the basis of each denial of a request. This frequently causes the answering party to admit the request, rather than attempt to justify the denial in the accompanying interrogatory answer.

§6.12. Supplementing discovery

Rule 26(e) imposes a duty to supplement and correct disclosures and discovery responses. This duty applies to required disclosures — initial, expert, and pretrial disclosures — and responses to discovery — interrogatories, documents requests, and requests to admit. The duty to supplement expert disclosures extends both to the expert's report and the expert's deposition.

The time requirements are unclear. Required disclosures must be supplemented "at appropriate intervals." Responses to interrogatories, documents requests, and requests to admit must be supplemented "seasonably." This duty to supplement arises when a party "learns that in some material respect" the disclosure or response is "incomplete or incorrect" and the "additional or corrective information has not otherwise been made known to the other parties during the discovery process or in writing." The Comment to Rule 26(e) notes that "supplementation need not be made as each new item of information is learned, but should be made at appropriate intervals during the discovery period, and with special promptness as the trial date approaches." The intent of the rule is fairness: parties must supplement periodically so the opposing parties are not unfairly disadvantaged, and they cannot withhold information to gain strategic advantages. Problems arise most frequently with experts, when experts develop additional opinions and bases for their opinions, but these new opinions and bases are neither in the expert's report nor were they brought out during the expert's deposition.

Failure to supplement can have drastic consequences. Under Rule 37(c), failure to disclose or supplement disclosures or discovery responses will result in the exclusion of the undisclosed information at the trial, hearing, or motion, "unless such failure is harmless." In addition, the court on motion and after a hearing may impose other sanctions, including reasonable expenses and attorney's fees.

The message of Rule 26(e) is clear: periodically review your disclosures and discovery responses, and if you have acquired material new information that has not been included in your disclosures and responses, and it has not yet been made known to the other parties, disclose it promptly, either by amending your disclosures and responses or notifying the other parties of the new information in writing.

§6.13. *Discovery motions*

Discovery under the federal rules is largely executed without judicial intervention. Except for physical and mental examinations, discovery before the parties have conferred to develop a discovery plan, discovery which would exceed the numerical limits on interrogatories and depositions, and discovery which would violate a court order regulating discovery entered under Rule 16, the parties can conduct discovery without prior judicial approval. Only when there is a dispute over discovery need the courts become involved.

Three points should be remembered. First, Rule 37(a) now requires the moving party's lawyer to certify what good faith efforts have been made to confer with the other party to resolve a discovery dispute informally before the courts will intervene. An appropriate certification must be signed by the lawyer and attached to the motion. The certification can also be made part of the motion, and this is the more common approach. Second, discovery abuse has probably been the subject of more controversy and proposals than any other aspect of the litigation process. Courts have responded to the problem by becoming more involved in discovery, particularly by having discovery plan conferences and by dealing more actively with abuses and imposing stiffer sanctions. Third, amendments to Rule 26 give courts additional powers to regulate discovery. Rule 26(b)(2) gives courts the power to limit discovery where it is unnecessarily cumulative or duplicative, or is obtainable from other sources with less effort and expense. Rule 16 gives courts power to hold discovery conferences and impose a discovery plan. Rule 26(g) parallels the Rule 11 requirements that the lawyer's signature is a certification that he has read the discovery document; has made a reasonable inquiry; and that the document is consistent with the rules and law, is not made for any improper purpose, and is not unreasonably burdensome or expensive. In today's climate, abusing discovery by filing frivolous, needless, or unduly burdensome discovery requests, responses, or motions can result in severe sanctions.

There are two principal types of discovery motions, those for protective orders and those for orders compelling discovery.

1. Protective orders[58]

Rule 26(c) and, in the case of oral depositions, Rule 30(d) govern protective orders. Whenever an entity or person from whom discovery is sought feels that it is being subjected to annoying, embarrassing, oppressive,

---

58. Wright §83; James & Hazard §5.13; Friedenthal §7.15; Moore's Manual §15.02(1)(d); Manual of Federal Practice §§5.94–5.105; Moore's Federal Practice §§26.67–26.79; Wright & Miller §§2035–2044.

unduly burdensome, or unduly expensive discovery demands, the appropriate procedure is to move for a protective order. Both parties and nonparty deponents can seek protective orders.

The motion must usually be brought in the district where the action is pending. However, where a deposition has been terminated so that a protective order can be obtained, the proper jurisdiction under Rule 30(d) is either the district where the action is pending or the district where the deposition is being taken. The latter may well be proper where a nonparty deponent is seeking the protective order, since the deposition is often taken where the deponent resides or does business.

Under Rule 26(c), the moving party must show "good cause." While grounds for protection are obviously numerous, the most common grounds are that the discovery requested is so lengthy and detailed that it is unduly oppressive and expensive; for example, discovery involving lengthy or repetitive interrogatories and depositions, and overly detailed documents requests and requests to admit. Another common ground is the serving of notice for "apex" depositions on high corporate officers who have no firsthand knowledge of any relevant facts. If the dominant purpose of the discovery is not to develop information reasonably necessary to prepare for trial or settlement, but to harass the corporate officer or force the opposition into submission, Rule 26(b)(2) is violated and the protective order is appropriate. Another common ground is serving interrogatories and documents requests that ask for disclosure and production of income tax returns, corporate financial data, and other proprietary information. Unless this information is relevant to claims of lost income or punitive damages, a protective order barring, limiting, or delaying such discovery is appropriate. Other motions frequently seek to limit disclosure, such as restricting persons present at depositions and preventing the disclosure of business secrets to persons outside the litigation, to limit the discovery methods which may be used, and to seal depositions and other discovery and require that they be unsealed only by court order.

In this computer age, an increasingly frequent topic for motions for protective orders is electronic data. While relevant information in electronic form is clearly discoverable through a properly worded Rule 34 production request, motions commonly seek protection on the ground that the discovery request is unduly burdensome in time and cost. These motions, of course, are directed to the sound discretion of the court. The general rule is that the producing party bears the cost of production. It is also a general rule that the producing party is only obligated to produce the requested information in the form in which it presently exists (paper or electronic, for example), and is under no obligation to convert the information into a form that is more useable to the requesting party (from paper to electronic, for example). When a documents request is broad, the likelihood of obtaining relevant information is low, and the burden on the disclosing party is high, the court may issue a protective order barring the request, limiting the request, ordering the requesting party to pay the cost of production, or ordering that the cost be shared. For example, a document request that asks for all e-mail between all company employees for a two-year period is exceptionally broad, the likelihood of finding relevant information (the "smoking gun") is low, and the expense to the disclosing party to find and retrieve the requested information will be high (particularly when compared to the money in dispute in the case); the court usually will balance the competing concerns (the "proportionality" of potential discovery yield with anticipated discovery cost) and may consider any of these options. As the requesting party, make your e-discovery request as focused and specific as possible to reduce the likelihood of successful objections and court ordered cost shifting.

Rule 26(c) also requires that the motion be accompanied by a certification from the moving party's lawyer that he has made a good faith attempt to confer with the opposing party and resolve the dispute without court action.

Keep in mind that many discovery matters come up by motions to compel after a party has objected to discovery requests. Objections are permitted in answers to interrogatories, document requests, and requests to admit. In these circumstances the objection protects the responding party. The requesting party must move for an order compelling discovery, and there is no need for the responding party to move for a protective order.

However, if you plan to move for a protective order, make the motion early. Do not wait until the other side moves to compel discovery. The judge will wonder how serious your motion for a protective order is if it follows on the heels of your opponent's motion to compel discovery. Hence, the better practice is to object to the discovery request and immediately file your motion for a protective order.

If a protective order is appropriate, Rule 26(c) provides a variety of remedies that can protect a party or person from embarrassment, oppression, and undue burden or expense. These include barring the requested discovery; regulating the terms, conditions, methods, and scope of discovery; limiting persons present at the discovery; requiring the sealing of depositions and documents; and regulating or barring disclosure of trade secrets and confidential information.

The motion for a protective order must be prepared like any other motion, and must include statements of the facts as well as a request for the relief sought.

Example:

[Caption]

MOTION FOR PROTECTIVE ORDER

Plaintiff Willard Johnson requests that this court enter a protective order pursuant to Rule 26(c) against defendant Clark Johnson, and in support of his motion states:

1. On August 8, 2004, defendant took plaintiff's first deposition. This deposition took approximately four hours and generated a transcript of 238 pages.

2. On April 15, 2005, defendant again took plaintiff's deposition without opposition by plaintiff. This deposition took approximately three hours and generated a transcript of 181 pages.

3. On July 2, 2005, plaintiff was served with a third notice of plaintiff's deposition.

4. This pending action involves a simple intersection collision. The two previous depositions have exhaustively covered what plaintiff knows about the collision, what happened afterwards, his medical treatment, and all claimed damages.

5. The notice for a third deposition, under these circumstances, violates Rule 30(a), constitutes an attempt to annoy, oppress, and place undue burdens on the plaintiff, and has no proper purpose. Since plaintiff lives out of state, another deposition will again impose significant financial and time expenses.

WHEREFORE, plaintiff Willard Johnson requests that this court enter a protective order barring defendant Clark Johnson from taking further depositions of the plaintiff.

_____

Attorney for Plaintiff

Each discovery motion must be accompanied with a certificate of compliance, either a separate document or contained within the motion. If a separate document, it should look like the following:

CERTIFICATE OF COMPLIANCE
WITH RULE 26

I, Allen Smith, attorney of record for Plaintiff Willard Johnson, certify that I have complied with the requirements of Rule 26(c) by doing the following:

1. On July 3, 2005, I sent a letter to defendant's counsel asking why a third deposition of the plaintiff was necessary. I received no written or oral reply to my letter.

2. On July 10, I called defendant's counsel and personally spoke with him. He stated that he noticed the plaintiff's deposition a third time to "make sure he'd covered all the bases," and gave no other reason for wanting a third deposition.

3. I requested that defendant's counsel withdraw the notice for the plaintiff's deposition, but he refused. Consequently the bringing of this motion for a protective order is necessary.

Dated:_____   _____

                                                Attorney for Plaintiff

Example:

[Caption]

MOTION FOR PROTECTIVE ORDER

Plaintiff Nancy Jones moves, pursuant to Rule 26(c), for a protective order against defendant XYZ Corporation, and in support of the motion states:

1. The pending case is a product liability case involving a rubber hose manufactured by defendant XYZ.

2. Plaintiff has previously served a motion to produce the rubber hose involved for the purposes of inspection and testing. Defendant's response stated that the rubber hose has already been shipped to ABC Laboratories for testing.

3. There is a substantial danger that any testing by ABC Laboratories will alter or destroy the rubber hose and forever prevent plaintiff from inspecting and testing it.

4. In compliance with Rule 26(c), I hereby certify that I telephonically conferred with the attorney for defendant XYZ Corporation. The attorney refused to delay the testing by ABC Laboratories, and specifically stated that the testing would go forward unless this court granted a protective order. Consequently, this motion for a protective order has become necessary.

WHEREFORE, plaintiff requests this court to enter a protective order against defendant as follows:

(a) prevent anything from being done with or to the rubber hose until plaintiff has had a reasonable opportunity to inspect and photograph it;

(b) prevent any tests that would destroy or affect the appearance and integrity of the rubber hose;

(c) if destructive testing is necessary, order that such testing be conducted at a time and place so that plaintiff's experts can be present, observe the testing procedure, and obtain a copy of all test results;

(d) award payment of reasonable expenses, including attorney's fees, to plaintiff incurred as a result of making this motion.

_____

Attorney for Plaintiff

A common practice is to prepare a proposed order and attach it to the motion. The proposed order should parallel the motion by setting out what information needs to be protected and how it will be protected.

After the motion is prepared and signed, a copy along with a notice of motion must be served on every other party under Rule 5. The original of the motion and notice of motion, with a proof of service, must be filed with the clerk of the court. Keep in mind that many federal district judges delegate discovery matters to magistrate judges, so make sure your notice of motion correctly specifies who will hear the motion.

2. Compelling discovery[59]

Rule 37(a) governs motions for orders compelling disclosure or discovery. A party seeking to compel discovery must move for an appropriate order in the district where the action is pending, except if the matters relate to discovery from a nonparty, in which case the motion must be brought in the district where the discovery is being sought.

The attorney for the moving party must attach a certification to the motion showing what good faith attempts to confer and resolve the dispute were made before filing the motion.

A party can move for an order compelling discovery whenever a party fails to answer or gives evasive or incomplete answers to proper discovery. Frequently the issue arises when a party responds by objecting to an interrogatory, request to produce, or request to admit. A motion to compel must then be made to determine whether the objection is proper. The issue also frequently arises when a party fails to answer interrogatories, produce documents after being served with a request to produce, refuses to designate a deponent on behalf of a corporate party, or, in the case of deponents, refuses to appear, be sworn, or answer questions. It also arises when a Rule 26(a) disclosure is claimed to be inadequate or not in compliance with the rule.

Under Rule 37(a)(4), the court has authority to award reasonable expenses, including attorney's fees, to the prevailing party, when a motion to compel is granted and also when the discovery sought is provided after the motion has been filed. Even if your motion is granted, the court may deny a request for fees and costs if it determines that no good faith effort to resolve the dispute was made prior to seeking court intervention.

Rule 37(c)(1) provides a self-executing sanction for failure to make the Rule 26(a) required disclosures. Unless you have substantial justification for failing to make the required disclosures, you will not be permitted to use at trial, at a hearing or in a motion, any witness or information that you did not disclose unless the failure to disclose was harmless. In addition to or in lieu of the preclusion sanction, the court may order other appropriate sanctions, including expenses or attorney's fees, and even informing the jury of the failure to make disclosure.

The most common motions to compel usually involve either a party's failure to respond to discovery at all, or responding with evasive or incomplete answers that do not fairly meet the substance of the request.

59. Wright §90; James & Hazard §5.13; Friedenthal §7.16; Moore's Manual §15.13; Manual of Federal Practice §§5.216–5.235; Moore's Federal Practice §37.02; Wright & Miller §§2281–2293.

Example:

[Caption]

MOTION TO COMPEL DISCOVERY

Defendant Alfred Jenkens moves that this court enter an order compelling plaintiff Thomas Smith to answer interrogatories, and in support of his motion states:

1. On June 5, 2005, defendant served his first set of interrogatories on plaintiff.

2. On July 15, 2005, defendant by letter reminded plaintiff's lawyer that answers to interrogatories were overdue and had not yet been received. A copy of this letter is attached as Exhibit A. No response to this letter has been received.

3. Over 100 days have passed since defendant served interrogatories on plaintiff and to date no answers have been received.

4. Defendant's counsel has called plaintiff's counsel three times since July 15, 2005, each time reminding him that the answers had not been received, and, during the last call, told counsel that a motion to compel would be filed unless answers were received immediately. That last call was made one week ago.

WHEREFORE, defendant requests the court to order plaintiff to serve interrogatory answers within five days and award reasonable expenses, including attorney's fees, to defendant incurred as a result of making this motion.

_____
Attorney for Defendant

After the motion is prepared and signed, a copy along with a notice of motion must be served on every other party under Rule 5. The originals of the motion and notice of motion, with a proof of service, must be filed with the clerk of the court. Keep in mind that many district judges delegate discovery matters to magistrate judges, so make sure your notice of motion correctly specifies who will hear the motion.

A good practice is to ask the court to set out in its order compelling discovery what the sanctions will be if the order is not obeyed. This makes it more likely that the opposing party will comply with the order.

As a matter of litigation tactics, however, always consider *not* moving to compel discovery. Under Rule 37(c), a party that fails to disclose information required to be disclosed under Rule 26 shall not be allowed to use as evidence such information at trial, a hearing, or a motion. Since this preclusion is automatic ("unless such failure is harmless"), you may be better off not seeking to compel discovery and instead moving to preclude the undisclosed information when the opposing party attempts to introduce it at trial.

3.   Sanctions for abuse[60]

Rule 37 provides for the enforcement of discovery orders by permitting a wide range of sanctions for discovery abuse on lawyers, parties, and individuals. Sanctions can also be imposed on lawyers under the broader authority of 28 U.S.C. §1927. In recent years courts have been much more active in imposing sanctions, a trend that has received support from the Supreme Court.[61]

Sanctions for discovery abuse are contained in Rule 37, and are of three basic types. The severity of the sanction should obviously be commensurate with the seriousness and impact of the abuse.[62]

First, under Rule 37(a)(4), sanctions "shall" be imposed, after a hearing, against the losing party or that party's lawyer, unless the moving party failed to make a good faith effort to resolve the dispute informally before bringing the motion, or other circumstances exist that would make the imposition of sanctions unjust. Sanctions against the losing party or lawyer can include the reasonable expenses incurred by the winning party in making or opposing the motion, including reasonable attorney's fees. If the discovery motion is denied, the court can also enter any appropriate protective order.

Second, under Rule 37(b), sanctions for discovery abuse can be imposed where a deponent or party fails to obey a previous court order regarding discovery. In this situation, the court can enter essentially any sanction appropriate to the level of misconduct involved. Such sanctions can include ordering that certain facts be deemed admitted, barring a party from presenting evidence, striking pleadings, dismissing all or part of the action, entering a default judgment, and treating a refusal to obey as a contempt of court.[63] Sanctions can also include awarding reasonable expenses, including attorney's fees, if appropriate under the circumstances.

Third, under Rule 37(c) the sanction for failure to make disclosures required under Rules 26(a) or 26(e)(1) without substantial justification will be that the party failing to disclose as required is barred from using the withheld witness or information at a trial or hearing, "unless such failure is harmless." The court can also impose other appropriate sanctions, including reasonable expenses and attorney's fees. Think of Rule 37(c) as an evidence rule; if you don't disclose as required under the various provisions of Rule 26, the required sanction is preclusion of that undisclosed evidence. The moral is clear: disclose fully, disclose early, and supplement early.

---

60. Wright §90; James & Hazard §5.14; Friedenthal §7.16; Moore's Manual §15.13; Manual of Federal Practice §§5.216–5.235; Moore's Federal Practice §§37.03–37.09; Wright & Miller §§2281–2293; Joseph, Rule Traps, Litigation (Fall 2003).

61. Roadway Express, Inc. v. Piper, 447 U.S. 752 (1980); National Hockey League v. Metropolitan Hockey Club, Inc., 427 U.S. 639 (1976); Societe Internationale v. Rogers, 357 U.S. 197 (1958).

62. Societe Internationale v. Rogers, 357 U.S. 197 (1958).

63. National Hockey League v. Metropolitan Hockey Club, Inc., 427 U.S. 639 (1976); note that an order imposing sanctions for discovery abuse under the rules is not a final appealable order. See Cunningham v. Hamilton, 527 U.S. 198 (1999).

Motions to compel directed to parties must be filed in the district in which the action is pending. Motions directed to nonparties must be filed in the district in which discovery is sought to be conducted.

Rule 37(c) also permits the award of reasonable expenses, including attorney's fees, incurred as a result of proving matters that were denied in a Rule 36 request to admit, unless there was a good reason for the failure to admit. A party denying a proper Rule 36 request does so at the risk of being responsible for the expenses later incurred to prove it. Reasonable expenses would include the attorney's time and witness expenses, such as travel and lodging, that are necessary to prepare and prove the denied fact at trial.

Finally, Rule 26(g) gives the court power to impose sanctions against the lawyer or party who signs, without substantial justification, a Rule 26(a) disclosure that violates the requirements of that rule. The sanctions can be imposed after motion of a party or on the court's own initiative, and include any appropriate sanction, including reasonable expenses and attorney's fees.

With the sanctions permitted by Rules 26 and 37, it should be obvious that the court has the power and discretion to impose such sanctions as will be an effective response to discovery abuse. The difficult decisions, however, involve those situations where the discovery abuse was not caused by the party itself, but by the party's lawyer. Under these circumstances, it may be unjust that a party who may have a meritorious claim or defense should suffer adverse consequences due to abuse by his lawyer. For that reason, Rule 37(b) also allows, as an alternative or additional sanction, the imposition of reasonable expenses, including attorney's fees, against the abusing party or his lawyer, or both, unless there was a substantial justification for the noncompliance. This permits the court to fine the lawyer directly if the lawyer was the principal cause of the failure to comply.

Conversely, a lawyer must protect himself from the possible imposition of sanctions when the client is the reason for a failure to comply with a discovery order. The common problem involves a client who fails to provide documents or information necessary to respond to discovery, or a client who fails repeatedly to submit to a deposition. When this occurs, the lawyer must make it clear to the judge and the other lawyers that his client is the cause of the problem. This can be done orally in conversations with the other lawyers, and perhaps through letters to them explaining what steps you have taken to try to comply with their discovery. If you do this, the other lawyers will probably ask for discovery abuse sanctions only against your client. If the other lawyers ask for sanctions directly against you, you must, both in a written response to the motion and at the hearing on the motion, detail the efforts you personally have made to comply with the discovery. Of course, if the client continues to refuse to cooperate with the lawyer, the lawyer may need to withdraw from the representation.

§6.14. Discovery review

Under Rule 16, judges may enter scheduling orders for, among other matters, the completion of discovery. Since most judges now actively participate in case management, they commonly set a discovery cutoff date at the scheduling conference. A cutoff date means that all formal discovery must be completed by that date. (Keep in mind that a request to admit facts is not usually considered discovery for this purpose.)

About three months before the cutoff date is a good time to review the status of discovery. Among the things you should consider are the following:

1. Required disclosures (Rule 26)
   a. Initial disclosures, expert disclosures, and pretrial disclosures received?
   b. Supplemental disclosures necessary?
   c. Motions pending?
2. Interrogatories (Rule 33)
   a. Answers to all interrogatories received?
   b. Supplemental answers necessary?
   c. Experts and opinions disclosed?
   d. Motions pending?
3. Documents requests (Rule 34)
   a. Responses to requests received?
   b. Documents and electronically stored information actually delivered?
   c. Supplemental responses necessary?
   d. Expert reports received?
   e. Motions pending?
4. Mental and physical examinations (Rule 35)
   a. Plaintiff's examination done?
   b. Medical report requested and received?
5. Depositions (Rule 30)
   a. All necessary witnesses deposed?
   b. Experts deposed?
   c. Ordered transcripts received?

Discovery in large part is making sure you get what you need and what you are entitled to. As the months pass, many loose ends appear. You never received all the documents and electronically stored information you were promised. You have yet to depose one of the experts. The other side never supplemented its interrogatory answers. A motion has never been ruled on. These kinds of loose ends tend to get lost in the shuffle as more immediate matters capture your attention.

Hence, about three months before the discovery cutoff date is a good time to review the status of discovery. Mark this date on your litigation calendar and docket control system. Why three months? It takes time to tie up the loose ends. You need to remind your adversary, first by letter and then by follow-up calls, that you have not gotten all your discovery. If resolving discovery disputes informally fails, you need to move to compel answers.

Taking these steps early makes good sense. The last thing a judge wants to hear on the eve of the discovery cutoff date is a motion to extend the time to complete discovery. The judge will naturally want to know what you have been doing in the preceding months. If your discovery activity has been low, or nonexistent, don't expect the judge to help you now.

VII

MOTIONS

§7.1.   Introduction

"Motion practice" is a significant part of the litigation process. Motions are used to regulate the routine "housekeeping" matters in litigation, such as the rescheduling of discovery, hearings, and other deadlines. Motions are also used to reach dispositive results, such as motions to dismiss or motions for summary judgment. Every litigated matter will involve motions, so knowing when and how to present appropriate, well-drafted motions and how to respond to them is an essential skill for every litigator.

A motion is simply an application to a court for an order. Presenting an effective motion, however, involves both technical requirements, such as format and service rules, and substantive requirements, which control how the body of a motion should be organized and constructed so that the motion will be persuasive to the judge. This chapter discusses both routine housekeeping and dispositive motions. However, pleadings motions, principally governed by Rule 12, are discussed in §5.4; discovery motions, principally governed by Rule 37, are discussed in §6.15.

§7.2.   General requirements for motions

Rules 5 through 11 govern how motions are made. However, local rules must always be checked because they often detail matters such as filing requirements, page size, page limitations, format, organization, supporting memoranda and exhibits, and special service times. While motions may present numerous matters and seek a wide variety of relief, their basic requirements are generally the same.

1. Form

Under Rule 7(b), a pretrial motion must meet three basic requirements. It must be in writing, must "state with particularity the grounds therefor," and must state the relief or order requested. A written notice of motion, which states what the motion is for, can also satisfy the requirement of a written motion. Within these broad requirements a great deal of flexibility is allowed, and how a particular motion is structured is controlled primarily by tactical considerations.

The format requirements for motions are identical to those for pleadings. A motion must have a caption showing the name of the court, the names of the parties to the action, and a designation of the motion involved. Where there are multiple parties, the name of the first party on each side, with an "et al." designation, is sufficient.

Every motion must be signed by a lawyer representing the moving party. The signature also constitutes a certification that the written motion complies with the Rule 11 requirements. The motion must show the lawyer's name, address, and telephone number. While some lawyers put the original of all court papers on a blue-backed sheet, Rule 7 does not require it, and local rules usually dispense with this formality.

Example:

UNITED STATES DISTRICT COURT
FOR THE DISTRICT OF IOWA

John Smith, Plaintiff	No. 05 C 100
v.	
Johnson Corporation, et al., Defendants	

MOTION TO RESET HEARING DATE

Plaintiff John Smith moves this Court for an order continuing the hearing on defendant's motion for discovery sanctions, presently set for July 1, 2005, for ten days. In support of his motion, plaintiff states:

      1. . . .
      2. . . .
      3. . . .

WHEREFORE, plaintiff John Smith requests the Court to enter an order continuing the hearing, presently set for July 1, 2005, to July 11, 2005.

           Attorney for Plaintiff
           Address
           Telephone

In many jurisdictions the practice required by local rule is to state only the motion itself and put all supporting points, legal authority, and exhibits on an attached memorandum. Where they exist, these format formalities obviously must be followed.

2. Notice, service, and filing

Rule 6(d) requires that a written motion, any supporting affidavits, and notice of the motion and hearing be served on every party at least five days before the hearing date, unless the federal rules or a court order alters the time requirement.[1] As a practical matter, all documentation that accompanies a motion should be attached to and served with the motion. Service can be made by any of the methods permitted by Rule 5 on every party presently in the case. The most common methods are service by mail or personal service, although service by electronic means is now permitted. The motion with proof of service must be filed with the clerk of court or, if permitted by local rules, with the judge.

Example:

[Caption]

NOTICE OF MOTION

To: Alfred Jackson
      Attorney for Johnson Corporation
      100 Madison St., Suite 1400
      Chicago, Illinois 60602

Please take notice that on June 15, 2005, at 9:30 A.M., plaintiff will appear before the Hon. Prentice Marshall in Courtroom No. 2303, United States Court House, 219 S. Dearborn St., Chicago, Illinois, and present a motion to reset a hearing date. A copy of

---

1. For instance, a motion for summary judgment must be served at least ten days before the hearing date. See §7.8.

the motion, with supporting memorandum and exhibits, is attached to this notice.

_____

Attorney for Plaintiff
Address
Telephone

For the convenience of the court and other parties, it is good practice to give more notice than the minimum required by Rule 6 when possible under the circumstances. It is also good practice to call the other lawyers to select a mutually agreeable hearing date, if possible, before sending out the written notices. This gives the court time to read the motion, avoids disputes over whether notice was adequate, minimizes continuances, and fosters a good working relationship with the other lawyers in the case.

A motion can be served in any of the ways set out in Rule 5(b). The standard methods are to mail the motion and notice of motion to a lawyer for each party or have the motion and notice delivered to them or someone at their offices. Following service, the originals of the notice and motion should be filed with the clerk of the court along with a proof of service. In many jurisdictions the motion and notice of motion are filed with the clerk of the judge who will actually hear the motion, as well as with the clerk's office. Filing must occur "within a reasonable time" after service, but obviously must be done before the date set for the hearing. The usual procedure is to file the originals immediately after service. Be sure you get a copy of the motion, notice, and proof of service stamped "filed" and dated by the clerk to keep in your files. Filing by facsimile or other electronic means is proper if permitted by local rule.

Proof of service is merely a certificate, issued by a lawyer or a nonlawyer, that states that service on the other parties has been made in a proper way. The federal rules do not define certificate of service, but local rules usually do. These should be checked since some rules provide for a certificate from an attorney, while a nonattorney may be required to make a declaration under penalties of perjury or a notarized affidavit of service. The certificate of service is usually attached to the end of the motion.

Example:

CERTIFICATE OF SERVICE

I, James Brown, served the above motion for a continuance by mailing a copy to Sharon Smith, the attorney for defendant Johnson Corporation, at 100 Madison St., Chicago, Illinois 60601 on June 7, 2005.

_____

Attorney for Plaintiff

How do you select the day for the hearing on the motion? Check with the clerk of the judge to whom the case is assigned to determine on what days the judge hears motions, since practices vary widely. Some judges hold daily court hearings; others hear motions only on designated days. Find out what your judge's practice is so that the date you select will be one on which the motion can be heard. Finally, check with the clerk the day before the hearing to make sure the case will actually appear on the next day's motion calendar and to find out when you should be in the courtroom. Many judges arrange their court calendars to hear uncontested and routine cases first and contested matters afterwards.

3.   Content of the motion

Under Rule 7(b), a motion must be in writing, must "state with particularity the ground therefor," and must state the relief or order requested. Since the Rule permits a great deal of flexibility, the content of a motion is principally governed by tactical considerations: What will be an effective way to present this motion?

The usual procedure, required by many local rules, is to draft a concise motion summarily setting out the matter and the relief requested, supplement it with a memorandum of law if appropriate, and attach any necessary exhibits and supporting documents. Some local rules also require that the motion state whether the other party opposes, or will not oppose, the motion. Call the other side's lawyer to find out her position. In this way a judge can scan the motion quickly, then review the more detailed supporting materials.

The usual practice must be modified, however, for the relative seriousness and complexity of the motion and for local practice. For example, a motion to reset a hearing date because you will be on trial in another case should be brief. The motion need only point out when the hearing is presently scheduled, state where and when the conflicting trial is scheduled, and how long that case will take to try, and then suggest a new date for the hearing. In this situation the judge will want brevity, and the factual representations by counsel in the motion should be enough.

At the other extreme, a motion for summary judgment will usually be a thorough presentation of both law and facts. You will probably need to make a motion that sets out the background of the case, the relief requested, and incorporates by reference a memorandum that thoroughly discusses the applicable law and existing facts. The memorandum should also contain excerpts from the pleadings and discovery, exhibits such as documents and records, and witness statements in affidavit form. The motion and accompanying materials should be a self-contained package having everything the judge will need to decide the motion.

Learn what your judge's personal preferences on oral argument are and modify your written motion accordingly. Some judges dislike oral argument, and prefer to get everything in writing; others at best skim the written motions, preferring to have oral argument set out the details. While you must always comply with the Rule 7 and local rule requirements and protect your record by having the essential matters in your motion, there is no point in not acceding to your judge's preferences.

In short, drafting a motion requires a flexible approach. The relative complexity of the motion, local custom in presenting motions, and even the preferences of the judge all come into play. Motions that are specifically tailored to these considerations, which do not mechanically follow a set blueprint, have a much better chance of succeeding.[2]

4. Responses to motions

Once served with a motion, the respondent has two choices: oppose or not oppose the motion. If the motion is a routine one, a common practice, if you do not oppose the motion, is to notify the opposing lawyer of your position, who will tell the judge at the hearing on the motion that you have no objection to the motion. This will eliminate your having to come to court. However, you should file a statement that says you have no opposition to the motion, since it is good practice to have a written record of your position, and this should eliminate the danger that your position is misrepresented.

Example:

[Caption]

STATEMENT OF NONOPPOSITION TO DEFENDANT'S MOTION FOR ADDITIONAL TIME TO ANSWER

Plaintiff John Smith does not oppose defendant's motion for 10 additional days to answer plaintiff's complaint, presently set before the Hon. Prentice Marshall on June 15, 2005, at 9:30 A.M.

_____
Attorney for Plaintiff

Another approach is to agree to a "consent order," in which both parties draft an agreed-upon order that disposes of the motion. While this does not guarantee that the judge will sign it, in practice the judge usually will. This approach is common in state courts, but not in federal court.

On the other hand, if you decide to oppose the motion, serve and file your response in advance of the hearing. Rule 6(d) requires service at least one day before the hearing. Make sure you file your response with the judge's clerk before the hearing. The response should set out the reasons for your opposition and include case law and other authority you will want the judge to consider.

---

2. The motion should be drafted with precision the first time, since no rule expressly allows amendments of motions; Rule 15 applies only to pleadings. In practice, however, amendments of motions are sometimes permitted.

Example:

[Caption]

DEFENDANT'S OPPOSITION TO PLAINTIFF'S MOTION FOR LEAVE TO FILE A SECOND AMENDED ANSWER

Defendant Wilbur Johnson opposes plaintiff's motion for leave to file a Second Amended Answer, presently set before the Hon. Prentice Marshall on June 15, 2005, at 9:30 A.M., for the following reasons:

    1. . . .
    2. . . .
    3. . . .

WHEREFORE, defendant Wilbur Johnson requests the Court to enter an order denying plaintiff's motion for leave to file a second amended answer.

Attorney for Defendant

5. Hearing and argument

On the date set for the hearing, check whether an order has already been entered. Many judges will enter orders granting routine and uncontested motions in advance of the hearing day. This is particularly likely where both parties jointly make the motion or the court has been notified in advance that the motion is unopposed. Check with the clerk before the motion calendar starts to determine if the motion has been ruled on. Some courts post a list of motions that have been ruled on outside the courtroom. If yours has already been decided, make sure you get a copy of the order from the court clerk. Most clerks mail copies of the order to the lawyers in the case.

If your motion is still pending, the case eventually will be called by the clerk. The usual practice is for the lawyers to approach the bench when their case is called, state who they are, and which party they represent. If the motion is a routine one, the judge will usually let the lawyers make brief comments, make a ruling from the bench, and immediately enter an appropriate order. If a significant motion is involved, the judge will probably permit lengthier arguments and take the case "under advisement," meaning the judge will research and consider the issues further before deciding the motion.

To prepare for oral argument at the hearing, it is critical to learn what your judge's practice is. Some judges disfavor oral argument and dispense with it altogether for routine motions or, for other motions, give the lawyers very little time to argue. In this situation you obviously must make all your points in the written motion. At the other extreme are judges who at best scan written motions and rely heavily if not exclusively on oral argument in deciding whether to grant a motion. Preparing for oral argument depends a great deal on knowing what the judge wants to hear. If you don't know, ask lawyers familiar with the judge, or watch a motion calendar in that judge's courtroom and see how the judge conducts hearings.

If the judge's practice is to allow substantial oral argument, you need to decide what will persuade the judge to rule in your favor. Sometimes the weight of prevailing law will be persuasive, at other times the facts. Whatever it is, don't repeat the contents of the motion unless the judge tells you he needs his memory refreshed. Many judges begin the hearing by telling the lawyers that they have read the motion and response, and then ask the lawyers if they have anything to add. Take heed of this request, since usually a motion has an important point that will persuade the judge. It may be the law, facts, basic fairness, or the result of a particular ruling. Basic fairness or the results of a ruling can frequently be argued more persuasively orally.

Regardless of what points you have selected to argue orally, act confident and professional. Address your comments to the judge, not opposing counsel. Above all, don't interrupt or argue with counsel. The judge will usually ask the movant to argue first, and then give the respondent an opportunity to argue. Nothing is as unprofessional and ineffective as two lawyers bickering with each other, yet unfortunately this is an all too common event during motion hearings.

As the movant, standard procedure is to approach the lectern positioned before the bench, or to stand at counsel table, introduce yourself, state what party you represent, give the other lawyers a chance to identify themselves and their parties, state what your motion is for, and then go immediately to the points you have selected to emphasize. When you are finished, the other lawyers can respond. When they are through, you may, depending on the judge's practice, have a short opportunity to rebut. Always be prepared to answer any questions the judge may ask.

Example:

> Judge: Call the next case.
>
> Clerk: Williams v. Louisiana Chemical Company. Defendant's motion to reset the trial date. (Lawyers for plaintiff and defendant come to the podium.)
>
> Defense Lawyer: Good morning, your honor. Dominic Gianna for the defendant.
>
> Plaintiff Lawyer: Lorna Propes for plaintiff Williams, your honor.
>
> Defense Lawyer: This is our motion to reset the trial date for this case. We filed our motion, and plaintiff filed a written response.
>
> Judge: I've read the motion and response.
>
> Defense Lawyer: Your honor, our motion to reset the trial date should be granted for three reasons. First, . . .
>
> Judge: Thank you. Plaintiff, do you wish to respond?
>
> Plaintiff Lawyer: Yes, your honor. We oppose the motion because . . .
>
> Judge: Thank you, counsel. The trial date previously set will be vacated, and the trial will be rescheduled for April 1, 2005.

The key to making effective oral arguments is always remembering that the argument must be thought through in advance, coordinated with the written motion, and must supplement the motion by emphasizing the important points that, in your judgment, will present your side in its best light.

6. Order

Regardless of when the motion is decided, the court will enter an order.[3] In federal court, routine motions are usually decided by a "minute order," which is merely a form on which the clerk makes an entry reflecting the ruling. The minute order is then signed by the judge or stamped with his signature, and a copy is mailed to the lawyers. If the motion is important, the judge may prepare a written opinion and order explaining the reasons for the ruling.[4] Since Rule 5(b) now permits local rules to allow service through the court's electronic transmission system, some courts are now posting orders and rulings only on the court's Web site. Make sure that every pending motion is ultimately decided by an order, that the order accurately reflects the court's ruling, and that you obtain a copy of the order.

The court may refer certain motions to a U.S. magistrate judge, since magistrate judges are empowered to hear routine civil pretrial matters.[5] In recent years it has become particularly common for magistrate judges to supervise the discovery process in civil cases. The motion procedure before a magistrate judge is identical to that before the district judge.

§7.3. *Extensions of time and continuances*

The kinds of motions that can be presented to the court are limited only by the movant's imagination. Practically, however, the routine housekeeping motions invariably deal with time and date modifications. These are the motions for extensions of time, continuances, and new hearing and trial dates.

Rule 6(b) governs extensions of time. If a motion to extend time is made before the expiration of the applicable time period, the court may grant the motion for "cause." However, if the motion is made after the applicable time period had expired, the court may grant the motion only where the failure to act timely was caused by "excusable neglect."

What constitutes "cause" or "excusable neglect" is addressed to the court's discretion, and must be evaluated in the context of the pending case. Courts have generally been realistic and accommodating in permitting extensions of time where the applicable period has not yet run. Usually any reason other than one involving bad faith and actual prejudice to an opponent will result in the court's granting a reasonable extension of time.[6]

3. See Rule 77(d).
4. This practice may differ from state practice, where the prevailing lawyer sometimes prepares a draft order reflecting the court's ruling, which the judge then signs.
5. See Magistrate's Act, 28 U.S.C. §§631 et seq.
6. See Wright & Miller §1165.

Excusable neglect, on the other hand, is judged on a substantially higher standard. Courts have usually denied extensions of time where the failure to act within the required time limitations was caused by the lawyer's inadvertence or ignorance of the applicable rule or by a lawyer's busy case load and other work demands.[7] It is usually an extraordinary situation involving good faith, such as the death or serious illness of a lawyer or a member of her family, a delay by a client in forwarding a complaint and summons, or difficulties in substituting proper parties or different lawyers, that must be present before a court will find excusable neglect and permit an extension of time.

Some time periods for post-trial matters usually cannot be enlarged. These include a motion for judgment after trial, motion for new trial (Rule 50(b)), motion to amend findings and judgment (Rules 52(b) and 59(e)), motion for a new trial (Rule 59(b)), motion to set aside a judgment for reasons such as mistake, fraud, or newly discovered evidence (Rule 60(b)), and appeals from magistrate judges' decisions (Rule 74(a)).

Make the motion and have it decided within the applicable time period. Give the court solid reasons why an extension is necessary, and ask only for such additional time as is reasonably needed. Above all, avoid missing a deadline. This is not a situation you want to find yourself in. The best way to avoid having these disasters arise in the first place is by creating, maintaining, and following a reliable docket control system, which will remind you of all significant dates for each case you are handling. These vary from simple calendars to sophisticated computer systems, but are critical for every litigation lawyer.

Routine motions for extensions of time or continuances should be structured simply. The pertinent information that forms the basis for the motion can ordinarily be put in the body of the motion.

Example:

[Caption]

MOTION FOR ADDITIONAL TIME TO ANSWER OR RESPOND

Defendant Robert Johnson moves this court for an order granting defendant an additional 10 days to answer or respond to plaintiff's complaint. In support of his motion defendant states:

1. Defendant was served with the summons and complaint on June 1, 2005. Under the rules defendant's answer is due on or before June 21, 2005.

2. Defendant's attorney received the complaint from the defendant on June 13, 2005.

3. Plaintiff's complaint has five counts and is based on an alleged series of contracts with the defendant.

4. To answer the complaint, defendant's attorney will have to evaluate numerous business records, which the defendant is presently locating, and review them with defendant.

---

7. See Wright & Miller §1165.

5. Defendant's attorney believes he can prepare and serve an answer or otherwise respond if an additional 10 days to answer or respond is granted.

WHEREFORE, defendant requests that this court enter an order extending defendant's time to answer or respond to July 1, 2005.

_____

Attorney for Defendant

Note that the motion asserts facts in the body of the motion that are based on the lawyer's own knowledge, or on information already contained in the court file. In this situation the facts do not need to be stated in affidavit form. Where the facts that are the basis of the motion are within someone's knowledge other than the attorney, the facts must be in affidavit form and attached to the motion.

§7.4. *Substitution of parties*

During the pendency of an action, events may take place that will require that a named party be replaced by another. Such a substitution of parties can be required when a party dies, becomes incompetent, or loses all legal interest in the action. A public official, named as a party, can die, resign, or be voted out of office. In these situations Rule 25 provides for substitution with a successor party. Unless death abates the action, the court, upon notification and demonstration of the change, will order a substitution. In the case of public officials, the substitution is automatic.

The usual procedure is to make a motion for substitution of parties, state the reason for the substitution in the body of the motion, and attach any necessary documents as exhibits. For example, if a party dies and will be substituted by the administrator of the estate, attach a copy of the death certificate and the probate court order appointing the administrator of the estate.

§7.5. *Temporary restraining orders and preliminary injunctions*

Injunctions are of three types: temporary restraining orders, preliminary injunctions, and permanent injunctions. A permanent injunction is a final remedy that can be ordered only after a trial on the merits of the case. Temporary restraining orders and preliminary injunctions, governed by Rule 65, are provisional remedies. A temporary restraining order can be granted without notice to the other side, and can be granted only until a hearing for a preliminary injunction can be held. Its purpose is to avoid an immediate irreparable injury to the petitioning party. A preliminary injunction, by contrast, can be issued only after an adversarial hearing; it maintains the status quo until the case is tried.

Both temporary restraining orders and preliminary injunctions are forms of injunctions. Since an injunction is an equitable remedy, it can only be granted if the legal remedies are inadequate. Accordingly, make sure that the underlying complaint asks for injunctive relief and that such relief would be proper if the complaint's allegations are ultimately proved. While Rule 65 governs temporary restraining orders and preliminary injunctions, local rules often have additional requirements that must be met.

1. Temporary restraining orders[8]

a. Law

A temporary restraining order (TRO) is governed by Rule 65(b). Since this is an extraordinary procedure, the Rule's requirements must be followed precisely.

First, a TRO can be granted without notice to the opposing party, but only if three requirements are met. These requirements reduce the risk that a TRO will be granted in error and cause an injustice to the other party. The motion must be supported by affidavit or a verified complaint alleging specific facts that show that "immediate and irreparable injury, loss or damage will result" unless the order is issued before the opposing side can be heard. In addition, the attorney representing the applicant must file an affidavit stating the "efforts, if any, which have been made to give notice" and the "reasons supporting his claim that notice should not be required." Finally, the applicant for a TRO must post security in an amount the court deems sufficient to cover the costs and damages that may be incurred if the party restrained is found to have been wrongfully restrained. All three of these requirements must be met. Although Rule 65(b) expressly requires only that an applicant for a TRO show an "immediate and irreparable injury," case law generally holds that the applicant must make the same showing, at least on a preliminary basis, as that required for a preliminary injunction.[9] That is, the applicant must show, in addition to an irreparable injury, that there is a likelihood of success on the merits of the case, that the threatened injury to the applicant exceeds any foreseeable injury to the adverse party if the order is granted, and that any order will not be against the public interest. As a practical matter, a court will not enter a TRO unless these considerations, taken as a whole, appear to weigh heavily in the applicant's favor. Keep in mind that jurisdictions differ on the relative weight to be put on these considerations.[10]

Second, if a TRO is granted, the order must specify the injury, why it is irreparable, why it was granted without notice, and describe in reasonable detail the acts that are enjoined. It is limited to the duration set by the court, which cannot exceed 10 days, although it can be extended for another 10 days for good cause.

---

8. Moore's Manual §10.07(2); Friedenthal §15.4; Manual of Federal Practice §7.101; Moore's Federal Practice §§65.05–65.08; Wright & Miller §§2951–2953.

9. Moore's Manual §10.07(2); Manual of Federal Practice §7.101; Moore's Federal Practice §65.06, Wright & Miller §2951.

10. See Gohn & Oliver, In Pursuit of the Elusive TRO, 19 Litigation (No. 4, 1993).

Third, the court must set a date for a hearing on a preliminary injunction at the earliest possible time whenever a TRO is granted without notice. The party against whom the TRO was issued can, with two days' notice, move to have the TRO dissolved.

b. *Practice approach*

Apply for a TRO only under appropriate circumstances. There is a great deal of work involved, and the court cannot properly issue a TRO unless an immediate and irreparable injury will occur without it. Since a TRO is a powerful and extraordinary judicial step, courts are necessarily reluctant to grant it except in the most compelling of circumstances.

Demonstrating an immediate and irreparable injury and an inadequate remedy at law is understandably difficult. The threatened harm must be both imminent and serious. Common situations involve threatened damage to unique property and proprietary interests. For example, if someone is about to cut down mature elm trees on another's property, if a magazine is about to release personal photographs of a private person without authorization, if a former employee is about to breach a covenant not to compete, or if a former employee is about to sell trade secrets to a foreign competitor, a TRO may be appropriate because in these situations the wronged party cannot be made whole through money damages. Make sure you know and can accurately describe both the threatened conduct and the persons and entities you seek to enjoin.

Second, make sure that the court has both subject matter jurisdiction over the claim and personal jurisdiction over the defendant. Lack of subject matter jurisdiction will result in dismissal of the complaint. Lack of personal jurisdiction will make any injunctive relief ordered unenforceable. Keep in mind that if you file in state court, the defendant may be able to remove to federal court if the requirements of 28 U.S.C. §1441 are met. If this happens, you may lose valuable time in actually obtaining the TRO, so it may make sense to file in federal court in the first place.

Third, moving for a TRO requires that you prepare, file, and ultimately serve several things at nearly the same time. These include:

- verified complaint, or unverified complaint with witness affidavits, and summons
- application for TRO and preliminary injunction
- attorney's affidavit of attempted notice
- witness affidavits
- security for costs and damages
- draft of proposed court order

i. Complaint and summons

Where a TRO is being sought, the allegations in the complaint will form the factual basis for the motion and must be coordinated with it. The relief requested should include a TRO, preliminary injunction, and permanent injunction. The factual allegations should, like any complaint, be specific enough to show that the pleader is entitled to the relief requested if the allegations are proved. Finally, although not required, the allegations should be verified by the party, since this has the same evidentiary effect as an affidavit. A complaint is verified when it contains a statement that the party has read the complaint, personally knows the facts, states that the facts are true, and the statement is sworn to before a notary public.

The complaint is usually filed at the same time as the application for the TRO. This means that the summons will not yet have been served. However, since the Rules require that the attorney state how notification on the adverse party has been attempted, you should always try to have service of the complaint and summons expedited, especially since Rule 4 permits service by any person not a party and at least 18 years old.

The complaint, application, and supporting documents are usually filed with the emergency judge, an assignment that is usually rotated among the active judges. Find out who the present emergency judge is, and notify the judge's secretary or clerk of the situation.

ii.   Application for TRO and preliminary injunction

The application for a TRO should be combined with a request for a preliminary injunction, since under Rule 65(b) a hearing on a preliminary injunction must be scheduled as soon as possible after a TRO without notice is granted.

The application must allege that an immediate and irreparable injury will occur unless the TRO is granted. Since the application must be supported by facts, it usually refers to the verified complaint and accompanying witness affidavits for factual support. As with motions generally, the application itself is usually drafted simply and refers to the supporting material for the substance.

Example:

[Caption]

APPLICATION FOR TEMPORARY RESTRAINING ORDER AND PRELIMINARY INJUNCTION

Plaintiff applies, pursuant to Rule 65, for a temporary restraining order and requests that a hearing for a preliminary injunction be set. In support of his application plaintiff states:

1. Plaintiff will suffer an immediate and irreparable injury unless his application for a temporary restraining order is granted.

2. In support of his application for a preliminary injunction and a hearing date, plaintiff states:

(a) defendant will perform the threatened acts, as more fully set out in the complaint, unless enjoined;

(b) defendant's threatened action, if carried out, will result in irreparable injury to plaintiff;

(c) a preliminary injunction will not injure or inconvenience the defendant.

3. In support of his application, plaintiff incorporates by reference the allegations of his verified complaint and the facts as set forth in the witness affidavits attached as Exhibits A through C.

4. Plaintiff's attorney's certificate showing her efforts to give notice to the adverse party, and why notice to the defendant should not be required, is attached as Exhibit D.

5. Plaintiff is ready to provide security in such amount as the court determines is necessary to cover the costs and expenses incurred by the defendant in the event the defendant is found to have been erroneously restrained and enjoined.

WHEREFORE, Plaintiff requests that the court enter a temporary restraining order against defendant and set a hearing for a temporary injunction at the earliest practical time.

_____
Attorney for Plaintiff

iii.   Attorney's certificate regarding notice

Rule 65(b) requires that the attorney for the moving party certify in writing "the efforts, if any, which have been made to give the notice and the reasons supporting his claim that notice should not be required." Notice here includes informal as well as formal notice. Courts clearly prefer any notice over none at all, such as a telephone call to the adverse party, his lawyer if known, or an agent. Accordingly, the lawyer's certificate should show all the steps she took to give some advance notice to the adverse party. A sound approach is to notify the defendant by whatever means are available, unless there is a clear danger that any notice would create an even more immediate danger of irreparable injury.

Example:

<u>CERTIFICATE OF ATTORNEY IN SUPPORT OF APPLICATION FOR TEMPORARY RESTRAINING ORDER WITHOUT NOTICE</u>

I, Terry Anton, attorney for plaintiff, make this certificate, in accordance with Rule 65(b), in support of plaintiff's application for a temporary restraining order without notice to the defendant.

1. On June 1, 2005, at approximately 1:00 P.M., I was first informed of defendant's imminent conduct as set forth in the complaint. I immediately began drafting the complaint, this application, and the supporting documents.

2. At the same time I telephoned defendant at his place of business to advise him of this application, but could not personally contact him. I left a message with his answering service, but have received no call from him.

3. I have attempted to locate the defendant's residence and present whereabouts without success.

4. I have no knowledge of any attorney who may presently represent the defendant, and have attempted to learn this without success.

_____

Attorney for Plaintiff

iv. Witness affidavits

Rule 65 requires that the applicant for a TRO show specific facts, through a verified complaint or witness affidavits, that demonstrate the required "immediate and irreparable injury." Accordingly, you should review the verified complaint and determine what additional facts must be shown, and put them in affidavit form. The affidavit should show who the witness is and demonstrate that the witness has firsthand knowledge of all the facts recited in the affidavit.

Example:

AFFIDAVIT

I, William Jones, having been first duly sworn, state:

1. I am the plaintiff in this action. I live at 123 Maple Lane, Denver, and am the owner of that property.

2. On June 1, 2005, at approximately 8:30 A.M. I saw the defendant . . .

3. . . .

4. . . .

I hereby declare, under penalties of perjury, that the facts stated in this affidavit are personally known to me, and that they are true.

_____

Name of Affiant

Signed and sworn to
before me on June 2, 2005.

_____

Notary Public

My commission expires on _____.

Note that 28 U.S.C. §1746 sets forth a procedure for making and using unsworn declarations under penalty of perjury, which can be used for witness affidavits.

v.   Security for costs

Rule 65(c) requires that a TRO cannot be issued unless the applicant provides adequate security to cover any costs and damages that may be incurred by the adverse party if the TRO is wrongfully issued. Accordingly, thought must be given to the likely security requirement. Ordinarily this means obtaining a bond from a surety or posting a cash bond with the clerk of the court, although the court can set any other security requirement. Since the court will not issue the TRO until the security has been set and met, you should always have the plaintiff prepared to deposit the likely cash bond immediately if the TRO is granted. Check with the clerk's office to determine its requirements for receiving bonds and other security. If you need a bond from a surety or fidelity company, call it immediately to find out what information and documentation it will require before issuing a bond. The cost of the bond is a litigation cost for which the client is ultimately responsible, regardless of the outcome of the case.

vi.   Hearing, order, and service

The necessary papers need to be presented to the assigned judge or the emergency judge, who will review the papers to determine if the Rule 65 requirements and standards have been met. This will usually be done in the judge's chambers on an ex parte basis, since the other side will probably not have received notice of the application for the TRO. The judge needs to be convinced that an irreparable injury will occur unless the TRO is granted immediately, until a hearing, with both parties present, can be held.

It is the usual procedure in federal court for the judge or his clerk to issue orders, either minute or full written orders. However, since with a TRO time is critical, it is useful to prepare a draft order for the judge in advance so that it can be immediately signed if the judge grants the TRO. Rule 65(b) requires that the order specify the date and time issued, define the injury, state why the injury is irreparable, state why the TRO was granted without notice, specify the terms and duration of the order, and set a hearing date for the temporary injunction at the earliest possible time.

Example:

[Caption]

ORDER

This cause being heard on the application of plaintiff for a temporary restraining order and preliminary injunction, the plaintiff appearing ex parte without notice to the defendant, the court having considered the verified complaint, witness affidavits, and the attorney's certificate attached as exhibits to plaintiff's motion,

THE COURT FINDS:

1. Plaintiff's threatened injury as described in the verified complaint is irreparable because. . . .
2. This order is being granted without notice to defendant because. . . .

THE COURT ORDERS:

1. The defendant is hereby restrained from. . . .
2. This order shall remain in effect until June 4, 2005, at 5:00 P.M.
3. A hearing on plaintiff's motion for a preliminary injunction is set for June 4, 2005, at 2:00 P.M. and the defendant is hereby ordered to appear in this courtroom at that time.
4. A copy of this order, along with copies of the complaint, summons, motion, and supporting documentation, shall be served forthwith on the defendant.

SO ORDERED:

_____
Judge

Date: _____

Time: _____

Since the court's order is not enforceable until the defendant receives actual notice of it, you should attempt to notify the defendant by telephone of the court's order and arrange for immediate proper service of a certified copy of the order under Rule 4. Make sure the order is filed with the clerk of the court.

2. Preliminary injunctions[11]

a. Law

Preliminary injunctions are governed by Rule 65(a), which has several requirements. The procedure is simpler than that for a TRO, because the crisis atmosphere of a TRO is missing.

---

11. Moore's Manual §10.07(2); Friedenthal §15.4, Manual of Federal Practice §7.100; Moore's Federal Practice §65.04, Wright & Miller §§2947–2950.

First, the Rule requires notice to the adverse party. Although it does not specify the necessary time period, it is likely that the usual five-day notice period for motions under Rule 6(d) applies. Also, notice of the motion must include service of the complaint and summons.

Second, the movant must post security in an amount the court deems proper for the payment of costs and damages that may be incurred if the party is found to have been wrongly enjoined.

Third, the movant has the burden of showing, through verified pleadings or testimony and other evidence at the hearing, that: (1) if the injunction is not ordered, the movant will suffer an irreparable injury; (2) the movant will likely succeed on the merits of his claims at trial; (3) the threatened injury to movant exceeds any threatened injury to the adverse party; and (4) a preliminary injunction would not be against the public interest. Various jurisdictions have different formulations of this four-part test, and of the required burden of proof, so jurisdiction-specific research will be necessary here.

Fourth, if the court orders a preliminary injunction, the order must be specific and state in reasonable detail what acts are enjoined. The order granting a preliminary injunction remains in effect until the court has a trial on the merits, although the court can modify or vacate the order if warranted.

The court can consolidate the hearing on the motion for a preliminary injunction with a trial on the merits. If consolidation is not ordered, evidence presented at the hearing on the motion for a preliminary injunction need not be repeated at the trial on the merits. Consolidation is frequently ordered where injunctive relief is the principal remedy sought and the evidence at the hearing for the preliminary injunction would be largely the same as at the trial.

An order granting or denying a preliminary injunction and permanent injunction is appealable. An order granting or denying a TRO is not appealable.[12] Since the issuance of injunctive orders is addressed to the court's discretion, the order will be reversed on appeal only if it was erroneous as a matter of law or the order was improvidently granted.

b. Practice approach

A preliminary injunction can come before the court in two ways. First, it can be set by the judge as part of an order granting an application for a TRO. Second, the plaintiff can move for a preliminary injunction.

The critical point to remember is that the hearing on the preliminary injunction is, as a practical matter, often the determinative proceeding in an injunction case. Proof presented at the hearing need not be duplicated at a later trial. Furthermore, the court can advance the trial on the merits and consolidate the trial with the hearing. Where injunctive relief is the sole or principal remedy sought, the court will often accelerate and consolidate the trial and hearing. In practice, the hearing is the trial and is conducted essentially like a bench trial. The court will frequently order

12. See Wright §102.

that discovery be expedited and state what discovery will be permitted under the circumstances. As the plaintiff's lawyer, you must be prepared to go to trial quickly and present your entire case on short notice. This means that you must have live witnesses prepared to testify, and essential documents that can be qualified for admission in evidence, at the hearing on the preliminary injunction. When the hearing has been consolidated with the trial, if the court rules in favor of the plaintiff, it will enter a permanent injunction rather than only a preliminary injunction.

Before moving for a preliminary injunction, assess the benefits and risks. On the plus side, moving for a preliminary injunction gets the court involved early and gets the defendant's attention quickly. If you want the case resolved quickly, either through a settlement or an early trial, or you want to reach a "standstill agreement" with the other party that will maintain the status quo while the case is pending, the motion may help accomplish these objectives. On the minus side, moving for a preliminary injunction is expensive because you may end up with two hearings — the hearing on the motion and the later bench trial. It also requires that you be prepared to present all your evidence on short notice. If you need substantial discovery to prepare for the hearing and expedited discovery is not practical, the motion may do more harm than good. Finally, the bond requirement the court will impose if a preliminary injunction is granted may be substantial, depending on the relief requested.

In many cases, it is simpler and cheaper for the plaintiff not to move for a preliminary injunction and instead ask for a prompt trial on the merits. The court may be receptive, especially if neither side has asked for a jury trial on any of the claims. This will give you more time to prepare fully, avoid the bond requirement, avoid the possibility of two rounds of discovery, and avoid the additional cost of preparing for both a full hearing and a trial.

As defendant, decide if you want to resist the preliminary injunction, especially if the plaintiff's burden of proof in that jurisdiction is low. Consider asking for a high bond requirement, which the plaintiff may have trouble meeting or be unwilling to post. Consider a standstill agreement until a trial on the merits can be held.

If you decide to present a motion for a preliminary injunction, it should be drafted both to allege the legal requirements for such relief and to specify precisely what acts are sought to be enjoined.

Example:

[Caption]

MOTION FOR PRELIMINARY INJUNCTION

Plaintiff moves for a preliminary injunction enjoining defendant, his officers, employees, agents and any persons working with him, until a trial on the merits is held and a final order is entered in this action. In support of his motion plaintiff states:

1. Defendant will act in the manner alleged in the complaint unless enjoined.

2. Defendant's threatened action if carried out will result in irreparable injury, loss and damage, as more fully alleged in the complaint.

3. The injury to plaintiff, if defendant is not enjoined, will substantially exceed any foreseeable injury to the defendant.

4. A preliminary injunction will not be against the public interest.

WHEREFORE, plaintiff requests that the court enter a preliminary injunction enjoining defendant from [specify and describe conduct sought to be enjoined].

_____

Attorney for Plaintiff

§7.6. Removal

1. Law

The right of a defendant to remove a case from state to federal court is a statutory right governed by 28 U.S.C. §§1441-1452 and the applicable law is discussed in §3.5 supra.

2. Practice approach

A defendant considering removal must ask several questions before preparing a petition for removal.

a. Can I remove?

Removal is a procedure by which a defendant can transfer, from state court to federal court, a case in which the plaintiff's complaint alleges a claim over which a federal court would have had original jurisdiction. The propriety of removal is based solely on the plaintiff's claims. Removal cannot be based on a defense or anticipated defense, even if the defense is based on federal law.[13]

b. Should I remove?

Removal is nothing more than a change from a state to a federal forum. Consequently, there is no point in removing unless the defendants will benefit from the change. The potential advantages include a quicker trial date since federal courts frequently have less of a backlog than state courts. Federal districts, however, give priority to criminal cases and usually

---

13. See Rivet v. Regions Bank, 522 U.S. 470 (1999).

make diversity cases the lowest priority on the trial calendar. Another potential advantage is the procedural differences that may exist between the state and federal courts. For example, the pleading possibilities may be greater and the discovery rights broader in federal court. Also, the Federal Rules of Evidence may be more relaxed on admissibility issues than state evidence rules. Removing to federal court is also a way of getting the case away from an unfavorable state judge. Finally, federal jury panels are usually drawn from a larger geographical pool and may have different characteristics than a state jury panel. These types of strategic possibilities must be carefully evaluated before proceeding further.

c. Can I get codefendants to remove?

Removal cannot be granted unless all defendants, except nominal or fraudulently joined ones, agree to remove. There is no point in filing a removal notice unless your codefendants agree to join in the removal. Defendants for this purpose includes only those defendants who have been served with the complaint and summons. Defendants named in the complaint who have not been served with the complaint and summons need not agree to removal, since they are not yet in the lawsuit. This "unanimity rule," when coupled with the 30-day time limit, can create problems when a case has multiple defendants who are not all served with the complaint at the same time. The traditional approach has been that the time the first defendant is served with the complaint starts the running of the 30-day period. This can be unfair if later defendants are served near the end of that 30-day period. Some courts now hold that the later-served defendants have 30 days from formal service of the complaint on them to file a notice of removal.[14]

d. Can I remove all claims?

The most common ground for removal is complete diversity between plaintiffs and defendants, and more than $75,000 in issue, so long as no defendant is a citizen of the state in which the action is brought, as provided by §§1332 and 1441(b). Also common is removal under federal question jurisdiction, as provided by §§1331 and 1441(b).

What happens if some, but not all, claims are explicitly removable under §1441? Under §1441(c) a defendant can sometimes have a nonremovable claim removed to federal court if such a claim is related to a removable claim. Such a determination is addressed to the discretion of the court, which can permit removal of the entire case or remand all matters in which state law predominates. However, §1441(c) now provides that if removal is based on a separate and independent claim, that claim must involve a federal question; separate claims based on diversity are no longer sufficient.

14. See Marano Enterprises v. Z-Teca Restaurants, 245 F.3d 753 (8th Cir. 2001).

When fewer than all claims are removable, you must decide whether removing some but not all claims is strategically advantageous and economically feasible. The advantages are the potential benefits of removal that were discussed previously. The disadvantages concern the time and costs expended in litigating in two different forums.

e. What are the procedural requirements for removal?

If after considering the relevant issues you decide that removal is the proper course, make sure you follow the procedure set out in 28 U.S.C. §§1446-1450, since case law requires that the procedures be closely followed. There are several basic steps that are requirements of the removal process.

i. Timing

The notice of removal must, under §1446(b), be filed in the federal district court in the division in which the state action is pending within 30 days after the defendant receives formal service of the complaint and summons.[15] If an amended pleading is the first indication that the case is removable, the defendant must file the petition within 30 days of the receipt of such pleading. Section 1446(b) imposes an absolute time limit of one year for removals based on diversity, measured from the commencement of the action.

ii. Notice of removal

Each defendant in the case who has been served, except nominal or fraudulently named defendants, must sign and file a "notice of removal." The notice itself must contain a "short and plain statement of the facts" entitling the defendant to removal. This necessarily means that the jurisdictional requirements for removal set out in §1441(b) must be alleged in the notice since plaintiff's state court complaint will not usually allege them. This is particularly important where diversity is the basis for removal, in which case the notice must allege the diversity jurisdiction requirements of both complete diversity and the jurisdictional amount, and that none of the defendants is a citizen of the state in which the action is brought. However, regardless of the jurisdictional basis, whether federal question, diversity, or actions against the federal government, it must be alleged accurately and completely since the appropriateness of the removal depends principally on this allegation. Where more than one ground for removal exists, each should be alleged.

---

15. See Murphy Bros. v. Michetti Pipestringing, 526 U.S. 344 (1999), holding that a defendant must remove the case within 30 days after being formally served.

Example:

[Federal Court Caption]

Mary Jones, Plaintiff	No. _____
v.	
John Smith, Defendant	

NOTICE OF REMOVAL

To: The United States District Court for the District of Arizona:

Defendant John Smith hereby gives notice that the above captioned case is being removed from the Superior Court of Pima County, Arizona, to the United States District Court for the District of Arizona. In support of this notice defendant states:

1. Plaintiff Mary Jones commenced this action against defendant John Smith in the Superior Court of Pima County under the caption of "Mary Jones, Plaintiff v. John Smith, Defendant," Docket No. 05 C 10478, by serving a copy of the complaint and summons on defendant on June 1, 2005.

2. The complaint alleges that [summarize each count]. A copy of the complaint and summons is attached. No other pleadings or other proceedings have been filed or taken to date.

3. This action is a civil action and is one over which this court has original jurisdiction under 28 U.S.C. §1331 [and/or §1332, etc.] and is an action that can be removed to this District Court pursuant to 28 U.S.C. §1441.

4. [If federal question:] This court has original jurisdiction over this action because it appears from plaintiff's complaint that this is a civil action that arises under the _____ Act, _____ U.S.C. §_____, [or Constitution or treaty] because plaintiff claims that. . . .

5. [If diversity:] This court has original jurisdiction over this action because it appears from plaintiff's complaint that this is a civil action, and:

(a) Plaintiff, both when this action was commenced and now, was and is a citizen of the State of California;

(b) Defendant, both when this action was commenced and now, was and is a citizen of the State of Nevada. Defendant was not, when this action was commenced, nor is he now, a citizen of the State of Arizona.

(c) The amount in controversy, exclusive of interest and costs, exceeds $75,000.

6. [If multiple defendants:] Each defendant served consents to the removal of this case.

7. [If no jury demand was made in the complaint, and you want one, add a jury demand and immediately comply with all federal jury demand requirements.]

_____

Attorney for Plaintiff

If the case has more than one defendant, the notice of removal should be signed by each defendant's lawyer, since each defendant must agree to remove.

iii. Notice to adverse parties

Section 1446(d) requires that each adverse party be notified promptly of the filing of the notice of removal. This is done in the same way that notice is customarily given.

Example:

[Federal Court Caption]

NOTICE OF FILING NOTICE OF REMOVAL

To: [_attorney for plaintiff_]

Please take notice that on June 10, 2005, defendant John Smith filed a Notice of Removal in the United States District Court for the District of Arizona. A copy of the Notice of Removal is attached to this notice.

_____

Attorney for Defendant

The original notice should be filed with the clerk of the court after copies of the notice have been sent to the attorneys of all adverse parties.

iv. File notice of removal in state court

The final step in the removal process is filing a copy of the notice of removal with the clerk of the state court. This act terminates the jurisdiction of the state court.

v. Further proceedings

Once the above steps are completed, removal is complete. There is no order required to effect removal. The federal district court retains jurisdiction, unless and until the case is remanded back to the state court, and can proceed as with any other case.

The usual state of affairs after a case has been removed is that the defendant who has been served has not yet responded to the complaint, and other defendants have not been served. The served defendant must, under Rule 81(c), answer or otherwise plead within 20 days of receipt of the initial pleading or summons, or within five days of filing the notice of removal, whichever is longer. The answer or other response must comply with the federal pleading rules. If plaintiff has not served all defendants before the notice of removal is filed, service must be made in compliance with Rule 4. In short, all action taken after removal must be taken under the federal rules.

vi. Motion to remand

If a removal of the case from state to federal court is improper, it must be alleged in a timely motion to remand under §1447(c). If the motion is based on a defect in the notice of removal, it must be raised within 30 days of the filing of the notice of removal. If the defect is based on lack of subject matter jurisdiction, it can be raised at any time. If the motion is granted, the order remanding the case may also order the payment of costs and actual expenses, including attorney's fees, incurred as a result of the improper removal.[16]

§7.7. Judgment on the pleadings[17]

Motions for judgment on the pleadings are governed by Rule 12(c). After the pleadings are closed, but sufficiently before trial so that trial will not be delayed, any party can move for judgment on the pleadings. The motion determines if, based on the allegations in the pleadings, the moving party is entitled to judgment. For purposes of the motion, the movant's well-pleaded allegations that have been denied are deemed false, while the opponent's allegations are deemed true. In short, the pleadings are viewed in the light most favorable to the opponent of the motion. It is only when the undisputed facts as pleaded show that the movant is entitled to judgment that the motion should be granted.[18] If a party presents matters outside the pleadings and the court decides to receive them, the motion is treated as one for summary judgment.

A motion for judgment on the pleadings under Rule 12(c) is different from a motion to dismiss under Rule 12(b)(6). The motion to dismiss

---

16. In Martin v. Franklin Capital Corp., 546 U.S. 132 (2005), the Supreme Court held that under the removal statute attorney fees "should not be awarded when the removing party has an objectively reasonable basis for removal."

17. James & Hazard §5.18; Friedenthal §9.1; Manual of Federal Practice §§4.31–4.34; Moore's Manual §16.01; Wright & Miller §§1367–1372; Moore's Federal Practice §12.15.

18. See Moore's Manual §16.01.

considers only if a claim in a complaint (or counterclaim, cross-claim, or third-party complaint) properly sets forth a claim upon which relief can be granted. The analysis is limited to the allegations in the claim. By contrast, the motion for judgment on the pleadings considers not only the complaint but also the answer.

The motion for judgment on the pleadings is usually made only in cases where "legal" defenses, such as the statute of limitations, are clearly shown to exist. Since under the federal rules answers need not be responded to, allegations in the answer cannot be the basis for judgment on the pleadings.

Example:

[Caption]

MOTION FOR JUDGMENT ON THE PLEADINGS

Defendant Johnson Corporation moves this Court to enter judgment on the pleadings in favor of the defendant. On the undisputed facts in the pleadings, defendant is entitled to judgment, under Rule 12(c), as a matter of law.

In support of its motion defendant states:

    1. . . .

    2. . . .

    3. . . .

WHEREFORE, defendant Johnson Corporation requests the Court to enter judgment on the pleadings in favor of the defendant.

_____

Attorney for Defendant

Rule 15 provides that motions to amend pleadings should be "freely given when justice so requires." Therefore, if it appears likely that a motion for judgment on the pleadings will be granted, the plaintiff should move for leave to amend, if the defect can be cured. Under these circumstances the motion for leave to amend should attach the proposed amended pleading. Where the motion is made before substantial discovery has been conducted, it should ordinarily be granted, despite the pendency of a motion for judgment on the pleadings.[19]

The motion for judgment on the pleadings is closely related to the motion to dismiss under Rule 12(b).[20] Of the seven grounds for a Rule 12(b) motion, the most commonly asserted one is Rule 12(b)(6): failure to state a claim upon which relief can be granted. A Rule 12(b)(6) motion should be made after the defendant has received the plaintiff's complaint and before answering. If the motion is granted, the plaintiff will usually be

---

19. See Manual of Federal Practice §4.33.
20. See §5.4.3.

given leave to file an amended complaint; usually the plaintiff can cure the defect. The litigation then continues.

By contrast, a motion for judgment on the pleadings is made after the pleadings are closed and it has become evident that there is a legal bar, such as an applicable statute of limitations, that will prevent plaintiff from recovering anything. For this reason, a motion for judgment on the pleadings should not be made unless it is clear from the facts in the pleadings, in light of applicable substantive law, that plaintiff cannot recover on his claim. Such motions are infrequently made.

§7.8. Summary judgment[21]

Summary judgment is governed by Rule 56. It is designed to be an efficient method of deciding a case when there are no genuine disputes over any material facts. A motion for summary judgment can be made on any claim — complaint, counterclaim, cross-claim, or third-party claim — and on a complaint for declaratory judgment. Partial summary judgment can be granted on fewer than all parties, fewer than all counts, or on one of several issues within a count, such as liability.

1. When made

A complaining party may move for summary judgment on its claim 20 days after the action has been commenced or after an adverse party has moved for summary judgment. A defending party on whom any such claim has been asserted may move for summary judgment at any time. A motion for summary judgment must be served on all other parties at least 10 days before the hearing date.

Since Rule 56(a) allows motions for summary judgment early in the litigation process, when to bring such a motion is principally a matter of litigation strategy. While the Rule permits early motions, as a practical matter they have little chance of success before the pleadings have been closed. The motion is usually made after substantial discovery has been conducted, the important facts become known, and it becomes increasingly apparent that there are no serious disputes over the essential facts.

2. Standards and matters considered

A moving party is entitled to summary judgment only if "there is no genuine issue as to any material fact" and "the moving party is entitled to a judgment as a matter of law." The motion merely asks the court to decide if there are any material facts in issue and whether the substantive law entitles

21. Wright §99; James & Hazard §5.19; Friedenthal §§9.1–9.3; Moore's Manual §§17.01–17.19; Wright & Miller §§2711–2742; Moore's Federal Practice §§56.02–56.04; Manual of Federal Practice §§4.35–4.42.

the moving party to judgment. It is not the court's function here to determine what facts are true. In deciding if material facts are in dispute, however, the court can consider the pleadings, discovery, exhibits, and witness affidavits.

What facts are material is determined by the claim involved and the allegations in the pleadings. The court will review the movant's motion and supporting matters and determine if any material facts remain disputed. The court will resolve any doubts against the moving party. Keep in mind, however, that the formal pleadings are not controlling. If the pleadings show a dispute, but the discovery and affidavits show that no dispute over any material fact exists, the motion should be granted.

If the motion fails to demonstrate that summary judgment should be granted, the opponent theoretically need do nothing. As a matter of practice, of course, the opposing party always responds to the motion with a memorandum and, if possible, affidavits showing why the motion should not be granted. However, if the motion with accompanying materials shows that the motion should be granted, the opponent ordinarily must, if able to, present a response and opposing affidavits to show that disputes over material issues still remain.[22] If the court then finds that disputed issues remain, the motion will be denied.

3. Hearing, order, and appealability

At the hearing on the motion for summary judgment the judge will usually allow oral argument, and then ordinarily will take the case under advisement and enter a written order at a later time. The order will set out whether the motion is granted or, if partial summary judgment is requested, on what issues the motion is granted or denied. It will also set out the findings and reasoning that are the basis of the order.

Appealability of the order depends on whether the order disposes of all or only part of the case. When an order granting the motion disposes of the entire case, the order is final and appealable.[23] Where the order grants only partial summary judgment, either for some but not all parties or for some but not all claims, the order may be appealable, depending on whether the court makes it an appealable one under Rule 54(b). That Rule permits the judge to make the order appealable "only upon an express determination that there is no just reason for delay" and the judgment is expressly entered.

---

22. See Celotex Corp. v. Catratt, 477 U.S. 317 (1986), where the Court rejected the notion that the moving party must always support the motion with affidavits showing the absence of a genuine dispute over a material fact. Where a party has the burden of proof on an essential element and fails to make a sufficient showing to establish that element after an adequate time for discovery, there is no genuine dispute over a material fact and the other party may be entitled to summary judgment without a further factual showing. See also the companion cases to *Celotex:* Matsushita Elec. Indus. Co v. Zenith Radio Corp., 475 U.S. 574 (1986), and Anderson v. Liberty Lobby, Inc., 477 U.S. 242 (1986).

23. See Moore's Manual §17.19(1).

When the motion is denied, the usual reason is that material facts are still in dispute. An order denying summary judgment on that basis is not final and cannot be appealed.[24]

4. Practice approach

Summary judgment motions have three important characteristics. First, a summary judgment motion, if granted, will terminate part — and sometimes all — of the litigation. Second, a summary judgment motion is time consuming and expensive for the client. Third, the summary judgment motion frequently may not succeed or, even if successful, the losing party may successfully appeal. Therefore, the threshold question any lawyer contemplating bringing a summary judgment motion must ask is: Does it make legal, factual, and economic sense for my party to bring the motion in this particular case?

a. Should I move for summary judgment?

Since summary judgment can only be granted under Rule 56 if "there is no genuine issue as to any material fact" and "the moving party is entitled to a judgment as a matter of law," the first step is to determine if the case is the kind of case that is suitable for disposition through summary judgment. Small cases, those involving one or two issues, are suitable candidates. Contract cases, such as suits on promissory notes where the signatures are conceded to be either genuine or fraudulent, are also good candidates. Cases involving affirmative legal defenses, such as a statute of limitations or res judicata, should be considered. In these kinds of cases the legal issues are frequently clear, the facts may be simple, and the motion, if successful, may terminate the entire litigation. While both plaintiffs and defendants may bring summary judgment motions, it is the defense that more commonly brings them.

Certain kinds of cases may also be suitable for partial summary judgment motions. In a case having numerous parties or claims, a summary judgment motion may eliminate one or more parties or claims, thereby simplifying the case. A partial summary judgment motion can be directed at a specific part of the case such as damages issues. For example, the motion can attack punitive damages or consequential damages claims. Partial summary judgment may be sought on liability issues, so that the trial will be limited to the issue of damages. While partial summary judgment motions often make sense only in larger cases, it can be extremely beneficial in those cases.

What kinds of cases are usually not suitable for summary judgment motions? Cases involving mental state issues, such as fraud and intentional tort cases, cases involving circumstantial evidence, and those involving witness credibility issues, such as eyewitness testimony, are poor candidates.

---

24. See Moore's Manual §17.19(2).

These cases invariably involve disputed facts and simply cannot be resolved by this motion.

There are other questionable reasons to pursue summary judgment. One reason frequently given is that the motion will expedite discovery. However, summary judgment is an expensive discovery vehicle, and motions to compel discovery are generally more efficient and effective. Another reason given is that the motion will force an earlier disclosure of the other side's experts. However, witness affidavits from experts are rarely from the experts who will testify if the case goes to trial. For example, the other side may obtain an affidavit from its consulting expert and "save" its testifying experts for trial. Yet another reason given is that the motion will "educate the judge." However, there are usually easier ways to accomplish this, such as a good pretrial memorandum. Finally, some argue that a summary judgment motion increases the pressure on the other side to settle. While this may be true, a party reluctant to realistically explore settlement will usually feel pressure only when the trial date draws near.

Finally, there are good reasons not to file a summary judgment motion. First, the motion educates your opponent, since the motion is essentially a condensed trial. An early motion educates your opponent earlier. Second, the costs associated in bringing a serious motion are substantial, since the motion will usually require at least 10-15 hours to prepare, and may require much more time. The cost of preparing exhibits and witness affidavits for the summary judgment motion can be substantial. The client must be advised what the expected costs are to bring the motion before the decision can be made. Third, most summary judgment motions fail. The client must also be advised of the likelihood of success or failure before an intelligent decision can be made to make the motion. You need to consider what will happen if you win the motion in the trial court, but lose it on appeal. This is principally a concern for plaintiff, who might be better off simply trying the case than winning a motion that might be reversed on appeal. Fourth, you may decide not to present a motion for partial summary judgment because that part of the case has strong jury appeal, and it will improve your entire case if it goes to trial. Finally, keep in mind that on appeal the appellate court reviews the trial court decision de novo, while on appeal from a judgment after trial the trial judge's findings of fact are reviewed on a clearly erroneous standard.

b. When should I bring a summary judgment motion?

One possibility is to bring the motion early in the litigation process, soon after the right to amend pleadings has passed but before substantial discovery has been taken. This can be effective in simple cases such as suits on contracts or notes, involving simple issues such as whether payment was made or whether the parties executed the contract. However, keep in mind that the opposing party may ask for a delay in the hearing on the motion and the right to take additional discovery before responding to the motion, which the judge may grant under these circumstances.

Most summary judgment motions are brought after substantial discovery has been done, but well in advance of the trial date. This has the obvious advantage of using the other side's discovery responses to demonstrate that there is no factual dispute over any material facts. Be sure to make the motion well before the trial date, or before a trial date is even set. Summary judgment motions filed on the eve of trial are usually viewed as a desperate attempt to avoid trial and will be poorly received.

If you decide to make a summary judgment motion, file and serve the motion well in advance of the hearing date. While Rule 56 permits service to be made only 10 days before the hearing, or 13 days if service is by mail, the court will need time to evaluate a serious motion. In addition, the opposing party has a right to respond. Setting a hearing date well in advance will allow the opposing party to prepare and present a response and will minimize continuances.

c. How should I organize a summary judgment motion?

Rule 56 has no technical requirements and states only that the movant show that she is "entitled to a judgment as a matter of law" and that there is no "genuine issue as to any material fact." Therefore, the movant must demonstrate that the law, and the facts, compel that the motion be granted. Hence, the two essential components of a summary judgment motion are:

1. the memorandum of law, which discusses the applicable substantive law, and
2. the statement of facts, which, with supporting exhibits, discusses the applicable facts.

d. How do I prepare the memorandum of law?

A good place to start is to get the pattern jury instructions used in your jurisdiction for the claims, or defenses, involved in the motion. The elements instructions will tell you what specific proof is necessary for each of those claims, or defenses, on which you are seeking summary judgment and is a useful blueprint for the specific contents of the memorandum of law. If your jurisdiction does not use pattern jury instructions, you must research the substantive law (which you should have already done before filing, or responding to, the lawsuit). Once you have done this, you can then easily draft a memorandum of law, which tells the judge exactly what must be proven to establish a prima facie case on each claim, or defense, involved.

Aim for brevity, both in the memorandum of law and the statement of facts. The motions most likely to be granted are usually the ones that can demonstrate that summary judgment is proper in a few pages. If it takes dozens of pages to accomplish this, the judge will usually find that the law is unclear or that some material fact is still in issue and deny the motion.

e. How do I prepare the statement of facts?

Summary judgment is a fact-driven motion, so how you organize and present your facts is critical. Your statement of facts must show that there is no material fact over which there is a genuine dispute. The statement of facts will contain the material facts that are necessary to the motion and will be annotated to the factual sources that support it. A good method is to use the elements instructions to determine what facts are material, then organize and state those material facts in paragraphs much like the factual allegations in a complaint. Each material fact stated must then be cross-referenced to the sources that prove that fact.

Keep in mind the hierarchy of factual sources necessary to demonstrate that no material facts are in dispute. There are three basic sources:

1. opponent's pleadings allegations and discovery responses
2. records and documents (yours and opponent's)
3. witness affidavits

Of these, your opponent's pleadings allegations and discovery responses will usually be the most persuasive, since it is more difficult for the opponent to contest the facts that come out of its own pleadings and discovery responses. Particularly persuasive are your opponent's responses to your requests to admit under Rule 36, since the matters admitted are deemed conclusively established for purposes of this litigation. Least persuasive are witness affidavits, since your opponent can usually attach contrary witness affidavits in its response, thereby creating a factual dispute over a material fact, and defeating the motion.

Example:

DEFENDANT'S STATEMENT OF FACTS

Defendant Alice Smith, through her attorney, submits this Statement of Facts pursuant to Rule 56 and local rules in support of her Motion for Summary Judgment on Count I of plaintiff's complaint alleging breach of contract.

1. Alice Smith, defendant, is the president, chairperson of the board of directors, and majority shareholder of Smith Optical Company. (Exhibit #1, Complaint, Par. 4; Exhibit #2, Answer, Par. 4)

2. James Woods, plaintiff, was hired as an employee of Smith Optical Company on June 1, 2000, and was terminated as an employee on December 1, 2004. (Exhibit #3, Woods deposition transcript, p. 14; Exhibit #4, Smith deposition transcript, p. 22; Exhibit #7, Termination letter dated December 1, 2004, attached as exhibit to Smith deposition)

3. When James Woods was first hired, he was given a copy of Smith Optical Company's Employee Personnel Manual. (Exhibit #3, Woods deposition transcript, p. 26)

4. The Employee Personnel Manual that James Woods was given when first hired provided that "The three-step procedure for terminating employees for inadequate performance shall NOT be applicable if an employee engages in criminal conduct, acts of

dishonesty, or acts which threaten the health or safety of other employees or customers." (Exhibit #5, Employee Personnel Manual, p. 7; Exhibit #6, Affidavit of Helen Griggs, custodian of records for Smith Optical Company)

    5. The termination of James Woods was approved at the board meeting of Smith Optical Company held on December 15, 2004. (Exhibit #4, Smith deposition, p. 44; Exhibit #8, Board minutes of 12/15/04 meeting; Exhibit #6, Affidavit of Helen Griggs, custodian of records)

Each exhibit cited must be attached to the statement of facts. The usual practice is to bind and tab the exhibits so that the judge, when reading the statement of facts, can quickly find the exhibit. Check both the local rules and the judge's rules since many of them are quite specific on how exhibits must be organized, bound, and tabbed.

These factual sources need to be presented properly in the motion. Pleadings and discovery present no problems, since they are part of the record and copies of, or excerpts from, the pleadings or discovery responses can be appended to the statement of facts. However, records, documents, photographs, and other demonstrative aids presented as exhibits, and witness testimony presented by witness affidavits, must be prepared carefully to meet the Rule 56 requirements.

f.   How do I prepare exhibits?

The principal concern with exhibits is that they are properly qualified, since Rule 56 requires that any facts presented in support of the motion must be admissible in evidence. For example, merely attaching a business record as an exhibit to the statement of facts will probably be deemed inadequate. The sounder practice is to determine what evidentiary foundation would be necessary to get this exhibit admitted at trial, then prepare an accompanying witness affidavit that establishes the proper foundation for that exhibit. For example, most documentary exhibits can be properly introduced as either business records or, if signed instruments, by authenticating the signatures of the persons signing the instruments. Finally, make sure that the exhibit contents do not violate other evidentiary rules. For instance, double hearsay problems are common in business records. The key point to remember is that the judge need not consider "evidence" that supports the summary judgment motion if that evidence would not be admitted at trial. Hence, it is your responsibility to demonstrate that each exhibit would be admissible at trial, through a carefully drafted affidavit from an appropriately qualified foundation witness.

Another useful approach is to send a request to admit facts, under Rule 36 to the opposing party, asking it to admit the evidentiary foundations for the exhibits you will use to support your summary judgment motion. If the opposing party admits them, it makes presenting the motion much simpler.

Since brevity is important, consider using summaries under Rule 1006 of the Federal Rules of Evidence to summarize voluminous records.

Sometimes this information can be presented in graphs and charts and still meet Rule 1006's requirements.

g. How do I prepare witness affidavits?

Drafting witness affidavits must also be done carefully. Rule 56 requires that affidavits be based on "personal knowledge," state only "such facts as would be admissible in evidence," and "show affirmatively that the affiant is competent to testify" to the matters contained in the affidavits. The standard practice is for the lawyer to draft the witness affidavit in consultation with the witness. Hence, you need to plan what the witness would testify about if she were testifying at the trial of the case and prepare the witness affidavit to recite that testimony. Have the affidavit read like a direct examination, using the witness' vocabulary, not legalese, so the affidavit shows the witness' own "testimony." Accordingly, the affidavit should first show that the witness is competent to testify and has personal knowledge of the facts recited in the affidavit. The affidavit should then set out the events and activities of which she has firsthand knowledge and show how she has acquired that knowledge. If the witness will qualify records, documents, or other exhibits, the affidavit must set out the proper evidentiary foundation for each exhibit's admission in evidence, and the exhibit should be attached to the affidavit as an exhibit. Finally, the affidavit should be sworn to before a notary public, and a suitable attestation should be at the end of the affidavit.

Example:

AFFIDAVIT IN SUPPORT OF
MOTION FOR SUMMARY JUDGMENT

I, Gloria Patterson, having first been sworn, state under oath:

1. I am a resident of Tucson, Arizona, and have resided there since 1988.

2. Since January 1, 1990, I have been the president of Cross-Country Transportation, an Arizona corporation having its principal place of business in Tucson, Arizona. As president, I have the overall responsibility for its operations, including entering into contracts on behalf of Cross-Country Transportation.

3. On June 1, 2005, at approximately 10:00 A.M., I was in the office of Smith Corporation at 100 Main Street, Tucson, Arizona, for a meeting with John Smith, the president of Smith Corporation, the defendant in this case. Also present was Adam York, the plaintiff in this case.

4. At that meeting, I saw John Smith sign his name to a contract, a copy of which is attached to this affidavit as Exhibit A. The signature at the bottom of page 5 of Exhibit A is that of John Smith, the defendant.

5. I have seen John Smith sign his name to various documents about 15 times over the past five years. Based on this previous

experience, I recognize the signature on page 5 of Exhibit A as that of John Smith, the defendant.

I hereby declare, under the penalties of perjury, that the facts stated in this affidavit are personally known to me, and that they are true.

_____

Gloria Patterson

State of Arizona
County of Pima

Signed and sworn to before me on _____

_____
Notary Public

My commission expires on _____

Note that 28 U.S.C. §1746 sets forth a procedure for making and using unsworn declarations under penalty of perjury, which can be used for witness affidavits.

Expert witness affidavits, which should be prepared in the same way, do involve one additional problem. Rule 56 (requiring personal knowledge) and Rule 703 of the Federal Rules of Evidence (permitting expert opinion testimony without first admitting in evidence the facts or data the expert relied on to reach the opinion) are seemingly in conflict. The logical answer is that Rule 703 should control. Experts rely on many sources that are not within their personal knowledge in evaluating problems and reaching opinions and conclusions, yet may, under Rule 703, testify about their opinions and conclusions at trial. Furthermore, it is obvious that Rule 56 did not intend to make affidavit requirements more stringent than the evidentiary rules applicable to trials.

The basic rule on expert witness affidavits is not to use one at all unless absolutely necessary. In most cases, one expert's affidavit will usually generate an opposing expert's affidavit, thereby probably defeating the summary judgment motion. An expert's affidavit is usually useful only when it contains principally factual matter and basic, indisputable matter that the other side cannot contest by an opposing expert's affidavit.

h. How does the summary judgment motion look when done?

Most effectively organized motions have several parts:

1. the motion itself, stating what relief is being sought
2. memorandum of law, setting out the applicable law
3. statement of facts, annotated to the pleadings, discovery, exhibits and witness affidavits

4. excerpts from pleadings and discovery, marked and tabbed
5. exhibits, marked and tabbed
6. witness affidavits, marked and tabbed
7. table of contents, if useful

Finally, the overall impression your summary judgment motion should convey is simplicity, clarity, and confidence because a motion that is verbose, complicated, and muddled has no chance of success. From your memorandum of law the judge must quickly understand the elements of the claims, or defenses, involved in the motion. From your statement of facts the judge must be convinced that these are in fact all the material facts necessary to decide the motion. Finally, from your supporting pleadings, discovery, exhibits, and witness affidavits the judge must be convinced that there is clear, sufficient, and admissable proof of each of these material facts.

Example:

[Caption]

MOTION FOR SUMMARY JUDGMENT

Defendant Albert Smith moves, pursuant to Rule 56, for an order entering summary judgment in his favor and against the plaintiff on:

1. Count I of the complaint;
2. Count II of the complaint on the issue of punitive damages only.

Defendant states that summary judgment is proper on these counts because there is no genuine issue as to any material fact in Count I, and no genuine issue as to punitive damages in Count II, and that defendant is entitled to summary judgment to the extent requested as a matter of law.

In support of his motion are the following attachments:

1. memorandum of law
2. statement of facts
3. excerpts from interrogatories and interrogatory answers
4. excerpts from depositions
5. excerpts from requests to admit facts and responses
6. three witness affidavits

WHEREFORE, defendant Albert Smith requests the Court to enter an order granting summary judgment on Count I of the complaint, and on Count II on the issue of punitive damages.

_____
Attorney for Defendant

However, not all summary judgment motions need to follow this item-ized structure. Remember that effective summary judgment motions are clear and simple, and the simplicity must be appropriate to the circum-stances. Therefore, if the motion can be made briefly, yet persuasively, so much the better.

For example, assume that defendant decides to move for summary judgment on the ground that plaintiff did not give the defendant, a municipal entity, proper notice of intent to sue within the required statu-tory period. Plaintiff's motion would only need to set forth the statutory notice requirement and cite the evidence, such as interrogatory answers or deposition transcripts, that shows that proper notice was not given within the required period. Such a summary judgment motion could probably be made in two or three pages and will be particularly effective because of its simplicity and brevity.

i. Common problems

What are the common problems that arise when drafting summary judgment motions? Remember that bringing a summary judgment motion takes time to do well and is expensive to the client. Therefore, the motion should not be made unless it has a realistic chance of success, is cost effective, and promotes the client's overall litigation strategy.

The most common drafting problem in bringing summary judgment motions is a lack of clarity and focus. Remember that the motion cannot be granted unless it demonstrates there is "no genuine issue as to any material fact and that the moving party is entitled to a judgment as a matter of law." This means that the motion must clearly set out both the applicable sub-stantive law and the material facts that have relevance to the issues raised in the motion. Confusion, complexity, and verbosity are the enemies of suc-cessful summary judgment motions.

Another common mistake is inadequate references to the factual proof contained in the motion's statement of facts. The statement of facts, and its support, are usually the most important part of the motion. Remember that the motion must establish what every necessary material fact is and show the admissible source of proof of each of those facts. If the motion alleges material facts without showing the source of proof or demonstrating that the source is admissible at trial, the judge can ignore the claimed facts and deny the motion on that basis. This means that each claimed material fact needs a citation to its sources of proof, much the way that a statement of facts in an appellate brief needs constant cross-references to the trial tran-script, and a showing that the source of proof is admissible in evidence.

Finally, motions for summary judgment frequently contain defectively drafted witness affidavits. Remember that the judge will not consider any "facts" unless the motion affirmatively shows that the claimed facts are actually admissible at trial. This means that witness affidavits must demon-strate that the witness has firsthand knowledge of the facts recited in the affidavit and will be able to testify to those same facts if called as a witness at trial. It also means that, whenever the motion refers to an exhibit such as a document, record, or diagram, the judge cannot presume its admissibility.

A witness affidavit from a competent witness must establish the evidentiary basis for the exhibit's proper admission in evidence at trial.

5. Opponent's responses

What should the opponent of a motion for summary judgment do? There are four basic things. First, if the summary judgment motion was brought early in the litigation, under Rule 56(f) the non-moving party can ask for a continuance to pursue discovery. This rule permits the non-moving party to "catch up" to the moving party as far as fact gathering is concerned, so that it will not be unfairly disadvantaged when the motion is heard. In this situation, the judge will probably order accelerated and focused discovery and defer hearing the motion for an appropriate period.

Second, the opponent should consider making a cross-motion for summary judgment. If such a motion can be made consistent with the requirements of Rule 11, it has the practical effect of opposing the original motion and frequently makes the judge inclined to deny both motions. This is frequently done in breach of contract cases.

Third, the opponent can actively respond to the motion. Rule 56(e) expressly states that an opposing party cannot rely on denials in the pleadings to resist the motion. Of course, if the motion on its face fails to show that the movant is entitled to relief, the opposing party theoretically need not do anything. In practice, however, the opponent must look at the motion, determine if it is defective on its face, and pinpoint the defects in its memorandum in opposition to the motion. If the motion incorrectly sets forth the applicable law, point it out. If the motion fails to state all the material facts necessary to decide the motion, point them out. If the motion fails to cite to the sources of proof of the material facts, point out where this occurs. If the witness affidavits are improperly drafted, fail to show the firsthand knowledge of the witness, fail to show the qualifications of the witness, or fail to establish an evidentiary foundation for the admission of exhibits relied on in the motion, point them out. If there are expert witness affidavits, review them carefully. Look particularly for things the expert would be expected to say but did *not* say; that's where the weaknesses are (and where your expert's countering affidavit should focus). In short, meticulously analyze the motion, statement of law, statement of facts, and supporting affidavits and exhibits to make sure that they are complete and proper.

Fourth, if there are no defects in the motion itself, you will need to oppose the motion by presenting exhibits and witness affidavits that contradict the movant's exhibits and affidavits on some material facts, thus creating factual disputes and issues of witness credibility. Since witness credibility issues and factual disputes over material matters can only be resolved at trial, the motion should be denied.

How the response is entitled and organized differs according to the lawyers and issues. The important point, however, is that the response clearly and efficiently demonstrates that summary judgment is inappropriate under the circumstances, either because of a fatal defect in the motion or because your response demonstrates that material facts necessary to the motion remain in dispute.

Example:

[Caption]

PLAINTIFF'S MEMORANDUM IN OPPOSITION TO DEFENDANT'S MOTION FOR SUMMARY JUDGMENT

Plaintiff Johnson submits this memorandum in opposition to Defendant Acme Corporation's motion for summary judgment on the claim for punitive damages. Since, as is demonstrated in this memorandum, and supporting exhibits and affidavit, there remain material facts in issue, defendant is not entitled to summary judgment as a matter of law, and the motion should be denied.

Law

Defendant incorrectly states the applicable law . . .

Facts

The facts essential to the question of whether a genuine dispute over material facts remain in issue are . . .

Argument

In this case, material facts are disputed by the parties . . .

Conclusion

Wherefore, Plaintiff Johnson requests that the court deny Defendant Acme Corporation's motion for partial summary judgment on the claim for punitive damages.

Dated:_____   _____

Attorney for Defendant

6.   Hearing on the motion

The court will usually schedule a hearing on the motion. How you prepare for the hearing and how you present your strongest points are much the same as for any hearing on an important motion. As the movant, keep in mind that simplicity and brevity are the key to a successful hearing. If it takes a long time to demonstrate that you are entitled to summary judgment, the very length of your argument will help to defeat your motion.

Plan on taking only a few minutes to demonstrate the key point: that since there are no material facts in dispute summary judgment should be granted. As the party opposing the motion, show how complex, convoluted, and contested the material facts are, so that the inevitable conclusion is that the dispute can only be resolved through a trial. How to argue at a hearing on a motion is discussed further in §7.2.

In most summary judgment motions the judge will take the motion "under advisement" after the hearing and issue a written order sometime later.

§7.9.   *Dismissals and defaults*[25]

Dismissals are governed by Rule 41. There are two types of dismissals, voluntary and involuntary. While the Rule speaks only of plaintiffs, it is clear that the Rule applies to any claimant and therefore to any claim, counterclaim, cross-claim, or third-party claim. It permits dismissals of fewer than all claims against fewer than all parties.[26]

1.   Voluntary dismissals

There are two ways to obtain a voluntary dismissal. First, if an answer or summary judgment motion has not yet been filed, a plaintiff can simply file a notice of dismissal with the clerk of the court. No court order is required. The rationale is that this Rule permits a plaintiff to withdraw a lawsuit that is ill-considered or prematurely brought without incurring penalties.

Example:

[Caption]

NOTICE OF DISMISSAL

Please take notice that on June 15, 2005, plaintiff Wilbur Jackson filed this Notice of Dismissal to dismiss plaintiff's complaint without prejudice, pursuant to Rule 41, with the clerk of the Court.

_____
Attorney for Plaintiff

---

25. Wright §97; James & Hazard §12.14; Friedenthal §§9.4–9.5; Manual of Federal Practice §§7.5, 7.63; Moore's Manual §§19.01–19.11; Wright & Miller §§2362–2376; Moore's Federal Practice §§41.02–41.07.

26. Rule 15, governing amendments of pleadings, and Rule 21, governing joinder, overlap Rule 41 and should always be checked. See Moore's Manual §19.04.1.

Second, if all parties who have appeared in the action agree on a dismissal, the plaintiff need only file with the clerk of the court a stipulation of dismissal signed by all parties. Again, no court order is required. This is the usual method for terminating a lawsuit following a settlement.

Example:

[Caption]

STIPULATION OF DISMISSAL

The parties, plaintiff Wilbur Jackson and defendant Frank Johnson, agreed on June 15, 2005, to dismiss the above-captioned action, with prejudice, and for each party to bear its costs of suit.

_____
Attorney for Plaintiff

_____
Attorney for Defendant

In all other circumstances, plaintiff may obtain a voluntary dismissal only by court order. The court has power to impose terms and conditions that are appropriate under the circumstances, which may include the payment of costs, expenses, and attorney's fees to the defendant. Under ordinary circumstances the motion should be granted, unless the defendant can show that some actual legal prejudice would result from a second lawsuit.

As a tactical matter, plaintiff should simply file and serve a motion for a voluntary dismissal of the action, stating reasons for granting the relief. If the court will only grant the motion upon terms that seem unduly harsh or expensive, plaintiff should consider withdrawing the motion and continuing with the action.

Regardless of whether the voluntary dismissal was obtained through a notice of dismissal or court order, the dismissal is without prejudice unless otherwise stated.[27] The claim can then be refiled later. However, under Rule 41(d), if a plaintiff later files the same claim against the same defendant, the court can order the plaintiff to pay the costs of the previously dismissed action to the defendant and can order a stay of the new action until plaintiff complies with the order for payment of costs.

Where the dismissal is made by notice of dismissal, the first one is without prejudice. However, to avoid abuse of this Rule by repeated filings and dismissals of actions, Rule 41(a)(1) has a "two dismissal rule." A notice of dismissal is with prejudice and constitutes an adjudication on the merits if the second dismissal is based on the same claim previously dismissed in any federal or state court.

27. See Semtek International v. Lockheed Martin Corp., 531 U.S. 497 (2001), for a discussion of the meaning of dismissal "on the merits."

The court ordinarily will not look into the plaintiff's motivation in seeking a voluntary dismissal. The only issues are whether a dismissal would create a legal prejudice to the defendant and what terms the order should include so that defendant's costs and expenses will be reasonably reimbursed. For instance, a plaintiff may dismiss an action that has been removed to federal court even if the only purpose of the dismissal is to defeat the removal and resulting federal jurisdiction, since a defendant has no absolute right to have a case tried in federal court.[28]

Under Rule 41(a)(2), a voluntary dismissal of a claim will not be allowed if a counterclaim has been pleaded before the plaintiff has served a motion for voluntary dismissal, if the counterclaim has no independent jurisdictional basis, or if the defendant objects to the dismissal. The reasoning behind this Rule is that the plaintiff, having previously decided to sue, cannot now use a voluntary dismissal to avoid the counterclaim. Where the defendant's counterclaim does have an independent basis for federal jurisdiction, the plaintiff may dismiss his complaint.

2. Involuntary dismissals

Involuntary dismissal provides a method for terminating a claim where a plaintiff has been guilty of misconduct. While the Rule mentions only a defendant's motion to dismiss, it is clear that the court may dismiss on its own motion.[29] There are several grounds for an involuntary dismissal.

First, a plaintiff's failure to prosecute a claim can result in dismissal. This depends on the nature of the case, but includes a plaintiff's lack of diligence in litigating, such as failing to respond to motions or to appear at hearings, and other repeated dilatory behavior. Involuntary dismissal is a drastic remedy and will normally not be imposed unless other remedies are inadequate. The difficult cases often involve situations where the plaintiff's inaction is a result of his attorney's misconduct, but the plaintiff may have a valid claim. In these situations the court will usually do something short of involuntary dismissal.

Second, the court can involuntarily dismiss where the plaintiff fails to comply with rules of procedure or with court orders. Keep in mind that most failures to comply involve discovery. The Supreme Court has held that only the discovery rules control sanctions for discovery abuse.[30] Hence, Rule 41 will govern situations involving failures other than in discovery.

Third, an involuntary dismissal may be entered at trial where the evidence presented by the plaintiff fails to demonstrate that the plaintiff is entitled to any relief. This is permissible only during a bench trial after plaintiff has rested his case in chief. This motion performs the same function as a motion for judgment as a matter of law in a jury trial. However, since the judge during a bench trial is also the trier of fact, the judge may evaluate the facts that the plaintiff has presented; while

---

28. See Moore's Manual §19.05.
29. See Moore's Manual §19.08.
30. See Societe Internationale v. Rogers, 357 U.S. 197 (1958).

in a motion for judgment as a matter of law under Rule 50, the judge must consider the evidence in the light most favorable to the plaintiff.

An involuntary dismissal is with prejudice unless otherwise ordered. Hence, it is a final and appealable order.

3. Defaults

Closely related to dismissals are defaults, governed by Rule 55. This Rule allows a plaintiff to obtain a default judgment against a party that fails to plead or take any steps to defend against the pending claim. The usual situation involves a defaulting defendant.

Defaults are allowed only when the claim seeks affirmative relief. If the claim is for a specific sum, or a sum that can be computed to a specific amount, a default judgment can be entered by the clerk of the court, provided the defendant is not an infant or incompetent. The plaintiff must present an affidavit to the clerk of the court setting out the facts showing default and the sum due. The affidavit should be in the same form as any notarized witness affidavit.[31]

In all other cases the claimant must make a motion for default at least three days before the hearing. If the defaulting party has appeared in the case, you must serve a notice of motion on that party at least three days before the hearing. Even if the defaulting party has never appeared in the case, it is a good practice to serve a notice of motion anyway. At the hearing the court will determine if the allegations of the claim are true and, if plaintiff is entitled to judgment, what the proper amount of damages is.

Example:

[Caption]

MOTION FOR DEFAULT

Plaintiff Joan Franklin moves for an order finding defendant Thomas Johnson in default, finding that the defendant owes plaintiff the sum of $84,246.80 plus costs, and for judgment against defendant in that amount. In support of her motion plaintiff states:

1. On March 1, 2005, defendant Thomas Johnson was personally served with the summons and the complaint, as shown by the affidavit of service on the summons.

2. Defendant has failed to answer the complaint, has failed to make an appearance, or in any way respond or defend, although over 90 days have passed since service upon him.

3. Defendant has not responded to three letters sent to him by plaintiff's attorneys. Copies of these letters are attached as Exhibits A, B, and C.

31. See §7.9.3.

4. Plaintiff is prepared to testify to her reasonable damages, which total $84,246.80.

WHEREFORE, plaintiff requests that the court find defendant Thomas Johnson in default, hold a hearing to determine the exact amount due plaintiff, and enter judgment for plaintiff and against defendant in that amount.

_____

Attorney for Plaintiff

Defaults are most commonly obtained in simple cases where a defendant who has been properly served fails to respond in any way to the lawsuit and enough time has passed so that it becomes obvious the defendant does not intend to defend against the claim.

If the sum due is clear, such as in a contract action for past due rent or in an action for an unpaid bill for purchased merchandise, an affidavit to the clerk of the court is appropriate. In many cases, however, the full damages can only be determined at a hearing, requiring that a motion for default be made.

At the hearing on the motion, sometimes called a "prove-up," you should be prepared to show that service on the defaulting party was proper, that the allegations of the complaint are true, and what the proper damages are. While judges vary on the formality of the prove-up hearing, you should have all your documentation available and any witnesses on hand that may be necessary to prove your case. For example, in an action on a contract, you should be able to prove proper service with the proof of service in the court file. If necessary, have the person who served the complaint and summons testify. You can prove the existence and execution of the contract by calling a witness who was present at its execution. Another witness along with exhibits can prove performance by the plaintiff, typically payment of the contract price. Other witnesses and records can show nonperformance by the defendant and the extent of the plaintiff's damages. Although the court may not require them, or permit witnesses to summarize what they know in a narrative fashion, it is always safer to have all your witnesses available and prepared to testify as if the proceeding were a trial.

A defaulting party can only have the default judgment set aside if any of the reasons under Rule 60(b), principally excusable neglect, are shown.[32] For that reason, you should take certain steps to minimize the chances that a default will be vacated. First, serve the defendant by the most direct of the permitted service methods. Second, wait an appropriate

32. What constitutes "excusable neglect" under Rule 60(b) is unclear, since the term is not defined in the rule, and the case law is hardly uniform. Some courts require a showing of culpable conduct or bad faith; others require only a showing of carelessness or negligence. The Supreme Court has not resolved the issue, although in Pioneer Investment Services Co. v. Brunswick Associates, 507 U.S 380 (1993), it considered what the term excusable neglect means under a bankruptcy rule. See Wright & Miller, §2851.

period of time, at least 60 to 90 days, before seeking a default. Third, during this time you should send the defendant periodic letters asking for a response and spelling out the consequences of a default. Finally, send the defendant a notice of motion for the default motion, even though this is required only if the defendant has previously appeared in the case. Taking these steps now will support the motion itself and will make it less likely that the defaulted defendant will succeed in having the default judgment set aside later. The defendant will usually try to vacate the judgment only when you take steps to execute the judgment against the defendant's property, such as garnishing a savings account, and the matter suddenly becomes "serious."

Moving for a default judgment as soon as permitted under the Rules usually has the effect of stimulating action by the defendant. If you think the defendant really wants to defend, but is just dragging his feet, making a quick motion for default is frequently an effective technique for getting the lawsuit going.

§7.10. *Consolidation and separate trials*[33]

Under Rule 42 the court may consolidate separate cases for trial, or have parts of a single case tried separately.

1. Consolidations

Consolidation is governed by Rule 42(a) and has several elements. First, actions can be consolidated only when all actions are "pending before the court." This means that the cases have all been filed and are presently pending in the same district court. Second, the actions must have "common questions of law or fact." Typical are personal injury actions by several plaintiffs arising out of a single accident. Third, the court may decide to consolidate only certain issues for hearing or trial, such as the liability issues. This is a discretionary matter for the court and is usually decided after discovery has been completed and the cases are scheduled on the trial calendar.

2. Separate trials

Under Rule 42(b), the court may also order separate trials. This is permitted where separation will create convenience, avoid prejudice, or permit a case to be tried more efficiently and economically. The court has broad authority to separate claims, counterclaims, cross-claims, and third-party claims and to separate issues in any claims, or to separate parties. The typical situation involves unrelated permissive counterclaims or third-party claims where it makes sense to try unrelated claims later or spin

---

33. Wright §97; Friedenthal §6.2; Manual of Federal Practice §§7.3–7.4; Moore's Manual §20.01; Wright & Miller §§2382–2390; Moore's Federal Practice §§42.02–42.03.

off third-party actions to keep the trials simpler. This decision is also usually made only when discovery is complete and the case is on the trial calendar. Frequently a decision to sever is made at the final pretrial conference.

While the court has authority to separate issues, a problem often arises because the Rule expressly reserves a party's rights to a jury trial. The case law is still unclear as to when a court may order separate trials of issues before different juries.[34] Separate trials on liability and damages issues before the same jury cause no problems, but there is some dispute over different juries deciding the separate issues.[35]

§7.11. *Interlocutory appeal*[36]

Motion practice can be a significant part of any litigation, and the trial court may rule on numerous motions — discovery and summary judgment motions, for example — as the litigation proceeds. Can the party that loses a motion immediately appeal the order, or must it wait until after the case ends and the trial court enters a final judgment?

A "final judgment" is a judgment order that decides the case on the merits and leaves nothing else for the trial court to do. While the distinction of what is final — and what is not final — is obvious in most cases, in some situations, usually involving complex litigation, uncertainty can arise because Rule 54 does not itself define what a final order is. Merely designating an order as a "final order" is not determinative of that fact. Rule 54(b) does eliminate much of the uncertainty over what constitutes a final order by providing that the trial court may enter a final judgment as to fewer than all parties and claims, so long as the trial court expressly determines that there is no just reason for delay and expressly directs that judgment be entered.

As a general rule, parties can only appeal from a final judgment of the trial court. The benefits of the general rule are obvious: it prevents piecemeal appeals; it allows an appellate court to consider all appellate issues in the context of a complete trial record; and the trial court will be correct in its rulings most of the time. On the other hand, there are situations where an earlier appeal is sensible, and rules, statutes, and case law have allowed interlocutory appeals in several situations.

First, interlocutory appeals may be taken as of right under 28 U.S.C. §1292(a) if:

> (1) the interlocutory order grants, continues, modifies or dissolves an injunction, or refuses to dissolve or modify an injunction;[37]

---

34. See Wright §97.

35. See Wright & Miller §2390.

36. Wright §§101–104; Wright & Miller §§3920–3930; James & Hazard §§12.9–12.12.

37. By case law a distinction has been drawn between preliminary injunctions and temporary restraining orders: an order granting or denying a preliminary injunction is appealable, but an order granting or denying a TRO is not.

(2) the interlocutory order appoints a receiver, or refuses to appoint a receiver or refuses to take steps to accomplish the purposes of a receivership;

(3) the interlocutory decree determines the rights and liabilities of parties in an admiralty case.

Second, interlocutory appeals are discretionary under §1292(b). This section, which is infrequently used, provides for interlocutory appeals if the trial court certifies in its order that the case "involves a controlling question of law as to which there is substantial ground for difference of opinion and that an immediate appeal from the order may materially advance the ultimate determination of the litigation." If the trial court issues such an order, the appropriate appellate court has discretion whether to permit the interlocutory appeal.

Third, courts have recognized an additional narrow class of special cases, the so-called collateral orders doctrine, that may also be appealed immediately, although the principal litigation is not completed.[38] These involve situations where the trial court has decided one issue of a case that is entirely collateral of the main litigation but too important to deny review until the entire case is decided.[39] The issue must be independent of the principal action, the order must completely dispose of that issue, and it must be effectively unreviewable if an appeal is allowed only after final judgment. These are also infrequent and are principally involved in complex litigation.

Fourth, the extraordinary writs of mandamus and prohibition may also be used to appeal the trial court's rulings in limited circumstances. For example, writs of mandamus are most commonly used to enforce a right to a jury trial where the trial court has improperly denied that right.

If you can properly take an interlocutory appeal, make sure you follow the applicable Federal Rules of Appellate Procedure, particularly Rule 5, which governs appeals by permission under 28 U.S.C. §1292(b).[40]

---

38. See Wright §101.

39. The leading case is Cohen v. Beneficial Industrial Loan Corp., 337 U.S. 541 (1949).

40. See Becker v. Montgomery, 532 U.S. 757 (2001), holding that failure to sign a notice of appeal is not a fatal jurisdictional defect, so long as the defect is promptly cured once the omission is called to the appellant's attention.

VIII

PRETRIAL CONFERENCES AND SETTLEMENTS

§8.1. Introduction

Over 95 percent of civil cases filed in court settle before trial. The law prefers settlement and has created several methods to accomplish it. Judges prefer settlement, and the trend has been toward greater judicial involvement, principally by using pretrial conferences to get the adversaries together to discuss settlement possibilities. Finally, most clients ultimately prefer settlement over the increased expenses and uncertainties of a trial. Small wonder, then, that lawyers settle most cases before trial.

This chapter discusses both pretrial conferences and settlement because the two are closely related in most cases. Judges are increasingly using pretrial conferences to force settlement discussions as a case nears trial. Although lawyers should and do discuss settlement at other times, once a case has been filed in court the most common point at which settlement is discussed seriously is after discovery has been completed but before trial preparations have begun. Since this is when pretrial conferences are commonly scheduled, it makes sense to discuss both pretrial conferences and settlements as interrelated parts of the litigation process.

§8.2. Pretrial conferences[1]

1. Procedure

Pretrial conferences are governed by Rule 16, which gives the trial court broad authority to hold pretrial conferences on a wide spectrum of matters and to enter comprehensive pretrial orders. Rule 16 is not mandatory, however, and trial judges vary widely in how they use the Rule. Many districts and individual judges have also adopted local rules and instructions further

---

1. Wright §91; James & Hazard §§5.16–5.17; Friedenthal §§8.1–8.3; Moore's Manual §§18.01–18.09; Manual of Federal Practice §§6.1–6.18; Moore's Federal Practice §§16.07–16.22; Wright & Miller §§1521–1530.

regulating pretrial conferences, and specifying the organization and contents of the pretrial memorandum. Hence, in preparing for a pretrial conference, you must comply not only with Rule 16, but also with applicable local rules, and be aware of your judge's special instructions on, and attitude toward, pretrial conferences. Note that Rule 16(f) authorizes sanctions for failure to participate in good faith in pretrial conferences.

There are three basic purposes for holding a pretrial conference. First, it is used early in the litigation process to develop a discovery plan. Second, it can be used to streamline the case for trial purposes. Third, it can be used to promote settlement of the case. This section discusses the second purpose; §8.3 discusses settlement conferences.

Under Rule 16(d), a final pretrial conference can force the parties to sit down with the judge and discuss settlement possibilities, force the parties to narrow the issues that will actually be tried, and streamline the presentation of evidence by obtaining stipulations, evidentiary rulings, and limitations on witnesses. The usual time contemplated by Rule 16(d) for the conference is a few weeks before trial. By this time pleadings will be closed, discovery completed, and most motions will have been ruled on.

Judges vary widely in how they conduct pretrial conferences. Some will merely have an informal meeting in chambers, without the court reporter, to discuss the general nature of the lawsuit. At the other end of the spectrum are judges who will hold a formal conference, sometimes in open court, and conduct a detailed review of the pretrial memorandum, make all possible rulings, and detail them in an extensive pretrial order. Some judges actively encourage settlements, others do not. Also, some judges are flexible and let the lawyers participate in deciding what type of conference would be most productive in a particular case. Learn how your judge conducts final pretrial conferences and prepare accordingly. If you do not know your judge's practice, ask around. The judge's law clerk is usually a good place to start.

2. Pretrial disclosures and memorandum

Rule 26(a)(3) requires that each party must disclose to the other parties certain information that it may present at trial other than solely for impeachment purposes. The information must be disclosed at least 30 days before trial, unless the court directs otherwise. The information required to be disclosed includes:

1. witnesses who are expected to testify at trial
2. witnesses who may be called "if the need arises"
3. witnesses who are expected to be presented through depositions (and a transcript of pertinent portions of the testimony)
4. each exhibit expected to be offered at trial
5. each exhibit that may be offered "if the need arises"

Parties receiving the pretrial disclosures can, within 14 days of receipt, file objections to the designated deposition transcripts and the exhibits list. All objections other than relevance are waived by failure to object.

These pretrial disclosures are usually made as part of a pretrial memorandum. How detailed to make the memorandum depends on local rules and the particular judge's procedures; some require only a short, general memorandum, while others expect a detailed review of the case. Some vary the requirements, depending on the complexity of the case. The trend is toward requiring a pretrial memorandum that is prepared jointly by the parties. Keep in mind that many jurisdictions have local rules concerning the organization and contents of the memorandum. Many judges have standing orders that specify the content and organization of the pretrial memorandum. The following subjects are ordinarily included in a pretrial memorandum and discussed at the conference.

a. Jurisdictional statement

Because federal courts are courts of limited jurisdiction and subject matter jurisdiction must be affirmatively shown by the plaintiff (and can be challenged at any time), the jurisdictional basis for the case is usually the first item in the pretrial memorandum.

b. Issues of law

A principal purpose of the pretrial conference is to reduce legal issues to those that will actually be tried. Pleadings often assert many possible claims and defenses against every possible party. In the pretrial memorandum the judge will usually require each party to state the claims and defenses that will actually be presented at trial. Keep in mind that the pretrial order, which reflects the pretrial memorandum, amends the pleadings. Therefore, if you decide to waive certain claims in the memorandum, they will be deemed waived for trial. At this time the judge may also permit amendments to the pleadings so that the pleadings accurately reflect the disputed trial issues.

Where multiple claims are involved, the judge has authority under Rule 42(b) to order separate trials when it will promote the orderly and efficient presentation of evidence. In addition, as a trial strategy matter it is often preferable to pursue only the strongest claims without presenting alternative theories of recovery, particularly if they are factually or legally inconsistent.

c. Uncontested and contested facts

To avoid unnecessary formal proof and to focus on disputed facts, the judge will usually require that each party state what facts it agrees to and what facts it contests. Where facts are agreed upon, they may be introduced at trial through stipulations. While a judge has no authority to force the parties to stipulate to facts, as a practical matter it is often in everyone's best interests to do so. Keep in mind that if you do not admit a fact, your opponent can then serve a request to admit. If you do not admit it in your response to the request and your opponent later proves that fact at trial, the court under Rule 37(c) may award costs and attorney's fees expended to prove it.

Some judges use the uncontested facts as an introduction to the case during jury selection. Therefore, a useful way to prepare the uncontested facts is to use storytelling to give a clear overview of the case, rather than to merely list the uncontested facts.

d. Witness lists

The judge will usually require a list of lay and expert witnesses that will be called in each party's case in chief. Be safe. List all witnesses you may call at trial, including the adverse party and the adverse party's witnesses. Remember that you are not required to call all the witnesses you list but you will be precluded from calling witnesses not listed. Judges also frequently require addresses and a summary of each witness' expected testimony and the qualifications of each side's experts. Under Rule 26(a)(3), this requirement does not extend to witnesses that are solely impeachment witnesses, but the rule covers witnesses "whom the party may call if the need arises," which should include rebuttal witnesses. Each party may be asked to state whether it intends to object to the subject matter of any witness' testimony or the qualifications of any expert; also, the judge may eliminate cumulative or repetitive witnesses.

e. Exhibit lists

Parties will usually be required to prepare lists of all exhibits they will introduce in evidence at trial. Again, be safe. You cannot introduce at trial an exhibit that was not listed in the pretrial memorandum. Pleadings and discovery usually are not considered exhibits, but deposition transcripts are. Under Rule 26(a)(3), the requirement extends to all exhibits the party expects to offer and exhibits the party "may offer if the need arises," and a "designation of those witnesses whose testimony will be presented through a deposition," unless the witness or deposition is to be used solely for impeachment purposes. The usual procedure is to list and describe each exhibit, and designate the sections of each deposition transcript by page and line number, and attach copies of the exhibits and the designated sections of each transcript to the memorandum. Opposing parties may be required to state whether they object to any of the exhibits and, if so, provide the legal basis for the objection. This requirement essentially operates as a motion in limine on objections to evidence. If there is no objection to an exhibit, the judge will usually treat the exhibit as admitted in evidence. Where objections exist, the judge may be able to rule on them before trial. Keep in mind, however, that some objections, such as foundation objections, cannot be ruled on in advance of trial. However, the judge is at least alerted to the objections that will be heard at trial and thus will be able to decide them more efficiently.

f. Damages proof

In certain types of cases the judge may direct that evidence on damages issues be presented separately. Other parties will be required to state whether they object to the evidence or the amounts asserted. Certain special damages, such as lost wages and medical bills, are often not contested and can be admitted at trial through stipulations.

g.   *Instructions of law*

The judge usually requires that each party submit proposed jury instructions and state whether it intends to object to the opponent's instructions, and, if so, provide the basis for each objection. While the judge often cannot decide whether to give an instruction before evidence has been presented at trial, the judge can usually rule on the wording of proposed instructions. Since this can be a time-consuming task, reviewing the instructions at a pretrial conference can often avoid substantial delay at trial. If the case is one in which special interrogatories or verdict forms will be submitted to the jury, the same procedure can be followed.

The usual practice is to put each instruction on a separate page, and show on the bottom of each instruction its number, which party requested it, and the legal basis for the instruction.

h.   *Voir dire questions*

The most common practice in federal court today is for the judge to ask all or most of the voir dire questions during jury selection. Where this is the practice, the lawyers are asked to submit proposed voir dire questions to the judge, who then decides whether to ask the questions during the jury selection process. Frequently judges will direct the parties to list their proposed voir dire questions in the pretrial memorandum.

i.   *Trial briefs*

Most judges today expect the parties to submit a trial brief discussing the applicable substantive law and likely evidentiary issues. Some judges want the parties to append their trial briefs to the pretrial memorandum; others ask for trial briefs only if settlement negotiations have broken down and a trial looks likely. The brief's complexity should reflect the relative complexity of the substantive and evidentiary issues. The trial brief alerts the judge and parties to anticipated procedural and evidentiary issues, reviews applicable law, and permits the judge to schedule hearings and make rulings. The advantage to both sides should be apparent, since each side has an interest in presenting its case in a smooth, uninterrupted way. Jurors are annoyed by constant side bar conferences and recesses. Trial briefs, coupled with pretrial motions and motions in limine, will minimize trial interruptions and benefit everyone.

A simple joint pretrial memorandum is usually drafted by the lawyers for each of the parties, with each party contributing those portions that reflect its own witnesses, exhibits, and objections to the other side's evidence. This has the obvious benefit of putting all the necessary information in one document. However, it's always a good idea to volunteer to do the final drafting work to make sure that it accurately contains all your material.

Example:

[Caption]

JOINT PRETRIAL MEMORANDUM

Counsel for plaintiff Frances Johnson, defendant Robert Jones, and defendant Lisa Roberts submit the following Joint Pretrial Memorandum:

I   Jurisdiction

Jurisdiction is based on diversity of citizenship under 28 U.S.C. §1332. Plaintiff is a citizen of California, defendant Jones is a citizen of Arizona, and defendant Roberts is a citizen of Nevada. The amount in controversy exceeds the sum of $75,000, exclusive of interest and costs.

II   Uncontested Facts

The collision involving two cars occurred on June 1, 2005, at approximately 2:00 P.M. Plaintiff Frances Johnson was a passenger in a 2000 Honda Accord owned and driven by defendant Robert Jones. Jones was driving north on Kolb Road intending to turn left (west) on 22nd Street. As he was executing this turn, the defendant Lisa Roberts, who was driving her 2002 Buick Skylark southbound on Kolb Road, struck Jones' car.

Kolb Road has two lanes of traffic in each direction, a left turn lane at the intersection, and a median strip. Twenty-second Street has two lanes of traffic in each direction, a left-turn lane at the intersection, and a median strip. The intersection of Kolb Road and 22nd Street is controlled by several traffic lights.

The weather on June 1, 2005, was sunny and clear. The road conditions were dry.

Plaintiff Frances Johnson was injured as a result of the collision. She was taken to St. Mary's Hospital emergency room for treatment and was admitted to the hospital for continued care. Plaintiff was discharged from St. Mary's Hospital on June 4, 2005. Plaintiff's hospital and physician bills for this period totaled $4,471.04.

Plaintiff was absent from work between June 1, 2005, and July 5, 2005, when she returned to her job as a bank teller at First National Bank.

III   Contested Facts

1. Which car had the right of way at the time of the collision?
2. What color were the traffic lights at the time of the collision?
3. What was the extent of the injuries to plaintiff?

4. Does plaintiff have any permanent injuries or disabilities as a result of this collision?

5. Will plaintiff need further medical treatment in the future and, if so, what treatment?

6. What amount of money will reasonably compensate plaintiff for the damages incurred as a result of this collision?

IV   Contested Issues of Law

1. Was defendant Robert Jones negligent?
2. Was defendant Lisa Roberts negligent?
3. If both defendants were negligent, what is the relative degree of negligence of each defendant?

V   Exhibits

A. *Plaintiff Johnson's Exhibits:*   *Objections to Admissibility:*

1. Medical expenses totaling $4,471.04 as evidenced by vouchers in support of each expenditure contained in a blue brochure with a cover sheet listing the medical expenses.   None.
2. The Police Department official report of the accident.   Objected to by defendant Jones on hearsay grounds.
3. St. Mary's Hospital emergency room records of the plaintiff.   None.
4. Photographs of the plaintiff showing her shoulder deficit.   None.
5. X rays taken of the plaintiff.   None.
6. Photographs and diagrams of the intersection involved.   None.

B. *Defendant Jones' Exhibits:*   *Objections to Admissibility:*

1. Plaintiff's hospital and medical records.   None.
2. X rays.   None.
3. Plaintiff's employment records.   None.
4. Bills concerning property damage.   None.
5. Time sequence of signal lights.   None.
6. Photographs of the vehicles.   None.
7. The police report as far as it is admissible.   None.

C. *Defendant Roberts' Exhibits:*	*Objections to Admissibility:*
1. Police report of accident.	Objected to by plaintiff and by defendant Jones, for the reasons stated in the attached Memorandum of Law.
2. Photographs of vehicles involved.	None.
3. Plaintiff's medical records.	None.

VI   Witnesses

A. *Plaintiff Johnson's Witnesses:*

1. Plaintiff.
2. Elizabeth Martin, M.D.
3. Ernest Jackson, M.D.
4. Philip Wigmore, a bystander.
5. Bernie Sullivan, plaintiff's supervisor at First National Bank.
6. Investigating police officer Frank O'Malley.
7. Defendants.

B. *Defendant Jones' Witnesses:*

1. The parties to this action.
2. Investigating police officer Frank O'Malley.

C. *Defendant Roberts' Witnesses:*

1. The parties to this action.
2. Doctors who have seen or treated plaintiff.
3. Richard Hollister, a bystander.
4. Officer Barbara Horn, Police Department.
5. Glenda Sylvester, accident reconstruction expert.

VII   Jury Instructions

Plaintiff and defendants' proposed jury instructions are attached.

Plaintiff Johnson objects to Jones' instructions numbers 4, 7, and 9, and objects to Roberts' instruction number 6 for the reasons stated in the attached Memorandum of Law.

Both defendants object to plaintiff Johnson's instructions numbers 6, 7, 8, and 13 for the reasons stated in the attached Memorandum of Law.

RESPECTFULLY SUBMITTED this 1st day of September 2006.

By _____
Attorney for Plaintiff Johnson

By _____
Attorney for Defendant Jones

By _____
Attorney for Defendant Roberts

3.   Pretrial order

Rule 16(e) requires that the judge enter an order reciting the actions taken at the pretrial conference, and local rules frequently specify how, and by whom, the order will be drafted. Practices vary widely. Some judges prepare the order, either by stating the results of the conference in open court so the court reporter will record it, or by preparing a written pretrial order. Other judges have the parties draft an agreed order, which the judge then reviews and signs. Some judges ask the parties to estimate the number of trial days necessary to try the case; in lengthy trials, judges may impose time limitations on the parties. The estimated length of trial and any time limitations are then included in the pretrial order.

The content of the pretrial order is critical, since the order controls the trial. If the pretrial order incorrectly recites the disputed issues, witnesses, exhibits, or other matters, it must be promptly corrected. The best time to do this, when possible, is while the order is in draft form and not yet signed by the judge. Once entered, the order can be modified "only to prevent manifest injustice."

A simple pretrial order might look like the following.

Example:

[Caption]

<u>FINAL PRETRIAL ORDER</u>

The following are the results of pretrial proceedings in this cause held pursuant to Rule 16 and IT IS ORDERED:

I

This is an action for damages arising out of a collision involving vehicles driven by defendant Jones and defendant Roberts, which occurred on June 1, 2005, at the intersection of Kolb Road and 22nd Street.

II

Jurisdiction is based on diversity of citizenship under 28 U.S.C. §1332. Plaintiff is a citizen of California, defendant Jones is a citizen of Arizona, and defendant Roberts is a citizen of Nevada. The amount in controversy exceeds the sum of $75,000, exclusive of interest and costs. Jurisdiction is not disputed.

III

The following facts are admitted by the parties and require no proof:

1. The collision occurred on June 1, 2005, at the intersection of Kolb Road and 22nd Street.

2. Defendant Jones was the owner and operator of a 2000 Honda Accord that was involved in the collision.

3. Defendant Roberts was the owner and operator of a 2002 Buick Skylark that was involved in the collision.

4. Plaintiff Johnson was a passenger in defendant Jones' vehicle at the time of the collision.

5. The weather on June 1, 2005, was sunny and clear. The road conditions were dry.

6. The intersection of Kolb Road and 22nd Street is controlled by several traffic lights.

7. Plaintiff was absent from work from June 1, 2005, through July 5, 2005.

8. Plaintiff was admitted to St. Mary's Hospital emergency room on June 1, 2005, and was discharged from the hospital on June 4, 2005.

9. Plaintiff's hospital bill was $2,492.83.

10. Plaintiff's doctor bills to date total $1,978.21.

IV

The following are the issues of fact to be tried and determined upon trial:

1. Whether the defendants used due care in operating their vehicles?

Plaintiff contends that both defendants were speeding, not driving safely, and not keeping a proper lookout.

Defendant Jones contends that he was driving within the speed limit and operating his vehicle safely.

Defendant Roberts contends that she was driving within the speed limit and operating her vehicle safely, and that defendant Jones failed to yield the right of way.

V

The following are the issues of law to be tried and determined upon trial:

1. Whether the defendants, or either one of them, were negligent?

Plaintiff contends that both defendants were negligent and that their negligence jointly and directly caused plaintiff's injuries.

Defendant Jones contends that he was not negligent, and that his conduct caused no injuries to plaintiff.

Defendant Roberts contends that she was not negligent, that she did not violate any statutes, and that her conduct caused no injuries to plaintiff.

VI

1. The following exhibits are admissible in evidence in this case and may be marked in evidence by the Clerk:

    a. Plaintiff's exhibits: (see attached List number 1)

    b. Defendants' exhibits: (see attached Lists numbers 2 and 3)

2. As to the following exhibits, the party against whom the same will be offered objects to their admission upon the grounds stated:

    a. Plaintiff's exhibits: (see attached List number 4)

    b. Defendants' exhibits (see attached Lists numbers 5 and 6)

3. The parties will offer the following deposition testimony and have the following objections:

    a. Plaintiff deposition excerpts (see attached List number 7)

    b. Defendants' deposition excerpts (see attached List numbers 8 and 9)

VII

The following witnesses will be called by the parties upon trial:

    a. On behalf of plaintiff: (see attached List number 10)

    b. On behalf of defendants: (see attached Lists numbers 11 and 12)

The following expert witnesses will be called by the parties at trial, with their areas of expertise and the subjects of their testimony:

    a. On behalf of plaintiff: (see attached List number 13)

    b. On behalf of defendants: (see attached Lists numbers 14 and 15)

VIII

A jury trial has been requested, and was timely requested. It is anticipated that the case will require five trial days.

IX

Each side has submitted a set of proposed jury instructions and verdict forms:

    a. On behalf of plaintiff: (see attached Set number 16)

    b. On behalf of defendants: (see attached Sets numbers 17 and 18)

APPROVED AS TO FORM:

_____

Attorney for Plaintiff Johnson

_____

Attorney for Defendant Jones

_____

Attorney for Plaintiff Roberts

The foregoing constitutes the Final Pretrial Order in the above case. All prior pleadings in the case are superseded by this Order, which shall not be amended except by consent of the parties and by order of this court.

_____

United States District Judge

Dated: _____

The pretrial order bars parties from raising any claims or defenses not permitted by the order, and restricts the witnesses, exhibits, objections, and any other matters to those contained in the order. While Rule 16(e) permits modification to prevent manifest injustice, the granting of such a motion is discretionary with the judge, and counsel must ordinarily present a persuasive reason for amending the order.

Since pretrial orders are not usually final orders, they cannot be appealed under 28 U.S.C. §1291 until the case is disposed of by a final judgment.[2] However, an appeal following a final judgment can raise errors in the pretrial order.

§8.3. Settlements[3]

Settling a case involves four basic steps: determining the case's settlement value, selling your assessment to the opposing side, having the client agree, and preparing and signing the settlement agreement. While a case can be settled at any time, settlement possibilities are almost always explored when a case nears the pretrial conference stage and a trial is just around the corner. Discovery will be complete at this point, and there is sufficient information to accurately assess the case.[4] If settlement before or at a settlement conference does not occur, they can, and often do, occur just

---

2. Under a few special circumstances an interlocutory appeal may be permitted. See §7.11; 28 U.S.C. §1292; Moore's Manual §18.08.

3. See G. R. Williams, Legal Negotiation and Settlement 90–109 (1983); J. Jeans, Trial Advocacy 425–465 (2d ed. 1993); R. Bastress & J. Harbaugh, Interviewing, Counseling and Negotiating (1990); S. Krieger et al., Essential Lawyering Skills (1999).

4. Obviously, settlement should be explored earlier as well, for instance just before or just after filing suit, or after the plaintiff's deposition has been taken, when the costs both in terms of time delay and litigation expenses can be held down.

before or during trial, particularly just after the jury is picked, opening statements are made, or after the plaintiff has testified.

For this reason, you should take stock of your case again when the final pretrial conference is first scheduled. Preparing the pretrial memorandum necessarily will involve reviewing the pleadings, discovery, contested issues, witnesses, exhibits, and potential factual and legal problems. You might as well review the case for its settlement potential in the same systematic way. Remember that the best way to prepare for settlement is to prepare for trial. This always sends positive signals to the other parties.

1.   Case evaluation[5]

You need to evaluate the case in a clear, progressive way so that you reach an accurate and realistic assessment of its strengths and weaknesses. The sequence to use for your case evaluation should include the following, which parallel the way you have used a litigation chart to structure your litigation plan.[6]

a.   List elements of proof

Look at the elements instructions for liability, special damages, general damages, and defenses for every claim you intend to pursue at trial. The elements instructions will itemize exactly what facts must be proved. This, of course, should already be on your litigation chart.

b.   List sources of proof

List all lay and expert witnesses, with a summary of their testimony; all exhibits; and any other anticipated proof, such as stipulations and judicial notice. Include only evidence that you reasonably believe will be admissible at trial.

c.   Relate proof to elements

Now list the various witnesses and exhibits with the specific facts that must be proved for each claim and defense. Do this for your opponent's proof as well. This approach will organize the evidence and show what evidence there is to prove and refute for each element of the claims and defenses.

d.   Review credibility of the proof

Once you have organized the evidence and related it to the elements of the claims and defenses, you must take the critical step of realistically assessing whether it will be considered credible to a jury. How persuasive will the witnesses be? How probative are the exhibits?

5. See J. Jeans, Trial Advocacy ch. 20 (2d ed. 1993).
6. See §2.2.

Assessing credibility of proof is largely a function of trial experience, but there are other ways to get a "feel" for your case. Do the witnesses have good personal, family, and employment backgrounds that will make them believable to a jury? Do they tell stories that make sense? What kind of impressions did they make when they were deposed? Are their stories consistent with our common experience in life? Are the witnesses consistent with each other? A good practice for any lawyer, regardless of experience, is to try out your case, giving an objective summary of your side's proof as well as the other side's proof. This can be done before experienced trial lawyers, colleagues, friends, and spouses. Their reactions to the case and assessment of the case's strengths and weaknesses will usually be good indicators of how the proof will be viewed by a real jury.

e. Evaluate your case's jury appeal

Cases, of course, are not presented in a perfect, dispassionate world. A major consideration is whether your case, or your opponent's, has jury appeal. This must be assessed whenever any party has made a jury demand. Granted, "jury appeal" is an elusive concept, but it is extremely important to consider both before filing a demand for a jury trial with your initial pleading and before reviewing the case for settlement purposes. The basic components of jury appeal are the claims, the parties, and the lawyers.

The claims have much to do with whether a jury will be sympathetic to, or offended by, the conduct of either side. For the most part, juries are sympathetic to the unassuming individual who has been victimized. For example, a simple negligence case involving property damage or a routine contract action usually has little jury appeal. A negligence case against a drunk driver, however, or a contract action by a home owner against a home builder charging faulty construction will have substantial appeal.

Jury appeal is influenced by who the parties are. Similar cases can have widely varying verdicts, depending on the appeal of the parties. A plaintiff who is physically attractive, speaks well, and has a middle-class background will have considerable appeal. A trial involving a wealthy defendant, or a corporate or government defendant, will usually generate substantially higher verdicts for the plaintiff.[7]

Finally, the particular trial lawyer will obviously have some impact. Experienced trial lawyers with a proven record for obtaining good verdicts in similar types of cases can be expected to get better verdicts than other lawyers. Accordingly, you should always investigate your opponent's actual jury trial experience and reputation as a trial lawyer, and add this information to the overall analysis.

f. Review jury verdict reporters

Most jurisdictions, particularly those with large metropolitan populations, have jury verdict reporter services that periodically report the facts of

---

7. There are numerous psychological studies that have identified factors that affect witness credibility. See, e.g, Applying Social Psychological Research to Witness Credibility Law, in 2 Applied Social Psychology Annual (1980).

cases tried and the verdicts obtained.[8] By researching these services, not only for your jurisdiction but similar ones, you can at least learn the range of verdicts realistically attainable in similar cases. Keep in mind, however, that verdicts can vary widely depending on the jurisdiction, judge, lawyers, and facts — factors not readily apparent in the reports.

g. *Review the trial expenses*

Trials are expensive, both emotionally and financially. The client must realize the emotional toll a trial can take, and must be aware of the significant demands a trial will make on his time, demands that must take priority over all other obligations. Give the client a projection of how much of his time you will need in order to prepare and try the case, and what he will be doing during those hours. Where a client is unwilling to make the necessary commitment, or is unprepared to handle the emotional stresses and uncertainties of a trial, settlement is the obvious course.

The client should also be aware of the trial expenses involved, because they can be substantial. This is a good time to review your litigation budget with your client.[9] If you are being compensated on an hourly basis, you should give the client a current estimate of the trial preparation and trial time involved. Experienced trial lawyers usually need at least one day of preparation for each day of trial, and often more. At hourly rates of $100 per hour, a five-day trial, requiring five preparation days, will cost a client over $10,000 in attorney's fees alone. Where a statute permits awarding attorney's fees to the winning party, this will significantly increase the costs to the losing side.

Witness fees, particularly for experts who must be compensated for their time and travel and housing expenses, can be substantial since medical and other technical experts usually command hourly rates comparable to that of lawyers. For example, doctors usually insist on being compensated at the same hourly rate they would receive in their practice; taking a doctor away from his practice for even half a day will cost at least a thousand dollars. Flying an expert in to testify at trial will obviously be substantially more expensive. Finally, court costs and other expenses cannot be overlooked, since they can add up during a protracted jury trial. Court costs, including the daily juror fees, can become substantial in any lengthy trial.

h. *Consider preparing a settlement brochure*

In recent years it has become common among plaintiffs' personal injury lawyers to prepare so-called settlement brochures in major cases. These brochures essentially set out the background of the plaintiff along with the evidence showing liability and damages. The fact summaries are usually supplemented by photographs, videotapes, and documents such as employment records, hospital and other medical records, bills, and medical and economic expert reports detailing the extent of injuries,

---

8. Frequently used national services are the ATLA Law Reporter and Jury Verdict Reports, which report the monetary range of successful plaintiff's verdicts.

9. See §2.2.5.

the degree of permanent physical losses, and the plaintiff's economic future. Some lawyers believe that developing such a brochure is the most effective way of presenting the plaintiff's case before trial and obtaining a favorable settlement, since it can graphically show the nature and extent of the injuries, summarize the quality of the plaintiff's case, and demonstrate the jury appeal of the plaintiff. Even if you are not preparing a settlement brochure, consider bringing graphic exhibits to demonstrate your proof on liability and damages at the settlement conference.

i. Determine the settlement value

Your case evaluation is not complete, of course, until you have determined dollar figures and terms that represent the highs and lows of your settlement range. The high figure will reflect the "best result" you can realistically expect to receive after trial. The low figure will be the amount your client is willing to receive (as plaintiff) or pay (as defendant) rather than go to trial. How do you determine this settlement range?

Begin by determining the "best result," also called the "target point," that you can realistically expect to get if the case goes to trial. If your liability and damages proof goes well, what is the jury verdict likely to be? This is the most optimistic verdict estimate for your side. This best result will be the basis for determining your first offer during the settlement negotiations. (Your first offer will typically be somewhat higher than your best result estimate.)

Next, determine the "worst result" if you go to trial and both the liability and damages proof goes poorly. In that case, what is the jury verdict likely to be? This is the most pessimistic verdict estimate for your side.

Once you have estimated your own best and worst results, you need to determine the client's "bottom line." What are your client's needs and expectations? What dollar amount and terms will the client be willing to accept rather than go to trial? This, of course, requires that you discuss thoroughly with the client all the risks of going to trial, the financial and psychic costs of the trial itself, the "time value" benefit to the plaintiff by receiving the settlement money now, and what the net amount is that the client will actually receive (after deducting, if plaintiff, the anticipated fees and costs). The client's bottom line, also called the "resistance point," will be the basis for determining your final offer during the settlement negotiations.

How do you actually estimate your best and worst results? First, you need to establish the dollar amount of a likely verdict if the plaintiff prevails on both liability and damages. In some cases, such as contract claims, it may be possible to reach a specific figure because the contract has a liquidated damages clause or the claim is over an unpaid debt. In most cases, such as personal injury cases, it is better to determine a range, depending on whether the case goes well or poorly (your best and worst results). In personal injury cases, some damages, such as already incurred expenses for hospital and doctor bills, car repairs, and lost wages (sometimes called "special" or "out-of-pocket" damages), may be easy to determine, but other damages, such as future medical expenses, lost future income, and pain and suffering may not be easy to value, and the range of possible damages may be substantial. For example, you may decide that the jury will award damages of $200,000 as a best result but only $40,000 as a worst result. Make the same kind of assessment of any counterclaims. The more common the facts of the case are, the more accurately you should be able to determine the verdict range. Review jury verdict reporters for similar cases in your jurisdiction.

Second, determine the probability that plaintiff will succeed on the issue of liability, expressed as a percentage. As with damages, it is better to determine a range, depending on whether the case goes well or poorly. For example, you may decide that the plaintiff has a 75 percent likelihood of prevailing on liability as a best result but only a 25 percent likelihood as a worst result. Make the same kind of assessment for any counterclaims. If a personal injury case is being tried under comparative negligence, you need to determine the likelihood that the jury will find the plaintiff was also negligent, again expressed as percentages to reflect the best and worst results.

Third, analyze the additional costs the client will incur if the case goes to trial. These costs will include attorney's fees and other trial expenses such as expert witnesses. Of course, if you are being paid on a contingency or flat fee basis, there will be no additional legal fees. When you are being paid on an hourly basis, however, you will need to estimate the hours likely required to prepare and try the case and then multiply that estimate by your hourly rate. Make the same estimate for your opponent. Those additional legal fees and trial expenses alter the net value of the case if it goes to trial and need to be factored into the settlement evaluation. (The fees and costs reduce the settlement value for plaintiffs and increase them for defendants.)

Fourth, you need to take into account the time value of money. Money received now is worth more than the same amount of money received at a later time. As plaintiff, you need to "discount" the value of the case to reflect the benefit of receiving an amount of money now rather than after a trial. (Defendant must do the opposite since deferring payment is a benefit.) This discount, expressed as a percentage, depends on how much sooner the plaintiff will get the money and the increased value of getting it now. For example, if a case will not be tried for one year and the yield on a prudent investment or bank deposit is 5 percent, an amount received one year from now will be worth about 5 percent less than that amount received now.

Finally, see if the defendant's insurance coverage or other ability to pay will create a practical limit on what the plaintiff can realistically hope to recover. When insurance coverage is low and the defendant has no other substantial assets that could help satisfy a judgment, the policy limit may be the only amount the plaintiff can ever recover. In this situation, the defense may simply "tender the policy" to settle the case.

Example:

You represent the plaintiff in a personal injury case on a contingency fee basis. The applicable state's law is comparative negligence.

Your settlement value analysis should proceed along the following lines:

1. Assuming liability, you assess the likely damages verdict at $100,000 as the best possible result and $50,000 as the worst possible result.

2. You assess the likelihood of obtaining a verdict finding the defendant negligent at 90 percent as the best possible result and 50 percent as the worst possible result. You assess the likelihood of a verdict finding the plaintiff also negligent at 0 percent as the best possible result and 50 percent as the worst possible result.

3. Since you are representing the plaintiff on a contingency basis, the trial will not generate additional legal fees. However, you estimate that the plaintiff will have to pay $5,000 for trial expenses, principally expert witness fees and costs.

4. You estimate that the case will not be tried for one year, and the current rate of return for safe investments is 5 percent.

The settlement range of the case computes as follows:

1. Under the best possible result analysis, the $100,000 damages estimate must be reduced by 10 percent (the chance the jury will not find the defendant negligent), to $90,000, and by the trial expenses of $5,000, to $85,000, and by 5 percent (the time value of money), to $80,750. That figure, $80,750, is your estimate of the best possible result after trial. (This means that the net to your client is approximately $54,000 after your 33 percent contingency fee is deducted.)

2. Under the worst possible result analysis, the $50,000 damages estimate must be reduced by 50 percent, to $25,000, and by another 50 percent (the possibility the jury also will find the plaintiff contributorily negligent), to $12,500, and by the trial expenses, to $7,500, and by 5 percent, to $7,125. That figure, $7,125, is your estimate of the worst possible result after trial. (This means that the net to your client is approximately $4,775 after your contingency fee is deducted.)

This outcome range, between $80,750 and $7,125, is what you must then discuss with your client to determine the client's bottom figure. Assume that the client says he would rather go to trial than accept a settlement of less than $35,000 (which would net the client approximately $20,000 after fees and costs are deducted). Your first offer to the defense should be somewhat higher than $80,750 (perhaps $90,000); your last offer cannot go below $35,000. This will be your negotiation range during the settlement meeting.

The defendant, of course, should be making the same kind of analysis. However, because the defendant will usually be paying legal fees on an hourly basis and can expect to pay additional legal fees of perhaps $20,000 if the case is tried, and trial costs of perhaps $5,000, that $25,000 must be *added* to the defendant's settlement analysis. For example, the defendant may have assessed the best possible outcome at zero dollars (a complete defense win at trial) and the worst possible outcome as a $30,000 verdict for plaintiff. This means that any settlement for less than $25,000 will still be financially attractive to the defendant because even winning the case at trial will cost the defense that much. Defendant should be willing to settle the case anywhere between $25,000 and $55,000, and the defendant's bottom line should be $55,000.

Since the plaintiff is willing to settle for between $80,750 and $35,000, and the defendant should be willing to settle for between $55,000 and $25,000, a negotiated settlement should eventually be reached somewhere in the $35,000 to $55,000 range.

During the past few years, litigation support firms have developed decision tree models to determine the settlement values of cases at various stages of the litigation process. A decision tree, a commonly used tool in the business world, divides the litigation process into its component parts and analyzes the risks that exist at each stage of the process. While assigning probabilities to each component of the process may be difficult — for example, what is the probability that summary judgment on plaintiff's punitive damages claim will be granted, or what effect will a ruling limiting expert testimony have on the trial? — this method does force you to analyze every possible influence on the settlement value of a case. In large and complex litigation, decision tree analysis is becoming common as lawyers increasingly understand that settlement analysis can, and should, be done systematically.

Settlements happen when both sides undertake reasonably objective case evaluations and reach reasonably justifiable estimates of verdict ranges and expenses if the case goes to trial, and bargain reasonably to achieve a compromise.

j.   Evaluate the tax consequences of settlement[10]

Finally, you must know the potential tax consequences of a settlement. The beginning point is 26 U.S.C. §104(a)(2), which excludes from income any damages received, through suit or settlement, for "personal physical injuries or physical sickness." This has been generally interpreted to mean damages received through a tort or tort-based claim. For example, a settlement of a negligence claim based on a vehicle collision in which the plaintiff received physical injuries will be excludable from plaintiff's income, even though part of the damages may reflect lost income.

Section 104(a)(2) makes clear that punitive damages received are taxable income. It also makes clear that compensatory damages for nonphysical personal injury cases, such as defamation and wrongful discharge, are also taxable income.[11]

10. See Robert W. Wood, Taxation of Damages Awards and Settlement Payments (3d ed. 2005); Robert W. Woods, Tax Deductions for Damage Payments: What, Me Worry? 110 Tax Notes 243 (Jan. 16, 2006).

11. See, e.g., the resolution of Murphy v. I.R.S., 493 F. 3rd 170 (D.C. Cir., 2007), where the D.C. Circuit reversed its prior decision and now held that nonphysical personal injury damages for emotional distress and injury to professional reputation were not excludable from gross income.

What should a plaintiff do to fall within the exclusion of §104? At the complaint drafting stage, plaintiff should bring tort, not contract, claims and allege damages for personal physical injuries whenever possible. At the settlement stage, the settlement agreement should state that the settlement is for the plaintiff's personal physical injury claims whenever possible. If the complaint alleges both tort and nontort claims, it may be possible to settle only the tort claims and dismiss the nontort claims. The agreement should characterize the settlement amounts as compensatory, not punitive, damages. However, keep in mind that while the characterization in the settlement agreement may be influential, it is not dispositive, and the IRS may challenge it later.

A defendant should not have a tax reason to resist characterizing a settlement as excludable under §104, since whether the defendant can deduct the settlement on his tax return (as a business expense, for example) will not be controlled by how plaintiff treats the settlement on his return. However, defendant does benefit in having any possible settlement treated early as excludable under §104, since the settlement ultimately agreed on should be lower if both sides agree that it will be nontaxable to the plaintiff.

The Supreme Court has now held that the gross amount of a settlement in attorney contingent fee cases (where the exclusion of I.R.C. §104(a)(2) does not apply) is includable in the plaintiff's gross income for federal income tax purposes. Commissioner v. Banks, 543 U.S. 426 (2005). Congress, however has acted to mitigate the problems, although some issues remain. See I.R.C. §62(a)(20).

In commercial litigation — involving such diverse claims as business torts, contract, antitrust, bad faith, and punitive damages — and in structured settlement agreement situations, the tax consequences of a settlement are complex, and a settlement should never be entered into unless you have determined the likely tax consequences to your client or have received the advice of an experienced tax specialist.

k. Marshall your facts

During the settlement negotiations, you will need to support your positions on liability and damages with facts. Taking positions without having credible facts to support those positions is merely posturing and will have no impact on the other side. Hence, you need to organize the facts that you will use to justify your positions and be ready to present them persuasively during the settlement meeting. Always ask: What are the strongest points of my case, and how can I most effectively present them?

Meanwhile, of course, your opponent will be doing the same thing. Therefore, you need to assess what your opponent's likely positions are on these liability and damages issues and what your opponent's likely factual arguments will be to support those positions. You then must be prepared to rebut them with credible facts. Always ask: What are the strongest points of my opponent's case, and how can I most effectively defuse them?

Finally, you need to determine how many of these facts you will disclose during the negotiations and what facts you will "save" for trial.

For example, you may have impeachment that will seriously erode the credibility of your opponent's key eyewitness, and your opponent doesn't know about it. There is always a possibility that your opponent is only attending the settlement conference to try to pump you for additional information that has not been disclosed during discovery, or is trying to learn your likely strategy if the case goes to trial. During settlement negotiations, each side is constantly trying to glean more information from the other side than it discloses. You need to decide whether you are better off disclosing such facts now (because they may push the other side into settling on more favorable terms) or withholding such facts (because the other side will then have an opportunity to obtain refuting evidence).

Remember the requirements of Model Rule 4.1, which provides: "In the course of representing a client a lawyer shall not knowingly: (a) make a false statement of material fact or law to a third person. . . ." The comment to that rule states: "This rule refers to statements of fact. Whether a particular statement should be regarded as one of fact can depend on the circumstances. Under generally accepted conventions in negotiation, certain types of statements ordinarily are not taken as statements of material fact. Estimates of price or value placed on the subject of a transaction and a party's intentions as to an acceptable settlement of a claim are in this category. . . ."

2.   Negotiating a settlement with opposing counsel

The dynamics of negotiation, in the litigation as well as other fields, has received increasing attention in recent years. This has occurred, in part, because litigation and trial costs have made settlement more desirable, but also because there is a growing awareness that learning negotiating methods can improve a lawyer's ability. The literature on negotiation methods for lawyers is rapidly expanding, and a number of books are particularly useful for litigators.[12] Although this text obviously cannot review this literature in detail, a summary about negotiations may still be useful.

Trying a case inherently involves risks since neither party can ever predict with absolute certainty what a jury will decide in a given case. Settlements are simply the way in which lawyers eliminate the risks in the litigation process. Since risks are at the core of that process, you need to do whatever you can to minimize them. This requires that you adequately prepare the case for trial since the more you know about the case, the fewer the uncertainties and unknown factors, and hence the less risk. It also requires that you realistically evaluate the case for settlement purposes. The more relative uncertainty there is in your opponent's mind, the

---

12. C. Craver, Effective Legal Negotiation and Settlement (2001); G. Bellow & B. Moulton, The Lawyering Process: Negotiation (1981); R. Fisher & W. Ury, Getting to Yes (2d ed. 1991); W. Ury, Getting Past No (1991); X. Frascogna & H. Hetherington, Negotiation Strategy for Lawyers (1984); R. Haydock, Negotiation Practice (1984); G. Williams, Legal Negotiation and Settlement (1983); S. Krieger et al., Essential Lawyering Skills (1999).

more flexible and compromising his position is likely to be. Factors that increase uncertainty in your opponent's mind are your own thorough preparation of the case, your willingness and ability to go to trial if necessary, and your client's willingness and preparedness for trial.

What negotiating approach should you use? Negotiation styles are as varied as lawyers are numerous. Nevertheless, there are two basic approaches that are followed today. The first is competitive: The lawyer makes an initial high offer, keeps the pressure on the opponent, and makes as few concessions as possible. The atmosphere is entirely adversarial, and the projected attitude is one of strength. This approach, perhaps the traditional way in which settlement negotiations were conducted, has benefits, principally that any settlement reached will probably be a good one for the lawyer with the more competitive lawyer. Its drawback is that probably a lower percentage of cases settle under this approach. A possible conclusion to draw is that this approach is effective where you have a strong case and don't need to compromise.

The other approach is cooperative: The lawyer emphasizes the parties' shared interests, shows a willingness to make concessions, and makes a more realistic initial offer. The atmosphere is conciliatory, and egos are kept on the sidelines. The benefit of this approach is that probably more cases get settled. On the negative side, the settlement may not be as good for your client since the other side may try to take advantage of your attitude. Accordingly, this approach is probably more effective when both parties are equally strong.

The cooperative approach is becoming more accepted, probably because it seems to improve the possibilities of reaching an eventual agreement. While it has several characteristics, the key to the cooperative approach is to avoid taking rigid positions. Instead, the lawyers who are negotiating focus on the mutual interests of their clients, avoid personalizing the conflicts, and expand the possible solutions before objectively reviewing the possible solutions to settle on a resolution of the conflict. This approach, by avoiding personalities and rigid posturing, becomes a joint effort to reach solutions.

Your settlement strategy, in addition to determining your negotiation style, also needs to include where and when the meeting will be held, who will make the first settlement overture and first offer, who will make the first concession, and the order in which the issues will be discussed. First, decide where and when the settlement meeting will take place because serious negotiations are usually conducted face-to-face. Most lawyers, of course, prefer to have the meeting in their own offices on the theory that they will have the "home court" advantage. This may be unacceptable to the other side, which may insist on a neutral site. Some lawyers like to start first thing in the morning; others like to start later and run late. These are all details, but they are important and need to be worked out in advance. Most lawyers do not bring their clients to the meeting because the client's presence is usually not conducive to the give and take atmosphere needed to have productive negotiations. However, the lawyers know where their clients can be reached during the meeting in case direct communication becomes necessary.

Decide whether you should make the first settlement overture and the first actual offer. Lawyers traditionally have been reluctant to initiate settlement discussions or to make the actual first offer on the theory that starting the process will be taken as a sign of weakness. Lawyers always want the other side to start the process and make the first offer. In recent years, however, there has been a change, with more lawyers recognizing that starting the process is hardly a sign of weakness, provided that the lawyer has prepared properly and has made a reasonable offer. The more important question is: Is this first offer realistic? If so, it will start the negotiation process. If not, the other side will summarily reject it and the process will be ended before it ever starts.

The initial offer should be somewhat higher (if plaintiff) or somewhat lower (if defendant) than that party's best result assessment. This allows for the possibility, although unlikely, that the other side has assessed the case differently and is willing to settle on the basis of that first offer. More commonly, this initial offer gives you leeway during the negotiation process, particularly since the other side will expect you to be flexible.

Decide on the first concession and whether you should make it. Like the first offer, lawyers have traditionally been reluctant to make the first concession on the ground that it signals weakness and an eagerness to settle. In recent years, however, there has been a change here as well, as lawyers realize that it is not the concession itself that conveys a weakness, so long as it is coupled with an insistence that the other side reciprocate with mutual concessions. If only one side is willing to make concessions, that is not a negotiation at all.

Decide on the order in which you plan to take up the various issues that need to be negotiated. Most lawyers prefer to tackle the smaller issues first, with the larger or more difficult issues left for later. The idea is that if the parties can resolve the small issues, it sets the groundwork for cooperation and compromise on the more difficult issues.

Settlement negotiation meetings, particularly if both lawyers genuinely cooperate to reach a compromise acceptable to both sides, follow a predictable course. The meeting usually starts off with the polite talk that breaks the ice and establishes an appropriate atmosphere. After that comes the information-exchanging stage, in which the parties try to learn the other side's concerns, needs, and interests. After that comes the position-taking stage, in which the parties state their own positions and make their offers, justify their positions with supporting facts, and challenge the other side's positions with contradictory facts. It is at this stage that the bartering process takes over, with mutual concessions triggering further compromises until an agreement is reached. Remember that most concessions are made either at the beginning (usually the small concessions) or near the end (usually the major concessions) of the negotiations, as each party realizes that the opponent is becoming resistant to further concessions and the alternative is to try the case. Remember that during the bartering process it is particularly important to watch the other side and listen closely for verbal and nonverbal cues that reveal the opponent's true position and attitude. Just as in playing poker, perception is important.

If an agreement is reached, it must be put in writing. It is important to review the details of the agreement before the meeting comes to an end so that there are no misunderstandings. Always volunteer to draft the actual settlement. If the other side insists, be sure to review the agreement carefully and change any language that does not accurately and fairly reflect the agreement.

Finally, if the parties were unable to reach an agreement at the settlement meeting, this does not mean the negotiations failed. It may have paved the way for future discussions. It may have provided the groundwork for mediation or arbitration. The last offers by each side may be the basis for a high-low agreement if the case goes to trial. And it may have given you some insight into how the other side intends to present its case if it proceeds to trial.

3.   Negotiating at a settlement conference

Under Rule 16(a), the court can direct that a conference be held to facilitate a settlement. The court may direct that parties, or representatives with settlement authority, attend the conference or be available by telephone. With consent of the parties, the court may engage in ex parte communications with the parties and their lawyers.

Settlement conferences with the court most commonly are held after discovery is closed but before final trial preparations begin. Settlement conferences may be held in conjunction with the final pretrial conference contemplated by Rule 16(d). A common practice is for a judge, other than the one before whom the trial will be held, to preside over the conference.

Settlement conference practices vary widely. Some judges actively promote settlement, others are passive about settlement. Some will meet with the lawyers only, others will insist that the clients be present. Some will meet collectively with the lawyers or parties, others will meet with each lawyer and party on an ex parte basis. Still others use both collective and ex parte meetings. Ex parte discussions with the judge can be important, particularly for parties involved in emotionally charged cases such as negligence and wrongful death, because it gives the parties a chance to express their feelings to the judge. Once they get the feelings off their chest, settling the case becomes possible. Some judges will review the court file before the conference, focusing on the pleadings and joint pretrial memorandum, while others expect the lawyers to tell them what the case is all about at the conference. Some judges require the parties to submit confidential settlement memoranda or letters containing the parties' positions on liability and damages, an assessment of their strongest and weakest facts, a justification of their settlement demands and offers, a history of their settlement negotiations, and their predictions of a likely verdict range if the case is tried.

Because practices vary widely, you must know the general procedures in your jurisdiction, as well as the specific practice of your particular settlement judge. If you don't know, ask the judge's clerk or secretary, or talk to lawyers familiar with the judge. Be prepared for the unexpected.

The judge may ask a lawyer to cut a legal fee to make settlement possible. The judge may ask the lawyer what the lawyer's fee is, or what the party's settlement authority is. The judge may want to talk to the client without the lawyer being present. The judge may propose settling the case using base-ball arbitration rules. The important thing to keep in mind is that anything can happen at a settlement conference. Your job as the lawyer is to learn what you can expect from the particular settlement judge and to prepare yourself and your client appropriately.

What does the judge want to know at the settlement conference? There are two principal concerns. First, the judge wants to know what the likely outcome of this case will be if it were tried before a jury. Second, the judge wants to learn which party is prepared and eager to try the case. These two concerns will shape the judge's attitude and recommendations during the conference.

As plaintiff, you will usually have the first opportunity during the conference to tell the judge "what the case is all about." Be an advocate, and project a winning attitude. Show that you are eager to try the case, yet remain willing to be reasonable. Decide how you would present your case to a jury, how you would justify the amount you are asking for, and then argue it to the settlement judge. Consider starting with damages proof, using exhibits to make them clear. For example, summarize your out-of-pocket expenses with the exhibits that support them. In a personal injury case, those expenses exhibits would usually include all medical bills, photographs of the plaintiff, and expert reports. This will give the judge a grasp of how "big" the case is and what proportion of the damages sought are concrete, out-of-pocket expenses, as opposed to intangible damages such as pain and suffering. Next, summarize your proof on liability, again using exhibits such as police reports, photographs, and diagrams to support it. Some plaintiffs' lawyers put together a settlement brochure that contains the key damages and liability information and supporting exhibits. As defendant, your job is to show that plaintiff's damages are overinflated and will not be convincing to a jury, that liability is questionable, and that your offer to settle is therefore reasonable.

Each side usually will have only a few minutes to present its best points on damages and liability, so your presentation will essentially be like a short closing argument in a bench trial, factually based and shorn of emotional rhetoric. Expect the judge to question your positions. After all, the judge will see her role as showing that plaintiff's demand is unrealistically high, while the defendant's offer is unrealistically low. If the judge can get the plaintiff to come down, and the defendant to come up, a settlement may be possible. Hence, your role as an advocate is to convey to the judge that you are prepared, that your figures are realistic and supportable, and that you and your client are ready and eager to try the case if the other side refuses to be "reasonable." While the expectation at the conference is that both sides will be flexible, your aim is to get the judge to adopt your position as the more reasonable, realistic one and then pressure the other side to accept it.

If the judge recommends that the case be settled for a certain amount, what should you do? Keep in mind that the decision to settle or go to trial is the client's. While you can, and should, advise the client whether the recommended settlement is reasonable, the client makes the final decision, and you must live with it. Be prepared for an unusual or creative settlement suggestion. For example, if the stumbling block in a medical malpractice case is the extent of future medical expenses, the judge might suggest settling for a given dollar amount coupled with a reservation of right to sue if a future medical contingency occurs.

Who should be the negotiator at the settlement conference? While traditionally the lawyer trying the case has also been the negotiator, in recent years lawyers have increasingly turned the job of negotiating a settlement, and attending the settlement conference, to a negotiating lawyer. The logic is that by getting someone else, other than the lawyer who has been managing the litigation, to negotiate, chances for a settlement are improved. This approach is becoming common in large commercial cases. However, if a settlement conference will be held as part of a final pretrial conference, Rule 16(d) requires that the lawyer trying the case attend the conference.

Finally, be patient. Experienced judges and litigators know that settlements often take time. A settlement may not be reached during the first settlement conference. However, the key concept is to get the parties talking about settlement. Once the ice is broken and the parties are talking, most cases seek their own pace, and most eventually settle.

4.   Client authorization

Before you begin negotiations on behalf of a client, you must have authority to settle. The law in almost all jurisdictions is that an agreement to represent a client does not confer authority to settle. Therefore, the client must expressly authorize his lawyer to settle.[13] A client cannot give a valid consent unless he is fully informed concerning the terms of the proposed settlement, understands the terms and the reasons for them, and expressly consents to them.

Involve the client in the decision making, and discuss the pros and cons of settlement options. This is best done by keeping the client well informed throughout the litigation and up to date on the status of the case. Schedule a meeting with the client to discuss the upcoming settlement possibilities, give him your best present assessment of the case, and explain what you believe would be a reasonable settlement and the reasons for your evaluation. Listen to the client's questions, and candidly address his concerns. If the client agrees to settle the case on those terms, obtain his written authorization for that settlement. This is best done by sending a letter that recites the terms of the settlement proposal to the client. He should sign and return a copy of the letter acknowledging and approving its terms. When time is short, authorization by phone will suffice, but this should be followed up with a letter reciting the details of the authorization, as in the example below.

13. 30 A.L.R.2d 944 (1953); 5 A.L.R.5th 56 (1992).

Example:

Dear Mr. Johnson:

As we discussed yesterday, the defendant's lawyer in your case asked us to consider the possibility of settling your case without a trial. I am writing to make sure you understand what is involved in a settlement and to obtain your permission to reach a settlement with the defendant.

Trials involve risks, and it is impossible to predict with certainty how your case will look to a jury and what verdict the jury will return. Nevertheless, based on the present state of your case, it is my judgment that if a jury were to find the defendant liable, it would return a verdict in the $30,000 to $40,000 range. However, I feel that there is perhaps an even likelihood that a jury would find no liability at all. In addition, we must consider that the expenses of going to trial will be in the $2,000 range, which primarily involves the costs of having the medical experts testify. Finally, keep in mind that my fee for representing you in your case is one-third of any recovery.

The "value" of your case for settlement purposes, then, is approximately as follows: a potential verdict of $30,000 to $40,000, discounted by 50 percent to reflect the possibility the jury will find that no liability exists, and reduced by the $2,000 trial expenses. This comes to a total in the $13,000 to $18,000 range. Of course, by settling the case, you will avoid having to pay the trial expenses.

Based on these considerations, I recommend that you settle your case for not less than the sum of $15,000, which, after deducting my fee, would result in your actually recovering $10,000. Each side will pay its own court costs, which for us have been approximately $150 to this date. Yesterday you told me to go ahead and try to settle your case for not less than $15,000. Of course, I will negotiate with the defendant's lawyer and try to get a higher settlement.

If you still authorize me to settle your case for not less than $15,000, please sign and date the copy of this letter in the spaces provided and return it to me as soon as possible. I will keep you fully informed of the settlement negotiations as they progress.

Sincerely,

_____

John Lawyer

Authorized:

_____

William Johnson

Date: _____

When representing a defendant where insurance coverage is involved, remember that your client is the party, not the insurance company. While insurance contracts customarily permit the insurer to select defense counsel and control the conduct of the defense, case law has increasingly upheld the client's right to authorize any settlement.[14] In short, you must represent the best interests of the insured, and the insurer usually cannot settle a case against the insured's wishes. If this occurs, the client can usually have the settlement set aside, since under these circumstances it is not binding.[15] Finally, keep in mind that when you represent more than one client, you have a professional responsibility to each client when settling the case.[16]

5.   Settlement agreements

Since settlements are simply agreements between parties, general contract law principles apply. Good practice generally requires that the agreement be in writing and signed by each party, and some local rules require it.

Settlements are generally made using either a release, a covenant not to sue, or a loan receipt. When the agreement has been executed, the case can be dismissed with prejudice. It is extremely important to understand the legal differences between the various settlement methods. The choice of method is influenced by the types of legal claims and the number of parties involved, whether the settlement is intended to be complete or partial, the type of court action or approval that may be necessary, and the applicable law of contribution. You must know the law of the jurisdiction that governs the settlement agreement because statutes and case law concerning releases, covenants not to sue, and loan receipts vary among the jurisdictions. Also, the drafting of the agreement is important, since you need to ensure that it is treated under the applicable law in the way you want it treated, and that it has the effect you intend. This is particularly important in cases with joint tortfeasors, where issues of contribution among the tortfeasors may arise.

a.   *Releases, covenants not to sue, and loan receipts*

A basic common law release operates as a discharge of all claims against the parties to the release as well as against any persons against whom the same claims are or could have been asserted. In short, a release is a complete discharge, or satisfaction, of an action. For this reason a release is used only when there is a settlement of the entire lawsuit involving every claim and every party.

---

14. See §8.3.4(g) on insurer good faith requirements.

15. This conflict between a client and the client's insurer is a complex area of law and must be researched thoroughly. See, e.g., R. Keeton, Basic Text on Insurance Law ch. 7 (1971); R. Keeton & A. Widiss, Insurance Law (1988).

16. See Model Rules of Professional Conduct, Model Rule 1.8(g) governing aggregate settlement of claims.

A covenant not to sue does not discharge any parties. It is simply a contract between two or more parties in which the plaintiff agrees not to sue or to pursue an existing claim against one or more defendants. For this reason a covenant not to sue is used when there is a partial settlement not involving every party.

The need for covenants not to sue has an historic basis. Since under common law a release was a discharge of all joint tortfeasors, a plaintiff could not use a release when he wished to settle a tort claim with fewer than all defendants. The covenant not to sue solved this problem. Today the effect of the common law release rule has been eliminated in those jurisdictions that have adopted the Uniform Contribution Among Joint Tortfeasors Act.[17] However, the laws of the states are not uniform, and the relevant laws must be understood to determine the effect on contribution whenever the settlement involves a tort claim having multiple joint tortfeasors. A simple covenant not to sue does not prevent a nonsettling defendant from later bringing a contribution claim against the settling defendant after a final judgment, unless a statute (like the Uniform Contribution Among Joint Tortfeasors Act) in the applicable jurisdiction prevents this result. Therefore, it is critical that you know how your jurisdiction deals with the question of contribution.

In recent years a third kind of partial settlement, the "loan receipt," sometimes called a "Mary Carter agreement,"[18] has been used to generate some contribution among joint tortfeasors. Under this settlement approach, one defendant agrees to "loan" a certain amount to the plaintiff. The plaintiff "settles" with that defendant, but that defendant remains in the case with his exposure limited to the loan amount, with a chance of recovering the loan amount if the plaintiff gets a recovery greater than a stated amount against the other defendants. Through the loan receipt approach a defendant can settle for a given amount, which might be recouped after trial. Plaintiff for her part gets an early partial recovery and a cooperative defendant. The legality of this basic settlement technique has been upheld in most jurisdictions over public policy objections, but courts have also generally required that the existence and sometimes the terms of a loan receipt be disclosed to the remaining defendants and have allowed it to be used to show the bias and interest of a witness who testifies at trial if the witness is associated with the settled defendant.[19] Because such an agreement is usually discoverable and admissible to show bias and interest if the settled party testifies at trial, the loan receipt is less used today.

Any number of variations of the basic loan receipt formula are possible. The choices are numerous and are affected by the extent to which the details of such arrangements are admissible at trial, and whether the

17. W. Prosser & P. Keeton, The Law of Torts §§49–50 (5th ed. 1984); D. Dobbs, The Law of Torts (2000).

18. Booth v. Mary Carter Paint Co., 202 So. 2d 8 (Fla. App. 1967). See also Vermont Union School Dist. No. 21 v. Cummings Const. Co., 469 A.2d 742 (Vt. 1983), City of Tucson v. Gallagher, 493 P.2d 1197 (Ariz. 1972).

19. See Reese v. Chicago, Burlington & Quincy R.R., 283 N.E.2d 517 (Ill. App. 1972), aff'd, 303 N.E.2d 382 (1973); held improper, see Elbaor v. Smith, 845 S.W.2d 240 (Tex. 1993); Dosdourian v. Carsten, 624 S.W.2d 241 (Fla. 1993).

jurisdiction's law of contribution among joint tortfeasors is affected by any particular agreement's structure. The jurisdictions vary widely on the validity and enforceability of the numerous variations of Mary Carter agreements. It should be apparent that you should never enter into a loan receipt agreement unless you are familiar with the particular jurisdiction's applicable law.

b. Drafting the agreement

Regardless of which type of settlement is used, care obviously must be taken in drafting the agreement to ensure that it is specifically tailored to the case involved. First, the agreement should clearly state whether it is a release, covenant not to sue, or loan receipt, and state what matters it does and does not resolve. Second, the agreement should describe the events involved in the case, since the discharge will only be for those events. Third, the agreement should recite the claims of liability and damages and the defendant's denial of them, since it is the compromise of these disputed claims that constitutes the mutual consideration in the agreement. Fourth, the agreement should specify how the pending court case is to be terminated. Fifth, the agreement can contain a choice of law clause and specify the details of any contribution in a covenant not to sue, if appropriate and permitted under the applicable jurisdiction's law. Finally, if the terms of the settlement are to remain confidential, the agreement must expressly provide for confidentiality. Most defendants, faced with other plaintiffs having the same or similar claims, will insist on confidentiality as a condition for settling the case. Historically, courts routinely approved settlements that included confidentiality agreements. However, in recent years some courts have rejected confidentiality agreements, particularly where the lawsuit being settled has substantial public interest.

The following are simple examples of a release and covenant not to sue. They should be modified to fit the facts of any particular situation and the particular law of the applicable jurisdiction.

Example:

SETTLEMENT AGREEMENT
AND RELEASE OF ALL CLAIMS

In consideration of the sum of $ _____, which Plaintiff acknowledges receiving, Plaintiff_____agrees to release Defendants_____and_____ and their heirs, survivors, agents, and personal representatives from all claims, suits, or actions in any form or on any basis, because of anything that was done or not done at any time, on account of the following:

All claims for personal injuries, property damage, physical disabilities, medical expenses, lost income, and all other claims that have been or could be brought, including all claims now known or which are presently unknown but in the future might become known, which arise out of an occurrence on or about ___(date)___, at ____*(location)*____, when Plaintiff claims to have been injured as a result of a collision between an automobile driven by Plaintiff and automobiles driven by the Defendants.

As a result of this collision, Plaintiff has brought suit against the Defendants for damages. The Defendants have denied both liability and the claimed extent of damages. This release is a compromise settlement between Plaintiff _____ and Defendant _____ and Defendant _____.

It is expressly agreed that this agreement is not an admission of liability or fault, but that this agreement and payment is made as a compromise to settle all claims arising out of this occurrence. The parties declare that they have voluntarily entered into this agreement in good faith, have read and understand it, and consider it to be a fair and reasonable settlement.

This agreement, which is a contract and not a mere recital, is a release and shall operate as a total discharge of any claims Plaintiff has or may in the future have arising out of the above occurrence against these Defendants and any other persons.

Plaintiff _____ and Defendant _____ _____and Defendant _____ also expressly agree to terminate any actions that have been filed, particularly a claim by this Plaintiff against these Defendants currently filed as civil action no. _____ in the United States District Court for the District of _____, in _____. Plaintiff and these Defendants agree to execute a Stipulation of Dismissal, with prejudice, and file it with the Clerk of the above Court, thereby terminating that action in its entirety, within seven days of the execution of this agreement. The Stipulation of Dismissal shall provide that each party shall bear its own costs, attorney's fees, and filing fees.

Date: _____   _____
                                                Plaintiff

                                                _____
                                                Defendant

                                                _____
                                                Defendant

Example:

COVENANT NOT TO SUE

In consideration of the sum of $ _____, which Plaintiff acknowledges receiving, Plaintiff _____ agrees not to institute, pursue, or continue any claim, suit, or action in any form or on any basis, because of anything that was done or not done at any time, against Defendant _____ and his heirs, survivors, agents, or personal representatives on account of the following:

Any claims against Defendant _____ for personal injuries, property damage, physical disabilities, medical expenses, lost income, and any other claims that have been or could be brought, including all claims now known or which in the future might become known, which arise out of an occurrence on or about ____*(date)*____, at ____*(location)*____, when Plaintiff claims to have been injured as a result of a collision between an automobile driven by Plaintiff and an automobile driven by Defendant.

As a result of this collision, Plaintiff has brought suit against Defendant for damages. Defendant has denied both liability and the claimed extent of damages. This covenant not to sue is a compromise settlement between Plaintiff _____ and Defendant _____.

This agreement is a covenant not to sue, and not a release or an accord and satisfaction. Nothing in this agreement shall operate as a discharge against any other persons, and Plaintiff _____ expressly reserves the right to pursue any claims against any other persons other than Defendant _____ and his heirs, survivors, agents, and personal representatives.

Plaintiff _____ and Defendant _____ _____ also expressly agree to terminate any actions between them, particularly a claim by Plaintiff against this Defendant currently filed as civil action no. _____ in the United States District Court for the District of _____, in _____. Plaintiff and Defendant agree to execute a Stipulation of Dismissal, with prejudice, and file it with the Clerk of the above Court, to terminate that action against this Defendant only, within seven days of the execution of this agreement.

Date: _____   _____
                                 Plaintiff

                                 _____
                                 Defendant

When drafting a settlement agreement, you must research the law of the applicable jurisdiction to determine the validity and effect of these settlement devices,[20] and you must keep the following basic concepts

20. For an excellent discussion of this area along with illustrations of potential problems, see Dewey, Traps in Multitortfeasor Settlements, 13 Litigation (No. 1, Summer 1987).

clear. First, the effect of a release under common law terminates all of plaintiff's claims against all existing and potential defendants, not just the settling defendant. This common law rule, however, may have been changed by statute. As a plaintiff, never agree to a release unless you fully understand the legal effect on all present and future litigation. Second, if the common law rule *is* still in effect, a covenant not to sue, first created to avoid the effect of the common law release rule, technically keeps the claims alive against the settling defendant since the plaintiff only agrees not to enforce the claims against that defendant. As a result a settling defendant is still exposed to contribution claims by the other defendants who are still in the lawsuit. As a defendant, never agree to a covenant not to sue unless you have adequate protection against later contribution claims, either by statute or by the settlement agreement. Third, remember that contribution among joint tortfeasors is not the same thing as indemnification. Contribution does not affect valid indemnification claims against any parties. Fourth, many states by statute protect a settling joint tortfeasor defendant by providing that any judgment against the non-settling tortfeasor be reduced either by the amount the settling defendant paid the plaintiff or by the percentage of fault subsequently attributed to the settling tortfeasor in a lawsuit against the non-settling defendants (see the Uniform Apportionment of Tort Responsibility Act, the successor to the Uniform Contribution Among Joint Tortfeasors Act). These statutes also typically discharge the settling defendant from any later contribution claims by non-settling defendants and other joint tortfeasors (see the Uniform Contribution Among Joint Tortfeasors Act). However, not all states have such statutes, so the settling defendant must know the applicable jurisdiction's law to assess his exposure to later contribution claims. Fifth, the settlement agreement can usually specify what jurisdiction's law will apply to the agreement. Such a choice of law clause can then apply more favorable law to the contribution issues. Sixth, jurisdictions vary in how they define a defendant's pro rata share of any judgment against joint tortfeasors.[21] If the jurisdiction does not protect a settling defendant from contribution claims, the defendant should make sure that the settlement agreement adopts the applicable jurisdiction's definition of a pro rata share and insist that the defendant get a "credit" for either the amount paid to the plaintiff to settle or a pro rata share, however defined, of any ultimate judgment plaintiff gets, whichever is greater. Finally, if the lawsuit involves both contract and tort claims, make sure you know how much of the settlement amount will be allocated to each type of claim. This is important, because contribution exists only in tort, not contract. Shifting the allocation of the settlement amount between the contract and tort claims will affect the amount of contribution the nonsettling defendants may be entitled to later.

It should be apparent that the drafting of a settlement can be complex, particularly in situations involving joint tortfeasors and depending on the applicable jurisdiction's law. In general, every plaintiff wants a guaranteed dollar amount from the settling defendant, wants to keep

21. The share may be the amount of money paid by the settling tortfeasor or calculated on a per capita or percentage of responsibility basis.

claims alive against the non-settling defendants, and wants no relief from contribution for the settling defendant. Every settling defendant, by contrast, wants to get out of the case with a guaranteed dollar amount to cap his exposure and wants adequate protection from later contribution claims, if a statute does not already provide it. A careful lawyer must know the legal effect and validity of these settlement devices, the contribution law that applies to the tort claims, and must prepare a carefully drafted instrument that fits the particulars of the case so that the final agreement achieves what the lawyer needs in order to adequately protect his client.

Most defense lawyers will insist on the settlement agreement containing a confidentiality clause. The following language is commonly used.

Example:

> The parties agree not to disclose to or discuss with any person, entity, or public news media, directly or indirectly, in whole or in part, the terms, conditions, content, or nature of this settlement agreement or settlement negotiations, including but not limited to the settlement amount or whether the settlement was favorable or unfavorable. The parties also agree that any documents, electronically stored information, or things obtained from or produced by the defendant during this lawsuit shall be considered confidential information and will not be disclosed to any person, entity, or public news media, directly or indirectly, in whole or in part.

In addition, consider submitting the settlement agreement to the court and asking the court to incorporate the settlement agreement in the order terminating the case and retaining jurisdiction over the settlement. Once the settlement agreement is signed by the parties, approved by the court, and incorporated into the final order, the parties can enforce the agreement through the court and seek the court's contempt power to punish any violations of the agreement.

c. Structured settlements

In recent years so-called structured settlements have become common, particularly in the personal injury area when plaintiffs have been seriously and permanently injured. A structured settlement is simply a settlement under which the plaintiff receives periodic payments rather than one lump sum or a combination of such payments. The benefit to the plaintiff of such a settlement is that she is assured of support over a period of years. Defendant's insurance companies also benefit, since paying a settlement over a number of years reduces the true cost of the settlement. Socially, structured settlements help ensure that the plaintiff will not become indigent and depend on the state for support. Under §104(a)(2) of the Internal Revenue Code, periodic payments when properly designed receive the same tax treatment as lump sum payments, and some states have legislation regulating them, often based on the Model

Periodic Payments of Judgments Act. Structured settlements are complicated and involve both statutory regulation and tax laws. This is an area where advice from someone experienced in this settlement method is warranted.

The most frequently used approach in structured settlements is to provide for an initial lump sum and a series of periodic payments. The lump sum is large enough to cover the plaintiff's attorney's fee, other legal expenses, and the plaintiff's unpaid bills. The periodic payments cover either a fixed period of years or the lifetime of the plaintiff; the periods are either annual or for a shorter time. If the payments extend over a number of years, they may be tied to the inflation rate by providing for increases based on the Consumer Price Index or other measure of inflation rates. The defendant's insurer usually funds the periodic payments by purchasing an annuity from an established life insurance company that will automatically make the payments required under the agreement.

Example:

SETTLEMENT AGREEMENT

    Plaintiff _____ and Defendant _____ are parties to a civil action, Case No. _____, presently pending in the United States District Court for the District of _____.

    Plaintiff and defendant wish to avoid the burdens and expenses that will be incurred in further prosecuting and defending this action, and wish to resolve and settle all disputes in this action. By entering into this settlement agreement neither party admits to any fault or liability.

    In consideration of the cash payments, mutual releases, and other obligations contained in this contract, the sufficiency of which both parties acknowledge, plaintiff and defendant agree to the following:

    1. Plaintiff fully releases and discharges the defendant from all liabilities, losses, costs, and expenses related to the subject matter of this action.

    2. Plaintiff will dismiss with prejudice its complaint in this action within 7 days of the execution of this agreement. However, the United States District Court before which this action is pending shall retain jurisdiction over this action to enforce the terms of, and resolve any disputes which may arise under, this agreement. The parties agree that the stipulation of dismissal shall contain the provision that the court shall retain jurisdiction over this action for the purpose of enforcing the terms of, and resolving any disputes arising under, this agreement, and that the court's order of dismissal shall incorporate the terms of this settlement agreement.

    3. Plaintiff and defendant will bear their own costs and attorney's fees arising out of this action and settlement agreement.

4. Defendant will pay plaintiff the total sum of $500,000, to be paid by cashier's checks payable to plaintiff, according to the following schedule:

a. $200,000 to be paid at the time this agreement is executed by the parties.

b. $30,000 to be paid each year for a total of 10 years, beginning in 2005 and ending in 2014. The first payment shall be made on or before June 1, 2005, and each successive yearly payment shall be made on or before June 1 of that year.

5. The parties agree that the payments described above shall be without interest, provided that the payments are timely made.

6. The parties agree that in the event the defendant fails to make payment of any of the above amounts on or before the required dates, the remainder of all the payments shall immediately become due and owing, and the plaintiff has the right to immediately apply to the United States District Court for a judgment for the entire amount that remains due and owing. The parties agree that interest on the amount due and owing will bear an annual interest rate of 10 percent from the date of the breach of this agreement.

7. If any action is commenced between the parties to this agreement to enforce any provisions of the agreement, the prevailing party shall be entitled to recover reasonable costs and expenses, including attorney's fees.

8. This agreement shall be governed and interpreted in accordance with the laws of the state of _____.

Date: _____   _____
                                   Plaintiff

                                   _____
                                   Defendant

The tax implications of structured settlements to both parties can be complex, particularly when future payments will be funded through annuities or other contracts with insurance companies. In these situations, a settlement should never be entered into unless you have determined the likely tax consequences to your client and have received the advice of an experienced tax specialist.

d.   High-low agreements

In recent years, high-low agreements have become common. While not a device that settles a case, it does have benefits for both sides. A high-low agreement is a contract between plaintiff and defendant that establishes the maximum and minimum recovery to the plaintiff and thereby eliminates the risk of either a complete win or loss. It is frequently used in personal injury cases involving large potential damages, where liability is seriously in issue, and in commercial cases having punitive or treble damages in issue.

For example, consider a personal injury case in which plaintiff is seeking damages in the millions, and defendant is contesting both liability and damages. Plaintiff's principal fear is that the jury may return a defense verdict on damages. Defendant's principal fear is that the jury may return a verdict in favor of the plaintiff on liability and award several million in damages. Accordingly, plaintiff and defendant agree that the case will proceed to trial, and that, regardless of the jury's verdict, plaintiff will not receive more than $2,000,000 and not less than $500,000. The $2,000,000 becomes the "high" and the $500,000 becomes the "low" in the high-low agreement. The agreement becomes a compromise eliminating the possibility of a catastrophic verdict for either side.

High-low agreements are negotiated much like a settlement agreement, but are usually made just before or during trial. This is because as the trial progresses, the parties have a greater sense of urgency in avoiding a disastrous result. Both sides have a mutual interest in reducing risk and achieving finality by avoiding an appeal. The parties' last demand and offer before settlement talks collapsed are a good starting point in reaching a high-low agreement, although the numbers will be modified by how the trial is progressing.

When negotiating such an agreement, be sure to consider all the possibilities that may arise and need to be included in the agreement. For example, will the agreement bar post-trial motions and any appeal? Will it bar an appeal of the verdict amount but not other issues? What happens in the event of a mistrial, caused either by events during the trial or by the jury's inability to reach a verdict on all or some counts? Who pays costs, and what are the included costs? Does the agreement cover prejudgment and post-judgment interest? When should the judge be informed that an agreement exists, since the existence of the agreement may influence how the judge conducts the trial? Must the judge approve the agreement?

In most cases, the lawyers will advise the judge of the agreement and its terms at the end of the trial, when the jury is ready to deliberate, and put on the record the terms of the agreement. When the jury returns its verdict, the judge later enters judgment consistent with the terms of the agreement and the jury's verdict. The jury, of course, is not told about the agreement.

e. Terminating the suit

After a settlement agreement has been reached, the lawsuit must be terminated. The standard method is to file a stipulation to dismiss with the clerk of the court. Under Rule 41 a court order is no longer necessary.

Make sure the stipulation to dismiss is with prejudice as to the settling defendant, since this bars the plaintiff from refiling the claim later. If the settlement is only partial, as is the case with a covenant not to sue, the stipulation must clearly show which party is being dismissed and which parties remain in the case. The stipulation is signed by the lawyers for the parties who have agreed to settle.

Example (complete dismissal):

[Caption]

STIPULATION OF DISMISSAL

Plaintiff _____, Defendant _____, and Defendant _____ agree to dismiss this action with prejudice, and each party will bear its costs and attorney's fees.

Date: _____

_____
Attorney for Plaintiff

_____
Attorney for Defendant

_____
Attorney for Defendant

Example (partial dismissal):

[Caption]

STIPULATION OF DISMISSAL

Plaintiff _____ and Defendant _____ agree to dismiss this action with prejudice as to Defendant _____ only, and the action shall continue as to the remaining Defendants.

Date: _____

_____
Attorney for Plaintiff

_____
Attorney for Defendant

A simple stipulation of dismissal will be adequate when the case will not be dismissed until the settlement has actually been carried out. For example, in a personal injury case the stipulation of dismissal is routinely filed with the clerk after the plaintiff has received and cashed the settlement check. In this situation, there is no danger that the defendant will breach the settlement agreement.

However, if the settlement agreement requires future performance, plaintiff will want the court to retain jurisdiction for the purpose of enforcing the terms of the agreement, should that ever become necessary. For example, a settlement agreement may require the other party to make future periodic payments, or contain a noncompetition clause. In this situation, you will want the court to retain jurisdiction after the case is dismissed. The safe approach is to have the agreement expressly provide for it and to have the court enter an order of dismissal expressly retaining jurisdiction. The Supreme Court has held that a district court retains jurisdiction over the case after a dismissal with prejudice only if the order of dismissal refers to and incorporates the settlement agreement or expressly reserves the court's jurisdiction to enforce the settlement agreement.[22] If the settlement agreement calls for continuing the court's jurisdiction, and the order of dismissal incorporates the terms of the settlement agreement, the court will retain jurisdiction. A party that violates the settlement agreement also violates the court order, and the district court will have ancillary jurisdiction to enforce the order.

Where you want the court to retain jurisdiction, make sure the settlement agreement has an appropriate clause.

Example:

> The parties agree that the court shall retain jurisdiction over this case and the parties for the purpose of enforcing the terms of the settlement agreement. The parties further agree that this case will be terminated only through an order of dismissal that expressly incorporates the terms of this agreement and expressly retains the court's jurisdiction over the case and the parties.

You will then need to prepare a draft order incorporating the agreement and retaining the court's jurisdiction and submit it to the court for signature.

In certain types of cases court approval is needed for any settlement. Settlements in class actions must have court approval under Rule 23(e). Also, settlements involving decedents' estates or incapacitated parties such as minors and incompetents usually require court approval. In these situations the action will be brought in the name of the representative party, such as a guardian, guardian ad litem, conservator, administrator, or executor. Local statutes and rules must always be checked to ensure compliance with technical requirements. The usual procedure is to present a petition to the court having jurisdiction over the party, usually a probate or family court, and to serve notice to all parties and other interested persons. A hearing is then conducted on the proposed settlement and, if approved, an appropriate court order authorizing the settlement will be entered.

f. Offers of judgment

Rule 68 provides that a party defending a claim can serve an offer of judgment upon the opposing party more than 10 days before the trial.

---

22. See Kokkonen v. Guardian Life Insurance Company of America, 511 U.S. 375 (1994), which makes clear that Rule 41(a)(2) permits a dismissal order that retains jurisdiction for the purpose of enforcing the settlement agreement if the parties wish this to occur.

The purpose of Rule 68 is to encourage settlements where reasonable offers to settle have been made. If the offer is refused and a judgment following trial is the same or less favorable to the plaintiff than the pretrial offer of judgment, the plaintiff becomes responsible for the defendant's "costs" incurred from the time of the offer. An offer of judgment can be made on any "claim," including the plaintiff's claims against the defendant, defendant's counterclaims against the plaintiff, cross-claims between defendants, or third-party claims against third-party defendants.

In recent years Rule 68 has become a prominent weapon in the settlement stage of the litigation process and has generated substantial case law. Rule 68 applies whenever a final judgment is in a plaintiff's favor but is the same or less favorable than the offer to settle made by a defendant.[23] The defendant's offer to settle must be reasonably certain in amount and must be unconditional, but there is no requirement that the settlement and cost amounts be itemized.[24]

The principal difficulty in applying Rule 68 has concerned the meaning of the term "costs." It is clear that costs include court fees, witness fees, and court reporter fees,[25] but less so concerning attorney's fees. In Marek v. Chesney,[26] the Supreme Court held that "costs" refers to all costs that can be awarded under applicable substantive law. In that case, a 42 U.S.C. §1983 civil rights action, §1988 allowed attorney's fees to the prevailing party. However, the plaintiff's judgment was not as favorable as the defendant's pretrial offer of judgment. Therefore, plaintiff could not recover as part of costs any attorney's fees incurred from the date of the defendant's offer, which included the attorney's fees for the entire trial.

Case law has generally rejected a similar argument, in attorney's fees cases, that the plaintiff who gets a judgment less favorable than a previous offer should also be required to pay defendant's post-offer attorney's fees.[27]

The present usefulness of Rule 68 to defendants depends largely on whether "costs" include attorney's fees. Where they include only court costs and the like, these are likely to be sufficiently small in most cases that they will not exert much pressure on a plaintiff to settle. Where costs include attorney's fees because a statute expressly so provides, Rule 68 affords substantial leverage against a plaintiff since, if the later judgment is less favorable than defendant's offer of settlement, the plaintiff will forgo recovering attorney's fees from the date of the offer. As Marek v. Chesney illustrates, this can be a substantial amount. As a defendant, always make sure the offer of judgment specifies whether attorney's fees are part of the

---

23. Delta Air Lines v. August, 450 U.S. 346 (1981).
24. Marek v. Chesney, 473 U.S. 1 (1985).
25. See 28 U.S.C. §§1920 et seq.
26. 473 U.S. 1 (1985).
27. Crossman v. Marcoccio, 806 F.2d 329 (1st Cir. 1986).

offer, since courts differ over whether an accepted offer bars a plaintiff from obtaining additional statutory attorney's fees.

If a defendant wishes to make an offer of judgment to the plaintiff, this must be done more than 10 days before trial begins. Make sure the offer is actually delivered to the plaintiff's attorney within the permissible time. Make sure every offer of judgment has a reasonable time limit. Do not file the offer in court at this time; otherwise the trial judge may see it and be influenced by it.

Defendants usually make settlement offers under Rule 68 when settlement negotiations have broken down and a trial is to begin soon. However, the offer can be made at any time, and you should consider making it earlier if you can realistically assess the case's value, particularly where attorney's fees are included as costs. The offer can be made in a letter, sent by registered mail or hand delivered, or in a formal offer with an attached proof of service.

The offer of judgment should be tied to your settlement approach and your earlier offers to settle, and accounts for the elimination of risk, time, costs of trial, and an appeal, so that it puts realistic pressure on the other side and later demonstrates to the settlement judge that you have been realistic in evaluating the case.

Example:

[Caption]

OFFER OF JUDGMENT

To: *(attorney for plaintiff)*

Defendant Johnson Corporation, pursuant to Rule 68, offers to allow judgment to be entered against it, in favor of plaintiff Frank Jones, in the amount of fourteen thousand ($14,000) dollars, and costs of suit incurred to the date of this offer.

This offer is made under Rule 68 of the Federal Rules of Civil Procedure and Rule 408 of the Federal Rules of Evidence, is made as a settlement offer, and is not to be taken as an admission of, or any indication of, liability on the part of this defendant.

This offer shall remain open for ten days after service of the offer.

Date: _____   _____

Attorney for Defendant
Johnson Corporation

If the plaintiff elects to accept the offer of judgment, he simply sends a notice to the defendant that he accepts the offer. The acceptance must be made and written notice served within ten days of when the offer is served. Judgment can then be entered on the accepted offer.

g. Evidence rules

Under Rule 408 of the Federal Rules of Evidence, compromises and offers of compromise are not admissible to prove liability or damages. Rule 408 is broadly drafted to bar settlement discussions from being introduced at trial on those issues. The Rule, however, does not prevent admission of such evidence for other purposes, principally to expose bias and interest of a testifying witness. The law is clear that a party that has settled and later becomes a witness at the trial of the same case can be cross-examined on the settlement.[28]

h. Insurer good faith requirements

In civil litigation a defendant will often have some insurance coverage. The insurance contract normally has language under which the insurer reserves the right to manage the defense and negotiate a settlement. However, courts have usually imposed a duty on the insurer to deal fairly and in good faith to protect the interests of the insured. This duty comes about because the interests of the insurer sometimes conflict with those of the insured. The insured naturally wants the company to stand behind her and defend vigorously or, if a settlement is reached, to settle within the policy limits. The insurer also has an interest in defending vigorously, but in a settlement situation only has a financial interest in settling the case under the policy limit. Hence, the insurer and insured's interests come most sharply in conflict where there is a risk of exposure over the policy limits since, once the policy limit is reached, only the insured has additional exposure. Because of this conflict, courts have imposed a good faith obligation on the insurer to defend the case fairly and to adequately protect the insured's interests. In other words, the insurer has a duty to defend and must conduct the defense in the best interests of the insured as though there were no policy limits.[29]

Any settlement offer from the plaintiff should be communicated to the insured, since the insured is the actual party. Case law is not uniform on whether failure to notify the party of a settlement offer is a breach of good faith, but some courts have so held.[30] It is obviously a good practice to notify your client of every settlement offer, regardless of how unrealistic it is. Where a duty to defend in good faith has been breached, the insurer is generally liable for the entire judgment, regardless of policy limits.[31]

For defense lawyers the message from case law should be clear. The defense lawyer's client is the insured, and the lawyer's professional and ethical obligation is to serve the best interests of the client. That the lawyer was selected, and will have fees paid, by the insurance company does not

---

28. Johnson v. Moberg, 334 N.W.2d 411 (Minn. 1983); Hegarty v. Campbell Soup Co., 335 N.W.2d 758 (Neb. 1983).

29. See G. Williams, Legal Negotiation and Settlement 105–106 (1983).

30. See L. Russ & T. Segalla, Couch on Insurance (3d ed. 1995).

31. See 49 A.L.R.2d 711 (1956).

alter the professional obligations. Where settlement negotiations are in progress, both the insured and insurer must be kept informed of its progress. Whenever possible, the insured and insurer should both agree in writing to any settlement. Since the lawyer serves the client, not the insurer, the lawyer must accept a reasonable settlement, even when it involves the policy limits, if it is in the best interests of the client. Where exposure above the policy limits is involved and you, as lawyer, cannot get both the insured and the insurer to agree to a settlement, you must always research the status of the law in your jurisdiction to determine what the rights, duties, and liabilities of the insured and the insurer are in such circumstances.

i.   Enforcing settlements [32]

Although uncommon, a party may sometimes breach a settlement. Since a settlement agreement is a contract, the settlement can always be enforced in a separate contract action, but this is not the preferred method. Under Rule 60(b), the wronged party can move to enforce the judgment, provided that, as discussed above, the order of dismissal previously entered expressly retained the court's jurisdiction for purposes of enforcing the settlement agreement. The motion must be made in the same court, preferably before the same judge to whom the case had been assigned, and must cite a permissible reason for obtaining relief from a final judgment. You may need to have the case restored to the court's active calendar before you make the motion. At the hearing on the motion, be prepared to prove up the breach of the settlement agreement.

j.   Settlement statement

When a plaintiff's lawyer has received a settlement check from a defendant or defendant's insurer in accordance with a settlement agreement, the check must be deposited in the client's trust account. The lawyer must then, if being paid under a contingency fee agreement, prepare a written statement showing what the outcome was, the amount to be remitted to the client, and how that amount was calculated.[33] This statement, commonly called a settlement statement or sheet, shows the gross amount received in settlement, costs, attorney's fees, and the net amount that goes to the client. The client needs to approve the accounting, and the funds are disbursed from the client's trust account in accordance with the statement.

32. Wright & Miller §§2860 et seq.
33. See Model Rules of Professional Conduct, Rule 1.5(c). Such a statement is required in every contingency fee case, whether the case is concluded by settlement, trial, or other means.

Example:

<u>SETTLEMENT STATEMENT</u>

June 1, 2005

Settlement amount	$100,000.00
Costs (per attached itemized list)	$10,000.00
Net amount (settlement amount minus costs)	$90,000.00
Attorney's fees (33⅓ percent of net amount)	$30,000.00
Net amount to client	<u>$60,000.00</u>

ACCEPTED AND APPROVED:

_____

[client's signature]

Date: _____

The statement should be modified to include other particulars of the case, such as other distributions for workers' compensation liens. It should also reflect, where pertinent, that the client is solely and completely responsible for any unpaid bills, such as medical bills.

APPENDIX

LITIGATION FILE: JONES v. SMITH

This appendix is part of the litigation file in Jones v. Smith, an automobile collision case. It illustrates each basic step in the pleadings, discovery, motions, and settlement stages of the litigation process.

FACTS

John Jones, a 23-year-old delivery truck driver, was involved in a collision with Susan Smith. The collision occurred on September 2, 2006, at the intersection of 40th Street and Thomas Road in Phoenix, Arizona. Jones injured his stomach, neck, back, a shoulder, and an ankle and was out of work for a month. His car was also damaged.

Jones brings suit in federal court in Phoenix, Arizona. He claims that Smith negligently ran a red light at the intersection and crashed into his car (he was not operating a delivery truck at the time). Jones is a citizen of Arizona; Smith is a citizen of Nevada. The lawsuit was filed on January 2, 2007.

UNITED STATES DISTRICT COURT FOR THE DISTRICT OF ARIZONA

John Jones, 　　　Plaintiff, 　　v. Susan Smith, 　　　Defendant	No._____ Civil Action **JURY TRIAL DEMANDED**

The "Caption" includes the Court, the parties, and the case number.

The court clerk will stamp the case number when the complaint is filed with the clerk. The jury demand is usually put in the caption as well as at the end of the complaint.

COMPLAINT

Plaintiff John Jones complains of defendant Susan Smith as follows:

1. Jurisdiction in this case is based on diversity of citizenship and the amount in controversy. Plaintiff is a citizen of the State of Nevada. The amount in controversy exceeds, exclusive of interest and costs, the sum of seventy-five thousand ($75,000) dollars.

2. On September 2, 2006, at approximately 2:00 P.M., plaintiff John Jones ("Jones") was driving a vehicle northbound on 40th Street toward the intersection of 40th Street and Thomas Road in Phoenix, Arizona. Defendant Susan Smith ("Smith") was driving a vehicle eastbound on Thomas Road toward the same intersection.

3. Smith failed to stop for a red light at the intersection of 40th Street and Thomas Road, and negligently drove her vehicle into Jones' vehicle.

4. As a direct and proximate result of Smith's negligence, Jones injured his stomach, neck, back, shoulder, ankle, and other bodily parts, received other physical injuries, suffered physical and mental pain and suffering, incurred medical expenses, lost income, and will incur further medical expenses and lost income in the future.

WHEREFORE, plaintiff John Jones demands judgment against defendant Susan Smith for the sum of $100,000, with interest and costs.

This is the standard jurisdictional allegation in diversity cases. It should be the first paragraph of the complaint.

The factual allegations should be clear and simple. This makes it more likely that they will be either admitted or denied outright, making the pleadings easier to understand.

The negligence and causation claims are kept simple. This is adequate under "notice pleading" requirements. The injury allegations are usually spelled out in some detail.

Many complaints simply ask for "a sum in excess of $75,000," the jurisdictional limit.

Dated: January 2, 2007

Anne Johnson

Anne Johnson
Attorney for Plaintiff
100 Congress Street
Phoenix, AZ 85001
882-1000

PLAINTIFF DEMANDS TRIAL BY JURY

This avoids requesting unrealistic damages. The danger of exaggerated damages is that, unless amended, the pleadings can be read to the jury at trial, making the plaintiff look greedy.

Most jurisdictions also require submitting a jury demand form and paying a jury demand fee to preserve the right to a jury trial.

UNITED STATES DISTRICT COURT FOR
THE DISTRICT OF ARIZONA

John Jones,
        Plaintiff,
      v.
Susan Smith,
        Defendant
	No._____

SUMMONS

TO THE ABOVE-NAMED DEFENDANT:
Susan Smith
200 Palmer Way
Las Vegas, Nevada

    You are hereby summoned and required to serve upon Anne Johnson, plaintiff's attorney, whose address is 100 Congress Street, Phoenix, AZ, 85001, an answer to the complaint which is herewith served upon you, within 20 days after service of this summons upon you, exclusive of the day of service

    If you fail to do so judgment by default will be taken against you for the relief demanded in the complaint.

Thomas Barber
_____
Clerk of the Court

[Seal of U.S. District Court]

Dated: <u>January 2, 2007</u>

A good practice is to give the person who serves the complaint and summons any additional information about the defendant that may help make an effective service.

In this case service is made under the Arizona long-arm statute. Service could also be made using the mail and waiver of service provisions of Rule 4.

The person making the service must prepare an Affidavit of Service showing how service on the defendant was actually made.

The Affidavit of Service form is frequently attached to the summons form.

UNITED STATES DISTRICT COURT FOR THE DISTRICT OF ARIZONA

John Jones,
          Plaintiff,
     v.   No. 07 C 1000
Susan Smith,
          Defendant

ANSWER

Defendant Susan Smith answers the complaint as follows:

1. Admit
2. Admit
3. Deny
4. Defendant denies plaintiff was injured as a result of any negligence by the defendant, and is without knowledge or information sufficient to form a belief as to the truth of all other allegations in Par. 4, and therefore denies them.

Simple responses are more likely to be made since the complaint's allegations are correspondingly simple.

First Defense

Each defense should be set out separately.

Plaintiff's claimed injuries and damages were caused by plaintiff's own negligence, which was the sole proximate cause of any injuries and damages plaintiff may have received.

WHEREFORE, defendant requests that plaintiff receive nothing, and that judgment be entered for the defendant, including costs of this action.

Dated: January 15, 2007

William Sharp

William Sharp
Attorney for Defendant
100 Broadway
Phoenix, AZ 85001
881-1000

AFFIDAVIT OF SERVICE

I, Helen Thompson, having been first duly sworn, state that I served a copy of defendant's Answer on plaintiff by personally delivering it to Anne Johnson, attorney for plaintiff, at 100 Congress Street, Phoenix, Arizona, on January 15, 2007.

Helen Thompson
Helen Thompson

Signed and sworn to before me on January 15, 2007.

Mary Ryan
Notary Public

My commission expires on December 31, 2007.

[Seal]

After the complaint has been served, every other court paper must be served on every other party in accordance with Rule 5. The usual service is personal delivery or mailing to the party's attorney of record.

An affidavit or certification of service should always be attached to every court paper showing how proper service was made.

All court papers must be filed with the court either before service or within a reasonable time after service.

In practice, court papers are usually filed with the court clerk the same day service is made.

UNITED STATES DISTRICT COURT FOR
THE DISTRICT OF ARIZONA

John Jones,
      Plaintiff,
   v.   No. 07 C 1000
Susan Smith,
      Defendant

PLAINTIFF'S INITIAL DISCLOSURES

Plaintiff John Jones makes the following initial disclosures to the defendant, pursuant to Rule 26(a)(1) of the Federal Rules of Civil Procedure:

(A) Individuals

The following individuals are likely to have information relevant to disputed facts:

1. John Jones, plaintiff
2. Susan Smith, defendant
3. Carol Brown
   42 East Cambridge Street
   Phoenix, AZ
   482-3737
4. Mary Porter
   42 East Cambridge Street
   Phoenix, AZ
   482-3737
5. Off. Steven Pitcher
   Phoenix Police Dept.
6. Lenore L. Lang, M.D.
   333 East Campbell Avenue
   Phoenix, AZ 85016
   482-6000
7. Frank Hoffman, M.D.
   222 West Thomas Road, Suite 100
   Phoenix, AZ 85013
   222-4000
8. J. Franks, D.C.
   55 North 27th Avenue
   Phoenix, AZ 85007
   881-9876

9. Diane Devo
    Devo Wholesale Florist
    3731 40th Street
    Phoenix, AZ 85007
    434-1000
10. John Jones, Sr., and Mary Jones
    1020 N. 50th Street
    Phoenix, AZ 85013
    332-8571

Witnesses #1-5 are occurrence witnesses; witnesses #6-10 are medical and damages witnesses.

(B) Documents and tangible things

The following documents and tangible things, which are attached, are relevant to disputed facts:

1. Devo Wholesale Florist employment records
2. Doctors Hospital medical records
3. Dr. Lang office records and bill
4. Dr. Hoffman office records and bill
5. Dr. Frank office records and bill
6. Walgreen Pharmacy bills
7. Phoenix Police Dept. accident reports
8. X-rays
9. Photographs of accident scene

(C) Damages computation

The following is the present computation of known damages:

1. *Medical and related expenses:*
Doctors Hospital bill	$1,257.18
Dr. Lang bill	339.70
Dr. Hoffman bill	340.00
Dr. Franks bill	697.80
Walgreen Pharmacy bills	83.13
2. *Lost wages:*
Devo Wholesale Florist	700.00
3. Property damages:
Toyota vehicle repair	1,213.00
4. *Other expenses:*
Broken wristwatch	75.00
College books	162.00

5. *Pain and suffering:*

Past	over 40,000.00
Future	over 30,000.00

The documentation of these damages is contained in the documents identified in section (B) above.

(D) Insurance

Rule 26(a)(1)(D) does not apply to the plaintiff since defendant has filed no counter-claims in this action.

Dated: January 20, 2007

Anne Johnson

Anne Johnson
Attorney for Plaintiff
100 Congress Street
Phoenix, AZ 85001
882-1000

UNITED STATES DISTRICT COURT FOR
THE DISTRICT OF ARIZONA

John Jones,
        Plaintiff,
    v.   No. 07 C 1000
Susan Smith,
        Defendant

DEFENDANT'S INTERROGATORIES TO PLAINTIFF

Pursuant to Rule 33 of the Federal Rules of Civil Procedure, defendant Smith requests that plaintiff Jones answer the following interrogatories under oath, and serve them on the defendant within 30 days:

1. Describe the personal injuries you received as a result of the occurrence described in the complaint (hereafter "this occurrence").

2. State the full names and present addresses of any physicians, osteopaths, chiropractors, and other medical personnel who treated you as a result of this occurrence, each such person's areas of specialty, the dates of each examination, consultation or appointment, the amount of each such person's bill, and whether each bill has been paid.

3. Were you confined to a hospital or clinic as a result of this occurrence? If so, state the name and address of each such hospital or clinic, the dates of your confinement at each facility, the amount of each such facility's bills, and whether each bill has been paid.

4. Have you incurred other medical expenses, other than these requested in Interrogatory Nos. 2 and 3, as a result of this occurrence? If so, state each expense incurred, the nature of each expense, when the expense was incurred, to whom it was incurred, and whether each expense has been paid.

5. Have you incurred any expenses as a result of this occurrence other than medical expenses? If so, state the nature of each expense,

Interrogatories will usually be the first discovery device the parties serve on each other.

In this example, the defendant served interrogatories on plaintiff two weeks after answering the complaint. (Many defendants serve interrogatories with the answer.)

Note how each interrogatory deals with a separate, defined category and asks for all relevant data for the category. This will usually generate more complete answers. It also gives the answering party the opportunity of answering the interrogatory by producing the relevant records that contain the answers.

the date incurred, the amount of each expense, the reason for incurring each expense, and whether each expense has been paid.

6. Were you unable to work as a result of this occurrence? If so, state the date during which you were unable to work, each employer during these dates, the type of work you were unable to do, and the amount of lost wages or income from each employer.

7. Have you recovered from the claimed injuries that resulted from this occurrence? If not, state the claimed injuries from which you have not recovered and any present disability.

The plaintiff's current condition and medical history are important areas that should be explored thoroughly. This can then be verified during the plaintiff's deposition.

8. During the 10 years preceding September 2, 2004, have you suffered any other personal injuries? If so, state when, where, and how you were injured and the name and address of each medical facility where, and physicians by whom, you were treated for these injuries.

9. During the 10 years preceding September 2, 2004, have you been hospitalized, treated, examined, or tested at any hospital, clinic, physician's office, or other medical facility for any conditions other than those requested in Interrogatory No. 8? If so, state the name and address of each such medical facility and physician and the dates of such services and the medical conditions involved.

10. State the full name and address of each person who witnessed, or claims to have witnessed, the collision between the vehicles involved in this occurrence.

Occurrence witnesses are obviously important in this kind of case. It's a good practice to break them up by category in appropriate cases.

11. State the full name and address of each person who has any knowledge of the facts of the collision other than those persons already identified in Interrogatory No. 10.

12. Describe your vehicle involved in this occurrence, any damages to your vehicle as a result of this occurrence, the name and address of any firm repairing your vehicle, the amount billed for repairs, when such repairs took place, and whether the repair bills have been paid. If your vehicle has not been repaired, state where it is presently located and its condition.

13. Identify, by date, description, and source any medical records and any other records or documents of any kind in your or your attorney's possession or control that relate in any way to this occurrence and the injuries

Medical records are obviously critical in this kind of case. The descriptions you get and damages you claim resulted from this occurrence.

14. For each expert expected to testify at trial, state:

(a) the expert's full name, address, and professional qualifications;

(b) the subject matter on which the expert is expected to testify;

(c) the substance of the facts and opinions to which the expert is expected to testify; and

(d) a summary of the grounds of each opinion.

Dated: February 1, 2007

William Sharp

William Sharp
Attorney for Defendant
100 Broadway
Phoenix, AZ 85001
881-1000

will be used to send production requests to the plaintiff and subpoenas to third-party sources.

This interrogatory tracks the language of Rule 33. Under Rule 26(a), expert disclosures will be made in accordance with Rule 26(a)(2) and the time-table set by the court.

A proof of service must be attached.

UNITED STATES DISTRICT COURT FOR
THE DISTRICT OF ARIZONA

John Jones,
      Plaintiff,

v.   No. 07 C 1000

Susan Smith,
      Defendant

PLAINTIFF'S ANSWERS TO INTERROGATORIES

Plaintiff John Jones answers Defendant's interrogatories as follows:

<u>Interrogatory No. 1</u>: Describe the personal injuries you received as a result of the occurrence described in the complaint (hereafter "this occurrence").

<u>Answer:</u> Cervical, dorsal and lumbar sprain and strain; cerebral concussion; multiple contraction headaches and concussion headaches; left hemiparesis with ataxia; ankle sprain; numbness; multiple contusions and abrasions.

<u>Interrogatory No. 2:</u> State in full the names and present addresses of any physicians, osteopaths, chiropractors, nurses, or other medical personnel who treated you as a result of this occurrence, each such person's areas of specialty, the dates of each examination, consultation, or appointment, the amount of each such person's bill, and whether each bill has been paid.

<u>Answer:</u>
Doctors Hospital
1947 East Thomas Road
Phoenix, Arizona 85016

Lenore L. Lang, M.D.
333 East Campbell Avenue
Phoenix, Arizona 85016

Frank Hoffman, M.D.
222 West Thomas Road
Suite 100
Phoenix, Arizona 85013

The usual way of answering interrogatories is to set out the questions and the answers, making it easy to correlate the two.

J. Franks, D.C.
55 North 27th Avenue
Phoenix, Arizona 85007

(See answer to interrogatory no. 4; answer may be supplemented as discovery and investigation continues.)

Interrogatory No. 3: Were you confined to a hospital or clinic as a result of this occurrence? If so, state the name and address of the hospital or clinic, the dates of your confinement at each facility, the amount of each facility's bills, and whether each bill has been paid.

Answer: No; treated, but not confined, at Doctors Hospital.

Interrogatory No. 4: Have you incurred other medical expenses, other than those requested in Interrogatory Nos. 2 and 3, as a result of this occurrence? If so, state each expense incurred, the nature of each expense, when the expense was incurred, to whom it was incurred, and whether each expense has been paid.

Answer:

Doctors Hospital	$1,257.18
Lenore L. Lang, M.D.	339.70
Frank Hoffman, M.D.	340.00
J. Franks, D.C.	697.80
Walgreen Pharmacy	83.13

Those bills have been paid.

(Answer may be supplemented as discovery and investigation continues.)

Interrogatory No. 5: Have you incurred any expenses as a result of this occurrence, other than medical expenses? If so, state the nature of each expense, the date incurred, the amount of each expense, the reason for incurring each expense, and whether each expense has been paid.

Answer:

Broken wristwatch	$ 75.00
College books	162.00

Wristwatch repair bill has been paid.

Here the plaintiff has prepared partial answers, and acknowledges that further information will generate supplemental answers later. However, these partial answers were prepared within the 30-day requirement of Rule 33.

Interrogatory No. 6: Were you unable to work as a result of this occurrence? If so, state the dates during which you were unable to work, each employer during these dates, the type of work you were unable to do, and the amount of lost wages or income from each employer.

Answer: Yes, September 2, 2006, to October 1, 2006. Devo Wholesale Florist. Delivery truck driver. $700 — one month's salary.

Interrogatory No. 7: Have you recovered from the claimed injuries that resulted from this occurrence? If not, state the claimed injuries from which you have not recovered and any present disability.

Answer: Plaintiff still experiences headaches, neck pain, and lower back pain.

Interrogatory No. 8: During the 10 years preceding September 2, 2006, have you suffered any other personal injuries? If so, state when, where, and how you were injured, and the name and address of each medical facility where, and physicians by whom, you were treated for these injuries.

Answer: No.

Interrogatory No. 9: During the 10 years preceding September 2, 2006, have you been hospitalized, treated, examined, or tested at any hospital, clinic, physician's office or other medical facility for any conditions other than those requested in Interrogatory No. 8? If so, state the name and address of each such medical facility and physician, the dates of such services, and the medical conditions involved.

Answer: No.

Interrogatory No. 10: State the full name and address of each person who witnessed, or claims to have witnessed, the collision between the vehicles involved in this occurrence.

Answer:
John Jones, plaintiff
Susan Smith, defendant
Carol Brown, 42 East Cambridge Street, Phoenix, AZ

This is a typical interrogatory answer. It provides all the facts requested, does so efficiently, and does not volunteer anything not asked for.

Mary Porter, 42 East Cambridge Street, Phoenix, AZ

Officer Steven Pitcher, Phoenix Police Department

(Answer may be supplemented as discovery and investigation continues.)

Interrogatory No. 11: State the full name and address of each person who has any knowledge of the facts of the collision, other than persons already identified in Interrogatory No. 10.

Answer: See persons listed in answer to Interrogatory No. 4; John Jones, Sr., and Mary Jones, plaintiff's parents; Diane Devo, plaintiff's employer.

(Answer may be supplemented as discovery and investigation continues.)

Interrogatory No. 12: Describe your vehicle that was involved in this occurrence, any damage to your vehicle as a result of this occurrence, the name and address of any firm repairing your vehicle, the amount billed for repairs, when such repairs took place, and whether the repair bills have been paid. If your vehicle has not been repaired, state where it is presently located and its condition.

Answer: 2001 Toyota Corolla four-door sedan. Extensive damage to left and front side of car. Jack's Auto Repair, 2000 East Valley Road, Phoenix. $1,213. Repair, completed about September 30, 2006. Repair bill has been paid.

Interrogatory No. 13: Identify, by date, description, and source any medical records, and any other records or documents of any kind in your or your attorney's possession or control, that relate in any way to this occurrence and injuries and damages you claim resulted from this occurrence.

Answer: Employment records of Devo Wholesale Florist
Doctors Hospital records
Dr. Lang's office records

Witness lists must frequently be supplemented over time, since the ongoing investigation will often uncover additional witnesses.

This is another typical answer. It provides the facts called for, yet does not volunteer anything.

Dr. Hoffman's office records
Dr. Franks' office records
Medical bills
X-rays taken by the above health care providers
Phoenix Police Department Accident Report
Photographs of the scene of the accident

(Answer may be supplemented as discovery and investigation proceeds.)

Interrogatory No. 14: For each expert expected to testify at trial, state:

    (a)   the expert's full name, address, and professional qualifications;

    (b)   the subject matter on which the expert is expected to testify;

    (c)   the substance of the facts and opinions to which the expert is expected to testify; and

    (d)   a summary of the grounds of each opinion.

Answer:
Frank Hoffman, M.D.
222 West Thomas Road
Suite 100
Phoenix, AZ 85013

J. Franks, D.C.
55 North 27th Avenue
Phoenix, AZ 85007

Lenore L. Lang, M.D.
333 East Campbell Avenue
Phoenix, AZ 85016

(Answers may be supplemented as discovery and investigation continues.)

Dated: February 25, 2007

John Jones

The initial answer to this standard interrogatory is frequently "None known at present—investigation continues," on the basis that the answering party has not yet decided who its testifying experts will be.

Here the treating physicians will obviously be witnesses at trial, so their names are disclosed, with supplemental answers to follow.

In federal court expert disclosures are usually made under Rule 26(a).

State of Arizona
County of Maricopa | SS.

I, John Jones, being first duly sworn, state that:

I am the plaintiff in this case. I have made the foregoing Answers to Interrogatories and know the answers to be true to the best of my knowledge, information and belief.

John Jones
John Jones

Subscribed and sworn to before me this 25th day of February 2007, by John Jones, Plaintiff.

Mary Ryan
Mary Ryan, Notary Public

My commission expires on
    December 31, 2007.

[Seal]

Interrogatory answers must be signed under oath by the party making them.

Like any court papers, the answers must be served on every party. A proof of service, showing how service was made, must be attached to the answer.

UNITED STATES DISTRICT COURT FOR
THE DISTRICT OF ARIZONA

John Jones,
          Plaintiff,
     v.   No. 07 C 1000
Susan Smith,
          Defendant

REQUEST FOR PRODUCTION OF DOCUMENTS

Pursuant to Rule 34 of the Federal Rules of Civil Procedure, defendant requests that plaintiff produce within 30 days, in the law offices of William Sharp, 100 Broadway, Phoenix, AZ 85001, the following documents and electronically stored information for inspection and copying:

1. All medical reports, records, charts, X-ray reports, and all other records regarding any medical examinations and treatment received by plaintiff for the injuries claimed in the complaint. If any such reports, etc., exist in electronic form, those records are to be produced in the native format in which the reports, etc., were created and stored.

2. All U.S. Income Tax Returns filed by plaintiff for the years 2001 through 2006.

Dated: February 1, 2007

William Sharp

William Sharp
Attorney for Defendant
100 Broadway
Phoenix, AZ 85001
881-1000

Note that this documents request was served at the same time as were the interrogatories.

Documents requests usually depend on interrogatory answers to identify the relevant documents. Here, however, what the defendant wants is both simple and obvious, so the defendant decides to serve the requests with interrogatories.

A proof of service must be attached.

UNITED STATES DISTRICT COURT FOR
THE DISTRICT OF ARIZONA

John Jones,
       Plaintiff,
       v.
Susan Smith,
       Defendant
	No. 07 C 1000

PLAINTIFF'S RESPONSE TO REQUEST FOR PRODUCTION OF DOCUMENTS

Plaintiff responds to defendant's Requests for Production of Documents as follows:

1. Plaintiff will produce copies of all reports in plaintiff's possession regarding medical examinations and treatment of plaintiff for his injuries. These copies will be delivered to defendant's attorney on or before March 1, 2007.

2. Plaintiff herewith produces his U.S. Income Tax Returns for the years 2001 through 2005. The return for 2006 has not yet been prepared.

Dated: <u>February 25, 2007</u>

Anne Johnson (signature)

Anne Johnson
Attorney for Plaintiff
100 Congress Street
Phoenix, AZ 85001
882-1000

A response to a production request should be filed so there is a court record that shows how and when the request was complied with. If photocopying will be expensive, the requesting party will usually have to pay for the photocopying charges.

A proof of service must be attached.

UNITED STATES DISTRICT COURT FOR
THE DISTRICT OF ARIZONA

John Jones,
       Plaintiff,
   v.   No. 07 C 1000
Susan Smith,
       Defendant

SUBPOENA DUCES TECUM

TO: Diane Devo, President
      Devo Wholesale Florist
      3731 40th Street
      Phoenix, AZ 85010

YOU ARE HEREBY COMMANDED to appear and give testimony under oath at the law office of William Sharp, 100 Broadway, Phoenix, AZ 85001 on March 15, 2007, at 1:00 P.M. You are also commanded to bring the following:

All records relating to the employment of John Jones at Devo Wholesale Florist, from the first day of employment through the present date, including but not limited to records showing wages received, hours worked, and the condition of John Jones' health.

A deposition subpoena that also requires the witness to bring specified records can be used to obtain records from nonparty witnesses. Under Rules 34(c) and 45, the records alone can be subpoenaed.

Make sure that you serve a Notice of Deposition on every other party, because other parties always have a right to attend any deposition and question the deponent.

Dated: <u>March 1, 2007</u>

[Seal]

Thomas Barber

Clerk of the Court

UNITED STATES DISTRICT COURT FOR
THE DISTRICT OF ARIZONA

John Jones,
                Plaintiff,
       v.
Susan Smith,
                Defendant
	No. 07 C 1000

NOTICE OF DEPOSITION

TO: PLAINTIFF JOHN JONES

Please take notice that the undersigned will take the deposition of John Jones, Plaintiff, on March 15, 2007, at 2:00 P.M. at 100 Broadway, Phoenix, AZ 85001. You are hereby notified that the plaintiff is to appear at that time and place of case and submit to a deposition under oath.

Two weeks' notice is appropriate in this type of case.

Dated: March 1, 2007

A subpoena is not necessary since the deponent is a party.

William Sharp

William Sharp
Attorney for Defendant
100 Broadway
Phoenix, AZ 85001
881-1000

A proof of service must be attached.

UNITED STATES DISTRICT COURT FOR
THE DISTRICT OF ARIZONA

John Jones,
      Plaintiff,
v.

Susan Smith,
      Defendant

No. 07 C 1000

DEPOSITION OF JOHN JONES

DEPOSITION OF John Jones, taken at
2:13 P.M. on March 15, 2007, at the law offices
of William Sharp, at 100 Broadway, Phoenix,
AZ 85001, before Mary Ryan, a Notary Public
in Maricopa County, Arizona.

Appearance for the plaintiff:

Anne Johnson
100 Congress Street
Phoenix, AZ 85001

Appearance for the defendant:

William Sharp
100 Broadway
Phoenix, AZ 85001

JOHN JONES

Called as a witness, having been first duly sworn,
was examined and testified as follows:

EXAMINATION BY MR. SHARP:

Q. This is the deposition of the plaintiff,
John Jones, being taken in the case of
John Jones v. Susan Smith, Case No. 07
C 1000 in the United States District
Court for the District of Arizona. It is
being held at the law office of William
Sharp, 100 Broadway, Phoenix, Arizona
85001. Today's date is March 15, 2007.
Present in addition to Mr. Jones are

This is a standard
introductory
statement.

myself, William Sharp, attorney for defendant Smith, Anne Johnson, attorney for plaintiff Jones, and Mary Ryan, a certified court reporter and notary public. Mr. Jones, you were just sworn to tell the truth by the court reporter, correct?

A. That's right.

Q. It's important that you understand the questions and give accurate answers. If there's anything you don't understand, or anything you don't know or aren't sure of, you let us know, all right?

A. Yes.

Q. Please tell us your full name.

A. John J. Jones.

Q. How old are you?

A. I'm 23.

Q. Are you married or single?

A. Single.

Q. Where do you live?

A. 1020 North 50th Street, Phoenix, Arizona.

Q. How far did you go in school?

A. I graduated from high school — Central High, 2002.

Q. What did you do after high school?

A. I joined the army.

Q. Tell us about your army experience.

A. After basic training, I was sent to an infantry division, and did most of my three years in Germany. I was a corporal when I received my honorable discharge. That was in August 2005.

Q. What did you do after that?

A. I came back to Phoenix, moved into my parents' house, and started working for Devo Wholesale Florist.

Q. Where is that located?

A. It's at 3731 40th Street, Phoenix.

Q. What kind of work do you do there?

A. I started as a sales clerk, then I became a driver on one of their trucks.

Q. What do you do as a driver?

A. I deliver flowers from the store to customers in the Phoenix area.

Q. What were your hours in August and September 2006?

a. Personal background
Note the form of the questions and the tone of the examination. The principal purposes of this deposition are to acquire information and assess the plaintiff as a trial witness. Accordingly, the questions are usually open-ended, designed to elicit information and have the plaintiff do the talking. The questions are asked in a pleasant, friendly way.

b. Work experience

A. It varied, but it was usually 6:00 A.M. to 2:00 P.M.

Q. Were those your hours the day of the accident?

A. Yes.

Q. Other than your job for Devo Florist, did you have any other jobs or activities in September 2006?

A. I didn't have any other job. I was a part-time student at Glendale Community College.

Q. Mr. Jones, were you ever involved in an automobile accident before September 2, 2006?

A. No.

Q. Did you ever have personal injuries of any kind before September 2, 2006?

A. No.

Q. During the past 10 years, other than for this accident, did you ever see a physician for any reason?

A. Well, our family doctor is Dr. Hoffman. I would see him from time to time for checkups, shots, and things like that. But I never had any serious injury or illness that I went to Dr. Hoffman for.

Q. Mr. Jones, tell me each injury you feel you've received as a result of the accident on September 2.

A. Okay. I hurt the left side of my neck, my lower back, my left ankle, my left shoulder, and my stomach.

Q. Let's start out with the left side of your neck. What injuries did you receive there?

A. I think I whipped my head to the side when the car crashed into me and I strained my neck. I had these shooting pains in my neck whenever I tried to move it.

Q. How long did that pain continue?

A. Well it was pretty severe about a week, and then it started getting better. I still get pains there from time to time.

Q. Tell me about the injuries to your lower back.

c. Accident and health history must be explored, since preexisting injuries would affect the damages pictures.

d. Each claimed injury should be explored in detail.

The "tell me" form of questions are used to get the witness to disclose everything.

If the plaintiff at trial tries to claim additional injuries, he can hardly say he didn't mention all his injuries during the deposition because the lawyer didn't give him a chance to do so.

Since pain and suffering will probably be the largest single element of damages, these questions are important to "pin down" the witness and prevent later exaggeration at trial.

A. Well, that was sort of the same thing. I must have wrenched my back from the force of the collision. Just like my neck, it was stiff and hurt for a while. After about a week it started getting better, and today I only get the pain from time to time, especially toward the end of the work day.

Q. Tell me about your left ankle.

A. I sprained my ankle during the accident. That was probably the worst injury. I had to stay off my feet for about two weeks, and I really couldn't start walking on it for three or four weeks. That's the injury that kept me out of work for a month.

Q. When did your ankle start getting better?

A. About a month after this happened it was well enough so I could start working, although I was still limping for quite a while. It probably took about four months before the ankle healed up completely.

Q. Tell me about the injury to your left shoulder.

A. I got some cuts and scratches and bruises on my left shoulder when I crashed into the dashboard of the car. That hurt for maybe two weeks, and then went away.

Q. Finally, tell me about the injuries to your stomach.

A. I guess I injured my stomach when I smashed against the steering wheel. It was just painful inside of my stomach. That went away after a few days.

Q. Other than these injuries to your neck, lower back, ankle, shoulder, and stomach, did you receive any other injuries?

A. Oh yeah. I received a concussion on the left side of my head. That's what the doctor told me.

Q. Mr. Jones, let's talk about the medical treatment you received for these injuries following the accident. First, how did you get to Doctors Hospital?

The "any other injuries" question is always useful. Again, it prevents later exaggeration.

e. Medical treatment

Note how this deposition is organized chronologically (with

A. An ambulance came to the intersection and they put me on a stretcher and drove me to the hospital.

Q. What happened when you arrived at Doctors Hospital?

A. The ambulance attendants took me into the emergency room, and some nurses checked me over, took my pulse and blood pressure, and stuff like that. After a while one of their doctors examined me. I think her name was Dr. Lang. I told Dr. Lang where I hurt and about the accident.

Q. What kind of treatment did you receive at the hospital?

A. Well, they examined me, x-rayed, cleaned up some of the cuts on my shoulder and chest, and put my ankle in a cast. It wasn't one of those big plaster casts, it was a cast that went around the back of my ankle and foot and was surrounded with an elastic bandage. I must have been there a couple of hours, and by that time my parents had come to the hospital, and they took me home.

Q. Did you receive any medication prescription?

A. The doctor gave a prescription for Tylenol with codeine, which my mother picked up at the drug store. The doctor told me to follow instructions on the bottle and take the medication if I needed it for the pain.

Q. Mr. Jones, tell us about the month you spent before you went back to work.

A. Well, the first week I pretty much spent in bed. Sometimes I got up and lay on the couch and watched TV. At that time everything was aching, my neck hurt, my head hurt, my stomach hurt, my ankle was swollen up. I spent all my time with my foot up to keep the swelling down, and I was taking the medicine to keep the pain down.

the exception of the accident itself). This is usually the best way to organize the questions, unless you have a specific reason for doing it another way.

f.   Recovery period

Q. How long was it before you were able to move around the house?

A. I'd say the first week or 10 days I pretty much spent on my back. After that period of time the pain in my head, shoulder and stomach started going away, and the swelling in my ankle was starting to go down. I got a pair of crutches and started moving around the house a little bit. I couldn't stay on my feet very long before the foot would swell up if I stood up for any length of time.

Q. At the end of September 2006, what was your physical condition like?

A. The scratches and bruises had gone away. The pains in my neck, shoulder, stomach and leg, and back, had started to get better. The only places that really kept on hurting was my lower back and my ankle.

Q. Tell me about those.

A. Well my back would have these stabbing pains from time to time. It felt real stiff. My ankle was stiff. My ankle was still swollen, and I couldn't walk on it yet. Dr. Hoffman, my family doctor, had removed the cast about three weeks after the accident and I could start walking without crutches, but I was still limping and the ankle would get sore if I walked on it for any length of time.

Q. When did you see Dr. Hoffman?

A. My mom took me to Dr. Hoffman about three weeks after the accident. He checked me out, removed the soft cast from my ankle, and told me it was okay to start walking around without the crutches if I could stand it.

Q. When did you stop using the crutches?

A. I stopped using them when I went back to work at the beginning of October.

Q. What did you see Dr. Franks, the chiropractor, for?

Since the defendant's purpose is to minimize the extent and length of the pain, these questions are important. Again, they prevent later exaggeration.

The history of the plaintiff's treatments is, of course, available from the medical records, which the defendant will have before the deposition. Nonetheless, these questions test the witness' recall and propensity to exaggerate.

A. Well, my mom thought that going to a chiropractor might help my back and ankle. My back still hurt, and my ankle was still sore. She thought that it might be a good idea to get some physical therapy to see if that might help. That's why I went to Dr. Franks.

Q. How many times did you see Dr. Franks?

A. I went to him for the first time around October 1st. I went to see him maybe twice a week for the next couple of months.

Q. What kind of treatment did Dr. Franks perform?

A. He would give me physical therapy. That involved bending my back, stretching it, applying heat treatments, things like that. The same thing was true for the ankle.

Q. Did it help?

A. Yes. About two months later, maybe by Christmas, most of the stiffness and pain had gone away.

Q. From December 2006 to the present day, describe your physical condition.

A. It's better. I still have pain from time to time in my back and ankle.

Q. When do you get the pain there?

A. Well, it depends on how much or how hard I work. The more I work the more likely I am to get those pains.

Q. How often do you get those pains?

A. It's maybe once a week for an hour or two, usually at the end of the work day.

Q. When was the last time you took Tylenol with codeine?

A. I took that stuff for maybe six weeks.

Q. Did you ever take any painkillers other than Tylenol with codeine?

A. I sometimes take aspirin when I get these pains.

Q. Other than what you've told me about, do you have any other injuries or problems that you feel were caused by this accident?

A. No, you pretty much covered it.

These questions effectively limit the damages.

Q. Mr. Jones, let's talk about some of the bills involved here. First the medical bills. Your interrogatory answers show that the bills from Doctors Hospital, Dr. Lang, Dr. Hoffman, and Dr. Franks have all been paid. Who paid those bills?

A. I'm not sure. I know they were paid by my health insurance. I think my mother paid the Walgreen pharmacy bill.

Q. Who paid for the wristwatch repair?

A. My mom paid that. I'm supposed to pay her back.

Q. You claim college books expenses in the amount of $162. Tell us about that.

A. Well, I was a part time student at Glendale Community College. I had already bought the books for the two courses I was taking. When I got injured, I couldn't take the courses I signed up for.

Q. Did you lose any tuition money?

A. No. The college said since I got hurt it wouldn't charge me for the courses I signed up for.

Q. How much income did you lose as a result of this accident?

A. I get paid $700 a month salary from Devo Florist. I went back to work October 1, 2006. The way I figure it, I lost one month's salary, or $700.

Q. The $700 is your gross income, isn't it?

A. Yes.

Q. What's your take-home pay?

A. We get paid on the first and fifteenth of the month. My take-home for half a month is about $270.

Q. Mr. Jones, let's talk about how this accident happened. Describe the vehicle you were driving.

A. It's a 2001 Toyota Corolla four-door. I bought it when I got out of the service. It was in really good shape, because I took good care of it.

Q. Is the title to that car in your name?

A. Yes.

---

g. Expenses and lost income

While the fact that most of the bills have been paid by insurance is not admissible at trial, it will have some effect on the settlement picture.

h. The accident

Note that here the questioner has saved the accident as the last topic. Some lawyers save the most important part of a deposition for the end, on the theory that the lawyer then has a better "feel" for the witness and the witness' guard will be down by that time.

Q. The accident happened around 2:00 P.M.?

A. Yes.

Q. At the time of the accident, where were you coming from?

A. I was coming from work at the flower shop.

Q. Where is that flower shop located?

A. On 40th Street and Thomas Road.

Q. 40th Street is the north-south street, correct?

A. Yes.

Q. Where is the flower shop in relation to the intersection?

A. It's not right at the corner. It's on 40th Street maybe 300 feet south of Thomas.

Q. Which side of 40th Street is the flower shop on?

A. It's on the east side.

Q. Tell me how you went from the flower shop north on 40th Street.

A. My car was parked in the lot next to the flower shop. When I got out of work, I pulled out of the lot and started going north on 40th Street.

Q. Describe what 40th Street looks like.

A. It's a pretty wide street. It has three lanes of traffic in each direction. In addition, it has left-turn lanes at the major intersections.

Q. There are traffic lights at the corner of 40th Street and Thomas, right?

A. Yes.

Q. Where are they located?

A. I think there's one at each corner and on the median strips.

Q. How many lights face the northbound traffic on 40th Street?

A. Probably around three.

Q. When you pulled onto 40th Street, which lane did you pull into?

A. I got into the inside lane, right next to the median strip.

Q. Mr. Jones, when was the first time you looked at the traffic lights at the corner of 40th Street and Thomas?

These scene description questions are useful to see how effectively the plaintiff can describe the scene, and are good questions to see how effective a trial witness he will make.

A. When I first pulled onto 40th Street and got in the inside lane.

Q. How far were you from the intersection at that time?

A. I guess around 100 feet.

Q. How fast were you going at that time?

A. Maybe 20 or 25 miles per hour.

Q. What was the color of the traffic lights at that point?

A. Green.

Q. What happened as you went northbound on 40th Street?

A. Well, it all happened really quickly. As I went north, the light turned yellow just before I got into the intersection. I was going through the intersection on the yellow light when suddenly I got smashed by another car from the driver's side.

Q. How long had the light been yellow at the time the other car collided widi you?

A. It couldn't have been more than two or three seconds.

Q. How fast were you going when you were hit?

A. Maybe 25 or 30 miles per hour.

Q. Did you ever see the car that hit you before the impact?

A. Not really. I first saw it just before it was about to smash into me. It couldn't have been more than 10 or 15 feet from me. Before I could even put on my brakes, the car hit me.

Q. Tell us what happened from the moment the two cars hit?

A. Well, I remember putting on my brakes, I kind of skidded in the intersection, and the other car seemed to be stuck against the side of my car. I can remember getting bounced around inside the car and smashing my head and chest against the inside of the car and the steering wheel.

Q. Were you wearing a seat belt at that time?

A. No.

Q. Did your car have seat belts?

A. Yes.

This is a useful answer since he was only about three seconds from the intersection before he looked at the lights.

This answer is also useful since it suggests that the plaintiff was not paying much attention as he entered the intersection.

Note how the questions become more specific. The questioner's purpose now is to "pin down" the witness to specific facts.

This is important, since in some jurisdictions this fact is admissible to show plaintiff's own negligence or failure to prevent damages.

Q. What happened when your car came to a stop?

A. I was pretty much numb. I can remember people coming up to me when I was in the car telling me not to move. I wasn't going to move anyway. I just hurt all over. I don't know how long it was, but after a while an ambulance came and they got me out of the car and put me on a stretcher.

Q. Mr. Jones, just before the impact, describe exactly what you were doing.

A. Well, I remember starting into the intersection. Since the light was yellow, I remember looking to the right to make sure that there weren't any cars taking a turn that might get in my way. I just looked to my right and then looked back up the road, then I saw the other car coming from my left just before it crashed into me.

Q. Did you ever put on your brakes before the impact?

A. No, I don't think so, there wasn't time to react.

Q. Mr. Jones, is there anything you remember about how this accident happened that you haven't told me about this afternoon?

A. No, nothing that comes to mind. I think I've pretty much told you everything.

Q. That's all the questions I have at this time. Do you have any questions, Ms. Johnson?

Ms. Johnson: No.

Mr. Sharp: Will you waive signature?

Ms. Johnson: No, we'll read and sign.

(The deposition was concluded at 3:06 P.M.)

John Jones
_____
John Jones

Some lawyers always ask this kind of question, since it's potential impeachment if the plaintiff "remembers" more at trial.

The party deponent should not waive signature, since he should review the transcript for accuracy.

Note that the plaintiff's lawyer asked no questions. This is the usual practice, unless the party gave incorrect or confusing answers that need to be corrected or clarified.

Note also that the plaintiff's lawyer made

State of Arizona
Country of Maricopa   SS.

no objections during the deposition. The questions were proper, so objections were unnecessary. The lawyer did not make objections for the purpose of coaching the plaintiff on desired responses, ethically questionable conduct some lawyers unfortunately engage in.

The foregoing deposition was taken before me, Mary Ryan, a Notary Public in the Country of Maricopa, State of Arizona. The witness was duly sworn by me to testify to the truth. The questions asked of the witness and the answers given by the witness were taken down by me in shorthand and reduced to typewriting under my direction. The deposition was submitted to the witness and read and signed. The foregoing pages are a true and accurate transcript of the entire proceedings taken during this deposition.

The court reporter must arrange a meeting with the deponent so he can review the transcript, note any claimed inaccuracies, and sign the transcript. Any claimed inaccuracies are usually put on a separate sheet and attached to the transcript.

Dated: April 1, 2007

Mary Ryan
Notary Public

My commission expires on
    December 31, 2007.

UNITED STATES DISTRICT COURT FOR
THE DISTRICT OF ARIZONA

John Jones,
        Plaintiff,
    v.   No. 07 C 1000
Susan Smith,
        Defendant

NOTICE OF MOTION

TO: Anne Johnson
     Attorney at Law
     100 Congress Street
     Phoenix, AZ 85001

PLEASE TAKE NOTICE that on June 10, 2007, at 9:00 A.M., or as soon as counsel can be heard, defendant in the above-captioned matter will present the attached Motion to Compel Discovery before the Hon. Joan Howe, Courtroom No. 4, United States Court House, Phoenix, Arizona.

Even with service by mail, this is adequate notice. As a professional courtesy, however, it's a good idea to call the opposing lawyer and let him know you're serving the motion.

Dated: June 1, 2007

William Sharp

William Sharp
Attorney for Defendant
100 Broadway
Phoenix, AZ 85001
881-1000

UNITED STATES DISTRICT COURT FOR
THE DISTRICT OF ARIZONA

John Jones,
            Plaintiff,
        v.   No. 07 C 1000
Susan Smith,
            Defendant

MOTION TO COMPEL DISCOVERY

Defendant moves for an order compelling plaintiff to answer in full interrogatories previously served on plaintiff, pursuant to Rule 37 of the Federal Rules of Civil Procedure. In support of her motion defendant states:

1. Defendant served interrogatories on plaintiff on February 1, 2007.

2. Plaintiff partially answered these interrogatories on February 25, 2007. Many of the answers are incomplete and do not provide the facts called for.

3. Plaintiff's answers to Interrogatory Nos. 2, 4,10,11,13, and 14 stated that "answers may be supplemented as discovery and investigation continues."

4. To date plaintiff has neither supplemented his interrogatory answers nor advised defendant that no additional answers will be forthcoming, although defendant has requested, by telephone and letter, that plaintiff submit supplemental answers.

WHEREFORE, defendant requests the court to order plaintiff to serve supplemental interrogatory answers within 10 days and award reasonable expenses, including attorney's fees, incurred by defendant as a result of this motion.

Since over three months have passed since plaintiff served incomplete answers to interrogatories, this motion should be brought.

In many jurisdictions local rules require that a motion must be supplemented by a memorandum of points and authorities. In other jurisdictions this is done only for complicated or contested motions, such as for summary judgment. You should always show what efforts you have made to get compliance before filing the motion.

Keep in mind that many jurisdictions require a lawyer to certify compliance with local rules that require that the parties first try to resolve discovery disputes informally.

Dated: June 1, 2007

William Sharp

William Sharp
Attorney for Defendant
100 Broadway
Phoenix, AZ 85001
881-1000

Note that Rule 37
allows the court to
award the reasonable
costs incurred in being
forced to bring this
motion. This includes
attorney's fees. Asking
for perhaps $200-500
here would
be reasonable.

AFFIDAVIT OF SERVICE

I, Helen Thompson, having been first duly sworn, state that I have served a copy of the attached Notice of Motion and Motion to Compel Discovery on plaintiff's attorney by mail at 100 Congress Street, Phoenix, Arizona 85001, on June 1, 2007.

Helen Thompson

Helen Thompson

Signed and sworn to before me on June 1, 2007.

Mary Ryan

Notary Public

My Commission expires on December 31, 2007.

[Seal]

UNITED STATES DISTRICT COURT FOR
THE DISTRICT OF ARIZONA

John Jones,
            Plaintiff,
        v.   No. 07 C 1000
Susan Smith,
            Defendant

REQUEST TO ADMIT FACTS
AND GENUINENESS OF DOCUMENTS

Plaintiff requests defendant, pursuant to Rule 36 of the Federal Rules of Civil Procedure, to admit within 30 days the following facts and genuineness of documents:

1. Defendant was the owner of a 2001 Buick Skylark sedan on September 2, 2006.

2. Defendant was driving the 2001 Buick Skylark sedan when the collision occurred on September 2, 2006.

3. Defendant was a driver licensed by the State of Nevada at the time of collision.

4. Each of the following documents, attached as exhibits to this request, is genuine and a business record of the entity it purports to be from:

If this case will go to trial, the plaintiff will need to establish basic facts. These requests cover facts that the defendent will probably not contest, and that will streamline the plaintiff's case during trial.

Exhibit No.   *Description*

1.   Phoenix Police Dept. accident report.
2.   Title and registration documents from Nevada Dept. of Transportation showing defendant to be the owner of a 2001 Buick Skylark sedan.
3.   Driver's license issued to defendant by the Nevada Dept. of Transportation.

Dated: June 1, 2007

Anne Johnson

Anne Johnson
Attorney for Plaintiff
100 Congress Street
Phoenix, AZ 85001
882-1000

A proof of service must be attached.

UNITED STATES DISTRICT COURT FOR
THE DISTRICT OF ARIZONA

John Jones,
         Plaintiff,

      v.   No. 07 C 1000

Susan Smith,
         Defendant

DEFENDANT'S ANSWER TO PLAINTIFF'S REQUESTS TO ADMIT FACTS AND GENUINENESS OF DOCUMENTS

Defendant answers plaintiff's Requests for Admission of Facts and Genuineness of Documents as follows:

<u>Request No. 1:</u> Defendant was the owner of a 2001 Buick Skylark sedan on September 2, 2006.

<u>Answer:</u> Admits.

<u>Request No. 2:</u> Defendant was driving the 2001 Buick Skylark sedan when the collision occurred on September 2, 2006.

<u>Answer:</u> Admits.

<u>Request No. 3:</u> Defendant was a driver licensed by the State of Nevada at the time of the collision.

<u>Answer:</u> Admits.

<u>Request No. 4:</u> Each of the following documents, attached as exhibits to this request, is authentic and a business record of the entity it purports to be from:

Exhibit No.	*Description*
1.	Phoenix Police Dept. accident report.
2.	Title and registration documents from the Nevada Dept. of Transportation showing defendant to be the owner of 2001 Buick Skylark sedan.

Like interrogatories, the usual practice in answering is to set out both the request and the answer. This avoids confusion.

3. Driver's license issued to defendant by the Nevada Dept. of Transportation.

Answer: Admits.

Dated: June 20, 2007

William Sharp

William Sharp
Attorney for Defendant
100 Broadway
Phoenix, AZ 85001
881-1000

A proof of service must
be attached.

UNITED STATES DISTRICT COURT FOR
THE DISTRICT OF ARIZONA

John Jones,
        Plaintiff,
    v.   No. 07 C 1000
Susan Smith,
        Defendant

OFFER OF JUDGMENT

Pursuant to Rule 68 of the Federal Rules of Civil Procedure, defendant offers to allow judgment to be taken against her in the amount of THIRTY THOUSAND DOLLARS ($30,000.00), and costs of suit incurred to the date of this offer.

This offer is being made under Rule 68 of the Federal Rules of Civil Procedure and Rule 408 of the Federal Rules of Evidence.

By this time defendant has sufficient facts to assess the case's settlement value. The offer of judgment will put additional pressure on the plaintiff to consider a realistic settlement.

Dated: August 1, 2007

William Sharp

William Sharp
Attorney for Defendant
100 Broadway
Phoenix, AZ 85001
881-1000

A proof of service must be attached.

UNITED STATES DISTRICT COURT FOR THE DISTRICT OF ARIZONA

John Jones,
| Plaintiff,
| v.   No. 07 C 1000
Susan Smith,
| Defendant

MOTION FOR ORDER TO COMPEL PLAINTIFF'S PHYSICAL EXAMINATION

Defendant moves under Rule 35 of the Federal Rules of Civil Procedure for an order compelling plaintiff to submit to a physical examination. In support of her motion defendant states:

1. Plaintiff's physical condition is genuinely in controversy since the complaint alleges a variety of physical injuries.

2. Plaintiff during his deposition stated that he still suffers from the consequences of the accident that is the basis for his complaint. These include periodic pain in his back and ankle.

3. There exists good cause, in light of the above, for a physical examination of the plaintiff to evaluate the plaintiff's current physical condition and prognosis.

4. Rudolf B. Anton, M.D., a board certified neurologist, has agreed to examine and evaluate the plaintiff at his medical office located at 4401 North Scottsdale Road, Scottsdale, Arizona, on September 15, 2007, at 5:00 P.M., or at another time, as directed by this court.

WHEREFORE, defendant requests that the court enter an order directing the plaintiff to be examined on the terms set forth above.

Dated: September 1, 2007

William Sharp

William Sharp
Attorney for Defendant
100 Broadway
Phoenix, AZ 85001
881-1000

Since plaintiff has not accepted the offer of judgment, defendant must continue her trial preparations. Getting a current evaluation of the plaintiff's medical condition and prognosis from a physician who has not previously seen the plaintiff is vital.

Keep in mind that many jurisdictions require a lawyer to certify that he has complied with local rules that require that the parties first try to resolve discovery disputes informally.

A proof of service must be attached.

UNITED STATES DISTRICT COURT FOR
THE DISTRICT OF ARIZONA

John Jones,
           Plaintiff,
       v.   No. 07 C 1000
Susan Smith,
           Defendant

JOINT PRETRIAL MEMORANDUM

Plaintiff and defendant submit the following joint pretrial memorandum:

Judges frequently have instructions on what the memorandum should contain and how it should be organized.

I   Jurisdiction

Jurisdiction of the court is based on diversity of citizenship under 28 U.S.C. §1332. Plaintiff is a citizen of Arizona. Defendant is a citizen of Nevada. The amount in controversy exceeds the sum of seventy-five thousand ($75,000) dollars, exclusive of interest and costs.

II   Uncontested Facts

Plaintiff Jones and defendant Smith were involved in a vehicle collision on September 2, 2006. The collision occurred at the intersection of 40th Street and Thomas Road in Phoenix, Arizona, at approximately 2:00 P.M. At the time of the collision Jones was driving his car, a 2001 Toyota Corolla four-door sedan, northbound on 40th Street; Smith was driving her car, a 2001 Buick Skylark sedan, eastbound on Thomas Road. The intersection is controlled by traffic lights.

On September 2, 2006, Jones was employed as a delivery driver by Devo Wholesale Florist and was being paid gross wages of $700 per month.

Jones received various physical injuries as a result of the collision. He missed one month's

These facts have all been admitted in the pleadings or during discovery.

work and wages from his job. His medical bills to date total $2,717.14. His vehicle repair costs totalled $1,213.00 His other out-of-pocket expenses totalled $237.00.

III   Contested Issues of Fact and Law

1. Did Smith run a red light?
2. Did Jones run a red light?
3. Was Smith negligent?
4. Was Jones negligent?
5. If both Smith and Jones were negligent, what is the degree of negligence of each of them?
6. What were the extent of Jones' injuries as a result of this collision?
7. What are Jones' reasonable damages?

IV   Exhibits

A.   *Plaintiff Jones'*   *Objections, if any*
     Exhibits

		Objections, if any
1.	Doctors Hospital records	None.
2.	Dr. Lang's office records	None.
3.	Dr. Hoffman's office records	None.
4.	Dr. Franks' office records	None.
5.	All bills for above	None.
6.	X rays taken by above	None.
7.	Devo Wholesale Florist employment records	None.
8.	Phoenix Police Dept. reports	Objection, for reasons stated in attached memorandum.

If any evidence is objected to, the judge may rule on the objections, if possible to do so, during the pretrial conference.

9.	Accident scene photographs	None.
10.	Jack's Auto Repair records and bill	None.
11.	Watch repair bill	None.
12.	Glendale Community College bills	None.
13.	Walgreen pharmacy bill	None.
14.	Accident scene diagrams	None.

If objections are made, the objecting party should state the basis for the objection, with supporting citations if necessary.

B. *Defendant Smith's Exhibits*   *Objections, if any*

1. Plaintiff's hospital and medical records   None.
2. Rudolf Anton, M.D., medical records   None.
3. Accident scene photographs   None.
4. Accident scene diagrams   Objection, misleading.
5. Phoenix Police Dept. reports to extent admissible   None.

V   Witnesses

A. *Plaintiff Jones' Witnesses*
1. Plaintiff
2. Carol Brown, 42 East Cambridge Street, Phoenix
3. Mary Porter, 42 East Cambridge Street, Phoenix
4. Dr. Lang
5. Dr. Hoffman
6. Dr. Franks
7. Diane Devo, Devo Wholesale Florist
8. John Jones, Sr., and Mary Jones, plaintiff's parents
9. Officer Steven Pitcher, Phoenix Police Dept.
10. Defendant
11. Personnel from Jack's Auto Repair, to qualify exhibits
12. Personnel from above hospitals and physicians, to qualify exhibits

B. *Defendant Smith's Witnesses:*
1. All of plaintiff's witnesses
2. Dr. Rudolf Anton

VI   Jury Instructions

Plaintiff's and defendant's proposed jury instructions are attached.

1. Plaintiff objects to defendant instruction nos. 6, 7, and 9, for the reasons stated in plaintiff's attached memorandum.

2. Defendant objects to plaintiff instruction nos. 2, 3, 4, and 6, for the reasons stated in defendant's attached memorandum.

RESPECTFULLY SUBMITTED,

Date: <u>November 1, 2007</u>

Anne Johnson

Anne Johnson
Attorney for Plaintiff

William Sharp

William Sharp
Attorney for Defendant

RELEASE

In consideration of the sum of thirty-six thousand dollars ($36,000), which plaintiff acknowledges receiving, Plaintiff John Jones agrees to release Defendant Susan Smith and her heirs, survivors, agents, and personal representatives from all claims, suits, or actions in any form or on any basis, because of anything that was done or not done at any time, on account of the following:

All claims for personal injuries, property damage, physical disabilities, medical expenses, lost income, and all other claims that have been

Pretrial memoranda frequently also contain a memorandum of law from each party that discusses any legal issues that the judge will need to resolve before or during trial.

The judge's final pretrial order will usually track the language and organization of the memorandum and contain all rulings on admissibility issues that were made at the conference.

A release would be the standard way of settling this case, since it is a complete settlement by all the parties.

or could be brought, including all claims now known or that in the future might be known, which arise out of an occurrence on or about September 2, 2006, at 40th Street and Thomas Road, in Phoenix, Arizona, when plaintiff claims to have sustained injuries as a result of a collision between an automobile driven by plaintiff and an automobile driven by defendant.

As a result of this collision plaintiff has brought suit against defendant for damages. Defendant has denied both liability and the claimed extent of damages. This release is a compromise settlement between Plaintiff John Jones and Defendant Susan Smith.

This agreement is a release and shall operate as a total discharge of any claims plaintiff has or may have, arising out the above occurrence, against this defendant and any other persons.

Plaintiff John Jones and Defendant Susan Smith also agree to terminate any actions that have been filed, particularly a claim by this plaintiff against this defendant currently filed as civil action No. 07 C 1000 in the United States District Court for the District of Arizona, in Phoenix, Arizona. Plaintiff and defendant agree to execute a Stipulation of Dismissal, with prejudice, and file it with the Clerk of the above Court, thereby terminating that action in its entirety, within five days of the execution of this agreement.

Date: December 1, 2007

John Jones
John Jones

The parties, not their lawyers, must sign the release.

Susan Smith
Susan Smith, Defendant

UNITED STATES DISTRICT COURT FOR
THE DISTRICT OF ARIZONA

John Jones,
       Plaintiff,
      v.
Susan Smith,
       Defendant
	No. 07 C 1000

STIPULATION OF DISMISSAL

Plaintiff John Jones and Defendant Susan Smith agree to dismiss this action with prejudice, and each party will bear its costs and attorney's fees.

The stipulation of dismissal terminates the lawsuit. No court order is necessary.

Dated: December 2, 2007

Anne Johnson

Anne Johnson
Attorney for Plaintiff

William Sharp

William Sharp
Attorney for Defendant

INDEX